The Jazz Collection

Made Possible By
THE GLORYA KAUFMAN FUND
and the Assistance
of Many Kind Friends

"Where d
dirty blues
ever jump
to the U.S

"[T]his is an entertaining must-read for music-loving travelers or for those who want to travel through the then and now of jazz and blues."

—New Orleans Times-Picayune

"Jazz . . . is an acquired taste, yet Christiane Bird engages us right off."

—The Washington Post

"The Jazz and Blues Lover's Guide to the U.S. is the best work of its kind I have ever seen. Christiane Bird knows and loves her subject. She's obviously done her background research, but more importantly, she's been to the places she writes about and manages to convey what it's like to be in a Mississippi Delta juke joint or an East St. Louis biker's bar. This is a great travel guide, but it should also be viewed as an important historical resource, since so much of the material about landmarks, local history, the clubs, and the people who run them has never appeared in any other book."

—Jim O'Neal, founding editor of *Living Blues* magazine

"Gives jazz lovers 'Landmarks and Legends' that could form the basis for walking tours in many United States cities."

—The New York Times

"Dig it!"

—Playboy

Christiane Bird

The
Jazz
and
Blues Lover's
G U I D E
to the U.S.

UPDATED EDITION

With More than 900

Hot Clubs,
Cool Joints,
Landmarks and Legends,

from

Boogie-Woogie

to

Bop

and Beyond

▲
▼▼

Addison Wesley Publishing Company

Reading, Massachusetts   Menlo Park, California   New York
Don Mills, Ontario   Wokingham, England   Amsterdam   Bonn
Sydney   Singapore   Tokyo   Madrid   San Juan
Paris   Seoul   Milan   Mexico City   Taipei

Cover design by Paul Bacon
Text design by Jennie Bush, Designworks, Inc.
Set in 9-point Bookman by NK Graphics, Keene, NH

Library of Congress Cataloging-in-Publication Data
Bird, Christiane.
     The jazz and blues lover's guide to the U.S.: with more than 900
hot clubs, cool joints, landmarks, and legends, from boogie-woogie
to bop and beyond / Christiane Bird.—Updated ed.
          p.   cm.
     Includes bibliographical references and index.
     ISBN 0-201-62648-9
     1. Jazz—History and criticism.   2. United States—Guidebooks.
3. Musical landmarks—United States—Guidebooks.   I. Title.
ML3508.B57   1994
781.65'0973—dc20   93-44290
                                                          CIP

1 2 3 4 5 6 7 8 9-ARM-97969594
First printing, March 1994

Contents

Acknowledgments vii

Preface ix

Introduction 1

How to Use This Book 10

National Sources 11

South

New Orleans *14*

Memphis *37*

The Mississippi Delta *58*

Atlanta *83*

Miami/Fort Lauderdale *94*

Northeast

New York *104*

Boston *152*

Philadelphia *161*

Pittsburgh *173*

Baltimore *184*

Washington, D.C. *193*

Midwest

Chicago *208*

Kansas City, Missouri *237*

St. Louis   *253*

Detroit   *266*

Indianapolis   *280*

Cincinnati   *289*

Minneapolis/St. Paul   *298*

Texas

Houston   *310*

Dallas   *321*

San Antonio   *331*

Austin   *340*

West Coast

Los Angeles   *354*

San Francisco/East Bay   *371*

Portland   *385*

Seattle   *391*

Appendix

A Brief History of Jazz and Blues   *400*

Major Festivals   *403*

Notes   *409*

Bibliography   *411*

Selected Index   *415*

Acknowledgments

In researching both the current and previous editions of this book, I depended heavily on the expertise of local critics, musicians, deejays, scholars, and music fans, many of whom gave most generously of their time and knowledge. In particular, I would like to thank Val Ginter in New York City; Harrison Ridley Jr. in Philadelphia; Bob J. Cohen in Boston; Keter Betts and the late Felix Grant in Washington, D.C.; Joe Jennings in Atlanta; Judy Peiser and the Center for Southern Folklore in Memphis; Jim O'Neal and the staff of Stackhouse Records, Bill Ferris, and Peter Lee in Mississippi; Don Marquis and Jan Ramsey in New Orleans; Ed Bell in Miami; Rick Mitchell, Lizette Cobb, and Noma Clay in Houston; Jim Beal and Little Neesie in San Antonio; Tary Owens in Austin; Tim Schuller in Dallas; Shirley Owens in Kansas City; Joel Slotnikoff in St. Louis; Melvin Ice, Clem Tiggs, and Mary Rose Niemi in Indianapolis; Ron Esposito in Cincinnati; Felix Wohrstein and David Whiteis in Chicago; Rich Johnson in Davenport, Iowa; Pat Collins, Leigh Kamman, Tom Surowicz, and Joel Johnson in Minneapolis/St. Paul; James Jenkins, Jim Dulzo, and John Sinclair in Detroit; Tina Mayfield in Los Angeles; and Philip Elwood and Pat Monaco in San Francisco. Thanks, too, to the Visitors and Convention Bureaus of many of the above cities.

In addition, in the South, in New Orleans, I would like to thank Bruce Raeburn and the Hogan Jazz Archive, George Buck, Al Rose, Kevin McCaffrey, and Johnny Donnels; in Memphis, David Nicholson, Wally Hall, Irwin Scheft, John Floyd, David Evans, and the Memphis Jazz Society; in Mississippi and the Delta, the Blues Archive at the University of Mississippi, Bubba Sullivan, and Malcolm Walls; in Atlanta, the staff of *Creative Loafing*, and Eric King; and in Miami, Lee Amlie, Greg Baker, Doug Adrianson, and Bob Perry.

In the North, in New York, I would like to thank Hugh Wyatt and David Hinckley, both ex-colleagues from the *New York Daily News*, the New York Public Library at Lincoln Center, the Schomburg Center for Research in Black Culture, and Margaret Davis; in New Jersey, the Institute for Jazz Studies at Rutgers; in Boston, Eric Jackson, Frederick J. Bouchard, Fred Taylor, Ed Henderson, Ernie Santosuosso, Ted Drozdowski, and Mai Kramer; in Philadelphia, Francis Davis, Teddy Royal, Tom Moon, Tom Cullen, Doug Waltner, and Bobby Zanzel; in Pittsburgh, Marty Ashby, Nelson Harrison, Tony Mowod, Bob Karlovitz, Sue Pellant and the Carnegie Library, and Nathan Davis; in Baltimore, Leonard Yorke, J.D. Considine, Dale Patton, Rosa Pryor, and the City Life Museums; and in Washington, D.C., Ron Weinstock, Willard Jenkins and the National Jazz Service Organization, Eddie McDermon, Louie Bellucci, Reuben Jackson, and Steve Hoffman.

In the Midwest, in Chicago, I would like to thank Michael

Frank, Harriet Choice, Bob Koester, Penny Tyler, Mwata Bowden and the Association for the Advancement of Creative Musicians, Joe Segal, Richard Wang and the Chicago Jazz Archive, and the Jazz Institute of Chicago; in Kansas City, Chuck Haddix and the Marr Sound Archive, Kathy Feist and the Jazz Ambassadors, Dick Wright, and the Kansas City Jazz Commission; in St. Louis, Harper Barnes, Bill Greensmith, Terry Perkins, Luana Hays, and Pauline Stark; in Detroit, Steve Sanchez and Michael Jewett; in Indianapolis, Tom Coombs, Elaine Anderson, the staff of the *Indianapolis Recorder,* Jim Clark, Dave Baker, and Wilma Gibbs and the Indiana Historical Society; in Cincinnati, Steve Tracy, Kitty Carson, Cal Collins, the late Jimmy McGary, and Paul Plummer; and in Minneapolis/St. Paul, Janis Lane-Ewart and Arts Midwest, Sarah Oxton, Jane Donahue, and Tim Bradach.

In Texas, in Houston, I would like to thank the Princess and the Houston Metropolitan Research Center; in Dallas, Russell Smith, Chuck Nevitt, Alan Govenar, Tom Guerin, and the Dallas Public Library; and in Austin, John Wheat and the Barker Texas History Center, Michael Point, John Conquest, L.E. McCullough, and Alex Coke.

On the West Coast, in Los Angeles, I would like to thank Dawan Muhammad, Don Muhammad and the musicians of the World Stage, Mary Katherine Aldin, Bill Kohlhaase, Fred Schuster, Richard Ginell, Don Snowden, Zan Stewart, Meg Sheehan, and Zack Staenberg; in San Francisco, Lee Hildebrand, Andrew O'Hehir, and Dr. Juba; in Portland, Bob Dietsche, Lynn Darroch, Rick Hall, Ardis Hedrick, Teresa Jordan, Rebecca Kilgore and Ron Steen; and in Seattle, John Gilbreath, Dave Hiscock, and Paul de Barros.

Finally, too, I would like to thank my family and Jerry Brown for their constant support; and my longtime friend and editor Nancy Miller, for her unfailing enthusiasm, generosity, and insight.

Preface to the 1994 Edition

Since researching the first edition of this book over three years ago, inevitable change has occurred. Some clubs have disappeared; others have risen to take their place. Some spots, previously known to only a handful of fans, have been "discovered"; others have altered the type of music they offer or the kind of clientele they attract. Interestingly enough, however, most of the old jazz/blues stand-bys—the Village Vanguard in New York, the Jazz Showcase in Chicago, the neighborhood juke joints in Mississippi—remain as they were and, seemingly, always have been.

The amount of club turnover has varied widely from city to city. A few places, such as Miami and Portland, have witnessed enormous change, with almost every venue that I visited in 1991 replaced by something new. Other cities, such as San Francisco and Chicago, have remained relatively stable.

Among the clubs that have, sadly, closed their doors for good are the warm and wonderful Glass House in New Orleans, the late-night Lou's in Memphis, and the high-spirited Brooklyn Bar & Grill in San Antonio. But each one of these unique clubs seems to have passed its legacy on to the next generation. Trombone Shorty's in New Orleans, the Blues City Cafe in Memphis, and Saluté in San Antonio all pick up where their predecessors left off.

From this, it's tempting to conclude that there are somehow a predetermined number of jazz/blues clubs in each city and that for every venue that goes out of business, another one rises to take its place. There is some truth to this, but after making hundreds of calls to cities all over the country, I can also cautiously conclude that jazz and blues is in a relatively healthy state, with more clubs in existence today than were three years ago. The cities of St. Louis, Atlanta, and Austin, which had no full-time jazz clubs in 1991, are now home to the nationally-known Just Jazz, the locally-known Just Jazz, and the Elephant Room respectively. Miami now has about twice as many jazz spots as it did three years ago, while numerous other cities, including Philadelphia, Pittsburgh, Baltimore, Washington, D.C., San Antonio, Kansas City, and Detroit all boast at least one new important jazz venue, and Los Angeles and New Orleans boast several new important jazz venues. As for blues, though the number of clubs has remained more or less the same in most major blues cities, such as Chicago and St. Louis, it has exploded in some unexpected spots. Three years ago, for example, neither Los Angeles nor Cincinnati had much in the way of full-time blues clubs; now, both are home to about a half dozen.

There also seems to be a slowly growing awareness regarding the importance of jazz and blues history. Memphis now has two new music museums, one devoted to the blues, the other to the Memphis sound, while the Delta Blues Museum in Clarksdale, Mississippi, has expanded its exhibits significantly, thanks in part to a grant from the National Endowment for the Humanities. Ma

Rainey's house in Columbus, Georgia, has been restored and will soon be turned into a museum; several handsome new grave markers honoring bluesmen have been erected in Mississippi, and a bill now pending before Congress proposes to create a national park dedicated to jazz in New Orleans.

Of course, however, the news from the jazz/blues front is hardly overwhelmingly positive. There are still many more fine musicians than there are venues to hire them, and the music still goes more or less unappreciated by most of the general public. Some important clubs have closed (J's and Condon's in New York, Baker's Keyboard Lounge in Detroit) or changed character (Caravan of Dreams in Fort Worth), and some cities have cumulatively less venues than they did three years ago. Most notable among these are Portland, which seems to be gradually losing its once unique and thriving local jazz scene; and Houston, the fourth largest city in the U.S., which has lost its one and only national jazz club.

Several trends already well apparent when the first edition of this book came out have become even more pronounced. Probably the most significant of these is the rising importance of the jazz concert venue. Large institutions such as Lincoln Center in New York and the Kennedy Center in Washington, D.C., now have extensive jazz programs, while numerous smaller cultural centers, such as the Manchester Craftsmen's Guild in Pittsburgh and the Sammon Center for the Arts in Dallas, bring more national jazz artists into their respective cities than do the local clubs. Jazz also continues to find itself paired with many strange bedfellows—everything from a sushi bar in Hollywood, Florida, to a wine store cum bar in St. Louis.

Meanwhile, in the blues world, the biggest news is the formation and rapid expansion of two major club chains. The most ambitious is the House of Blues, which is also a foundation dedicated to the preservation of the music, primarily through education (see Boston, p. 158). Founded by Isaac Tigrett, who started up the Hard Rock Cafe, the House of Blues opened its first club and educational project in Boston in 1992, and will be opening similar clubs and projects in New Orleans, Los Angeles, New York, and Chicago in 1994 and 1995. The second chain is Billy Blues, a Texas-based operation that within the past three years has established thriving venues in San Antonio, Dallas, Houston, Austin (merging with the legendary Antone's), Denver, and Heidelberg, Germany. Obviously, these large, commercial chains can never replace the holes-in-the-wall in which the blues was born, but with any luck, they will be intelligently run and provide both more work/revenue for the musicians and more live music for the fans.

Finally, a note on researching this edition: Although I visited most of the clubs included in the 1991 edition in person, such extensive travel was not possible the second time around. I did manage to get to a number of major cities and locales (Memphis, the Mississippi Delta, New Orleans, Los Angeles, San Francisco,

Portland, Seattle, Boston, and New York), but for others, I had to rely heavily on telephone interviews with local critics, deejays, musicians, club owners, and fans. Such an approach obviously has its pitfalls, but I tried to speak to as many people as possible so as to present as accurate a picture as possible. This second edition has also allowed me to include a number of unusual clubs that I missed the first time around (the Sandbar in New Orleans, the Flamingo Lounge in Brooklyn, H&M Bar-B-Q in Kansas City), fine-tune some of my earlier entries, and go into greater depth in several cities (most notably Seattle and Miami) that received short shrift in the first edition.

—*Christiane Bird*
New York City, 1993

The
J a z z
and
Blues Lover's
G U I D E
to the U.S.

Introduction

I wish I could say that after four months spent traveling around the country compiling information for this book, I had discovered dozens upon dozens of hitherto unknown jazz and blues clubs; that deep in the bowels of Atlanta or Indianapolis were holes-in-the-wall that rocked until dawn; or that way down on some back alley in Houston or Los Angeles were juke joints packed with mind-blowing musicians the likes of which the world had never heard. This, of course, is not exactly the case—the golden era of jazz and blues is over (at least for now). But in some ways, the truth is almost as exciting, and certainly as interesting, for in every major American city—even those with no commercial jazz or blues club, and a general population that could care less about either—the music is being kept very much alive, sometimes through small African-American neighborhood clubs, sometimes through sophisticated concert series, sometimes through enthusiastic restaurateurs. There is a tremendous number of talented musicians out there and—among a limited audience at least—a tremendous enthusiasm for the music.

To bemoan the condition of jazz and blues in this country (despite what seems to be a current renaissance of interest) has become commonplace, and with good reason. Jazz and blues is America's most original art form, and yet it's woefully neglected by the mainstream. Many people barely know who Duke Ellington or Charlie Parker are, let alone Charlie Christian or Sonny Boy Williamson (I or II), or newer stars such as Lester Bowie or David Murray. The Europeans and the Japanese, who flock to jazz and blues concerts by the thousands, may appreciate the music's enormous beauty and complexity, but in general, we Americans do not. One of the saddest things about working on this book—and there were many sad things, as the history of jazz and blues is in many ways the history of the oppression of blacks in America—lay in realizing how many talented musicians have no place to play. I can think of no city that has "enough" clubs, especially for the younger or lesser-known player.

Some of this may be inevitable. There's always been something underground about jazz and blues anyway, and perhaps that's the way it always will be, even should be. Art of all types seems to need a certain amount of neglect to grow. But in the jazz and blues world, even artists who have come into their own rarely receive full-scale recognition, and many musicians working today have a hard time making a living.

Most major cities have two basic types of clubs, those that bring in national talent, and those that feature local players. The national clubs have the best musicians, the best acoustics, and the best sight lines; but the local clubs, though much more erratic, are often more atmospheric and more fun. Some national clubs are one-of-a-kind spots that shouldn't be missed—the Village Vanguard in New York, Tipitina's in New Orleans, Baker's Keyboard Lounge in Detroit; but the same can also be said of some tiny local joints such as the Glass House in New Orleans (where the Dirty Dozen got their start), Green's Lounge in Memphis (a 20-year-old juke joint), and Babe & Ricky's in Los Angeles (the last of the Central Avenue clubs).

Local clubs are like families. Everyone knows everyone else, and people stop by to gossip, play cards, and watch television, as well as to drink and hear music. This is especially true in the poorer, African-American communities, where there is almost always a club or two that never advertises and is generally unknown to the rest of the city but that has been offering music at least once a week for 10, 20, even 30 years. It was in little joints such as these that jazz and blues was born, and even today, there's a certain magic about the neighborhood place. Never mind that it's often built of cement blocks or located in a dangerous part of town, never mind that its talent is usually unknown (and sometimes deservedly so). On a Friday or Saturday night, when the notes start to circle and soar, these places are the musical centers of the universe.

Among club owners on both the local and the national level, rich and poor, black and white, I found a predictable mix. Some were running their establishments for the love of the music, some were operating purely as efficient businessmen (these were the majority), and some were looking to make a quick buck (though this seldom works for long in the jazz-blues world, where there's not that much money to begin with). Usually, though not always, it was surprisingly easy to tell which was which simply by walking into a place. There's a certain indescribable feeling about a good club, whether its decor is upscale or down. Good times, good spirits, good sounds seem to vibrate off the walls, even in the daytime, when all that's tangibly evident is the smell of last night's beer.

To book known musicians nowadays is tremendously expensive, which helps account for the relative decline in the number of pure music clubs today as compared to 20 or 30 years ago, and the relative rise in the number of concert-type venues and restaurants that also feature jazz and blues. To survive in the modern world, many establishments have to be two things at once. Nonetheless, just because a club is also a restaurant doesn't mean its sounds are any less fine.

As a white woman exploring an art form that is predominantly black, I was constantly aware of the slippery, cumbersome issue of race. For all the strides that have been taken in civil rights over the past three decades, very few music venues in this country are truly integrated. Every establishment that I visited was either white, or it was black, and though many did have a somewhat mixed audience, there was often depressingly little real interaction between the races. As everyone knows yet seldom acknowledges, integration may be in effect on legal and institutional levels, but on a social level, not too much has changed. Even finding out about the

African-American clubs if you are from out of town can be a difficult process: most aren't covered by the mainstream press.

This black/white dichotomy seems especially true in the blues world, where most clubs are either trendy air-conditioned white establishments charging $10 to $20 a head, or poor cement-floored black juke joints with no cover charge. Jazz venues are usually more mixed, but the upscale African-American clubs attract even fewer whites—sometimes deliberately so—than do the poor juke joints. R&B is yet another story. There's still a "chitlin circuit" out there, featuring such stars as Tyrone Davis and Denise LaSalle, and these audiences are almost always 99 percent black.

And then there's the thorny question of the relationship between jazz and blues. Most people acknowledge that blues predates jazz and that the two forms borrow frequently from each other, but beyond that all agreement ends. Many see the two sounds as totally different and totally incompatible. Today's burgeoning number of young white blues fans often dismiss jazz as sophisticated cocktail chatter, while many jazz musicians still equate bluesmen with raw and unsophisticated country folk. Club owners even say that the crowds' drinking habits differ. Blues fans drink beer; jazz fans drink hard liquor. Blues fans drink a lot; jazz fans sip. This kind of thinking gets extended even further by audiences who describe jazz as *only* the sounds of the 1920's and '30's, or *only* those that are post bebop.

Part of the problem is that jazz is a complicated music that requires listening. Appreciating it takes time and effort, and since few people take that time or effort, or even get exposed to the music in the first place, it often gets left by the wayside, or else stuck in definitions and settings so formal that it scares people off. Blues, being more accessible, has a somewhat easier time of it, yet many white audiences still have no real idea of where it comes from. I think of the strange irony of one enthusiastic club owner who told me in one proud breath that he featured "nothing but the blues," and then, in another, whispered that I ought to skip the next stop on my list because it was, "you know, *black*."

Despite such muddled thinking, and our still ugly, much-segregated world, jazz and blues have probably done more to further integration than any other single art or entertainment form. One of the most wonderful things about the music is how it has brought together so many different people from so many different worlds—if not always physically, at least spiritually. I spent many amazing nights traveling from poor juke joints to plush hotel lounges to pretty yuppie-buppie clubs; and on some level, the audiences were always the same. The club business may be extremely volatile, susceptible to everything from social whim to changes in the drinking laws, but the appeal of the music itself is stable and timeless. A song or riff heard in a black club today will be heard in a white club tomorrow, just as it was heard in the Cotton Club in the '20's or on 52nd Street in the '40's.

Many of the smaller clubs located in run-down districts are managed by women, usually motherly or grandmotherly sorts striving to provide something "nice for the neighborhood," and it is largely their care, I think, that makes the poorer places, often impeccably kept, so appealing. They're not only entertainment centers, they're also living rooms, and homes. Usually all gray and nondescript on the outside, looking more like storage sheds than anything else, they are all explosive beauty on the inside, alive with more color, sight, and sound than can be found in a dozen more upscale clubs put together. A woman dressed in high, high heels and a sequined skirt hugs the arm of a man dressed in a white three-piece suit with an elegant hat. A middle-aged stud with sunglasses dances next to a grandfather with a cane dances next to a young gyrating woman in a red slinky dress. Meanwhile, a tuxedoed musician with diamonds on his fingers and gel in his hair moans out the blues; and chicken wings and pig-ear sandwiches are for sale behind the bar. It's all a very private, self-contained world completely apart from mainstream American life, a world that despite its poverty seems rich and warm and real and makes the late twentieth century, with its constant emphasis on materialism and success, seem even more vapid than usual.

But as warm and real and exciting as the smaller, poorer clubs are, they're also far too easy to romanticize. As an outsider, I had the option of leaving when I was ready, of going back to a plusher, more open world; for many of the neighborhood people I met, their Friday or Saturday nights were it, the high point of their week. They'd just spent their extra cash and tomorrow would be another day. Nowhere was this brought home to me more powerfully than in a small club in Memphis. Upon hearing that I was from New York, a tiny African-American woman dressed completely in black and wearing a big cowboy hat gripped my arm. "Take me with you," she said, her voice heavy with a yearning that is surely impossible for me or any other middle-class person to truly understand. For her, going to New York was as distant a dream as winning the lottery is to most Americans.

As a single, middle-class woman visiting clubs in poorer neighborhoods, I never had any trouble and only once or twice encountered a hostile remark. Instead, most people were extremely gracious and hospitable. Interested that I was interested, they were pleased and proud to show off their clubs and their music. I must also quickly add that although on any given night I may have been the only out-of-towner in the crowd, I am hardly the only middle-class person "foolish" enough to venture into run-down districts. In every major city, there exists a hard-core group of musicians, deejays, critics, and music enthusiasts who make regular forays to the "wrong side of town" to catch those hot jam sessions that can somehow never quite be duplicated at the commercial clubs. It was, in fact, this group who directed me to many of the clubs I visited, and always, there had been many other out-of-towners there before me. I was especially struck by this in Mississippi, when in some tiny, hole-in-the-wall joint, looking for all the world as if it had never had *any* visitor of *any* kind, the owner would bring out a scrapbook filled with pictures and letters from Norwegians, Japanese, Germans, and Swedes, all of whom had passed through his place in earlier years.

All the clubs included in this book are friendly and safe places, but the streets themselves are something else. One thing that a visitor learns right away is that in a rough neighborhood, people take care of their own. At first when someone graciously offered to walk me to my car whenever I left a club, I thought it was because I was a single woman and a stranger in town. I soon realized, however, that almost everyone was walked to his or her car—it's an ordinary precaution in neighborhoods where trouble may always be lurking.

As for the more established, nationally known clubs, many have long and proud histories. Often started up by jazz and blues fanatics while they were still in their early twenties (Joe Segal of the Jazz Showcase in Chicago, the late Max Gordon of the Village Vanguard in New York, Clifford Antone of Antone's in Austin), they've played an important role in bringing top musicians to the attention of the general public. Max Gordon was one of the first to present everyone from Dinah Washington to Sonny Rollins, while Clifford Antone has helped launch the careers of innumerable Texas bluesmen, including the late Stevie Ray Vaughan, his brother Jimmie Vaughan, and Angela Strehli.

Like the local clubs, the national clubs have a regular clientele, and it often includes well-known musicians who hang out in the joints after their gigs elsewhere are done. Bradley's is a favorite among musicians in New York; the Blue Wisp is a favorite in Cincinnati. Nowadays, too, the nationally known spots attract numerous foreigners, who seem to come straight from the airport to the clubs and then, suffering from jet lag, fall asleep during the second set.

Located somewhere between the two extremes of the spectrum represented by the poor neighborhood clubs and the nationally known ones are the newer yuppie and buppie establishments. Music in these pretty watering holes, which tend to live short lives, is usually more of an afterthought than anything else, but the musicians themselves, when allowed to stretch out, are often quite good.

And then there is the upscale hotel, which has played a surprisingly significant role in jazz history. During the big-band era, numerous posh hotels such as the Pennsylvania in New York, the Adolphus in Dallas, and the Peabody in Memphis were instrumental in first exposing white, middle-class audiences to jazz. Nowadays, all that most hostelries have to offer is insipid cocktail music in overly air-conditioned lounges, but there are a few notable exceptions—the Grand Avenue Bar in the Biltmore Hotel in

Los Angeles, the Regattabar in the Charles Hotel in Boston—and the hotels, no matter what their music policies, do still remain one of the few steady avenues of employment for jazz musicians.

A new trend also seems to be emerging in the jazz and blues world: ethnic restaurants now turned quasi-club. When these restaurants are African, African-American, or even Japanese, the connection seems understandable enough, but sometimes the music can also be found in the most unexpected of places: a classy Chinese restaurant in Boston (the Lai Lai), a Middle Eastern restaurant in Detroit (the Gnome), and a small Italian bistro in Philadelphia (J.J.'s Grotto). Once again, it seems, jazz and blues defy categorization.

But clubs and live music are only part of the story. Today's music was shaped by yesterday's musicians, and one of the joys of working on this project lay in seeing the very direct connections that exist between the present and the past, reality and legend. To see the hospital where Bessie Smith died, the house where John Coltrane lived as a young man, the building where Charlie Parker first played with Dizzy Gillespie, the graveyard where Howlin' Wolf is buried—all this contributes to a vivid picture of the music and its culture as an integral part of the American scene.

For the most part, historic jazz and blues sites go unrecognized by the general public and officialdom. Some of this has to do with ignorance and racist attitudes, but there are also some very real physical problems. Most jazz and blues artists grew up in ramshackle houses or tenement buildings that now look more ready for the wrecker's ball than for a historic plaque, and many legendary nightclubs and theaters have been torn down. Some states and cities have found ways around this. Mississippi, despite its racist reputation, has several historic blues markers (the site of W. C. Handy's former home, the site where the "Southern crosses the Dog"); and Kansas City has done a wonderful job of mapping out the 18th and Vine Historic District. Baltimore has a museum devoted to Eubie Blake and a statue honoring Billie Holiday, and New Orleans also has a jazz museum and a statue honoring Louis Armstrong. Texas has placed an historic marker by Blind Lemon Jefferson's grave, and the National Park Service has designated a number of jazz- and blues-related buildings National Historic Landmarks (Duke Ellington's home in New York, Scott Joplin's apartment in St. Louis).

Back in the days before desegregation, nearly all American cities had one main drag that was the black community's business and entertainment center. Sometimes these streets were big and elaborate affairs, like Seventh Avenue in Harlem or 47th Street in Chicago; sometimes they were tiny and rather rural—Nelson Street in Greenville, Mississippi, East 11th Street in Austin, Texas; but always, they housed important theaters and nightclubs bursting with sound. Even today, when you mention U Street in Washington, D.C., Pennsylvania Avenue in Baltimore, Decatur or Auburn Avenue in Atlanta, Beale Street in Memphis, Elm

Street (Deep Ellum) in Dallas, or Hastings Street in Detroit, some-one's eyes will light up.

All of those once-splendid avenues are gone now, replaced by abandoned lots and boarded-up buildings. Most fell into decline in the early 1960's with urban renewal, the building of the super-highways (which often cut through the heart of African-American neighborhoods), desegregation, and the advent of rock. Urban re-newal not only destroyed the fabric of black neighborhood life by demolishing old familiar buildings and replacing them with cold edifices, but also cut jazz and blues to the quick by removing the grass-roots clubs where both children and adults first learned about the music. In addition, when African Americans were finally allowed to frequent the white clubs, many formerly successful black businessmen who had been catering exclusively to black customers went bankrupt as their clients went elsewhere.

Traveling through these poor neighborhoods by day, when there's no live music or liquor to help smooth the rawness, is even sadder than it is by night. In terms of pure acreage alone, the amount of devastated urban landscape in this country is appalling. It's one thing to live in a big city such as New York, and to be vaguely aware of Harlem or the South Bronx, perhaps occasion-ally venturing to a specific address therein, and quite another to drive through mile after mile after mile after mile—will it never end?—of East St. Louis, South Dallas, the South and West sides of Chicago, the Mississippi Delta, Watts, southwest Atlanta, parts of northwest Washington, east Kansas City, Detroit. Boarded-up building follows boarded-up building, empty lot follows empty lot, and how anyone or anything can emerge from this ravaged land with any sense of self or soul intact—let alone an artistic vision—is truly remarkable.

Only a few historic jazz and blues landmarks are left, and visit-ing them is an emotional thing, even for one who wasn't around back then. To see the old Minton's in New York, the old Cherry Blossom in Kansas City, or the old Cosmopolitan Club in St. Louis, after all the stories and all the songs—once such hotbeds, now such shells—"That, my love," said bass player Keter Betts, as he helped me locate some of Washington, D.C.'s, old U Street sites, "is like seeing a long-ago love. You see them again years later, and . . ." He shrugged. "Nothing."

Some cities, most notably Memphis, are trying to bring back their rich musical past by revitalizing historic clubs and neighbor-hoods. Others, most notably Kansas City, have created all sorts of music commissions, boards, and societies to help preserve the music. So far, none of these schemes seems to be working terribly well: hanging on to heritage is a tricky thing. Bygone eras cannot be recreated, and sometimes the stamp of approval destroys the very thing that it is trying to preserve. (The same could be said of this book, which by directing readers to out-of-the-way places could help to dilute the very atmosphere that makes those places special.)

On the other hand, recognition is necessary for survival. Without it, much of the richness of jazz and blues history could be lost forever. Throughout my travels, I met numerous people who are desperately working against time to interview dying generations of jazz and blues artists, or to otherwise preserve and promote the music. Many are toiling unofficially, without pay or promise of publication: I think particularly of Harrison Ridley, a deejay in Philadelphia who is compiling a five-volume history of jazz in that city; and of Nelson Harrison, a trombone player and educator in Pittsburgh who spends much of his spare time (what spare time?) traipsing around the city with a tape recorder. Even more particularly, I think of James Jenkins, a retired bus driver in Detroit, who has put almost all of his pension into starting up a national jazz museum. He got the idea on the day Duke Ellington died. "I just had to do something," he says.

In the jazz and blues world, people are always scraping, always just getting by. There's never enough money, never enough manpower, never enough popular interest. Nonetheless, in this same world, people are always dreaming. Most operate completely outside the mainstream, where strokes of serendipitous fortune are hard to come by (few poor neighborhood clubs are going to be "discovered," few jazz or blues musicians are going to "make it") but they believe too passionately in what they are doing to let this bother them.

Every city that I visited differed completely from the next in ways that are hard to pinpoint. Despite the homogenization of America—which certainly does exist—each city, beneath its McDonald's and Kentucky Fried Chickens, has its own distinct rhythms, flavors, and values. Washington, D.C., felt wide and windswept and heavy, with music clubs floating like flotsam on a sea of monuments. Houston also felt wide and windswept, but here, everything was flotsam *except* the small African-American music clubs with their roots reaching deep into the past. Austin and Minneapolis/St. Paul seemed packed with aging "ex-hippie" guardians of the blues, while Indianapolis—a city that refuses to go on daylight saving time—seemed filled with earnest, well-meaning folk. All of this gets translated directly into the music: during my travels, I heard David "Fathead" Newman give two completely different performances, one in Austin, where he blew wild and blue with a big all-out Texas sound, the second in Chicago, where he was more elegant, sophisticated, and refined.

Wherever I went, people would ask the same questions: What's the best city for jazz? Where are the most blues? My answers are not particularly startling. With an enormous number of great clubs and great musicians, New York is by far and away the best jazz town. Yet, at the same time, the city's music scene seems to have lost some of its soul. Spontaneity has been replaced by formality, enthusiasm by high prices and tightly controlled sets. Easy, relaxed jam sessions—so wondrous in other cities, where they charge *maybe* $2 to $4 a head—are few and far between; and audiences are often so tightly packed in that it's hard to breathe, let alone feel comfortable.

At the other extreme, there's Portland, Oregon, which also has a very unusual jazz scene, quite unlike that of any other city in the United States. While there's no club here bringing in national talent on a nightly basis, there are nearly a dozen solid local clubs featuring top-caliber area players (some of whom have national reputations) six or seven nights a week. Even more startling for a small city of under 500,000 is the local community's active involvement in the music—they come out to hear their favorite players again and again.

As for the blues, they really are thriving. Chicago is on fire these days with nearly a dozen first-rate clubs smoking seven nights a week, and a hundred others happening at least some of the time. St. Louis and Kansas City have strong underground blues scenes that are just now becoming recognized, while Houston has a strong underground blues scene that is still largely unrecognized. Memphis and Austin are also hot with the music, while L.A. and San Francisco/Oakland both have a smattering of strong blues clubs.

Being alone and on the road for a long period of time is a strange and isolating experience. I lost much sense of myself as a person, and became, in a sense, the project. I was no longer male or female, black or white, but rather, a human tape recorder, seeing but somehow not being seen (at least to myself). Nothing mattered except that I interviewed the person I had to interview, got where I had to get. I no longer had a sense of place, becoming unbearably anxious every time I tackled a new city (how am I going to find my way around *this* time?) and forming strong attachments to little things (my car packed with research, those blessedly cheap Motel 6's, the weekly phone calls home). Driving hundreds of miles in a day became second nature, as did bopping around to four or five clubs a night or eating sandwiches out of 7-Eleven's. Many people were extremely helpful, fascinating, and kind, and although I appreciated it enormously, part of me was always detached—even when I was most touched—worrying about the next interview, the next stop. Beneath it all, however, I was always aware that I was immensely privileged, that I was seeing worlds that few outsiders ever see.

Nearly every day brought with it some unusual club or some unusual happenstance. There was the Bach Dancing and Dynamite Society, a homey bungalow and jazz joint on the beach just outside San Francisco; the Green Mill, an old gangster hangout and jazz club in Chicago; Po' Bob's, a friendly black bikers' blues club near St. Louis; Caravan of Dreams, a plush Fort Worth club reminiscent of a sultan's tent; and Twins, a hot Ethiopian restaurant and jazz club in Washington, D.C. There was the night at the Brooklyn Street Bar & Grill in San Antonio, Texas, when dozens of first-rate, mostly Mexican-American jazz musicians blew time and space away; and the afternoon at the Mutual Musicians Foundation in Kansas City when I was shown the very special piano—shut up in a closet—that Scott Joplin and Count Basie once played. There was also the night I got lost on the eerie black-and-blue back roads of the Delta beneath a huge orange moon, and thought how the Mississippi nights—so different from the Mississippi days—still belong to the poor and to the blues.

And then there were the people: music business people (critics, deejays, musicians) without whose help this book couldn't have been written, and grass-roots people without whom there would be no music business. I think of Mr. Morse Gist in Helena, Arkansas, who once sold Sonny Boy Williamson (II) his harmonicas; Noma Clay, a manager in a small Houston club who took me out at two a.m. one morning to hear some of the meanest, baddest blues around; Rich Johnson, who showed me Bix Beiderbecke's home and grave in Davenport, Iowa; Tina Mayfield, Percy Mayfield's wife, who welcomed me into her home in Los Angeles; and Mrs. Z. L. Hill, who runs the boardinghouse in Clarksdale, Mississippi, that once housed the hospital where Bessie Smith died.

Just where is jazz and blues going? I'm really not scholar or critic enough to say. All I know is that the music is out there, and will always be out there.

It's time to give it its due.

—Christiane Bird
New York City, 1990

How to Use This Book

Each chapter in this book is divided into two sections: one that briefly covers the history of jazz and blues in that city and mentions a few music landmarks, and one that covers the current music scene. Neither category pretends to be definitive, but is a sort of musical potpourri compiled from my own experience and information given to me by local experts. All pertinent omissions are sincerely regretted.

The main danger in writing a book like this is high club turnover. Places come and go at an alarming rate, and by the time this guide is published, some of the establishments listed herein will be no more. On the other hand, for every club that dies a quick death, there are many others that have been around for decades (predicting which clubs are which is next to impossible; ironically, it is often the smallest, poorest club that lasts the longest). It is therefore imperative to call all clubs before visiting, or in the case of the Delta juke joints that have no phone, to stop by in the afternoon. Throughout the listings, I have also included information on when music is offered, what kind of music is offered, cover charges, food, etc. This has been included as a general guideline, rather than for strict informational purposes and should be checked in advance. CALL, CALL, CALL.

The section called "Sources," which lists local publications, etc.

that give day-to-day music listings, will help you orient yourself in the jazz and blues scene of each city (see also "National Sources," below). At the end of each chapter, the sections "Radio" and "Record Stores" contain specific information on jazz/blues programming and the best places to buy the music.

Especially for the smaller cities, I have mentioned numerous places that aren't, strictly speaking, clubs, or even regular music venues. Some of these are primarily restaurants; others just offer live entertainment once or twice a week. I have felt it important to include these spots, however, as they are often local institutions that have been the mainstays of their respective jazz and blues communities for years and years. I have also used the terms "local" and "national" musicians rather loosely, and more as a way of indicating whether a club books touring talent or not than as a way of measuring the quality of its music. Many cities are home to "local" musicians who are nationally or even internationally known.

Not all of the clubs in the following pages are for everyone. Some are extremely informal; some are extremely expensive. Still others are located in rough neighborhoods, and should be visited with caution. If you do venture into a rough neighborhood, it's a good idea to arrive early so that you can park near the door. Also, inquire about parking or cab service when you call. Surprisingly enough, some of the tiniest and most unassuming of clubs— Checkerboard's on Chicago's South Side, Eli's Mile High Club in West Oakland—have become so well known that they now offer security parking. Others, located in neglected neighborhoods in major cities, such as Showman's in Harlem, are happy to call cabs for their patrons.

As for the sites mentioned under "Landmarks and Legends," many are abandoned buildings that will be of interest only to a handful of fans, or to the armchair traveler. Others are private homes, and the privacy of their residents should be respected.

Key

Dollar signs are used throughout the book to indicate cover charges and other prices:

$ = inexpensive ($1–$6)
$$ = moderate ($7–$15)
$$$ = expensive ($16–$25)
$$$$ = very expensive ($26 and above)
CC = credit cards accepted

National Sources

Jazz Times (7961 Eastern Ave., Suite 303, Silver Spring, Md. 20910-4898; 301-588-4114 or 800-866-7664) is a monthly available on newsstands that includes some current information on jazz clubs and events in various cities. *Living Blues* (The Center for the Study of Southern Culture, University of Mississippi, University,

Miss. 38677-9990), a bimonthly magazine available by mail only, does the same for blues. *Living Blues* also puts out an inexpensive biannual national blues directory listing club addresses, blues society addresses, booking agents, and more.

Please send all corrections, updates, and suggestions to Christiane Bird, c/o Addison-Wesley, 170 Fifth Avenue, New York, New York, 10010.

The Preservation Hall Jazz Bands have been a New Orleans staple since the 1960's.

Jazz Club Collection, LSM

South

New Orleans

> One of my pleasantest memories as a kid growing up in New Orleans was how a bunch of us kids, playing, would suddenly hear sounds. It was like a phenomenon, like the Aurora Borealis—maybe. The sounds of men playing would be so clear, but we wouldn't be sure where they were coming from. So we'd start trotting, start running—"It's this way!", "It's that way!"— And, sometimes, after running for a while, you'd find you'd be nowhere near that music. But that music could come on you any time like that. The city was full of the sounds of music. . . ."
>
> —*Danny Barker in* Hear Me Talkin' to Ya

The list of New Orleans jazz, blues, and R&B greats is tremendously impressive, beginning with Buddy Bolden, King Oliver, Jelly Roll Morton, Sidney Bechet, Johnny Dodds, and Louis Armstrong, and continuing in more recent times with Professor Longhair, Fats Domino, Dr. John, Allen Toussaint, the Marsalis family, Irma Thomas, and Harry Connick, Jr. In between are scores of other internationally renowned artists playing in a wide variety of styles.

As far as music historians can tell, jazz was first heard on the streets of New Orleans in the late 1800's. A strong African influence (see Congo Square, page 18), combined with Creole and Anglo elements, led to the development of the new sound, which was played in the open air by the city's countless brass bands. Parades, picnics, "lawn parties," and especially funerals—to an early New Orleanian, all called for music.

In 1898, the city's notorious Storyville district was created, and suddenly there were hundreds of jobs for all kinds of musicians. Classically educated Creole musicians, representing the cream of black society, mixed with uneducated musicians playing a more raw, more emotional sound, and "jass," as it was then called, evolved yet further.

Storyville was closed in 1917, the same year a group of white New Orleans musicians, the Original Dixieland Jazz Band, recorded the first jazz record. In 1918, Louis Armstrong began testing his chops by playing on the Streckfus riverboats that plowed the Mississippi, but by 1922 he was gone, up to Chicago to join King Oliver's band.

During the 1920's and '30's, Milneburg on Lake Pontchartrain, 10 miles from downtown New Orleans, was one of the best places in the city to hear jazz. Back then, the shoreline was lined with hundreds of fishing camps built out onto piers over the water, where the town's citizens would come for the weekend, bringing with them food, friends, and private jazz bands. On any given weekend, there might be as many as 50 or 60 jazz groups playing up and down the docks. "We'd hire Papa Celestin's band for thirty-five dollars for the weekend and bring the cook," says jazz historian Al Rose, who lived through those days. "We'd buy a two-hundred-pound green turtle. The Creole word for turtle, 'cawein,' also means picnic, and we'd get on a railroad train that took us to the lake. The train had an empty car on it for the drunks coming back, and they'd be loaded on like cordwood."

The late 1940's, '50's, and '60's brought with them a new urban sound, best represented by the blues and R&B music of such masters as Fats Domino, Professor Longhair, Huey "Piano" Smith, Dr. John, and Irma Thomas. Though less known for its blues than for its jazz, New Orleans has always had a strong blues sensibility, as can be heard in its gospel choirs and honking saxes.

In the 1980's, jazz in New Orleans went through another renaissance, this one led by trumpet player Wynton Marsalis. Along with Wynton came his brothers Branford on sax and Delfeayo on trombone, trumpeter Terence Blanchard, saxophonist Donald Harrison, pianist Harry Connick, Jr., the Dirty Dozen Brass Band, the ReBirth Brass Band, and others.

Sources

Offbeat (522-5533) is an excellent free monthly music guide, written especially for out-of-towners. *Gambit* (486-5900), a free weekly, also has listings, as does the Friday section of the *Times-Picayune* (826-3464). The Basin Street Press publishes a "Jazz Map" of New Orleans, by Dr. Karl Koenig. (For details, write to 1627 S. Van Buren, Covington, La. 70433.) *Offbeat* also publishes the *Louisiana Music Directory,* which includes extensive listings of bands, musicians, booking agents, record labels, clubs, and festivals in Louisiana. (Available in New Orleans bookstores, or write 921 Canal St., Suite 900, New Orleans, La. 70112.)

For general maps and other information, contact the Greater New Orleans Tourist and Convention Commission, 1520 Sugar Bowl Dr., 566-5011, or stop by the Tourist Information Center at 529 Ann St. in the French Quarter.

The area code for New Orleans is (504).

A Note on Neighborhoods

New Orleans is a city deeply rooted in its past. Nothing seems to change here, not the old French Quarter, not the fine Creole cooking, not the love of good times. Tourists may come and go by the thousands, but New Orleans never changes.

"Uptown" New Orleans means anything west of Canal Street, while "Downtown" includes, among other neighborhoods, the historic French Quarter. The Garden District, located Uptown, is an elite nineteenth-century residential neighborhood; Faubourg Marigny, near the French Quarter, is a young, nontourist area known for its avant-garde theaters, art galleries, and music clubs. Tremé, also near the French Quarter, is one of the oldest African-American neighborhoods in the city.

Pete Fountain blows at his namesake club.

Courtesy New Orleans Hilton

Traffic in the French Quarter is often heavy, but otherwise, driving in New Orleans is relatively painless.

Landmarks and Legends

IN AND AROUND THE FRENCH QUARTER

(The following sites can be viewed on foot. The route below begins at the northwestern end of the Quarter, proceeds east and south, and then circles back around to the Uptown side of Canal Street. As of this writing, there are several proposals in the works to create a jazz park, complete with museums and performance venues, in the Canal Street—Basin Street—Armstrong Park area. Hopes are that the proposals will result in federal and/or state funding and the redevelopment of these neighborhoods.)

Storyville, *once bounded by Basin, Robertson, St. Louis, and Iberville streets.*

Storyville, the notorious red-light district whose reputation has taken on mythic proportions over the years, was once located adjacent to the French Quarter, just north of Basin Street. Today, the 16-block area is occupied by the Iberville housing projects and it is marked by an historical plaque on the Basin Street traffic island, near Iberville Street.

Created on January 1, 1898, Storyville was an urban planning experiment designed to stop the spread of whorehouses throughout the city. But much to the chagrin of the city alderman, Sidney Story, for whom it was named, it quickly evolved into virtually a self-contained kingdom of vice. It even had its own mayor, state legislator Tom Anderson, who was also its foremost pimp.

The streets of Storyville were lined with huge, ornate brothels, cabarets, honky-tonks, gambling dens, and dance halls. At one time there were over 2,000 prostitutes working the District, as it was called, and typical prices ranged from as high as $50 in the brothel-mansions, of which there were 30 to 40, to as little as 50 cents in the "cribs," small rooms with doors facing the streets for seductive posturing.

The District provided musicians with a wealth of employment opportunities. All the dance halls needed bands, and all of the major whorehouses had their own steady "professor" or house piano player. Jelly Roll Morton, Tony Jackson, Clarence Williams, and King Oliver were among the hundreds of musicians who once played Storyville.

In 1917, the Secretary of the Navy decreed that the vices of Storyville constituted a threat to America's military forces and shut the District down. Some of its madams moved to the French Quarter, and some of its musicians moved north in a migration that had already begun before 1917.

In addition to this official Storyville, which employed whites, blacks, and octoroons, there was also an unofficial Black Storyville, located just uptown of Canal. Louis Armstrong grew up in Black Storyville.

Lulu White's Saloon, *NW corner of Bienville and Basin streets.*

Lulu White was the most famous madam of Storyville, and Mahogany Hall was the most notorious brothel, with a mirrored parlor that alone was estimated to have cost $30,000. Among the many things White, the aunt of composer Spencer Williams, was famed for were the diamond rings she wore on all her fingers, including her thumbs. She also employed some of the finest piano players in the city, including Jelly Roll Morton and Tony Jackson.

Mahogany Hall is gone now, replaced by a parking garage, but Lulu White's Saloon, a windowless brick building on the corner of Bienville and Basin streets that was once attached to the hall, still stands. The building once had a third floor (torn off by a storm not too long ago) and that's where the legendary "Blue Book," a guide to the ladies of Storyville, was published. It listed its subjects by name, address, and color, with the 1915 edition including nine octoroons, 254 blacks, and 464 whites. The publication also contained advertisements; a sample read:

"Of all the landladies of the Tenderloin, there are few better known or admired than Grace Lloyd. Grace, as she is commonly called by all who know her, is a woman of very rare attainments and comes of that good old English stock from across the waters.

"Grace is regarded as an all-round jolly good fellow, saying nothing about her beauty. She regards life as life and not as a money-making space of time."[1]

Old Storyville cribs, *Bienville between Basin and Crozat streets.*

Of all the hundreds of "cribs" that once existed in Storyville, these are the only ones still standing. According to jazz historian Al Rose, each one of the six compartments in the small two-story building would be rented out to different women for $3 per eight hours, thereby allowing landlords to earn what was then a substantial $12 a day.

Frank Early's Saloon, *SW corner of Bienville and Crozat streets.*

A wonderful old wooden building with shutters and a rickety second-floor balcony, Early's Saloon is now a convenience store for the Iberville projects. Tony Jackson, flamboyant and homosexual and one of the best piano players in the District, was playing here when he wrote the song "Pretty Baby." It was written about another man.

Louis Armstrong Park, *N. Rampart and St. Ann streets.*

Dedicated in 1980 to New Orleans's most famous son, the Louis Armstrong Park today is sadly deserted and run-down, with the sign over its arch in a state of disrepair. Once, however, this whole area (torn down in the 1950's and left abandoned for years), housed dozens of important jazz spots: San Jacinto Hall, the Gypsy Tea Room, Economy Hall, the Frolic, Globe Hall.

Louis Armstrong's solemn statue now stands in a shallow pool to the right of the entrance. The Municipal Auditorium, the Theatre for the Performing Arts, Beauregard Square, and Perseverance Hall are also located here, but the park is no place for a lazy afternoon stroll. It is unpatrolled and should be visited with caution.

Congo Square, *now Beauregard Square, in Armstrong Park.*

In the left-hand corner of the park, near the entrance, is a square lined with dark shiny bricks arranged in dizzying circles. Nowadays the square is usually completely silent, swept clean by the wind, but somehow, as you stand listening, you can almost hear and see it all again . . . the drums, the dancing, the horns, the chanting—the endless lines of people swilling and swirling—the parades, the masks, the mysteries of *voodoo* . . .

Congo Square is the place before the place, the actual spot where, many experts believe, jazz was born. Back in the 1800's the square was the Sunday-afternoon gathering place for African slaves and one of the only spots in the New World where blacks could legally play and dance to the complex polyrhythms of Africa (drum playing was against the law in most parts of the United States, as slave owners felt it led to rioting). Through the performances at the square, the African sounds were not only preserved but also gotten out into the open where they could both influence and be influenced by European music (i.e., become jazz).

Perseverance Hall, *NE corner of Armstrong Park.*

Perseverance Hall, with its imposing Greek Revival facade, is the oldest Masonic Temple in Louisiana, dating back to 1820. During its early years it was both a meeting place for the Masonic Lodge and a sort of civic center for the "free men and women of color" who lived in the nearby Tremé district.

Later the hall was known for its dances. The crowds were white but the bands were black, and the Captains Streckfus, riverboat captains who hired jazzmen to play on their steamboats, would come here looking for players. Buddy Bolden and Kid Rena were among the musicians who played the hall.

The New Orleans Jazz Club Collections, *Louisiana State Museum, United States Mint, 400 Esplanade Ave., 568-8215.*

Started in 1961 by the New Orleans Jazz Club, the collections have had a variety of homes over the years, finally moving into the old United States Mint building as part of the Louisiana State Museum in 1983. The exhibits, which cover one wing of the museum, are large and well presented, with plenty of blown-up photos and memorabilia. Sidney Bechet's soprano sax is here; so are Baby Dodds's drumsticks and Papa Jack Laine's cowbell. One whole case is devoted to Armstrong: highlights are the cornet he learned to play on in the Municipal Boys' Home in 1913 and the bugle he played at home, also in 1913. Another case contains the cuff links Bix Beiderbecke wore shortly before his death, and his handkerchief. These were donated to the museum by Hoagy Carmichael, with a note saying, "You may launder the handkerchief if you wish, but perhaps it is better to display it in its present state of age."

New to the museum in 1993 is a letter of admiration written by Harry Connick, Jr., age ten, to Eubie Blake, age 84. Other new additions in the works include an exhibit on the Marsalis family, and another on the history of New Orleans women in jazz.
Open: T–Su, 10 a.m.–5 p.m. *Admission:* $.

Odd Fellows Masonic Hall, *1116 Perdido St. near S. Rampart St., and* **Eagle Saloon,** *401 S. Rampart St.*

On the second floor of this long, gray building, whose entrance was once through 1116 Perdido, was the Masonic Hall, a popular dance site. The legendary Buddy Bolden was a regular here from 1900 to 1906, as was a floorwalker named Bob Foots, who wore size 14 shoes and carried a nightstick. Beneath the hall was the Eagle Saloon (401 Perdido), from which Frankie Dusen's Eagle Band took its name.

It was in front of the Odd Fellows one Labor Day that Louis Armstrong first heard Sidney Bechet play. All the musicians were working in parades that day, but somehow Bechet had fallen between the cracks. Then Henry Allen, Red Allen's father, spotted him standing near the hall and immediately put him to work. "Bechet joined the band," writes Armstrong in his autobiography

On a summer's day,
young brass bands
take to the streets
in and around Jack-
son Square.

Satchmo, "and he made the whole parade, blowing like crazy. . . . I followed him all that day. There was not a cornet player in New Orleans who was like him. What feeling! What soul! Every other player in the city had to give it to him."

Jane Alley, *between Loyola and S. Rampart streets, directly opposite City Hall.*

Jane Alley, the one-block street where Louis Armstrong was born, supposedly on the Fourth of July, 1900 (though music historians have since established that his true date of birth was August 4, 1901), is now part of an empty lot marked CENTRAL PARKING SYSTEM. On the north side of the lot is a brick wall, over the top of which you'll see a tree, where Armstrong's house once stood (it was torn down in 1964).

In Louis's day the area was known as Black Storyville, or "the Battlefield," and it was a tough part of town, crowded, writes Armstrong in *Satchmo,* with "gamblers, hustlers, cheap pimps, thieves, prostitutes and lots of children." At the age of 12 or 13, Armstrong fired a pistol during a New Year's Eve celebration and was hauled off to jail by a policeman. Two days later, he was sentenced to the Colored Waifs' Home for Boys. All was not lost, however, because he joined the home's brass band and was quickly made its leader.

Red Onion, *762 S. Rampart St. at Julia.*

Back in the 1910's and '20's, the then seedy Red Onion, now a well-kept office building, was a mecca for black and white musicians alike. Jelly Roll Morton, Louis Armstrong, Johnny Dodds and Sidney Bechet all played here; later, in New York in 1924, Louis recorded with several groups called the Red Onion Jazz Babies, one of which included Sidney Bechet. Johnny Dodds also recorded a tune called "Red Onion Blues."

DOWNTOWN

(These sites are best toured by car. The following route begins near the Quarter, and proceeds north and then east, crossing a bridge into the Ninth Ward.)

Jack Laine's home, *2401–2405 Chartres St. at Mandeville.*
Laine, one of the first white jazz musicians, lived in this big white and sky-blue house, complete with a balcony and, today at least, orange trees out front. Laine was a popular bandleader who sometimes had as many as four jobs in one day and is said to have had the first ragtime marching band in the city.

Italian Hall, *1020 Esplanade Ave., near N. Rampart St.*
A handsome mauve-and-white building with lions at its door, the Italian (now condominiums) was a popular dance hall during the 1920's. The first racially mixed recording in the South was made here when a white clarinetist sat in with a black band called the Jones and Collins Astoria Hot Eight.

Sidney Bechet's home, *1507 Marais St., near St. Bernard.*
Bechet, the Creole clarinetist and soprano saxophonist who would later go on to become a national celebrity in France (Nice has a statue dedicated to him), grew up in this small, somewhat dilapidated wooden house with the big front porch. As a young boy, Bechet began playing with his brother's Silver Bells Band, but even back then he knew he wanted a different sound. "I could see there was other bands who were doing more to advance ragtime, playing it with a better feeling," he writes in his autobiography, *Treat It Gentle.* "I'd listen and I'd get the feeling terrible strong that I wanted to play how they were playing." Before long, young Bechet, then only about 10, formed his first band, the seven-piece Young Olympia Band, with trumpet player Buddy Petit. The young men had considerable success, playing many kinds of engagements—balls, banquets, and parades—all over the city.

The Alley, *off Claiborne Ave., near St. Bernard St.*
Just west of the Circle Mart located at the southwest corner of Claiborne and St. Bernard is an extremely narrow alleyway. Back in the 1910's, before unions, this tiny space was usually jammed with musicians looking for work. A prospective employer would come here and shout out what he wanted—a drummer, a trumpet player, a piano player; $4 for the night—and would often conduct an audition right on the spot.

Edward Boatner's home, *2139 Ursulines Ave., at Galvez.*

This large, two-story, green building with columns and a gate was once home to Detroit preacher and composer Edward Boatner, who wrote not only the religious classic "He's Got the Whole World in His Hands" but also the jazz classic "When the Saints Go Marching In." According to jazz historian Al Rose, "Saints" was first published in a Baptist hymnal in 1916 and it was Louis Armstrong who first turned it into a jazz hit in 1936. Boatner's son was the jazz saxophonist Sonny Stitt.

Jelly Roll Morton's home, *1441–1443 Frenchmen St., at Robertson.*

This very attractive dark-red house, built in the traditional mid-nineteenth-century Creole style, was the boyhood home of composer and piano player Jelly Roll Morton (Ferdinand La Menthe). Born into a well-educated family, Morton learned to play a number of instruments as a child, eventually settling on the piano.

In *Mister Jelly Roll,* by Alan Lomax, Ferdinand states that he was first exposed to music at the age of six months. A "sporting woman" to whom his godmother had "loaned" him was arrested and thrown into jail, along with her young charge. "The inmates were singing and making a lot of noise . . ." says Jelly Roll, "and, as long as they would sing, it would keep the baby happy."

Fats Domino's home, *NW corner, Caffin Ave. and Marais St.*

Antoine Domino grew up in this working-class neighborhood in the lower Ninth Ward, located just beyond the Industrial Canal, and even after making it big, he vowed he'd never leave. The house where he now lives, just a few streets away from his boyhood home, surely stands out, though: it is three times bigger than anything else in sight, a tan-brick 1950's-style residence with a peaked roof, pink and yellow trim, a white wrought-iron fence with pink and green roses, and surveillance cameras.

Inside, rumor has it, there are crystal chandeliers, four ivory dominos set into the tile of a white marble floor, and closets filled with hundreds of wonderful suits in all colors of the rainbow. Fats's favorite room is said to be the kitchen, for he loves to cook, and even when he travels, packs hotplates and cooking gear along with his clothes and musical equipment.

UPTOWN

(The following route, best toured by car, begins at Constance Street and proceeds as far north as La Salle Street and as far west as Webster.)

Nick LaRocca's home, *2216 Constance St. near Philip.*

LaRocca, the leader of and cornet player for the Original Dixieland Jazz Band (the group that made the first jazz recording in

1917), had a musical staff imprinted on his front door. The notes, still there today, spell out the beginning of the jazz classic, "Tiger Rag."

Professor Longhair's home, *1740 Terpsichore St. near Baronne.*

The house is brown, wooden, and typically New Orleans, this last abode of the Professor, who lived here for only a short period prior to his death. That period was one of the few happy ones of his life.

Fess's story is an all-too-familiar one. Born Henry Roeland Byrd in 1918, he grew up haunting the clubs of Rampart Street and did some recording for Atlantic in the early 1950's. Nothing really took off, though, and Fess sank into a long and impoverished obscurity until 1970, when a British blues journalist, Mike Leadbitter, found him sweeping out the floor of a record shop. After this, a New Orleans promoter, Quint Davis, set about resuscitating his career. "He was in a totally depreciated state physically, . . ." Davis once said. "When he sat down, he couldn't get up. When he did stand up, his knee would rattle around until it set into a groove so he could walk. He had a vitamin deficiency, he had no teeth, no digestion, and he couldn't go to the bathroom."[2]

One of Davis's first moves was to book the Professor into the New Orleans Jazz and Heritage Festival (an event that Davis had helped launch), and from then on, Fess's luck began to change. He

Basin Street was once lined with innumerable dens of iniquity, from whose windows poured "jass."

Jazz Club Collection, LSM

BASIN St

began playing at local clubs and international festivals, released two albums and became part owner of the club Tipitina's (see "Clubs, etc.," page 34).

In 1980, shortly after moving to this house, Fess was on the brink of national stardom. His concerts were attracting more and more attention; he was scheduled to be taped for a television documentary; and his already sold-out album, *Crawfish Fiesta,* was about to be released. But it was not to be. On the morning of January 30, the Professor died in his sleep. He is buried beneath a piano-shaped tombstone in the Mt. Olivet Cemetery in Gentilly, a parish of New Orleans.

Dew Drop Inn Café and Bar, *2836 La Salle St., near Washington.*

In the 1940's and '50's, the Dew Drop Inn was the most famous African-American nightclub in New Orleans. Known for its R&B talent, it featured everyone from national names like Big Joe Turner, Little Richard and Dinah Washington to local up-and-comers like Guitar Slim, Charles Neville, and Allen Toussaint. Big-name entertainers—Duke Ellington, Ray Charles, Ella Fitzgerald—also stopped in whenever they were in town.

According to *Up From the Cradle of Jazz* by Berry, Foose, and Jones, the club was started by chance by a barber named Frank Painia, who began selling refreshments out of his shop when city workers building a nearby housing project needed a place to buy lunch. The shop eventually grew into a restaurant, which grew into a nightclub.

Because it was the late '40's and the Dew Drop was an African-American club, it was against the law for whites to enter. As word about the Dew Drop spread, however, whites began frequenting the club, with owner Painia welcoming everyone. This led to periodic raids. One case in 1952, involving white movie star Zachary Scott, made the papers, and as late as 1964, Painia, who was still being harassed, filed suit in federal court to challenge the constitutionality of the law. The passage of the Civil Rights Act by Congress that same year made the case moot and it was dropped.

The Dew Drop closed in 1972, following the death of Frank Painia, but the place (now an empty building, though the sign DEW DROP INN. HOTEL/LOUNGE/RESTAURANT is still intact) lives on in memories and in the words of the song "Jumpin' at the Dew Drop," by Ivory Joe Hunter: "Jumping at the Dew Drop, meet you down there / Jumping at the Dew Drop, really send you / They swing and they boogie and they groove some, too / If you don't enjoy, there's something wrong with you."

Buddy Bolden's home, *2309 First St., just off La Salle St.*

Of all the figures in jazz history, Buddy Bolden is the most elusive. One of the first jazzmen—some say *the* first—and idolized by musicians and audiences all over the city, he is shrouded in legend.

They say that he could memorize music instantly; that the ladies followed him wherever he went; that he drank heavily; that he was never slow to pick a fight.

Some things, however, are known to be fact: Bolden did blow a mean cornet, he did die in a mental institution, and he did live at 2309 First from 1887 to 1906. In fact, he used to sit on the front steps of this small yellow house with the red trim and play jazz duets with Harry Shields, a white clarinet player who lived down the street.

By the time Bolden went insane in 1906–7, he had left this house and moved in with his mother and sister at 2302 First. As he became increasingly violent and incoherent, his family, not knowing what else to do, called the police. They placed him first in a common jail cell, then in the Jackson State Hospital for the insane, where he died, oblivious to his surroundings, nearly 20 years later.

OTHER NEARBY SITES

New Orleans Fairgrounds, *near Gentilly Blvd. and Esplanade Ave., not far from City Park (5 min. N of Quarter).*

The premier music festival in the United States takes place every late April on the grassy grounds of the New Orleans race track (see "Major Festivals," page 403). Now ten days in length, the extravaganza presents more than 3,000 musicians playing jazz, blues, R&B, gospel, zydeco, Cajun, Afro-Caribbean, ragtime, folk, country-and-western, Latin, and more. The event is also known for its food—boiled crawfish, jambalaya, gumbo, etc.—and its crowds, a total of about 360,000 at last count.

The first forerunner of today's New Orleans Jazz & Heritage fest took place in May 1968, as part of the 250th birthday celebration of the city. Back then, the events were free and held downtown on Canal Street and in what is now Armstrong Park. Louis Armstrong, Dave Brubeck, Duke Ellington, Pete Fountain, and Woody Allen (who flew in from filming *Bananas*) were among the headliners.

Marsalis Motel, *corner of Shrewsbury and River roads (25 min. W of French Quarter).*

Ellis Marsalis, Sr., father of Ellis Marsalis, Jr., and grandfather of Wynton, Branford, and Delfeayo, once ran a motel out of this one-story brown building in a residential area of Jefferson Parish. Ellis Sr. was an influential local businessman who did much to promote civil rights in New Orleans, but he reportedly was none too happy when his son, Ellis Jr., began running a jazz club out of the family motel in the 1950's. Ellis Jr. has since served as a sort of mentor and role model to dozens of today's New Orleans musicians.

Lake Pontchartrain and **Milneburg Lighthouse** *(10 min. N of Quarter)*.

Many visitors to New Orleans never make it out to the lake, and that's a shame because it's a beautiful sight (even though the lake is polluted), a pale blue expanse stretching as far as the eye can see. Fishermen sit along its edges, casting their lines; sailboats tack gently in the wind, their bright sails billowing in the breeze.

During the early years of jazz, the lake resounded with music. First there was the West End, where from the late 1890's to 1910 or so public concerts were held in large outdoor bandstands. Then there was Spanish Fort, which was basically an amusement park with entertainment stages. Finally, on the eastern end of the lake, there was Milneburg, a mind-boggling place where 50 to 60 top-quality bands played up and down the docks.

All of that is gone now, replaced by landfill and the University of New Orleans, but the names of two of the lake's three main resorts, Milneburg and West End, remain as a sort of legacy, along with the Milneburg Lighthouse. Spanish Fort is no more.

A scenic lakeshore drive follows the shoreline between West End and Milneburg.

Clubs, etc.

Jazz and blues still flourish in New Orleans, though they're neither as plentiful nor as concentrated as one might wish. The French Quarter, once a mecca for jazz fans, now has very few good jazz spots, and those that do exist are on the area's fringes. Bourbon Street itself has become a wasteland, lined with sex shows, souvenir shops, and third-rate music clubs, all of which loudly hawk their wares to the droves of tourists, who stroll, drinks in hand, from one amusement to another. At its best, the street feels like a seedy carnival filled with characters; at its worst, it's a cheap, exploitative tourist trap.

To find good jazz and blues in New Orleans, as elsewhere in the country, you have to look. Most of what you'll hear here is New Orleans–style jazz, in both its traditional and contemporary forms, but modern jazz can also be found. Touring blues acts are most frequently booked into **Tipitina's** and **House of Blues.**

Some of the many players to watch out for include oldtime veterans Danny Barker, the Humphrey Brothers, Wendell and John Brunious, and Pud Brown; pianist Ellis Marsalis; bassist Walter Payton; trumpet players Wallace Davenport and Nicholas Payton; bluesmen Bryan Lee, Walter Washington, and George Porter; Tuba Fats; Snooks Eaglin; clarinetists Pete Fountain and Chris Burke; sax player James Rivers; vocalist and bandleader Banu Gibson; vocalists Charmaine Neville, Irma Thomas, and Marva Wright; the ReBirth Brass Band, the Olympia Brass Band, the Young Olympians Brass Band, Trombone Shorty's brass band, and Tony Dagradi & Astral Project.

Many clubs in New Orleans are open until 4 or 5 a.m. on the weekends, but live music generally stops at 2 a.m.

Personal Choices

Best club for New Orleans music: *Tipitina's*
Best-known jazz club: *Preservation Hall*
Best modern jazz club: *Snug Harbor*
Best traditional jazz club: *Maxwell's Toulouse Cabaret*
Best jazz restaurant: *Palm Court*
Best neighborhood jazz joint: *Trombone Shorty's*
Best (and oddest) blues club: *Mid-City Lanes*
Most atmospheric jazz/blues spots: *Warehouse Café, Columns Hotel*

FOR JAZZ

IN AND AROUND THE FRENCH QUARTER

Preservation Hall, *726 St. Peter St., 523-8939.*

Well, here it is, the most famous jazz joint in New Orleans. Too bad it's so crowded, too bad it's so hot, too bad the musicians all seem so tired.

Preservation Hall has contributed much to New Orleans's music history. In 1961, when it was founded by Allan and Sandra Jaffe, there was no place in the whole city of New Orleans in which to hear authentic jazz played by its originators. Oh, sure, there was *jazz*, in fact there was lots of *jazz*, all up and down Bourbon Street, but most of it was young and most of it was white.

Preservation Hall (which many skeptics predicted would die an early death) and the Jaffes, through much personal sacrifice, changed all that. They gave the older traditional African-American jazzmen—Kid Thomas, Punch Miller, George Lewis, Willie and Percy Humphrey—a forum in which to play; and before long, the place began attracting national attention. The Jaffes' next step was to book their bands out of town, and eventually they developed a highly successful touring schedule placing three Preservation Hall bands on the road at the same time.

Preservation Hall is still a must stop, especially if Pud Brown or the Humphrey Brothers are playing (many of the other older musicians have passed away). But a visit here does come as a disappointment. The cover is so blessedly low that it means there's always a wait (an hour or more isn't unusual), and it's always jammed with chattering tourists. Also, the decor is almost too simple for a place so successful—a few battered wooden benches and peeling, dingy walls—and the musicians, old masters though they are, all too often seem bored.

Music: nightly. *Cover:* $.

The "ladies" of Storyville once hawked their wares from "cribs" facing the street.

Club Second Line, *216 Bourbon St., 523-2020.*
Dixieland can be heard most afternoons and evenings at this large, neat club, furnished with lots of small round tables and chairs. Though the club caters primarily to tourists and tour groups, the music is usually quite good, thanks to the house band, the Crescent City Five. Some weekend nights feature top blues or R&B acts such as Luther Kent or Marva Wright.
Music: daily, M–F from 5 p.m., Sa–Su from 1 p.m. *Cover/minimum:* $, $$–$$$ for special acts.

Jelly Roll's, *501 Bourbon St., 568-0501.*
Back in the 1960s and '70s, No. 501 Bourbon was the home of trumpet player Al Hirt. Today, the legendary New Orleanian takes up residence in the club once again, this time playing upstairs in "Jumbo's Room" (named after him; Jumbo is his nickname) on Saturdays and Mondays, while the Dukes of Dixieland play downstairs. The club is large and spacious, and geared primarily toward tourists. Hirt's shows last exactly one hour and 15 minutes; R&B is often featured late nights.
Music: most nights. *Cover:* $ downstairs, $$$ upstairs. Reservations highly recommended upstairs.

Maison Bourbon, *641 Bourbon St., 522-8818.*
A pleasant club with pleasant jazz, the Maison started out 22 years ago as a sidewalk cafe and still has that casual outdoor feel.

The tables and chairs are lined up in rows beneath hanging plants, and there's a sultry mural of a Bourbon Street parade on one wall.

The club has a longstanding tradition of featuring outstanding trumpet players. Names from the past include Thomas Jefferson and Wallace Davenport, who still plays here on occasion. A traditionalist's complaint: there's no standard front line.
Music: daily, from mid-afternoon on. *Cover/minimum:* $.

Maxwell's Toulouse Cabaret, *615 Toulouse St., 523-4207.*

Traditional jazzman and big-band leader Jimmy Maxwell, long the musician of choice at the city's most exclusive Carnival balls, now runs his own jazz joint, together with his brother and sister, John and Peggy. The club is located in the old Toulouse Theatre, where the Broadway hit *One Mo' Time* originated and the legendary piano player James Booker once performed.

In addition to Jimmy and his orchestra, regulars at Maxwell's include Rene Netto & the Sounds of New Orleans and the Milneburg Joys. On Sunday nights, New Orleans District Attorney Harry Connick, *Sr.* (that's right), sings standards along with Jimmy's band. According to a local reporter, the father's voice is somewhat reminiscent of the son's, but "more mature and less nasal."

The Maxwells have converted the building's former lobby into a bar, complete with Second Line umbrellas (HAND DECORATED BY MOTHER MAXWELL) hanging from the ceiling, and a souvenir shop. The music room in back is all done up in black, and sight lines are excellent. Shows last exactly one hour, but there's no additional cover for the second set unless a crowd is waiting outside.
Music: nightly. *Cover:* $$$, includes one cocktail. CC. Reservations recommended.

Palm Court Jazz Café, *1204 Decatur St., 525-0200.*

Nina Buck, wife of George, founder of Jazzology (the world's oldest independent jazz record label), GHB, and other record labels, opened this winsomely pretty restaurant in 1989 and it's been a local favorite ever since. Recently expanded into an enormous back room, complete with high ceilings, lace curtains, and slowly spinning fans, it is one of the few places in New Orleans where you can dine while listening to jazz. Veteran musicians such as Pud Brown or Percy Humphrey are often on tap, and the Creole food is both delicious and reasonably priced. George Buck's records are for sale along one wall.
Music: W–Su. *Cover:* $. *Food:* Creole. CC. Reservations recommended.

Snug Harbor Jazz Bistro, *626 Frenchmen St. (Faubourg Marigny), 949-0696.*

The best place in the city for modern jazz, Snug Harbor is a spacious club-restaurant with brick floors, blond wood, and a young urban crowd. Dinner is served in the front rooms, by big picture windows and a blue aquarium, while the music takes place out back in a large, high-ceilinged space rimmed with a balcony. There's also a friendly bar area up front, lined with stools, mirrors, and hanging plants. Charmaine Neville, Walter Washington, and Ellis Marsalis are regulars here.

Music: nightly. *Cover:* $$. *Food:* Creole. CC. Advance music ticket sales available; no reservations taken for dinner.

Horizons, *New Orleans Hilton, 2 Poydras St., 561-0500.*

High atop the Hilton, on the edge of the Mississippi River, is one of the city's most upscale clubs. Recently done over to the tune of half a million, it boasts a lot of comfortable black booths, tables and chairs, a polished dance floor, and spectacular views of the city. Saxman James Rivers and vocalist Luther Kent, both Crescent City favorites, are regulars here, along with vocalist Estella Denson.

Music: F–Sa, M, Tu, some other nights. *Cover:* $.

Pete Fountain's, *New Orleans Hilton, 2 Poydras St., 561-0500.*

The famous jazz clarinetist, who used to run his own place on Bourbon Street, now has a jazz club on the third level of the Hilton Hotel. The new place—all brown and deep red decor—is a snazzy reproduction of the old. Fountain's shows, which seat 500, are enjoyable but tightly controlled and no bargain. He starts each night at 10 and ends at 11:15 sharp.

Music: Tu, W, F, Sa. *Cover:* $$$. Amex only. Reservations required.

Also

Café Brasil (Frenchmen St. at Chartres, 947-9386), a hip, eclectic club best known for its Brazilian and world music, often has jazz on Mondays and Thursdays in the early evening. Outdoor afternoon jazz can be heard at the **Gazebo** (1018 Decatur St., 522-0862), a pretty little place with dainty green tables, pink-cushioned chairs, and a simple, imaginative menu. **Fritzel's** (733 Bourbon St., 561-0432), a casual, comfortable bar, located somewhat off the tourist track, also offers worthwhile jazz, usually on the weekends.

ELSEWHERE IN THE CITY

Trombone Shorty's, *1533 St. Philip at Robertson (Tremé, 5 min. from Quarter), 523-1481.*

A one-room neighborhood joint with its doors usually left wide open to let in some air, Trombone Shorty's packs them in on Sunday nights when young, handsome James Andrews and his brass band (including his 11-year-old trombone-playing brother, Troy Michael, after whom the band and club are named) take to the stage. Dancers go crazy, spinning and swirling, as soon as the music starts, while the band members themselves weave in, out, and about the crowd. Musicians from all over the city, including students from the University of New Orleans, often come by to sit in.

For the most part, the club's clientele is young, black, and neighborhood hip, but a few white and older folk are always among them. Outside and up and down the street there's usually a lot of cruising going on.

Lois Andrews, James's mother, is the brains behind the place, and she can usually be found working the bar. Photographs of musicians plaster the stark white walls and ceiling; other bands, such as the Soul Rebels, also play here.
Music: Su, many Sa. *Cover:* none.

Joe's Cozy Corner, *1532 Ursulines Ave., at Robertson (Tremé, 5 min. from Quarter), 561-9216.*
Just down the street from Shorty's is another hot neighborhood joint, this one catering to a slightly older and more sedate crowd. Run by Joe Glasper and his family, the club is long, neat, and compact, with a bar in the front room and music in the back. Pictures and photographs hang from the walls, and pink tablecloths drape the tables.

The legendary bassist Walter Payton is a regular here, as is Smokie Johnson, who once played with Fats Domino. Other musicians often sit in, and well-known professionals such as Wynton Marsalis have been known to stop by. On Monday nights, the club gives away free plates of its "Blue Monday Special"—red beans and rice.
Music: Su–Tu, mostly jazz, some R&B. *Cover:* none.

Columns Hotel, *3811 St. Charles Ave. (10 min. from Quarter), 899-9308.*
Built in 1881 and on the National Register of Historic Places, the Columns is one of those lovely Southern mansions with big white pillars and enormous spreading trees out front. Over the last three years, it has also developed a reputation for presenting first-rate jazz (albeit only once a week). The music usually comes compliments of Tony Dagradi & Astral Project, who play a contemporary New Orleans sound that attracts a large and enthusiastic following. The music's setting is magnificent: a pale blue and pink ballroom with 20-foot-high ceilings and marble fireplaces.
Music: Th. *Cover:* $. *Food:* Creole, Cajun, Continental; available in the Patio Tea Room across the hall. CC.

Sandbar, *University of New Orleans campus at the Cove (on shore of Lake Pontchartrain, near corner of Elysian Fields Ave. and Leon C. Simon Dr.; 15 min. from Quarter), 286-6381.*
A small and unassuming pub with low lighting, cork walls, and excellent acoustics, the Sandbar is one of the best places in the city to hear up-and-coming talent. Students enrolled in the university's

jazz studies program (directed by Ellis Marsalis) play here regularly, and the club is also a favorite haunt of UNO's jazz faculty and visiting professionals. Some of the many who've performed at the Sandbar include Marcus Roberts, Ed Blackwell, Harold Battiste, and Donald Harrison.
Music: W and occasional other nights, during the academic year only. *Cover:* $.

Winnah's Circle, *2169 Aubry St. (just off St. Bernard, at Galvez; 10 min. from Quarter), 948-2212.*
There's no sign outside this small trim house—just a window pulsating with light—but inside, Ms. Sylvia Crier runs a sophisticated neighborhood club that presents a mix of jazz, pop, soul, and R&B. Crier, who's a high school economics teacher and the former owner of a race horse, named the club after her favorite sport in hopes that her horse would finally win a race. (He did, she says, shortly after she opened the club.) Bright red tablecloths adorn the tables, and tiny red Christmas-tree lights decorate the walls. Regulars include vocalist Big Al, and Walter Payton. A security guard stands outside, keeping watch over the parking lot.
Music: Tu, F–Su. *No cover.*

Also

The **Warehouse Café** (see "For Blues" page 34) frequently presents many of the city's top younger brass bands. **Kemp's** (2720 La Salle St., bet. Washington and Fourth, 891-2738), a neighborhood club similar in spirit to Trombone Shorty's and Joe's Cozy Corner, presents jazz on Sundays and Mondays.

Jazz Brunch

The jazz brunch was supposedly originated by Ella Brennan of the famous Brennan restaurant family. Since then, the idea has spread all over the city, and although the music is usually only pleasant background sound, the food—this being New Orleans— is always first-rate. Some of the more popular spots are listed here.
The Commander's Palace (1403 Washington Ave., 899-8221), in the Garden District, is an amazing bright blue Victorian mansion and 1920's bordello turned restaurant. Run by the Brennan family. Jazz brunches Sa–Su. $$$. CC. Reservations recommended, jackets required on Sundays.
Arnaud's (813 Bienville St., 523-5433), one of the most famous fine Creole restaurants in the French Quarter, serves a Sunday brunch accompanied by a jazz trio. Brunch $$$. CC. Reservations recommended.
Mr. B's (201 Royal St., 523-2078), one of New Orleans's "best-kept secrets," is also run by the Brennan family. Brunch on Sundays often features the Original Crescent City Jazz Band. $$$. CC. Reservations recommended.

La Gauloise in the Meridien Hotel (614 Canal St., 527-6712) is a "true" French restaurant with a Sunday buffet jazz brunch. $$$. CC. Reservations recommended.

Other restaurants offering jazz brunches include the medieval-like **Court of Two Sisters** (613 Royal St., 522-7261), the **Top of the Dome Restaurant** in the Hyatt Regency (500 Poydras Plaza, 561-1234; during football season only), **Kabby's** in the Hilton (2 Poydras St., 561-0500), and **Le Jardin** at the Westin (100 Iberville St., 566-7006).

FOR BLUES

IN AND AROUND THE FRENCH QUARTER

Old Absinthe House Bar, *400 Bourbon St., 525-8108 (not to be confused with the Old Absinthe House at 240 Bourbon).*

With its fine house band, Bryan Lee and the Jump Street Five, this is the only club on Bourbon Street that offers decent blues on a regular basis. Lee, a blind white bluesman from Minnesota, has been playing here five nights a week for the past 11 years, and he always puts on a tight show. B. B. King and Robert Plant have been visitors here; Cyndi Lauper sat in with the band once.

The Absinthe House dates back to 1806, when it served as a coffeehouse for area businessmen and planters, some of whom posted their "dueling cards" up on the wall, near the ceiling. Back in those days, duels—which were common in Louisiana—got started with a polite exchange of these cards, and though the cards have since turned black from years of rising nicotine, they're still up there. The lower walls are covered with a modern-day substitute: business cards.

Meanwhile, the wall behind the bar, not to be outdone, is padded with a three-inch layer of dollar bills. During World War II, men going off to war put their name and date of departure on these bills as a sort of good luck charm. The tradition has continued up to today and there's an estimated $2,200 up there now, some of it dating back to the war.

Music: nightly. *Cover/minimum:* $.

House of Blues, *225 Decatur St. (French Quarter).*

The second House of Blues (see Boston, page 158) opened at this location on New Year's Eve 1993–94. Check the local papers for updated information.

Vic's Kangaroo Cafe, *636 Tchoupitoulas St. (1½ blocks from Poydras), 524-4329 or G'DAY.*

Located in the rapidly gentrifying Warehouse District, Vic's is a little bit of the Land Down Under transported to New Orleans. A hopping joint on a hopping corner, the place—long and narrow, with a bar to one side, a step-up stage on the other—is usually packed with an enthusiastic 20-something crowd. Australian flags, stuffed koala bears, and pictures of kangaroos seem to be everywhere.

Blues-rock happens here on Saturday nights, and jazz is sometimes presented during the week. Vic's is also known for its Australian wines and bar food, including "dog's eye" (meat pie) and "snag roll" (sausage roll). The kitchen remains open until 3 a.m.

Music: Sa, some other nights. *Cover:* none. *Food:* Australian, etc.

ELSEWHERE IN THE CITY

Warehouse Café, *1179 Annunciation (10 min. from Quarter), 586-1282*

Further west in the Warehouse District, in an old "cottage" dating back to the 1860's, is the creaky, comfortable Warehouse Café which seems tailor-made for jazz and blues. On one side is a beer-soaked bar; on the other, a stage, wooden dance floor, fireplace, and scattered tables and chairs. Crooked brick walls, huge exposed beams, old carousel horses, and tiny colored lights complete the club's hodgepodge feel.

Regulars at the Warehouse include many of the area's better-known young brass bands, including the ReBirth Brass Band and the Young Olympians Brass Band.

Music: F–Sa. *Cover:* $–$$. *Food:* Creole, Cajun.

Tipitina's, *501 Napolean Ave. (Uptown, 15 min. from Quarter), 895-8477.*

Simply to call Tip's one of New Orleans's best nightclubs would be to do it a disservice. It is that, but it's also much more. This is not just another successful music club.

Named after the song by Professor Longhair, Tipitina's was founded in 1977 by a group of New Orleanians who saw a need for a large music hall featuring all kinds of sound—blues, R&B, rock, jazz, reggae, Cajun, alternative. Professor Longhair, a close friend of the group's, was in the midst of his comeback then, and there was no place in New Orleans for him—or anyone like him—to play. There was also no place for the city's many different ethnic populations to mix.

After much searching the group found its current cavernous location (previously a livery, bordello, boxing gym, bar room, and meeting place for the Ku Klux Klan), and almost immediately the place took off. It became, and still is, home base for the Neville Brothers, the Radiators, and Dr. John, not to mention Professor Longhair himself, who as part owner played here several times a month while he was still alive.

Most major blues acts have passed through Tipitina's, where they play on a big black stage, surrounded by balconies, while the crowd dances the southern nights away. Makers of the film *The Big Easy* even came here, hoping to catch some of the club's magic on celluloid, but Tip's was temporarily closed at the time and so the movie—rumors to the contrary—was actually shot at a nearby dance hall.

Music: nightly. *Cover:* $–$$$. Amex.

Mid-City Lanes, *4133 S. Carrollton Ave. (Uptown, 15 min. from Quarter), 482-3133.*

Everything's painted pale blue and pink inside this creaky old 18-lane bowling alley, built in 1941, that's recently become one of the hottest, and weirdest, blues joints in the city. Where else can you listen to the honks, riffs, and howls of the likes of Snooks Eaglin, the Iguanas, or George Porter while picking up a 7–10 split?

Even so, the history behind the place is even stranger. It all began back in 1988, when owner John Blancher, then in his mid-thirties, went on a pilgrimage to the city of Medjugorje, in what was then Yugoslavia, with the hopes of seeing an apparition of the Virgin Mary (reports of such apparitions were in the news at the time). He had no such luck, but while there placed a wish in a mountainside altar asking that he find something that his whole family could get involved in. One week later, back in New Orleans, someone asked him if he wanted to buy a bowling alley.

Blancher, who'd worked as a teacher, insurance agent, and caterer, but never as anything remotely resembling a bowling alley owner, gamely put in his bid, and three months later, Mid-City was his. Today, he can be found working most nights alongside his wife, Deborah, his parents, his sister, and his kids.

There are two music stages at Mid-City (two bands play most nights), one on either side of the bar/shoe rental shop, and lots of ceiling fans. In one corner is a small café with muraled walls depicting 1950's New Orleans.

Music: W–Sa, some Su, much blues. *Cover:* $.

Muddy Waters, *8301 Oak St. (Uptown, 15 min. from the Quarter), 866-7174.*

A large neighborhood club near Tulane University, Muddy Waters features blues approximately two days a week and rock-and-roll the rest of the time. Run by the Sullivans, an Australian family who came to New Orleans expressly for the purpose of opening a music club, it has a relaxed, friendly feel. Several nights of the week are devoted to "new" bands, while one or two nights a month feature "jazz and poetry" sessions. Some of the better-known blues artists who've performed here include Snooks Eaglin, Marva Wright, and Walter Washington.

Music: nightly, some blues. *Cover:* $.

Maple Leaf Bar, *8316 Oak St., 866-9359 or 866-LEAF.*

Located in two adjacent narrow buildings across the street from Muddy Waters, the Maple Leaf is better known for Cajun and zydeco than it is for pure blues. Inside, the old buildings have tin

ceilings, revolving fans, and a small balcony; outside, there's a patio that's open during the summer months.
Music: nightly. *Cover:* $.

Also

Carrollton Station (8140 Willow St., 865-9190) is a friendly neighborhood bar, partly done up in a nautical motif (the owner is a sailor), that features blues on the weekends. **Madigan's** (800 S. Carrollton Ave., 866-9455), located just down the street from Carrollton Station, has blues on Sunday nights. Blues and/or R&B can also be heard at many of the jazz clubs listed above.

Other Venues and Special Events

On any given Saturday or Sunday, the streets of the French Quarter, especially Jackson Square and Royal Street, are bursting with music. Up to 35 groups—some jazz, some folk, some blues—perform. Some of it is quite good, but most of it is mediocre to awful.

Street music has such a history in New Orleans, beginning with its early marching brass bands and funeral processions, that it's hard to believe it was ever frowned upon. Yet from the 1930's to the '70's, the streets of the city were almost musically dormant, so much so that when, in 1973, trumpet player Scotty Hill (then newly returned from San Francisco, where street music was everywhere) started playing on a local corner, he was arrested.

Eventually, of course, the case was resolved, permits were issued, and a new era of New Orleans street music began. Hill still plays the streets on occasion with his six-piece traditional French Market Jazz Band. (Watch for a Scottish-looking guy dressed in plaid). Others worth watching out for include Anthony "Tuba Fats" Lacen (who also plays at Preservation Hall) and the talented high-school-aged brass bands who usually play in Jackson Square.

The *Creole Queen* (524-0814), leaving from the Poydras Street Wharf near Riverwalk, offers a jazz dinner cruise every evening. The *Steamboat Natchez* (586-8777), which leaves from the Toulouse Street Wharf behind Jackson Brewery, offers day and nighttime Dixieland cruises.

Photographer Johnny Donnels, who runs a gallery at 634 St. Peters St. (525-6438), specializes in jazz and New Orleans photography.

In addition to the world-famous **New Orleans Jazz and Heritage Festival** (see "Major Festivals," page 403), the three-day **French Quarter Festival** (522-5730) is held every April, and the **Tomato Festival,** featuring brass bands and Caribbean music, is held in early June.

Radio

WWOZ/90.7 FM (568-1238). Premier station for New Orleans sounds. Noncommercial.

WWNO/89.9 FM (286-7000). NPR affiliate, run by the University of New Orleans. Jazz late nights; blues, M nights.

WTUL/91.5 FM (865-5887). Student-run station, affiliated with Tulane University. Some jazz and/or blues daily.

Jazz and blues can also be heard occasionally on **WYAT/990 AM** and **WYLD/940 AM**.

Record Stores

The **Louisiana Music Factory** (225 N. Peters, 523-1094) specializes in Louisiana music. **Tower Records** (Jackson Brewery, 408 N. Peters St. at Decatur St., 529-4411) and the **Sound Warehouse** (231 N. Carrollton Ave., 484-7200, or 5300 Tchoupitoulas, 891-4026) also offer a good selection of local artists; the **Palm Court Jazz Record Center** (Palm Court Café, 1204 Decatur St., 525-0200) offers much in the way of traditional jazz. Other stores include **Hot Wax** (722 Orleans St., 525-4249), which specializes in New Orleans R&B; **Jim Russell Rare Records** (1837 Magazine St., 522-2602), which specializes in New Orleans and hard-to-find artists; **Record Ron's** (1129 Decatur St., 524-9444), **Record Ron's Too** (407 Decatur St., 525-2852), and **Record Ron's Stuff** (239 Chartres St., 522-2239), carrying new, used, and rare records, tapes, and CDs.

Elsewhere in Louisiana

Just over an hour away from New Orleans, in the city of Baton Rouge, is one of the best blues joints around, **Tabby's Blues Box & Heritage Hall** (1314 North Blvd., 387-9715). It's run by Rockin' Tabby Thomas, a singer-guitarist–keyboard player whose last album was *King of the Swamp Blues* (Maison de Soul label). There's music at Tabby's most weekend nights.

Mem phis

Of all the cities in the United States, none is closer to the blues than Memphis, Tennessee. From the early 1900's on, blues musicians from all over the South and especially the Mississippi Delta came here to seek their fortunes after leaving small poverty-ridden homes in farming and plantation communities. W. C. Handy, Bukka White, Furry Lewis, Memphis Slim, Memphis Minnie, Big Joe Williams, Riley "B.B." King, Bobby "Blue"

Bland—they all came here, some to stay for good, others to begin a journey that would eventually take them around the world.

The central gathering spot for blues musicians in Memphis was Beale Street (see "Landmarks and Legends," page 39). Here, they could play for tips on street corners, or—if they were lucky—perform in the local theaters and clubs. From 1912 to 1918, W. C. Handy published the first commercial blues music from an office on Beale; by the 1920's, nationally known artists such as Ma Rainey and Bessie Smith were coming to town specifically to perform in theaters on Beale.

As the century progressed and the music world became more complex, so did the Memphis sound. In 1949, Sam Phillips opened a studio on Union Avenue, where he would record not only such blues greats as Howlin' Wolf and Ike Turner, but also the King of Rock-and-Roll, Elvis Presley. In the early 1950's, B. B. King and Bobby "Blue" Bland helped to urbanize the traditional blues sound by using gospel and jazz elements. In 1958, Stax Records recorded the R&B and soul sounds of Otis Redding, Rufus and Carla Thomas, Booker T. and the MG's, and Isaac Hayes.

Memphis also has a lesser-known but important jazz history. Alberta Hunter was born here in 1895, and Jimmie Lunceford, who is buried in the city's Elmwood Cemetery, taught at a high school in the city for years. Other nationally known jazz musicians who have come out of Memphis include a long line of piano players, among them Lil Hardin (who later married Louis Armstrong), Phinaes Newborn, Jr., Donald Brown, and James Williams; drummer Jimmy Crawford; trumpet players Booker Little and Marvin Stamm; multi-instrumentalist Frank Strozier; saxophonists George Coleman, Hank Crawford, and Sonny Criss; and guitarist Calvin Newborn.

Sources

The best music source is *The Memphis Flyer* (521-9000), a free weekly with excellent listings. Other sources include the Friday section of *The Commercial Appeal* (529-2211), *Shake, Rattle & Roll* (276-1770), a free monthly guide to Memphis music, and *Memphis Magazine* (521-9000), a slick monthly.

WEVL/90 FM frequently announces music happenings around town, with the show "Up On Memphis" (Friday, 8:30 a.m.) giving detailed information. Kreature Comforts' *Lowlife Guide to Memphis* ($), available at the Center for Southern Folklore and Shangri-La Records (see "Record Stores," page 56), is a quirky, irreverent guide to such essential attractions as the sites where Jim Jarmusch's *Mystery Train* was filmed and the barbershop where Elvis got his hair cut.

For maps and other general information, contact the Memphis Visitor Information Center, 340 Beale St., 576-8171, or the Memphis Convention & Visitors Bureau, 47 Union Ave., 543-5300.

The area code for Memphis is (901).

A Note on the Neighborhoods

Sitting on the bluffs overlooking the Mississippi River, Memphis is a sprawling fan-shaped city with a population of about 610,000. Downtown, where Beale Street and most of the city's oldest buildings are located, is situated on the edge of the river. Through its center runs Third Street, which becomes the legendary Highway 61 south of the city.

Midtown is located about 15 minutes east of downtown, and then the city fans out to its suburbs, East Memphis and Germantown. Pinch is a 12-block district just north of downtown, and Whitehaven (once exactly what its name implies, but now a mixed neighborhood) is located 20 to 30 minutes south of the city. Many of Memphis's older African-American neighborhoods, where figures such as Alberta Hunter and B. B. King once lived, have disappeared, victims of urban renewal.

Getting around in Memphis is easy, although a car is essential if you're planning on leaving the downtown. There's little traffic and parking is plentiful.

Landmarks and Legends

(With the exception of the old WDIA building, the old Stax Recording site, and Graceland, all of the locations below are within walking distance of downtown, although Sun Studio and the Mallory-Neely house, both east of downtown, are a hike.)

Beale Street

If Beale Street could talk
If Beale Street could talk
Married men would have to take
their beds and walk
Except one or two
Who never drink booze
And the blind man on the corner
Who sings the Beale Street Blues . . .

—W. C. Handy, "Beale Street Blues"

By the early 1900's, Beale Street was the African-American capital of both Memphis and the Mid-South. A bustling street lined with everything from stores to banks, it was nonetheless best known for its nightlife: theaters, taverns, nightclubs, and bordellos. For many of the blacks in the area, almost all of whom lived in abject poverty, Beale Street was *their* street, an unreal world to which they could escape, if only for an evening. Whites were rarely even allowed on Beale after dark.

W. C. Handy arrived on Beale in the early 1920's, and he was followed by everyone from Bukka White and Furry Lewis to Ar-

Veteran Mose Vinson plays a mean blues piano.

Center for Southern Folklore Archives

nold "Gatemouth" Moore and Albert King. During the 1940's, a band called the "Beale Streeters" was formed by B. B. King, Bobby "Blue" Bland, Johnny Ace, Roscoe Gordon, Willie Nix, and others.

Bluesmen were not the only musicians to roam Beale. Jug bands were once an institution in what is now Handy Park, while in the 1920's and '30's, jazz and swing dominated the clubs. The "zoot suit," that emblem of the jazz and gangster era, was also invented here, by Louis Lettes, a Beale Street tailor. Its long jacket was originally designed not for fashion, but for practicality—to keep the suitpants from wearing out.

Part of the reason that Beale Street was so wide open to everything from gambling to prostitution was politics. Under Memphis's then mayor, E. H. "Boss" Crump, anything could—and often did—go down. In the first decade of the century, Memphis was the murder capital of the country, with 556 homicides per annum, most of them involving African Americans. In the 1950's, however, bad publicity caused the mayor to clamp down on all forms of vice, and many Beale Street establishments were closed for good.

It was the beginning of the end for Beale. One by one the remaining legitimate businesses moved elsewhere, and by the 1960's, after the Civil Rights movement provided new opportunities for blacks in other parts of town, the old Beale Street was completely gone.

Today, the entire area is a National Historic District filled with restaurants, clubs, and shops.

W. C. Handy's Home, *352 Beale St., 527-BLUE*.

W. C. Handy lived in this simple shotgun house in the early 1900's. It is now both a museum and the headquarters of the Blues Foundation, a nonprofit organization dedicated to preserving the blues. Here Handy wrote many of his most famous works—"Yellow Dog Blues," "Beale Street Blues," "Ole Miss Blues"—and raised six children before moving to New York to start his own publishing company.

Today, copies of Handy's sheet music lie strewn about the one-room museum (moved here from its original location at 659 Jennette Pl.), along with an old rocking chair, a piano, and plenty of photos.

Open: May 1–Labor Day, Tu–Sa, 10 a.m.–5 p.m., Su 1–5 p.m. The rest of the year by appointment. *Admission:* $.

The Monarch Club, *340 Beale St.*

Also known as the "Castle of Missing Men" because gunshot victims killed here could be quickly disposed of at the undertaker's place out back, the Monarch was nonetheless one of the classiest joints on Beale. Mirrored walls decorated its lobby and there were black-cushioned seats built into its walls.

Beale Street Blues Museum, *329 Beale St., 527-6008*.

Located in the Old Daisy Theatre and opened in early 1993 by lawyer and blues aficionado John Montague, the museum traces the history of blues on Beale from the 1890's to the present. Included in the museum are exhibits on ragtime, W. C. Handy, Furry Lewis, Memphis Minnie, and the Hooks Brothers, once the street's premier photographers. The exhibits are somewhat statically laid out behind glass cabinets, and organization is not what it could be (placards giving an historical overview are sorely lacking), but there are lots of fascinating memorabilia, including dozens of old Okeh records, Furry Lewis's "shine box," and a sign from the old Beale Street reading SPITTING ON SIDEWALKS PROHIBITED. PENALTY $5–$10.

Montague also owns the **Memphis Music Hall of Fame** (97 S. Second St., 525-4007), which features exhibits on Stax artists, among others.

Open: M–Sa, 10 a.m.–6 p.m.; Su, 11 a.m.–5 p.m. *Admission:* $.

Palace Theater, *318 Beale St. (NE corner of Hernando St.)*.

Now demolished, the Palace was once one of the most important places on Beale for aspiring young blues musicians. A Wednesday night amateur show, hosted first by deejay-schoolteacher/newspaper columnist Nat Williams and then by blues veteran Rufus Thomas, gave many musicians—B. B. King, Johnny Ace, and Bobby "Blue" Bland among them—their first shot at stardom. Rufus was especially partial to B.B., whom he allowed to come back time after time so that the young man could earn the one-dollar prize that would help keep him fed.

PeeWee's, *315 Beale St.*

PeeWee's was once a favorite hangout among blues artists because the proprietors, two Italians, were always willing to take messages over the phone from promoters and anyone else booking musicians. Many of the bluesmen checked in here daily for messages and while they were waiting for work, rolled dice in the backroom.

W. C. Handy wrote the first commercially successful blues—"Mr. Crump's Blues," later retitled "Memphis Blues"—at Pee-Wee's. The song was originally meant to be a campaign tune for mayoral candidate E. H. "Boss" Crump.

Mitchell's Hotel, *207 Beale St.*

From the 1940's to the 1960's, Andrew "Sunbeam" Mitchell and his wife, Ernestine, ran a hotel and upstairs club in this gray building, now a tourist information center. Sunbeam was a sort of godfather to the struggling bluesmen, giving them a bed when they were homeless, a bowl of chili when they were hungry, and a place to jam after the other clubs had closed. He also encouraged younger musicians by buying them instruments and, during the Civil Rights era, made his hotel available for meetings and rallies.

Over the years, Sunbeam ran a number of clubs on Beale, including the Club Handy, the Domino Lounge, the Flamingo Room, and the Hippodrome. The list of blues, soul, R&B, and jazz artists who passed through them is enormous, including Count Basie, Lionel Hampton, Johnny Ace, and Bobby "Blue" Bland. When B. B. King was just starting out and needed a manager, Sunbeam was on hand; when Little Richard couldn't get work during the 1950s, Sunbeam hired him to wipe down tables to keep him near the music.

Sunbeam, who died in 1989, managed clubs up to the end, his last being the still-operating Club Paradise (see "Clubs, etc.," page 48).

Handy Park, *NW corner of Beale and Hernando streets.*

Located across the street from the old Mitchell's, the small bench-lined park, once a marketplace, was created in 1931. W. C. Handy came down from New York to be on hand for its dedication, and a statue of him was added in 1960, two years after his death.

For years the park was a primary gathering place for country bluesmen arriving from the Delta, and even today, the park draws musicians, some of them officially, through concerts put on by the Blues Foundation, and some not so officially, some playing the blues and some just playing. Gospel singers can also often be heard here on weekends.

A. Schwab's Dry Goods Store, *163 Beale St., 523-9782.*

The oldest continuously operating business on Beale, A. Schwab's, founded in 1876, is the kind of place that isn't supposed to exist anymore. Sprawled over three stories, with creaky wooden floors and even creakier wooden staircases, it's jammed full of all the essentials and nonessentials of life. "If you can't find it at Schwab's, you're better off without it" is the store's motto, and it's one that's hard to refute. Ketchup bottles sit next to magic potions sit next to 99-cent ties sit next to a pair of size 74 blue jeans. Meanwhile, overhead, swings a bunch of gloves bearing an uncanny resemblance to a bunch of grapes.

On Schwab's second floor is an old-fashioned record player spinning out the blues: Bessie Smith, Muddy Waters, B. B. King. Schwab's, it turns out, may have been the first business in the country to sponsor a blues radio program; called "Bluestown," it was aired for an African-American audience from 1943 to 1947 by WHBQ. In those years, the radio station had few records of its own, so Schwab's graciously lent them a varying selection, 25 at a time.

For many years, Schwab's was also one of the only places in town where blues records were sold. Back then, nobody knew the names of recordings—they just referred to songs by their number on the local jukebox, a confusing matter since jukebox numbers were hardly interchangeable.

"We sold those records three for a dollar, right next to the nightgowns," says Mr. Schwab, a talkative, ruddy-faced man with twinkling eyes who's usually roaming about in a green apron. "We played them there, too, and sometimes the crowd got so big, nobody would do any shopping. That's when we'd put on a spiritual record—that weeded out the listeners from the buyers in a hurry." *Open:* M–Sa, 9 a.m.–5 p.m.

Center for Southern Folklore, *130 Beale St., 525-3655.*

Recently relocated into this roomy ground-floor office, shop, and exhibit space, the center is a wonderful not-for-profit institution that has been documenting the grass-roots culture of the South through films, records, oral histories, books, and festivals for over two decades now. Their informal exhibits—which often feature people as well as things—change every six months or so, and last year they sponsored a Stax and Soul music exhibit that the locals still remember. On sale in the gift shop is everything from quilts and "Elvis dolls" by area artists to W. C. Handy tapes and films on "praying pigs." *All Day and All Night: Memories from Beale Street Musicians* is screened regularly at the Center, which also sponsors daily walking tours of Beale Street and periodic cultural tours of the Delta.

Open: M–Sa, 9 a.m.–5:30 p.m., Su, 1–5 p.m. Blues piano player Mose Vinson performs every Sa, 12–4:30 p.m. *Admission:* $.

The Peabody, *149 Union Ave., 529-4000.*

For nearly 70 years, the Peabody has been Memphis's most elegant hotel, a luxurious establishment frequented by the elite of the South that is on the National Register of Historic Places. It is perhaps best known for its marching ducks, who descend from their penthouse on the roof every morning to swim and play in the lobby fountain all day, and for historian David Cohn's comment, "The Mississippi Delta begins in the lobby of the Peabody Hotel and ends on Catfish Row in Vicksburg."

During the 1930's and '40's, the Peabody was also known for its big band sounds. A national CBS radio program was broadcast by local station WREC from the swish Skyway ballroom, where for as little as $5 young white audiences could hear such stars as Paul Whiteman, Tommy Dorsey, and Harry James. An interesting aside: the man who set up the remote hookup for CBS was Sam Phillips, later the founder of Sun Studio.

Several early blues musicians (Speckled Red, Tommy Johnson, Willie Brown) were recorded at the Peabody, thanks to field units sent out by various record companies, and later, in 1969, a performance at the hotel marked a turning point in B. B. King's career. Up until then, B.B., like most African-American artists, had been performing primarily on the chitlin circuit, a loose connection of black nightclubs scattered across the country. Then, after his hit "The Thrill Is Gone," he was invited to showcase at the Peabody for a group of social chairmen from college campuses. He was an instant success and college concerts quickly became a staple in his schedule.

The Memorabilia Room, situated on the second floor of the hotel, documents some of its history. Items on display include programs from the Skyway and a copy of "Rhapsody in Blue" autographed by George Gershwin for W. C. Handy.

WDIA/1070 AM, *112 Union Ave., 529-4300.*

In February 1989, WDIA, the nation's first all-black-format radio station, celebrated its fortieth anniversary. It's still on the air 24 hours a day with talk, news, and a mix of oldies, blues, and gospel, having changed its programming little from its earliest days.

Many a famous blues deejay has come through WDIA, including Nat D. Williams, A. C. Williams, the Reverend "Gatemouth" Moore, Robert "Honeyboy" Thomas, Theo "Bless My Bones" Wade, B. B. King, and Rufus Thomas, who still has a Saturday morning blues show. WDIA is also known as the "Goodwill Station." Over the years, it has helped find lost children, cats, and dogs; gotten help for people whose homes have burned, bused the handicapped, and built a center for African-American children from broken homes. WDIA has a small museum documenting these and other events.

Open: By appointment. *Admission:* free.

**Beale Street once
teemed with shops,
banks, theaters,
taverns, nightclubs,
and bordellos.**

*Hooks Brothers' Col-
lection, Center for
Southern Folklore
Archives*

Stax Recording Studios, *926 McLemore Ave., now a vacant lot.*

The old Stax Building (large and white with a huge orange arrow on its side), demolished in late 1989, was to have been rebuilt inside the Pyramid in downtown Memphis. Those plans seem to be on indefinite hold, however. Meanwhile, souvenir bricks from the old studio are on sale at Shangri-la Records (see "Record Stores," page 56).

Stax Records, established by Jim Stewart and Estelle Axton in 1960, made a major contribution to the world of soul and R&B. During the sixties, it recorded everyone from Otis Redding and Rufus Thomas to Sam and Dave and Booker T. and the MG's.

Sun Recording Studio, *706 Union Ave., 521-0664.*

Sam Phillips, probably best known for discovering Elvis Presley, first rented this modest space—now a museum—in 1949. Phillips, who was working as a sound engineer for local radio station WREC, had been listening to black musicians for years and was determined to record them. "I thought it was vital music," he tells writer Robert Palmer in *Deep Blues*, "and although my first love was radio, my second was the freedom we tried to give the people, black and white, to express their very complex personalities, personalities these people didn't know existed in the fifties."

Some of the blues artists Phillips recorded include Howlin' Wolf, Muddy Waters, Ike Turner, Little Milton, B. B. King, James Cotton, Junior Parker, and Walter Horton. Rufus Thomas's "Bear Cat" was Sun's first hit, and "Rocket 88," believed by some to be the first rock-and-roll song ever, was recorded here by Ike Turner, Jackie Brenston, and others in 1951.

In the early days, anyone could walk into Sun and cut a record for a mere $4. One of the musicians who did so in 1954 was 18-year-old Elvis Presley, who subsequently remained with Phillips for approximately one year before switching to the bigger RCA Victor label. Other white artists recorded by Sun included Johnny Cash, Carl Perkins, Roy Orbison, Conway Twitty, and Jerry Lee Lewis.

Today, Sun Studio is a modest one-room museum. A tour guide gives a brief history of the place (complete with cuts from songs) and then leaves visitors alone to examine the pictures on the wall, the mobile recording unit near the door, and the WHGO mike used the first time one of Presley's songs ("That's All Right, Mama") was aired. Next door to the studio is a café, once the hangout of the Sun Studio artists, that serves "Hound Dogs" and grilled peanut-butter-and-banana sandwiches, "You-Know-Who's favorite snack."

Sam Phillips still lives outside Memphis, and there's a recording facility down the street run by his sons. It's also possible to record in the original Sun Studios, which has been equipped with state-of-the-art tracks. Some of the recent artists who have done so include Ringo Starr and U2.

Open: daily, 10 a.m.–6 p.m., tours every hour on the half hour.
Admission: $.

Mallory-Neely House, *652 Adams Ave. (midtown),*
523-1484.

W. C. Handy used to play for parties given by a Mrs. Frances Neely in this historically preserved 25-room Italian-style Victorian home, located on Memphis's "Millionaire's Row." He and other African-American musicians played in a small room in back, where they could be heard but not seen. Many years later, when Handy was famous and living in New York, he sent Mrs. Neely a letter consoling her for a broken leg, and the letter is now on display in the mansion turned museum.

Open: Tu–Sa, 10 a.m.–4 p.m.; Su, 1–4 p.m. Closed Jan.–March.
Admission: $.

Old WDIA Building, *2267 Central Ave.*

Before WDIA moved to Union Street it was housed in this nondescript tan-brick building (now home to KFTH-FM), and it was here that Riley "B.B." King came in 1948, having heard of the new African-American station and hoping it would give him a break. Station owner Bert Ferguson listened to the young man, decided he was unpolished but "wholesome," and gave him a job as the "Pepticon Boy." It was Riley's job to advertise a new health tonic ("Pepticon, Pepticon, sure is good / You can get it anywhere in your neighborhood") during a 10-minute spot for which he could sing and play anything he liked. On weekends he was required to drive around town and play from the top of a Pepticon truck while someone sold the tonic out the back. There was no pay involved in any of this, but Riley was allowed to advertise a gig he then had in West Memphis.

Riley's popularity grew steadily, and the station soon gave him a new full-fledged show. They also gave him a new name, "Beale Street Blues Boy," soon shortened to "Blues Boy King" and finally to "B.B." King.

Graceland, *3734 Elvis Presley Blvd. (Whitehaven), 332-3322 or 800-238-2000.*

The home of the King of Rock-and-Roll is bigger and more tourist-oriented than ever, with packed vans leaving for the mansion every few minutes, a new ultrasophisticated car museum, and umpteen souvenir shops. Everything from the King's favorite sequined costumes to his half dozen Harley Davidsons are on display, while everything from velveteen portraits of Elvis to Graceland dinnerware is for sale. It's all fascinating, somehow, and well worth the steep ticket price. More people visit Graceland than any other private home in the United States except the White House.

Elvis was deeply influenced by the blues. Many of his early hits were blues songs that he'd first heard performed by black artists—songs for which he received millions while the originators received next to nothing (Arthur "Big Boy" Crudup's "That's All Right, Mama," Big Mama Thornton's "Hound Dog").

As a young man, Presley spent much time on Beale Street, listening, watching, talking. While there, he met deejay and emcee Nat Williams and badgered him into letting him perform along with the black contestants at amateur night at the Palace Theater. "We had a lot of fun with him," Nat Williams tells Margaret McKee and Fred Chisenhall in *Beale Black and Blue,* "Elvis Presley on Beale Street when he first started was a favorite man. When they saw him coming out, the audience always gave him as much recognition as they gave any musician—black. He had a way of singing the blues that was distinctive. He could sing 'em not necessarily like a Negro, but he didn't sing 'em altogether like a typical white musician. . . . Always he had that certain humanness about him that Negroes like to put in their songs."

Open: daily, 9 a.m.–5 p.m. *Admission:* adults, $$–$$$, children, $–$$ (depending on tour chosen).

Also

Albert King, the "Godfather of the Blues" (and no relation to B.B.), who died in December 1992, is buried just over the river from Memphis in the Paradise Gardens cemetery, Edmondson, Arkansas (501-735-2552). Following King's funeral services, which were held in Memphis, the hearse took a short detour down Beale Street, led by the Memphis Horns playing "When the Saints Go Marching In."

Blues legend Furry Lewis, who died in 1981, is buried in the Hollywood Cemetery, 2012 Hernando Road (774-0260), on the outskirts of Memphis. Fans raised the money for his impressive headstone, inscribed with a guitar, in 1983.

Clubs, etc.

Today, Memphis is trying to recapture the magic of its music past by revitalizing Beale Street. Over the past ten years, a multitude of new clubs—most notably, the new **B.B. King's**—have opened up, and new festivals or music projects seem to be inaugurated almost monthly. Unfortunately, much of this activity, well intentioned though it is, has a hollow feel. Things are too sanitized, too sanctified, and everyone seems to be trying too hard.

This is not to minimize the Memphis scene. There are a number of fine musicians performing around town regularly. The present can never be the past, however, and it pays to venture beyond the commercial Beale Street area to some of the lesser-known clubs such as **Green's** or the **North End.**

Some of the blues and R&B talent that can be heard in Memphis today includes veteran bluesman Rufus Thomas, harmonica player Mojo Buford, piano players Booker T. Laury and Mose Vinson, the Fieldstones, the Hollywood All-Stars, white bluesmen Don McMinn and Sid Selvidge, and vocalists Ruby Wilson and James Govan. Some of the jazz figures include the veteran Fred Ford–Honeymoon Garner Trio, saxmen Zaid Nasser and Emerson Able, bass player Rodney Jordan, vocalist Joyce Cobb, pianist James Hurt, the groups Jungle Dust and the Midtown Jazzmobile, trumpet player Scott Thompson, and guitarists Calvin Newborn and Girard McVey.

Blues in Memphis can be heard a healthy seven days a week, especially during the spring and summer, when Beale Street flourishes and outdoor festivals and concerts abound. The jazz scene is much more confined, with the only truly rich day for the music being Sundays.

Generally speaking, bars and clubs in Memphis stay open until 2 a.m., but some, like **Blues City Café/Band Box,** have late licenses that allow them to operate until 3 a.m. and beyond.

Alberta Hunter made a triumphant homecoming appearance at the Orpheum In 1978.

Personal Choices

Best upscale blues club: *B.B. King's*
Best late-night blues club: *Blues City*
Best juke joints: *Green's, Junior Kimbrough's (near Holly Springs, Miss.)*
Best jazz spot: *Joyce Cobb's*
Best jazz jam: *Huey's*
Most atmospheric jazz bar: *Mallard's*

F O R   J A Z Z

Joyce Cobb's, *209 Beale St., 525-0484.*

A large and elegant room with flickering candlelights on shiny tabletops, hanging ivy, and black-and-white photographs, this is the only club on Beale that offers jazz on a regular basis. Even so, the jazz is mixed in with plenty of blues, soul, pop, and R&B. Joyce Cobb, one of the city's premier vocalists, can do it all.

A 17-piece big band, playing the music of the 1930's and '40's, is often featured on Monday nights, while Cobb and her band, Cool Heat, play Wednesdays through Saturdays. Sundays are usually devoted to a talent competition, and nationally known artists playing elsewhere in town sometimes stop by. Isaac Hayes and Al Jarreau are but two recent examples.

Barbecue is the club's specialty—there's a $20,000 smoker pit out back.
Music: nightly, some jazz. *Cover:* $–$$. *Food:* barbecue, etc. CC.

The North End, *346 N. Main St. (Pinch district), 526-0319.*
Tucked away from mainstream Memphis, the North End is a tiny gem of a place that features both jazz and Delta blues. The red-brick building is old and feels it, with creaking wooden floors, exposed brick walls, and dark green oilcloth tablecloths. Lots of old signs hang from the walls: DRINK COCA-COLA, GRAPETTE SODA, PAUL BEAR BRYANT BLVD., while the menu ranges from wild rice blended with everything imaginable (mushrooms, chicken, cheddar cheese) to tamales and stuffed potatoes.

Jungle Dust, the jazz group that's here on Sundays, plays "mainstream jazz on the modern side," and often other talented local musicians show up late in the evening to jam with the group. Fridays are usually devoted to bluesman Sid Selvidge.
Music: W–Su, some jazz and blues. *Cover:* $. *Food:* sandwiches, etc.

Huey's, *1927 Madison Ave. (midtown), 726-4372.*
The Midtown Jazzmobile, a shifting amalgam of top Memphis-based players that usually includes ex-Staxman Erroll Thomas, has been playing at this midtown bar every Sunday afternoon for the past 16 years, and sometimes the place is so crowded, it's hard to get in. Later on in the evening, the mood switches to blues, with groups arriving from all around the region. During the W. C. Handy Awards (see "Other Venues and Special Events," page 55), anyone—including B. B. King—is likely to stop by.

Huey's is a big friendly place with a solid, beer-soaked bar, booths with red-and-white-checkered tablecloths, and thousands of toothpicks stuck in its ceiling. There are also a few bedraggled plants near the window, looking for all the world as if someone tried to yuppify the place and then gave up on what would surely be an impossible task.

A second Huey's, **Huey's East,** (2858 Hickory Hill, 375-4373) has recently opened up in the suburbs. Similar to the original, it also offers jazz on Sunday afternoons.
Music: Su. *No cover. Food:* American.

Mallard's, *Peabody Hotel, 149 Union Ave. (downtown), 529-4140.*
Everything from rock to blues and R&B has been featured at this beautiful Old World bar, done up in heavy dark wood and engraved glass. Lately, however, the emphasis has been on the veteran jazz musicians Fred Ford and Honeymoon Garner, who play here most weekends.
Music: F–Sa, occasional weekdays. *No cover.*

Also

Marmalade's and **Blues City** (see "For Blues," below) feature jazz regularly, as does the **Escape Lounge** of the **Admiral Benbow Inn** in midtown (1220 Union Ave., 725-0630). Though the lounge—an old club, recently revamped—is run by black country-and-western singer J. P. Netters, her husband, jazz vocalist James Austin, often performs with his band on the weekends. Well-known jazz names touring the area also stop by on occasion.

Jazz can be heard once a week or so at **Club Memphis** (2790 Park Ave., 323-1394), a big and modern neighborhood club with lots of neatly aligned tables and chairs, a disco ball, and blue lights; and **Newby's** (539 S. Highland, 452-8408), a suburban club catering to a somewhat older crowd.

Some of the area's best-known jazz musicians occasionally play the city's hotel lounges. Calvin Newborn, for one, is often at the **Days Inn,** downtown. Watch the local papers for listings.

F O R B L U E S

BEALE STREET AND DOWNTOWN

B. B. King's Blues Club & Restaurant, *143 Beale St., 524-KING.*

B.B. was 20 years old with $2.50 in his pocket when he arrived on Beale in 1946 to make a name for himself, and 65 years old with over 50 albums to his credit when he returned in 1991 to open this large and friendly, two-storied club, always rocking with fine sounds. Purists may object to the club's well-scrubbed and somewhat touristic atmosphere, but it's done a lot to bring much-needed business to Beale and give the whole Historic District a more permanent feel.

Ruby Wilson, a big-throated Dallas schoolteacher who came to Beale Street when it reopened to pursue her lifelong dream of becoming a singer, is a regular here, and she performs with a band called the King B's. Other regulars include the rapidly up-and-coming Little Jimmy King, the adopted grandson of Albert King, and Preston Shannon. National acts are also booked twice a month or so, and B.B. plays the club four or five times a year.

Featured items on the club's menu include an Itta Bena salad, *blues*berry cheesecake, a Lucille burger, and a King steak. The club also has its own *Blues Beat* newsletter and souvenir shop. *Music:* Tu–Su. *Cover:* $; more for national acts. *Food:* American, Southern. CC.

Blues City Café/Band Box, *138-140 Beale St., 526-3637.*

Located directly across from B.B.'s, Blues City has such a grungy, low-down, comfortable feel that it's no wonder it's the best spot on the street for late-night blues. One side of the club is a simple café serving catfish, steak, ribs, and the like until 2:30 a.m.; the other is a bar and music room where the brick walls seem to lean in at odd angles and tiny Christmas lights twinkle up near ceiling fans. The club is home to a spirited house band, the Blues City All Stars, and on a typical night all kinds of players are likely to show up, from the young and handsome Little Jimmy King—gold tooth flashing—who plays his guitar upside down and left-handed, like his namesake, to a middle-aged drummer dressed in a three-piece suit. National artists such as John Hammond and Mose Allison are also booked on a regular basis, and roots bluesmen Booker T. Laury and Memphis James frequently perform in the early evenings.

Following Albert King's death, Blues City held an all-day memorial tribute to raise money for his tombstone. Over $5,000 was raised, $3,000 from the unlikely source of the Splash Casino in Tunica, Mississippi.

Music: nightly. *Cover:* $; more for national acts. *Food:* Southern.

Rum Boogie Café, *182 Beale St., 528-0150.*

Whoever designed this two-level place, connected by an iron circular staircase, did one terrific job—there are guitars donated by big-name artists (the late Stevie Ray Vaughan, The Radiators, Kenny Loggins) hanging from the ceiling, and rusting signs from Highway 61 and Stax hanging from the walls.

The Rum Boogie features music seven nights of the week, usually compliments of Don McMinn and the Rum Boogie Band, and the club is always packed with a young crowd drinking, dancing, listening, and eating. Booker T. and the MG's and Bon Jovi have been known to put in surprise appearances.

Music: nightly. *Cover:* $. *Food:* American. CC.

Blues Hall, *184 Beale St., 528-0150.*

Adjacent to the Rum Boogie—and covered by the same admission price—is a small dusty hall filled with a hodgepodge of mismatched tables and chairs. There are no fancy guitars hanging from the ceiling here, just an old battered guitar case with the words FURRY LEWIS in thick, white-paint brushstrokes.

Blues Hall tries to be Memphis's answer to Preservation Hall in New Orleans by booking artists who tend to play roots blues. The hall also provides a sometimes welcome relief from the craziness next door: the mood is quiet and the audience listens well.

Music: F–Sa. *Cover:* $. *No food.*

Marmalade, *153 E. Calhoun St. (downtown), 522-8800.*

R&B is the staple here, along with first-rate Southern-style cooking. The place is large and rambling, with a bit of a homey rec-room feel, perhaps because of the college pennants pinned to one wall and the game boards in the backroom. Pictures of Memphis artists—B. B. King, Alberta Hunter, Phineas Newborn—hang in

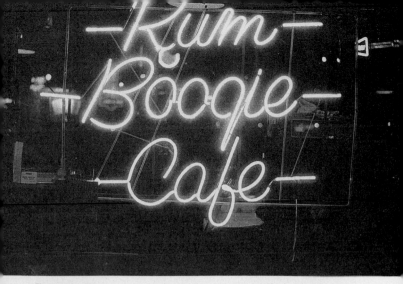

The popular Rum Boogie features a house band led by Don McMinn.

the hall, and a wide-screen TV provides entertainment before the music starts.
Music: F–Su. Cover: $. Food: Southern.

Ernestine's and Hazel's, *NW corner of S. Main and Calhoun streets, 523-9722.*
Ernestine Mitchell, wife of Sunbeam (see **Mitchell's Hotel,** page 42), and her sister Hazel (who "passed" shortly after Sunbeam) opened up this scruffy lunch counter on the edge of downtown back in 1967, and it's since become a neighborhood institution. "Neck bones, beets, chitlins, ham hocks, buffalo fish, any kind of peas, beans, all kinds, meatloaf, cornbread . . ." answers Ernestine, a heavy-set woman who seems half asleep but is undoubtedly not missing a beat, when asked what she serves.
Ernestine's only began offering blues a year ago, and its music, usually compliments of the Hollywood All-Stars or the Beale Street Cadillac Blues Band, is still somewhat sporadic.
Music: most Sundays. Cover: $. Food: Soul.

Elsewhere in Memphis

Green's Lounge, *2090 Person Ave. (between midtown and East Memphis, near Defense Depot), 274-9800.*
For over 18 years, Rose Green has been running one of the hottest juke joints in Memphis. Located in an obscure cement build-

ing painted pale green, it's just a neighborhood place, but what a neighborhood place. . . .

The Fieldstones, led by electric bass player Lois Brown and drummer Joe Hicks, are regulars here and so was Evelyn Young, the sax player who taught B. B. King many of his changes, before her death in 1991. The Fieldstones play a Memphis sound that is alternately scorchingly hot and achingly blue, and when they really get down, the whole building seems to rock.

On a typical night, Green's, a rough room lined with rickety tables and colored Christmas tree lights, fills quickly with smoke and dancing figures dressed in weekend finery. Men in big white hats gyrate alongside women in sequined dresses, while the music pounds out, intoxicating, hypnotizing. A young man holds his girlfriend close while two elderly men talk at the bar. A large woman in shiny blue rotates, rotates, rotates, in front of a small muscular man wearing a baseball cap. A tiny woman who looks as if she's been crying slips out the front door into a night that is dark and enormously quiet.

Music: Sa. *Cover:* $.

The Place 2-B, *1035 E. Brooks Rd. (S of Downtown, near the Memphis airport), 396-6739.*

Former Stax-man Ollie Nightingale and his band, the Nightingale Express, are regulars at this long, neat, neighborhood club equipped with tiny sparkling lights, multicolor streamers, plenty of tables and chairs, and a large rectangular bar. Run by Imogene Miller, an elegant middle-aged woman who was inspired to open her club by her friend Albert King shortly before his death, the Place 2-B has presented all the Beale Street regulars, including Rufus Thomas and Preston Shannon, as well as out-of-towners such as Chick Willis.

Music: F–Su. *Cover:* $. *Food:* soul, short order.

Brittenum's Corner Lounge, *1300 Airway Blvd. (bet. midtown and East Memphis), 458-2655.*

Almost every Sunday night for the past 20-odd years, the Hollywood All-Stars have been putting on a fine blues show in Brittenum's neighborhood bar. This juke joint is very simple but very pretty, with pink walls, black beams, a pool table, juke box, and lattice-work windows. A sign outside reads: "If you don't abide by house rules, pass it up. Don't take glasses from building. This is a nonviolent business."

Music: Su. *No cover.*

Club Paradise, 645 Georgia Ave. (10 min. S of downtown).

A huge club with a somewhat rough reputation, the Club Paradise was the last Memphis establishment owned by the late Sunbeam Mitchell (see **Mitchell's Hotel,** "Landmarks and Legends," page 42). Open only when major blues and R&B acts such as Little Johnnie Taylor or Denise LaSalle are booked, the

Paradise, its facade alive with graffiti'd color, is housed in a converted bowling alley that's part of a run-down shopping center near the Foote Homes housing project.

Music: most weekend nights. *Tickets:* $$–$$$.

Also

Blues can be heard at **The North End, Huey's, Club Memphis,** the **Admiral Benbow Inn** (see "For Jazz," page 49) and the **King's Palace Café** (162 Beale St., 521-1851), a supper club that usually attracts a large number of tourists. A number of downtown restaurants also offer blues on the weekends, including **Automatic Slim's** (83 S. Second St., 525-7948), an airy Southwestern-looking restaurant (though its menu is mixed) lined with works of art, and **The Brewery** (235 Union, 526-BEER), which has its own beer vats.

Other Venues and Special Events

The Reverend Al Green has a ministry at the **Full Gospel Tabernacle** (787 Hale Rd., 396-9192) in Whitehaven, and when he shows up, there's nothing quite like hearing that huge soul voice shake down this evil world. The only trouble is, there's no telling when he'll appear, and since he took over the church nine years ago, the congregation has been steadily dwindling. Sometimes there seem to be almost as many tourists and curiosity seekers in the church as bona fide members.

Even without the reverend, the modern, octagonal tabernacle is worth visiting. Its choir, though small by gospel standards, has a full, powerful sound and is accompanied by drums, a piano, and tambourines. Services start at 11 a.m.

Built in the late 1920's for vaudeville and movies, the **Orpheum Theater** (203 S. Main St. at Beale, 525-7800), recently restored to the tune of $5 million, is a glittering palace complete with immense chandeliers, ornate tapestries, and triple balconies. Once host to everyone from Harry Houdini to John Philip Sousa, it now features cultural events ranging from the opera to the blues.

Alberta Hunter, who spent a tough, poor childhood in some of Memphis's meanest neighborhoods (so much so that she ran away to Chicago at the age of 16), made a triumphant return to her hometown in 1978. Her performance at the Orpheum attracted over 2,000 people, many of whom were shocked when the spirited lady, instead of mouthing the expected gracious remarks, blasted the South for its still apparent racist attitudes.

Producer Irwin Scheft and the **Jazz Foundation of Memphis** (725-1528) sponsor approximately eight jazz concerts a year at different locations, featuring national artists. Watch the local papers for listings.

One of the best barbecue places in town (look for the building with the smoking chimney) is the **Cozy Corner Restaurant** (745 N. Parkway, 527-9158), which also features great jazz and blues in the form of tapes played over a loudspeaker. Owner Raymond Robinson has recorded everyone from Louis to Dinah.

Every November, the entire blues world descends on Memphis for a four-day conference and celebration that culminates in the **W. C. Handy Awards,** a national blues awards show. Begun in 1980, the program, sponsored by the Blues Foundation (174 Beale St., 527-BLUE), gives out W. C. Handy Awards to performers in approximately 20 categories and "Keeping the Blues Alive" Awards to seven or eight industry promoters, clubs, and societies.

During the week of the conference, all the major clubs in Memphis present special performances of the blues. The three-hour ceremony itself features live acts and is open to the public. General admission tickets are limited; advance reservations highly recommended. The foundation also sponsors a National Amateur Blues Talent Night in early September at the New Daisy Theater (330 Beale St., 525-8979).

Periodically, the Beale Street clubs join forces to offer one low cover price for a general-admission ticket or wristband that's good for all. The music on these festival days starts in the midafternoon and lasts until 2 or 3 a.m. Sometimes the festivals have official names—the **Beale Street Music Fest,** the **Memphis Music Fest** (Memphis artists only)—and at other times they're more informal.

The Center for Southern Folklore presents the three-day **Memphis Music and Heritage Festival** every July (usually the second weekend) with music, crafts, Southern cooking, and more. A local writer calls the event the "best-kept secret in the country for regional Southern music."

"Blues on the Bluff" is a series of fund-raising concerts held by WEVL in July and August on the meadow outside the National Ornamental Metal Museum (374 W. California Ave., 774-6380). The concerts offer spectacular views of the Mississippi River.

Radio Stations

WEVL/90 FM, (528-1990). Jazz and blues daily. Of special note: "Cap'n Pete's Blues Cruise," "Memphis Beat" with Wally Hall, both F nights.

WDIA/1070 AM, (529-4300). Blues all day Sa. Of special note: "Rufus and Jaye" with Rufus Thomas and Jaye Michael Davis, Sa morning.

WSMS/92 FM, (678-3692). Student-run jazz station connected with Memphis State University.

Record Stores

Schwab's (163 Beale St., 523-9782) still sells a small selection of rare blues 45's, along with a few albums featuring Memphis musicians. **Boss Ugly Bob's Tapes and Records** (726 E. Mc-Lemore Ave., 774-6400) specializes in R&B and has a good selection of blues and jazz. **Shangri-La Records** (1916 Madison Ave., 274-1916) specializes in Memphis music and has a mail-order catalogue. **Poplar Tunes** (308 Poplar St., 525-6348) also has a good selection of Memphis artists.

Other Nearby Locations

Junior Kimbrough's houseparty, *Chulahoma, Miss. (About 40 miles SE of Memphis and 12 miles W of Holly Springs, Miss. Heading south on Hwy. 7 from Holly Springs, turn west onto Highway 4. Junior's is about 10 miles down on the right. Look for lots of parked cars.)*
Junior Kimbrough's houseparty, now in its eighth year, is a legendary event, one that blues enthusiasts throughout the state love to talk about. It happens every Sunday afternoon (and often Friday and Saturday evenings as well), in a weatherbeaten house that was once a church, surrounded by trees and fields. The neighbors start arriving about 3 p.m., and they sit on the steps, their legs dangling, or inside the living room with its peeling wallpaper, sagging sofas, and wonderful glittering folk paintings based on *Ebony* magazine covers.

From the early afternoon on, everyone is talking, laughing, and drinking, but when Junior and his sidemen begin to play—their first few electrified notes stinging the air—the whole audience seems to freeze in midsentence.

Kimbrough, who says he plays the "cotton patch blues," was born and raised in Holly Springs. He's been playing since he was 8, and has traveled to festivals all over the world. Bluesman R. L. Burnside lives right next door and often plays the houseparty as well.

To find out when Kimbrough and friends are playing call Fat Possum Records in Oxford, Miss., 601-236-3110.

W. C. Handy's Birthplace, *620 W. College St. (downtown), Florence, Ala., 205-760-6434.*
Located approximately 125 miles southeast of Memphis in the town of Florence, Alabama, is the log cabin where W. C. Handy was born in 1873. The son of a Methodist minister, W.C. lived here until he was 19, attending the local school (where he also taught for a time) and playing the organ in his father's church. His father did not approve of his son's interest in music and, when W.C. came home with a guitar one day, demanded that he turn it in for a dictionary.

The log cabin is furnished with period pieces, and adjacent to it is a museum filled with Handy memorabilia, such as the piano on which he wrote "St. Louis Blues," his trumpet, schoolbooks, family albums, and awards. Especially interesting is the Braille sheet music that Handy used during the last 15 years of his life, after losing his sight.

A weeklong W. C. Handy festival featuring concerts, art exhibits, and more is sponsored by the Music Preservation Society in Florence every August (P.O. Box 1827, Florence, Ala. 35631; 205-766-7642). Started up by bass player Willie Ruff 13 years ago, the festival presents a multitude of musical events (jazz, blues, gospel), and 80 percent of the concerts are free. Roberta Flack, Manhattan Transfer, and the late Dizzy Gillespie have all played the fest, and there's even music in the church where Handy's father and grandfather once preached, the Greater St. Paul AME.

Open: Tu–Sa, 10 a.m.–4 p.m. *Admission:* $.

The Mississippi Delta

The Mississippi Delta is generally believed to be the place where the blues originated. A wedge-shaped region of land lying in northern Mississippi between the Mississippi and Yazoo rivers, it has spawned an enormous number of musicians, many of whom now have international reputations.

Some scholars pinpoint Dockery Farms near Cleveland as the actual birthplace of the blues.[1] From this area came such early musicians as Charley Patton, Tommy Johnson, and Willie Brown. Later, musicians could be heard in tiny juke joints throughout the region: Muddy Waters in Clarksdale; Sonny Boy Williamson* in Helena, Arkansas; Son House and Robert Johnson in Robinsonville; and dozens upon dozens of others. Even a partial list of the Delta's bluesmen is overwhelming in its musical importance: Howlin' Wolf (Chester Burnett), James Cotton, Willie Dixon, Memphis Minnie, John Lee Hooker, Mississippi John Hurt, Elmore James, Bukka White, Albert King, B. B. King, Jimmy Reed, Houston Stackhouse.

The conditions that gave birth to the blues—poverty, racism, and inhumane working situations—led many musicians to leave the state as soon as they could. Most traveled North, heading first to Memphis and then to urban centers such as Chicago, St. Louis, and Detroit. Nonetheless, the blues hardly vanished from the Mississippi countryside, and even today—though much diminished in scope— the music can still be heard in a number of juke joints in a number of towns, its raw hypnotic sound reaching deep into the night.

---

*The Sonny Boy Williamson referred to throughout this chapter is Rice Miller, also sometimes referred to as Sonny Boy Williamson II to distinguish him from John Lee "Sonny Boy" Williamson.

General Sources

The best center for blues information throughout the Delta is the Stackhouse/Delta Record Mart (232 Sunflower Ave., Clarksdale; 627-2209), run by Jim O'Neal, founder of *Living Blues* magazine. Stackhouse sells a "Delta Blues Map Kit" ($$) with updated information on historical blues sites and juke joints, and a blues roadmap. Telephone poles are another good informational source, where ads for the chitlin circuit are often placed.

For maps and other information, contact the local Chambers of Commerce.

The area code for Mississippi is (601).

A Note on Mississippi

Something surprising is happening in Mississippi. After decades of ignoring—virtually denying—the existence of that "devil's music," the blues, the state is beginning to acknowledge its importance. In Clarksdale, the Chamber of Commerce puts out a map pinpointing blues sites. In Greenville, local entrepreneurs promote "blues breakfasts" and "blues happy hours" during the Delta Blues festival. In Moorhead, a state historic plaque marks the spot where the "Southern crosses the Dog" (see Tutwiler, "Landmarks and Legends," page 73).

It is uncertain how much of Mississippi's changing attitude is due purely to economics. This is a poor state, and blues fans bring in much-needed tourist dollars. But the Mississippi of 1990 is not the Mississippi of 1960. Racially and economically, things are changing around here.

Just what this will mean for the blues is hard to tell. Too much commercialization of the music will surely dilute its power. On the other hand, blues fans coming into Mississippi (and they're still not exactly arriving in droves) help to keep the music alive.

Juke Joints

Visiting juke joints takes time and patience. Most feature live music only once a week, on Friday or Saturday nights or Sunday afternoons, and there are no set times for performances. Also, since many places don't have phones, it's hard to find out what's happening in advance.

One way around this is to stop by the juke joints in the afternoon. Many are hard to find, anyway, and it helps to scout them out during daylight hours. In all likelihood, someone will be around then to answer questions, and if they're not featuring music that night, they'll be able to direct you to some place that is.

Most juke joints are poor, simple, windowless affairs, built of cement or tin. There are usually a few rickety tables, a makeshift bandstand, a large dance floor, and Christmas-tree lights and ornaments to brighten the place up. Sometimes there's a nominal

$2–$3 cover; and beer and soda and setups (i.e., cups and ice for hard liquor, which must be brought in) are for sale.

According to the people at Stackhouse Records, three of the most active jukes in Mississippi today are **Margaret's Blue Diamond Lounge** and the **South End Disco,** both in Clarksdale, and **Junior Kimbrough's** near Holly Springs (see Memphis, page 57). Artists to watch for in the Clarksdale/Helena area include Big Jack Johnson, Sam Carr, Frank Frost, Little Jeno, Lonnie Shields and Wesley Jefferson; J.B. & the Midnighters, with guitarist Johnny Billington; harpman Arthneice "Gas Man" Jones; and the blues-soul group Delta Blues Brothers. In the Greenville area, there's T-Model Ford, Abie "Boogaloo" Ames, John Price, and Willie Foster; in Indianola, look for Bobby Whalen and the Ladies Choice Band.

HIGHWAY 61

WELCOME TO MISSISSIPPI reads the sign with the huge magnolias, and almost immediately, the hills give way to a flat green land stretching fine as a wire beneath the Southern sun. Already there's the sound of a freight train far in the distance, while cotton fields appear to the left and the right.

Driving south from Memphis to Clarksdale on Highway 61—once the black man's lifeline to the North—is a strange, lonely experience. The ache of the blues seems to hover in the air as the familiar names flash past: Walls, where Memphis Minnie was born; Robinsonville, where Robert Johnson grew up; Tunica, where James Cotton was born; Lula, where Charlie Patton and Robert Nighthawk once lived.

For all the apparent lushness of the fields, the towns are small and poor. All is quiet and peaceful, though it's a peace that one senses can be easily snapped. Outsiders are watched here—respectfully watched, but watched nonetheless.

Truckstops selling catfish appear from time to time, along with strange farm vehicles looking like giant flies. Reminders of the blues are everywhere. The old Highway 61 parallels the new and is lined with miles of rusting red Illinois Central railroad cars. Crossroads, often marked with official highway signs, appear out of nowhere, and in the evening, driving beneath a midnight-blue sky gradually turning black, it's easy to imagine the Devil lounging against a tree somewhere, waiting.

> I went down to the crossroads, fell down on my knees,
> I went down to the crossroads, fell down on my knees,
> Ask the Lord above for mercy, say boy, if you please.
> Mmm . . . standing at the crossroads I tried to flag a ride
> Mmm . . . standing at the crossroads I tried to flag a ride
> Ain't nobody seem to know me, everybody pass me by.
>
> —*Robert Johnson, "Crossroads Blues"*

ROBINSONVILLE

At one end of town are a few big homes, surrounded by cypress trees. At the other end are small, rickety buildings, their roofs held up by spindly sticks of wood. In between is a simple post office building, its American flag hanging limp, and a huge nightclub called the Hollywood. Behind everything, overwhelming the day, are the cicadas, their harsh chirping voices canceling out words and thought.

Robert Johnson, one of the most enigmatic of blues singers, spent much time in and around Robinsonville. He grew up on plantations located nearby and may have gone to school in Commerce, the next town over. He started playing the jukes as a young man and, according to fellow musician Son House, was reasonably good on the harmonica and a disaster on the guitar. "Such a racket you never heard," Son House once said, "It'd make people mad, you know."

Johnson left Robinsonville at about 20, only to return a year later. Son House recounts their reunion:

"He spoke, and I said, 'Well boy, you still got a guitar, huh? What do you do with that thing? You can't do nothing with it.' He said, 'Well, I'll tell you what.' I said, 'What?' He said, 'Let me have your seat a minute . . . So he sat down there and finally got started. And man! He was so good! When he finished, all our mouths were standing open. I said, 'Well, ain't that fast!' He's gone now."[2]

Johnson, according to Son and others, was gone in more ways than one. There was only one way he could have learned the guitar so quickly—by selling his soul to that Devil waiting by the crossroads.

CLARKSDALE

From the '30's on through the '40's and '50's, Clarksdale was a major blues town. John Lee Hooker was born here, and so were Ike Turner, Little Junior Parker, and Sam Cooke. Robert Nighthawk, Bukka White, "Gatemouth" Moore, Eddie Boyd, Son House, and Charley Patton all once lived in the area, and Muddy Waters, who moved here at a young age, may have gotten his nickname from going fishing on Fridays (getting "muddy") and selling his catch on Saturdays at the town's then-legendary fish fries.

Fourth Street, a short street on the other side of the tracks, is the main drag of black Clarksdale. Most of the blues joints were located here, and several, including the **Blue Diamond** and **Smitty's,** are still situated nearby. The street itself, however, has seen better days. Crack has been a problem since early 1989.

Otherwise, Clarksdale is a quiet, low-slung town of one- and two-story buildings. Small shops and banks line the downtown streets, and traffic lights (despite the fact that there's very little traffic) seem to be everywhere.

Sources

The Coahoma County Chamber of Commerce (1540 De Soto St. at Highway 49S, 627-7337) puts out a free map pinpointing blues sites. See also Stackhouse/Delta Record Mart (see "Record Stores," page 68).

Landmarks and Legends

WROX, *Alcazar Hotel, Corner of Third and Yazoo streets, 627-7343.*

The first floor of this building feels hollow and abandoned. A creaky elevator leads up to the second and shakes to a stop. The door opens, and way down at the end of a huge dark empty hall is a sagging couch and a sign that reads: "WROX, Clarksdale's Only Full-time Full-service Radio Station."

WROX is the home of Early Wright, one of the first black dee-jays in the South. A large, slow-moving man with a serious smile, Mr. "Soul Man" Wright, now in his seventies, has been spinning his blues and gospel shows since 1947.

Wright began his career as a mechanic and part-time manager of a local gospel group. His rich heavy voice caught the ear of the station manager of WROX, who offered him a job. "He begged me for two weeks," says Wright, "so I went to my pastor and asked him, would it hurt me any in the church to do the show? He said no, and I been here ever since."

Today, Wright's shows are the same as they always have been—wonderfully loose and even-flowing. He says anything and everything that comes to mind, and dead air space—which happens sometimes when he has to fetch something from the other room—doesn't phase him. Visitors, no matter who they are, are always welcomed and interviewed on the air.

"I never had a manager to interfere with my show," Wright says with one of his serious smiles. "I just play what I think."

Wright's blues shows run M–F, 6–8 p.m.; his gospel shows, M–F, 8–10 p.m. and Su, 5–10:45 p.m. It's best to get there a few minutes before 6 p.m. on weekdays and before 5 p.m. on Sundays.

Delta Blues Museum, *Carnegie Public Library, 114 Delta Ave., 624-4461.*

Follow the faded blue line to the library's second floor, where director Sid Graves and his staff, with the help of the National Endowment for the Humanities and monies raised by Z. Z. Top and others, have put together a series of exhibits honoring the blues. To the right of the museum's entrance sits a life-size figure of Muddy Waters overlooking a changing exhibit space that's usually devoted to a living Delta musician, while to the back is "All Shook Up," a display that chronicles the "Mississippi Roots of American Popular Music" (including gospel, rockabilly, jazz, R&B, and the blues). Among the many fascinating bits of memorabilia in the mu-

Mississippians get
down in Clarks-
dale's Blue Dia-
mond Lounge.

Jim O'Neal

seum are an early microphone from **WROX** radio (used by Ike
Turner), a Sonny Boy King Biscuit flour bag, the huge charred
sign from the store at Three Forks behind which Robert Johnson
reportedly died (see "Quito," page 77), skull sculptures by Son
Thomas, one of B.B.'s "Lucilles," a bottle-top slide donated by
Bonnie Raitt, and a harmonica signed by James Cotton. The museum is also packed with lots of wonderful photos, some by the
well-known Mississippi photographer William Eggleston.

In addition, the museum houses a blues library, screening and
listening areas, where visitors can peruse through books, newslet-
ters, CD's, and video tapes; and a small book and gift shop.
Open: M–F, 9 a.m.–5 p.m. *Admission:* free.

Stovall plantation, site of Muddy Waters's home,
*Oakridge Rd., 8 miles from downtown (home is on the left-
hand side, just past a row of brick houses).*

Located on a pretty country lane just outside town is the enormous Stovall plantation, where Muddy Waters (McKinley Morganfield) grew up. The plantation, stretching out to the horizon
and beyond, is a kingdom unto itself, complete with cotton fields,
an irrigation plant, a general store, and a church.

Muddy came to Stovall's with his grandmother when he was
three years old. By then, he was already beating on anything and

everything he could find, "trying to get a new sound," and by the time he was seven, he had mastered the harmonica.

When Muddy was 26 and making 22½ cents an hour driving a tractor for Stovall, two folksong collectors working with the Library of Congress, Alan Lomax and John Work, came through Clarksdale. They were directed to Waters's home (which was also a juke joint on the weekends), where they recorded him playing his bottleneck guitar. A few months later Muddy left town on the Illinois Central, headed for Chicago.

At the moment, Muddy's former home is still located on Stovall's and a small sign commemorating the site is located across the street. Eventually, however, the Clarksdale Historical Society hopes to take it apart and partially reconstruct it inside the Delta Blues Museum.

Wade Walton's barbershop, *317 Issaquena Ave.*

A young black man dressed completely in red is sitting in a pale green barber chair getting his hair cut. His baseball cap hangs on the hatstand; a guitar hangs over the mirror. A sign on the wall reads: "Profanity will not be tolerated."

Meanwhile, Mr. Wade Walton, barber-musician, clips quietly away. A meticulous man given to wearing suspenders and bow ties, he's known for his harp, for his "Talking Straight Razor," and for his guitar.

Born the sixteenth of 17 children, Walton started playing music as a young boy, putting rattlesnake tails inside his guitar to make it sound louder. He's recorded an album, *The Blues of Wade Walton*, and is occasionally invited to play a festival in Europe.

As a barber, Walton has seen some famous heads. "I used to cut Sonny Boy's hair before he went across the bridge to KFFA," he says. "It took thirty minutes to get there and he was always late. I cut Charlie Pride's hair too." Walton also remembers Muddy Waters, who used to play his guitar on the corner of Sunflower and Fourth.

Sometimes, if he has a moment, Wade will play his guitar for casual visitors; sometimes he won't. He does, after all, have a business to run.

Open: Tu–Sa, 10 a.m.–6 p.m.

W. C. Handy's home, *Issaquena St., near Third St.*

Handy lived in Clarksdale from 1903 to 1905. His house once stood on the site now occupied by Walton's Shop, and a plaque out front commemorates the spot: "In Clarksdale, Handy was influenced by Delta blues which he collected and later published. . . ."

Riverside Hotel, *615 Sunflower Ave.*

September 26, 1937: A car crashes into a truck parked alongside Highway 61. One of the passengers, a woman, is severely injured; her arm is nearly severed. Bleeding profusely, she is rushed to a nearby hospital, but it is too late, and she is dead before morning.

The woman is Bessie Smith, about whose death so much controversy once raged. An early article, written by John Hammond in *Down Beat,* stated that Bessie bled to death while waiting for treatment at a white hospital, and despite Hammond's later retraction (his apology stated that he'd been writing primarily on hearsay), white liberals reading the story became enraged and turned her death into a cause célèbre[3] that refused to die. As late as 1960, Edward Albee was writing a play about it.

All this was doubly ironic, both because Hammond frequently denounced much real racial injustice that most liberals conveniently ignored, and because later evidence showed that Bessie was *not* taken to a white hospital, but to a black one: the G. T. Thomas Hospital located at 615 Sunflower Avenue, Clarksdale.

Today, the Thomas Hospital has become the Riverside Hotel, a modest establishment of some 25 rooms, and Bessie Smith is far from the only blues artist connected with it. During the '40's, shortly after it had become a hotel, a whole host of musicians— Sonny Boy Williamson, Robert Nighthawk, Kansas City Red, Jackie Brenston, and others—called this place home.

Mrs. Z. L. Hill, a lovely, articulate woman, her gray hair in a bun, owned the hotel back then and she owns it today. All of the above blues musicians have signed her register, and she still has Robert Nighthawk's suitcase, which was left here when he died in 1967.

Another musician connected with the hotel is Ike Turner, who was born and bred in Clarksdale. Says Mrs. Hill with a sniff, "When he was old enough and thought he was a man—he wasn't, but he thought he was—he quit school and come to the hotel and got him a room."

Before long, Ike also got him a band, and one of the songs the group both wrote and rehearsed while staying here was "Rocket 88" (see Sun Studio, page 45). Mrs. Hill was in on the tune from the very beginning, and she sewed little ROCKET 88 badges onto the band members' ties before sending them on their way to the recording studio. "They were the prettiest things," she says.

Bell Grove Baptist Church, *831 Garfield St. (just S of Highway 61), 624-2920.*

One of Muddy Waters's cousins, the Reverend Willie Morganfield, still preaches at this big brick church with the square white steeple. Morganfield is reputed to be an impressive and inspiring preacher, and is also a recording artist in his own right, with several records and tapes to his name.

Morning worship: Su, 11 a.m. *Prayer meeting:* W, 6:30 p.m.

Clubs, etc.

Margaret's Blue Diamond Lounge, *Fourth and W. Tallahatchie streets.*

When Margaret Palmer's man walked out on her a few years ago, she decided to keep running their lounge—a long rough cement-floored room just off Fourth Street—on her own. Since then, the place has become a local favorite and was featured on ABC-TV's "Nightline" in January 1989.

One of the most active joints in the Delta, the Blue Diamond, dark and sad by day, glitters with Christmas ornaments and the sound of the blues by night. Music happens here regularly on Saturdays, often thanks to Arthneice "Gas Man" Jones or Wesley Jefferson, and sometimes on Fridays as well. Local filmmakers recently made a video at the place called *Juke Joint Saturday Night* and it can be screened at the Delta Blues Museum.

South End Disco (a.k.a. Red's), *395 Sunflower Ave. at Fourth St., 627-3166/627-1367.*

Red Paton has been running this scruffy brick blues club, painted gunmetal gray, for the past 20 years now, but it's just recently that the place has been marked (however discreetly) with a sign out front, near its big cylindrical barbecue smoker. Inside, the club boasts a hodgepodge of mismatched tables and chairs, a pool table lit by blue lights, and a small disco ball. Big Jack Johnson, Willie Cobbs, and Lonnie Shields are some of the musicians who occasionally perform here, and the place is always packed on Friday and Saturday nights, whether there's live music or not.

Mr. Johnnie's Place, *347 Issaquena St.*

Blues guitarist Johnnie Billington runs blues workshops for the youth of Clarksdale out of this big, no-frills box of a room with signs reading NO DRUGS posted on every wall. Billington, who used to work as a mechanic for the Mississippi school system, wants to pass the blues heritage on to the next generation, as well as give the kids somewhere to go besides the streets. He's a strict teacher, though, who tolerates no fooling around. "I want kids who'll stick through it," he says.

Informal blues jams and workshops can be heard at Mr. Johnnie's most weekend nights and many afternoons after school. Billington, who's usually nattily dressed in a white shirt and tie, also hopes to set up a more formal concert series in the near future.

Born about 35 miles east of Clarksdale, Billington has an unusual theory about the blues. "The Delta blues comes from the birds," he says. "Each bird had a different sound and they would be beeping each other. The blues comes from that."

Smitty's Red Top Lounge, *377 Yazoo Ave., 627-4421.*

James Smith, a.k.a. "Smitty," has been running his lounge for the past 27 years, and some years have been better than others.

Dockery's, once home to Charlie Patton, may be the actual place where the blues were born.

Frank Frost and the Jelly Roll Kings posed for an album cover here once, and the place has been written up in a Swedish magazine. Most years, however, have been uneventful, hard and lean. Not that it's affected Smitty's personality much. A tall and gangling man, usually wearing a baseball cap, he's always willing to pass the time of day with friends and strangers.

Smitty's is a dark windowless room. Junk is stored in the corners and the floors are uneven. None of this matters when the band begins to play, but the music is extremely sporadic—call ahead.

Thomas's Lounge, *2025 Fourth St., 624-2140*.

Thomas's is a big, crooked house in need of a few repairs, but it has a fresh country-air feel. The owner, L.S., a gentle man who works in a garage by day, once wanted to be a musician himself, but he had two daughters and "couldn't go around." He now lives in rooms above the club.

Big Jack Johnson, who lives in the neighborhood, sometimes plays here, as does the Wesley Jefferson Band. Again, however, the music is sporadic—call ahead.

Also

Live blues can be heard many weekends at the **Country Blues Lounge** (1695 Robertston Rd., 624-8171) in Lyon, a tiny town located just northeast of Clarksdale. (Heading north on Highway 61 out of Clarksdale, *don't* take the road to the left pointing to Lyon. Instead, turn right on the only paved road along that stretch of highway and drive for about two miles). The lounge is run by veterinarian Dr. Tyrone Powell.

The **River Mount Lounge** (911 Sunflower Ave., 627-1971), the **Pastime Lounge** (426 DeSoto Ave.) and the **Fantasy Lounge** (505 DeSoto Ave.) are three more upscale clubs that occasionally feature live blues, while the **VFW** on Highway 49S at the edge of town presents touring R&B acts.

Every August, the Sunflower River Blues Association (P.O. Box 1562, Clarksdale, Miss. 38614) puts on a two-day **Sunflower River Blues Festival** featuring music, workshops, lectures, and films.

Record Stores

Stackhouse/Delta Record Mart, *232 Sunflower Ave., 627-2209.*

Jim O'Neal, one of the foremost authorities on the blues, runs a record store out of this odd-looking building, shaped like a riverboat and located in the heart of Clarksdale's downtown. The store specializes in the Delta Blues, naturally, and O'Neal also runs his record label, Rooster Blues Records, from this address. The label's been around for well over a decade, but the store opened in 1988 on Muddy Waters's birthday, April 4.

Recently, too, O'Neal has started up the Stackhouse Recording Studio, built by bluesmen Lonnie Pitchford, Lonnie Shields and others, to pursue his longtime determination to record some of the area's musicians. Thus far, Stackhouse has recorded Willie Cobbs, John Hurt, Jr., and Lonnie Pitchford, among others.

Stackhouse has a mail-order catalogue, which can be ordered from the above address.

Open: M–Sa, 10 a.m.–6 p.m.

Radio

WROX/1450 AM (627-7343). Early Wright, M–F nights.
WWUN/101.7 FM (627-1113). Blues, M nights.
WQMA/1520 AM (326-8642). Daily, 6 a.m.–6 p.m.

HELENA, ARKANSAS

Located across the Mississippi from Clarksdale, Helena was a thriving wide-open port town during the '30's and '40's. The main street, Cherry, which paralleled the levee, had dozens of white saloons, while Elm Street, running just behind, had dozens of black. Bluesmen from all over—Johnny Shines, Robert Johnson, Howlin' Wolf, Sunnyland Slim, and Roosevelt Sykes (born in Helena)—congregated here by the dozens, knowing they could get work. Roosevelt Sykes wrote a song called "West Helena Blues," and Memphis Minnie sang about "Reachin' Pete," an unpopular policeman who patrolled Cherry Street.

"Most everywhere you'd go back then, you'd step into them blues," says one longtime Helena resident.

Today, Helena is a sad little place trying to get its feet back on firm economic ground. Cherry is still the main street—and it's lined with some wonderful pre–World War I buildings, but many stand abandoned. Some hope does seem to be in the air, however, thanks largely to the small but growing tourist industry that's now being generated by the Mississippi River steamboats that just started making regular stops here, the new **Delta Cultural Center** (see page 70), and the **King Biscuit Blues Festival**.

One of the best blues festivals around, the King Biscuit Blues Festival, is held every October (see "Major Festivals," page 403) in honor of Sonny Boy Williamson. Williamson was the town's most famous resident, and even though most of Helena's citizenry were or are oblivious to the blues, those who knew him still talk about him with amazement.

Sources

For blues information, visit Blues Corner (see "Record Stores," page 72). For maps and general information, contact the Phillips County Chamber of Commerce (111 Hickory Hill, 338-8327) or the Tourist Information Center (Highway 49 bypass, 338-7602).

The area code for Helena is (501).

Landmarks and Legends

KFFA Radio, *1360 Radio Drive, 338-8361*.

In the annals of blues history, there's nothing quite like KFFA's "King Biscuit Time," which over the 28 years it was broadcast live probably had more impact on the blues than any other radio program.

It all started back in 1941, when the station's owner was approached by Sonny Boy Williamson (then known as Rice Miller) and Robert Lockwood, Jr., who sold him on the then novel idea of playing on the air in return for the chance to advertise their gigs. The owner agreed and they lined up a sponsor, Interstate Grocer Co., distributor of King Biscuit Flour.

The show, broadcast Mondays through Fridays from 12:15 p.m. to 12:30 p.m. (later 12:15 p.m. to 12:45 p.m.), was an instant success, almost immediately expanding to include other musicians such as Pinetop Perkins, James "Peck" Curtis and Houston Stackhouse. Sonny Boy's picture was plastered onto cornmeal bags, sales soared, and the show went on the road, playing from the back of Interstate's delivery trucks.

Other businesses, impressed with King Biscuit's profits, soon followed suit, hiring blues singers to advertise a wide range of products. Before long, too, radio shows dedicated exclusively to the blues (nonexistent before then) started up around the country.

Williamson left KFFA intermittently throughout his career but remained affiliated with it all his life. He was not an easy man to work with. "He was a mean SOB," says Sonny Payne, the announcer who broadcast thousands of Sonny Boy's shows. "Twice a month we had to get him out of the clink. He'd been taken advantage of so many times, he started fighting back. That's what got him in trouble all the time."

"King Biscuit Time" switched from a live to a record format in 1969, and the show went off the air completely in 1980. Revived again in 1986, it is now running in its old time slot, with its old announcer, Sonny Payne. Nowadays, however, the show, which won the prestigious Peabody Award in 1992, is being broadcast out of the Delta Cultural Center (below).

Meanwhile, KFFA, basically a country music station that has moved several times over the years, is currently housed in this small building surrounded by tall grasses on the outskirts of town. A rusting Interstate truck with the KING BISCUIT FLOUR logo sits outside its front door, and souvenirs such as KFFA mugs and bumper stickers are on sale inside.
Open: M–F, 8 a.m.–5 p.m.

Delta Cultural Center, *95 Missouri St. (at the end of Cherry St., by the river), 338-8919.*

Dedicated to the heritage of the Arkansas River Delta, this well-conceived nonprofit center includes exhibits on everything from the Civil War to the Mississippi River. Near the back of the museum is a small display featuring some of the blues, gospel, and country artists who have come out of the state (including Johnny Cash, Al Green, and Conway Twitty) and a room with a rough wooden floor from which "King Biscuit Time" is broadcast. Visitors are welcome to listen in on the broadcast, which takes place every weekday at 12:15 p.m.
Open: M–Sa, 10 a.m.–5 p.m., Su, 1–5 p.m. *Admission:* free.

Helena National Bank Building, *302 Cherry St.*

KFFA was broadcast from the fifth floor of this, the tallest building in Helena, during the mid-sixties. On May 25, 1965, Williamson failed to show up for work, and Sonny Payne sent Peck Curtis out to find him. "When he got back," says Payne, "We had already started the show. 'Mr. Sonny,' Peck says to me, 'Sonny Boy's dead.' 'Dead?,' I said, 'you joshing me?' 'No sir.' 'Get on in there and let's play.' That's all I said."

Gist's Music Company, *307 Cherry St., 338-8441.*

Gist's is a huge barn of a place, with the wooden floors, hanging fans, and dusty smell of another era. Harmonicas fill the old glass cases, guitars hang from the walls, and a bell tinkles every time someone steps over the well-worn threshold.

Proprietor Mr. Morse Gist, called "Mr. Guitar" by his customers, is a tall quiet-spoken man. He once owned the building where Williamson lived and died, and sold the musician and his band their instruments and guitar strings.

"It would take Sonny Boy a long time to buy a harmonica," says Mr. Gist, "and one time he stormed back in, wanting to return one he'd bought that morning. Now he knew that wasn't allowed, it wasn't sanitary, and I got angry, he got angry, it was hot. Finally, I grabbed another harmonica off the shelf and told him never to come back. I threw the old harmonica away, but later I took it back out and put it in the back drawer. I needed something to remind me not to get angry. Darned if some museum people didn't come by a few years back and ask me for it."

While Mr. Gist is talking, Richard Jackson, a former friend of the blues musician, comes in. When he hears the subject at hand, he nods gravely. "Sonny Boy was a lovely fellow to meet," he says. "He always had a smile on his face and I hate to say it, but he changed suits every day. He didn't wear no rags. His house was the same way, just like a woman stayed there, he kept it that clean." *Open:* M–Sa, 10 a.m.–5 p.m.

Interstate Grocer Company, *Walnut Street between Missouri and Phillips streets.*

Located three blocks from Sonny Boy's boarding house, Interstate Grocer had introduced King Biscuit Flour two years before the founding of KFFA. The product was doing well, but not that well, and the owner, Max Moore, jumped at the chance to sign up the "King Biscuit Entertainers."

Today, another distributor, Helena Wholesale, sells Sonny Boy meal throughout Arkansas and Mississippi.

Sonny Boy Williamson's Boarding House, *427½ Elm St. at the corner of Pecan St., now an empty lot.*

A large brick building once stood on this site that over the years housed a chicken-processing plant, an auto-repair shop, and, upstairs on the second level, a half dozen "rooms" available for rent (they were actually more like cubicles built of two-by-four's). Sonny Boy Williamson first came here in 1941, and even though he would be gone for years at a time, recording up North or touring in Europe, the landlord always kept his room intact.

In 1964, the 65-year-old musician returned to Helena one last time. Though virtually unknown in the United States, he was a star in Europe. He'd been the hit of several blues festivals and had recorded with The Yardbirds and Eric Clapton, among others. The Helena townspeople were therefore surprised to see him back in town, resuming his old duties at KFFA. The explanation that he gave them was that he'd come home to die. "We're like elephants," he said. "We knows." Eight months later he was dead.

No. 427½ was still standing until late 1989, when it was severely damaged by lightning and high winds, and was torn down. The Sonny Boy Williamson Society salvaged many of the original bricks, and they hope one day to erect a museum on this site. The project has been actively supported by a number of musicians, including spokesman Kim Wilson, and several clubs have held benefits to raise money (Antone's in Austin, B.B.'s in Memphis, Legends in Chicago). Donations can be sent c/o the Sonny Boy Blues Society, P.O. Box 237, Helena, AR 72342.

Clubs, etc.

Eddie's Café, *corner of Yazoo and Missouri streets (one block behind Blues Corner record store).*

Frank Frost's girlfriend, Eddie Mae, runs a sociable café out of this dilapidated corner building many weekend evenings, and sometimes, when Frost feels like it, he and his friends put on a show. FRESH WHITE RIVER FISH HOT TO GO DAILY reads the sign outside the café. Fishing is Frost's other great passion.

Record Stores

This Little Pig Antiques and Gifts, and **Blues Corner,** *105 Cherry St., 338-3501.*

Bubba Sullivan of the Sonny Boy Blues Society runs a first-rate blues record shop in a large room next to his wife's sprawling antique store. Sullivan, a lifelong blues enthusiast who turned to the record business when he lost his farm a few years ago, is one of the few people in town—black or white—who really appreciates its music history, and he's constantly struggling to get it more recognition.

In addition to being a motherlode of Delta blues recordings, Blues Corner is a hangout for area musicians. Sam Carr, Frank Frost, Lonnie Shields, and John Weston all stop by here regularly. Blues Corner also has a mail-order catalogue.

Open: M–Sa, 9 a.m.–6 p.m., Su, 1–5 p.m.

Radio

KFFA/1360 AM (338-8361). "King Biscuit Time" with Sonny Payne, M–F, 12:15–12:45 p.m. "Blues Hour," Tu nights.

FRIAR'S POINT

Between Clarksdale and Helena is Friar's Point, Mississippi, once the Coahoma County seat and the site of the ferry crossing, which was the only way to cross the Mississippi before the mid-1950's. More than one blues musician on his way to a gig screeched onto a soon-to-depart ferry in the nick of time; and Eddie Condon's jazz tune "Friar's Point Shuffle" was named after this place.

Today, Friar's Point is a forsaken little town with a few nice homes, a few not-so-nice homes, and an historic museum featuring, rather surprisingly, artifacts of Native Americans.

The Queen of Hearts in Jackson is as known for its barbecue as for its blues.

MERIGOLD

South of Clarksdale and Merigold on Highway 61 is the Rushing Winery, founded by the Rushing family. Three generations ago, in the 1920's, Tom Rushing was the town's deputy sheriff, and was the subject of "Tom Rushen Blues," (a misspelling of "Rushing") recorded by Charley Patton: "When you get in trouble, it's no use to screamin' and cryin' / When you gets in trouble, it's no use to screamin' and cryin' / Tom Rushen will take you back to the prison house flyin'."

TUTWILER

Right through the middle of Tutwiler cut the railroad tracks. A tight line of brick buildings line either side, but the town feels empty, almost abandoned, even at high noon on a hot summer's day, and it's easy to imagine how eerie the place must seem at night.

W. C. Handy was sitting in the old Tutwiler railroad depot (no longer standing, although the foundation is still visible), waiting for a train that was nine hours late on that fateful night in 1903 when he first heard the blues. "A lean, loose-jointed Negro had commenced plunking a guitar beside me while I slept," Handy writes in his autobiography, *Father of the Blues*. "His clothes were rags; his feet peeked out of his shoes. His face had on it some of the sadness of the ages. As he played, he pressed a knife on the strings of the guitar. . . . The effect was unforgettable."

One of the phrases that the man repeated three times was "Goin' where the Southern cross the Dog." Handy asked what it meant and the man explained that he was headed to Moorhead, farther south, where the tracks of the Southern Railroad cross the Yellow Dog, a local name for the Yazoo and Mississippi Valley Railroad.

This was the first documentation of the blues and the slide guitar. As far as music historians can ascertain, blues did not exist much before 1900.

Sonny Boy Williamson's grave, *cemetery, Whitfield Church, just outside Tutwiler. Heading south, take Highway 49W ⁷⁄₁₀ mile to a paved road on right. Go about ¹⁄₂ mile, then turn left. Go another 1¹⁄₂ miles, past houses and fields, and watch for the abandoned church on right.*

Sonny Boy's gravestone is impressively large, unusual for a blues musician's (their graves are usually unmarked), but depending on the season, it can be extremely difficult to find as it's often covered over with brambles and vegetation. Look for the gleam of harmonicas—offerings left by earlier passersby—that surround the stone.

Parchman Penitentiary, *Highway 49W between Tutwiler and Drew.*

Before there were blues there were work songs, call-and-response chants used to coordinate groups of workers. Work songs were common among railroad workers and at penitentiaries, where prison gangs would sing while cutting wood or hoeing cotton.

Many bluesmen found themselves in Parchman at some point in their careers, and the penitentiary has been celebrated in a number of songs, including Bukka White's "Parchman Farm Blues." According to one legend, White was involved in a bar fight in which someone was killed. Rather than face charges, he fled to Chicago. He landed a recording session with Lester Melrose and was sitting in front of a microphone, singing, when the sheriff's deputies from Mississippi arrived, arrested him, and took him back to Parchman. His time here was not a total waste, however. While at the prison, he was recorded by Alan Lomax, who came to Parchman in 1939 to gather material for the Archive of American Folk Song in the Library of Congress.

Parchman is still operating as a state penitentiary today. Signs on either side of the institution say "Emergency Stopping Only Next Two Miles" but the prison itself—surrounded by dry, dusty fields—is located rather near the highway, where a red-and-white railroad crossing stick is raised and lowered to admit visitors, volunteer or otherwise.

Bluesmen are still incarcerated here, too. In 1992, Peter Lee and Fat Possum Records recorded David Malone, Junior Kimbrough's son, in the penitentiary (see **Junior Kimbrough's Houseparty,** page 57). Malone, who has since been released, was serving time for burglary; his was the first recording done at Parchman since the 1950s, and he was backed up by the Parchman Band, mostly made up of trustees, which tours the state from time to time.

DREW

Howlin' Wolf used to play in Drew's central square, while Charlie Patton, Tommy Johnson, and other musicians often gathered here to talk, swap stories, and sing the blues.

Today, the small town is home to the **Music Mart** (161 N. Main St., 745-6576), a record store owned by Drew native Marvin Flemmons, which carries a good selection of R&B and some blues. Flemmons grew up listening to the big bands, playing in his own high school band, and spinning records for local events, but it wasn't until he was listening to the radio one day in 1972 that he learned that the number one song of that year, "I'll Take You There," was by a group from his hometown, the Staple Singers. "I thought, 'How can they be from *Drew?*' " he says.

Today, Flemmons organizes the one-day **Staples Park Festival,** featuring Pops Staples and local blues musicians, the first Saturday of June. The festival is scheduled to coincide with the **B.B. King Homecoming Concert,** held in Indianola the Friday night before, and the **Mississippi Crossroads Blues Festival,** held in Greenwood the Saturday before.

DOCKERY

Dockery Farms, *Highway 8 between Cleveland and Ruleville.*
The Dockery Service Station is shut down. So, it appears, is the Dockery Baptist Church. But there's fresh hay in the barn with its fading DOCKERY FARMS sign, and someone is still working the fields out back.

Music critic Robert Palmer writes in *Deep Blues* that Dockery's—a huge plantation that's a town unto itself—may have been the actual place where the Delta blues originated. Charley Patton, one of the earliest bluesmen, once lived here, as did his teacher, a man named Henry Sloan, about whom almost nothing is known, but who was playing the blues as far back as 1897.

Patton lived in the Dockery area most all his life, attracting a coterie of imitators, and many of his songs reflect his life there. "Pea Vine Blues," for example, was written about the railroad, nicknamed the "Pea Vine" because of its circuitous route, that Dockery's men built in the late 1920's. Two of Patton's most famous students were Son House and Howlin' Wolf, and the first song the Wolf ever played was "Hitch Up My Pony, Saddle Up My Black Mare," Patton's showpiece.

INDIANOLA

The road leading into Indianola, once home to both B. B. King and Albert King (no relation), is a pretty one, long and winding. It follows the banks of a wide, dark river on whose surface float dozens of ducks.

Indianola's downtown consists of a small park and short main street. Though the town has yet to really acknowledge its best-known sons, there are two concessions to their fame: a B. B. King Street, and B.B.'s half-forgotten handprints, stamped into the cement sidewalk on the southwest corner of Second and Church streets. The location is an interesting one: a little farther on, just over the tracks, is the poor, black section of town, but this corner falls—just barely—within the boundaries of middle-class "respectability."

Unlike many musicians, B. B. King has never forgotten his hometown. He returns to Indianola every June to give a free concert in Fletcher Park (and elsewhere in the state) and a paying one in his old haunt, the Club Ebony. He also sponsors a local baseball team, the B. B. Kings.

Sources

The Chamber of Commerce (887-4454) is located at 104 E. Percy St.

Clubs, etc.

Keyhole Inn, *Church Street.*

The cozy two-room Keyhole, located just over the railroad tracks, features live bands many weekend nights. Bobby Whalen and the Ladies Choice Band are regulars, and the music can last until the wee hours, depending on "how good things be going."

Owner Mary Price, who works as a housekeeper by day, has been running the Keyhole for the past 21 years, and that includes cooking—catfish, buffalo fish, hamburgers, and bologna sandwiches—as well as tending bar. She's put a lot of time into the place: there are pictures of Africa and blinking Christmas lights, a pool table, and a blues jukebox.

Club Ebony, *404 Hannah St., 887-9915.*

The Club Ebony used to be Jones' Night Spot, and it was here that a young B. B. King first heard Sonny Boy Williamson, Robert "Junior" Lockwood, and Louis Jordan, among many others. Some years later, B.B. met his second wife, Sue Carol Hall, here while playing a gig of his own. Hall's mother, Miss Ruby, managed the place back then.

Today, the club is run by Mary Shephard, a charming grand-mother (though she hardly looks it) who's had the Ebony for over 16 years. B.B. still does an annual show here, and other big names, such as Bobby "Blue" Bland and Little Milton, come by regularly as well. The Ebony, however, is no longer really a blues club. Disco bands are usually the featured entertainment ("It's what the young people want"), although there is a blues deejay on most Wednesday nights.

Music: live blues twice a month. *Cover:* $$.

Also

There are no longer any blues at the 40-plus-year-old **Club Indianola** (409 Second St.), but it's worth driving by just to see the club's beautifully painted window. **Chevy's Four Seasons Restaurant** (Highway 82E, 887-6413) is one of the few white blues clubs in the Delta.

MOORHEAD

Like many of the towns in the center of the Delta, Moorhead has a different feel from the towns farther north. Things are greener and lusher here, and catfish farms—neat little man-made tracks of water—abound.

Moorhead is a simple one-street town, and right through its middle run the tracks of the Southern and the Dog (see Tutwiler, page 73), around whose gleaming, pragmatic lines so much lore has arisen. An historical marker marks the juncture.

Clubs, etc.

Cotton Inn, *Olive Street (Highway 3), downtown, across from the gas station.*

Sometimes, on Friday or Sunday nights, John Price and the Wonders, or T-Model Ford, take to the stage of this small, dark, unmarked joint with its painted pink walls. The place is rough-looking even for the Delta—the cement floors are uneven, the light bulbs are exposed and the seats are cracked—but that's because it's been around forever. For decades, people working the fields picking cotton used to come here to celebrate on the weekends. "A man worked five days a week, he want to come in and kick up his legs," says John Price.

QUITO *(about 4 miles south of Itta Bena on Highway 7)*

The how, where, and why of Robert Johnson's death continues to fascinate. Some say he was stabbed, some say he was poisoned, some say he died on all fours, barking like a dog.

> You may bury my body, ooh, down by the highway side,
> So my evil spirit can get a Greyhound bus and ride.

The latest chapter in the mystery surrounding the bluesman's death has resulted in the erection of two different markers, one in

Quito, the other near Morgan City. Both purport to indicate John-son's gravesite.

Quito's **Robert Johnson tombstone** stands near the Payne Chapel M.B. Church (on Highway 7 south from Itta Bena, turn right onto a dirt road marked "Leflore Co. #512 West"; the church is a few hundred yards down on the right and the tombstone is to the left of the church in the back of a small cemetery abutting a field). It was donated by an Atlanta rock group, appropriately called the Tombstones, who'd read about the supposed burial site, as identified by an ex-girlfriend of Johnson's, in *Living Blues* (No. 94). The stone was erected in late February 1991.

Johnson reportedly died behind the **Three Forks Store;** al-though no one seems to be quite certain where that site was, either, some believe that it was the brown building at the bridge in Quito (on the right just before reaching the Payne Chapel), moved here from a mile or so farther down the road sometime after Johnson's death.

MORGAN CITY

The **Robert Johnson Memorial Monument** at the Mt. Zion M.B. Church (heading north on Highway 7 from Morgan City, turn right onto Leflore Co. #511, toward the National Wild-life Refuge; the church is on the left) is an impressive affair, with inscriptions on all four sides. Funds for the memorial, dedicated on April 20, 1991, were donated by Columbia Records, thanks to the efforts of organizer Skip Henderson. Columbia, which also paid off the church's debts (again thanks to Henderson) was to have erected Johnson's tombstone as well, but when the stone was de-livered, a deacon at the church refused to accept it because one already stood in Quito.

To make things even more confusing, the Zion Church *is* John-son's official burial site, according to his death certificate. *But,* writes Jim O'Neal in his "Delta Blues Map Kit," "a number of peo-ple, including Honeyboy Edwards, have said that Johnson's sister had Robert's body moved to another cemetery" (the Payne Chap-el's?).

Whatever the truth may be, the Mt. Zion church itself stands simple, lovely, and serene, a small white clapboard building with a cross on top overlooking lush green fields.

BELZONI

Merigold (see page 73) was not the only place where Charley Patton got in trouble. He also spent a few nights in the Humphreys County Jailhouse. Today, the courthouse and jail, built of yellow brick, are both still standing and both still in use. The jailhouse—a very small affair, located just behind the imposing courthouse—seems to be a casual sort of place, with basketball courts, and laun-dry hanging on the line.

HOLLY RIDGE

Charlie Patton's grave is located in the tiny, dusty one-street town of Holly Ridge, just off Highway 82 between Leland and Indianola. Coming off the highway, turn left onto the main street and look for the New Jerusalem M.B. Church (on the left), where Patton once performed religious songs back in the 1930's. The church's graveyard is located two lots farther down, also on the left, opposite the last house in town, and Patton's grave is near the back. It went unmarked until July 20, 1991, when funds for the impressive headstone—complete with an inscribed guitar and a photo—were raised, mainly by Creedence Clearwater great John Fogerty, through the efforts of Skip Henderson.

Behind the graveyard, empty fields stretch out, dotted with abandoned railroad cars.

GREENVILLE

Greenville, population 50,000, is one of the few cities in the Delta. It's also Mississippi's largest river port and is home to many manufacturing, towboat, and barge-construction companies.

Nelson Street has traditionally been the town's blues street, renowned not only in Greenville but also elsewhere in the Delta. "When you're on Nelson Street on a Saturday night, you're as deep in the blues as you can get," Jim O'Neal once wrote.

At one time, the music could be heard everywhere along Nelson—in the cafés, in the liquor stores and bars—but today, **Perry's Flowing Fountain** is the street's only real club, and it features live blues only occasionally. Nelson Street's growing drug problems haven't helped matters any either, although a neighborhood revitalization program led by MACE (Mississippi Action for Community Education), a nonprofit organization founded by civil rights activists in 1967, is in the works.

Sources

The Chamber of Commerce (378-3141) is located at 915 Washington Ave.

Clubs, etc.

Perry's Flowing Fountain, *816 Nelson St., 335-9836.*
In Perry Payton's neat, cozy club are two rows of tables and chairs, dozens of tiny Christmas lights, and a bright mural on the wall depicting a purple-clad lady in a fountain. One side of the club is "Annie Mae's Café," which is mentioned in a Little Milton song (this was once his hangout and he still stops by occasionally when he's in town), and T-shirts are for sale behind the bar.

Payton, a mortician by day, knew all the big names—Ray Charles, B. B. King, Little Junior Parker, Howlin' Wolf—back when they were first coming up because he used to book them into

Mary Price has been running Indianola's Keyhole Inn for over 20 years.

the old Elks Club for about $300. Those who are still alive play for him whenever they're in town, but in general, the only blues that can be heard here are the ones the deejay spins.

Also

Lillo's Restaurant (Highway 82E in nearby Leland, 686-4401), a family-run place that's been around since 1948, often books piano player Boogaloo Ames with a jazz trio on Thursday nights.

Radio

WESY/1580 AM (378-9405). Blues M, F, early afternoon.
WIQQ/102 FM (378-2617). Blues, M night.

VICKSBURG

Best known as the site of the battle that turned the tide of the Civil War, Vicksburg, which marks the end of the Delta, has its own surprising share of jazz and blues history. African-American brass bands were common in the city as far back as the 1880's, and from 1953 to 1973, one of the Mid-South's most popular dance bands, the Red Tops, headed by drummer Walter Osborne, was based here. Vicksburg, which was also the hometown of Willie Dixon, even has a rather tenuous claim to being the site where the word "jazz" originated: in 1924, the *Vicksburg Evening Post* quoted a *New York Times* critic as saying that the word was coined to refer to a black drummer named Chaz (short for Charles) Washington who was known for his syncopated beat.

And then, there was the Blue Room. Ah, the Blue Room! Mention that name in Vicksburg and eyes will light up. From 1937 to 1972, the Blue Room, located at the corner of Clay and Mulberry streets, was one of the best clubs around, featuring the finest that jazz and blues had to offer: Louis Armstrong, Dinah Washington, Louis Jordan, Count Basie, etc.

It was the club's owner, Tom Wince, however, who really made the place unforgettable. The legends that surround him are endless: half black, half Jewish, he had 13 wives, one child by each; his bronzed baby shoes were his most prized possession and they hung in his club; he owned a huge diamond ring, reaching to his knuckle, that he kept wrapped in tissue paper in his pocket, ready to be taken out upon request; he drove a pink Lincoln with leopard-skin upholstery; he allowed whites into his club only on special occasions; he didn't allow visiting from one club table to another, as he felt it led to fighting.

Tom Wince's flamboyance didn't end with his death in 1972, either. His grave in the city cemetery (where part of the movie *Mississippi Burning* was filmed) is an amazing affair—a huge star, flanked by two urns, bearing the epitaph: "An internationally known night club owner who established and operated the famous Blue Room Night Club."

Radio

WQBC/1420 AM (636-1108). Blues, Sa nights.

JACKSON

Technically speaking, Jackson, the state capital, is too far south and west to be located in the Delta. Nonetheless, it's played an important role in Delta blues history. During the late 1920's and '30's, H. C. Speir, a Jackson music store owner, was a talent scout for all the major record companies and was responsible for getting many of the early Mississippi bluesmen—Charley Patton, Tommy Johnson, Skip James, and Robert Johnson, among them—recorded. Later, in the 1950's, Lillian McMurry, who owned a furniture store and record shop, launched the Trumpet label, and Johnny Vincent launched Ace. Nowadays, Malaco Records, a major contemporary African-American label, is headquartered here.

McMurry's store was located on Farish Street, which was and is the main artery of the city's African-American community (although some white store owners, such as McMurry, also had businesses here). During the '20's and '30's, the street also housed the second-story Crystal Palace (538 N. Farish, now above a bar called Birdland), a jazz club that brought in all the big acts of the day. Right across the street from the Crystal was the Alamo Theater, now marked with a neon sign, where Otis Spann won a talent concert at the age of eight.

Sources

The local paper, the *Clarion-Ledger* (961-7000) does a good job of listing music events. The Chamber of Commerce (948-7575) is located at 201 S. President St., and Rand-McNally city maps are available in local convenience stores.

Landmarks and Legends

Trumpet Records, *309 N. Farish St.*

In 1950, Lillian McMurry, who ran a furniture and record store out of this gray building near the intersection of Amity Street, founded Trumpet Records. One of the first artists she wanted to record was Sonny Boy Williamson, whom she had heard over KFFA radio. She and her brother and a friend set out to comb the Delta to locate Williamson, but no one would tell them where he was. Finally McMurry realized that the two white men were hindering rather than helping her cause. As Mike Rowe relates in *Chicago Blues,* she went into the next shack alone, introducing herself as a record company owner, "and this lady grinned and said, 'Why, come right in, Mrs. McMurry, he's right in the back room.' "

Ace Records, *209 W. Capitol St.*

Founded in 1955 by Johnny Vincent, Ace was best known for rock-and-roll, mainly the group Huey Smith & the Clowns, but the label also recorded a few R&B artists such as Earl King and Frankie Ford. Vincent closed down Ace in the early '60's but recently started it up again.

Clubs, etc.

Hal & Mal's, *200 S. Commerce St., 948-0888.*

Located near the railroad tracks, this long brick building houses a large and friendly commercial club that features both local and national talent. Blues and rock-and-roll is the focus, but all sorts of other music—jazz, folk, country—can also be heard. B. B. King, Tyrone Davis, and Lionel Hampton have played here, as have local groups such as the Tangents and Charlie Love & Night People.
Music: F–Sa. *Cover:* $–$$. *Food:* American, soul. CC.

Queen of Hearts, *2243 Martin Luther King, Jr., Dr., 366-2311.*

Owner Chellibe Lewis is as well known for his barbecue as he is for his juke joint, and the mouth-watering smell of chicken and ribs cooking outside on the open fire seeps through the walls of this small, makeshift neighborhood place, whose walls are lined with bits of broken mirror. The music is somewhat sporadic, but King Edward, one of the city's hottest guitar players, often plays on Sunday nights.

Red, Hot & Blue, *1625 E. County Line Rd. (at city limits), 956-3313.*

Owned by Thomas Couch, Sr., and his son, who also own Malaco Records, this Red, Hot & Blue franchise is one of a chain of 12 "Memphis-style barbecue" restaurants, only some of which feature live music. Blues comes to this location on the weekends only, and it's often (no surprise here) courtesy of Malaco recording artists such as the Beat Daddys or Mike Griffin & the Unknown Blues Band. The club's walls are decked out with lots of blues paraphernalia.

Music: F, Sa. *Cover:* $. *Food:* barbecue, grilled items, etc.

Also

The Subway Lounge (619 W. Pearl St.), one of the city's oldest clubs, often has live blues on the weekends, sometimes compliments of King Edward, performing with five or six of the city's top singers in a blues vocalists' jam.

Jackson hosts a number of festivals, including the one-day **Zoo Blues** (352-2582) fest in April, the **Farish Street Festival** (960-1557) over Labor Day weekend, and the two-day **Jubilee Jam** (960-1557), held in May.

Radio

WJSU/88.5 FM (968-2140). Affiliated with Jackson State. Jazz and some blues daily.

WMPR/90.1 FM (956-0212). Affiliated with Tougaloo College. Contemporary blues daily.

Atlanta

For a major city with a large African-American population, Atlanta, surprisingly, has never had a particularly strong jazz history. Probably the best-known name to come out of here was composer and arranger Duke Pearson. Others include saxophonists George Adams and Marion Brown, singer-pianist Perry Bradford, pianist Eddie Heywood, trombonist J. C. Higgenbotham, and in more recent years, the Harper Brothers. Fletcher Henderson is also associated with the city—he studied chemistry at Atlanta University before pursuing a music career.

Among the local groups, the Peachtree Strutters, playing an early New Orleans style, have been a popular band in Atlanta for years and years. Though now somewhat diminished in size—only a few of the once-large band's members remain—they still play around town on special occasions.

Blues played a prominent role in Atlanta in the first half of the century. Back then, the city served as a communications center connecting the South with the Northeast, and numerous record labels, including Columbia and Okeh, set up field recording units here. The hub of the city's blues activity was Decatur Street, once home to Blind Willie McTell, Peg Leg Howell, and Georgia Tom Dorsey. Bessie Smith also spent much time in Atlanta in the early part of her career.

Sources

Two excellent music sources are *Creative Loafing* (688-5623), a free weekly, and *The Hudspeth Report* (255-3220), a free monthly. The Friday and Saturday editions of the *Atlanta Journal-Constitution* (526-5151) also contain listings. The City of Atlanta runs an arts hotline (853-3ART) that includes music listings.

For maps and other information, contact the Atlanta Convention and Visitors Bureau, 233 Peachtree St., NE, Suite 2000; 521-6600.

The area code for Atlanta is (404).

A Note on the Neighborhoods

Atlanta is a sprawling metropolis made up of a small downtown, a few major streets, and a multitude of suburbs. Buckhead is an affluent neighborhood located to the north; Virginia Highland (centering around Virginia and Highland streets) is a young, trendy area in an older part of town to the east. Five Points, so named because five streets converge here, is another entertainment district near the downtown, while Little Five Points is a more eclectic entertainment area somewhat south of downtown. The Underground is a new Rouse Company development whose entire basement floor (Kenny's Alley) is devoted to music clubs. Patrons here shop from one sound to another as if they were shopping for clothes, but some of the music is actually quite good. Southwest Atlanta is home to a large African-American community.

Since many of Atlanta's clubs and historic sites are located in or near the downtown, it is possible to navigate the city by taxi. If you are driving, traffic is usually light, and parking spaces plentiful.

Landmarks and Legends

(With the exception of the Waluhaje Club, all of the sites below are near the downtown and can be toured on foot.)

Auburn Avenue, *from Peachtree Street east.*
Nearly two miles long, Auburn Avenue was the heart of Atlanta's African-American commercial district from the turn of the century to the 1960's. The nation's oldest black daily, the *Atlanta Daily World,* was founded here in 1928, and Martin Luther King, Jr., was born here in 1929. In 1957, *Fortune* magazine called the avenue "the richest Negro street in the world."

Some of the establishments located along Auburn in days gone by include the Gate City Colored School (the first public school for blacks in Atlanta) and the European Hotel (the first hotel for blacks). Auburn never acquired the nightlife reputation of nearby Decatur Street, but two important theaters-nightclubs, the Royal Peacock and the Top Hat Club, were located here in the 1950's.

The avenue, which begins in the heart of Atlanta's downtown, went into a steep decline following the Civil Rights riots of the '60's, but the area is now being revitalized. The African-American Panoramic Experience (APEX) Museum, a sophisticated black-history museum, opened up several years back, and the Historic Facade Program, designed to help local businessmen renovate their establishments, is now in effect. The Martin Luther King, Jr., Historic District, which includes King's grave and a small museum, is also located on the far eastern end of the avenue. For a leader of such magnitude, the museum is much too small and haphazardly put together, but at least it's there.

Royal Peacock, *186 Auburn Ave., 880-0745.*
The Royal Peacock was opened in 1949 by a Ms. Carrie Cunningham and quickly became the social and cultural center of Auburn Avenue. Nat "King" Cole, Lucky Millinder, Cab Calloway, Sam Cooke, and many others performed here; Little Richard got one of his first big breaks here.

The Royal Peacock reopened several years ago, and though now operating primarily as a lounge and bar, it does present live music, including blues and reggae, from time to time. Outside, the original marquee and neon theater sign are still in place.

WERD, *330 Auburn Ave.*
No longer in business, but once located in a mustard-colored building that now houses Atlanta's Southern Christian Leadership Conference, WERD was the first African-American-owned radio station in the country, founded by Jesse B. Blayton in 1947. The station's sign still hangs out front.

The APEX Museum *(African-American Panoramic Experience), 135 Auburn Ave., 521-2654.*

A sophisticated, well-lit museum dedicated to African-American history and culture, the APEX changes its exhibits from month to month, but always on view are historical photos and a short film describing the history of the area. The exceptional film *Sweet Auburn Avenue,* narrated by Cicely Tyson and Julian Bond, is alone well worth the visit; a $25 million expansion project is in the works, to be completed in 1995.

Open: T–Sa, 10 a.m.–5 p.m. *Admission:* $.

Decatur Street, *near Peachtree Street.*

During the early 1900's, the downtown end of Decatur Street (where Georgia State University is now located) was the heart of Atlanta's black nightlife, filled with saloons, pool halls, taverns, and theaters. The street was also overrun with gangsters, both black and white, and a "normal" Saturday night brought with it at least six "razor operations."[1]

Before World War I, Decatur was famous for its blues piano players. Later, it became filled with musicians from all over Georgia, Alabama, and the Carolinas, many of whom played the lighter sound of the Piedmont blues. One of these new arrivals was Blind Willie McTell, whose name later became synonymous with Atlanta blues. Blind Willie—who could be heard on the streets of the city as late as the early '60's—was fiercely independent, breaking record contracts whenever he felt like it.

Another famous Decatur Street bluesman was Peg Leg Howell. Peg Leg turned to blues in 1916 after his brother-in-law shot him in the leg and he had to give up farming. One of the first Atlanta musicians to be recorded, Peg Leg usually worked the streets with other musicians where, according to Giles Oakley in *The Devil's Music,* "they generated a wailing excitement, singing together with extrovertedly exaggerated voices."

Decatur Street was home to two major theaters, the "81" and the "91," named after their respective street numbers (and since replaced by the university's auditorium). The "81" was the larger and more prestigious of the two. Georgia Tom Dorsey worked there as a boy, selling soda pop, and Bessie Smith was "practically raised" in its backyard.

Film actor Leigh Whipper remembered Bessie from those early days back in 1913: "She was just a teenager and she obviously didn't know she was the artist she was. She didn't know how to dress—she just sang in her street clothes—but she was such a natural that she could wreck anybody's show."[2]

By 1924, Bessie, returning to the "81" after a national tour, was not only fashionable but famous. People lined up three abreast to buy tickets to her shows and a special performance was put on for whites only. This was common practice at the time—whites might adore black artists, even purchase their albums, but when it came to seeing them in concert, the musicians were still booked almost

Blind Willie's is named after Atlanta's best-known bluesman, Blind Willie McTell.

exclusively into all-black theaters, which usually reserved a night or two for an all-white audience.

Underground Atlanta, *Martin Luther King, Jr., Dr. and Peachtree Street*

Today's Underground is a vast new shopping and entertainment complex in downtown Atlanta. Opened in 1989, to the tune of $142 million, it is yet another Rouse Company project, complete with the usual cute boutiques and pricey restaurants.

What makes the Underground unique, however, is that it is built on the historic city viaducts that were constructed between 1893 and the 1940s to route street traffic over congested railroad lines. Back then, merchants located on the lower levels promptly moved their stores up to the street to be near traffic, and left abandoned buildings behind. Some of these buildings became homes for the city's poorer folk; others became prostitution houses or blues bars.

In "Preachin' the Blues" Bessie Smith describes those days: "Down in Atlanta, G.A. / Under the viaduct every day / Drinkin' corn and hollerin' hooray / Pianos playing 'til the break o' day."

Despite the celebratory words of Bessie's song, the underground must have been a horrible place, cold in the winter, hot in the summer, dirty, airless, rat-infested. It's hard to get a true feeling for all of that in today's squeaky-clean Underground, but at the nearby Mitchell Street viaduct (which is actually the one referred to in Bessie's song), conditions back then are all too easy to imagine. The place, now a parking lot located near the junction of Martin Luther King, Jr., Drive and Butler Street, is ugly, cavernous, and threatening—not an area to wander around alone in late at night.

The Waluhaje, *West Lake Ave., on the left, heading from Simpson Street (it's the only large building in the area).*

Now a Job Corps training center, this big red-brick building, looking stern and institutional behind a pillared fence, was once a luxury hotel housing the Waluhaje Club. During the '50's, clubs and fraternities held dances here, and famous performers such as Dinah Washington, Tony Bennett, and Ella Fitzgerald were regulars.

Dizzy Gillespie played the Waluhaje in December 1956 shortly after making an enormously successful State Department tour to Africa, the Near East, the Middle East, and Asia. The date was an important one to both him and other African-American musicians, as he explains in his autobiography *To Be or Not to Bop.* "This was still a mixed band with a black leader playing in Georgia where whites were still struggling to hold on to segregation. One of the reasons we'd been sent around the world was to offset reports of racial prejudice in the United States, so I figured now we had a chance to give the doctor some medicine. . . . We opened at the black-owned Waluhaje, a beautiful new luxury apartment and entertainment complex in Atlanta, and, of course, a lot of whites there wanted to come to see us and they did, with no segregation."

Clubs, etc.

Atlanta has two top jazz spots: **Just Jazz,** a club that books both national and local talent, and the **Atlanta Renaissance Hotel,** known for its presentation of local talent. The city also has two strong, serious blues clubs, **Blind Willie's,** which concentrates on roots blues, and **Blues Harbor,** which leans more toward national touring acts.

Some of the local jazz talent to watch for includes saxophonist Joe Jennings and his band Life Force, the Paul Mitchell Jazz Trio, Rodrick Smith and the New Jazz Collective, trumpet player Dave Ferguson, keyboard player Mose Davis, piano players Ojeda Penn and Dan Mattrazzo, alto player James Hudson, trumpeter and pianist Danny Harper, and jazz singers Audrey Shakir, Bernadine Mitchell, and Crystal Fox. Blues players include sax player Grady "Fats" Jackson, Luther "Houserocker" Johnson, Lotsa Poppa, Sandra Hall, and Chicago Bob Nelson.

Most bars and clubs in Atlanta stay open until two a.m. (three a.m. on Fridays).

Personal Choices

Best jazz club: *Just Jazz*
Best hotel for jazz: *Atlanta Renaissance*
Best blues club: *Blind Willie's*
Best upscale blues club: *Blues Harbor*
Most historic club: *La Carrousel*

F O R   J A Z Z

Just Jazz, *2101 Tula St., NW (midtown), 355-5423*
The only real jazz club in town, Just Jazz is a second-story, worn-around-the-edges lounge that books both national and locally based talent. Some of the many who have appeared in this long, low-lit room with an enthusiastic audience and lots of antique instruments and jazz portraits hanging from the walls include Ramsey Lewis, Freddie Hubbard, Lionel Hampton, Joe Jennings, and Freddie Cole.
Music: W–Su. *Cover:* $–$$$.

Atlanta Renaissance Downtown Hotel, *590 W. Peachtree St., NW, 881-6000.*
The second most consistent spot for jazz in Atlanta, the Renaissance Hotel offers live music about three nights a week. Top local artists are usually featured, with the Clark College radio station, WCLK/91.9 FM, broadcasting a weekly show from here on Friday nights. The jazz lounge, divided into three sections with a fireplace and bar, is located on the hotel's twenty-fifth floor and offers glorious panoramic views of the city.
Music: W, F, Sa. *Cover:* $. CC.

Dante's Down the Hatch, *3380 Peachtree Rd., N.E. (Buckhead), 266-1600.*
Dante's Down the Hatch, *Underground Atlanta, 577-1800.*
For years, Dante's has been touted as the oldest jazz club in Atlanta. As such, it's a depressing statement on the times. Both uptown and downtown Dantes are primarily touristy restaurants built to look like the hulls of ships, complete with portholes, wooden booths, fishnets, anchors—even live crocodiles.

Jazz does happen at Dante's—again both uptown and down—but it's usually a predictable mix of standards and contemporary tunes designed to please a largely indifferent crowd. Paul Mitchell, the city's elder statesman of jazz, who has performed at Dante's almost every night for over 20 years (he is currently at the Buckhead location) says, a bit sadly, "Times have changed, people have changed. Once, when I played a ballad, people would say, 'Shsh.' Now, they talk. It used to bother me, but it doesn't anymore. There's still a kind of communication going on—I don't know what it is, but it's there."

For all its drawbacks, Dante's is an Atlanta institution—owner Dante Stephensen is no fool, and no doubt it's the club's commercial bent that has helped it survive. Consequently, it has attracted many well-known artists passing through: Gladys Knight, Max Roach, Keith Jarrett, and Chuck Mangione among them. Both clubs have similar music and pricing policies.

Music: nightly. *Cover:* $. *Food:* fondues and salads. CC.

La Carrousel, *at Paschal's Motor Hotel and Restaurant, 830 Martin Luther King, Jr., Dr. SW (Southwest Atlanta, 10 min. from downtown), 577-3150.*

Miss Rose Phillips, a gracious, soft-spoken schoolteacher, has been tending bar at La Carrousel in Paschal's Motor Hotel for over 18 years. When she was a little girl and came in with her parents, she heard Ramsey Lewis play. Later there were Dizzy Gillespie, Jimmy Smith, Count Basie, Cannonball Adderley, and others.

La Carrousel, located in an African-American commercial district, is one of the oldest still-operating clubs in Atlanta. A big long room filled with low tables and red swivel chairs, it's lined with oil paintings of the circus: Emmett Kelly, the big top, a merry-go-round. Two painted horses greet guests at the door and the bar itself is a mock carousel, twinkling with red lights.

At one time, La Carrousel was *the* jazz room in Atlanta, attracting music fans of all ages and races. Today, however, things aren't what they used to be. Jazz still happens here every Friday and Saturday night, but the place, the players, and the crowd are older, grayer, and more cynical than they once were.

Things aren't what they used to be at the Paschal Motor Hotel, connected to La Carrousel by a skyway, either. An ineffable sadness seems to hang over the place, perhaps because, back in the '60's, the hotel and its restaurant was a place of such hope. Martin Luther King, Jr., Ralph Abernathy, and Andrew Young were regulars here; the Selma march was planned from here; Robert Kennedy, following King's assassination and before his own, set up an office here.

Today, all that fervor and expectation are gone, long gone. The halls at the hotel are dim and half empty, smelling of stale air and tired lives. Voices echo down from the restaurant; newspaper odes to the past are mounted on the wall. . . .

Paschal's, their words read, is a rags-to-riches tale. Opened in 1947 by two brothers who came from a tiny Georgian town, it started out as a chicken shack. Back then, a full meal cost a mere 52 cents, and before long, the place became so popular that it expanded into a restaurant. Next came the hotel and La Carrousel.

Modern-day Paschal's may have lost much of its earlier fire, but it's still well worth visiting—for its history, for its fried chicken (still a favorite among local politicians), and for its jazz, featuring established local musicians.

Music: F–Sa. *No cover.*

The Ritz-Carlton, Buckhead, *3434 Peachtree Rd., NE,*
237-2700.

"I could never understand jazz," says William Noll, conductor
and musical director of the elegant Ritz Carlton, Buckhead.
"Nothing was ever written down. But then I began to see that jazz
musicians are like symphony orchestras. They have a batlike
radar, they really read each other."

Noll, a classically trained musician with 28 years of professional experience, started studying jazz only about seven years
ago, but it's because of him and his enthusiasm for the music—
which seems to be bursting him apart at the seams—that the Ritz-
Carlton instituted a steady jazz program. First, there's the Ritz-
Carlton Orchestra, playing the big-band sounds on special occasions. Then there's a weekend jazz program in the Café, and jazz,
compliments of the William Noll Duo or Quartet, weekday evenings in the lobby lounge.
Music: daily. *No cover.*

Café 290, *290 Hilderbrand Rd. (Sandy Springs, 20 min. N of
downtown), 256-3942.*

Located in the Balcony Shopping Center on the outskirts of
town, Café 290, with its low ceilings, flickering candles, and suburban feel, offers local jazz ranging from traditional to bop. Sundays
are devoted to the blues. Across the street from the Café is the famous **Punch Line** comedy club, and well-known comics, Robin
Williams and Eddie Murphy among them, have been known to
stop by.
Music: nightly. *No cover. Food:* American. CC.

FOR BLUES

Blind Willie's, *828 N. Highland Ave. (Virginia–
Highland), 873-2583.*

Small and friendly, with an exposed brick wall, a great blues
jukebox, and high revolving fans, Blind Willie's concentrates on
roots blues. A poster of Blind Willie McTell, the club's namesake
(see Decatur Street, "Landmarks and Legends," page 85), hangs
to one side, and Mardi Gras beads are draped over the bar.

Once a hardware store, the club usually features its house band,
the Shadows, backing up local blues veterans such as Grady
"Fats" Jackson, or Luther "Houserocker" Johnson. Nationally
known names—Rufus Thomas, Lonnie Mack, Johnny Copeland,
and Taj Mahal—also come through on a regular basis.
Music: nightly. *Cover:* $–$$.

Blues Harbor, *2293-B Peachtree Rd., (Buckhead)
605-0661.*

Located in a building with large windows overlooking a creek,
Blues Harbor is one fancy blues bar, equipped with blue-and-

white Laura Ashley–type curtains, lots of nice posters—even a carpet on the floor. Well, at least the chairs are mismatched.

Blues Harbor books only out-of-town talent, most of which comes from the West Coast, Washington, D.C., or Chicago. Some of the artists who've been here include the Mighty Flyers, Roomful of Blues, and Mack "Guitar" Murphy. Guitar player Ray Chesna plays in the early evenings on Fridays and Saturdays.

Food is also an important part of the club, and the place is famous for its "Blues Plate Special," lobster and prime rib.
Music: nightly. *Cover:* $–$$. *Food:* American. CC.

Fat Matt's Rib Shack, *1811 Piedmont Rd., 607-1622*.
Primarily a barbecue restaurant, Fat Matt's also serves up local blues every night of the week. Regulars include such bands as Jelly Roll, Chicken Shack, and the Lee Griffin Band.

Fat Matt's only seats about 40 people, and its walls are hung with photos of blues greats. On the small makeshift stage in the corner is a beat-up drum kit and an old piano that was once used at the Royal Peacock.
Music: nightly. *No cover. Food:* barbecue.

Dr. Rib, *1174 Euclid Ave. (Little Five Points), 525-5525*.
A sort of upscale sibling of Fat Matt's (the owners are brothers), Dr. Rib features a dining room to one side, a bar to the other. Lava lamps hang from the walls and a colorful mural swirls behind the stage. Many of the bands that play Fat Matt's also play here, while Frog McWilliams (who once played with Fats Domino) and the New Blues Crew are regulars on weekend afternoons.
Music: nightly, weekend afternoons. *No cover: Food:* barbecue.

Also

Blues and R&B can occasionally be heard at the **Royal Peacock** (880-0745; see "Landmarks and Legends," page 85), which reopened for business a few years ago. **Café 290** (see "For Jazz," page 91) and **Red, Hot & Blue** (3880 Roswell Rd., 814-0066), a "Memphis-style barbecue restaurant" that is one of a chain, offer blues on the weekends.

Other Venues and Special Events

One of the five sister festivals to the world-renowned event produced in Montreux, Switzerland, each July, the **Montreux Atlanta Music Festival** (853-3ART, ext. 223) takes place in late August. The 11-day fest, held at various venues throughout the city, features lots of jazz and blues, both national and local, as well as other types of music. The 10-day **Atlanta Jazz Festival,** one of the largest free jazz festivals in the world, is held in late May–early June. Both local and national artists are presented.

The **Spivey Hall Jazz Series,** featuring touring artists, is held every July and August at Spivey Hall (5900 N. Lee St., Clayton State College, 961-3683).

Nationally known jazz and blues performers can also be heard occasionally at the **Fox Theatre** (660 Peachtree St., 881-2100), a lavish 1929 former Shriners temple whose architecture is half Moorish, half Egyptian; the **Center Stage Theater** (1374 W. Peachtree St., 681-2100); the **Omni Coliseum** (100 Techwood Dr. NW, 577-9600), and the **Lakewood Fairgrounds/Coca-Cola Amphitheater** (627-5700), which also hosts an annual blues festival.

Radio

WCLK/91.9 FM (880-8273). A 24-hour jazz station affiliated with Clark College and the NPR network. Blues, Sa afternoon.

WRFG/89.3 FM (523-3471). Blues, M–F mornings; W, Th evenings. Of special note: "True Blues," Th evenings with Eric King.

WOKS/1340 AM (706-576-3565). Much blues daily.

Jazz and blues can also be occasionally heard on **WREK/91.1 FM** and **WRAS/88.5 FM.**

Elsewhere in Georgia

Gertrude "Ma" Rainey's home, *805 Fifth Ave., Columbus, Ga.*

The "Mother of the Blues" lived in this small two-story row house 90 miles south of Atlanta for the last five years of her life. For years, the house stood unoccupied and in dilapidated condition, but in 1992, thanks largely to the efforts of the Columbus African-American Heritage Preservation Society and the City of Columbus, the home's exterior was restored to the tune of $76,000. Work is now underway to turn the building into a museum.

Once a performer with the Rabbit Foot Minstrels, Ma Rainey cut numerous best-selling blues records, and, legend has it, kidnapped Bessie Smith and taught her how to sing the blues. (Many dismiss this story as apocryphal; others say that Ma and Bessie were lovers.) By the time she returned to Columbus, the city of her birth, Rainey had stopped performing, but she kept her hand in the entertainment business by owning and operating two theaters in nearby Rome. Nonetheless, when she died in 1939 at the age of 53, her death certificate listed her occupation as "housekeeper."

Fletcher Henderson's home, *1016 Andrew St., Cuthbert, Ga.*

Approximately 120 miles south of Atlanta is the house where Fletcher Henderson and his brother Horace, also a jazz musician, grew up. A one-story Victorian dwelling, the house was built in

1888 and was the home of Professor Fletcher Hamilton Henderson, Sr., a leading black educator, until his death in 1943.

While living here, both Fletcher and Horace attended the school where their father taught, and studied piano. Fletcher then moved to New York, where he led the house orchestra at the Roseland Ballroom. Horace moved to Ohio, where he formed his own ensemble, which was noted, back then, for its progressive sound.

Miami/Fort Lauderdale

Miami has produced only a handful of nationally recognized jazz and blues artists over the years, but from the 1930's through the '60's, the city had an active and sophisticated jazz scene, catering largely to the tourist trade. Overtown Square in the African-American section of town was once renowned for its glittering black-and-tan clubs featuring artists such as Nat "King" Cole, Louis Armstrong, and Lena Horne. Meanwhile, over in lily-white Miami Beach, many of the posh hotels had showrooms presenting black entertainers and Las Vegas stars. The "Jackie Gleason Show" in particular, taped at the Miami Beach Auditorium (now the Theater of the Performing Arts) in the 1960's, brought in many of the biggest jazz names of the day.

Some of the musicians born in Miami include drummer Panama Francis, bassist Jimmy Garrison, saxophonist George Kelly, and trumpeter Blue Mitchell. Musicians born in other parts of the state—Fats Navarro in Key West, the Adderley brothers in Tampa—once spent much time in the city, as did, and does, Ira Sullivan, the great trumpet player who's lived here for decades now.

Sources

New Times (372-0004), a free weekly, has excellent listings. Other sources are the Friday editions of the *Miami Herald* (350-2111) and the Fort Lauderdale *Sun Sentinel* (761-4000), and *XS Magazine* (356-4943), a free Fort Lauderdale weekly.

The Sunshine Jazz Organization runs a jazz hotline at 382-3938. The city also has a blues hotline: 666-MOJO. WLRN/91.3 FM announces calendar listings on "Lunchtime Miami," Fridays, 11 a.m.–1 p.m.

The Greater Miami Convention & Visitors Bureau is located at 701 Brickell Ave., Suite 2700; 539-3063 or 800-283-2707. The Greater Fort Lauderdale Convention & Visitors Bureau is located at 200 E. Las Olas Blvd., Suite 1500, 765-4460 or 800-22-SUNNY.

The area code for Miami/Fort Lauderdale is (305).

A Note on the Neighborhoods

Eleven million tourists fly south to Miami each year, many of them heading for the sun-and-fun communities of Miami Beach, (including South Beach), Coral Gables, and Coconut Grove. South Beach, 15 minutes from downtown, is filled with luscious pastel-colored Art Deco buildings, most of them renovated and housing trendy restaurants, boutiques, and clubs, one or two still untouched by modern times and home to silver-haired retirees with walkers who play bingo in their lobbies late at night. Coral Gables, 15 minutes southwest of downtown, was the nation's first planned city, and it's a moneyed land filled with fine hotels and restaurants. Coconut Grove, also to the southwest, is billed as Miami's "Bohemia," but it's usually packed with tourists on the make.

Carol City, 20 minutes north of downtown, is home to a large African-American community as well as to recent immigrants from the Caribbean. Fort Lauderdale, a mecca for tourists from the North, is approximately 40 minutes north of Miami; Hollywood is located between Miami and Fort Lauderdale.

Landmarks and Legends

Overtown Square, *N.W. Second St. bet. Sixth and Tenth streets.*

Originally settled by workers for the Flagler railroad system, Overtown, adjacent to the downtown, was once the largest and most vibrant African-American community in Miami. Through its heart ran Avenue G (now Second Avenue), which was also known as "Little Broadway" or the "Great Black Way." Lined with jazz clubs, hotels, and theaters of all sorts, it attracted both blacks and whites and actively courted the tourists from up North with promises of "exotic" foods and entertainment.

The tallest building in Overtown was the Mary Elizabeth Hotel (now torn down), which hosted everyone from Supreme Court Justice Thurgood Marshall to Adam Clayton Powell. Many of the black artists who were then performing on Miami Beach but were not allowed to overnight there also stayed at the Mary Elizabeth. Other important Overtown spots included the Lyric Theater, one of the most elegant theaters in town; the Harlem Square Club, where Sam Cooke recorded his memorable album; and the Sir John Hotel, in whose basement was the Knight Beat club, run by Clyde Killens.

As was the case with many other early African-American communities, Overtown was destroyed in the process of "urban renewal" and the construction of expressways. Now, however, the area, which is filled with abandoned buildings, is being revitalized.

The 16,500-seat Miami Arena was built here a few years back (it's home to the Miami Heat, the city's basketball team), and a Historic Overtown Folklife Village, highlighting black history, is in the works. The Folklife Village will include a "Jazz Walk of Fame" and studio spaces for the performing arts.

Lyric Theater, *N.W. Second Ave. and Ninth St.*
The Lyric, built in 1913 by a wealthy black businessman, may have been the first legitimate theater in Overtown. Once described as "possibly the most beautiful and costly playhouse owned by colored people in all the Southland," it presented all the greats, including Count Basie, Lena Horne, Ella Fitzgerald, and Nat King Cole. Converted into a church around 1960, it stood vacant for a few years in the 1980's and is now being restored to its former grandeur. It is expected to reopen as a theater in 1996.

Clubs, etc.

With its large Latin population, Miami is a melting pot of sounds. There's lots of reggae, lots of salsa, lots of dance music—all of which has its effect on jazz. The city is also home to the University of Miami, which has one of the most respected jazz programs in the country.

Downtown Miami has little to offer in the way of nightlife, most clubs and restaurants being located in Miami Beach, Coconut Grove, Coral Gables, and Fort Lauderdale. The majority of these cater to a tourist clientele.

Though the Miami area has no steady club venue for national touring jazz acts, the city does have a large number of fine restaurants and clubs that present first-rate, locally based talent. Foremost among these are the **MoJazz Café, Rose's, O'Hara's Pub** (in Fort Lauderdale), and the **Sushi Blues Café** (in Hollywood). **Tobacco Road** brings in national blues acts on a regular basis, while the **Musicians Exchange Cafe** (in Fort Lauderdale) and **Stephen Talkhouse** feature national acts of all kinds, including some blues, occasional jazz.

Some of the many top-caliber jazz musicians playing in the Miami/Fort Lauderdale area today include trumpet players Ira Sullivan and Pete Minger; pianist Dr. Lonnie Smith; jazz and blues vocalists Alice Day and Toni Bishop; Latin/jazz flautist Nestor Torres; saxmen Ed Calle, Kenny Millions, and Gary Campbell; contemporary funk saxman Arthur Barron; vocalist and violinist Nicki Yarling (who also fronts a blues band, Little Nicki and the Slicks); Caribbean jazz steel drummer Othello; viola player Debbie Spring; and Japanese vibraphonist by way of Hawaii, Tom Toyama. Two top big bands in the area are the University of Miami Concert Jazz Band and Atlantean Driftwood.

Blues and R&B talent worth looking out for include Roach Thompson, IKO-IKO, the Blind Tigers, Fleet Starbuck Blues Band,

Nightstalkers, Big Mama Blu, Good Rockin' Johnny & the Wise Guys, and Little Nicki and the Slicks.

Bars and clubs close anywhere between 2 and 5 a.m.

Personal Choices

Best jazz clubs: *MoJazz Café, Rose's, O'Hara's Pub*
Most unusual jazz/blues spots: *Sushi Blues Café, Bread of Life*
Best blues club: *Tobacco Road*

F O R   J A Z Z

MoJazz Café, *928 71st St., Miami Beach, 865-2636.*
Owned by Mo Morgan, a musician who used to run the Jazz-mania Society (a 1970's jazz loft) in New York City, the MoJazz Café features top locally based jazz musicians every night of the week. Some of the many who have played here include Ira Sullivan, Pete Minger, Alice Day, Little Nicki Yarling, and Gary Campbell; and there's also a house band, the MoJazz Band, and a Latin group, Saoco, that usually plays once a week.

The club is small, informal, and simply laid out, with wood paneling and high ceilings. A bar area is to one side, chairs and tables to the other, and jazz posters and photos hang from the walls.
Music: nightly. *Cover:* none at the bar, $ at the tables. *Food:* American and Cuban.

Rose's, *745 Washington Ave., South Beach, 532-0228.*
One of the newest jazz clubs in town, this cozy spot offers up a steady mix of jazz, blues, and R&B, along with some world music. Owned by jazzman Arthur Barron, who also plays at the club on a regular basis, Rose's is trying to revive the jazz tradition on South Beach, which was once a hotbed of the music (see chapter introduction, page 94).

The club seats about 200, and out back are pool tables. Early in the week, the club is closed for special events, such as record release parties, films, and fashion shows.
Music: Th–Sa. *Cover:* $–$$.

O'Hara's Pub & Sidewalk Café, *722 E. Las Olas Blvd., Fort Lauderdale, 524-1764.*
A small pub with exposed brick walls and mirrors all around, O'Hara's features a fine house band, O'Hara's All-Stars, led by Dr. Lonnie Smith. The band also includes drummer Danny Burger, and usually plays with a featured guest sax such as Bobby Pines. On the first Sunday of every month, a big band is presented.

Located on one of Fort Lauderdale's most upscale thoroughfares, O'Hara's is an informal place with wooden tables, a central stage, and two bars. Outdoors there's a patio.

Music: nightly and Su afternoons. *Cover:* none. *Food:* pizza, sandwiches, etc.

Bread of Life Natural Food Market and Restaurant, *2388 N. Federal Hwy. (Capital Bank Plaza), Fort Lauderdale, 565-RICE.*

Jazz has its share of strange bedfellows, and in this case, it's natural foods. Bread of Life owner Richie Gerber, who is also a saxophonist, heads up a group called, ahem, the Nutrients ("Music You Can Assimilate") and brings in a different guest artist every weekend. The music's always straight-ahead, with lots of bebop and swing, and some who have played here include Pete Minger, Milton Mustafa, Ira Sullivan, and Eddie Higgins.

The restaurant, with the food market next door, is located in one of the city's newest shopping centers. Done up in a low-lit tropical decor, it features an indoor Art Deco–esque fountain, a shiny black mica bar, and lots of Art Deco prints on the walls.

Music: F, Sa, 7–10 p.m. *No cover. Food:* natural foods, including fresh fish and chicken.

Music Room, *Ocean Manor Hotel, 4040 Galt Ocean Dr., Fort Lauderdale, 566-7500.*

A cozy lounge with a beautiful view of the ocean, the Music Room often presents the duo pianos of the Baker Brothers in the early part of the evening, and trios, quartets and/or vocalists as the night wears on. Vocalist Yvonne Brown and her five-piece orchestra, featuring pianist Jon Frangipane, are regulars. Equipped with lots of pastel-colored couches, plants, and flickering candles, the lounge serves no food but is located across the hall from the hotel's restaurant, Vesuvio's.

Music: duo pianos nightly; larger groups, W–Sa. *No cover.*

Sushi Blues Café, *1836 Young Circle, Hollywood, 929-9560.*

In yet another weird musical combination, this tiny sushi spot, reputed to have excellent food, offers up much jazz and blues, usually compliments of Kenny Millions and friends, who include Randy Bernsen and Mick Taylor, of Rolling Stones' fame. Millions, who is a world-renowned "avant-garde scholar of the saxophone," with 19 recordings to his credit, owns the club along with his wife, Junko, who is also the restaurant's cook. The club is all wood and tile, with seats for about 50 customers, and lots of posters from Millions's tours on the walls.

Music: W–Sa. *Cover:* $. *Food:* sushi, etc.

Studio One 83, *2860 N.W. 183rd St., (Carol City, North Miami), 621-7295 or 621-7625.*

Located in what was once a J.C. Penney Shopping Center, Studio One 83 is a multientertainment complex with a main hall capable of seating up to 2,500 people (R&B concerts featuring the likes of Tyrone Davis are held here); a state-of-the-art disco called Miami Nights, and an intimate Studio Jazz Room, done up in modern black and white. Top area musicians often play here on the weekends.

Music: Th–Sa. *Cover:* $ for jazz; $$ for R&B.

Also

Doc Dammer's Saloon, Bar & Grill in the elegant Colonnade Hotel, Coral Gables (180 Aragon Ave., 441-2600), offers fine jazz on Saturday nights, usually compliments of the Vince Maggio Trio featuring Eric Allison on sax and flute. On the opposite end of the luxury scale is **Kelly's Pub** in Hollywood (1832 Harrison, 929-7940), described by one habitué as a "dim, workingman's bar" that has been presenting the Hollywood Jazz Quintet every Sunday night for nearly ten years.

Greenstreets in the Holiday Inn in Coral Gables (2051 LeJeune Rd., 443-2301) has been booking solid, mainstream jazz groups for years and years. The **Sea Siam Restaurant** in South Miami (12735 S. Dixie Highway, 233-5599) is a Thai seafood restaurant that offers jazz several nights a week. The **Krystal Restaurant & Lounge,** Fort Lauderdale (451 N. State Road 7, 792-4111), is a large West Indian–American restaurant and club that presents jazz jams on Monday nights, reggae on the weekends. **Tavern 213,** a dark, wood-paneled bar, also in Fort Lauderdale (213 S.W. Second St., 463-5213), has jazz on Fridays and Saturdays, often compliments of the Randy Bernsen Trio.

Among the blues bars listed below, **Tobacco Road** has a popular jazz jam on Wednesday nights, usually led by the Roadkill Orchestra; **Club M** also presents some jazz.

F O R   B L U E S

Tobacco Road, *626 S. Miami Ave. (near downtown), 374-1198.*

At over 80 years old, Tobacco Road's liquor license is the oldest in Miami. Even better, the long, narrow (it's only 24 feet wide) club—built of Dade County pine—is a first-rate blues joint, one of the best in the country. IKO-IKO is its house band, and a whole host of national talent, including the late Albert Collins, B. B. King, Taj Mahal, and Charlie Musselwhite, have passed through its doors.

The current incarnation of Tobacco Road was started up six years ago by Kevin Rusk and Patrick Gleber, two young men then not long graduated from college. At the time, everyone thought they were crazy: the club and its neighborhood had fallen on dirty, drug-infested times. But the two ignored public opinion—first cleaning the place up, then serving food, then adding music—and today the club is usually packed with a young, urban crowd. A few

years ago the city even named the street running along outside Tobacco Road.

The club is laden with stories. At one time, rumor has it, Al Capone hung out here, and upstairs there's a fake bookshelf built for
hiding booze during Prohibition. Also upstairs—reached by
climbing a circular staircase lined in red—is the **McClain Cabaret,** named after the half sister of Bessie Smith. A Miami resident,
"Diamond Teeth" Mary McClain is now in her 80's, but she still
performs at the club from time to time.

Music: nightly. *Cover:* $–$$. *Food:* burgers, etc.

Musicians Exchange Café, *729 W. Sunrise Blvd., Fort
Lauderdale, 764-1912.*

What started out in the '70's as a small music store and a musicians' referral service has since grown into a sprawling multifa-
ceted organization housing a unique club called the Exchange
Café. A place made more for listening than for drinking, the Café
has featured many greats such as Buddy Rich, Stan Getz, James
Cotton, and John Lee Hooker, along with local talent. Today, classic rock, folk music, and "original music" are what's usually on tap,
but blues and some jazz can also be heard on a regular basis.

The Café is located on the second story of the Exchange building (which now also includes rehearsal studios, recording studios,
music stores, and a booking agency), and resembles an old-style
Greenwich Village club. The ceiling is low, the lighting dim, and
the atmosphere laid back.

Music: W, F–M, some blues, occasional jazz. *Cover:* $–$$$. *Food:*
Italian, American.

Stephen Talkhouse, *616 Collins Ave., South Beach,
531-7557.*

Owned and operated by the same people who own the Talk-
house in Amagansett, Long Island, New York, the new Talkhouse
is much like the old in style: unpretentious, intimate, eclectic. All
kinds of music is presented here, from rock to country, Latin to
folk, and some of the jazz and blues artists who have appeared re-
cently include George Porter, the Dirty Dozen, John Hammond,
and Taj Mahal.

The club is located in the Art Deco district, in a gray-and-white
Mediterranean-style building with a courtyard and patio. Inside,
there's a long bar, separate from the seating/stage area, 20-foot-
high ceilings, and lots of good sight lines.

Music: nightly, some jazz/blues. *Cover:* $–$$$$. *Food:* American.

Shucker's, *Inn on the Bay, 1819 79th St. Causeway, North
Miami, 865-7100.*

Located in a hotel on the edge of a beautiful bay, Shucker's is a
large, two-story indoor/outdoor restaurant/club with a waterfront

bar, volleyball courts, pool tables, and live reggae and blues. Weather permitting, the music is usually presented outdoors. *Music:* W–Sa, much blues. *No cover. Food:* American.

Club M, *2037 Hollywood Blvd. (near Young Circle), Hollywood, 925-8396.*

Housed in one of the oldest buildings in town, the Club M is all dark wood and exposed ceilings with lots of local artwork and diving relics (helmets, masks, etc.) hanging from the walls. A smallish neighborhood joint with a long bar and pool table, it features live blues three days a week, and a jam session on Thursday nights. Triple Threat, the Nightstalkers, and Roach Thompson are among the musicians who play here.

Music: Th–Sa, blues, occasional jazz. *Cover:* $. *Food:* Colombian.

Other Venues and Special Events

The **Gold Coast Jazz Society** in Fort Lauderdale (524-0805) sponsors monthly concerts, September through May, in the small, European-style Riverside Hotel (620 E. Las Olas Blvd., Fort Lauderdale, 467-0671). Both national and local artists are featured, and nonmembers are welcome. The **Sunshine Jazz Organization** in Miami (696-0805) also sponsors events open to the public at various venues around town.

The **Sun Bank Sunday Jazz Brunch** (761-5703) happens the first Sunday of every month along Riverwalk, a bricked walkway that runs through downtown Fort Lauderdale, along the New River, to the Broward Center for the Performing Arts. Three outdoor stages are set up, and all kinds of regional jazz musicians are presented, along with gourmet brunches offered by area restaurants.

The **Riverwalk Blues Festival,** sponsored by the Musicians Exchange Café, is usually held on the first weekend of November. The café also sponsors a two-day **Music Expo,** which is a sort of birthday celebration held in its parking lot, in early May. The **Tobacco Road Blues Festival** is a day-long affair held at the club every mid-October.

Now over ten years old, **Festival Miami** is a month-long event featuring classical, chamber, and jazz music that's put on every fall by the University of Miami School of Music (284-4940). About 25 concerts are presented, most at the Maurice Gusman Concert Hall on the University of Miami Campus, Coral Gables. The University also presents numerous jazz concerts by students and faculty throughout the year. Some are free and outdoors, others are held in Gusman Hall, and all are open to the public.

National acts also sometimes come through the **Gusman Center for the Performing Arts** (174 E. Flagler St., 372-0925), the **James L. Knight International Center** (400 S.E. Second Ave., 372-0929), and the **Cameo Theater** (1445 Washington St.,

532-0922), a wonderfully restored auditorium in the historic Miami Beach area.

Radio

WLRN/91.3 FM (995-1717 or 995-2236). NPR affiliate, licensed by Dade County school system. Much jazz daily. Of special note: "Lunchtime Miami," with Ed Bell or Len Pace, midday, M–F.

WDNA/88.9 FM (662-8889). Public access station with much jazz, 7 a.m. to midnight, some Latin and blues.

WLVE/93.9 FM (654-9494). Contemporary jazz.

WTMI/93.1 FM (856-9393). Jazz and blues, midnight to early morning, Tu–Sa.

Record Stores

Two of the best stores in the area are **Blue Note Records** in North Miami Beach (16401 N.E. 15th St., 940-3394) and **Sid's Records & Tapes** in Fort Lauderdale (3251 University Drive, 345-7111).

Back in the late
'30's, Count Basie
packed them into
52nd Street's
Famous Door.

*Frank Driggs
Collection*

Northeast

New York has been the international center of jazz for so long that it's hard to believe things were ever otherwise. But compared to New Orleans and Chicago, New York came relatively late to jazz. Although there were stride piano players in the city in the late 1910's and early 1920's, and the Original Dixieland Jazz Band played to packed houses at Reisenweber's Restaurant in 1917, it was only in the late 1920's—largely because of the growing importance of its radio and recording industries—that New York began attracting large numbers of musicians.

New York's first major jazz center was Harlem, which already by the mid-1920's was filled with clubs, theaters, dance halls, and speakeasies, all exploding with sound. Many were located along Seventh Avenue in the 130's and Lenox Avenue in the 140's. Chick Webb was playing for thousands of "happy feet" at the Savoy Ballroom, while Count Basie, then known as "Bill," was lying on the floor of the Lincoln Theater, trying to learn how Fats Waller worked the organ pedals. Some blues could be found, too, at theaters such as the Apollo and the Alhambra, but New York never was—or is—much of a blues town.

As exciting though all this activity was, however, it was nothing compared to the 1930's, when New York, along with the rest of the country, witnessed an unprecedented rise in the popularity of jazz. As the big band era began in earnest, crowds black and white flocked to dance halls and ballrooms all over the city to hear the then new swing sounds of bands led by Fletcher Henderson, Lionel Hampton, Paul Whiteman, Benny Goodman, Tommy Dorsey, and many others. "Battles of the bands," in which two competitive big bands were pitted against each other on opposite sides of a huge dance floor, became commonplace, with many of the best-known groups showcasing top vocalists such as Ella Fitzgerald and Billie Holiday.

In the 1940's, Harlem again became hot as Minton's and Monroe's, two tiny clubs known for their jam sessions, gave birth to modern jazz through the experimentations of Charlie Parker, Dizzy Gillespie, Thelonious Monk, Kenny Clarke, and others. Their new bebop sound spread quickly, igniting audiences throughout the city, and soon, 52nd Street, whose Prohibition-era speakeasies had turned into jazz clubs, became the new center for the new music. The Onyx, the Three Deuces, and the Famous Door were among "the Street's" most famous clubs; then, on nearby Broadway, there was Birdland, named after Charlie Parker, and the Royal Roost, reputedly the first modern sit-down jazz club. Prior to the 1940's, jazz had been played mostly for the dancing.

Fifty-second Street began to decline in the early 1950's, as the old jazz clubs turned into strip joints and the music's center moved downtown once again, this time to Greenwich Village. Clubs such as Café Society, the Five Spot, Café Bohemia, and the Village Vanguard, which had already been thriving in the 1940's, began featuring musicians like Miles Davis, John Coltrane, Charles Mingus, Ornette Coleman, and Sonny Rollins. Audiences queued up round the block to hear the hottest new talents, and New York garnered the reputation of being the only real city in the country where top-caliber music could be heard in dozens of top-caliber clubs every night of the week.

Sources

The best music source is the weekly *Village Voice* (475-3300), where all the major clubs advertise and the critics highlight a few choice acts each week. The *New Yorker* magazine (536-5400) presents a good, selective, critical listing, and *New York* magazine (880-0700) presents a selective, not so critical, listing. The *New York Daily News* (210-2100) has music listings on Fridays and Sundays; the *New York Times* (556-1234) has listings on Sundays and its critics make music recommendations on Fridays. The *New York Post* (815-8000) has listings on Fridays. Other good sources, especially for smaller venues, are the many free alternative or neighborhood publications, most notably the *New York Press* (941-1130).

The Jazz Foundation of America, a nonprofit organization, runs a Jazzline at 718-465-7500.

For maps and other information, contact the New York Convention and Visitors Bureau at 2 Columbus Circle (at W. 59th St.), 397-8222.

The area code for Manhattan is (212). Queens, the Bronx, and Brooklyn are (718).

A Note on Neighborhoods

Despite its enormous size, New York is an easy city to navigate. Fifth Avenue divides the city into the East and West sides, and except in Greenwich Village and a few other areas, streets are laid out in numbered grids. The even-numbered streets run east, the odds, west. The even-numbered avenues run north, the odds, south.

Harlem, the city's historic African-American neighborhood, is located in northwest Manhattan, above W. 110th Street. Greenwich Village, the fabled Bohemian district now usually filled with tourists, is to the southwest, between West 14th and Houston streets. As used here, "Downtown" refers to addresses below 34th Street, and "Midtown," to the city's business center between 34th and 57th streets. The Upper West Side, known for its performing arts, lies above West 57th Street, and the Upper East Side is a well-heeled area above East 57th Street.

New York's public transportation system is excellent, and all of the spots listed below can be reached via subway, bus, or taxi.

Driving should be avoided, as street parking is difficult to find and lot parking, expensive.

Landmarks and Legends

HARLEM AND UPPER MANHATTAN

The following sites are all located within walking distance of each other. As outlined below, the tour starts at 142nd Street and Lenox Avenue, heads west to Adam Clayton Powell, Jr., Blvd. (Seventh Avenue), and then north to 156th Street before circling back downtown to 118th Street. (See also "Tours," page 151.)

Cotton Club, 644 Lenox Ave., at 142nd Street

This most famous of the big three Harlem Renaissance nightclubs (the other two were Connie's Inn and Smalls' Paradise) was torn down in the 1950's to make way for a housing project. The plush club, which once catered to a whites-only, cream-of-society and gangster crowd, was Duke Ellington's home base for four years and Cab Calloway's for three. All the other top entertainers of the day—Louis Armstrong, Ethel Waters, and Ivie Anderson, among them—also performed here.

The Cotton Club started as the Club Deluxe, owned by former heavyweight boxing champion Jack Johnson. Owney Madden's gang took the place over in 1922, hiring Andy Preer's Cotton Club Syncopators and "high-yaller" chorus girls, who had to be under 21 and at least 5 feet 6 inches tall. In 1927, Preer died and Madden recruited Ellington up from Philadelphia, demanding that he break his contract there. "Be big," Madden's henchman allegedly told Ellington's boss, "or you'll be dead."[1]

Duke Ellington then was still an unknown, but before long his name became a household word. He and his Jungle Band, as they were called, were broadcast on radio stations across the country, and the nightclub became a "must" stop for every out-of-towner visiting New York.

The Cotton Club moved from Lenox Avenue to West 48th Street in 1936, following the Harlem race riots. The new location lacked the magic of the old, however, and closed a few years later.

Savoy Ballroom, 596 Lenox Ave., near 140th Street

Now demolished (a Woolworth's marks the spot), the second-story Savoy once covered an entire city block and featured a large dance floor, two bandstands, and a retractable stage. In the 1920's and '30's, it was the most popular dance hall in Harlem, accommodating crowds of up to five thousand.

Drummer and bandleader Chick Webb, with his star singer, Ella Fitzgerald, was the acknowledged "King of the Savoy," and any visiting band had to take up battle against him, playing on the other bandstand at the opposite end of the hall. These "battles of the bands" attracted tremendous crowds, and once when Fletcher Henderson and Chick Webb (representing New York) were pitted against King Oliver and Fess Williams (representing Chicago), the riot squad had to be called in. Another famous battle took place during the Swing Era when Benny Goodman took on Chick Webb. Goodman was then at the height of his career, but the crowd cheered loudest for Webb.

Billie Holiday's first New York apartment, *108 W. 139th St., near Lenox Avenue*

Billie Holiday and her mother moved into a railroad apartment in this solid five-story building shortly after Billie arrived in New York. The Depression was then on and Billie walked Seventh Avenue every day trying to find work. Finally, she was auditioned as a dancer by the manager of a small club called Pods' and Jerry's (168 W. 132 St.), but when he found out that she only knew two dance steps, he angrily tried to throw her out. The piano player took pity. "Girl, can you sing?" he asked. "Sure I can sing," she said, "What good is that?"

Holiday quickly found out. The piano player started in on "Trav'lin' All Alone," and by the end of the song, the young singer had a new job. That job led to other jobs, which led to a review by music critic John Hammond and a debut at the Apollo.

As Billie settled into her new life, so did her mother, Sadie, who took up her favorite occupation—cooking. Before long, Holiday writes in *Lady Sings the Blues,* their apartment became known as "a combination YMCA, boardinghouse for broke musicians, soup kitchen for anyone with a hard-luck story, community center, and after-after-hours joint where a couple of bucks would get you a shot of whiskey and the most fabulous fried-chicken breakfast, lunch, or dinner anywhere in town."

Lincoln Theater, *58 W. 135th St., near Lenox Ave.*

The Lincoln, opened in 1915, was one of Harlem's earliest theaters, and unlike many other uptown venues, it catered to an African-American audience from the very beginning. Fats Waller was the theater's house organist for years, pounding out tunes to accompany silent films, and a young Bill Basie used to come in from his home in Red Bank, New Jersey, to watch the more established musician play. Fats got used to seeing Basie, and before long, the future Count was literally lying at the maestro's feet, watching how he used the pedals.

The Lincoln is now a church.

Smalls' Paradise, *2294½ Adam Clayton Powell (Seventh Ave.) Blvd., at W. 135th Street*

Opened in 1925 and closed in 1986, Smalls' Paradise was originally a long basement room capable of holding 1,500. During Prohibition it attracted a large downtown crowd and was famous for its

Sunday morning breakfast dances, which featured customers in glittering evening dress and waiters doing the Charleston while balancing trays of bootleg liquor. (Unlike the Cotton Club, Smalls' did admit blacks, but prices were so high that most were unable to afford it.) Later, during both the Depression and the war years, Smalls' continued to function as a smaller music spot, drawing everyone from Duke Ellington to Benny Goodman; in the '60's, it became "Big Wilt's" in honor of its new owner, basketball player Wilt Chamberlain.

Ed Smalls, the original owner, was a former elevator operator who had previously run the Sugar Cane Club (2212 Fifth Ave. at 135th Street), the first Harlem club to attract a large white crowd. Today, Smalls' is a boarded-up building with a fading sign.

Abyssinian Baptist Church, *132 W. 138th St., near Adam Clayton Powell Blvd., 862-7474*

Charlie Parker's funeral was held at the Abyssinian. Fats Waller's father was a minister here.

The Gothic and Tudor structure, with its marble pulpit and stained-glass windows, was opened in 1924, but the church itself dates back to 1808, when a few members of the First Baptist Church, then located on Gold Street, refused to accept that church's racially segregated seating policy and broke off to form their own congregation.

Today, services at the airy, red-carpeted church, laid out in circular pews, are held every Sunday at 9 a.m. and 11 a.m. and visitors are welcome. A small memorial room, dedicated to the Adam Clayton Powells, Sr. and Jr., who were both pastors here, is located in the community house; the church's five-keyboard organ is the largest in New York City.

Renaissance Ballroom and Casino, *150 W. 138th St.*

Right next door to the Abyssinian is a two-story red-brick building that was once the Renaissance, a ballroom offering gambling, dancing, and cabaret acts from the 1920's through the early '50's. Among the jazz musicians who performed here were Chick Webb, Lester Young (then playing in Al Sears's big band), and Fletcher Henderson, who packed the place in 1925, just after a highly successful tour of New England.

Striver's Row, *138th and 139th streets, between Adam Clayton Powell Blvd. and Frederick Douglass Blvd. (Eighth Ave.).*

The King Model houses, built by developer David King in 1891, are two of the most stunning blocks in Harlem. Three different sets of architects designed the development, with the most impressive row, the northernmost one, done by McKim, Mead & White. Both blocks (which acquired their nickname when they became the preferred address of early, ambitious African Americans) are immaculately kept, with service alleys running behind and flower boxes out front. According to Val Ginter, an urban historian with a strong interest in jazz, Fletcher Henderson once lived at 224 West 139th.

James P. Johnson's residence, *267 W. 140th St. near Frederick Douglass Blvd.*

In the early 1920's, the great stride piano player James P. Johnson moved into his sister's apartment in this now boarded-up building. A friend introduced J.P. to Fats Waller, then just a youngster, and Fats became Johnson's star pupil. The two of them often worked together in J.P.'s home on two pianos, and Johnson's sister became Fats's surrogate mother (his own had recently died), buying him his first pair of long pants.

"It was one big headache for me," May Wright Johnson says in *Hear Me Talkin' to Ya,* edited by Nat Shapiro and Nat Hentoff. "Fats was seventeen . . . and [he] would bang on our piano till all hours of the night—sometimes to two, three, four o'clock in the morning. I would say to him, 'Now go on home, or haven't you got a home.' "

Our Lady of Lourdes Church, *472 W. 142nd St., bet. Convent and Amsterdam avenues.*

In the 1950's, pianist Mary Lou Williams, depressed and dispirited, left music for a period of about three years. Turning to religion, she spent most of her days in Our Lady of Lourdes, meditating and talking to the needy. "I became a kind of fanatic for a while," she tells Whitney Balliett in *American Musicians: 56 Portraits in Jazz.* "I'd live on apples and water for nine days at a time. I stopped smoking. I shut myself up here like a monk. Father Woods got worried and he told me, 'Mary, you're an artist. You belong at the piano and writing music. It's *my* business to help people through the church and your business to help people through music.' He got me playing again."

Mary Lou Williams's apartment, *63 Hamilton Terrace.*

Williams lived just down the street from the church in this handsome apartment building. In the '40's, musicians such as Thelonious Monk, Dizzy Gillespie, and Charlie Parker stopped by—day or night—to try out their new ideas on her. In the '60's, Williams devoted much of her time to launching a foundation for helping musicians down on their luck.

Dinah Washington's apartment, *Bowery Bank Building, 345 W. 145th St.*

Dinah Washington moved into this big boxy Harlem landmark in early 1963. Most of her biggest hits, including "What a Difference a Day Makes," were recorded while she was living here, in a twelfth-floor penthouse. "It was a gorgeous place," says Lorraine Gordon of the Village Vanguard, "like the inside of a jukebox."

"A" Train, *145th Street near St. Nicholas Ave. (among other stops).*

The "A" Train subway line had just been built when Billy Strayhorn wrote the composition that Duke Ellington made famous. New, fast, and strong, it was the quickest way to get to Harlem.

Duke Ellington's apartment, *935 St. Nicholas Ave., near West 156th St.*

Although born in Washington, D.C., the Duke spent 22 years of his life, 1939 to 1961, in Apartment 4A of this handsome Harlem Gothic apartment building that's now a National Historic Landmark. While living here, he wrote many of his most famous compositions, performed at the Cotton Club, and premiered his controversial "Black, Brown and Beige," which he called a "tone parallel to the history of the American Negro," at Carnegie Hall.

Living with the Duke during this time was Beatrice Ellis, more often known as Evie Ellington, even though the two never officially married. They were still together when they moved downtown in the 1960's, but by that time they were seeing little of each other, as Ellington was constantly on the road and Evie had become reclusive.

Monroe's Uptown House, *198 W. 134th St., corner of Adam Clayton Powell Blvd.*

An important spawning ground for modern jazz (see Minton's Playhouse, page 113), Monroe's was opened by Clark Monroe in the 1930's. Billie Holiday sang here for three months in early 1937, and Charlie Parker played a central role in the club's cutting contests. On one legendary night, just before coming to Monroe's, Parker was jamming at a chili parlor up the street between 139th and 140th. "I was working over 'Cherokee,' " he said later, "and, as I did, I found that by using the higher intervals of a chord as a melody line and backing them with appropriately related changes, I could play the thing I'd been hearing. It came alive."[2]

Today, the former Monroe's is a deli.

Lafayette Theater, *2227 Adam Clayton Powell Blvd. at 132nd St.*

In the 1920's, the Lafayette, now a church, was one of two major theaters in Harlem (see Lincoln Theater, page 107). Located on the entertainment esplanade that was then Seventh Avenue, it hosted all the major talent of the day, including Duke Ellington, who made his first New York appearance here in 1923 as a member of Wilbur Sweatman's band, and Fats Waller—until he got fired, that is. An item in the New York *Age* on October 1, 1927, reported: "Fats Waller, who has been playing the organ at the Lafayette Theatre, was paid a visit by his wife one afternoon. She sat on the same stool with Fats as he was playing. The management objected. Words. Fats quit there and then."[3]

The Lafayette was twice as big as the Lincoln, and was best-known for its impressive variety shows and revues. *Shuffle Along* by Noble Sissle and Eubie Blake, the first major African-American review to make it to Broadway, was first produced at the theater in 1913; and it was followed by the *Plantation Revue* with Florence Mills, *The Chocolate Dandies,* also by Sissle and Blake, and Lew Leslie's *Blackbirds.*

Connie's Inn, *2221 Adam Clayton Powell Blvd., at 131st St.*

Located right next to the Lafayette was Connie's Inn. Originally called the Shuffle Inn in honor of the Sissle-Blake production, the swank basement club was opened in 1923 by two men in the delicatessen business, Connie and George Immerman (they had once hired Fats Waller as a delivery boy). Connie's Inn featured many major performers, including Fletcher Henderson, Zutty Singleton, Billie Holiday, and Louis Armstrong, who performed here in a show called "Hot Chocolates," written by Fats Waller and Andy Razaf.

One of the more infamous events in New York's gangland history took place right outside Connie's. "Mad Dog" Vincent Coll, wanted by both the mob and the law, kidnapped George "Big Frenchy" DeMange and George Immerman late one night and held them for ransom. Eventually, his demands were met, the two were released, and a gala celebration was held at the club. Later, "Mad Dog" was gunned down in a 23rd Street phone booth by Dutch Schultz's gang.

Connie's wasn't the only hot spot at 131st and Seventh, once known as "The Corner." There were also the Band Box, the Barbeque, the Hoofers' Club, and more. "This wasn't just one more of them busy street crossings, with a poolroom for a hangout. Uh, uh," writes Mezz Mezzrow in *Really the Blues,* "On The Corner in Harlem you stood with your jaws swinging wide open while all there is to this crazy world, the whole frantic works, strutted by."

The Tree of Hope, a famous Harlem talisman, once stood outside Connie's. Back then, legend had it that to rub the tree's bark brought luck, and many a musician stopped by, hoping for his or her big break. Later, when Seventh Avenue was widened, Bill "Bojangles" Robinson had the tree transplanted to the median strip that now runs down the parkway.

Today, Connie's Inn is a discount store. Directly across the street is Reid's Cleaners, Tuxedos for Hire, a shop that has been making costumes for the Apollo entertainers for years.

Alhambra Theater, *2110 Adam Clayton Powell Blvd., at 126th St.*

It was to the Alhambra that the future record producer and jazz critic John Hammond, then 16, slipped away one evening to hear his first blues singer, Bessie Smith. He told his family that he was going out to practice music with friends. Across the street from the theater, at number 2120, once stood the Alhambra Grill, where Billie Holiday sang before moving on to the Hot-Cha Bar and

Grill, at 134th and Seventh, where Ralph Cooper of the Apollo discovered her. Holiday also headlined at the Alhambra in the early 1930's.

The Alhambra is now an office building for the Department of Motor Vehicles.

Hotel Theresa, *2090 Adam Clayton Powell Blvd., at 125th St.*

The Theresa, once Harlem's largest and most famous hotel, is now an office building. A beautiful white-brick edifice that glistens in the sun, it played host to everyone from singer Lena Horne and guitarist Jimi Hendrix to boxer Joe Louis and Cuban leader Fidel Castro. Lester Young lived here until Billie Holiday invited him to move in with her and her mother; bandleader Andy Kirk, according to urban historian Val Ginter, managed the place in the late 1950's.

Cab Calloway's band also frequented the Theresa, and they stayed here one week while playing the State Theatre in Hartford, Connecticut, located about three hours away. Dizzy Gillespie, Jonah Jones, Cozy Cole, and Milt Hinton were all members of the band back then; they had a habit of throwing spitballs at each other when the Cab wasn't around. They were doing exactly that, while waiting for the State Theatre concert to start, when a spitball landed, *plunk,* right in the spotlight. Cab was furious, and after the show he accused Dizzy (Jonah Jones was actually the culprit), who in response drew a knife and cut the bandleader in the thigh. Cab fired Diz on the spot, and Diz took the bus home. But when the band pulled up to the Theresa that night, the trumpet player was there to meet it, and he and Cab sheepishly made up.

Apollo Theatre, *253 W. 125th St., 749-5838.*

Perhaps the single most important landmark in the history of African-American music, the Apollo has hosted nearly every major jazz or blues artist to come along. Bessie Smith, Ella Fitzgerald, Billie Holiday, Duke Ellington, Louis Armstrong, Count Basie, Lil Armstrong, Fats Waller, Pearl Bailey, Ray Charles, and James Brown all played the Apollo, and the list could go on and on. It is said that when a teenage Elvis Presley first came to New York, the one place he wanted to see was the Apollo. The same was later said of the Beatles.

Originally built in 1913, the Apollo was once Hurtig & Seamon's New Burlesque Theatre, known for presenting vaudeville to a Harlem that was then predominantly white. Back in those days, the best seats in the house cost a whopping $1.65. Frank Schiffman and Leo Brecher took the place over in 1935, by which time the neighborhood's racial mix had shifted to predominantly black.

Under its new management, the two-balconied theater, capable of seating two thousand, soon became especially famous for its Amateur Nights, in which new talent was presented to a highly critical audience that either applauded or booed the performers off the stage. Sarah Vaughan and Billy Eckstine made their New York debuts that way, as did Ella Fitzgerald (who was hired by Chick Webb that very night) and Billie Holiday.

Not all major entertainers had such positive experiences at the Apollo. Alberta Hunter opened on December 6, 1946, for what was to be a one-week engagement, but the show was abruptly "closed out," much to her hurt feelings. Lena Horne had a similar experience—the audience drove her offstage by throwing pennies at her.

Closed down in the late 1970's, the Apollo was completely refurbished in the early 1980's. Now a not-for-profit enterprise, it still reigns in regal splendor over 125th Street, and presents a weekly amateur night (see "Other Venues," page 149).

Baby Grand, *319 W. 125th St., near Frederick Douglass Blvd.*

Once a stylish club, now a clothing store, the Baby Grand was one of the last of the Harlem clubs to go, closing its doors for good only in 1989. For 42 years the cabaret had been home to musicians such as Jimmy Butts and Joe Turner as well as comedians such as Manhattan Paul and Nipsey Russell. In 1988, Ruth Brown taped a birthday show here for national television.

2040 Adam Clayton Powell Blvd. *(Seventh Ave.), near 124th St.*

Now being renovated after many years of dissuse, 2040 Seventh was once an apartment house filled with musicians. Dizzy Gillespie and his wife lived here shortly after they were married, and so did Billy Eckstine and his wife. The two musicians became close friends, and according to Eckstine, Dizzy was constantly studying, working out chord progressions and countermelodies on an old piano. Other residents living at number 2040 at that time or shortly thereafter included Erroll Garner, Clyde Hart, Buck Clayton, Harry Edison, and Don Byas.

Dewey Square, *Adam Clayton Powell Blvd. and 118th St.*

A small triangular park with the old Dewey Square Hotel (now a residential building) located on the north side, Dewey Square is where Charlie Parker developed his famous number of the same name. Today the park is called A. Philip Randolph Triangle.

Minton's Playhouse, *Cecil Hotel, 210 W. 118th St.* *864-5281.*

One of the greatest revolutions in jazz, the birth of bebop, was spawned in this neighborhood club run by onetime bandleader Teddy Hill in the Cecil Hotel. In 1941, Hill hired a house band that included Thelonious Monk and Kenny Clarke, and soon the small, dark place was packed every night with talent eager to jam. Dizzy Gillespie, Charlie Parker, Charlie Christian, Max Roach, and Tadd Dameron, were among the regulars; Monday nights, the traditional night off for musicians, brought big band talent such as Teddy Wilson and Roy Eldridge as well.

The Minton sessions—spontaneous, informal and often after-hours—gave the musicians a chance to explore new ideas, such as the flatted fifth. Everyone sat in in Minton's, including some who had no business doing so, and for them, the insiders would play their new complex ideas, forcing the incompetents off the stage.

According to Oran "Hot Lips" Page in *Hear Me Talkin' to Ya*, the word "bop" was coined at the club by Fats Waller. Often, when the younger musicians were fooling around trying out some of their new bop runs, Fats would shout at them, "Stop that crazy boppin' and a-stoppin' and play that jive like the rest of us guys."

Today, the recently restored Cecil houses "model" apartment units for the elderly, and attempts are being made to reopen Minton's. The club's magnificent mural depicting four musicians (two of which have been identified as Tony Scott and Charlie Christian) has been restored, and there's talk—pending funding—of starting up jam sessions. T-shirts are even for sale at the hotel's front desk.

UPTOWN, WEST

(The four sites below are spread over a 50-block area, but they could be walked on a nice day.)

George Gershwin's home, *316 W. 103rd St., near Riverside Dr.*

George Gershwin, the composer whose work had such an enormous impact on jazz, once lived (1925–31) in this small stone house near the Hudson River. He and his family had originally moved here so that he could have more privacy in which to work, but things didn't work out quite that way. When his friend S. N. Behrman came to visit one day in the late '20's, he found a group of strange young men playing billiards on the first floor and another group lounging on the second. Behrman finally found George's brother, Ira, and asked who the men were. Ira had no idea. "There's a bunch of fellows from down the street who've taken to dropping in here every night for a game," he said.[4]

The Gershwin building is marked with a plaque honoring the two brothers, who "created many memorable works here," and the awning out front reads GERSHWIN HOUSE.

Billie Holiday's last New York apartment, *26 W. 87th St.*

The last year of Billie Holiday's life was sad and lonely. Her health was poor, her career was at a low point, and days would go by without her seeing anyone. Says fellow singer Annie Ross in *Billie's Blues* by John Chilton: "She sat alone watching television night after night. She sat in an armchair puffing away at a marihuana 'joint' . . . just staring at the screen, shuffling the pages of the papers, making sure that she had planned her viewing schedule in such a way so that she didn't miss a single cartoon film."

On May 31, 1959, Billie collapsed and sank into a coma. Luckily, a friend was present, and he immediately rushed her to the hospital, where her case was diagnosed as "drug addiction and alcoholism." A few rough days passed and she was just beginning to recover when the police burst into her room, allegedly found a small envelope of heroin, and posted a guard outside her door. (Some, pointing out that the singer was too sick to leave her bed, said that the drugs had been planted; others believed that a well-wisher had brought them by.) Billie's books, flowers, and radio were confiscated, and she was "mugged" and fingerprinted while still in bed.

Meanwhile, her physical condition deteriorated. Cirrhosis of the liver and a serious kidney ailment were now diagnosed; a few weeks later, on the morning of July 17, she died. She was buried in St. Raymond's Cemetery in the Bronx, beside her mother.

Miles Davis's apartment, *312 W. 77th St.*

Davis moved into this handsome red townhouse, a former Russian Orthodox church that he had extensively remodeled, in the early '60's. In the basement he installed a gym and a music room where he could rehearse without disturbing anyone, and out back there was a garden. With him at first were his wife, Frances Taylor, and their children, but their marriage fell apart, as did Davis's subsequent marriage to Betty Mabry.

Davis recorded many important albums, including *Miles Smiles*, *In a Silent Way*, and *Bitches Brew*, while living at number 312. Nineteen sixty-nine and '70 were particularly productive years, and by 1971 Davis was not only making about $400,000 annually but had also been voted Jazzman of the Year by *Down Beat* magazine.

Nonetheless, by 1975, owing to health problems, disillusionment with the music industry, and an extensive cocaine habit, Miles's life had fallen apart. "From 1975 until early 1980 I didn't pick up my horn," he says in his autobiography, *Miles*. "For over four years, didn't pick it up once. I would walk by and look at it, then think about trying to play. But after a while I didn't even do that. . . . Mostly during those four or five years that I was out of music, I just took a lot of cocaine (about $500 a day at one point) and fucked all the women I could get into my house."

Eventually, through the help of George Butler at Columbia Records, Davis pulled himself out of his depression and drug habit and back into the world of music. He sold the house at number 312 in the early '80's when he and Cicely Tyson started living together.

Thelonious Monk's apartment, *243 W. 63rd St.*

For most of his life, Thelonious Sphere Monk lived in this red-brick building, now a boarded-up section of an otherwise vibrant apartment complex behind Lincoln Center. A gentle, introverted and eccentric man, Monk was long regarded by critics and club owners as unpredictable and unemployable, and was one of the last of the modern jazz pioneers to receive recognition.

Monk was a private man who seldom visited others and, upon answering the phone, often said, "Monk's not home." He spent most of his days playing and writing, and—despite periodic hospitalizations for mental illness—living a remarkably stable life with his family and wife, Nellie.

From 1951 to '57, Monk's cabaret card—this card was then a prerequisite for a musician working in New York—was taken from him when he was found sitting with a friend in a car that contained narcotics. Monk could have cleared himself by informing on his friend, who owned the dope, but he refused. He also refused to work outside New York or outside music, and spent those six years just barely surviving on scant income from rare recording dates.

In 1976, six years before his death, Monk withdrew from public performing. He is buried in Ferncliff Cemetery in Hartsdale, New York.

UPTOWN, EAST

Ellington Statue, *Central Park, Fifth Ave. and 110th St.*

A 20-foot-high statue of Duke Ellington, to be erected in October 1994, was commissioned for the park by the Duke Ellington Memorial Fund, an organization spearheaded by Bobby Short. The statue's design, by Los Angeles artist Robert Graham, was unveiled to the public in 1990, and it met with considerable controversy. Sexist and tacky is what then New York *Daily News* columnist Bob Herbert called the proposed statue, which showed nine nude women (supposedly the Muses) standing with a baby grand piano and an elegantly dressed Duke Ellington on their heads.

Stanhope Hotel, *995 Fifth Ave., across from the Metropolitan Museum of Art at 82nd St., 288-5800.*

On the night of March 12, 1955, Charlie Parker died in the hotel apartment of the Baronness "Nica" de Koenigswarter while watching jugglers on the "Tommy Dorsey Show." The Baroness, who was a friend and patron of many jazz musicians, had called a doctor upon Bird's arrival three days earlier, and he had warned her that the musician could die at any time. No attempt was made to move Parker, however, and none of his friends or wives were notified, although Bird did call his mother in Kansas City, who begged him to come home and not die in a hospital.

Parker was only 34 when he died, but his death certificate estimated his age to be 53. Drugs and alcohol had so ravaged his body that he seemed much older. A great deal of controversy also surrounded his death. The tabloids had a heyday with the fact that he had died in the Baronness's apartment, and there was an ugly tug-of-war between his wives over where he should be buried.

John Hammond's home, *9 E. 91st St.*

John Hammond, the record producer and writer who was responsible for discovering, recording, and promoting so many major musicians (Billie Holiday, Count Basie, Bessie Smith, Benny Goodman, Benny Carter, Teddy Wilson, Charlie Christian and, later, Aretha Franklin, Bob Dylan, and Bruce Springsteen, to name but a few) grew up in this luxurious six-story mansion. The son of a wealthy lawyer and a Vanderbilt, Hammond, born in 1910, could have chosen an easy and pampered life. Instead, he discovered jazz and blues—listening to early records when he was 8, slipping away from prep school to hear Bessie Smith in Harlem at 16—and spent a lifetime doing everything within his power to further the music. Hammond was also an ardent civil rights activist, covering the Scottsboro trial for the *Nation;* fighting for the rights of miners in Harlan County, West Virginia; and serving as an early board member of the NAACP.

MIDTOWN

(The following tour starts at West 58th Street and Eighth Avenue and proceeds south down the West Side, before cutting over to the East Side and heading north again.)

Reisenweber's Restaurant, *W. 58th St. and Eighth Ave., S.W. corner, just south of Columbus Circle.*

Though no longer standing, Reisenweber's was the spot where the Original Dixieland Jazz Band appeared in 1917, a sensational event that is generally credited with ushering jazz into New York. Shortly after appearing here, the ODJB, a New Orleans band led by cornet player Nick LaRocca, made the very first jazz recordings ever, cutting "Livery Stable Blues" and the "Original Dixieland One-Step" on February 26, 1917, at the Victor Studios.

Carnegie Hall, *W. 57th St. and Seventh Ave.*

New York's premier concert auditorium, built in 1891 in an Italian Renaissance design, has been featuring jazz ever since the musical form emerged. James Reese Europe, the country's first African-American bandleader, who used jazz elements at times, organized events here from 1912 to 1914, and in 1928, jazz pianists James P. Johnson and Fats Waller played a tribute to W. C. Handy. Then there was the historic "From Spirituals to Swing" concert organized by John Hammond in memory of Bessie Smith on December 23, 1938. Backed by *New Masses,* a Marxist publication (and a supporter that Hammond had some doubts about), the event was the first major concert produced in New York for an integrated audience. Hammond traveled all over the country collecting talent for the show, and among the many who played that night were Sidney Bechet, Meade "Lux" Lewis, Albert Ammons, Big Joe Turner, Big Bill Broonzy, the Mitchell's Christian Singers, the Kansas City Six (including Buck Clayton and Lester Young), and the Basie band. Benny Goodman also gave a highly acclaimed concert performance in 1938, and a released recording of the event brought to him a wide audience.

Other historic concerts followed. Norman Granz used the hall for his "Jazz at the Philharmonic" concerts between 1949 and 1953; and Duke Ellington presented his suite "Black, Brown, and Beige" in 1943. Charlie Parker played the hall in the late '40's, and Miles Davis and the Gil Evans orchestra performed here in 1961. Major jazz talent is still being presented by Carnegie Hall, and the JVC Jazz Festival sponsors events here every summer.

Park Central Hotel *(now the Omni Park Central Hotel), 870 Seventh Ave., near W. 55th St., 247-8000.*

In 1928, the Ben Pollack band, which then included an all-star cast of Jack Teagarden, Benny Goodman, and Jimmy McPartland, opened at the Park Central, which was once known for its big bands. The reviews were ecstatic and every night the hotel was packed with audiences eager to see the hot new group. Nonetheless, there was a lot of friction in the band. McPartland kept skipping rehearsals, and an ambitious Goodman—according to Pollack—kept taking too many solos.

Finally, tempers snapped. McPartland appeared on stage one night without garters, and his socks slipped down around his ankles. Pollack scolded him after the show, saying that wrinkled socks didn't look good on stage, and McPartland flew into a rage, quitting on the spot. Goodman, hearing the shouting, quit a moment later.

To add insult to injury, when Pollack stopped by the Park Central the next season to talk about his contract, he learned that Goodman and McPartland had already offered the hotel the entire band, *sans* Pollack, at a bargain price. Pollack eventually got the gig back and hired new men, but his band never regained its old popularity.

Fifty-second Street, *between Fifth and Sixth avenues.*

Back in the 1930's and '40's, more great musicians congregated on this one small block than any place else in the world, before or since. Art Tatum, Billie Holiday, Coleman Hawkins, Oran "Hot Lips" Page, Roy Eldridge, Teddy Wilson, Fats Waller, Erroll Garner, Mary Lou Williams, Dizzy Gillespie, Charlie Parker, Miles Davis, Sarah Vaughan, Count Basie, Woody Herman, Charlie Barnet, Buddy Rich, Dave Tough, George Shearing—all were here.

Fifty-second Street's magic began just after Prohibition, when New York's jazz center began shifting from Harlem to downtown. "The Street" at that time was lined with dark and smoky speakeasies, all housed in dilapidated brownstones with tiny vestibules, long bars, pressed-tin ceilings, and water-stained walls. The street's real heyday came about 10 years later, however, with the arrival of modern jazz (see Minton's, "Landmarks and Legends," page 113).

The music on 52nd Street ranged from New Orleans and Chicago jazz to bebop and early cool, and the musicians moved from one club to another with an ease that seems incredible today. In a single night, for the price of a few drinks, one could hear the same musician playing in three or four different clubs with three or four different bands.

The first music club to open on the Street was the Onyx, later dubbed the "Cradle of Swing." Then there was the Famous Door, named for the door inscribed with autographs of the famous that sat on a small platform near the bar; the long-running Hickory House, located on the next block, between Sixth and Seventh avenues, where Art Tatum often played during intermission; the Downbeat, a regular gig for Dizzy Gillespie; Kelly's Stable, where Coleman Hawkins recorded his famous 1939 "Body and Soul"; the Three Deuces, where Erroll Garner and Charlie Parker were regulars; and Jimmy Ryan's, known for its Dixieland.

The street began to decline after World War II, when its jazz clubs turned into striptease bars and clip joints. Today, all the old brownstones (with the exception of the 21 Club) have been torn down, to be replaced by towering glass-sheathed buildings. The only reminders of the past are the street signs that read SWING STREET (52nd St. between Fifth and Sixth avenues) and W. C. HANDY PLACE (52nd St. between Sixth and Seventh avenues). There are also small sidewalk plaques on the 52nd Street side of the CBS Building at Sixth Avenue honoring some of the jazz greats.

Ed Sullivan Theater, *1697 Broadway, near 53rd St.*

Ed Sullivan, a former sports columnist, began broadcasting his famous variety show, which quickly became a sort of arbiter of popular taste, from here in 1949. B. B. King, like Elvis Presley and the Beatles before him, played the theater. With him on the bill on October 18, 1970, were the Carpenters. (Benny Goodman also played the venue, when it was known as the Billy Rose Casino.) The theater is now home to the "David Letterman Show," and has been extensively restored.

Roseland Ballroom, *239 W. 52nd St.*

This Roseland Ballroom, opened in 1956, has been home to some jazz greats—Count Basie, among others—but it was the old, now destroyed Roseland at 1658 Broadway near 51st Street that had the legendary past. One of the largest ballrooms in New York from the '20's through the '40's, it was lavishly decorated and known throughout the country for its hot jazz and dancing. Fletcher Henderson's band (which included Louis Armstrong for a time, as well as Billie Holiday's father, who wanted nothing to do with either her or her mother) played a long and important residency there, while Jean Goldkette's band with Bix Beiderbecke performed at the ballroom in the late '20's.

Men never hurt for dancing partners at Roseland, where the "taxi" dance may have originated. Patrons rode up to the ballroom in cabs and bought rolls of 10-cent tickets that allowed them to dance with the hostesses, whose income depended on the tickets they collected. Roseland was also a segregated hall. No African Americans were admitted in the audience and even Hispanics were discouraged.

Today's ballroom still has a sort of dusty grandeur. Big band dancing is featured weekly (see "Clubs, etc.," page 140).

Birdland, *1674 Broadway, near 52nd St.*

Now a topless bar, Birdland was once located in the basement of this stolid building. Named after Charlie Parker, who opened the club in December 1949, it was an important center for bop.

Like the Royal Roost (then located at 1580 Broadway at 47th St., now the site of the Ramada Renaissance Hotel), which was the first sit-down club for jazz, Birdland had tables on the dance floor, bleachers for those who wanted to pay only the cover charge, and a milk bar for nondrinkers. Unlike the Royal Roost, it also had parakeets in bird cages (who were soon killed off by the air conditioning and smoke), its own radio wire and booth, manned by the renowned disc jockey Symphony Sid Torin, and a midget emcee named Pee Wee Marquette.

It was in front of Birdland one night that Miles Davis, then working the club, was badly beaten by two cops who challenged his right to "loiter" on the street. Miles, who would later need five stitches, was then taken to jail, where he was charged with disorderly conduct. A crowd of supporters gathered in protest, and the incident was covered by newspapers around the world. The charges were eventually dropped.

Charlie Parker, then suffering badly from drug addiction, also had his share of troubles here. One night he arrived at the club in pajamas, having just snuck out of a hospital where he was taking a cure. Another evening he fired the entire string section backing him, and then later that night, despondent, tried to commit suicide by swallowing iodine. He also had a bitter argument on stage with band member Bud Powell, causing Charles Mingus, who was also in the band, to step up to the mike and say, "Ladies and Gentlemen, I am not responsible for what happens on the bandstand. This is not jazz."[5]

Eventually, sadly enough, Parker was banned from the club that bore his name.

Metropole, *725 Seventh Ave., near 48th St.*

The Metropole featured afternoon and evening jazz through the 1950's and '60's. Writes trumpet player Buck Clayton in his autobiography, *Buck Clayton's Jazz World,* "The bandstand was behind the bar. It was only about four feet wide and many cats would fall off of the bandstand and down into the bar below if they were too tipsy. It was a long bar and as one group would finish their set the other group would come up. . . . We called the whole show 'Wall to Wall Jazz.' . . . You'd see about fourteen or fifteen musicians elevated on the stand behind the bartender and all swinging away on the closing number."

Scott Joplin's boardinghouse, *252 W. 47th St.*

From 1911 to 1915, Scott Joplin and his wife, Lottie, ran a boardinghouse out of this small residential building just down the street from the Hotel Edison, where many of Ellington's sidemen would later stay. (The boardinghouse was later moved to 133 W. 138th and then to 163 W. 131st St.)

Joplin had a difficult time of it in New York. His classic piano rags were selling poorly, he was quarreling with his publisher, and no one was interested in publishing his opera, *Treemonisha*. Finally he published the 230-page score himself, and for a period, it looked as if the Lafayette Theater might produce it, but nothing ever came of it.

Dispirited, Joplin went through long periods of depression and began playing badly. Often he had trouble remembering his most popular compositions. There was no private studio at the boardinghouse—just a piano in the front parlor—and he would become acutely embarrassed whenever his playing slipped.

In 1917 Joplin was admitted to Ward's Island for mental trouble, and three days later he was dead. He was buried in St. Michael's Cemetery in Astoria, Queens (72-02 Astoria Blvd., East Elmhurst, 718-278-3240). The grave went unmarked until 1974, when a simple plaque reading SCOTT JOPLIN, AMERICAN COMPOSER was laid.

Whitby Apartments, *325 W. 45th St.*

Now a coop apartment building, the Whitby was once the home of Gil Evans, composer, pianist, and arranger, who lived here throughout the '50's and '60's. Evans did much of his finest work with Miles Davis while living in this building, including the albums *Miles Ahead, Porgy and Bess,* and *Sketches of Spain*.

Blue Room, *Lincoln Hotel, 700 Eighth Ave., at 44th St.*

Now the middle-brow Milford Plaza, this solid brown-brick building was once the Lincoln Hotel, where the Blue Room nightclub was housed. Count Basie played here in the 1940's, and Billie Holiday—then with the Artie Shaw band—was given the backdoor treatment here in 1938. "Gee, it's funny," she told Bill Chase of the *Amsterdam News* the following year, "we were really a big hit all over the South and never ran into the color question until we opened at the Lincoln Hotel here in New York City. I was billed next to Artie himself, but was never allowed to visit the bar or the dining room, as did the other members of the band. Not only was I made to enter and leave the hotel through the kitchen but had to remain alone in a little dark room all evening until I was called. . . ."[6]

Town Hall, *123 W. 43rd St.*

Opened in 1921 as a public meetinghouse, Town Hall was the site of Bird's last public concert, held on October 30, 1954. According to his producer and biographer, Robert Reisner, the musician played magnificently throughout, despite the fact that the concert—owing to limited advertising—was poorly attended.

Town Hall began featuring jazz concerts in the early 1940's, when Dixieland jazz master Eddie Condon organized a regular series of jam sessions, featuring such artists as Oran "Hot Lips" Page, Pee Wee Russell, and Zutty Singleton. The sessions were informal—the musicians lounged, smoked and whispered to each other on stage—which was unusual at the time, and they met with great critical acclaim.

Today, the hall is still known for its jazz concerts.

Aeolian Hall, *33 W. 42nd St., near Sixth Ave.*

Now completely absorbed by the CUNY Graduate Center (only a few elevator doors, old walls, and ceiling details are left), Aeolian Hall was the site of the "First American Jazz Concert" presented by Paul Whiteman on February 12, 1924. Whiteman had set out to prove to the world that jazz has as much validity as classical music, a notion that many dismissed as "Whiteman's Folly" until they heard the concert's twenty-second selection, "Rhapsody in Blue," performed on the piano by its composer, George Gershwin.

Hotel Pennsylvania *(now the Penta Hotel), 401 Seventh Ave., near 33rd St.*

The Hotel Pennsylvania was once a popular spot for all the major swing bands. Glenn Miller's signature song, "Pennsylvania 6-5000" (still the hotel's phone number), was named after the place.

Hotel Roosevelt, *Madison Ave. and 45th St.*

In 1934, the Benny Goodman Orchestra played its first dance-hall engagement at the Roosevelt. The event was a disaster. The Roosevelt was Guy Lombardo's home base, and the waiters kept motioning to Goodman to tone it down. Some even requested a transfer to another room, and the customers sent caustic notes to the band.

Waldorf Astoria, *Park Ave. at E. 49th St.*

There was a time when the Waldorf was known for its jazz. Many major big bands, including those led by Benny Goodman and violinist Leo Reisman, played the Waldorf's Empire Room during the '30's and '40's, and Charlie Parker and Sidney Bechet performed for a youth conference sponsored by the hotel in 1949.

Louis Armstrong gave his last concert at the Waldorf in 1971. Then already in poor health, he insisted on playing despite the warnings of his doctor, who later reported that the following incident had taken place at his office two weeks earlier:

" 'Louie,' [I said,] 'you could drop dead while you're performing.' He said, 'Doc, that's all right, I don't care.' . . . And he sat there for a moment sort of removed and went through the motions of blowing that horn. 'I've got bookings arranged and the people are waiting for me.' "[7]

Armstrong went through with the concert (which got lousy reviews), and then checked into Beth Israel Medical Center, as he had promised his family and doctor. He died a few months later.

DOWNTOWN

(The following route, which can be toured on foot, begins in the East Village, on Second Avenue near 10th Street, and proceeds east and then south before heading west to Greenwich Village.)

Stuyvesant Casino, *140 Second Ave.*

Now a Ukrainian hall and restaurant, the Stuyvesant was once known for its dancing and jazz. New Orleans musician Bunk Johnson made his New York debut here in 1945; and others who played the hall included Sidney Bechet, Art Hodes, Henry "Red" Allen, and Buck Clayton.

The Stuyvesant and its music were also the objects of some controversy. When Bunk was brought up from New Orleans, bebop was in its infancy on 52nd Street, and many writers and critics, unable to understand the new sound, heralded Johnson's group with fulsome reviews, calling them the only band left playing "true jazz." Naturally, this did not sit well with the newer players.

Charlie Parker's apartment, *151 Ave. B, bet. Ninth and Tenth streets*

In 1951, Bird moved downtown into a solid four-story white stone building looking out onto Tompkins Square Park. With him were his girlfriend, Chan, and her daughter, Kim. "I like the people around here," he said once to his biographer Robert Reisner. "They don't give you no hype."

The apartment, large and comfortable, was filled with castoff furniture and Kim's toys, including a five-foot rabbit that Parker had given her. While here, the musician kept his life middle-class and respectable, greeting Chan's relatives in a suit and tie, and taking walks with Kim in the park. Later, Chan said that if it hadn't been for his talent, race, and drug addiction, Charlie could have lived out his days on Avenue B as a "happy square."[8]

The city renamed this block "Charlie Parker Place" in 1993.

Five Spot, *2 St. Marks Pl. (SE corner of Third Ave.).*

It was at the Five Spot, originally located at 5 Cooper Square, that Thelonious Monk finally became recognized in the late 1950's. A shadowy figure up until then, known mostly as the eccentric who'd written " 'Round About Midnight," he brought with him to the club a quartet that included John Coltrane. Their impact was enormous, and before long, the club was packed every night. "Trane was the perfect saxophonist for Monk's music because of the space that Monk always used," says Miles Davis in *Miles.* "Trane could fill up all that space with all them chords and sounds he was playing then."

From the beginning, the Five Spot was known for its serious commitment to music. Before Monk, there had been Cecil Taylor; after him came Ornette Coleman, who made a controversial New York debut at the club, and Eric Dolphy, who gave some of his most inspired performances there. Charles Mingus, who destroyed his $2,000 bass in anger at two hecklers one night, was also associated with the Five Spot.

Charles Mingus's loft, *5 Great Jones St., near Lafayette St.*

Mingus, his nerves frayed through career disappointments and personal problems, lived at this address for a turbulent period in 1966. While here, he worked at the Village Gate, where he threw a drum at Herbie Mann and wore a little but very real pistol (a Derringer with two bullets in it) around his neck as a charm.

On November 22, 1966, Mingus was evicted from his loft-apartment for alleged nonpayment of rent. The event was documented in the film *Mingus* by Tom Reichman, in which Mingus gives a long and bitter soliloquy and fires his shotgun at the ceiling.

Number 5 now houses a storefront on the first floor, with living quarters up above.

The Cookery, *21 University Pl. at E. Eighth St.*

Alberta Hunter, who had entered show business at the age of 16 and had had more than her share of ups and downs, suddenly quit music, without fanfare, in the mid-1950's. For the next 20 years she worked as a nurse at the Goldwater Hospital on Roosevelt Island. This was *after* going back to school for both her high school diploma and her nursing diploma, which she received at 62, having lied about her age to get into the program.

Then, in 1977, through a mutual friend, Hunter came to the attention of Barney Josephson, (see Café Society, page 125), who was running a restaurant-club called The Cookery. Josephson booked Hunter, and before long, at age 82, she was in the midst of a tremendous comeback.

The Cookery building now houses a barbecue joint.

Café Society (Downtown), *2 Sheridan Sq. (where Barrow St. runs into W. Fourth St., now the Ridiculous Theatrical Co.)*

Opened in 1939 by Barney Josephson, then a 36-year-old former shoe manufacturer, Café Society was one of the first truly integrated clubs downtown. Whites and blacks could sit and dance together—a courageous innovation for the time—and anyone who made a racial slur was immediately asked to leave.

Billie Holiday opened the L-shaped basement club, lined with quirky murals, and the engagement marked the turning point of her career. It was also here that her song "Strange Fruit" was born. The song came out of a poem written by poet Lewis Allen, whom Billie first met at the club.

Lena Horne followed Billie, and then there was Sarah Vaughan, Mildred Bailey, Joe Turner, Josh White, Big Bill Broonzy, Teddy Wilson, Art Tatum, James P. Johnson, Lester Young, Django Reinhardt, and many more. Fletcher Henderson played his last gig here in 1950.

Josephson opened a second Café Society Uptown (128 E. 58th St.) in 1940. Both clubs closed down in 1950.

Café Bohemia, *15 Barrow St., near Fourth St.*

Now a local watering hole, the Café Bohemia opened in 1955 with Oscar Pettiford as musical director. Saxophonist Cannonball Adderley, then a 26-year-old high school teacher up from Florida, made a New York debut here that same year that launched his career.

"Great night!," said Cannonball's brother Nat in a 1984 interview with Phil Schaap of WKCR radio. "We'd just come into town because my brother was going to do some work at NYU. He was gonna get his master's. And we went down, the first night, to Café Bohemia. . . . Oscar Pettiford was playing. . . . Charlie Rouse was there as well, he recognized Cannonball from Florida and one thing led to another. Cannon sailed through the first couple of tunes and then I went up and played and two nights later, we had a job. . . ."

Nick's, *170 W. 10th St. at Seventh Ave. S.*

One of the earliest spots in the Village for jazz, Nick's (now the Riviera Café) was a Dixieland haunt during the '30's. The club's resident band, led by Bobby Hackett, featured Eddie Condon, Pee Wee Russell and Zutty Singleton. Sidney Bechet also put in numerous appearances, as did Meade "Lux" Lewis, Muggsy Spanier, and Wild Bill Davison.

Electric Lady Studios, *52 W. Eighth St., near Sixth Ave.*

In early 1970, Jimi Hendrix completed his splendid Electric Lady Studios, shaped like a giant guitar, built into a row of four-story brownstones. He wanted the studios to be as beautiful physically as the music that would be created within, and so outfitted the place with state-of-the-art equipment, curving passageways, a

Fat Tuesday's, housed in an old German beer hall, still has a sort of oompah feel.

giant multicolor space mural, and walls of white carpet that reflected muted lights.

Hendrix recorded some 600 hours of tapes at the studios, but died on September 18, 1970 (from inhalation of vomit following barbiturate intoxication), before anything was released. Later, the Jimi Hendrix Estate hired an independent producer to put together albums from the raw, unedited tapes. The results didn't measure up to Hendrix's earlier work and ignited much controversy, largely because of the producer's decision to erase tracks featuring the original sidemen and replace them with Los Angeles studio musicians.

Before the Electric Lady Studios were created, 52 Eighth St. housed the Generation, a music club where Hendrix, B. B. King, and Buddy Guy played on the night that Martin Luther King, Jr., was killed. Today, the building's ground floor is still rounded like a guitar and there's a shiny ELECTRIC LADY plaque at the door.

Elsewhere in the City

Louis Armstrong's home, *34–56 107th St., Corona, Queens.*
The great Satchmo lived in this attractive red-brick building with beautiful gardens out back from the early 1940's until his death in 1971. It was his longest stay in one abode, and tales are

often told of how he used to sit on the front steps with his trumpet and entertain the neighborhood kids, some of whom came by with horns of their own. Lots of musicians also stopped by, and then there'd be the private jam sessions, especially on the Fourth of July (Armstrong's alleged birthday), when Louis would throw giant parties in the backyard.

The Corona house was actually bought by Louis's wife, Lucille. Upon their marriage, he had told her that he did not want a home, that he was content to live in hotels, but she went ahead and bought one anyway and he grew to like it, holing up here whenever he was off the road and refusing to move even after the neighborhood had deteriorated.

Today, the Armstrong home is on the National Register of Historic Places and is owned by Queens College, which plans to turn it into a museum. The house remains as the Armstrongs left it and is filled with priceless memorabilia: journals, letters, photos, Armstrong's private compilations of ribald jokes and tales (some of which are typed out on yellow "Satchmo" stationery and date back to Storyville days), 500 to 1,000 reels of tape-recorded TV and radio broadcasts, unreleased recordings, six trumpets, and boxes and boxes of sheet music, some of it annotated. To get everything in order for public viewing will take several more years; in the meantime, the college produces occasional concerts in the backyard.

Flushing Cemetery, *163-06 46th Ave., Corona, Queens, 718-359-0100.*
The great Satchmo is buried in this cemetery, located not far from his former home. On his tombstone, on which his epitaph is etched in gold, is a sculpture of a trumpet draped in cloth.

Jazzmen Johnny Hodges, Charlie Shavers, and Dizzy Gillespie are all buried here as well, Dizzy in a family plot where his name remains unmarked on the tombstone, as per the request of his family. After a private ceremony for the late great trumpet player (who died in 1993), held at St. Peter's Lutheran Church in Manhattan, a 14-car cortege drove along 52nd Street and up Broadway, past the sites of Birdland and the Royal Roost, and then on up into Harlem, past the site of Minton's Playhouse and the Apollo Theatre.
Open: daily, 8 a.m.–4:30 p.m.

Woodlawn Cemetery, *Webster Ave. and 233rd St., the Bronx, 718-920-0500.*
Duke Ellington, W. C. Handy, Joseph "King" Oliver, and Miles Davis are all buried in Woodlawn Cemetery, an idyllic park that's recognized as one of the most beautiful cemeteries in the world. Dating back to Civil War days, it's built on rolling hills with lots of shady trees and a shimmering sky-blue lake.

Ellington's grave is located in a corner plot, beneath a large tree, while Miles is buried less than 10 yards away, beneath a shiny black granite stone that reads IN MEMORY OF SIR MILES DAVIS. Handy's grave, with its lyre design, is also impressive, and all three sites are marked on the cemetery map.

Oliver was not so fortunate. Once "King" of the Chicago jazz scene, he died poverty-stricken and alone and is buried in an unmarked grave in the Salvia section. In 1927, Oliver—who had all of Chicago eating out of his hand—turned down an offer to headline at the Cotton Club in New York. (Duke Ellington took the job, which sprung him into stardom.) It proved to be a fatal mistake. By 1928, he was having a hard time finding work, and following the Depression, he lost his band. By the mid-1930's he was running a fruit stand in Savannah, Georgia. Later, he took a job as a janitor in a pool hall, but although he worked from early morning until midnight, he couldn't earn enough money to care for his worsening health. In one heartbreaking letter to his sister, who lived in the Bronx, he wrote that he had finally saved $1.60 and was coming to New York. He only made it in a casket.

Open: daily, 9 a.m.–4:30 p.m.

Williamsburg Bridge, *near Delancey St.*

One of three suspension bridges that span the East River, linking Manhattan with Brooklyn, the Williamsburg was Sonny Rollins's private retreat from 1959 to 1961, when he withdrew from a successful career to further explore the world of music. "I found it's a superb place to practice," he tells writer Whitney Balliett in *Dinosaurs in the Morning.* "Night or day. You're up over the whole world. You can look down on the whole scene. There is the skyline, the water, the harbor. . . . It makes you think."

Clubs, etc.

For an out-of-towner, the jazz scene in New York can come as a shock. Prices are often extremely high ($15–$35, plus a two-drink minimum) and the clubs, small and crowded. The quality of the music is almost always superb, but because many of the better-known places have become so formal, a certain energy sometimes seems to be missing. Good hangout-type places are few and far between, and making a spontaneous stop is often impossible in a city that's become more and more dependent on reservations.

There are some ways around this. The Village, where most of the jazz clubs are located, should be avoided on the weekends, when it's packed to capacity with tourists. The later shows are often better than the earlier ones: the musicians are warmed up then and you don't have to worry about being whisked out for the second set. For those on a budget, there are options (see below).

Despite its drawbacks, New York is far and away the jazz capital of the world. On any given night there's so much talent to choose from that it's hard to know where to go first. Below, find a few guidelines. Generally speaking, music in the city stops at 2 a.m., but there are places that keep going until 4 a.m. Many clubs have set showtimes each night; call for information.

THE QUINTESSENTIALS: The **Village Vanguard,** the oldest jazz club in New York; the **Blue Note,** the city's premier jazz supper club, known for mainstream acts; **Sweet Basil,** especially good for straight-ahead and avant-garde jazz; **Bradley's,** an acoustically perfect piano/bass room, now also featuring many trios and quartets; **Fat Tuesday's,** for mainstream acts; the **Knitting Factory,** for jazz on the cutting edge; **Red Blazer Too,** for traditional jazz; the **Village Gate,** for big acts, Latin jazz, and some blues; the **Bottom Line,** for eclectic acts, and the **Chestnut Room** in the Tavern on the Green, New York's newest jazz club for nationally known talent.

THE BARGAINS: **Showman's** and the **Cotton Club,** the last of the Harlem clubs; the **Louisiana Community Bar & Grill;** the **Five Spot; Red Blazer Too** and the **Cajun,** two traditional spots; **55 Bar** and **Arthur's Tavern,** two historic Village spots; **Dan Lynch's** and **Downtime** for blues; and many of the smaller clubs listed below presenting lesser-known talent. Also the "Terrace" at the **Village Gate,** the bar areas at **Birdland** and **Yardbird Suite, Sweet Basil** for weekend brunch, and the **Blue Note,** after hours.

FOR BRUNCH: **Sweet Basil, Birdland, Blue Note, Red Blazer Too,** the **Cajun,** the **Cotton Club, The Squire, Fat Tuesday's,** the **Sazerac House,** the **Village Corner,** and **Jimmy Walker's.**

FOR DANCING: Events sponsored by the **New York Swing Dance Society, Red Blazer Too,** the **Cotton Club,** the **Rainbow Room,** and **Roseland.**

FOR BLUES: For a city of its size, New York has very little in the way of blues clubs. The only three consistent spots for national acts are **Tramps** and the **Lone Star,** both presenting a variety of solid roots music, including blues, and **Manny's,** presenting exclusively blues. **Dan Lynch's, Downtime,** and **Terra Blues** are good clubs for local blues.

FOR JAZZ

GREENWICH VILLAGE

Village Vanguard, *178 Seventh Ave. S., 255-4037.*

A narrow staircase leads down, down into a dark wedge-shaped room filled with rickety tables. Along the walls, at odd angles, hang fading pictures of the greats—Thelonious Monk, Gerry Mulligan, Dexter Gordon—while up front is a crowded stage with a few battered chairs and a big piano.

Welcome to the private musical world of the Village Vanguard. For fifty-odd years, this tiny club, once run by the legendary, now deceased jazz impresario Max Gordon, has seen them all come and go. There was Miles Davis—"He was always tough," Gordon once said. "Always full of his own juice"; John Coltrane—"A very shy man, very much involved with his work"; Charles Mingus— "One time he was looking for an advance and I didn't have it. He ripped the front door off the hinges and threw it down the stairs." There was also Dinah Washington, who insisted on performing in a big blond wig, and Sonny Rollins, who simply disappeared one night after playing a superb first set and never came back.

Gordon, born in Lithuania, moved to New York from Oregon in 1926, planning to attend Columbia Law School. Instead, six weeks later, he was down in the Village, where, he later said, he'd been headed ever since setting foot in New York.

The Vanguard, opened in 1934, started out as a simple hangout for writers and artists, but Gordon soon began booking such then unknown talent as Leadbelly, Josh White, the Weavers, Lenny Bruce, Eartha Kitt, Woody Guthrie, Woody Allen, and Burl Ives. Later, in the mid-fifties, he started specializing in jazz, and since then virtually every major musician has played here, from Thelonious Monk to Chick Corea.

Today, the Vanguard is the oldest jazz club in New York, and it's often filled with jet-lagged but enthusiastic foreigners, who come here right off the plane. Now operated by Gordon's wife, Lorraine, who's always had input into the place (she was responsible for Monk's first booking here), it still features all the greats, from veterans such as Illinois Jacquet and Lou Donaldson to younger artists such as Terence Blanchard and Geri Allen. Cutting-edge sounds are seldom heard at the Vanguard, however; the emphasis is on jazz of the '40's and '50's. Meanwhile, the Vanguard Jazz Orchestra (formerly the Mel Lewis Big Band) has been jamming at the Vanguard every Monday night for over 20 years. *Music:* nightly. *Cover/minimum:* $$$. Reservations recommended.

The Blue Note, *131 W. Third St., 475-8592.*

Much of the time, the Blue Note, New York's premier jazz supper club, is an annoying place: commercial, expensive, crowded. Sometimes, though, the atmosphere is just right. This is most likely to occur at a late show during the week, when the crowd level is down and the intimacy level is up.

The Blue Note, a large rectangular place all done up in glitzy blues with mirrors (there's even a souvenir room upstairs), is known for its upscale mainstream sounds. Most of the biggest names in jazz have played here, including the late Dizzy Gillespie, Oscar Peterson, the Modern Jazz Quartet, Toshiko Akiyoshi, Lionel Hampton, Ray Charles, Dave Brubeck and Max Roach. Monday nights are often reserved for up-and-coming talents, and brunches are featured on the weekends.

A well-kept secret is the club's after-hours shows, which begin after the last set and last until four a.m. There's no additional cover for patrons already in house; $ for newcomers.
Music: nightly. *Cover/minimum:* $$$–$$$$, Tu–Su; $$, M; $, after-hours. *Food:* American. Amex only. Reservations recommended.

Sweet Basil, *88 Seventh Ave. S., 242-1785.*

One of the most wonderful things about Sweet Basil is that it's not predictable. One night the sounds will be straight-ahead—McCoy Tyner, Art Farmer; the next night things will be more progressive—Steve Lacy, the World Saxophone Quartet. And then there are the Sunday brunches, often featuring the legendary trumpet player Doc Cheatham, now in his eighties, who once played with Ma Rainey and Cab Calloway.

Another wonderful thing about Sweet Basil is that it's a good, comfortable place, intimate but not too intimate, crowded but not too crowded, with lots of light-colored pine and brick. Jazz photos hang from the walls; candles flicker on the tables. There's a small bar near the back, and a section built out onto the street for diners.

Started up in 1981 by an unlikely trio (a jazz promoter from Berlin, a singer from the Bronx, and a former high school principal), Sweet Basil is now under Japanese ownership. Numerous albums have been recorded here, and Gil Evans, during the last five years of his life, led his orchestra here every Monday night. Those sessions were legendary, with the rock star Sting, who'd recorded with Evans, so taken with the master that he often came down to listen and occasionally sit in. Nowadays, Monday nights are devoted to an electrified big band, playing Evans's music under the direction of his son, trumpeter Miles Evans.
Music: Tu–Su. *Cover/minimum:* $$$, nights; $ for brunch. *Food:* continental. CC. Reservations recommended.

Village Gate, *Bleecker and Thompson streets, 475-5120.*

Back in the '60's, 160 Bleecker Street was a sleazy derelict hotel with 1,400 rooms catering to winos and prostitutes and a laundry in its basement. Today, it's part luxury apartment building, part the Village Gate, one of the largest, oldest, and most respected jazz/cabaret clubs in New York.

Owned by impresario Art D'Lugoff, the Village Gate is actually a triple-decker affair, with three shows sometimes running simultaneously. The downstairs room, "The Gate," which seats 450, often presents well-known mainstream jazz, blues, Latin and world music acts; the "Top of the Gate" runs cabaret and revues; and the street-level "Terrace" showcases up-and-coming duos and trios nightly and on weekend afternoons, when college students jam.

The basement Gate still has a bombed-out laundry-room feel. Cavernous and dark, it's filled with long, scarred wooden tables arranged around the metal poles that support the building. Sight lines aren't always what they should be, but the list of greats who've performed here is long and mean: Miles Davis, Horace Silver, Dizzy Gillespie, Dexter Gordon, Charles Mingus, Albert King, Memphis Slim, John Lee Hooker. Over 60 albums have been recorded in this room; here, B. B. King gave one of his first performances before a white audience, in 1968, and Otis Rush's career was revived, in 1979. Monk made his last nightclub appearance at the Gate; and Red Garland was lifted off the stage once by two men in blue (he was being sued for alimony).

Although recently in a period of financial difficulty, the Gate got a new lease on life in late 1993 when it won court approval to turn itself into a nonprofit jazz museum. Exhibits, educational programs, and fund-raising events are now being planned, and the Gate also hopes to soon re-institute its legendary Monday night "Salsa Meets Jazz" program. The series, over 20 years old, was once run by Symphony Sid Torin, and has featured everyone from Willie Colon to Tito Puente.

Music: nightly. *Cover:* none at Terrace, $$$ at Gate and Top of Gate; CC. Reservations recommended except at Terrace.

Bradley's, *70 University Pl., 473-9700.*

With its dark, denlike feel, Bradley's is the sort of place that legends are made out of. Once run by the beloved, now deceased Bradley Cunningham (who, in his notorious passion for music, often kept the musicians after-hours for his own private sessions), it is now operated by his wife, Wendy.

Bradley's is the city's premier piano-bass room—the best in the world, according to *Newsday* jazz critic Stuart Troup. The piano, donated to the club by Bradley's old friend Paul Desmond, is tuned every day, and the room's acoustics are such that, conversation levels permitting, you can hear every note.

All the top piano and bass players have played at Bradley's, with Tommy Flanagan, Hank Jones, Dave McKenna, and Charles Mingus, before his death, having a particularly strong affiliation. Nowadays, trios or quartets are also often featured, and Sunday nights are usually reserved for new names in jazz.

Musicians often hang out at Bradley's after their gigs elsewhere are done. With a 2 a.m. set, one of the latest in the city, the music usually runs until 4 a.m. and the kitchen is open until 2:30 a.m.

Music: nightly. *Cover/minimum:* $$$. *Food:* American. CC. Reservations recommended weekends.

Arthur's Tavern, *57 Grove St., 675-6879.*

Housed in a building dating back to the early 1800's, Arthur's has been a jazz joint since the 1940's. Tiny and dark, with a beaten-up wooden bar and lots of Christmas-tree lights, it once saw the likes of Charlie Parker and Wild Bill Davison on its stage. Nowadays the place is home to Al Bundy, the George Stubbs trio, and the Grove Street Stompers, a traditional band here since 1961.

The Stompers, who play on Monday nights, are an enthusiastic six-piece band of both professional and "avocational musicians" (one's a commercial artist, another's in finance) led by piano player Bill Dunham (in real estate). The band's players have changed over the years, but the gig hasn't, and it's the longest-running same club, same night, same band act in the city.

Music: nightly. *No cover.*

Village Corner, *Bleecker Street and LaGuardia Place ("Corner of Walk and Don't Walk"), 473-9762.*

Housed in a nineteenth-century building that was first a bank, then a hotel, then a speakeasy with a fake soda-fountain facade, the Village Corner is now an atmospheric old bar featuring mainstream piano jazz during the evenings and trios on weekend afternoons. A pretty place with maroon walls, tin ceilings, revolving fans, and a big wooden bar, the club is located at the corner of "Walk and Don't Walk," for legend has it that on the night of Aug. 3, 1951, when the city first turned on those then new street signs, a man named Oliver Atwell had had a few too many. He called his wife to come to take him home, and when she asked where he was, he looked up, saw the new sign, and answered, "The corner of Walk and Don't Walk." Other establishments claim that they are located at that very same address, but according to New York Telephone and the U.S. Post Office, the Village Corner was the first. It's even listed that way in the phone book.

Music: M–Sa, Sa and Su afternoons. *No cover. Minimum:* $$. *Food:* burgers, etc.; brunch on weekends.

The Bottom Line, *15 W. Fourth St., 228-6300.*

Known for its eclectic booking, the Bottom Line is a big, comfortable Village institution, filled with a crowded sea of tables. The range of talent that has performed here is mind-boggling: Dr. John opened the place in 1974 with Stevie Wonder sitting in late that night to jam; Bruce Springsteen, then just on the cusp of fame, played a legendary five-night stand in 1975; and Dolly Parton was at the club in 1977, in a concert that drew both Andy Warhol and John Belushi. Then, too, there's been Patti Smith, Lou Reed, the Talking Heads, Graham Parker, Elvis Costello, Prince, and Suzanne Vega; and Miles Davis, B. B. King, Muddy Waters, George

Benson, Grover Washington Jr., John Mayall, and Robert Cray. *Music:* most nights, some jazz/blues. *Cover:* $$–$$$. *Food:* burgers, pizza, etc. Reservations recommended on weekends.

Visiones, *125 MacDougal St., 673-5576.*

Started up in the early 1940's as a Spanish restaurant, Visiones is a small and friendly family-run club with a dining area, a tiny bar, and stucco walls of white. A wide spectrum of jazz is featured (straight-ahead to fusion, big-band to progressive), but lately, thanks to its new one-of-a-kind, nine-foot-long German Steinway D-Model 320 piano, the place has been attracting lots of top pianists, including Johns Hicks, Mulgrew Miller, Harold Mayburn, and Barry Harris. Monday nights are usually reserved for the 17-piece Maria Schneider Orchestra, and the place is a late-night hang, with late shows starting at two a.m. on Fridays and Saturdays.
Music: nightly. *Cover/minimum:* $$–$$$. *Food:* Spanish, American bistro. CC. Reservations recommended on weekends.

55 Bar, *55 Christopher St., 929-9883.*

Two doors down from the well-known Lion's Head, long a favorite hangout among writers, is the dingy 55 Bar, an old dive that dates back to Prohibition. Regulars at this tiny hole-in-the-wall that's reached by descending three well-worn steps include guitarist Mike Stern and drummer Jim Mason. One of the bar's trademarks is its free popcorn, and its jazz jukebox, filled with old classics, is the best in town.
Music: nightly. *No cover.* Two-drink minimum.

Zinno, *126 W. 13th St., 924-5182.*

A spacious multiroomed restaurant all done up in peaches and creams, Zinno's specializes in piano-bass duos and piano trios. Milt Hinton, George Cables, Sonny Fortune, and Cecil McBee are among the many who have played here, in this upscale "casual but romantic" spot. Jazz lovers should request a table in or near the piano room; the back rooms are far removed from the music.
Music: nightly. *Cover:* $. *Food:* northern Italian. CC.

Knickerbocker Restaurant, *33 University Pl., 228-8490.*

A place for the "novice jazz listener" is the way management bills this historic restaurant with its heavy mahogany bar, brass railings, Hirschfeld drawings, and 28-ounce Porterhouse steaks, and that seems a fair assessment, although some top people, usually in the form of piano-bass duos, can be caught here. Harry Connick, Jr., played here for two years for no cover before going on to win fame and fortune at the Algonquin Hotel.
Music: W–Sa. *Cover:* $. *Food:* American. CC.

Zanzibar, *73 Eighth Ave., near 13th St., 924-9755.*

Billing itself as a "1940's supper club," Zanzibar is a pretty little room with a handful of plush red booths, a smattering of tables, and walls covered with bright, sunny murals of tropical life. Monkeys swing from tree to tree; gyrating figures kick up their heels.

Opened in 1993, the club offers up a mix of contemporary, fusion, R&B, Latin, and funk. Hiram Bullock inaugurated the place, and since then, a wide variety of acts have appeared, including Ray Barreto, Hugh Masekela, Junior Walker, Steve Coleman, and the World Flute Choir, a "12-flute big band." Sundays are usually preserved for big bands, Mondays for young fusion players, Wednesdays for Brazilian music, and weekends for headliners. "It's all high-energy stuff," says owner Eric Fuchsmain.
Music: nightly. *Cover:* $$–$$$. *Food:* light international.

Also

Poetry readings, new writings, new theater, and much jazz come to the long white-brick-walled basement of the **Cornelia Street Café** (29 Cornelia St., 989-9319) most every night of the week. Now over 16 years old, the café features a little bit of many things, including vocalists, bebop, and Latin jazz. The food here (contemporary American) is also quite good.

The **Sazerac House** (533 Hudson St., 989-0313), serving Cajun-influenced American food, offers up weekend jams featuring young musicians from the New School, and a Sunday jazz brunch. **5 & 10 No Exaggeration** (77 Greene St., 925-7414), a show and supper club filled with antiques, also has jazz on a weekly basis.

ELSEWHERE DOWNTOWN

The Knitting Factory, *47 E. Houston St., 219-3055.*

Ever since opening in 1987, the quirky, second-story Knitting Factory (located in a building that once actually was a knitting factory) has featured a little bit of everything: funk, rock, free improvisation, world music. But the simple, minimalist club with its comfortable, quasi-intellectual feel is really best known for its cutting-edge jazz. John Zorn, Elliott Sharp, Wayne Horvitz, the Microscopic Septet, the Jazz Passengers, and Tim Berne are among the many innovative musicians associated with the club.

The Knitting Factory was started up by two transplanted Wisconsinites, Michael Dorf and Bob Appel, when they were both in their twenties and it has had considerable success. The club has released over fifty CDs on its Knitting Factory Works label, and also produces a series for New York's JVC Jazz Festival.
Music: nightly. *Cover:* $–$$.

Fat Tuesday's, *190 3rd Ave., 533-7902.*

Fat Tuesday's is housed in what was once a German-American hall, built in 1894, and it still has a sort of oompah feel, especially upstairs, where mock Tiffany lamps hang above wooden booths, vaudeville photos, and red tablecloths. Most of the music takes

Hiram Bullock inau-
gurates Zanzibar,
one of Manhattan's
newest clubs.

place downstairs in a claustrophobic, *very* low-ceilinged basement
with subdued red lights, crowded tables, and crooked mirrors on
the walls. All sorts of major mainstream acts perform, including
Jimmy Smith, Jimmy Witherspoon, and Grady Tate, while Monday nights are devoted to the legendary guitarist Les Paul, who's
attracted a fair number of rock celebrities over the years: David
Bowie, Joan Jett, Steve Miller, the Beach Boys. Recently, too, the
club has begun featuring lesser-known acts upstairs, weekdays
early evenings, and Sundays, during brunch.
Music: nightly, Su afternoons. *Cover/minimum:* $$$. *Food:*
American. CC. Reservations recommended weekends.

Yardbird Suite, *35 Cooper Sq. (Third Ave. near Sixth St.),
228-5800.*
One of the newest clubs in town, and "sister" to the well-estab-
lished **Birdland** uptown (see page 142), the long and simple Yard-
bird Suite is a serious listening spot. Expressly built for sound, and
all done up in industrial blacks and grays, it's not so much about
atmosphere as it is about music. Many nights are devoted to
younger, lesser-known acts who the owner feels are about to make
names for themselves, while the weekends usually feature heavier
hitters, often playing jazz that's more on the cutting edge. Some
who have appeared here include David Murray and Dave Burrell
(on a double bill), Hammiet Bluiett, George Coleman, Kenny Bar-
ron, the Sun Ra Arkestra, and Roy Hargrove. Brazilian jazz can

often be heard on Mondays, while big bands are featured on Wednesdays. Once a month there's a jazz jam.

Music: nightly. *Cover/minimum:* $$–$$$. *Food:* light American.

Time Café, *380 Lafayette St., 533-7000.*

One of the most unusual jazz events in the city, the gathering of the Mingus Big Band, takes place once a week in a basement club located deep inside the Time Café. For one of those odd, inexplicable reasons, the weekly concert (now over a year old) has become a hip downtown happening, a place to see and be seen, whether a person has ever heard of Charles Mingus or not. The 14-piece band, playing the rambling, cacophonous, often astonishing music of the late composer, often with Randy Brecker on trumpet, puts on a good show, and though those at the door can be snooty, even downright rude, the room is casual and comfortable.

Music: usually Th (call ahead). *Cover:* $$$. *Food:* upscale burgers, pizza, etc. Reservations recommended.

Smalls' Paradise, one of the big three Harlem Renaissance clubs, was still going strong in the '40's.

Frank Driggs Collection

Louisiana Community Bar & Grill, *622 Broadway, near Houston St., 460-9633.*

A cavernous, candlelit place with a long, long, long front bar, peanut shells on the floors, and giant Mardi Gras masks on the walls, the Louisiana is primarily a restaurant/bar, but it does present some good jazz and blues, usually for no cover. One of the oldest bands in the city, the Harlem All-Stars (whose members have played with everyone from Fats Waller to Dizzy Gillespie), appears here weekly, and R&B and country can also be heard.
Music: nightly. *No cover. Food:* Louisiana. CC.

The Squire, *216 7th Ave., 727-8387.*

A Chelsea institution and neighborhood hangout, the Squire is one of the older jazz spots in New York. Long and low and filled with wooden beams, wooden barrels, and wooden booths, it usually presents lesser-known mainstream acts, especially quartets. A champagne brunch is served on Sundays.
Music: nightly, Su brunch. *Cover:* $–$$. *Food:* burgers, etc. CC.

S.O.B.'s, *204 Varick St., 243-4940.*

What began as a Brazilian nightclub ("Sounds of Brazil") has since become a multiethnic sort of place that emphasizes "tropical music" (African, Caribbean, reggae, Latin). Jazz can also be heard at this stylish club-restaurant outfitted with straw huts, bamboo, and fake palm trees; it ranges from Latin (Eddie Palmieri, Gato Barbieri) to South African (Hugh Masekela) to American (Gil Scott-Heron, Betty Carter). Most of the bands are dance-oriented, and there's a small dance floor that's almost always packed with beautiful bodies.
Music: M–Sa. *Cover/minimum:* $$$. *Food:* "Tropical." CC. Reservations for dinner only.

Cajun, *129 Eighth Ave., at 16th St., 691-6174.*

Traditional jazz and Dixieland bring the regulars back again and again at this brightly lit, boisterous place with the red-checked tablecloths, long wooden bar, and no cover charge. The quality of the music varies widely from night to night, but this is the spot where members of the Preservation Hall Jazz Band hang out when in town for a concert.
Music: nightly, Su brunch. *No cover. Food:* Cajun.

Also

Vocalist Deanna Kirk and friends appear most nights at **Deanna's Café** (130 E. Seventh St., 505-5288), a hip, tiny downtown spot that's usually packed. The decor inside is well-worn Victorian; outside, weather permitting, are a handful of tables. **Caliban** (360 Third Ave., near 27th St., 689-5155) is a long and cavernous neighborhood bar with mirrored windows that features up-and-coming talent on the weekends. Jazz sometimes comes to **Chelsea**

Commons (242 Tenth Ave., near 27th St., 929-9424), a neighborhood spot that's a bit off the beaten track, but of at least equal interest to jazz fans is the fact that the club's handsome, polished bar once stood in the original Five Spot.

The **Ballroom** (253 W. 28th St., 244-3005) is a comfortable nightclub, all done up in green and brass, that's best known for its tapas and cabaret, but it also presents much jazz. The **Hors d'Oeuvrerie** at Windows on the World (1 World Trade Center, 938-1111) features jazz, dancing, "international hors d'oeuvres and the world's greatest view."

MIDTOWN

The Five Spot, *4 W. 31st St., 631-0100.*

Opened with great fanfare in early 1993, the Five Spot was to have become another Blue Note. David Sanborn opened the place to the tune of $37.50 cover/$15 minimum, and other equally pricey acts soon followed. But the high-end-of-the-market approach didn't work, and the club is currently experimenting with a new policy: presenting lesser-known jazz, blues, R&B, and soul acts for no cover. Recent performers include Philip Hamilton, the lead singer for Special EFX, Joe Caldezo, who plays piano with the Brecker Brothers, and the great soul singer Irene Reid.

The room is a visual delight, housed in an elaborate neo-baroque ballroom with 25-foot-high ceilings, crystal chandeliers, and lots of gold leaf. Designed in 1890 by architect Stanford White as part of the Hotel Walcott (then the sister hotel to the Waldorf Astoria), the ballroom hosted both inaugural balls of Mayor La Guardia.

The sound system is impressive, and the food excellent (chef T. Joseph O'Brien once worked for Lutèce), making the Five Spot, for the moment at least, a bargain. Call ahead, though, as this policy may change.

Music: nightly. *No cover. Food:* contemporary American. CC.

The Rooftop at B. Smith's, *771 Eighth Ave., at 47th St., 247-2222.*

Located upstairs from the upscale namesake restaurant owned by the former model who once appeared on the covers of *Essence* and other high-fashion magazines, the Rooftop usually presents jazz on weekends only. A spacious contemporary place with a high slanted ceiling and skylight, the club is elegant but comfortable, with a stage built out over the street, shiny copper-colored columns, and candles flickering on white tablecloths. Sight lines and acoustics are excellent.

Much of the jazz at B. Smith's is fusion/contemporary, though straight-ahead and Caribbean sounds are also featured. The club books big names such as Ramsey Lewis on occasion, but its mainstay is high-quality, lesser-known talent.

Music: F, Sa. *Cover/minimum:* $$–$$$. *Food:* international. CC.

Rainbow Room and **Rainbow & Stars,** *30 Rockefeller Plaza, 632-5000.*

A New York institution located high above Midtown, the Rainbow Room sparkles with night views of the city, ladies in exotic dress, and big bands in sequined costumes. Over half a century old, this is the place to go to be wined and dined, and to dance the rhumba, the lindy, and the waltz. Waiters glide by in pastel tails, the polished dance floor slowly revolves, and colored lights twinkle across the domed ceiling.

Right next door to the Rainbow Room is a snazzy cabaret–supper club called Rainbow & Stars. Here, tables are draped in glittering silver and gray, and a multicolor rainbow shines across the door. Singers of all types are featured, some with a jazz bent, some without.

Dining at the Rainbow, which was completely renovated in 1987, doesn't come cheap. The average dinner check is $100 per person, the average supper check (supper is served 10 p.m.–midnight), $75.

Music: Tu–Sa. *Cover/minimum:* $$$$, Rainbow Room; $$$$, Rainbow & Stars. Amex only. Reservations required.

Red Blazer Too Restaurant, *349 W. 46th St. (bet. Eighth and Ninth avenues), 262-3112.*

The best place in the city for traditional jazz, the Red Blazer is a well-lit, old-fashioned, drinking-man–friendly type of place that presents a mix of big-band swing and Dixieland, along with some ragtime piano. Stan Rubin's Big Band has been playing here for years and years; other regulars include Lew Anderson's big band, and Jim Lawyer & the Bluebird Orchestra. On Sundays, during the club's jazz brunch, some of the regular customers, who've been coming here so long they're almost band members themselves, get up and sing along with the scheduled acts.

Located in the theater district, the Red Blazer is big and square with slatted wood walls, a striking musical mural, and a loyal, mostly middle-aged crowd. Dancing is featured most nights.

Music: nightly, Su brunch. *Cover/minimum:* $$. *Food:* American, continental. CC. Reservations recommended.

Roseland Ballroom, *239 W. 52nd St., 247-0200.*

Yesterday's magic (see "Landmarks and Legends, " page 119) may be gone, but twice a week, from early afternoon on, there's still big-band dancing on Roseland's polished floors. On a typical afternoon, a few older couples dance beneath the domed ceiling dotted with lights, while singles in their sixties and seventies sit on little red chairs watching. One older woman wrings her hands; an older man, stunningly dressed in black with patent-leather shoes and striped socks, adjusts an enormous red carnation in his lapel.

Much of the music at Roseland is not jazz, but swing tunes are played. Out front is a plaque listing MARRIED COUPLES WHO FIRST MET HERE. Some date back to the early '20's, others to the late

'80's. Also out front is a "Dance City Hall of Fame," filled with the dusty dancing shoes of everyone from Bill "Bojangles" Robinson to Gregory Hines.
Music: Th, Su. *Cover:* $-$$.

UPTOWN EAST

Café Carlyle and **Bemelmans Bar,** *Hotel Carlyle, Madison Ave. at 76th St., 744-1600.*

High society's favorite jazzman Bobby Short has been playing at the posh Café Carlyle for almost 25 years now, making two appearances annually, one in the spring, one in the fall. At other times, other classic cabaret acts or jazz groups such as Eartha Kitt or the Modern Jazz Quartet perform.

The Carlyle is an elegant, intimate, cocoonlike place with pink tablecloths, low red lights, ever-so-discreet waiters and ever-so-high prices. Delicate Vertes murals that evoke bygone splendours line the walls, while just across the hall is Bemelmans Bar, a similarly outfitted place usually featuring solo piano artists.
Music: Tu–Sa. *Cover:* $$$$ ($ for Bemelman's Bar). *Food:* bistro continental. CC. Reservations required.

Michael's Pub, *211 E. 55th St., 758-2272.*

For the quintessentially rude New York experience, it's hard to beat Michael's Pub, where if you call for reservations, someone may hang up on you, and nobody tells you that if you come for drinks only, you'll be stuck in a dusty area without stools behind a partition where you can't see the show. But . . . Michael's is the only place in the city where you can hear Woody Allen blow Dixieland away with the New Orleans Funeral and Ragtime Orchestra. The Monday-night gig, featuring Allen on clarinet, has been going on for 23 years now, come what may. Other nights, the club features classic cabaret acts, including some jazz.

Michael's is large and well lit, decorated in Tudor style, with lots of green, and heavy brown wood. Much of the crowd are tourists.
Music: Jazz M, some other nights. *Cover/minimum:* $$$$. *Food:* American. CC. Reservations recommended.

Also

La Cave on First (1125 First Ave., at 62nd St., 759-4011) is a lively and unpretentious spot, located beneath a Mexican restaurant, where much jazz and blues can be heard. Most of the performers are unknowns, but "names" such as Houston Person and Dakota Staton appear regularly. French and soul food is served.

The posh **Sign of the Dove** restaurant (1110 Third Ave. at 65th St., 861-8080) presents jazz in its Café Bar, where a simpler sandwich menu is available most nights of the week. **Jimmy Walker's** (245 E. 55th St., 319-6650) features a Dixieland brunch on Sundays, as well as traditional jazz one or two nights a week.

UPTOWN WEST

The Chestnut Room, Tavern on the Green, *Central Park West, at 67th St., 873-3200.*

Preeminent among New York's newer jazz spots, the Chestnut Room books many fine impressive acts such as Illinois Jacquet, Dr. Billy Taylor, Sir Roland Hanna, Hank Jones, and Jimmy Scott. The comfortable room is moderately sized, with an intimate feel, and sight lines and acoustics are quite good. Cover charges are also reasonable, especially given the caliber of the talent, and there is no minimum (although drinks and food are expensive).

There is a down side, however, The Tavern on the Green is a restaurant first and foremost, and a tourist attraction, and the Chestnut Room, like all the other rooms, is a glittering extravaganza, packed to the bursting point with mirrors, gilt, and wood. Elaborate chandeliers hang from the ceilings, and a multitude of lights flicker on the walls. Tourists, seemingly by the hundreds, stream by in the corridors outside, and for a person intent upon the music, it's all a bit distracting, although the room is quiet once the doors are closed.

Music: Tu–Su. *Cover:* \$\$–\$\$\$. *Food:* Continental, American. CC.

Birdland, *2745 Broadway at 105th St., 749-2228.*

There are a lot of nice touches in this long, high-ceilinged spot with its big picture windows, polished light-brown bar, and strips of neon light. First, there are pictures on the wall: jazz portraits done "in concert" at the club by artist Joanna Ashe. Second, there is the friendly atmosphere: the restaurant attracts a loyal neighborhood crowd. Third, there is the cover/minimum at the bar: low even for the likes of Sonny Fortune, Clark Terry, and Jaki Byard. Sight lines are not what they should be, however, and sometimes, during the week, the club's performers are mediocre at best. The bigger names usually perform on the weekends; most of the music here is straight-ahead.

Music: nightly, Su brunch. *Cover:* \$\$–\$\$\$. *Food:* Cajun American. CC. Reservations recommended weekends.

West End Gate, *2911 Broadway at 114th St., 662-8830.*

A modernized descendant of the old West End Café, a Columbia University hangout, the new West End presents jazz in the early part of the week. Top musicians from the city's colleges and universities are usually on tap, though "names" such as Jimmy Nepper or Thelonious Monk, Jr., also perform from time to time.

To get to the Gate, you have to go through a brightly lit brick-walled restaurant packed with students. The jazz room itself is dark and comfortable, with black tables, black curtains, and a big neon swiggle on a black wall.

Music: Su–W. *Cover:* \$–\$\$. *Food:* burgers; etc.

Augie's Pub, *2751 Broadway at 105th St., 864-9834.*

A tiny hole of a storefront restaurant with big picture windows and old brick walls, Augie's has quite by accident (the owner doesn't even *like* jazz) become a good spot in which to catch new talent. Young musicians congregate here for jam sessons that last until 3 a.m., and established musicians such as Roy Haynes sometimes stop by to hear their students play.

Music: nightly. *No cover. Food:* burgers.

Also

One of New York's older cabarets and supper clubs, **Sweetwaters** (170 Amsterdam Ave., 873-4100) is an elegant spot that presents everything from comedy and gospel to pop and R&B. Ruth Brown often appears here. **Cleopatra's Needle** (2485 Broadway, at 94th St., 769-6969) is a seafood and Middle Eastern restaurant that has recently been booking much solid jazz for no cover.

HARLEM

Showman's Café, *2321 Frederick Douglass Blvd. (Eighth Ave.), near 125th St., 864-8941.*

The only real jazz club left in Harlem, Showman's was once located next to the Apollo, and all the greats performing there used to stop by: Count Basie, Lionel Hampton, Dizzy Gillespie, Nat "King" Cole.

Nowadays, Showman's, relocated just around the corner, is a neat, simple, congenial place with wood paneling, hanging plants, and a marble bar. Everyone knows everyone, and there's a great sense of continuity as the club fills up with musicians young and old, old hoofers from the Copacetics, and men and women on their way home from work. "We're like a family here," says Mona Lopez, the club's friendly manager. "We know everyone who comes through that door."

Regulars at the club include vocalist Irene Reid, who once sang with Count Basie, Jimmy "Preacher" Robins, Lonnie Youngblood, and Frank Dell. Not many white New Yorkers make it up this far (this club is happy to call cabs for those who do), but once or twice a night, the place fills up with busloads of Europeans and Japanese who stay for 45 minutes or so and then leave. The regulars watch them come and go with great amusement.

Music: Th–Sa. *No cover:* F–Sa. *Food:* Southern.

La Famille Restaurant, *2017 Fifth Ave. at 125th, 534-9909.*

For over 30 years, La Famille has been serving up some of the best soul food in Harlem. For over 10 years, it's also been serving up one of the oldest jam sessions in the city. The quality of the music varies, but there's always plenty of enthusiasm, as, on a typical night, 15 to 20 people take to the stage. An older African-

American saxophonist gives way to a young Japanese guitarist gives way to an even younger white keyboard player, who's brought along his wide-eyed father.

Music at La Famille happens downstairs at an intimate bar, while dining takes place upstairs in three small but spacious and cheerful rooms. Some of the tables overlook the streets.
Music: most nights. *No cover. Food:* soul food.

Cotton Club, *666 W. 125th St., between Broadway and Riverside Dr., 663-7980.*

Dining and dancing, jazz, blues, and gospel, are mainstays at the Cotton Club, a nicely outfitted place complete with a cozy balcony overlooking the bandstand and portraits of jazz greats. One night a week is usually devoted to Doc Wheeler (now in his mid-eighties) and his swinging 16-piece big band, while blues bands often play on Monday nights, and weekends feature a gospel brunch.
Music: M, W–F; Sa–Su gospel brunch. *Cover:* $–$$$. *Food:* American. Reservations recommended for brunch.

Also

Sylvia's (328 Lenox Ave., near 126th St., 996-0660), Harlem's other soul-food institution, also offers jazz, usually on one or two weekday nights.

BROOKLYN

Flamingo Lounge, *259-A Kingston Ave., 718-493-7200.*

A neighborhood joint that's been keeping the music hot and alive for well over a decade, Flamingo's is one of the few spots in Brooklyn that offers live jazz on a regular basis. Long, dark, and well worn with embossed red wallpaper, fading pictures of jazz greats, and a comfortable bar strewn with shiny Christmas-tree garlands, it's the sort of place that's seen plenty of hard times, but always manages to hang in there. "Music is what this place is all about," says Mr. Levi, the owner. Most of the regulars, including Bobby Forrester and Nat Dixon, are musicians who live in the neighborhood, but bigger names such as Dakota Staton and Harold Mayburn also occasionally stop by.
Music: F, Sa. *No cover.*

Royston's, *63 Lafayette St. (1½ blocks from the Brooklyn Academy of Music), 718-243-0900.*

Much thought and care have gone into making this spot both casually elegant and neighborhood friendly. Started up by two old friends—one a former music teacher for the New York public schools, another an expert in the patent business—it's the sort of place that will serve up a little R&B, reggae, or a cappella music one night, an "R&B, jazz, and poetry" open mike the next, and a top jazz artist such as Cassandra Wilson, Donald Harrison, or Terence Blanchard on the weekends. Many jazz musicians, including Wilson and Harrison, live in the area, making it a natural spot for them to include on their performance schedules. Onaje Royston, nephew of one of the owners and longtime deejay (now at WNWK), books the place.

Open just over two years, Royston's features an attractive bar area up front, complete with lots of chrome and glass, and a comfortable listening room all done up in blues and Venetian pink with a stained-glass skylight in the back. Much original artwork hangs from the walls, including a series of striking African batiks and an original Saul Steinberg. The sound system is state-of-the-art.
Music: Tu–Su; jazz F, Sa, some other nights. *Cover:* $–$$$. *Food:* Southern style and "nouvelle soul food."

FOR BLUES

DOWNTOWN

Tramps, *45 W. 21st St., 727-7788.*
Five years ago, Tramp's was a steamy hole-in-the-wall bringing in the best of the blues. Today, it's a big, well-kept club with a beautiful old wooden bar, tablecloths, and a sizable dance floor, but it still brings in much blues. The acts (Charlie Musselwhite, Johnny Copeland, Dr. John) tend to be better known than earlier acts were, however, and other kinds of music, including zydeco, rockabilly, and Cajun, are also featured. Next door, too, is a smaller venue called **Tramps Café** that books somewhat smaller acts.

Irish owner Terry Dunne started up the old Tramps back in 1975 and, soon thereafter, sublet an apartment from a friend who had a huge collection of rare blues records. Dunne, always interested in the blues, was fascinated to discover such lesser-known artists as Big Jay McNeely and Nappy Brown and decided to track them down and bring them to New York. In 1978 he found Brown running a hog farm and church in North Carolina and, a few years later, McNeely, working in a post office in L.A. Dunne also reunited soul singers Don Covay, Wilson Pickett, and Solomon Burke, and provided a home for David Johansen's Buster Poindexter.
Music: W–Su, much blues. *Cover/minimum:* $$–$$$. *Food:* regional American. CC. Reservations recommended weekends.

Dan Lynch's, *221 Second Ave. at 14th St., 677-0911.*
The oldest local blues bar in the city, Dan Lynch's is long and funky, all done up in brown wood with worn tables, low red lights, and a beer-soaked bar. But for all its apparent raw, rough atmosphere, the place is a congenial spot basically run by women, who both handle the bar trade and book the bands. Local groups pre-

dominate, with Jon Paris and Popa Chubby especially worth catching.

Dan Lynch's was originally owned by two Irish brothers. A photograph of one of them hangs behind the bar, along with a 1934 newspaper clipping that reads DRINKING AT BARS SET FOR APRIL 1ST. The newspaper was found in the bar, which dates back to Prohibition days, when the brothers took it over.

A second **Dan Lynch's on 10th Avenue** (10th and 38th St., 502-5525) was opened just over a year ago. Laid out and made up to look virtually identical to the first, it books many of the same bands.

Music: nightly, both locations; Sa and Su afternoon jams, Second Ave. only. *Cover/minimum:* $–$$.

Downtime, *251 W. 30th St., 695-2747.*

Located on the ground floor of a building that houses many recording and rehearsal studios, Downtime, not surprisingly, is a music industry hangout. All kinds of music can be heard here, including rock, country, acoustic, and jazz (usually on Mondays), but blues and blues-rock play the biggest role. Regulars include bluesmen Jimmy Vivino and Michael Powers, who often plays the daily happy hour.

The bar is an easygoing, unpretentious place with a mural along one wall, a bar along the other, Art Deco lamps here and there, and a small balcony area up above. B. B. King kicked off his last tour here, and celebs such as Stephen King and Paul Schaffer have been known to stop by.

Music: nightly, late afternoons. *Cover:* $.

Terra Blues, *149 Bleecker St., 777-7776.*

Located deep in the heart of Bleecker Street madness (the thoroughfare is packed cheek-by-jowl on the weekends, with music blasting everywhere), Terra Blues nonetheless has its share of good blues bands. Most of those who perform are local favorites such as Michael Powers or Moe Holmes, but better-known acts such as Mack "Guitar" Murphy also appear from time to time. Located upstairs, the room is all red and white, with a stuccoed ceiling, figureheads mounted on the walls, and picture windows overlooking the street.

Music: nightly. *Cover:* $.

Mondo Cane, *205 Thompson St., near Bleecker St.,* *254-5166.*

Also located in the midst of Bleecker Street madness, Mondo Cane ("dog's world" in Italian) is a small, dark, second-story joint whose walls are painted with tiny, quirky, childlike figures. A favorite spot among young blues musicians, the club features a wide variety of local bands, some quite good, others not. Just around the

Dizzy blows for the Blue Note's anniversary celebration in 1984.

Courtesy Blue Note

corner is a sister club (**Mondo Perso,** 167 Bleecker St., 477-3770) which presents much funk, rock, some R&B. *Music:* nightly. *Cover:* $.

House of Blues, *Union Square East and 15th St.*

The fourth House of Blues (see Boston, page 158) is scheduled to open in the former American Savings Bank, an impressive neo-classical building that's been empty for years, sometime in 1994. The club will include a 300-seat restaurant.

MIDTOWN

Lone Star Roadhouse, *240 W. 52nd St., 245-2950.*

Back when the Lone Star was a young Texas upstart, occupying a Village address with a huge green iguana on top, it was an irksome spot: there was never enough *room,* you couldn't really *see.* Nonetheless, the club was one of the best in town: it had good times, good music, real soul.

Since moving uptown five years ago, the Lone Star, though still filled with checkered tablecloths and Texas paraphernalia, has changed character. The new spot is bigger and in some ways better—there's almost always *room,* you can always *see*—but some of the old excitement is gone. Middle age has set in.

Still, when it comes to roots American music, the Lone Star has much to offer. The first New York club to bring in national country headliners like Johnny Paycheck, it has also always featured

MANNY'S CARWASH
LIVE BLUES APPEARING TONIGHT
FROM CHICAGO
JIMMY ROGERS

Manny's Carwash plays nightly host to blues.

bluesmen such as James Cotton, Albert Collins, and Dr. John. Robert Cray played here while still an unknown, and the Blues Brothers did their first live show here. The night before the Live Aid concert, Lonnie Mack, the Rolling Stones, and Bob Dylan jammed at the Lone Star. Roy Orbison played his last gig at the club. Today, Texas blues stars—Lou Ann Barton, Marcia Ball, Kim Wilson—are regulars, along with rockabilly, zydeco, and regional blues talent such as Roomful of Blues.

Music: nightly, some blues. *Cover/minimum:* $$$. *Food:* regional American. CC. Reservations recommended weekends.

UPTOWN

Manny's Car Wash, *1558 3rd Ave., 369-BLUE.*

Patterned after the Chicago blues clubs, Manny's is trying to create what the Lone Star and Tramps have lost: intimacy. Small and dark, with exposed brick walls, tile floors, drink rails, and neon beer signs, it's only partially successful in its goal, but it does feature much in the way of the blues. Local (Popa Chubby, Jon Paris), regional (Duke Robillard, Bobby Radcliffe), and national artists (Lonnie Mack, "Gatemouth" Brown) are all featured, and there's usually a jam on Sunday nights.

Music: nightly. *Cover:* $–$$. *Food:* White Castle hamburgers.

Also

Nationally known blues artists can also be heard in several of the jazz venues mentioned in "For Jazz," most notably the **Village Gate,** and the **Blue Note.** Local blues of varying quality can be heard at a number of informal, mostly downtown clubs that charge little or no cover, including the **Rodeo Bar** (375 Third Ave., 683-6500), a big Western-style place done up in rough wood and animal heads (it's part of **Albuquerque Eats,** a restaurant serving Southwestern cuisine). For others, check the *New York Press* and *Village Voice.*

Other Venues and Special Events

The Reverend John Garcia Gensel was pastor to the New York jazz community at **St. Peter's Lutheran Church,** a big, modern sanctuary with towering ceilings and cubist colors (54th St. and Lexington Ave., 935-2200), for over 25 years. Duke Ellington wrote a joyful tone poem in his honor, "The Shepherd Who Watches Over the Night Flock," and Billy Strayhorn donated his Steinway to the church. Musicians turned to Gensel in times of celebration and grief and he buried almost all the important jazz figures of the last few decades, including Thelonious Monk, John Coltrane, Eubie Blake, Alberta Hunter, and John Hammond. His funerals became legendary: like the New Orleans funerals of old, they were more like big musical celebrations than anything else.

The Reverend Gensel retired in December 1993, but the many jazz events at St. Peter's continue, now under the leadership of the Reverend Dale Lind. Every Sunday afternoon at 5 p.m. there's jazz vespers, followed by a jazz concert at 7 p.m. Most Wednesdays September through June, 12:30 to 1:30 p.m., free jazz concerts are held in the Living Room; and every October, there's All-Nite Soul, a 12-hour jazz jam that runs from 5 p.m. Sunday to 5 a.m. Monday. All sorts of legends turn up for the All-Nite event, begun in 1970: Eubie Blake was there just before he turned 100, and Teddy Wilson appeared the year before he died.

The **Apollo Theatre** (253 W. 125th St., 729-5838) still presents a Wednesday "New Amateur Night at the Apollo," and other blues and R&B events are featured other nights of the week. **Town Hall** (123 W. 43rd St., 840-2824), **Carnegie Hall** (881 Seventh Ave., 247-7800) and the **Beacon Theater** (2124 Broadway, 496-7070) host frequent jazz concerts.

Jazzmobile (154 W. 127th St., 866-4900) is a rolling bandstand, cofounded by jazz pianist–composer-educator Dr. Billy Taylor, that brings free jazz to the inner city every summer. Many of the 70-odd concerts, featuring greats such as Jimmy Heath and Horace Silver, are held uptown, but some are presented in Midtown, Downtown, and in the other boroughs. The biggest concerts are held at Grant's Tomb (122nd St. and Riverside Dr., 666-1640).

The **New York Swing Dance Society** (696-9737) presents big-band dancing at the Continental Club, Irving Plaza, every Sunday night (17 Irving Pl., 533-0453; $$). A different band performs each week, and one, the Harlem Blues and Jazz Band, features musicians who played at the Savoy over 50 years ago. The Society also sponsors practice sessions on Fridays, and a free hour of dance lessons on the first Sunday of every month. Nonmembers are welcome.

Giant Step (hotline: 714-8001), where jazz meets rap, is a traveling weekly event ($$), now over three years old, that's been hosted by a variety of clubs. As a deejay spins records, jazz musicians and rappers take turns playing and improvising, and some heavy hitters (Roy Hargrove, Digable Planets, Sheila Jordan, Living Colour) have at times appeared.

Started up in 1973, **Highlights in Jazz** is the longest-running jazz concert series in the city. Now held at the Pace University Downtown Theatre (3 Spruce St., 346-1715; $$) September through May, the monthly event always features several first-class "official" performers and at least one surprise guest (Eubie Blake, Dizzy Gillespie, Branford Marsalis, Billy Taylor, and Stan Getz are but a few who have appeared over the years). "Sometimes I don't even know who's going to show up," says producer Jack Kleinsinger.

The **JVC Jazz Festival** (see "Major Festivals," page 403) takes place every summer, and the **Central Park Conservancy** (315-0385) presents many free concerts ranging from world music to jazz at the Central Park Band Shell each July through September. The "Classic Jazz Festival" has been an annual summer offering at **Lincoln Center** for years, and the performing arts complex now also features an extensive "Jazz at Lincoln Center" program yearround. Call Alice Tully Hall at 875-5050 for details. The **92nd Street Y** (1395 Lexington Ave., 996-1100) is known for its "Jazz in July" series.

The **Schomburg Center for Research in Black Culture** (515 Lenox Ave. at 135th St., 491-2200), a branch of the New York Public Library, presents frequent jazz concerts, films, and other events. The **World Music Institute** (545-7536) does a wide variety of imaginative bookings at various venues throughout the city. The **Cathedral of St. John the Divine** (1047 Amsterdam Ave. at 112th St., 662-2133), **St. Mary's Episcopal Church** (521 W. 126 St. at Broadway, 864-4013), and **St. Ann's Church** in Brooklyn Heights (157 Montague St., 718-834-8794) are also known for their jazz concerts.

For more on these and many other events—too numerous to mention—watch the papers.

Record Stores

Three chains with truly astounding selections are **J & R Music World** (Jazz Outlet, 33 Park Row, 349-8400), **Tower Records**

(692 Broadway, 505-1500; 1691 Broadway, 799-2500), and **HMV** (86th St. and Lexington Ave., 348-0800; 72nd St. and Broadway, 721-5900). Smaller stores include the **Jazz Record Center** (236 W. 26th St., 675-4480) and the **Golden Disc** (239 Bleecker St., 255-7899), both good spots for hard-to-find jazz records; the **Rainbow Music Shop** (102 W. 125th St., 864-5262), which specializes in R&B and gospel; and **Footlight Records** (113 E. 12th St., 533-1572), which has a good used-CD section. For others, check the New York Yellow Pages.

Radio

WBGO/88.3 FM (201-624-8880). A 24-hour jazz station affiliated with NPR. Blues Su morning, F evening, M–F at noon.

WKCR/89.9 FM (854-5223). Affiliated with Columbia University. Much jazz daily, some blues.

WQCD/101.9 FM (955-9123). Contemporary jazz station.

Other radio stations broadcasting some jazz and blues include **WBAI/99.5 FM, WBLS/107.5 FM, WNYC/93.9 FM, WEVD/ 1050 AM,** and **WQXR/1560 AM.**

Tours

Several companies offer tours of Harlem that include some of the sites described in this chapter. **Harlem Tours** (410-0080), the oldest and first African American–owned Harlem tour company, offers three-hour walking tours, some with a gospel service, some without. **Harlem Spirituals, Inc.** (302-2594/5) features a four-hour bus tour that includes a gospel service, a four-hour bus tour that includes a soul-food lunch, and a night tour that includes dinner and a visit to a jazz club. **New Harlem Renaissance Tours** (722-9534) offers various tours for groups of ten or more. **Gray Line New York** (397-2600) offers Sunday morning gospel tours and tours of the Upper West Side, including Harlem.

Val Ginter (496-6859), an urban historian and former jazz accordionist, conducts the city's only in-depth jazz tours. He covers Harlem and other jazz-related neighborhoods for groups of six or more.

While Boston has never been a major jazz or blues town, it has made a strong, steady contribution to the music. George Wein, the dean of festival producers (from the first Newport Festival in 1954 to a good dozen events around the country today), grew up here, attending Boston University and opening his famed Storyville in 1950, and Sonny Stitt, Paul Gonsalves, Dave Lambert, Serge Chaloff, and Roy Haynes were all born in Boston. Others connected with the city include Pat Metheny, George Russell, and Dave McKenna, all of whom now live in or near Boston, and Jaki Byard and Keith Jarrett, who went to school here. Present-day Boston continues to be an important jazz education center, home to the Berklee College of Music and the New England Conservatory of Music, among others.

Like many other cities, Boston was red-hot during the late '40's and early '50's. At that time, the Massachusetts Avenue–Columbus Avenue area on the edge of Roxbury near the downtown was lined with six or seven different clubs, resembling a mini-52nd Street; the Hi Hat, the Savoy Café, the Big M, Wally's Paradise (now Wally's Café, see "Clubs, etc., page 155"), Estelle's, and the Pioneer. The Savoy Café at 410 Massachusetts Avenue was a short-term home to Sidney Bechet's New Orleans Rhythm Kings, who made a number of broadcasts from here in 1945, and the Hi Hat was the first club to offer bop to Boston. Charlie Parker played the Hi Hat in 1953, and sometimes, after work, he and a friend would wander around Boston Common until dawn, making birdcalls with little wooden gadgets from the Audubon Society.

The city's first major uptown club was George Wein's Storyville, which specialized in Dixieland and swing. Opening first in Kenmore Square, it later moved to the Copley Square Hotel and brought in many nationally known names, ranging in sound from Wild Bill Davison and Pee Wee Russell to Count Basie and Duke Ellington.

Later, in the 1960's, there was Lennie's on the Turnpike (actually in Peabody, Mass.), which presented major artists such as Miles Davis, Charles Mingus, and Thelonious Monk; and the two-sided Jazz Workshop/Paul's Mall, owned by Fred Taylor and Tony Mauriello. The Jazz Workshop was dedicated solely to serious jazz, while Paul's Mall offered up everything from soul to fusion. "We launched a lot of new artists who are superstars today," says Fred Taylor, "Herbie Hancock, Bruce Springsteen, Keith Jarrett—Keith was our house pianist when he was going to Berklee."

Also flourishing in the '60's was Club 47, a tiny Cambridge coffeehouse that was instrumental in bringing the urban blues to Middle America. Its owner, folksinger Jim Rooney, presented Muddy Waters, Howlin' Wolf, Junior Wells, Buddy Guy, and many others to a hitherto unexposed audience (along with some jazz artists) and the response was tremendous. Fans lined up around the block, and soon other coffeehouses in other cities were presenting the urban blues.

Boston—thanks in large part to nearby Providence, Rhode Island, which gave birth to Roomful of Blues and Duke Robillard, among others—continued to be known as a good blues town through the '70's and '80's. One especially legendary club, in operation up until five years ago, was the 1369 Club in Cambridge (1369 Cambridge St.), which presented many major blues and jazz artists.

Sources

The weekly *Boston Phoenix* (536-5390) has excellent listings. Or pick up the Thursday section of the *Boston Globe* (929-2000) or the Friday section of the *Boston Herald* (426-3000).

For maps and other information, contact the Greater Boston Convention and Visitor Bureau (536-4100) at Boston Common, near the State House (Park and Tremont streets), or at the Prudential Center, near the entrance to the Sheraton-Boston Hotel.

The area code for Boston is (617).

A Note on Neighborhoods

Surrounded by island-studded Boston Harbor and other bays and rivers, Boston, which was already 145 years old when the Civil War began, can be a confusing place. Its downtown is a jumble of crowded streets, historic buildings, and glittering high-rises, while its outskirts are an equally confusing mass of districts and suburban towns, all with seemingly interchangeable names. Two of these, mentioned below, are Allston and Brookline, both located about 20 minutes west of the harbor.

Driving in downtown Boston is difficult. There's much congestion, and parking is generally available only in expensive lots. As soon as you leave the city's center, however, which is quite small, the streets open up and parking is plentiful. Two major arteries connecting almost everything are Commonwealth Avenue, running east-west, and Massachusetts Avenue, called Mass. Ave. by locals, running north-south.

Cambridge, located on the north side of the Charles River, is a short and easy bridge ride away from Boston proper. Though best known for its students, who congregate around Harvard Square, the city also houses large ethnic populations, many of whom live near Central Square. The heart of the city's business district, Central Square is also a haven for ex-hippies, free thinkers of all kinds, and the homeless. Inman Square, once known for its jazz clubs (now only Ryles is left) is just north of Central Square. Somerville is just north of that. All addresses in Cambridge are within 20 minutes of each other and street parking is usually available.

The Ray Brown Trio
plays the Regatta-
bar in the Charles
Hotel.

Clubs, etc.

Boston has two upscale hotel-based clubs that bring in national jazz (and occasional blues) talent: the **Regattabar** in the Charles Hotel and **Scullers** in the Guest Quarters Suite Hotel. **House of Blues** brings in national blues acts, and **Johnny D's** features an eclectic mix of touring talent, including jazz and blues. The **Middle East Restaurant** presents national jazz acts weekly. Boston also has a large number of strong local clubs, and a blues jam can be found somewhere every night of the week.

Some of the top jazz musicians and bands playing in the Boston area today include vibraphonist Gary Burton; keyboard player Mark Rossi; drummer Alan Dawson; trumpet player Tiger Okoshi and his group, Tiger's Baku; Frank Wilkins's Visions; pianists Bob Winter, Ray Santisi, and Dave McKenna; trumpet player Ruby Braff; vocalists Semenya McCord and Rebecca Parris; the Boston Jazz Orchestra; the Either/Orchestra; Orange Then Blue; the Boston Jazz Composers' Alliance; and the New Black Eagle Jazz Band. Some of the top blues artists are Roomful of Blues, Sugar Ray and the Bluetones, Luther "Guitar Junior" Johnson, Ronnie Earl and the Broadcasters, "Earring" George Mayweather, Joe Cook, and vocalist Shirley Lewis.

Generally speaking, clubs in the Boston area close at 2 a.m. though the music usually stops around 1 a.m.

Personal Choices

Best national jazz club: *Regattabar*
Best local jazz club: *Ryles*
Best historic jazz club: *Wally's*
Best national blues club: *House of Blues*
Best local blues club: *Johnny D's*
Best eclectic club: *Middle East*
Best neighborhood music bars: *Plough & Stars, Cantab Lounge*

FOR JAZZ

Regattabar, *Charles Hotel, 1 Bennett St., Cambridge (Harvard Sq.), 937-4020 (concert line) or 864-1200 (hotel).*

Housed in an upscale hotel in the heart of Cambridge, the classy Regattabar is the city's premier club for national acts. Mainstream jazz is what's usually featured (Stanley Turrentine, Benny Carter, Freddie Hubbard), but fusion, blues, and traditional jazz are presented on occasion; local stars such as Rebecca Parris and the Heavy Metal Horns appear in the early part of the week.

Located on the hotel's third floor, the Regattabar, best reached by a lighted, glass-walled elevator, is big but low-ceilinged, with lots of small, round, crowded tables. Sight lines are generally good, and the front rows are but an arm's length away from the players. *Music:* Tu–Sa. *Cover:* $$–$$$. *Food:* light supper fare. CC. Reservations recommended.

Ryles, *212 Hampshire St., Cambridge (Inman Sq.), 876-9330.*

The oldest jazz club in Cambridge and the second oldest in the Boston area, Ryles is known for its local talent. Many of the best Berklee students and professors perform here, and big names—Pat Metheny, Robben Ford, Grover Washington Jr.—make occasional surprise visits. Olga Roman, a popular local Latin vocalist who's since moved to Spain got her start here, as did the 11-piece group, Heavy Metal Horns. Ryles presents most every kind of jazz, but shies away from the avant garde.

Once an Italian restaurant, Ryles is large and well lit with skinny pillars, plants, and a sea of battered wooden tables. There's a second room upstairs, smaller and windowless, that showcases somewhat lesser-known groups, while downstairs stands a great jazz jukebox, stocked with vintage 45's from the 1940's. *Music:* nightly. *Cover:* $–$$. *Food:* burgers, etc.

Wally's Café, *427 Mass. Ave., Boston (Back Bay), 424-1408.*
Wally's was there, back in the days when Mass. Ave.–Columbus Ave. was a happening thing. Originally housed in a large room

across the street from its tiny current location, it was started up in 1947 by one Joseph Walcott, now in his nineties, who used to drive a cab for Boston's Mayor Curley. The mayor helped Wally procure his first club, and soon thereafter, the young entrepreneur started presenting jazz, sometimes booking acts in conjunction with his old friend Eddie Smalls of Smalls' Paradise in New York (see "New York, Landmarks and Legends," page 107).

Once a mainstay in the African-American community, Wally's now draws a racially mixed crowd of older black neighborhood residents and fresh-faced Berklee students, who take to the stage most every night. The jazz is not always the best in town, but there's a great sense of tradition in the air. Wally, who's still around, frequents the simple, brick-walled place—outfitted only with a bar and a few tables—during the day, while his grandsons take over at night. A blues jam is featured on Monday nights.
Music: nightly. *No cover.*

Willow Jazz Club, *699 Broadway, Somerville, 623-9874.*

A longstanding wood-paneled neighborhood bar, the Willow is a big rectangle, cut neatly in half. On one side is a bar, lined with trophies, where the locals come to drink and play cards; on the other side is a red room, filled with tables, where first-rate local and regional jazz can be heard. An avant-garde trio called The Fringe are regulars here; and then there are the players who come up from New York: saxophonist Bill Evans, pianist Kenny Werner, guitarist Mike Stern, and the James Williams Band. Tiger Okoshi also plays on occasion.
Music: nightly. *Cover:* $–$$.

Scullers, *Guest Quarters Suite Hotel, 400 Soldiers Field Rd., Allston (where the Mass. Turnpike meets Storrow Drive), 783-0811 (jazz line) or 783-0090 (hotel).*

The Boston area's *other* major hotel club opened up in 1990, and it's a plush, cushiony affair with floral-patterned fabrics, small marble tables, mahogany walls, and a glorious view of the Charles River. The jazz is mainstream, and somewhat more sedate than that of the Regattabar: there's an emphasis on jazz legends and vocalists (Dakota Staton, Jimmy McGriff, Herb Ellis, Mark Murphy, Jimmy Witherspoon), and horns are rarely heard. Local stars are presented in the early part of the week, and dinner packages are available in conjunction with the next-door Scullers restaurant, which serves international cuisine.
Music: Tu–Sa, Su brunch. *Cover:* $$–$$$. Reservations recommended.

Middle East Restaurant, *472 and 480 Mass. Ave., Cambridge (Central Sq.), 497-0576 (concert line) or 492-9181.*

A funky, well-lit restaurant with arched windows and lots of hanging plants, the storefront Middle East has been something of a community center for left-leaning Central Square for over two decades now. For the past six or seven years, it's also been known for an eclectic, often cutting-edge booking policy that presents everything from grunge rock and ethnic music to jazz and blues.

The Middle East has three music rooms, all of which operate most nights. "The Bakery" is a small stage on the ground floor that's likely to feature anything from a jazz guitarist to a belly dancer. Also on the ground floor is a back room equipped with long tables where jazz artists, both local and national (Joanne Brackeen, Henry Threadgill), perform on Monday nights, and a blues jam is usually held on Saturday afternoons. Downstairs is a remodeled bowling alley where bigger-name jazz acts (the World Saxophone Quartet, the Either/Orchestra) are presented on Wednesdays.

Music: nightly; jazz M, W; blues Sa afternoon. *Cover:* $–$$.
Food: Middle Eastern.

The Roof Restaurant, *The Ritz-Carlton Hotel, 15 Arlington St., Boston (Back Bay), 536-5700.*

Prior to 1946, the "Ritz Roof" was known throughout Boston as an elegant eatery where one could dine and dance the night away while listening to the likes of Artie Shaw, Benny Goodman, and Tommy Dorsey. Then came World War II, when too many GI's were getting drunk on the rooftop to suit the Ritz-Carlton's taste and image, and on top of that the building was hit by a destructive hurricane. The restaurant was shut down, apparently for good.

In 1993, however, the "Ritz Roof" reopened and once again there is dining and dancing beneath the stars. Appropriately enough, the band on tap is usually the Dick Johnson Swing Shift. Johnson leads the Artie Shaw Orchestra when it is on the road, and the Swing Shift is a scaled-down version of that 17-piece band.

Music: F–Sa, seasonal. *Cover:* $$. *Food:* New England, seafood.
CC.

Also

The **Western Front** (343 Western Ave., Cambridge, 492-7772), though primarily a reggae club, features jazz of the cutting-edge variety on occasion. The **Bristol Lounge** of the Four Seasons Hotel (200 Boylston St. at Arlington St., Back Bay, 338-4400) presents some of the city's finest piano players. The **Marketplace Café** in Boston's Faneuil Hall (227-9660) has jazz on Thursdays, usually compliments of the Brian Walkley Band.

Jazz can also be heard regularly at **Johnny D's, The Tam,** and the **Cantab Lounge** (see "For Blues," page 159).

FOR BLUES

House of Blues, *96 Winthrop St., Cambridge (Harvard Sq.), 491-BLUE.*

What is undoubtedly the most ambitious blues club ever opened in 1992 in this historic wooden house, which dates back to the 1800's. Painted blue and white on the outside and packed with blues memorabilia and Southern folk art on the inside, the House of Blues is a sort of upscale urban jukejoint, or "juke mansion," as its owners like to call it.

The ground floor is a restaurant, with rough-hewn wooden booths, blue-checked tablecloths, and video monitors describing various blues artists as their recordings come over the loudspeakers. Upstairs is the music room, with a state-of-the-art sound system, a peaked wooden ceiling, and more exquisite folk art (but few seats, a serious drawback when the place gets crowded). In the basement is a shop selling posters, books, T-shirts, and House of Blues leather jackets. You can bet Robert Johnson never saw anything like this.

The House of Blues is the brainchild of Isaac Tigrett, the man who started up the Hard Rock Café in London in 1971. Tigrett, who grew up in Memphis, has been a blues devotee ever since he worked as a chauffeur for Furry Lewis and Bukka White. Dan Aykroyd is also an investor, which accounts for the club's Blues Brothers logo.

But the House of Blues is more than just a club. It's also a foundation whose mission is to educate and raise cultural awareness. Groups of schoolkids are brought through here regularly to learn about the blues, African-American folk art, and Southern culture. The House of Blues is also working closely with the University of Mississippi and Harvard University to develop a curriculum that they can take directly into the schools. Other future projects include a resource center and scholarship program.

Purists may complain that the House of Blues is too commercial, and though the place does have a somewhat corporate feel, surely that is beside the point. The club is doing the community a service and with any luck, a more educated public will help the blues in general and the city's other, smaller blues rooms in particular.

The club usually features local and regional artists at the beginning of the week and national artists on the weekends. Other House of Blues clubs are scheduled to open in New Orleans, Los Angeles, and New York in 1994, and in Chicago in 1995.

Music: nightly. *Cover:* $–$$$. *Food:* Southern, American. CC.

Johnny D's Uptown Restaurant and Music Club,
17 Holland St., Somerville (Davis Sq.), 776-9667.

Run by a mother-daughter-son team, Johnny D's is a large and square-shaped neighborhood place, with a big dance floor and a step-up stage. Big comfortable booths line some of the walls, and there's a friendly bar at the back.

National acts playing a wide variety of music—blues, R&B, jazz, zydeco, reggae, world—perform most nights of the week, while the best of the local bands fill in on the off nights. Some of the many musicians who have appeared during the last year include Marcia Ball, Charmaine Neville, the Jazz Passengers, Maynard Ferguson, and Hugh Masekela. Sunday afternoons are devoted to blues jams, and by day the club is a restaurant.

Johnny D's won the W. C. Handy "Keeping the Blues Alive" Club of the Year Award in 1992.

Music: nightly, much blues and R&B, some jazz. *Cover:* $–$$.

The Tam, *1648 Beacon St., Brookline, 277-0982.*

Although located near Boston College, the Tam is not so much a college hangout as a neighborhood restaurant-bar. A large wood-framed suburban place that functions as a restaurant until 10 p.m., it's a Brookline institution (at one time, WGBH radio broadcast a live blues show from here) that today offers up a mix of blues, country, funk, folk, "original" rock, and reggae. Jazz or blues jams often take place on Mondays.

Music: nightly, some jazz and blues. *Cover:* $–$$.

Harper's Ferry, *158 Brighton Ave., Allston, 254-9743. Concert line: 254-7380.*

When it comes to character, Harper's Ferry hasn't got it. A modern, cavernous place that feels more like a college cafeteria than a club, it's dominated by a huge rectangular bar and filled with young athletic-looking types on the make. The stage is stuck way down at one end, making the music seem like an afterthought, even though the musicians are often first-rate. Rick Russell, the Stovall Band, and Heavy Metal Horns are regulars.

Music: nightly. *Cover:* $–$$.

The Plough & Stars, *912 Massachusetts Ave., Cambridge (bet. Central and Harvard squares), 492-9653.*

Named after a play by Sean O'Casey, the Plough & Stars is a Cambridge institution, a small and well-lit Irish pub that's always packed to the bursting point with students and locals, professors and office workers, writers and would-be writers, talking, talking, talking. Co-owned by novelist Padraig O'Malley and carpenter George Crawley, the Plough serves up a stick-to-the-ribs pub lunch during the day, and music of all types at night. Madeline Hall & the Rhythm Hounds is the bar's regular blues act.

Music: nightly, some blues. *No cover. Food:* pub fare.

Cantab Lounge, *738 Massachusetts Ave., Cambridge (Central Sq.), 354-2685.*

A worn and friendly neighborhood bar that attracts everyone from students to locals, Asian Americans to African Americans, the Cantab offers live music six nights a week, much of it blues, some of it jazz. Students from Berklee play here, as does veteran bluesman Joe Cook. The lounge is equipped with cement floors, ceiling fans, and the prerequisite bar TV; and it's named after "Cantabrigia," the Latin name by which Cambridge (England) was known in the Middle Ages.

Music: W–M, much blues, some jazz. *Cover:* $.

Sticky Mike's, *21 Boylston Pl. (in the alley), Boston, 426-BLUE.*

One of a row of upscale new bars catering to young urban professionals, Sticky Mike's nonetheless has atmosphere. Small, crowded, and dark, with exposed brick walls and red chili-pepper lights lining its bar, it features such popular local blues acts as Kat in the Hat and Double Cross.

Music: Tu–Sa. *Cover:* $.

Midway Café, *3496 Washington St. (near Williams St.), Jamaica Plain, 524-9038.*

A square-shaped neighborhood bar with scuffed wooden floors and a step-up stage, the Midway has an easy, laid-back, off-the-beaten-track feel. Located in a part of J.P. that's half blue-collar, half artists/writers/musicians, it features blues or R&B once or twice a week and a blues jam on Sunday nights. The bar dates back to 1934, when it catered to the workers of the Boston Gas Company, then situated across the street; today, it's owned by two young brothers, David and Jay Balerna, who bought the place five years ago, when they were just out of college.

Music: W–Su, much blues. *Cover:* $.

Also

There's usually a blues jam going on in at least one club every night of the week. In addition to the jams mentioned above, **Wally's** (see "For Jazz," page 155) and the **Boston Beach Club** in Boston's Faneuil Hall (227-9660; run by Silus Hubbard, who once ran the blues jams at the old 1369 Club) have jams on Monday nights, and the **Black Rose** in Cambridge (50 Church St., 492-8630) has a jam on Tuesday nights (as well as occasional other nights). **The 11th Chapter Saloon** in Somerville (366A Somerville Ave., 628-4300) also has blues, usually about once a week.

Other Venues and Special Events

The Berklee College of Music presents frequent faculty-student concerts at the **Berklee Performance Center** (136 Mass. Ave., Boston, 266-7455). The concerts are open to the public. **The New England Conservatory of Music** also presents some jazz at Jordan Hall (30 Gainsborough St., 536-2412).

Nationally known jazz and blues figures can occasionally be

heard at **Symphony Hall** (301 Mass. Ave., Boston, 266-1492), home of the Boston Symphony Orchestra. The **Charles Ballroom** at the Charles Hotel sometimes brings in big names, and tries to book them in some sort of meaningful conjunction with acts appearing in its Regattabar (Stan Getz and Astrud Gilberto, Gary Burton and Pat Metheny).

In addition to the **Boston Globe Jazz Festival** and the **Newport Jazz Festival** (see "Major Festivals," page 403), an outdoor jazz series featuring both local and national artists is held in the **DeCordova Museum** (Sandy Pond Rd., Lincoln, Mass., 259-8355; 30 minutes from downtown Boston) every summer.

For more information on these and other special music events, check the local papers.

Radio

WGBH/89.7 FM (492-2777). Affiliated with NPR. Jazz daily, including weekday evenings with Eric Jackson. Blues F, Sa nights with Mai Cramer.

WBUR/90.9 FM (353-2790). Affiliated with Boston University. Jazz late-late nights.

WERS/88.9 FM (578-8890). Affiliated with Emerson College. Jazz weekdays, midday. Blues late weekday nights.

WHRB/95.3 FM (495-4818). On the Harvard University campus. Jazz weekdays, 6 a.m.–2 p.m. Some blues.

WMBR/88.1 FM (253-4000). Affiliated with MIT. Jazz most weekday afternoons, blues Sa midday.

Record Stores

Stereo Jack's (1704 Mass. Ave., Cambridge, 497-9447) specializes in jazz and blues, and **Tower Records** (360 Newbury St., Boston, 247-5900) has a good jazz-blues department. **Cheapo Records** in Cambridge (645 Mass. Ave., 354-4455) and **Looney Tunes** in Boston (1106 Boylston St., 247-2238) have good used-record selections.

Philadelphia

Philadelphia's musical roots—in gospel, in soul, in rock and especially in jazz—run strong and deep. Over the past 100 years, the city, which was home to one of the earliest pre–Civil War communities of free African Americans, has produced some of the finest musicians in the world. Dizzy Gillespie lived here as a boy, John Coltrane as a young man, Bessie Smith as a mature artist. McCoy

Tyner graduated from West Philadelphia High School; Archie Shepp and Stanley Clarke graduated from Germantown High School; David Amram spent his childhood in nearby Feasterville; and Lee Morgan grew up in North Philadelphia. Then there were the Heath brothers (Jimmy, Percy, and "Tootie"), Philly Joe Jones, Jimmy McGriff, Ethel Waters, Bill Doggett, Red Garland, Sunny Murray, Sonny Fortune, Benny Golson, Bobby Durham, Bobby Timmons, Kenny Barron, Jabbo Smith, Jimmy Oliver, Mickey Roker, Grover Washington Jr., Shirley Scott, Sun Ra, and many others, all of whom lived in the city at one time or continue to live there.

During the 1920's and '30's, Philadelphia's African-American nightlife centered around South Street (see "Landmarks and Legends," page 163). There were the Dunbar, the Lincoln, and the Pearl, big theaters featuring name talent, along with numerous taverns and nightclubs. But it was from the '40's to the '60's that the city, along with New York, became one of the most significant centers for jazz in the country. Some of Philadelphia's most important clubs, including Pep's Musical Bar, the Blue Note, the Showboat, the Downbeat Club, and the Aqua Lounge were operating at that time, attracting musicians from all over the country. In the mid-fifties, Miles Davis came to Philadelphia to pick three of the four musicians (Philly Joe Jones, Red Garland, and John Coltrane) for his famed quintet, and during that same era, major musicians developing the "hard bop" style—Clifford Brown and Richie Powell among them—were living and working in town. Philadelphia is also known for its long line of great saxophonists, including John Coltrane, Jimmy Heath, Sonny Fortune, Odean Pope, and many others.

Sources

The *City Paper* (732-5542), a free weekly, has excellent listings. Other sources are the Friday sections of the *Philadelphia Inquirer* and *Philadelphia Daily News* (854-2000), and *Jazz Philadelphia,* published by the Mill Creek Jazz and Cultural Society (473-4273).

Temple University's WRTI-FM runs a jazz hotline at 204-JASS.

For maps and other information, contact the Philadelphia Visitors Center, 1525 John F. Kennedy Blvd., 636-1666.

The area code for Philadelphia is (215).

A Note on Neighborhoods

With a population of 1.6 million, Philadelphia is the fifth largest city in America. Laid out in four quadrants, each with its own park, its heart is Old City Hall. Market Street divides the city into east and west, and Broad Street divides it into north and south.

The Old City is an historic neighborhood just north of Market

Street, where Betsy Ross and Benjamin Franklin once lived; Northern Liberties is a former industrial neighborhood, now undergoing restoration, located just north of that. Society Hill, also near the downtown, is a restored cobblestoned area filled with fashionable restaurants and shops, while lower South Street is Philly's answer to Greenwich Village. Germantown is a residential neighborhood 20 minutes north of downtown.

Driving and parking in Philadelphia are difficult. Be prepared for much congestion and high parking fees.

Landmarks and Legends

(With the exception of the last two sites, all of the locations below are situated in or near the downtown and can be toured on foot.)

South Street, *Tenth to 17th streets.*

From the 1920's through the '50's, South Street was the main drag of black Philadelphia, and many of the city's most important theaters and nightclubs were located on or near it. Among the top spots were the Dunbar Theater, near 15th Street, where Sidney Bechet and Bessie Smith once starred together—and perhaps had a love affair—in a show called *How Come?;* Gibson's Standard Theater at 12th Street, where a then unknown Duke Ellington was playing just before he was hired by New York's Cotton Club; the Paradise Theater at Fitzwater and 16th streets; the Lincoln Theater and the Showboat at Broad and Lombard streets; and Pep's Musical Bar at Broad and South, where everyone from Dinah Washington to Yusef Lateef once performed. Of the above, only the Paradise Theater (now a housing project for the elderly) and the Showboat are still standing.

Showboat, *1409 Lombard St., near Broad St.*

Back in the 1950's, this somber gray building was the site of the famous Showboat, where Coltrane, Dizzy, Monk, Jamal, Miles, Getz, and Rollins all performed.

In *Chasin' the Trane* by J. C. Thomas, Jimmy Cobb tells of how one night while he and Coltrane were working here, a narc came in, took them to the men's room, and had them take off their shirts. Jimmy's arms were clean but Trane's had marks. "Those are birthmarks," he told the cop, "I've had them as long as I can remember." Evidently he was convincing, because the man let him go.

Located across the street from the Showboat, in what is now a parking lot, was the Lincoln Theater.

Kater Street

Bennie Moten wrote his "Kater Street Rag" about this tiny alleyway that runs east-west, parallel to South Street, from the Delaware River to the Schuylkill. Ethel Waters lived here when it was

The Earle Theater,
now demolished,
was to Philadelphia
what the Apollo is
to New York.

*Frank Driggs
Collection*

a red-light district, and Bessie Smith purchased homes for her family here. Dizzy Gillespie also lived on Kater at one time.

Bessie Smith's family's home, *1147 Kater St.*

Bessie Smith bought this now-abandoned house and the one nearby at 1143 Kater (no longer standing) for her family when she moved them up from Chattanooga, Tennessee, to Philadelphia in 1926. Her husband, Jack Gee, was reportedly not at all happy with the idea of having her family so close, but Bessie apparently appeased him by buying him a Cadillac for $5,000—an enormous sum at the time—for which she paid cash. She wanted her sisters and their children near her, partly, at least, to help her care for her adopted son, Jack, when she was out of town.

According to Bessie's biographer, Chris Albertson, Bessie, for all her wild ways, was a surprisingly devoted mother and sister. She doted on her son and supported all seven members of her transplanted family, none of whom worked, handsomely.

Academy of Music, *Broad and Locust streets.*

The opulent nineteenth-century Academy, styled after La Scala in Milan, is one of the finest theaters in Philadelphia. Built in the mid-1850's to the tune of $240,000, it stood roofless for one year, exposed to the elements, so that its walls would "settle."

Concerts of all types are put on at the Academy, and it was here that, quite accidentally, Coltrane first heard Bird. He and Benny Golson had gone to the Academy to catch Dizzy Gillespie, as Golson recalls in *Chasin' the Trane,* when "this short, squat guy in a pin-stripe suit stepped on stage. The band took the break and he started playing alto while coming out of a crouch. John just sat there, taking it all in. . . . Imagine being a saxophonist and never having heard this kind of music before."

Stars honoring Philly musicians stud the Broad Street sidewalk outside the building. Among those so honored are John Coltrane, Dizzy Gillespie, Bessie Smith, Marian Anderson, and Pearl Bailey.

Earle Theater, *SE corner of 11th and Market streets.*

The famous old Earle Theater, where everyone from Jack Teagarden to Louis Armstrong performed, once stood at this corner, and it was here that Lucky Millinder, who had a propensity for firing people (see Crystal Caverns, page 195), gave Dizzy Gillespie two weeks notice. "He just fired me," Dizzy writes in his autobiography *To Be or Not to Bop,* "and I don't know what his actual reasons were. He didn't have a reason. . . . He just had this firing syndrome."

Dizzie didn't let his notice bother him. Instead, during his last week with the band, he played his heart out until Lucky, impressed, called him to his dressing room and said to forget about the firing, he'd like him to stay. Diz said he was sorry, but no, he already had another job lined up. Lucky promptly offered him a five-dollar-a-night raise. "That was unheard of, man!" Dizzy writes, "I already had a salary of eighteen dollars a night. . . ."

Post Office and **Old Court House,** *Ninth and Market streets.*

A lovely Art Deco building with bas-relief sculptures depicting "Justice" and "The Law," the Old Courthouse now houses a rather sleepy-looking state superior court. Back in the 1940's, however, it was home to the intimidating federal courthouse, where Billie Holiday (who had just been playing the Earle Theater) was arraigned on May 27, 1947, for the concealment of narcotics.

Billie, broke and acting without a lawyer, pleaded guilty and was sentenced to a year and a day in the Federal Reformatory for Women at Alderson, West Virginia. The sentence was insignificant compared to what the verdict meant—that she could no longer work the New York clubs. A city regulation forbade the issuance of cabaret cards to anyone convicted of a felony. The press also treated her badly, and one leading radio station banned her records from the air.

John Coltrane's home, *1511 N. 33rd St. (20 min. NW of downtown).*

This three-story red-and-brown wood framed house with dormer windows and a peaked roof was Coltrane's home throughout most of the '50's. Today, it's still the residence of his cousin, Mary Alexander, for whom he composed "Cousin Mary."

Coltrane moved to N. 33rd Street in 1951, following a stint on the road with Dizzy Gillespie. He had decided to spend a year at home with his family in order to attend music school and get the formal training he felt he lacked. Enrolling in the Granoff School of Music, he studied theory, saxophone, and classical music, taking weekend playing jobs whenever he could.

Today, Mary Alexander has established a children's music workshop in the building next door to number 1511. Eventually, she also hopes to raise enough funds to restore the house and open it to the public.

Bessie Smith's grave, *Mt. Lawn Cemetery, 84th St. and Hook Rd., Sharon Hill (near the airport), 586-8220.*

When Bessie Smith died in 1937, following a car accident in Clarksdale, Mississippi (see "Riverside Hotel," page 64), all of black Philadelphia turned out to pay her homage. Her days of prosperity were long over by then, but thanks to an insurance policy, she was buried in a grand metallic coffin trimmed in gold and lined with pink velvet. Her beloved adopted son was absent from the funeral because her estranged husband, Jack Gee, driving down from New York, had found no room for him in the car.

Bessie's funeral cost approximately $1,000 but her insurance policy did not cover the cost of a headstone, and her grave went unmarked for 33 years. During that time, Columbia Records made a handsome profit on her reissues, and the funds raised by two benefits held to finance a tombstone mysteriously disappeared (some said into the pockets of Jack Gee).

It took a Philadelphia housewife, Mrs. Barbara Muldow, writing a letter to the *Philadelphia Inquirer's* Action Line in 1970, to make Bessie's headstone a reality. Reporter Frank Coffey followed up on Mrs. Muldow's letter by contacting Janis Joplin, an outspoken Bessie admirer, and Mrs. Juanita Green, a registered nurse and owner of two nursing homes who had worked for Bessie as a girl. Between the two of them, according to Chris Albertson in *Bessie*, the women pledged enough to buy a $500 tombstone.

Today, Bessie's stone, dark and solemn, sits proudly in a small African-American cemetery on the outskirts of Philadelphia. The epitaph reads: "The greatest blues singer in the world will never stop singing. Bessie Smith. 1895–1937."

Open: M–F, 9 a.m.– 4 p.m., Sa, 9 a.m.–noon.

Trane lived on North
33rd Street while at-
tending the Granoff
School of Music.

Clubs, etc.

For a grand old city of music, Philadelphia has very little in the
way of jazz and blues clubs. Only two clubs present jazz full time:
Zanzibar, the city's premier club for local and national acts, and
Ortlieb's, which features mostly local artists. Three cultural organizations, the **Afro-American Historical and Cultural Museum,** the **Painted Bride,** and the **Mill Creek Jazz and
Cultural Society** also present national artists on occasion.

The city has no full-time or even serious part-time blues club.
National blues acts can sometimes be heard at the **Chestnut
Cabaret** and **Red, Hot & Blue,** while the Philadelphia Blues
Machine (a blues society) also brings in national artists.

Some of the best-known musicians living in Philadelphia today
include pianist Shirley Scott; saxophonists Bootsie Barnes, Odean
Pope, and Jimmy Oliver; drummer Mickey Roker, and blues
great Sonny Rhodes. Other jazz players well worth catching include pianist Dave Burrell; keyboard player Trudy Pitts; drummers George "Butch" Ballard and Ralph Peterson, Jr.; violinist
John Blake; vibraharpist Khan Jamal; guitarists Jimmy Bruno and
Monette Sudler; Bayard Lancaster, known by his friends as "Mr.
Philadelphia Jazz" because of his love for the city; bagpipe player
Rufus Harley; the pop-jazz-funk Posmontier Brothers; and vocalist Evelyn Sims. Other blues players include Steve Guyger, the

Dukes of Destiny, Little Red Rooster, Crossharp Sharp, Crosscut Saw, and Blues Deluxe.

Most bars and clubs remain open until 2 a.m.

Personal Choices

Best jazz restaurants-clubs: *Zanzibar Blue, J.J.'s Grotto*
Best jazz jams: *Blue Note, Bob & Barbara's*
Best national blues club: *Chestnut Cabaret*
Best eclectic club: *North Star*

FOR JAZZ

Zanzibar Blue, *301-5 S. 11th St. (downtown), 829-0300 (tape) or 829-1990.*
A warm and lively downtown restaurant all done up in blue, Zanzibar features live jazz every night of the week, with locally based musicians playing most of the time and national acts brought in on selected Sundays. Some of the club's regulars include the Dennis Fortune Trio, Arpeggio, and the Colonel Byrd Quartet with Juanita Holiday. "Names" who've appeared here include Joshua Redman, Don Pullen, and Joey DeFrancesco.

Divided into three small rooms, Zanzibar features a dining room, a Jazz Café, and a Blue Bar. The Jazz Café is intimate and low-lit, filled with lots of wood and brass, while the Blue Bar, located upstairs, is patterned after a Harlem Renaissance club and boasts a large jazz-theme mural. Jazz can also be heard at the Blue Bar on the weekends.
Music: nightly. *No cover/$$ minimum* ($$$ for national acts). *Food:* international. CC.

Ortlieb's Jazz Haus, *847 N. Third St. (Northern Liberties), 922-1035.*
Once the lunch hall of a large brewery, Ortlieb's still feels like an old-fashioned German gasthaus, complete with mounted animal heads, beer advertisements, rotating fans, and heavy wooden tables and chairs. The building itself is long and narrow, because before it was a lunch hall, it was a bowling alley.

The Mickey Roker Quartet are regulars at Ortlieb's, as is Bootsie Barnes, and jam sessions led by the "Haus" Band are usually held on Tuesdays. It's all a bit predictable, but reliable as well, and sometimes known out-of-towners (Sonny Rollins, Frank Morgan) playing the area stop by. Ortlieb's is run by Pete Souders, a former Sun Oil executive who also often plays sax with the band, and his wife, Margaret, who was once a nurse.
Music: Tu–Su. *No cover. Food:* Cajun American. CC.

J.J.'s Grotto Restaurant, *27 S. 21st St. (at Chestnut, near downtown), 988-9255.*

J.J.'s started out as a cozy Italian bistro with black-and-white-tiled floors, a few simple tables, and checkered tablecloths. Five years ago, however, they started serving up jazz with their pasta and pizza, and it's all serious, thoughtful stuff. Guitar player Jimmy Bruno plays most nights, hosting a jam session on Thursdays, and bringing in featured guests on Fridays and Saturdays. Some of those guests include Dave Liebman, Larry McKenna and Chris Potter, and Herb Ellis and Tal Farlow have also played here.

Music: W–Sa. *Cover:* $–$$. *Food:* Italian. CC. Reservations recommended.

Chris' Café-Bar, *1421 Sansom St. (downtown, bet. Broad and 15th streets), 568-3131.*

A friendly, wood-paneled bistro serving "Southwestern cuisine with an Oriental flavor," Chris' is home to the Larry McKenna Quartet, who play here most Wednesdays through Saturdays. McKenna is a first-class tenor saxman who's opted not to leave Philadelphia for the big time, and well-known musicians such as Randy Brecker and Danny Turner often sit in with him when passing through town. Sundays, guitarist Jimmy Bruno is usually featured.

Chris' is housed in an old three-room building all done up in green, with green tablecloths, walls, and ceilings.

Music: W–Su. *Cover:* $. *Food:* Southwestern, Oriental.

Morgan's, *17 E. Price St. (Germantown), 844-6067.*

Opened in 1985 as one of Philadelphia's most prestigious African-American clubs, Morgan's has featured many of the biggest names in jazz, including Art Farmer, Wynton Marsalis, George Coleman, Jimmy Heath, and Benny Carter. Recently, however, its shows have been erratic, and the club has been operating more as a bar, lounge, and disco, than a jazz room.

The listening room is upstairs in a long, thin space lined with a bar and comfortable booths, while downstairs there's a dance floor whose walls are lit up with a mock Manhattan skyline. The club itself is housed in a nineteenth-century building that was once a private home, and on a dark summer's night, the neighborhood seems more rural than urban, with lots of rustling trees and restless crickets.

Music: sporadic. *Cover:* $$.

The White Horse Café, *408 S. Second St. (Society Hill), 829-9113.*

The White Horse is a genteel restaurant–jazz club that's all Victorian in feel, with pink tablecloths, ornate rattan chairs, a circular staircase, and huge lithographs of Parisian singers. The building itself once housed the oldest bar in Philadelphia, but all

signs of those raucous days have been completely eliminated. Today, the club specializes in local female vocalists with backup groups.
Music: Th-Sa. *Cover:* $. *Food:* International. CC. Reservations recommended.

Blue Note, *7400 Limekiln Turnpike (near Washington Lane, 30 min. N of downtown), 924-7324.*

There was a time when the Blue Note was the most famous jazz joint in Philadelphia, home to Dizzy Gillespie, Miles Davis, Clifford Brown, and others. This Blue Note is not that Blue Note—it's in a different location, under different management—but it's still doing its best to keep the music alive. A hot jam session has been held here every Monday night for years, featuring the Blue Note All Stars led by Tony Williams on alto sax. Local bands—sometimes jazz, sometimes not; sometimes with a vocalist, sometimes not—perform on Fridays and Saturdays, while national talent—Donald Byrd, James Moody, Dakota Staton—comes through occasionally.

The club is located on the outskirts of town in a quiet middle-class African-American community, and it's a friendly, attractive place built around an S-shaped, mosaic-studded bar. The waitresses wear elegant cocktail dresses, while the crowd ranges in style from blue jeans to sequins.
Music: M, F–Sa. *Cover:* $.

Bob & Barbara's, *1509 South St. (near downtown), 545-4511.*

A vibrant neighborhood bar, Bob & Barbara's is long and narrow, dominated by a huge red-padded bar and lots of blinking Christmas-tree lights. Many local jazz musicians stop in here on weekend nights to jam with the scheduled artists, jazz guitarist Teddy Royal, and organist Nate Wiley. Their music, hot and bebop, bursts out into the deserted, sometimes not-so-safe streets, while inside, a bartender moves slowly to and fro below a lowered ceiling. Behind him, by the cash register, is a picture of a young woman, perhaps his granddaughter, in a crisp, white graduation gown.
Music: M, F–Sa. *No cover.*

Natalie's Lounge, *4003 Market St. (West Philadelphia), 222-8633.*

Every Saturday for the past decade or so, Natalie's, a smallish, neighborhood club with lots of booths and tables and chairs, has been holding an afternoon jam that starts at about 4 p.m. and sometimes lasts until midnight.
Music: Sa afternoons. *No cover.*

Also

Jazz can also be heard at a number of restaurants in town, including the **23rd Street Café** (23rd and Race streets, 561-2488), an unpretentious eatery with a lively, weekly jam; the **Serengeti Café and Jazz Club** in nearby Camden (4901 Chapel Ave., 609-486-9888); and **Cafe Einstein** (208 Race St., 625-0904), which offers a jazz brunch on Sundays. The **Chestnut Cabaret** (see "For Blues," below) sometimes brings in touring jazz acts.

F O R   B L U E S

Chestnut Cabaret, *38th and Chestnut streets (University City), 382-1201.*
Large and square, with a big wooden dance floor and two immense bars, the 10-year-old Chestnut features a wide variety of national talent, ranging from reggae to rock. Blues plays a major role here: past performers have included John Lee Hooker, James Cotton, Willie Dixon, Buddy Guy, and John Hammond. The late blues guitarist Albert Collins, trailing his 400-foot-long cord, once walked out the Chestnut's door and around the block, followed by the crowd.

Everything at the Chestnut, from the sound system to the large-screen TV's, is top quality. The crowd ranges from college students (the University of Pennsylvania and Drexel University are nearby) to Rastas in dreadlock.
Music: most nights, some blues. *Cover:* $$.

North Star Bar, *27th and W. Poplar streets, 235-7827.*
An eclectic restaurant and club that serves up everything from Southwestern to Italian, jazz-rock-fusion to singer-songwriter-folk, the North Star also features some blues, both national and local. The Iguanas, California bluesman Robert Lucas, and the Dukes of Destiny, a regional R&B group, have all played here.

The North Star is housed in two two-story buildings, one new and one old, with the music room situated on the ground floor of the new building. Out back is a greenhouse area that's used for dining, and upstairs is the Green Room, where poetry readings are held.
Music: W–Sa, some blues. *Cover:* $–$$. *Food:* eclectic.

Red, Hot & Blue, *Rt. 70 and Sayer Ave., Cherry Hill (15 min. from Philadelphia), 609-665-7427.*
One of a chain of "Memphis-style barbecue restaurants," Red, Hot & Blue offers live blues two nights a week. Some of the artists who've played this suburban club include Sonny Rhodes, Floyd Hunter, and Johnny Copeland. The club is a square-shaped affair

with a bar to one side and a seating area to the other, and there are lots of blues memorabilia on the walls.
Music: Tu, Sa. *Cover:* $–$$. *Food:* barbecue, etc.

Tin Angel, *20 S. Second St. (downtown), 928-0770.*
Mostly a singer-songwriter haven presenting only acoustic musicians, the Tin Angel does feature blues musicians such as John Hammond on occasion. Long and narrow, the second-story club is equipped with a dropped tin ceiling, and tapestries and "pastel panels" on the walls. Tiny tin angels with wingspans of about 10 inches are suspended overhead.
Music: Tu–Sa, occasional blues. *Cover:* $–$$.

Also

Maggie's (624 N. Front St., 592-1645), which is primarily a rock club and restaurant, has blues on occasion. Blues can also be heard at some of the jazz clubs listed above.

Other Venues and Special Events

The Painted Bride (230 Vine St., 925-9914), now over two decades old, is a multiarts, multicultural organization dedicated to presenting "artists on the cutting edge." This is the place to go to hear players such as David Murray or Julius Hemphill, as well as younger artists such as Terence Blanchard. Concerts are held about twice a month in the center's aesthetically spare but comfortable auditorium.

The **Afro-American Historical and Cultural Museum** (Seventh and Arch streets, 574-0380) sponsors frequent jazz concerts often featuring Philadelphia artists who have gone on to win national acclaim: Milt Jackson, Jimmy Heath, Benny Golson, etc.

The **Mill Creek Jazz and Cultural Society** (4624 Lancaster Ave., 473-4273 or 473-2880), located in West Philadelphia, is a combination community center, jazz education center, and performance space. The Society puts on 24 concerts a year, featuring both local and national artists, and each guest musician who appears also conducts a workshop for the area's youth. Some of the many who have done so include Odean Pope, Bobby Watson, and David Newman. Concerts are held in an upstairs loft.

The **Academy of Music** (Broad and Locust streets, 893-1930) also features jazz on occasion, as does the **Theatre of the Living Arts** (334 South St., 922-1011), and the **Mann Music Center** (Fairmount Park, 878-7707).

In addition to the **Mellon Jazz Festival** and **RiverBlues** held in the city each summer (see "Major Festivals," page 403), **Penn's Landing/WRTI-FM** (636-1666) presents a free summertime jazz series in the historic 37-acre park on the Delaware River where William Penn stepped ashore in 1682. Then there's the **Presidential Jazz Weekend** (636-1666), offering about 90

Carl Arter and
friends play Eileen's
Zebra Room, one of
Pittsburgh's oldest
jazz joints.

Fred Kenderson

A Note on Neighborhoods

Pittsburgh, with a population of 1.5 million, may once have
been the ugly, polluted steel capital of the Northeast, but times
have changed. The steel industry has declined, *Fortune* 500 companies have moved in, and the environment has been cleaned up.
Pittsburgh is now a surprisingly pretty place surrounded by glis-
tening rivers and tree-covered mountains. Bridges seem to be
everywhere.

The city's downtown is the Golden Triangle, so named because
the Allegheny and Monongahela rivers come together here to
form the Ohio River. Adjacent to the Triangle is the Strip District,
a restored warehouse area now known for its nightlife. The Hill
District is an historic African-American neighborhood just north
and east of the downtown, while East Liberty and Homewood are
two other important African-American neighborhoods located yet
farther east. Between the Hill District and East Liberty is Oakland, home to the University of Pittsburgh, and Shadyside, once
known for its Bohemian atmosphere and now a trendy area filled
with boutiques and restaurants.

The North Side and the South Side are residential, predominantly working-class communities located across the Allegheny and Monongahela rivers respectively. Both are within ten minutes of the downtown.

Although the city has relatively little traffic, except in the Golden Triangle, driving is tricky. Hills and bridges pop up unexpectedly, and one wrong turn can send you over a river or into a neighborhood you never intended to visit.

Landmarks and Legends

(The route below starts in the Golden Triangle, proceeds to the Hill District and the University of Pittsburgh, and ends in Homewood. A car is necessary.)

The William Penn Hotel, *now the Westin William Penn, 530 William Penn Place, 281-7100.*

The William Penn, a sedate and luxurious landmark hotel in downtown Pittsburgh, had never had either an African-American patron or an African-American band when the then unknown Count Basie and his orchestra arrived there in 1936. The gig was an important one, according to John Hammond in *John Hammond on Record,* not only because the hotel had a network-radio wire, which would give the band national exposure, but also because it could lead to bookings in other William Penn–type establishments.

Alas, things did not go smoothly. First of all, though Basie tried to tone them down, the band couldn't help but swing. Second, the reviews (Hammond had invited several critics down from New York who had never heard the Basie band) were terrible.

Third, and potentially most disastrously, a major player went crazy one night after the show, attacking people in a local nightclub and knocking out two policemen. He was immediately taken to a nearby asylum, where he was placed in the violent ward, in a straitjacket, and allowed no visitors. He might have been lost in that institution were it not for the efforts of Hammond, who managed to talk the much more humane Neurological Institute of New York, which at that time did not treat African Americans, into accepting the musician. The man was found to have a secondary stage of syphilis (which, when combined with marijuana, can greatly disturb the nervous system), and three weeks later, following treatment, he was back with Basie, playing the Apollo.

Lower Wylie Avenue, *now the Civic Arena, just south of the Hill District.*

All of lower Wylie Avenue has been torn up and rebuilt, but back in the '20's and '30's, when Earl Hines was coming up, many major clubs and theaters were located here: the Collins Inn and the Grape Arbor, the Star Theatre and the Leader House.

Hines began playing at the Leader House regularly when he was still underage. Singer and house bandleader Lois Deppe, impressed with the boy's talent, convinced Hines Sr. to let his son join his band, and Earl moved in—literally—playing, eating, and sleeping at Leader's for the next two years. While there, he studied fellow piano players Jim Fellman, who had a "wonderful left hand" that stretched to make tenths, and Johnny Watters, who had a wonderful right hand that did the same.

Crawford Grill, *2141 Wylie Ave. (Hill District), 471-1565*

By the late '30's, lower Wylie Avenue had peaked. The action was now farther uptown, still on the avenue, but in the Hill District. A whole new generation of clubs emerged, including the Rhumba Theatre, the Bamboola, the Birdie, the Hurricane, and the Crawford Grill, number two (the Crawford Grill, number one, had been located on lower Wylie Avenue and was demolished for urban development).

Today, only the Crawford Grill, number two, is still standing. During its heyday in the '40's and '50's, it was a jazz mecca where all of the greats played—Charles Mingus, Clifford Brown, Nat King Cole, Maynard Ferguson, Thelonious Monk, and Max Roach. It was also here that three young Pittsburgh men got their start—George Benson, Stanley Turrentine, and Walt Harper, a household name in Pittsburgh circles.

After the riots of 1968, the Wylie Avenue community crumbled, to be replaced by abandoned buildings, drugs, and crime. Somehow, though, the Crawford Grill managed to survive, and even today, it operates as a neighborhood bar. A beautiful place—long, dark and cool—it's a sad oasis in the desperate streets around it. Exquisite African art is everywhere: masks and carvings line a shelf above the booths and there's a floor-to-ceiling totem pole in one corner. The artwork belongs to owner William "Buzzy" Robinson, who began placing it in the Grill after he'd run out of room at home.

Schenley High School, *N. Bellefield and Centre avenues (near the Hill District).*

Earl Hines attended Schenley High School back in the '20's, when he was living with his aunt, Sadie Phillips. Sadie performed in light opera and knew many of the name musicians of the day— Eubie Blake, Noble Sissle, Luckey Roberts—whom she'd invite over and make wait around until her nephew came home from school so that he could hear them play.

While at Schenley, Hines got his first taste of Wylie Avenue. An older cousin and a next-door neighbor dressed the 15-year-old up in long pants and a "big old diamond ring" and took him out for a night on the town to repay him for all the times he had entertained them and their girlfriends on the piano. "We were sitting in a restaurant," says Hines in *The World of Earl Hines,* "eating big steaks like I'd never had before . . . when I heard this music upstairs. It had a beat and a rhythm to it that I'd never heard before.

'Oh,' I said, 'if only I could just get upstairs and see what they're doing—see what kind of music that is!' "

Art Blakey and Ray Brown were two other Schenley High School graduates who went on to achieve fame.

International Academy of Jazz Hall of Fame, *University of Pittsburgh, William Pitt Student Union, Fifth and Bigelow, 648-7815.*

Founded in 1977, the Academy occupies approximately one fourth of the union's ground floor and is the oldest jazz hall of fame in the country. Plaques honoring notables such as Charlie Parker and Dizzy Gillespie line the walls, along with instruments donated by Sonny Rollins, Grover Washington, Jr., Clark Terry, and others.

Open: daily, 9 a.m.–11 p.m.

Westinghouse High School, *1104 N. Murtland St. (Homewood).*

The list of great piano players who came out of this solid old high school is breathtakingly impressive: Mary Lou Williams, Ahmad Jamal (Fritzy Jones at the time), Errol Garner, Billy Strayhorn. Many studied with one teacher, Carl McVicker, Sr., a tall, refined, Anglo-Saxon trumpet player who came to Westinghouse in 1927. "Jazz was a dirty word then," McVicker told *Pittsburgh* magazine in 1979. "The people in the educational system thought it was dangerous to encourage jazz bands, but it was a way of interesting kids."

One of McVicker's finest, and most difficult, students was Erroll Garner. "The other teachers told me I was foolish to waste my time with him," he said. "They said that with his IQ, he was too stupid to get up to the microphone, much less do anything. . . . He was 12 or 13 and very small. He sat on two telephone books when he played. I could see how much talent he had, but he couldn't play in the band because he couldn't read music. Still he had perfect pitch and could memorize instantly. . . . He had his own style even then."

Cardwell Dawson School of Music, *7101 Apple St. (Homewood).*

During the 1930's, pianist Mary Cardwell Dawson, founder of the National Negro Opera Company, ran a music school out of this now somewhat dilapidated 21-room house, equipped with a ballroom and servants quarters. Ahmad Jamal was one of her prize students, and for him and each of her other special students, she planted a tree in the front yard.

Dawson founded the National Negro Opera Company in Chicago in 1941 and soon thereafter established guilds in Pittsburgh, New York, and Washington, D.C. The National Negro Opera Company is the only opera company besides the Metropolitan

During the '40's and '50's, the Crawford Grill was exploding with talent.

Janinalyce

Opera Company to have appeared at the Metropolitan Opera House in New York's Lincoln Center.

Clubs, etc.

Though Pittsburgh has no club that brings in national jazz artists on a regular basis, there are a number of fine, smaller clubs and restaurants that feature top local and regional talent most nights, and national artists a few times a month. Among these are the **Shadyside Balcony, Rosebud, Stolen Moments,** and **Ramsey's II.** The **Pittsburgh Jazz Society** and the **Manchester Craftsmen's Guild** also bring in national acts on a regular basis. National blues artists can most frequently be heard at the **Decade.**

Some of the jazz artists and groups to watch out for include organist and local personality Walt Harper; veteran pianist Carl Arter; drummer Roger Humphries; piano player Frank Cunimondo; guitar players Jimmy Ponder, Joe Negri, Rodney McCoy, and Martin Ashby; trombone player Nelson Harrison; trumpet player Danny Kahn; vocalist Etta Cox; Dr. John Wilson's Big Band; the Balcony Big Band; Trio Grande, and the brother-and-sister team of Maureen and David Budway. The top blues singers and groups in town include Chismo Charles, Sandy Staley, Billy Price and the Swingtime Five, the Blues Orphans, the Blues Burners, and the Mystic Knights of the Sea.

Most clubs and bars in Pittsburgh close at 2 a.m.

Personal Choices

Best jazz restaurant-clubs: *Shadyside, Stolen Moments*
Best jazz "coffeehouse": *Rosebud*
Best cultural centers for jazz: *Ramsey's II, Manchester Craftsmen's Guild*
Best blues club: *The Decade*

F O R   J A Z Z

Shadyside Balcony, *5520 Walnut St. (Shadyside), 687-0110.*

At first the music seems incidental at this large upscale restaurant on the third floor of a commercial building. There are the prerequisite plants, the singles bar, the neat tables placed a discreet distance apart.

But first impressions can be wrong, and the Balcony, it turns out, offers up serious music ranging from swing to fusion in the form of vocalists, duos, trios, and the 17-piece Balcony Big Band. First-rate, local musicians such as Dave and Maureen Budway appear here most nights, while nationally known names such as Mark Murphy and Mose Allison are brought through about once a month. On Wednesdays in the early evenings there's a "Jazz for Juniors" program aimed at the under-12 set.
Music: M–Sa, Su brunch. *Cover:* $–$$. *Food:* American. CC.

Stolen Moments, *3239 Brighton Rd. (North Side), 766-4770.*

Started up by veteran jazz pianist-composer Carl Arter, record producer Michael Frank, and bassist-physician Sunny Sunseri, Stolen Moments is a tiny, homey place that until recently was just a neighborhood bar. Now remodeled, with a small stage at the far end, a kitchen out back, and lots of vintage jazz posters on the wall, it aims at serving up serious music, as well as good food, until the wee hours of the morning. Arter usually plays two or three nights a week. "We wanted to feature Carl because we feel that he's one of the great, unrecognized jazz artists of Pittsburgh," says Frank, founder of Earwig Records.
Music: W–Sa. *No cover, except for special events. Food:* American.

Foster's Bar & Grill, *Holiday Inn at University Center, 100 Lytton Ave. (Oakland), 682-6200.*

Home to the Pittsburgh Jazz Society (343-9555), which meets and presents concerts here every Sunday evening, Foster's also features top local talent such as Walt Harper, Trio Grande, or Harold Betters on Friday and Saturday nights. The jazz society's meetings often include performances by nationally known acts (Barney Kessel, Mark Murphy), and afterward there's a jam.

Unfortunately, however, for all its good music, Foster's has little to offer in the way of atmosphere. The large window-lined lounge, which can seat up to 400, feels like what it is—a sterile room in a Holiday Inn. Adjacent to the lounge is a restaurant.
Music: F–Sa. *No cover. Food:* American.

Rosebud, *1650 Smallman St. (Strip District), 261-2221.*
Located in the same building as the Metropol, one of Pittsburgh's biggest nightclubs, the Rosebud is a large coffeehouse and supper club that presents both regional and national artists. Equipped with wooden floors, seats for about 350 people, and local artwork, it bills itself as having a blend of "European flavor and eclectic style." The menu includes light entrées and a large variety of coffees and desserts.
Music: W–Sa, some jazz and blues. *Cover:* $–$$$. *Food:* American.

Ramsey's II, *7310 Frankstown Ave. (Homewood), 371-3445.*
With some of the best acoustics in the city for jazz, Ramsey's II is a sort of African-American cultural center that features jazz on the weekends; poetry, dramatic readings, fashion shows, and special events during the week. A number of fine local artists have appeared here (Jimmy Ponder, Bobby Jones), and the club has also sponsored some of the most unusual jazz events in the city, including a concert that paired a young Polish jazz orchestra with a young Pittsburgh jazz orchestra called the Kehonia Koncept, made up of 15- to 18-year-olds. Many "names," such as George Benson, Roy Ayers, and Mrs. Richard Wright (the wife of the former novelist; now living in Paris) stop by here when in town.

Ramsey's is run by John Brewer and his wife, Christina, who is both a fiber artist (her work is often displayed on the walls, along with that of other local artists) and the club's cook.
Music: F, Sa. *No cover, except for special events. Food:* Cajun, Jamaican, African.

Club Café, *56–58 S. 12th St. (South Side), 381-3777.*
A small and modern café with a streamlined aluminum bar, star-shaped lamps, and neon strips of light, the Club Café started out as a duo piano bar that, according to one local critic, appealed to a "furs and diamonds" crowd. Since then it's evolved into a more varied jazz club, with talent such as Etta Cox, Jimmy Ponder, or Kevin Black performing most nights. The club still maintains its somewhat sleek and sophisticated air, however.
Music: W–Sa, Sa afternoons. *Cover:* $. *Food:* Louisiana. CC.

Westin William Penn, *530 William Penn Pl., 281-7100.*
Jazz comes to the hotel's elegant Palm Court Lobby two evenings a week, thanks to a series called "Piano Plus." A piano plus other instruments are always featured and guitar player Joe Negri

(who can often be seen on the children's TV show "Mr. Rogers," which is filmed in Pittsburgh) is a regular. The William Penn, built in 1916, is a National Historic Landmark, and its plush, delightful lobby is filled with chandeliers, glass tables, overstuffed chairs, and tall palm trees (hence the name).
Music: Th–F. *No cover. Food:* appetizers.

James Street, *422 Foreland St. (North Side), 323-2222.*

For the past six years, James Street, once a sports bar, has been presenting some of the better-known names in Pittsburgh jazz, including Harold Betters and Rodney McCoy. But no matter who's playing, James Street, housed in a 100-year-old building, remains primarily a restaurant. The upstairs, elegantly decorated with etched glass, mirrors, and wooden paneling, is devoted to dining only, while the music takes place on a makeshift stage in the equally pretty basement level.
Music: F–Sa. *No cover. Food:* New Orleans. CC.

Eileen's Bar & Zebra Room, *708 N. Dallas Ave. (Homewood), 361-9503.*

For over 20 years, the friendly Zebra Room with its striped walls and red-black-white decor has been a steady neighborhood haven for jazz. Located in a basement room beneath Eileen's Bar, it's a small, cozy lounge filled with a handful of tables, a step-up stage, and a revolving mirrored globe. Jazz veteran Carl Arter played here on and off for years, and even though he now has his own club (Stolen Moments) he still comes by from time to time, as do Roger Humphries and Peetie Henderson.
Music: F–Sa. *No cover. Food:* American.

Too Sweet, *7101 Frankstown Ave. (Homewood), 731-5707.*

A large modern club with a dance floor and portable stage that's brought out for the jazz shows, Too Sweet presents a jazz jam most Saturday afternoons with top veteran player Roger Humphries and his band, R. H. Factor. Saturday nights are also devoted to jazz.
Music: Sa afternoons and nights. *Cover:* $. *Food:* simple American.

FOR BLUES

The Decade, *223 Atwood St. (Oakland), 682-1211.*

Started up in 1973, the Decade is Pittsburgh's premiere rock-and-roll saloon, but the blues are also featured on a regular basis. This is the place where touring acts such as Buddy Guy, Charlie Musselwhite, James Cotton, and Duke Robillard play when they come to town. Local blues are also presented regularly, while a house band called the Mystic Knights of the Sea (voted one of the "best bar bands" by *Details* magazine in 1993) hosts a popular blues jam every Sunday night.

Located near the University of Pittsburgh, the Decade is a "rough, hypermasculine place," filled with lots of wood, music memorabilia, and Pittsburghiana.

Music: nightly, some blues. *Cover:* $–$$.

Anthony's South Side, *1306 E. Carson St. (South Side), 431-8960.*

Once a small and funky neighborhood bar, Anthony's has been somewhat spiffed up in recent years. There are now picture windows facing the street, a jukebox, and black-and-white photos on the wall. Nonetheless, the place hasn't lost its friendly, unprepossessing air, and all sorts of local music (from reggae to alternative, fusion to blues) can be heard here. Some of the jazz and blues acts who play the club include electric violinist Rodney McCoy, duo jazz guitarists Rizzuto & Petroff, and the R&B group James King & the Usual Suspects.

Music: nightly, some blues and jazz. *No cover. Food:* appetizers.

Also

Blues acts can sometimes be heard at **Graffiti** (4615 Baum Blvd., 682-4210), a showcase venue in Oakland, **Metropol** (1600 Smallman St., 261-2221), a large, predominantly rock nightclub in the Strip District, and some of the jazz clubs listed above.

Other Venues and Special Events

Crafts and jazz don't usually go together, but then the **Manchester Craftsmen's Guild** (1815 Metropolitan St., 322-0800) isn't a usual sort of place. Founded in 1968 to provide apprenticeships to inner-city high-school students in ceramics and photography, the school has since grown to include jazz. In addition, the Guild, which is housed in a modern brick building on the edge of town, is home to a fine state-of-the-art auditorium that brings in national talent. Max Roach has recorded an album here, and Ahmad Jamal picked out the stage piano. A free reception, complete with coffee and baked goods, follows each show. The Guild also puts on a **Winter Jazz Festival** during the third week of January.

Along with its Sunday-evening concerts at Foster's (see "For Jazz," page 180), the **Pittsburgh Jazz Society** (343-9555), founded by WDUQ-FM deejay Tony Mowod, sponsors other, inexpensive jazz events around town, sometimes compliments of its Pittsburgh Jazz Society Big Band (composed of high school and college students). Watch the papers.

Heinz Hall (600 Penn Ave., 392-4800), where the Pittsburgh Symphony Orchestra performs, presents occasional jazz events, as do the **Civic Arena** (300 Auditorium Place, 333-7328) and the **I. C. Light Ampitheater** (1 Station Sq., 562-9900).

In addition to the **Mellon Jazz Festival** (see "Major Festivals," page 403), the 17-day **Three Rivers Arts Festival** (481-7040), one of the largest and oldest free festivals in the United States, is held in the city every June and features both national and local jazz and blues artists. The **South Side Summer Street Spectacular** (481-0651), the largest neighborhood festival in Pittsburgh, is a four-day event held in late July that features both jazz and blues. The **Shadyside Arts Festival** (681-2809), which includes some jazz, is held the first weekend in August.

Radio

WDUQ/90.5 FM (434-6030). Affiliated with Duquesne University and NPR; jazz every midday and evening.

WYEP/91.3 FM (661-9100). An independent, listener-supported station. Blues and R&B all day Saturday.

Bal timore

Despite its small size, Baltimore has had its share of jazz history. For many years it served as a feeder line for musicians on their way to New York while at the same time developing a strong jazz environment of its own. Pennsylvania Avenue and the Royal Theatre were particularly popular spots, attracting talent from all over the country, many of whom took up residence for weeks. Local musicians tended to play on "the Block," a red-light district then located on Baltimore Street between Gay and Calvert streets.

Baltimore has also produced a number of legendary musicians, including Eubie Blake, Billie Holiday, and Chick Webb. Cab Calloway spent his boyhood in the city, while Blanche Calloway, his sister and one of the nation's first women bandleaders, was born here. Later, there were guitarist Elmer Snowden, pianist Dick Katz, saxophonist Gary Bartz and vocalist Ethel Ennis, who once ran her own club on Cathedral Street (now Spike and Charlie's, see "For Jazz," page 190) and still resides in the area.

Many of Baltimore's earliest jazz musicians from the west side, Cab and Blanche Calloway among them, studied at Douglass High School under the tutelege of an earlier jazz and classical organist and cello player named William Llewellyn Wilson. Wilson was also the conductor of Baltimore's first African-American symphony orchestra.

Sources

The City Paper (523-2300), a free weekly, has excellent listings. Other sources are the Friday edition of *The Baltimore Sun* (332-6000), and Rosa Pryor's column in the *Baltimore Times* (225-3600).

For maps and other information, contact the Baltimore Visitor Information Center, which is located at 300 Pratt St. in the Inner Harbor area; 837-4636, 800-282-6632, or 800-837-INFO.

The area code for Baltimore is (410).

A Note on Neighborhoods

Over the past decade or so, ever since the opening of the Rouse Company project Harborplace and the acclaimed National Aquarium, Baltimore has become a tourist destination. Its formerly decrepit and abandoned downtown is now filled with glittering restaurants, high-rise hotels, and expensive boutiques.

Once away from the Inner Harbor, however, Baltimore reverts back to its true self: a solid city of neighborhoods, divided into north and south by Baltimore Street, and into east and west by Charles Street. Fells Point, lined with cobblestone streets and Colonial buildings, is a former shipbuilding and maritime center that dates back to the 1730's. Federal Hill is another cobblestone area near the downtown. Both are known for their nightlife.

Driving in Baltimore is easy. Traffic is light, and parking, except weekends in the Inner Harbor area and in Fells Point, is plentiful.

Landmarks and Legends

(The sites below are best toured by car. Pennsylvania Avenue starts near the downtown; East Baltimore is about 15 minutes east of downtown; the Famous Ballroom and the Cab Calloway Room are to the north.)

Pennsylvania Avenue

From the 1920's through the 1950's, Pennsylvania Avenue, stretching 23 blocks from Franklin Avenue on the south to Fulton Avenue on the north, was *the* avenue of black Baltimore. Lined with shops, restaurants, schools, churches, theaters, nightclubs, taverns, and businesses, it provided the city's largest African-American community with everything it needed.

More than anything else, though, Pennsylvania Avenue was renowned for its entertainment. The first African-American-owned hotel in Baltimore, the Penn Hotel, was built here in 1921, and by 1945, in the 14 blocks between Biddle and Baker streets alone, there were 47 liquor licenses, most of them issued to nightclubs. Among these were the Comedy Club and Wendall's Tavern, Gamby's and Dreamland, the Ritz, and the Sphinx Club. Live

**Fats Waller opened
the Royal in 1925.**

*Courtesy
Peale Museum*

music was everywhere, and even the bars and taverns without formal stages had a solo piano or organ player.

Pennsylvania Avenue became a victim of urban renewal in the mid-seventies. The lower half or "the bottom," which stretched from Franklin to Dolphin Street, was completely demolished, to be replaced by an occasional dispirited church, apartment building, or school. The upper half fared a bit better, and though considerably more dangerous now than it once was, is still lined with a hodgepodge of dilapidated buildings.

Royal Theatre, *1329 Pennsylvania Ave.*

Today, there's just an ugly 12-by-16-inch commemorative plaque standing on steel pipes in front of a fenced-in playing field, but the Royal Theatre was once one of the major stops on a black entertainment circuit that included the Apollo in New York, the Howard in Washington, the Earle in Philadelphia, and the Regal in Chicago. It was here that Billie Holiday got booed by her own hometown (the Royal was reputedly even tougher than the cold-hearted Apollo; "They would throw anything," says one Baltimorean) and here that Pearl Bailey gave her first performances—as a chorus girl.

The Royal, which seated about 1,350 people, opened in 1921 as the Douglass Theater, the "finest colored theatre in America, owned and controlled by colored people." Four years later, however, it went bankrupt and reopened under white management as the Royal. The Royal's first performer was Fats Waller.

The theater was demolished in 1971.

The Sphinx Club, *2107 Pennsylvania Ave. (near downtown).*
In operation until the early 1990s, the Sphinx was one of the oldest minority-owned clubs in the country, dating back to 1946 and the heyday of Pennsylvania Avenue. A well-known landmark in Baltimore's African-American community, it was founded by businessman Charles Phillip Tilghman and later run by his children.

Billie Holiday, Dinah Washington, and Sam Cooke were among the many who played the Sphinx, but the club never really had a true entertainment policy. Music was an informal thing. Anyone who wanted to play on the instruments lying around could, and often did. Today, the Sphinx has been replaced by a neighborhood bar.

Statue of Billie Holiday, *Pennsylvania Ave. bet.*
Lanvale and Lafayette streets.
She stands tall, strong, and lovely, this 8½-foot-high bronze statue of Lady Day. A gardenia blooms in her hair; a long gown rustles to her feet; her face is filled with confidence and joy. The inscription on a nearby plaque reads: "I don't think I'm singing, I feel like I am playing a horn. I try to improvise. What comes out is what I feel."

The Eubie Blake National Museum and Cultural Center, *396-8128.*
Eubie Blake is one of Baltimore's most famous sons, born in 1883 to former slaves whose previous 10 children had all died at birth. He grew up an only child and his musical talent was first noticed when, at age six, he climbed up onto an organ stool in a local department store while shopping with his mother and began to pick out a melody. Mrs. Blake bought a $75 organ, paying a quarter a week, and Eubie took lessons from a next-door neighbor. Soon, much to his mother's consternation when she finally found out, he was sneaking out of his bedroom window at night to play ragtime at a nearby brothel.

Up until the summer of 1993, the Eubie Blake Museum was located in a beautiful white townhouse at 409 N. Charles Street. Owing to a devastating fire, however, the museum (which did full justice to its subject's extraordinary life) is now closed. Plans are in the works to reopen; call the above number for updated information.

East Baltimore, *centering around N. Eden Street.*
Chick Webb, Billie Holiday, and Eubie Blake all once lived in this working-class neighborhood located not far from downtown. Webb was born at 1313 Ashland Ave., while Blake lived for a time at 414 N. Eden St. and Holiday at 200 S. Durham St. Webb's home has been replaced by an attractive row house; Blake's house

has also been torn down; Holiday's home is still standing, but is in dilapidated condition.

Today, in the center of East Baltimore, stands the well-worn Chick Webb Memorial Recreation Center (623 N. Eden St.), named after the legendary drummer whose life was the stuff that movies are made of. Born poor and hunchback in 1909, Webb became a cripple at the age of 5 after falling down the stairs. Nonetheless, four years later, he was out on the street selling newspapers so that he could buy his first set of drums.

Webb, who later led the house band at New York's Savoy Ballroom, was responsible for discovering Ella Fitzgerald. He first heard the then-shy girl sing at amateur night at the Apollo in 1934, and was so impressed that he hired her on the spot and brought her home to live with him and his wife.

Famous Ballroom, *1717 N. Charles St.*

For years, Baltimore's Left Bank Jazz Society held weekly concerts featuring all the big names in jazz—Dizzy Gillespie, Count Basie, Duke Ellington—at this former downtown ballroom. The society recorded all of its events, including Coltrane's last public performance, but owing to legal complications, the tapes have never been released. They are currently stored at Morgan State University.

The Left Bank, founded in 1964, scaled down its operations in 1980, because of escalating costs. The society still exists (see "Other Venues and Special Events," page 192), but it's less active and under different directorship.

Cab Calloway Room, *Parlett L. Moore Library, Coppin State College, 2500 W. North Ave., 383-5926.*

Although not born in Baltimore, Cab Calloway spent much of his boyhood here, and when it came time to decide how to dispose of his personal papers, he chose to donate them to this teacher training college, founded at the turn of the century. Some of the items on display in the Calloway Room, located in the college library, include a Hirshfeld caricature, the gold record received by the artist for his music for the movie *The Blues Brothers,* and his baton.

"Some artists make you think, others make you dream and still others like me want to entertain," reads a quote from the musician.

Open: M–F, 8 a.m.–5 p.m. or by appointment. *Admission:* free.

Clubs, etc.

Baltimore has few full-time jazz or blues clubs. Nonetheless, there are plenty of talented local musicians, and the music can be found in various neighborhood bars and restaurants. Nationally known jazz artists are occasionally brought in by the Left Bank Jazz Society, the **New Haven Lounge,** and the **King of France**

Tavern in the Maryland Inn in Annapolis, 45 minutes away. National blues artists are sometimes presented by **8X10** and **Max's.**

Some of the Baltimore-area players to watch out for include elder statesman and tenor saxman Mickey Fields; jazz-blues singer Ethel Ennis; Vernon Wolst and his Big Blues Band; blues pianist Steve Kramer; organist Sir Thomas Hurley; jazz guitarists Paul Wingo and Carl Filipiak; saxmen Gary Thomas and Gary Bartz (both ex-Baltimoreans now living in New York who still play their hometown); Harold Adams and the Moon August Band; bebop trumpeter Allen Houser; alto saxophonist Thomas Whit Williams and his son, drummer Tom Williams; bluesman Red Jones; and vocalists Sheila Ford, Aletta Green, and Dolores King Williams. D.C.-based talent such as bluesmen Tom Principato and Linwood Taylor, Big Joe & the Dynaflows, the Uptown Rhythm Kings, and Deanna Bogart can also be heard in the city regularly.

Most bars and clubs in Baltimore remain open until 2 a.m.

Personal Choices

Best jazz spots: *Bertha's, New Haven Lounge*
Best area jazz club: *King of France Tavern (in Annapolis)*
Best jam session: *The Sportsmen's Lounge*
Best club for blues: *8X10*
Best neighborhood blues bars: *Full Moon, Café Tattoo*

FOR JAZZ

New Haven Lounge, *1552 Havenwood Rd. (Northwood Shopping Center, near Loch Raven Blvd., 15 min. NE of downtown), 366-7416.*

Though the New Haven only presents jazz three nights a week, it's currently the most serious club in town for straight-ahead sounds. Gary Bartz, Ralph Moore, Steve Wilson, Joey De-Francesco, Paul Bollenback, and Sonny Fortune are among those who have appeared here.

Also a restaurant, the New Haven is housed in a smallish, high-ceilinged room that is part of one of the city's older shopping centers. Dark wood and comfortable booths line its walls, and candles light its tables.
Music: W, F, Sa. *Cover:* $. *Food:* American.

Bertha's, *734 S. Broadway (Fells Point), 327-5795.*
Bertha's is most famous for its mussels, which it serves up every which way: with garlic butter, with anchovies, with Spanish sauce. The building itself—long, thin, dark, and creaky—is as old as the neighborhood and, with its lanterns and round porthole windows, sometimes feels more like a ship than an edifice.

Despite its emphasis on food, music plays an integral role at Bertha's. Four nights a week, musicians crowd onto its tiny stage near the front door and play to a listening audience (the talkers sit farther back or in a second, separate room). Regulars include Paul Wingo, Allen Houser, and Big Bertha's Rhythm Kings, a Dixieland band that somehow manages to squeeze itself onto the stage. *Music:* Tu–W, F–Sa. *No cover. Food:* mussels, etc. CC.

Cat's Eye Pub, *1730 Thames St. (Fells Point), 276-9085.*

Once best known for its Irish music, the Cat's Eye now devotes most of the week to jazz, blues, acoustic folk, and " '70's rock." Traditional jazz bands play on Mondays and Thursdays, while Steve Kramer has been playing blues piano on Sunday afternoons for years.

The Cat's Eye, located on a cobblestone street on the edge of the harbor, is long and narrow and packed with enough "antiques" to keep anyone's grandmother happy. Maps and paintings hang on the walls, flags from the ceiling. The stage is rather oddly situated behind a big wooden partition that runs the length of the pub, and there's a second bar in the back.

Music: nightly, Sa–Su afternoons. *No cover.*

The Sportsmen's Lounge, *4723 Gwynn Oak Ave. (15 min. NW of downtown), 664-1041.*

Walter "Chappy" Chapman, a graphic artist with a Fu Manchu beard, has been coming to this neighborhood club every single night for 30 years. A slight man who usually nurses one drink the entire evening, he sits in a corner and watches and listens. He has seen many of the greats come and go that way—Count Basie, Dexter Gordon, Sonny Stitt, Gene Ammons—and except for the time when he broke his leg, has never missed a jazz set. "I come here because it's a peaceful place," he says. "Everyone knows each other, it's like a family." He pauses. "And because the music's very meaningful."

The heyday of the Sportmen's was the sixties, when it was owned by football player Lenny Moore and jazz in Baltimore was a happening thing. Those days are over, but the best jam session in the city still takes place here every Monday night. The sessions are usually led by jazz veteran Mickey Fields on tenor sax, and national talent passing through town sometimes stops in.

Located in a quiet middle-class African-American neighborhood, the Sportsmen is simple-looking on the outside, but inside it's quite plush, with rows of mirrors, comfortable swivel chairs, and a big stage.

Music: M, F–Sa. *No cover.*

Spike and Charlie's, *1225 Cathedral St., 752-8144.*

Voted one of Baltimore's 10 best restaurants by the *Baltimore Sun,* Spike and Charlie's houses a club on its lower level that offers a mix of R&B, blues, straight-ahead, and fusion. National artists such as Delfeayo Marsalis play here on occasion, but most of the talent is local. The club is intimate and dark, with a large stage and exposed brick walls.

Music: F, Sa. *Cover:* $–$$. *Food:* full-service American upstairs; light fare in the club. CC.

FOR BLUES

8X10, *10 E. Cross St. (Federal Hill), 625-2000.*

Named for the two buildings in which it is housed, numbers 8 and 10 Cross Street, 8X10 features a broad mix of music, including blues, zydeco, reggae, and progressive rock. Some of the blues artists who've performed here recently are James Cotton, James Harman, and Duke Robillard.

8X10 is housed in spic-and-span nineteenth-century buildings and is a well-lit multiroomed place with exposed brick walls, tile floors, and a balcony. During the 1940's and '50's, long before the present owners came on the scene, it was a famous neighborhood bar known as the Dew Drop Inn.

Music: nightly, occasional blues. *Cover:* $–$$.

Full Moon Saloon, *1710 Aliceanna St. (Fells Point), 558-2873.*

The long, thin Full Moon, with its brick walls, scarred wooden bar and milky-white glass fixtures, dates back to the 1700's. It's a neighborhood bar with a neighborhood feel. A doctor sits next to a biker who sits next to a construction worker who orders a glass of milk. There's a moosehead mounted on the wall, a jar of pickled eggs on the counter, and a big white kitchen sink behind the bar.

Local and regional blues and R&B acts come to the Full Moon every night of the week as well as Saturday and Sunday late afternoons. Thursdays, there's a blues jam.

Music: nightly; Sa, Su, 4–8 p.m. *Cover:* $. *Food:* raw bar/seafood.

Café Tattoo, *4825 Belair Rd., 325-RIBS.*

A friendly barbecue joint that's won all sorts of prizes for its sauces, chili, and beer (including the number two spot in the American Royal International Barbecue Sauce contest), Café Tattoo has local blues bands most nights of the week. Fat Tuesday and Loaded Roller are regulars, along with jazz guitarist Carl Filipiak, who plays solo on Tuesdays and with his big band on occasional Sundays. Housed in a 1922 building, the club features a glass-brick front window, tin ceilings, tables along one wall, bar stools along another.

Music: Tu–Su. *Cover:* none. *Food:* barbecue, chili.

Also

National and local blues acts are presented several times a month by **Max's** (735 S. Broadway, 675-MAXS), a large, predominantly rock venue in Fells Point. Blues can also be heard occasionally at the **New Haven,** the **Sportsmen's Lounge,** and the **Cat's Eye Pub** (see "For Jazz," page 190).

Other Venues and Special Events

The **Left Bank Jazz Society** (945-2266) sponsors approximately eight concerts a year, along with two jazz boat rides to Annapolis and back in the late summer. Food is included in the ticket price and nonmembers are welcome. **Jazz Expressways** (377-1331), another community jazz organization, sponsors concerts and Sunday jazz brunches featuring local artists. Again, nonmembers are welcome.

Joseph Meyerhoff Symphony Hall (1212 Cathedral St., 783-8110) occasionally presents top-name talent, while jazz and blues performers appear at the **Pier 6 Concert Pavilion** during the summer months (Pier 6, Inner Harbor, 625-1400). The **Blazz Festival** is a one-day event held on the Pier in June; the Baltimore Blues Society (444-1716) sponsors occasional special events, including an "**Eat the Rich**" picnic in September.

Radio Stations

(See also Washington, D.C., listings.)
WEAA/88.9 FM (444-3564). A 24-hour contemporary jazz station. Affiliated with Morgan State University.
WJHU/88.1 FM (516-9548). Jazz every evening.
WTMD/89.7 FM. Blues, Sa afternoons.

Other Nearby Locations

King of France Tavern, *Maryland Inn, 16 Church Circle, Annapolis (45 min. from Baltimore), (301) 263-2641.*

A 1784 tavern with original stone walls, brick arches, and huge wooden beams, the King of France, located in one of Annapolis's five historic inns, seems like an unlikely place for jazz. Nonetheless, many top area musicians, including Deanna Bogart, Ethel Ennis, and Charlie Byrd, play here regularly, and a jam session is held on Monday nights. The Crabtown Big Band plays on Wednesdays.
Music: W, F–M. *Cover:* $$. *Food:* light American. CC. Reservations recommended.

Washington, D.C.

It's hard to imagine Washington, D.C., as a dynamic music town, but it has considerably more jazz history than one might suspect. Duke Ellington, Mercer Ellington, Buck Hill, Jimmy Cobb, Claude Hopkins, Andy Razaf, Charlie Rouse, and Ira Sullivan were all born here, while James Reese Europe, Billy Taylor, Jelly Roll Morton, Ben Webster, and Benny Carter lived here either as children or adults. Many musicians once used Washington as a sort of base of operations providing easy access to other cities on the "black entertainment" circuit—Philadelphia, New York, Baltimore, Atlanta—while at the same time frequenting the capitol's U Street area (see "Landmarks and Legends," page 194).

From the 1920's through the 1950's, U Street was the hub of black Washington's commercial, professional, and artistic worlds. The famous Howard Theater, the Lincoln Theater, the Majestic Theater, the Crystal Caverns (later the Bohemian Caverns), the Jungle Club, and the Club Bali were all located here in the northernmost section of the original city of Washington. "U Street was one of the best-kept secrets in the world," said the late Felix Grant, a longtime D.C. deejay, in an interview in 1990.

By the mid-sixties, U Street's activity had diminished considerably (the Bohemian Caverns was the only large club left), and after the race riots of '68, the area went into a steep decline. Jazz moved elsewhere, most notably Georgetown, where Blues Alley had been operating since 1965.

A number of blues artists are also associated with Washington, D.C. Among them are rock-bluesman Tom Principato, the acoustic blues team of John Cephas and Phil Wiggins, Jimmy Thackery and the Nighthawks, Big Chief Ellis, and the R&B group the Clovers.

Sources

The best sources for music listings are *City Paper* (628-6528), a free weekly, and the Friday section of the *Washington Post* (334-6000).

For maps and other information, contact the Washington, D.C., Convention and Visitors Association, 1212 New York Ave., NW, Suite 600, or the Washington, D.C., Visitor Center at 1455 Pennsylvania Ave., NW (789-7000; same number for both).

The area code for Washington is (202).

A Note on Neighborhoods

Because so much of downtown Washington is devoted to government, there is little there in the way of entertainment—with a few exceptions, noted below. Georgetown has long been considered the place to go for nightlife in the capital, but in recent years, the historic area, known for its cobblestone streets and Federal-style buildings, has been overrun with college students, forcing older audiences to move elsewhere. The Adams Morgan neighborhood, centering on 18th Street and Columbia Road, is now a trendy favorite, as is nearby Alexandria, Virginia, another historic area, this one usually filled with tourists dressed in brilliant greens, yellows, and pinks. Both areas are better equipped with restaurants than music spots, however.

Driving in Washington is difficult—diagonal streets and frequent traffic circles make the city confusing to navigate—and parking is limited, especially in the downtown area.

Landmarks and Legends

(The following sites, most of which are located in northwest Washington, near the downtown, are best toured by car.)

U Street, *between Ninth and 17th streets, NW*

Today, much of the once-prosperous U Street area is sad, depressed, and dangerous, empty except for a few idle men sitting on stoops or wandering aimlessly about. This is changing, however. Thanks in part to the completion of the green subway line, which runs beneath U Street, the area is being revitalized. As of this writ-

Blues Alley, D.C.'s best-
known jazz club, began
as a Dixieland haunt.

Courtesy Blues Alley

ing, many of the jazz sites are still standing—the Majestic Theater at 1632 U St., the Club Bali at 1901 14th St. (now a theater), and others, listed below—but most are in dilapidated condition.

Crystal Caverns *(later Bohemian Caverns), SW corner of 11th and U streets, NW*

The Crystal Caverns was an important jazz spot from the mid-twenties through the '60's. A basement club, it was decorated by Italian craftsmen to resemble a cave.

It was at the Crystal Caverns that blueswoman Ruth Brown got her first real break. She had come to Washington from Virginia with Lucky Millinder's band, and one night while in the capital, two of the musicians in the band asked her to bring them some Cokes. She obliged, and when Lucky saw her, he went wild, saying he had hired her as a vocalist, not a waitress, and since she couldn't sing anyway, he was firing her.

"I think I must have had about four dollars if I had a penny," Brown told Arnold Shaw, author of *Honkers and Shouters*. "I stood there in disbelief. . . . I was pretty close to home—about two hundred miles. But my Dad had said, and how could I forget those words: 'Once you leave, don't call back here for anything.' "

Luckily, Brown went on to find a job at the Crystal Caverns, then being managed by woman bandleader Blanche Calloway, who told her she could sing there for a week, long enough to earn her fare back home. During that week, Brown was noticed by a talent scout who eventually landed her a record contract with Atlantic. Even so, it took another year for her luck to turn: en route to the studio in New York, she was in a car crash that hospitalized her for 12 months.

Lincoln Theater, *1215–19 U St., NW*

Now in the process of being restored to its former grandeur and scheduled to reopen soon, the Lincoln was once a favorite among the residents of U Street. Built in 1921 in the Georgian Revival style, it showcased both movies and live entertainment, including jazz and blues musicians.

Jungle Club, *1200 block, U St., NW*

Just west of the Lincoln (on the right, when facing the box office) is the run-down red-brick building that once housed Jelly Roll Morton's Jungle Club, also known at various points as the Music Box and the Blue Moon Inn. This was one of the last places where the musician played professionally before he went to the West Coast and died.

Jelly Roll (Ferdinand La Menthe) had come to Washington, D.C., in 1936 at the height of the Depression, leaving his wife, Mabel, behind in New York. He opened the club with his lover, Cordelia, and from the beginning the place brought him nothing but trouble. He and Cordelia fought constantly, patrons com-

plained about the club's high prices, and the swing era was beginning, leaving Jelly Roll behind.

Then, for a while at least, his fortunes changed. Jazz fans, many
of them white, discovered the club, and suddenly Jelly Roll was
hot once more. He would play "by the hour . . . smiling, with the
world again in a jug and the stopper in his hand," writes Alan
Lomax in *Mister Jelly Roll*.

Alas, the era of plenty did not last. An angry patron stabbed
Jelly Roll above the heart one night, and by the time he'd recovered, he'd decided to leave Washington. Nineteen thirty-nine
found him in New York with a bad heart; in 1940, he was poverty-
stricken on the West Coast. He died on May 1, 1941, in Los Angeles.

Howard Theater, *620 T St., NW*

The Howard, opened in 1915, was to Washington what the
Apollo was to New York or the Royal to Baltimore. *Everyone*
played here: Ethel Waters, Alberta Hunter, Duke Ellington, Pearl
Bailey, Lena Horne, Billy Eckstine, Dinah Washington, Sammy
Davis Jr. Ella Fitzgerald won an amateur contest here once; while
a few white musicians, Woody Herman, Stan Kenton, and Artie
Shaw among them, put on shows as well. There was a house or-
chestra, manned by musicians of many races—black, Cuban, and
Puerto Rican—and a bouncer called "Big Dog."

"Back then, people would be lined up all the way down the
blocks on both sides," says D.C.-based bass player Keter Betts.
"When Pearl Bailey was performing, she would have tables out
serving hot dogs and coffee. The place was completely alive. It was
the corner of Washington."

By the late '50's and '60's, the golden age of jazz had ended and
rock-and-roll took over the theater. The Howard closed its doors
for good after the race riots of 1968.

Corner of Seventh and T streets, NW

Right around the corner from the Howard were three jazz
joints—Gene Clores', the Offbeat, and the Club Harlem—located
at numbers 1855, 1851, and 1849 Seventh St. All the musicians
who performed at the Howard would come here to eat and jam
after the show. On the opposite side of the street, now torn down,
was a popular after-hours place called Old Rose's.

Also on the corner was the first of the *Waxie Maxie* record
stores (later a chain in the D.C. area), owned by Max Silverman.
Ahmet Ertegun, who would later found Atlantic Records, used to
sleep on a cot in Max's backroom in his younger, poorer days,
when he didn't feel like going home.

Duke Ellington's boyhood home, *1212 T St., NW*

Shortly after the Duke was born (given name, Edward Kennedy Ellington), his family moved to this lovely three-story tur-

Two sidemen from Lucky Millinder's band shoot the breeze on or near U Street, circa 1939.

Frank Driggs Collection

reted house in a quiet middle-class neighborhood. Ellington himself once wrote that he was "pampered and pampered, and spoiled rotten by all the women in the family." He attended the local Armstrong High School, got a job selling refreshments at a baseball park, and read all the mystery books he could get his hands on.

Ellington's musical talents took a while longer to assert themselves. His mother had signed him up for piano lessons with a local teacher named, all too appropriately, Mrs. Clinkscales, but he missed more lessons than he took. "At this point," he writes in his autobiography, *Music Is My Mistress,* "piano was not my recognized talent. Why, I thought, take it so seriously? After all, baseball, football, track and athletics were what the real he-men were identified with. . . ."

One summer, however, Ellington heard Harvey Brooks, a young piano player out of Philadelphia, and was so impressed that he decided he just *had* to learn how to play. Shortly thereafter he came up with his first piece, "Soda Fountain Rag," and at the next high-school party, an impressed "rather fancy" friend pushed him to the front of the room, saying that his buddy, "the Duke," would be happy to play for his classmates.

Thereafter, Ellington not only had a new nickname but also a new passion. "From then on," he writes, "I was invited to many parties, where I learned that when you were playing piano there was always a pretty girl standing down at the bass clef end of the piano. I ain't been no athlete since."

James Reese Europe's home, *1008 S. St., NW*

Just around the corner from the old Ellington residence is the former home of James Reese Europe. The Reese family moved here from Alabama in the early 1880's, and James and his sister, Mary Lorraine, a musician in her own right, grew up in this solid red-brick building with a garden full of flowers.

Europe was the nation's first African-American bandleader, and he is best remembered as the band master of the famous all-black 369th Regiment's Band in World War I, which was assigned to the French Army. (Noble Sissle was its drum major.) Reese played traditional band music, but he was the first to draw heavily on black musical styles: ragtime, jazz, blues, and spirituals.

Europe died tragically, stabbed to death by a member of his own band, a snare drummer who was known for his hot temper. It happened one night in 1919, when the band was appearing at the Mechanics' Hall in Boston. Europe had sent for the drummer to reprimand him over some small wrongdoing, and the man sprang at him, stabbing him in the neck with a penknife. Not realizing that he'd been seriously hurt, Reese calmly made arrangements for someone else to take over the band and then made his way to the hospital. He died a few hours later: his jugular vein had been severed.

Reese is buried in Arlington National Cemetery.

Charles Hotel, *1338 R St., NW*

"A man can leave home one morning and come home that night whistling and singing to find there ain't nobody there but him. I left two men like that," writes Billie Holiday in *Lady Sings the Blues.*

One of the men Billie left was Mr. John Levy, and they were staying at the Charles Hotel at the time. "There was snow up to your panties over the capital," she writes. Nonetheless, while Mr. Levy was out, she found her mink coat that he had hidden under the mattress, put her last few dollars in a bag (she had over $2,000 with her but Mr. Levy had locked them up in a safe downstairs), grabbed her dog, and walked down the fire escape in her stocking feet. A few hours later, she was in New York.

Duke Ellington's birthplace, *2129 Ward Pl., NW*

Now there's nothing here except a modern, sterile-looking post office building, but it was on this short street that Duke Ellington was born. A simple plaque marks the spot, while words above it read DUKE ELLINGTON BUILDING.

Even this much recognition for one of the greatest musicians of our time was hard-won: the late Felix Grant, a local deejay and the man responsible for the plaque's installation, worked on the project for 15 years before it became a reality.

Library of Congress, *First St. near E. Capitol St., SE,*
707-5000.

Into this impressive marble Italian Renaissance building—
heralded as the largest and costliest library in the world when it
was built in 1897—strode Mr. Jelly Roll Morton, musician and
persona extraordinaire, in May 1938 to prove to the world that he
and *not* W. C. Handy, as had been broadcast on a radio program,
was the father of jazz. Morton came to the Library's Coolidge Auditorium to record for folklorist Alan Lomax, who describes the
scene in *Mister Jelly Roll:* "With his long black Lincoln, his diamonds, and his high-class clothes, he scarcely looked like a good
source for folklore. . . . Unimpressed by the austere setting of the
most exclusive chamber-music recitals in the world, [he] tossed his
expensive summer straw on the bench of the Steinway grand,
raised the lid to stash away the bourbon bottle, and then fell to lar-
ruping away at *Alabama Bound.* . . . The plaster busts of Bach,
Beethoven, and Brahms looked sternly down, but if Jelly noticed
them, he probably figured they were learning a thing or two."

Clubs, etc.

Washington's premier jazz clubs for out-of-town talent are
Blues Alley and **One Step Down** (which also features top local
artists). The **Evening Star Jazz Bar** is a top spot for first-class
Washington-based talent, while several restaurant-clubs—most
notably **Twin's** and **Takoma Station**—are also known for local
jazz. **Tornado Alley** is the area's premier blues club, but there are
also numerous small bars and restaurants that feature blues.

Jazz artists to look out for in Washington today include Butch
Warren, who once played bass with Thelonious Monk, vibraphonist Jon Metzger, tenor saxophonists Buck Hill and Larry Seals,
bassist Steve Novosal, guitarists Kenny Definis and Paul Bollenback, pianist Reuben Brown, trumpet and flugelhorn player
Bobby Sanchez, multireedman Byron Morris, saxophonists Andrew White and Marshall Keys, keyboard player Lawrence
Wheatley, and vocalists Mary Jefferson, Deanna Bogart, Beverly
Kosham, and Ronnie Wells. Latin jazz groups include Paul Hawkins and La Jazz, featuring Maria Rodriquez; the Rhumba Club,
and Latin Five.

Three of the most popular blues groups playing in the D.C. area
are Tom Principato, the Uptown Rhythm Kings, and John Cephas
and Phil Wiggins. Other talented artists include soul-bluesman
Bobby Parker, Archie Edwards, Ben Andrews, Bruce Ewan & the
Solid Senders, Big Joe Maher and the Dynaflows, the Night-
hawks, the Persuaders, Jimmy Thackery, Danny Gatton, Jesse
Yawn, Little Sonny Warner, Robert Lighthouse, Warner Williams, Linwood Taylor, jazz-blues-gospel singer Sedatrius Brown,
Nap Turner (who also hosts a radio show on WPFW-FM), and Saffire, The Uppity Blues Women.

In general, the D.C. clubs stay open until 2 a.m. during the week, 3 a.m. on weekends.

Personal Choices

Best jazz club: *One Step Down*
Best jazz supper club: *Blues Alley*
Best jazz jam: *Twin's*
Best blues club: *Tornado Alley*
Best soul-blues joint: *New Vegas Lounge*

FOR JAZZ

Blues Alley, *1073 Rear Wisconsin Ave., NW (Georgetown), 337-4141.*
Ever since 1966, Blues Alley, the best-known club in Washington, has featured all the top names in jazz and then some. Located in a former carriage house, the place is elegant, yet sturdy and low-slung, with exposed brick walls, a wrought iron staircase, and lots of little tables covered with blue cloths. It really is located in an alley. Tobacco merchants once parked their buggies here when they came to the Georgetown wharf to buy and sell.

Despite its name, Blues Alley has always emphasized jazz, with blues being only an occasional thing. In fact, in the club's earliest days, it was primarily known for Dixieland.

Part of what makes Blues Alley so appealing is its small size (it seats only 125). It also has an excellent sound system, and an outstanding Creole menu, with every dish named after an artist. Part of what makes it not so appealing is its high prices.

A second Blues Alley is located in Tokyo, Japan, and the club also sponsors several community outreach programs, including the Blues Alley Youth Orchestra, whose members are promising young musicians.
Music: nightly. *Cover/minimum:* $$$–$$$$. *Food:* Creole. CC. Reservations recommended.

One Step Down, *2517 Pennsylvania Ave., NW (downtown), 331-8863.*
Take one tiny step down, and a few steps back. Out of the darkness, a long thin room opens up. Booths equipped with jukebox selectors, catsup, and A-1 Sauce bottles line one wall, while a bar, groaning with the weight of its liquor, lines the other. Near the entrance is a beautiful stained-glass window, aswirl with green, red, yellow, and purple.

For over 20 years now, the Cohen brothers have been operating one of the best clubs in Washington. One Step Down is everything a jazz joint should be: intimate, crowded, and smelling of the alcohol of time. Red candles flicker on the tables; tarnished horns hang over the bar. Local groups like the Lennie Cuje–Steve

Novosel Quartet and the Larry Camp Trio are featured during the week while the weekends are devoted to top out-of-town talent—Benny Carter, Art Farmer, Carmen McCrae, etc. A jazz jukebox lights up the place in the off hours, playing the likes of Duke Ellington, Dakota Staton, Stan Getz, and Oscar Peterson.
Music: Th–M, weekend afternoons. *Cover:* $$. *Food:* American. CC.

Evening Star Jazz Bar, *1200 19th St., NW (downtown), 785-STAR.*

Located adjacent to Sam and Harry's, one of D.C.'s finest steakhouses, the Evening Star is known for its top-quality straight-ahead jazz. Ron Holloway, who played with Dizzy Gillespie for years and years, is a regular here, as is Dick Morgan, who has long been a fixture on the D.C. jazz scene.

The jazz club is separate from the restaurant, but it still serves a light fare. A smallish place, it features a marble-topped bar that seats about 20 and tables and chairs for about 100 more. Old photos of jazz legends line the walls.
Music: Tu–Sa. *Cover/minimum:* $$. *Food:* light American.

Twin's Restaurant & Lounge, *5516 Colorado Ave., NW (at Longfellow, 20 min. from downtown), 882-2523.*

For the past seven years, some of the hottest jazz in D.C. has been steaming out of this tiny Ethiopian-American restaurant located on a quiet street lined with trees. Regulars include Bob Butta, Peter Edelman, and Buck Hill, and name musicians are sometimes brought in from New York or Philadelphia. Sunday nights there's a jam session that attracts musicians from all over the city.

Through it all, the two Tesfaye sisters move elegantly from table to table. They've put a great deal of care into their restaurant, and the place really feels more like a home than a commercial establishment. There are flowers and candles on the tables, baskets and neatly framed photos on the walls.
Music: Th–Sa. *Cover/minimum:* $. *Food:* Ethiopian-American.

Takoma Station Tavern, *6914 Fourth St., NW (20 min. from downtown), 829-1999.*

Located on D.C.'s far north side, near the Takoma Metro Station, the Takoma is an attractive, modern restaurant-club catering primarily to a young African-American professional crowd. There are a lot of good-looking people here dressed in good-looking clothes, and the music, though usually top notch, is most definitely secondary to the scene. The club is large and often noisy, with dozens of tables, exposed brick walls, a solid bar, and a tiny stage. Some of the regulars include the Marshall Keys Quintet and Marlon Jordan, and national artists such as Gil Scott-Heron are also presented from time to time.
Music: nightly. *No cover,* except for big acts. *Food:* American. CC.

Kala-Kala, *2439 18th St., NW (Adams Morgan), 232-5433.*

Booked by Paul Milesi, who used to book Twin's, Kala-Kala is one of D.C.'s newest jazz clubs. A long and narrow room with a bar to one side, a seating area and stage to the other, it's adorned with lots of African artifacts, including carved figures and masks, and statues of Kala, a Balinese god. Straight-ahead jazz is what's usually on tap, and there's a great jazz jukebox as well. "Lebanese finger food" is served.

Music: Tu–Sa. *Cover:* $. *Food:* snacks.

Café Lautrec, *2431 18th St., NW (Adams Morgan), 265-6436.*

As atmospheric as a French bistro, the charming Café Lautrec pays homage to its namesake with pictures of can-can dancers and the artist himself tucked away in unexpected corners. The walls are painted pink, and there are pretty wooden revolving fans everywhere, along with a cozy balcony area. Most nights trios and vocalists perform contemporary, Brazilian, and classic jazz, and tap dancers—who kick up their heels on *top* of the bar—also appear regularly.

Music: nightly. *Cover/minimum:* $$. *Food:* simple French. CC. Reservations recommended.

219 Restaurant/Basin Street Lounge/Bayou, *219 King St., Alexandria, Va., 703-549-1141.*

On a first visit, this place is confusing, with a restaurant on the first two floors, a lounge on the third and a ratskeller in the basement. Getting from one section to another is not easy—there's no telling where *this* staircase will lead—because number 219 was built as a mansion, not a commercial establishment.

In the end, though, it's the mansion atmosphere that gives the place its charm. Wonderfully Victorian, with elaborate floral wallpaper, antique furniture, and crystal chandeliers, it seems only appropriate that the local jazz featured here is usually light and frothy vocalese. Trios also perform regularly.

Music: W–Sa. *Cover:* $. *Food:* Southern provincial Creole. CC.

Also

Busara's Siamese Cuisine (2340 Wisconsin Ave., NW, 337-2340) in Upper Georgetown offers jazz in a room above the restaurant Wednesdays through Saturdays. Traditional Thai appetizers and drinks are served, and there's no cover.

The District also has several clubs that present Latin jazz and salsa. **Chelsea's** in Georgetown (1055 Thomas Jefferson, NW, 298-8222) has live Latin bands on Fridays and Saturday nights, and **Tullio's** (2020 K St. NW, 466-2020) features the same on Fridays. **Habana Village** in Adams Morgan (2467 18th St., NW, 462-6310) has a deejay Thursdays through Saturdays who plays an extensive selection of Latin jazz recordings past and present.

Colonel Brooks's Tavern (901 Monroe St., NE, 529-4002) is a small bar and restaurant that offers Dixieland every Tuesday night, compliments of the Federal Jazz Commission band; the **Market Inn** (200 E. Market St., SW, 554-2100) is an old Washington spot that features New Orleans jazz and Dixieland daily. Jazz can also be heard at **City Blues Bar** and other blues clubs mentioned below.

FOR BLUES

Tornado Alley, *11319 Elkin St., Wheaton, Md. (10 min. from downtown D.C.), 301-929-0795.*
A large square-shaped club with a big dance floor, blue-and-white-checked tablecloths, and posters all around, the Tornado presents a variety of national, regional, and local acts. Some of the many who've played here over the past year include Son Seals, Danny Gatton, Pinetop Perkins, and Roomful of Blues, and zydeco is also frequently on tap. The club serves up barbecue and cajun cuisine, and pool tables are located in a second room out back.
Music: Tu–Sa. *Cover:* $$. *Food:* barbecue, Cajun.

City Blues Bar, *2651 Connecticut Ave., NW (5 min. from downtown), 232-2300.*
Housed in what was once an old townhouse with arched doorways and moldings, the City Blues Bar is a restaurant-club featuring blues and some jazz every night of the week. Bluesmen Robert Lighthouse and Ben Andrews, and jazzmen Sydney Banda and Jacques Johnson are regulars, while the 54-item menu serves up everything from Jamaican jerk chicken to crab cakes. The walls are covered with murals depicting musicians; outside is a patio.

City Blues is owned and operated by an unusual trio: Jimy Brown, his mother, Teri Brown, and his wife, Lu Ann Brown. Teri Brown had worked as a waitress at the nearby Zoo Bar (see below) for 15 years when she and a partner bought the place in 1986. When her partner passed away, her son took his place and they opened up City Blues several years ago.
Music: nightly. *Cover:* $. *Food:* American, Caribbean, Italian.

Zoo Bar, *3000 Connecticut Ave., NW, 232-4225.*
Though its official name is the Oxford Tavern, everyone knows this small, well-worn, neighborhood watering hole—one of the oldest pubs in Washington—as the Zoo Bar. Located right across the street from the city's zoo, it's been attracting the same clientele for years and years. Everyone knows everyone here, and there's live music three nights a week, often courtesy of the same musicans who play City Blues.
Music: W, Th, Sa. *Cover:* $. *Food:* burgers, pizza, quesadillas, etc.

New Vegas Lounge, *1415 P St., NW (near downtown),* *483-3971.*

Located on the corner of 14th Street, which back before the 1968 riots was known for its hole-in-the-wall blues clubs, the Vegas is the best place in the city to hear soul- and R&B-tinged blues. A small club that also serves up "Vegas burgers" and "Vegas soul ribs," it's managed by singer Dr. Blues, who once performed at the 14th Street clubs and still takes to the stage on occasion.

The club's mostly a word-of-mouth spot, but it has attracted its share of out-of-towners and Europeans. Rock musician Stephen Stills also comes by from time to time.

Music: Tu–Su. *Cover:* $. *Food:* burgers, ribs, etc.

Fat Tuesday's, *10673 Braddock Rd., Fairfax, Va. (15 min. from downtown D.C.), 703-385-5717.*

A smallish place done up New Orleans style, with peanut shells on the floor and Mardi Gras paraphernalia (masks, beads, posters) on the walls, Fat Tuesday's presents a mix of local blues, progressive rock, and reggae, with blues featured about a third of the time. Every Sunday is blues, compliments of the Fat Tuesday Blues Band featuring Danny Morris of the Nighthawks and Kevin McKendree, who plays with Tom Principato.

Music: W–Su, some blues. *Cover:* $–$$. *Food:* Cajun.

The Wharf, *119 King St., Alexandria, Va., 703-836-2834.*

Everything in tourist-oriented Alexandria seems to be built of red brick with white trim, and The Wharf is no exception. The downstairs has been a seafood restaurant for two decades now, while the spacious upstairs, with its old exposed beams and brick walls, has been offering music for almost as long. Tom Principato plays here regularly, and jazz is also featured most weeks.

Music: nightly, much blues, some jazz. *Cover:* $. *Food (upstairs):* simple seafood and snacks. CC.

Also

Ben Andrews, a Delta-style blues slide guitarist, plays every Tuesday at the **Grog and Tankard** (2408 Wisconsin Ave., NW, near Georgetown, 333-3114). Blues and some jazz can be heard at the **Birchmere** (3901 Mt. Vernon Ave., Alexandria, Va., 703-549-5919), a club that features much acoustic music. Three large predominantly rock venues that occasionally bring in national blues talent are the **9:30 Club** (930 F St., NW, 393-0930), one of D.C.'s oldest rock clubs; the **Roxy** (1214 18th St., NW, 296-9292); and the **Bayou** (3135 K St., NW [Georgetown], 333-2897), which was once one of the best places in town in which to hear big bands.

For more information on blues in the D.C. area, contact the D.C. Blues Society (P.O. Box 77315, Washington, D.C. 20013-7715; 202-828-3028). The Society puts out a monthly newsletter and will be happy to send you a copy if extras are available.

Other Venues and Special Events

Since 1987, April has been **Duke Ellington Month** in Washington, D.C., and the Charlin Jazz Society (331-9404) sponsors events throughout the month, concluding with a free outdoor concert the last Saturday of April, featuring at least 20 regional artists. The Society also sponsors a jazz concert series at the **Kennedy Concert Center** (off Virginia Ave. near the intersection of F St. and New Hampshire Ave., NW, 467-4600).

A **D.C. Free Jazz Festival,** usually held over the Fourth of July weekend, is sponsored by District Curators (783-0360), a producer-presenter of multidisciplinary stage works. The group also sponsors occasional jazz concerts.

A free one-day **D.C. Blues Festival** is held in September; **Wolf Trap's Preservation Jazz & Blues Festival** (703-255-1900) takes place in June; and the two-week **Smithsonian Festival of American Folklife** (357-1300), featuring numerous blues artists, is presented every June–July. Old Town Alexandria sponsors a **Memorial Day Jazz Festival** (703-838-4200) featuring big bands.

The **Potomac River Jazz Club,** based in Falls Church, Va., has been presenting and preserving traditional jazz for over two decades, and their hotline (703-698-7752) provides extensive information on what's going on, traditionally speaking, in the Washington-Baltimore area.

Jazz and blues concerts can also be heard at **Wolf Trap Farm Park** in Vienna, Va. (703-255-1900), a national park for the performing arts; **Constitution Hall** (1776 D St., NW, 638-2661); and **Coolidge Auditorium** (in the Library of Congress, 707-5502).

Radio

WDCU/90.1 FM (282-7588). A 24-hour jazz station, affiliated with the University of the District of Columbia. Of special note: "The Blues Experience" with Steve Hoffman, Su nights.

WPFW/89.3 FM (783-3100). Jazz and public-affairs station. Some blues. Of special note: "The 'Bama Hour" with Jerry Washington, Sa midday; "Turner's Arena" with Nap Turner, W mornings.

Jazz and blues can also be heard occasionally on **WAMU/88.1 FM, WCXR/105.9 FM, WHFS/99.1 FM** and **WOL/1450 AM.**

Record Stores

Three good sources are **Olsson's Books and Records** (1200 F St., NW, 393-1853; 1307 19th St., NW, 785-2662, and other branches throughout the city); **Tower Records** (2000 Pennsylvania Ave., NW, 331-2400), and **Melody Records** (1623 Connecticut Ave., NW, 232-4002).

A tribute to Louis and friends graces a wall outside Chicago's New Regal Theater.

Chicago

The first jazz musicians from New Orleans began arriving in Chicago in 1915, and by the mid-1920's, the city was packed with both jazzmen and clubs. King Oliver, Freddie Keppard, Jelly Roll Morton, Lil Hardin, Alberta Hunter, Johnny Dodds, Baby Dodds, and Tom Brown (heading what was probably the first white band to come North) were among the first to arrive. Among the early clubs were Lamb's Café, the Royal Gardens, the De Luxe Café, the Lincoln Gardens, the Pekin, and the Vendome. The musicians were only one small part of a huge African-American migration North that began around World War I and was due primarily to the economic draw of the munitions, auto, and meat-packing industries.

Joe Oliver was the undisputed king of the early Chicago jazz scene, and there was much excitement when a young Louis Armstrong, who had played with Oliver in New Orleans, arrived at the Illinois Central railroad station on July 8, 1922, to join his mentor. Among those who flocked to see Oliver and Armstrong over the coming months were the city's young white musicians: Jimmy McPartland, Bud Freeman, Benny Goodman, Hoagy Carmichael, Eddie Condon, and Bix Beiderbecke. McPartland, Freeman, and others later formed the Austin High School Gang, which came to epitomize the hard-edged sound of "Chicago jazz."

Most of Chicago's early African-American population settled into a narrow corridor along South State Street between 16th and 39th streets. East 35th became the city's black entertainment district, and it was lined with posh theaters and black-and-tan clubs— the Sunset, the Apex, the Plantation. The time was the Roarin' Twenties, an era of drinking, dancing, and abandonment; and there were constant clashes between the gangsters, who controlled many of the clubs, and the police. On December 25, 1926, for example, two South Side establishments run by the mob were raided by 40 policemen who arrested 500 blacks and whites for doing an "immoral" dance called "the black bottom."

In 1928, with the opening of the splendid Savoy Ballroom, "black Broadway" shifted from 35th to 47th Street, and soon that street was lined with a whole new generation of theaters and clubs, including the Regal Theater, Gerri's Palm Tavern, and the Dreamland Café. Forty-seventh Street remained a center for black nightlife until well into the '50's, but during the Depression, many of the clubs were closed down by a reformist government, popular interest in jazz declined, and, as Milt Hinton put it, "Chicago just went down."[1] By the 1930's, the center of jazz had moved to New York.

During the '40's and '50's, bebop flourished both on Chicago's South Side and in the downtown. The corner of 63rd Street and Cottage Grove was a particularly important spot, and then there were the Gate of Horn, the Sutherland Show Lounge, and the Bee

Hive, where Charlie Parker played his last gig. In the mid-1960's, Chicago was again on the forefront of the music with the founding, by Muhal Richard Abrams, of the Association for the Advancement of Creative Musicians (AACM), an organization that has produced such cutting-edge artists as Roscoe Mitchell, Anthony Braxton, Henry Threadgill, and Ed Wilkerson.

Along with Chicago's earliest jazz musicians came its earliest blues musicians. By the time Lester Melrose began recording for RCA Victor and Columbia in the mid-1930's, the city was bursting with blues talent. Big Bill Broonzy, Tampa Red, Arthur "Big Boy" Crudup, John Lee "Sonny Boy" Williamson, Big Maceo, Memphis Minnie, and Lonnie Johnson were only a few of the many names that Melrose handled between 1934 and '51.

In the beginning, the Chicago blues had a simple, rhythmic country sound, but by the late '30's and '40's, things were taking on a distinct urban edge. There was a new intensity and excitement to the music, and a new sophisticated sound, most notably heard in the addition of the electric guitar, which first came to widespread attention through "Louisiana Blues," a hit recorded by Muddy Waters in 1950.

Early bluesmen arriving in Chicago usually headed for Maxwell Street (see "Landmarks and Legends," page 220), where they would meet other musicians and learn about Chicago's blues clubs, most of which were located on the South Side or along Lake and Madison streets on the West Side. Some of the best-known of these early clubs were Gatewood's Tavern, the Square Deal Club, and the 708 Club.

The Chicago blues scene reached its peak in the post–World War II years. All the top talent was living here then: Muddy Waters, Howlin' Wolf, Bo Diddley, Willie Dixon, James Cotton, and Sunnyland Slim; and Chess Records was recording prodigiously. It took a long time for the mainstream community to catch on, however, and as late as the early 1970's, it was still possible to hear such masters as Howlin' Wolf or James Cotton perform in a South or West Side club for as little as $2.

Sources

The best source is *The Reader* (828-0350), a free weekly, which lists hundreds of clubs all over the city. For blues, *The Original Chicago Blues Annual* ($, Straight Ahead International, 1133 N. Damen Ave., Chicago 60622; 342-0390) is an excellent guide, containing dozens of listings, along with information on the players. It is available at the Chicago Tourism Center and various bookstores, along with *Blues World Digest*, a free paper with listings, put out by the same company. The Friday and Sunday sections of the *Chicago Tribune* (222-3232) and the *Chicago Sun-Times* (321-3000) also contain listings.

The Jazz Institute of Chicago runs a hotline at 427-3300.

For maps and other information, contact the Chicago Tourism Council's Visitor Information Center at 78 E. Washington St. (also home of the Chicago Cultural Center) or 163 Pearson St., near the historic Water Tower, 744-2400.

The area code for Chicago is (312).

A Note on Neighborhoods

Chicago, city of ethnic neighborhoods, is spread along 29 miles of gray-blue Lake Michigan shoreline. The downtown centers on the Loop, Chicago's historic business district, which is still encircled by the tracks of the elevated train, the El.

Lincoln Avenue, on the North Side, is the current center for nightlife and it's always packed, especially on weekends, when finding a parking space is a problem. Rush Street is a somewhat older entertainment district, also on the North Side. The South and West Sides are the city's oldest African-American communities.

Because Chicago is so spread out, getting from one end to another can take time, despite the city's efficient system of encircling highways. Finding parking downtown, except in expensive lots, is often difficult.

Landmarks and Legends

F O R   J A Z Z

SOUTH SIDE

(The following route starts at E. 14th Street and proceeds south. A car is necessary.)

Coliseum, *E. 14th St. and S. Wabash Ave. (now an empty lot).*

The Coliseum was the site of the first jazz concert ever, organized by Okeh Records on February 27, 1926, for a crowd of several thousand. "Okeh Race Records Artists Night" the advertisements read, and the event brought together an amazing roster of talent: Clarence Williams, Louis Armstrong, Sara Martin, Chippie Hill, Blanche Calloway, Sippie Wallace, Bennie Moten. Later that same year, on June 12, Okeh sponsored a second concert, this one an immense "battle of the bands" led by such notables as King Oliver, Louis Armstrong, Al Wynn, and Erskine Tate.

Sunset Café/Grand Terrace Ballroom, *315–17 E. 35th St. at S. Calumet Ave.*

Now a hardware store, the Sunset Café, opened in 1921 under the control of Al Capone, was once one of the most popular black-and-tan clubs in Chicago. Louis Armstrong and Earl Hines were members of its house band, and Hines later became the club's musical director.

Open seven nights a week until 3:30 or 4 a.m., the Sunset was a major hangout for musicians, who would drop by after their gigs elsewhere were done. Benny Goodman would come with his clarinet in a sack, while Tommy Dorsey arrived with either a trumpet or a trombone, because he hadn't yet decided which one he wanted to play.

After the Sunset closed in 1937 it became the Grand Terrace, which had previously been located on the second floor of 3955 S. Parkway Blvd. (now Martin Luther King, Jr., Dr.—look for mock columns on the second floor). The Grand Terrace was also controlled by Al Capone, who would come into the club with his henchmen, order all the doors closed, and have the band play his requests. Everyone at the Grand Terrace, including the waiters, carried guns, and Earl Hines recalled a time when one gangster, shouting "the heat's on," tossed a package containing $12,000 into his lap and ran out the door. Hines, knowing that he would have to return the money eventually, hid it and was rewarded with $500 for his trouble.

When Count Basie first started playing at the Terrace, he was, according to record producer–music critic John Hammond, just awful. The ballroom, with its elaborate floor shows, demanded intricate musical arrangements, which Basie simply did not have at that time. Fletcher Henderson, in one of the more generous moves in music history, saved Basie's skin by allowing him to use half of his own arrangements.

Lil Hardin's home, *421 E. 44th St.*

Lil Hardin, a piano player and Louis Armstrong's second wife, had a decisive influence on her husband's career. Without her help and encouragement, Armstrong, then a shy and unassertive young man, might never have gone beyond playing second cornet in King Oliver's band. It was Lil who prodded Louis into leaving Oliver, and Lil who encouraged him to go to New York.

Lil and Louis separated in 1931, and Lil remained in their home, this row house built of gray stone. She never remarried and, according to some, was in love with Louis all her life. She never took off the rings he had given her, and carefully preserved his old cornet, letters, and photographs.

Then, on August 27, 1971, in what must surely be one of the saddest ironies in jazz history, Lil suffered a massive heart attack while playing a memorial concert for Louis in Chicago. In the middle of her solo, she simply fell off the piano bench and died.

Gerri's Palm Tavern, *446 E. 47th St., 373-6292.*

Back in the days when everyone was playing the Regal (see New Regal Theater, page 213), they all stopped in at Gerri's after the show. Louis "Scotty" Piper, the mayor of 47th Street, would be there, along with fighter Joe Louis and all the jazz and blues stars. "This was their home away from home," says Gerri Oliver, who has owned the tavern since 1957. "They would all leave messages here for their wives. It was a focal point for the community."

The Palm was a very elegant affair. Waiters dressed in tuxes and there was a big grand piano and a polished dance floor. Today, the club is still open for drinking, record spinning, and occasional live jazz.

Sutherland Show Lounge, *Sutherland Hotel, E. 47th St., near Drexel.*

During the late 1950's and 1960's, the Sutherland, which had a huge bar stretching from one end of the hotel's lobby to the other, featured performances by such greats as Cannonball Adderley, Nancy Wilson, Rahsaan Roland Kirk, and John Coltrane. In 1960, Miles Davis played to a packed audience so entranced, it didn't even budge when a fire broke out in the next room. "The firemen were outside the door putting out this fire," says Jimmy Cobb in *Miles Davis: A Biography,* by Ian Carr, "and nobody left! Smoke was all in the joint and nobody left. . . . Yeah, Miles was very popular."

Golden Lily, *309 E. 55th St. (also called Garfield Blvd.).*

Now part of a store with iron grills across its front, the Golden Lily was once a second-floor Chinese restaurant known for its jazz.

In the early 1930's, the Louisiana Stompers, led by drummer Francois Mosely with sidemen Teddy Wilson, Albert Ammons, and Punch Miller, played a long residency here; and in 1941, Coleman Hawkins packed the place (then called White's Emporium) with his immortal rendering of "Body and Soul."

Today, the only reminder of the building's earlier days is the vaguely Oriental white-and-yellow-tile trim that runs just beneath the roof.

Roberts Hotel, *301 E. 63rd St.*

In 1959, comedian Dick Gregory called Roberts Show Club at 6222 South Parkway Blvd. (now MLK Drive) "the biggest Negro-owned nightclub in America." Owned by a former taxicab entrepreneur, Herman Roberts, who had turned his 55-cab garage into a social hall for his friends (shortly thereafter opening it to the public), it featured everyone from Dinah Washington to Count Basie.

Sammy Davis, Jr., appeared at the club for a five-day stint in the late '50's, and it was due to him that Roberts, tired of picking up the entertainer downtown, expanded into the hotel-motel business. The hotel is now abandoned, but the marquee is still there.

New Regal Theater, *1645 E. 79th St. (near Stony Island Ave.), 721-9301.*

The old now demolished Regal Theater, which once stood at 4719 South Parkway Blvd., was at one time both a center for black nightlife in Chicago and a magnificent sight to behold. A 1928 edifice built in Moorish style, it could seat 3,500 and was opulently decorated with balconies, chandeliers, and velvet drapes. In its earliest days, it hosted variety acts by performers such as Josephine Baker, Buck and Bubbles, and the Mills Brothers; in the 1930's and '40's, it featured big bands and orchestras led by everyone from Duke Ellington to Woody Herman. Dinah Washington won an amateur contest there when she was 15, and in the 1950's and '60's, Miles Davis, Dizzy Gillespie, Wilson Pickett, and James Brown were featured entertainers. B. B. King's landmark album, *Live at the Regal,* was recorded at the theater.

The New Regal, which opened in 1987, has no real connection to the old. Nonetheless, its architecture is also opulent and Moorish, echoing its famous predecessor, and it features occasional jazz concerts by the likes of Bobby McFerrin. A splendid jazz mural covers one wall of a nearby parking lot.

WEST SIDE

Austin High School, *231 N. Pine Ave.*

In 1921, a group of young white students would stop in after school at a place called the Spoon and Straw for ice cream and soda. The parlor was equipped with a Victrola and the teenagers would sit around listening to records. One day, there were some new Gennett records on the table. . . .

"They were by the New Orleans Rhythm Kings," says trumpet player Jimmy McPartland in *Hear Me Talkin' to Ya*, edited by Nat Shapiro and Nat Hentoff, "and I believe the first tune we played was 'Farewell Blues.' Boy, when we heard that—I'll tell you we went out of our minds. Everybody flipped. . . .

"We stayed there from about three in the afternoon until eight at night, just listening to those records one after another, over and over again. Right then and there we decided we would get a band and try to play like these guys."

That was the beginning of the famous Austin High School Gang, who came to epitomize the Chicago sound during the 1920's. Benny Goodman, Eddie Condon, Dave Tough, and others were also later affiliated with the group.

Today, Austin, a big yellow building still operating as a high school, is located in a rough, run-down section of town.

IN OR NEAR DOWNTOWN

Congress Hotel, *520 S. Michigan Ave.*
In 1927, a young man named Francis "Cork" O'Keefe booked the Fletcher Henderson band into the prestigious Congress Hotel, much to the fury of the city's white musicians' union, which refused to accept the contract. An all-black band at a major hotel was still unheard of at that time. O'Keefe then threatened to take the contract to the black local, forcing the white local's hand, and that August, Henderson played an extended, and very successful, engagement.

The Congress, a magnificent hotel still in operation, witnessed a second racial breakthrough in 1935, when an interracial trio, led by Benny Goodman and including Gene Krupa and Teddy Wilson, played in a large commercial venue for the first time. The performance, sponsored by the Hot Club of Chicago, took place in the Urban Room at the corner of Michigan Avenue and Congress Parkway (now a cocktail lounge), and was so successful that Goodman (no crusader for civil rights; he had used Wilson purely for musical reasons) hired Wilson as a regular member of his organization.

Jane Addams's Hull-House Museum, *800 S. Halsted St. at Polk, 413-5353.*
Jane Addams's settlement house once consisted of 13 buildings covering an entire city block. Immigrants then living in the area took classes here in sewing and cooking and theater, and some of the boys played in the settlement's Boys' Band. Among them were Benny Goodman, his brother Freddy Goodman, and Art Hodes.

"At Hull House we weren't playing jazz," Freddy Goodman says in *The World of Earl Hines.* "Most of the music was marches, small overtures, primer-type things. . . . The way we first heard jazz was when we'd be passing a ballroom. . . . We'd hear music. It would be real exciting, and we'd sneak in. . . . One time Benny just jumped up onstage, grabbed the guy's clarinet and started to play. He was a natural, that's all."

Today, only two of the original settlement buildings are left. Operated as a museum by the University of Illinois at Chicago, they are open for touring and often present special exhibits.
Open: M–F, 10 a.m.–4 p.m.; in summer, Su, noon–5 p.m. *Free admission.*

Clark and Randolph streets.

Art Hodes's Chicagoans named a tune after this intersection, where the Lamb's Café and the Sherman Hotel (housing both the College Inn and the Panther Room) were once located. Three other pieces, Woody Herman's "Herman at the Sherman," Duke Ellington's "Sherman Shuffle," and Fats Waller's "Pantin' in the Panther Room," came out of this corner as well.

The Lamb's Café was one of Chicago's earliest venues for jazz. Tom Brown's Ragtime Band, probably the first white jazz band to appear in Chicago, was playing here before 1920. Later, the café featured Jabbo Smith and Johnny Dodds.

The Apartment Lounge once played host to everyone from Sonny Stitt to Clark Terry.

Both the College Inn and the Panther Room were important in the 1930's and '40's. Paul Whiteman's band was resident in the College Inn in 1933, and most of the big bands of the day played the Panther Room (decorated for its namesake), along with smaller groups led by artists such as Bud Freeman and Hot Lips Page. A young Bix Beiderbecke, sneaking out of Lake Forest Military Academy in Chicago's suburbs, sometimes visited the place. Says friend and fellow musician Sid Stewart in *Bix: Man and Legend,* "We sat there for hours and just listened. We thought it was wonderful . . . and it quickly became clear to me that Bix was destined for a career in professional music. It was as inevitable as death."

Civic Opera House and Theater, *20 N. Wacker Dr., 346-0270.*

Built in 1929, the stunning Civic Opera House, which together with the Civic Theater takes up an entire city block, sometimes sponsors jazz concerts. In one especially historic 1946 event, Dizzy Gillespie, Sidney Bechet, Jimmy McPartland, Gene Sedric, and Bud Freeman all appeared together. The Chess brothers also rented space in the building in their early days, the results of which were their first recordings: "Union Man Blues" and "Bilbo's Dead" with vocalist Andrew Tibbs.

Club Alabam, *747 N. Rush St.*

The building has been completely remodeled into a trendy sandwich shop, but a symbol of another era remains: the dark maroon CLUB ALABAM sign which still broods above the building. Visible only from the Division Street side, the sign, juxtaposed with light, airy neon below, seems heavy and mournful.

The Club Alabam featured jazz in the 1920's; Eddie South's Alabamians played here in 1927.

Grant Park, *Soldier Field.*

It was near the Buckingham Fountain that Mezz Mezzrow and Frank Teschemacher once played late, late-night clarinet duets "in the style of Jimmy Noone and Doc Poston getting high on gauge and blowing until we were blue in the face." One night, a motorcycle cop approached and the twosome, already hounded elsewhere by the police, was sure it was the beginning of the end. Instead, the cop just nodded approvingly and motioned them to keep playing. "After that," writes Mezz Mezzrow in *Really the Blues,* ". . . night after night, Bud [Freeman], Dave [Tough], Tesch and as many others as could squeeze in my car would broom over to this hide-out in Grant Park and blow our tops under the twinklers, shooting riffs at the moon. . . ."

London House, *360 N. Michigan Ave.*

Now, rather ironically, housing a Burger King, this solid building was once the London House, an elegant dinner club that flourished in the 1950's and '60's. It was well known for its piano trios, and Oscar Peterson and George Shearing were regulars.

Oriental Theater, *20 W. Randolph St.*

Now home to an appliance store called Oriental Electronics, the Oriental was once a spectacular theater that featured all the big bands of the 1930's. Duke Ellington appeared here in 1930 and 1934, Earl Hines in 1939.

NORTH SIDE

Aragon Ballroom, *1100 W. Lawrence Ave., 561-9500.*

Once known as one of the best dance spots in town, the Aragon, still a beautiful and ornate if somewhat run-down building with a towering marquee, started presenting jazz in the mid-1920's. Wingy Manone and his band—including Art Hodes, Bud Freeman, Floyd O'Brien, and Gene Krupa—were the first jazz group to appear here, and during the swing era, performances of big bands were often broadcast live. Today, the Aragon is used for pop and rock concerts.

Webster Hotel, *W. Webster Ave. and N. Lincoln Park West.*

It was at the Webster Hotel, now a residential building located across the street from the Lincoln Park Zoo, that Jelly Roll Morton and his Red Hot Peppers recorded for Victor Records in 1926. Despite being almost universally disliked among jazzmen (for his arrogance, for his lack of humor), Jelly Roll was apparently an agreeable musician to record with. Says Johnny St. Cyr, one of his sidemen, in *Mister Jelly Roll* by Alan Lomax, "He'd never give you any of your specialties, he'd leave it to your own judgment. . . . [He] was always open to suggestions."

F O R   B L U E S

SOUTH SIDE

(The following route starts near 21st Street, proceeds south to 35th Street and then east to Lakeland Avenue, before returning west to Indiana Avenue. A car is necessary.)

Chess Records, *2120 S. Michigan Ave.*

Started by Phil and Leonard Chess, two young immigrant brothers from Poland, Chess Records recorded nearly all of the blues—and many of the jazz—musicians of note working the Midwest in the '50's and '60's. Among their most famous artists were Muddy Waters, Howlin' Wolf, Otis Rush, Bo Diddley, Willie Dixon, Little Walter, Chuck Berry, Gene Ammons, James Moody, Sonny Stitt, and Kenny Burrell.

For most of the company's existence it was located in this sturdy three-story building on Chicago's South Side, which has been designated a Chicago landmark. Willie Dixon's Blues Heaven Foundation bought the building in 1993, and plans to convert it into a combination education center, art gallery, museum, and retail store.

The Chess brothers actually started out as nightclub owners of a place called the Macomba (39th Street and Cottage Grove), where everyone from Louis Armstrong to Ella Fitzgerald once performed. They launched their first label, Aristocrat, in 1947, recording in the back of a street-level store, where they hung an open microphone in a tiny toilet to add echo. One of their first recording artists was Muddy Waters.

The brothers changed the name of their company to Chess in 1950, but it wasn't until 1955, when they released Chuck Berry's hit, "Maybellene," that they achieved any real success. They then bought a radio station called WVON ("Voice of the Negro").

Twice a year, Leonard Chess traveled down South, seeking new talent, and legend has it that he sometimes set up his tape recorder in a cotton field, running a long extension cord into the plantation house. Howlin' Wolf and Arthur "Big Boy" Crudup were "discovered" on two such trips; another visit resulted in the acquisition of Jackie Brenston's "Rocket 88" from Sam Phillips of Sun Records (see Sun Studio, page 45).

Leonard Chess died in 1969, and Phil left the company shortly thereafter. During their tenure, they were frequently criticized for a lack of sensitivity. Etta James, according to Arnold Shaw, writing in *Honkers and Shouters,* was particularly outspoken. "The Chess brothers didn't know A from Z in a beat," she told him. "Leonard Chess would get in the booth with me while I was recording and when I would get to a part where he thought I should squawl or scream 'wheeawow!' he'd punch me in the side."

Site of John Lee "Sonny Boy" Williamson's death, *S. Giles Ave. bet. 31st and 32nd streets.*

Somewhere on this block Sonny Boy Williamson was fatally stabbed on the morning of June 1, 1948. He had just left the Plantation Club on East 31st Street and was heading toward his home at 3226 South Giles Avenue (now torn down), when he was maliciously attacked, and his wallet, wristwatch, and harps were stolen. Bleeding from the head, he stumbled home to his wife, who, thinking he'd just been in a drunken brawl, didn't call the ambulance until 5 a.m. He was DOA at Michael Reese Hospital.

Smitty's Corner, *NW corner of 35th St. and Indiana Ave.*

Though now completely remodeled and part of a liquor store, Smitty's Corner was Muddy Waters's home base throughout the mid- and late 1950's. During those years, he left town only to do a regular Wednesday-night gig in Gary, Indiana.

All this changed in the fall of 1958, when, through an offer to tour with an English traditional jazz group led by Chris Barber, Muddy Waters became one of the first blues artists to break through to a white audience. Big Bill Broonzy, who was known for assisting younger artists, had helped pave the way by recommending Muddy for the job. (Broonzy had already made several trips to Europe himself, but by the late '50's he was in poor health).

Muddy Waters's home, *4339 S. Lake Park Ave.*

The small three-story building is still occupied, but there is plastic over its windows, and the screen door, which was once inscribed with Muddy's name, is gone. Muddy lived here during the '50's and '60's, until the death of his wife.

"This was the house of the blues in the fifties," says Muddy's son, Charles Morganfield, a quiet-spoken man who moved back to the house some time ago. "We got them all, down there in the basement—B.B., John Lee, Chuck Berry. I had to get out of bed one time to get Chuck Berry down to Chess just before he made 'Maybellene.'"

Muddy is buried in the Restvale Cemetery in Worth (117th St. and Laramie, just west of Cicero, 708-385-3506; open M–F, 8 a.m.–4 p.m., Sa, 8 a.m.–3 p.m.).

The Checkerboard on the South Side has become so well known that it now has security parking.

708 Club, *708 E. 47th St.*

Bo Diddley played his first major gig at this small storefront club (now an abandoned shop, protected by an iron gate). Though originally from Mississippi, Diddley spent his youth in Chicago, playing the streets for about 12 years before appearing at the 708.

The 708 Club was a favorite among bluesmen in the '40's and '50's because its bandstand was located behind the bar, giving the musicians some protection from the club's wild audience. The South Side back then, writes Mike Rowe in *Chicago Breakdown,* was renowned for its "Saturday night tavern brawls, Sunday morning visits to the Provident Hospital emergency room and Monday morning appearances in the Fifth District Police Court at 48th and Wabash, 'the busiest police station in the world.' "

Theresa's Tavern, *4801 S. Indiana Ave.*

Formerly located in the basement of this brown corner building, "T's Basement," run by Theresa Needham, was once a South Side institution. "World-renowned Theresa's Tavern has more charisma or atmosphere than any other club in Chicago," reported *Living Blues* in 1973.

Opened in 1949 and closed in 1983–4, Theresa's started offering live music in 1953, much against the instincts of its owner, who once said she hated music. Buddy Guy was associated with the club for seven years, and Little Junior Wells for 18. Others who played here included Little Walter, James Cotton, Sunnyland Slim, and Otis Rush.

A "small, dark and generally cheerful" place with no special lights for the band and no dance floor, Theresa's was one of the first South Side clubs to start attracting a white audience in the early 1960's (many were college students from the nearby University of Chicago). The place was also famous for giving away food to the needy on Sundays. Each customer got pig feet and pig ears, two slices of bread, and hot sauce.

WEST SIDE

Maxwell Street, *between S. Halsted and S. Morgan streets.*

During its heydey in the early to mid-1900's, Maxwell Street (or "Jew Town") on a Sunday afternoon was a mile-long extravaganza of a bazaar filled with peddlers, pushcarts, and wooden stalls selling everything from spices and vegetables to clothes and appliances. Also to be seen everywhere, trying to attract passersby with their wares, were Gypsy fortune-tellers, dope dealers, and blues musicians.

For a newly arrived blues singer in Chicago, Maxwell Street was the primary meeting ground. Hound Dog Taylor played here, and so did Little Walter, Big Walter Horton, Honeyboy Edwards, Big Bill Broonzy, Floyd Jones, and Snooky Pryor. As Hound Dog Taylor tells Ira Berkow, author of *Maxwell Street,* "You used to get out on Maxwell Street on a Sunday morning and pick you out a good spot, babe. Dammit, we'd make more money than I ever looked at. Sometimes a hundred dollars, a hundred twenty dollars. Put you out a tub, you know, and put a pasteboard in there, like a newspaper? . . . When somebody throw a quarter or a nickel in there, can't nobody hear it. Otherwise, somebody come by, take the tub and cut out. . . ."[2]

Today, two blocks of Maxwell Street, between Halsted and Morgan, still function as a flea market on Sunday afternoons, and, during the summer months, the Maxwell Blues Band plays. The area is constantly being threatened with urban development, however, and there's no telling how much longer it will stand.

1815 Club, *1815 W. Roosevelt Rd.*

Once home base for Howlin' Wolf, and owned by his saxman Eddie Shaw, the 1815 was a regular gig for innumerable West Side bluesmen, including Magic Sam and Otis Rush. Shaw, who had sold the place in the 1970's, bought it again in the early 1990's, hoping to resurrect his old club. Alas, the project did not take off and the building stands abandoned once more.

Before the 1815 was the 1815, it was the Club Apex, where the owner was killed in 1970 while trying to stop a knife fight between two women on the dance floor.

IN THE SUBURBS

Howlin' Wolf's grave, *Oakridge Cemetery, Roosevelt Rd. and Oakridge Ave., Hillside (30 min. W of downtown), 708-344-5600.*

In the early 1970's, Chester Burnett, then in his sixties, suffered a series of heart attacks. Then, in 1973, he was in an automobile accident that resulted in severe kidney injury. Still, he continued to play in public, even though he could "no longer make his trademark entrance: crawling on all fours with a wolflike gleam in his eyes."[3] He died on January 10, 1976, and is buried beneath an impressive gravestone, engraved with flowers and an electric guitar.

Open: M–Sa, 9 a.m.–4 p.m.; Su, 10 a.m.–4 p.m.

Clubs, etc.

Chicago has one premier room that brings in out-of-town jazz talent, the **Jazz Showcase,** and numerous other clubs that feature top-caliber area musicians. **Andy's** is a particularly good place to hear traditional and mainstream jazz, the **Get Me High** is a haven for bebop, and **Hothouse** and the **AACM's** headquarters (see "Other Venues," page 235) are top spots for progressive jazz. The **Green Mill** features both bebop and progressive, and **The Bulls** and **Bop Shop** offer a little bit of many things. One of the city's most unique offerings is the fine late-afternoon jazz that can be found at **Andy's.**

Blues in Chicago is thriving. Its center has moved from the South Side to the North Side, and Lincoln Avenue especially is lined with one club after another, all offering music most nights. On the weekends, it's best to avoid the most famous clubs, **B.L.U.E.S.** and **Kingston Mines,** and head for lesser-knowns such as **Rosa's** and **Lilly's,** which also offer first-rate talent.

Although the blues joints on the South and West sides are not nearly as active as they once were, many still feature live entertainment at least once a week. Often the music, technically speaking, is not as good as that on the North Side (the top musicians are hired by the better-paying clubs), but the clubs' atmosphere—enthusiastic, friendly, and real in a way that a commercial place can never be—more than makes up for it.

Numerous top-caliber jazz and blues musicians play around Chicago today, and to select even a representative sampling is difficult, to say the least. Some of the top jazz musicians who appear most regularly, however, are veteran saxophonists Franz Jackson and Von Freeman, bassist Truck Parham, the Brad Goode Quintet, pianist Jodie Christian, violinist Johnny Frigo, bassist-multi-instrumentalist Malachi Favors, the Mike Smith–Ron Friedman Quintet, the Ed Peterson Quintet (sometimes with Fareed Haque), Mike Finnerty & the Heat Merchants, the Jeff Newell Quartet, the Kimberly Gordon Trio, the Rob Parton Quartet, the Barrett Deems Big Band, and the Big Band of Chicago.

Among the many blues musicians with which Chicago abounds are Sunnyland Slim, Koko Taylor, Buddy Guy, Junior Wells, Billy Branch, Joanna Connor, Jimmy Walker, Magic Slim & the Teardrops, Son Seals, Johnny B. Moore, Johnny Laws, Sugar Blue, and Willie Kent & the Gents.

Generally speaking, clubs have either 2 a.m. or 4 a.m. licenses.

Personal Choices

Best national jazz: *Jazz Showcase*
Best local jazz: *Andy's, Bop Shop*
Best progressive jazz: *Hothouse, Velvet Lounge*
Best North Side blues club: *B.L.U.E.S.*
Best historic club: *Green Mill*
Best South Side clubs: *New Checkerboard, Lee's Unleaded Blues, Brady's Lounge, Cuddle Inn*

FOR JAZZ

IN OR NEAR DOWNTOWN

Jazz Showcase, *Blackstone Hotel, 636 S. Michigan Ave., 427-4846.*
Joe Segal's Jazz Showcase, located in the august old Blackstone Hotel (on the National Register of Historic Places), is one of the

best clubs in the city and in the nation. Segal, who has been producing jazz concerts since 1947, has worked with all the greats (Max Roach, Dizzy Gillespie, Ira Sullivan, Dexter Gordon, Yusef Lateef, Sun Ra, the Art Ensemble of Chicago) and he emphasizes much mainstream and straight-ahead.

Segal put on his first jazz sessions when he was still in college, studying at Roosevelt University on the G.I. Bill. Those sessions, which took place in a student lounge, continued for 10 years, and Segal never did graduate. In 1957, he moved the sessions—which he had dubbed the Jazz Showcase, based on his initials—to the Gate of Horn folk club, and in 1960, to the Sutherland Show Lounge on the South Side (see "Landmarks and Legends," page 212). Later, the Showcase moved again and again, to such now-legendary spots as the Plugged Nickel, the Hungry Eye, and the Happy Medium, before settling down at the Blackstone in 1980.

Today's Showcase is both an acoustic and a visual gem, almost wedding cake–like in appearance, with lavender-blue walls, white moldings, and little green candles. Huge pictures of jazz musicians line the walls, and many of the tables are set up for couples, with both seats facing straight ahead. Sight lines are excellent.

The Showcase was the first jazz club in the country to institute a no smoking policy, and it's one of the few that actively welcomes children (Su matinees only; those under 12 admitted free).

Music: Tu–Su, Su matinee. *Closed:* Jan.–Feb. *Cover:* $$–$$$. CC. Reservations recommended.

Andy's, *11 E. Hubbard St., 642-6805.*

Back in 1978, Andy's started what has since become a Chicago tradition, "Jazz at Five." Every afternoon after work, middle-aged businessmen and young professionals traipse down to this large old room, once frequented by newspaper pressmen, to relax with a drink and some of the finest traditional jazz and bebop around. Regulars include Von Freeman, Mike Smith, and Barrett Deems, who once played with Louis Armstrong.

Andy's is filled with lots of heavy wood, old-fashioned hanging lamps, silhouetted pictures of jazzmen, and revolving fans. An enormous rectangular bar is situated near the front of the club, while small tables, set with red plastic tablecloths and flickering candles, are placed near the back. Andy's also features a "Jazz at Noon" series for the lunchtime crowd, and more jazz in the evenings after 8:30 p.m..

Music: M–Sa. *Cover:* $. *Food:* American. CC.

Cotton Club, *1710 S. Michigan Ave., 341-9787.*

The premier African-American club and disco in town, the Cotton Club—large, modern, and elegant—features jazz in the front room, and dancing in the back. An Art Deco–esque skyscraper adorns the facade, while inside, the decor is all black and white, exposed brick, and chrome.

Most of the jazz talent that appears here is high-caliber, and national talent like Stanley Turrentine, Pieces of a Dream, and Charlie Byrd comes through about once a month. The house band, Jazz Friends, leads a jam session weekly.

Music: W–M. *Cover:* $–$$, except for big acts (includes both rooms). Jackets required. Valet parking available. CC.

Jazz Oasis, *343 W. Erie, 787-7788.*

A candlelit restaurant with a large horseshoe-shaped bar in the middle, maroon-and-black booths along the sides, and a stage up front, the Jazz Oasis features much local and occasionally national talent. Some of the regulars who perform here include Ghalib Ghallab, Carmen Stokes, and Ray Silkman. Along the walls hang original paintings of jazz artists.

Music: Tu–Su. *Cover:* $–$$. *Food:* Cajun, Creole. CC.

Underground Wonder Bar, *10 E. Walton, 266-7761.*

A dark, candlelit basement club with black walls, pink ceilings, and a handful of tables (equipped with paper and crayons for creative adults), the Underground is owned by Lonie Walker, a jazz vocalist and piano player who has been performing in the Chicago area for over 15 years. Walker usually takes to the stage of her club about three nights a week, and she's often joined there by members of her kitchen and wait-staff; nearly everyone who works at the club is also an aspiring musician or actor. Other regulars include Elaine Hamilton and Peven Everett, and fans of the club buy memberships that allow them to get in for free.

Music: nightly. *Cover:* $. *Food:* homemade Mexican, pizza, etc.

Moosehead Bar & Grill, *240 E. Ontario, 649-9113.*

Filled with absolutely everything—stuffed animal heads, model ships, vintage posters, photos of Mayor Daley, a hooked-rug portrait of JFK, boxing gloves, an old-fashioned sleigh—the Moosehead also has jazz. Regulars include Milt Trenier, who usually appears (on a busman's holiday from his own club, see page 225) with a guest, and vocalist Catherine Whitney.

Music: Th–Sa. *No cover. Food:* American. CC.

At the Tracks, *325 N. Jefferson St., 332-1124.*

An eclectic place on the edge of town near the railroad tracks (watch for the green-windowed double-decker commuter trains that pass in the distance), At the Tracks is a big building made of yellow brick. A revolving sculpture hangs from its facade, while inside is a stairwell shaped like a big blue cube.

At the Tracks presents music of all types—jazz, R&B, alternative, world, rock. Latin jazz is often featured on Mondays, and a poetry-jazz series on Thursdays.

Music: M–Sa, some jazz. *Cover:* $. *Food:* sandwiches, etc. CC.

Gold Star Sardine Bar, *680 N. Lake Shore Dr., 664-4215.*

So tiny and perfect that it seems like a sleek dollhouse, the Sardine Bar, located in a posh office–residential building near the lake, is part-owned by Bobby Short, who has let all his friends play here: Tony Bennett, Frank Sinatra, Stan Getz, and even (it's hard to believe they got them all in) the Woody Herman band. The Sardine, which the *New York Times* has called the best cabaret in America, is mostly done up in black and white with mirrors and booths. One surprising note: the food in this sophisticated place, catering to 30- to 50-year-olds, is White Castle hamburgers, served with linen tablecloths.

Music: nightly. *No cover.* CC. No reservations.

Milt Trenier's Lounge, *610 N. Fairbanks Ct., 266-6226.*

Nearly every major Las Vegas performer of note has appeared at Milt Trenier's, a Chicago institution since 1977. Located in the basement of the plush Schatz Building (look for the trompe l'oeil out front), the low-ceilinged club is small and draped in blue satin, with a tiny dance floor, a revolving disco globe, and a low ceiling. Milt Trenier himself, "the entertainers' entertainer," usually performs weekends, and due to the plethora of hotels nearby, the place is usually 85 percent tourists, most over 40.

Music: Tu–Sa. *Cover/minimum:* $–$$. CC. Reservations recommended.

Dick's Last Resort, *435 E. Illinois St. (North Pier), 836-7870.*

One of a chain, Dick's is large, loud, and obnoxious: "No cover; no dress code; no class" is its motto. Still, the club features some of the best Dixieland and traditional music in town, and it's worth a visit if you can stand the frat-house chatter. Regulars include Jim Beebe's Chicago Jazz, Jim Clark's Jazz People, and Dave Remington's Dixie Devils.

Music: nightly. *No cover. Food:* catfish, ribs, shrimp, etc.

Also

Cricket's in the Tremont Hotel (100 E. Chestnut, 280-2100) hosts some fine Chicago musicians in the late afternoons and evenings. The **Hana Lounge** in the Hotel Nikko Chicago (320 N. Dearborn, 744-1900) also has jazz late afternoons and evenings. **River West** (see "For Blues," page 232) features a jazz big band weekly.

NORTH SIDE

Green Mill, *4802 N. Broadway, 878-5552.*

The Green Mill is the oldest nightclub in Chicago, dating back to 1907. Once owned by Machine Gun Jack McGurn (one of Al Capone's henchmen, and the leader of the St. Valentine's Day massacre), it was home to singer Joe E. Louis for years. Then Louis, getting a better job offer, left the place. McGurn, outraged, had the singer's vocal chords slashed, and left him for dead. Louis survived, however, and went on to become a successful comedian.

At one time the Green Mill was a big complex, occupying nearly an entire city block. There were gardens, gazebos, a dance hall out back, and a green windmill (hence the name) up top. All the major swing bands played here, and then there were Billie Holiday, Anita O'Day, Jack Teagarden, and Claude Thornhill. The legendary Texas Guinan was once the Green Mill's hostess. The movie *Thief,* with James Caan, was filmed here, and Hey Hey Humphrey, a great drummer down on his luck, froze to death in the club's basement.

Today, the Green Mill still feels like a creaky old-time speakeasy. The booths are covered with the original itchy horsehair and there are huge murky paintings on the walls. The jazz is topdrawer and it ranges in sound from the progressive Edward Petersen Quintet (sometimes with Fareed Haque) to the Big Band of Chicago. National talent is occasionally featured as well, and Miss Eve, a piano player who's been with the place since 1941, plays the cocktail hour. An "Uptown Poetry Slam," in which poets are either hissed at or applauded, is held on Sunday nights.
Music: nightly. *Cover:* $.

Hothouse, *1565 Milwaukee (NW of Loop), 235-2334.*
The place in the city for the progressive arts, Hothouse presents many post-1960's jazz artists such as David Murray, Roscoe

The Aragon Ballroom was once one of the best swing dance spots in town.

Mitchell, and Trevor Watts. African, Caribbean, European, and other international music traditions also play a large role, and the weekends are usually devoted to dance music. Poetry events frequently take place here as well.

Housed in a converted storefront, Hothouse is a small, warm, and casual place with terra cotta–colored walls, a mural swirling with jazz musicians, a large stage, and tables equipped with "antique" tablecloths. Because of the club's booking policy, it attracts a large international clientele.

Music/events: nightly, much jazz. *Cover:* $–$$.

Bop Shop, *1807 W. Division St. (NW of Loop), 235-3232.*

An eclectic hodgepodge of a club housed in what was once the old Schlitz brewery, the Bop Shop features much jazz, along with some poetry (one night a week) and rock-and-roll (usually during the day on weekends). The Jeff Newell Quartet, the Kimberly Gordon Trio, and the Von Freeman Quartet play here, and on Tuesdays, there's usually an open jazz jam that draws many musicians from DePaul, Northwestern, and other universities. Top-draw acts such as Anita O'Day are also brought in from time to time.

In the Bop Shop's front room is a small stage and bar; out back is an art gallery with a bigger stage; next door are No Palace and Leo's, two other venues where food and music are also served up. On any given night, four or five bands can be heard at the complex.

Music: nightly. *Cover:* $–$$. *Food:* sandwiches, etc.

Get Me High Lounge, *1758 N. Honore St., 252-4090.*

A local haven for bebop, the Get Me High is a tiny, laid-back hole-in-the-wall whose black walls are covered with chalked graffiti. "Willow weeps for no one," reads one quip; "Make money, not love," reads another.

Jimmy Carter once called the Get Me High his favorite jazz club (his son was going to Northwestern at the time), and some fine bebop players perform here. Among the regulars are Mike Finnerty and Jim Christopher. Big-name talent also stops by on occasion.

The club is so small (it accommodates only about 25), that to get to the restrooms, you have to climb up onto the high stage and go past the musicians. No one seems to mind.

Music: nightly. *Cover:* $.

The Bulls, *1916 N. Lincoln Park West, 337-3000.*

At over a quarter-century old, the friendly Bulls is one of the oldest music clubs in Chicago. In the '60's, it was known for folk and rock-and-roll; today it features mostly contemporary with some traditional and R&B thrown in for good measure. Bill McFarland & the Chicago Horns usually play on Monday nights.

Located in the basement of an apartment building, the Bulls looks like a mock Spanish cave. Its low ceiling is covered with

swirling plaster, and behind the stage is a mural depicting the skyline of Chicago. Old brass instruments are hung on the walls.
Music: W–M. *Cover:* \$–\$\$. *Food:* pizzas, snacks. CC.

Pops for Champagne, *2934 N. Sheffield Ave., 472-1000.*

Reminiscent of an English gentleman's club, with lots of heavy wood and dark-toned paintings, Pops presents many well-known Chicago-based musicians, including Franz Jackson, Von Freeman, and John Young. The club's real specialty, however, is its champagne; 150 varieties are available by the bottle, 12 by the glass. A jazz brunch is served on Sundays, and out back there's a garden that is open from spring to late fall.
Music: nightly. *Cover/minimum:* \$–\$\$. *Food:* appetizers, desserts. CC.

Also

The Big Band of Chicago plays once a week at the **Deja Vu Bar Room** (2624 N. Lincoln, 871-0205), a large and high-ceilinged place that also presents other jazz groups such as the Jeff Newell Quartet or saxophonist Lin Halliday.

A number of restaurants feature jazz, including **Tania's** (2659 N. Milwaukee, 235-7120), a two-story Cuban-Mexican-Spanish eatery that has much Latin jazz; and **Java Jive** (4242 W. Irving Park, 545-6200), a "minimalist" coffeehouse-café serving up homemade foods, much Brazilian jazz, and a Sunday jazz brunch (often with flautist Denuzio Lima). The **Elbo Room** (2871 N. Lincoln, 549-7700), a club with much alternative music, presents the Barrett Deems Big Band once a week.

SOUTH SIDE

New Apartment Lounge, *504 E. 75th St., 483-7728.*

Every Tuesday night for the past seven years, veteran saxman Von Freeman has been appearing at this small neighborhood club with its polished, sinuous bar, deep blue carpeting, and tiny colored lights. When out-of-town talent such as Etta Jones and Houston Person appear, the club's large backroom is also opened up.

Though now somewhat sleepy and low-key, the New Apartment has an impressive history. Sonny Stitt, Gene Ammons, Zoot Sims, Clark Terry, Sonny Criss, and Buddy Tate all played here at one time.
Music: Tu, some weekends. *Cover:* \$, except for out-of-town acts.

Velvet Lounge, *2128 S. Indiana Ave., 791-9050.*

You never know what you're in for at the Velvet, a cavernous old club with fading striped wallpaper, crooked paintings, and extra tables and chairs piled up in the corners. Sometimes the music, local young artists of all persuasions, is great, sometimes it isn't, but it's always interesting. On a typical night, a woman conga

player pounds away next to a singer who's making amazing gorilla sounds next to a sax player bent double over his instrument. The club is run by tenor saxophonist Fred Anderson.
Music: every other Sunday (watch *The Reader*). *No cover.*

Alexander's Steak House, *3010 E. 79th St. (at Exchange), 768-6555.*

A Chicago institution when it comes to steak and prime rib sandwiches, the 30-year-old Alexander's began featuring jazz about a year and a half ago. Thus far, the music only takes place once a week, usually compliments of Jazz Unites, with pianist John Young, bassist Eddie de Haas, tenor saxophonist Eddie Johnson, and others. The restaurant is a modern, upscale place with dining only in the main room, and jazz in the back, but it's possible to eat in the jazz room as well.
Music: Th. *Cover:* $. *Food:* steak, seafood. CC.

Also

Jazz can sometimes be heard at the historic **Gerri's Palm Tavern** (see "Landmarks and Legends," page 212) and at the **New Ritz Blue Room** (3949 S. King Dr., 924-8136).

SUBURBS

Fitzgerald's, *6615 W. Roosevelt Rd., Berwyn (30 min. W of downtown), 708-788-6670.*

An authentic roadhouse that dates back to 1917, Fitzgerald's is a large warm hall with maplewood floors, cypress-wood paneling, and excellent sight lines. An eclectic mix of music is presented, and the acts are often big names—Koko Taylor, the Kinsey Report, the Count Basie Band. The local Jazz Members Big Band also plays here regularly.

Before Fitzgerald's was Fitzgerald's, it was the Deer Lodge and the Hunt Club, where Lil Hardin Armstrong once played. Al Capone ran the place during Prohibition; parts of the movie *The Color of Money,* with Paul Newman, were filmed here.
Music: T–Su. *Cover:* $–$$.

FOR BLUES

NORTH SIDE AND DOWNTOWN

B.L.U.E.S., *2519 N. Halsted St., 528-1012.*

Probably the best-known blues club in Chicago, B.L.U.E.S. is small and dark, paneled with old black wood and strewn with Christmas-tree lights. All of the greats—Sunnyland Slim, Koko Taylor, Big Walter Horton, James Cotton, Pinetop Perkins—

have played on its tiny, rickety stage, which is only a few feet away from the audience.

B.L.U.E.S. was started up in 1979 by Bill Gilmore and Rob Hecko. Back then, their address wasn't quite so trendy and their crowd wasn't quite so big, but the music was the same.

Nowadays, B.L.U.E.S. has at least three or four different top-caliber acts every week. Especially wonderful are those nights when blues godfather Sunnyland Slim, now in his eighties, sits hunched over his piano, pounding the keys and smiling out at the crowd through deep-set eyes.

Music: nightly. *Cover:* $–$$.

B.L.U.E.S., Etc., *1124 W. Belmont Ave., 525-8989.*

Under the same ownership as B.L.U.E.S., B.L.U.E.S., Etc., located nearby but blessedly removed from the Lincoln Avenue madness, was built to handle the larger crowds that couldn't fit into the old place. Consequently, the artists here tend to have bigger names: Bo Diddley, Otis Rush, Magic Slim, Son Seals. Unfortunately, however, B.L.U.E.S., Etc., lit by an eerie blue light, is somewhat cold and lacking in atmosphere. Wednesday nights there's usually a blues jam.

Music: nightly. *Cover:* $–$$.

Kingston Mines, *2548 N. Halsted St., 477-4646.*

The other best-known blues club in Chicago, Kingston Mines is located just across and down the street from B.L.U.E.S. With two stages and a license that allows it to remain open until 4 a.m., it attracts a crowd that swells and shrinks and swells again as the night progresses. Despite the club's fame, it has a somewhat sleazy feel.

The 20-year-old Kingston has its own impressive list of names—Junior Wells, Son Seals, Otis Rush, Jimmy Johnson, Koko Taylor—and is housed in two 120-year-old buildings located right next door to each other. Music on the North Stage, as it is called, alternates with music on the South Stage, and the audience shifts accordingly, leaving room behind for people who wish to talk. A third room has also been recently added to accommodate overflow.

Lots of celebrities have stopped by the Kingston. Mick Jagger has been here four times, and other visitors include Chuck Berry, Gregg Allman, Eric Clapton, and Bob Dylan.

Music: nightly. *Cover:* $$. *Food:* pizza.

Rosa's, *3420 W. Armitage Ave., at Kimball, 342-0452.*

A blues bar run by Italians in an Hispanic neighborhood . . . hmm. At first, it's hard to know quite what to make of the concept, but as soon as owner Tony Manguillo starts to explain, things fall into place. It seems that when Tony was a teenager growing up in Italy, he got hooked on the blues. He went to every blues festival he could afford, and somewhere along the way, he met Junior Wells, who encouraged him to come to Chicago.

Soon thereafter, Manguillo, then in his twenties, arrived. "I felt like a Christian going to Jerusalem," he says. His first stop was the famous Theresa's on the South Side, and he liked it so much that he went back night after night for weeks.

Meanwhile, back in Italy, Mama Manguillo was getting worried. Finally she heard from her son. He had an extraordinary proposition: he wanted her to come to Chicago to help him open a blues bar. Then, Mama, who'd always wanted to come to America, did something even more extraordinary. She agreed.

Today, Rosa's—a spacious old club with wooden floors, a long bar, and a high stage—features blues nightly. Billy Branch, whom Tony met years ago at Theresa's, plays regularly, as do Buddy Scott, Otis Clay, and Sugar Blue. The club is a bit off the beaten track, making it a good place to hit on the weekend.
Music: nightly. *Cover:* $–$$.

Lilly's, *2513 N. Lincoln Ave., 525-2422.*

With uneven brick floors, arched doorways, hanging plants, and adjacent small rooms, Lilly's feels a bit like a sunny Spanish villa magically transported to chilly Chicago. Some fine blues acts—Jimmy Rogers, Johnny B. Moore, Johnny Laws—appear here, but alas, the very decor that makes the place so charming also makes it a difficult music venue. The acoustics are far from great and the sight lines can be poor, unless you're in the front room.
Music: Th–Sa. *Cover:* $.

Blue Chicago, *937 N. State St., (near the Loop), 642-6261.*

The only blues club located near the north side of downtown, Blue Chicago is the club of choice for out-of-towners without wheels staying at one of the many nearby high-rise hotels. A spacious, modern place with a triangular bar and large stage, Blue Chicago has featured everyone from Lonnie Brooks and Son Seals to Koko Taylor and Gloria Hardiman. The club makes a special effort to book female talent, and hosts a "Blues Women Weekend" annually.
Music: M–Sa. *Cover:* $.

Buddy Guy's Legends, *754 S. Wabash Ave., (South Loop), 427-0333.*

For years, Buddy Guy ran the tiny Checkerboard Lounge on the South Side (see New Checkerboard Lounge, page 232). A few years ago, however, he opened up this huge blue-and-white-tiled club that features a big open floor, a state-of-the-art sound system and a large-screen TV airing blues videos. There's even a special VIP section for famous guests.

Legends is about as far away from an old smoky blues bar as you can get, but that's the whole point. "We thought there was a

need for something big and modern," says one of the managers. A similar line of thinking has led the club to book a healthy mix of old legends and young, up-and-coming talent. Buddy Guy plays whenever he is in town, and sometimes there are acoustic and after-work blues sets in the early evenings.
Music: nightly. *Cover:* $–$$.

Brother Jimmy's BBQ, *2909 N. Sheffield, 528-0888.*

A large and friendly place that "looks like the inside of a barn," complete with high ceilings, a big skylight, unfinished wooden walls, and a concrete floor, Brother Jimmy's is primarily a southern barbecue joint that also presents blues. Eddie Clearwater, Magic Slim & the Teardrops, Jimmy Dawkins, and Big Time Sarah are among the musicians who've played here. The walls of the restaurant are covered with license plates and posters from North Carolina (among other things) because two of the owners went to Duke University, where they fell in love with barbecue and decided to bring it back home to Chicago.
Music: Th–Sa. *Cover:* $. *Food:* Southern barbecue.

River West, *1860 N. Elston, 276-4846.*

All kinds of music can be heard at River West, a club and bar "much like Cheers" that's filled with lots of wood, brass, and stained glass, including an eight-foot-square stained glass memorial to Elvis. Blues usually turn up about once a week or so, as does jazz (usually compliments of the Chicago Grandstand Big Band), and then there's reggae, rock, and a weekly acoustic open jam. Weekends are usually devoted to bigger acts, such as Mr. Blotto or Sugar Blue.
Music: nightly, some blues and jazz. *Cover:* $–$$.

Also

Blues can be heard at **Fitzgerald's** and some of the other jazz spots (see "For Jazz", page 229).

SOUTH AND WEST SIDES

New Checkerboard Lounge, *423 E. Muddy Waters Dr. (43rd St., South Side), 624-3240.*

The old Checkerboard Lounge, run by Buddy Guy, was once one of the hottest word-of-mouth joints on the South Side. Blue Mondays, when everyone from James Cotton to Carey Bell appeared, were especially popular.

Today, the New Checkerboard, under new management, is a much more commercial affair. A large room filled with long thin tables, it attracts a very lively crowd made up of blacks and whites, Americans and Europeans. Middle-aged couples in bright colors sit next to trendy Italians in designer chic sit next to college kids in

B.B. King and
Lucille appear in
concert.

Phillip Wong

blue jeans. Meanwhile, in a corner, near the bar, four poker-faced men, looking older than the century, play cards.

Regulars at the New Checkerboard include Johnny Laws and Magic Slim & the Teardrops.

Music: nightly. *Cover:* $. *Security parking available.*

Lee's Unleaded Blues, *7401 South Chicago Ave. (South Side), 493-3477.*

Once the legendary Queen Bee, where everyone from Junior Wells to James Cotton played, Lee's, now under different management, is still one of the best and most authentic blues bars on the South Side. A cozy, half exotic, half suburban place with red lights, mirrors, and red carpeting on the walls, it centers around a tiny stage and a polished serpentine bar. Buddy Scott plays here regularly.

Music: F–Su. *No cover.*

Cuddle Inn, *5317 S. Ashland (South Side), 778-1999.*

A neighborhood lounge with a carry-out liquor store and pool room in the front, the Cuddle Inn has been home to the soulful blues singer Johnny Laws for over seven years. According to a recent article in *Living Blues* (July–August 1993), Laws usually begins the evening by singing the blues of Howlin' Wolf, Muddy Waters, and others, but by the end of the night he puts down his

guitar and "stands in the middle of a throng of writhing dancers, singing, eyes closed as he digs deep into his music."
Music: F–Su. *Cover:* $.

Brady's Blues Lounge, *525 E. 47th St. (South Side), 536-6326.*
Friendly, nicely laid out, and all done up in blue, Brady's also features a carry-out liquor store up front, and a small lounge equipped with four booths and a bar out back. Some of the many musicians and bands who've played here include Roy Hightower, the Chicago Players, Willie Kent & the Gents, Vance Kelly, and Buddy Scott. In front, near the liquor store, is a video jukebox.
Music: Tu, Su. *Cover:* $.

Artis's, *1249 E. 87th St. (South Side), 734-0491.*
A bright and modern club equipped with a dance floor, a horseshoe-shaped bar big enough to accommodate three bartenders, and a crystal chandelier, Artis's frequently presents such blues acts as Billy Branch & the S.O.B.'s (Sons of Blues) or J. W. Williams & the Chi-Town Hustlers. The stage is situated in the center of the club, which accommodates about 150 people.
Music: Su–M. *Cover:* $.

Also

There are literally dozens of other South and West Side bars and clubs that offer blues periodically, some most weekends, some once a month. Among the more regular of these are **Mr. Tee's** (3500 W. Lake St., 638-2838), where Jumpin' Willie Cobbs often plays; the **Celebrity Lounge** (4830 S. Cottage, 538-4283), a large-ish club where the Checkmates play; the **Guess Who Lounge** (3800 W. Ohio St., 265-9831) where Jumpin' Willie Cobbs and Little Howlin' Wolf sometimes perform; and the **New Excuse Lounge** (5944 S. Halstead, 488-1189) and the **Tam Tam Lounge** (10914 S. Michigan, 928-1015), two clubs where L. V. Banks & His Swinging Blues Band can often be heard.

East of the Ryan (914 E. 79th St., 874-1500) is an upscale ballroom located in a hotel of the same name that often brings in large touring blues and R&B acts such as Bobby "Blue" Bland, Denise LaSalle, and Solomon Burke.

The *Chicago Blues Annual* (see "Sources," page 210) contains a more detailed listing, with addresses of close to 100 clubs.

Record Stores

At 3,000 square feet, the **Jazz Record Mart** (11 W. Grand Ave., 222-1467) owned by Bob Koester, founder of Delmark Records, is an amazing place. The "World's Largest Jazz and Blues Store," nearly one half of its floor space is still devoted to LP's, although there is also a sizable CD section. Koester also owns the

Collector's Record Mart (4243 N. Lincoln, 528-8835), housed in the old Delmark Records building, which carries only LP's. Both locations are much more than just stores; they're joints where musicians hang out, jazz and blues films are occasionally screened (at the Lincoln St. address), and artists hold autograph parties.

Two branches of **Rose Records** (214 S. Wabash Ave., 987-9044; 3259 N. Ashland, 880-0280) also have good jazz and blues selections, as does the branch of **Tower Records** on Clark Street (2301 N. Clark, 477-5994).

Other Venues and Special Events

The **Association for the Advancement of Creative Musicians** (7047 S. Crandon, 752-2212) presents three jazz concert series annually, featuring different faculty ensembles, at its School of Music and at other venues (museums, art galleries, etc.) around the city. The **AACM,** whose main focus is its educational center, where volunteer faculty teach area youth (about 75 each semester) in a tuition-free program, is also preparing for its thirtieth anniversary celebration. To take place in 1995, the fete will kick off with big-name concerts in Chicago, and then move on to perhaps five other cities in the United States and Europe.

In addition to the **Chicago Jazz Festival** and the **Chicago Blues Festival** (see "Major Festivals," page 403), two of the largest free jazz and blues festivals in the world, the **Annual Concerts in the Park Series** (294-2320) presents some free jazz and blues concerts during the summer. **"Weekend Jazz Parties"** are put on by the Jazz Showcase in the Blackstone Hotel (427-4300). These three-day affairs feature three nights of music, jazz videos, brunches, and more; hotel packages are available. The Jazz Institute of Chicago (427-1676) hosts an annual one-day **Jazz Fair,** also in the Blackstone, during which a variety of different bands play, and a sort of "jazz midway," selling records, T-shirts, etc., is set up.

Rosa's (342-0452) sponsors two unique (midnight–4 a.m.) **Blues Cruises** every summer. The **Maxwell Street Market** (Maxwell and Halsted streets) features street blues, weather permitting, Sundays, 8 a.m.–3:30 p.m.

Concert venues sometimes presenting jazz or blues include the **Erie Crown Theatre** (2301 S. Lake Shore Dr., 791-6190) and the **New Regal Theater** (1647 E. 79th St., 721-9301). For others, check the local papers.

Radio

WBEZ/91.5 FM (460-9150). NPR affiliate. Jazz weekday evenings, Sa and Su. Blues, Sa and Su early morning.

WNUR/89.3 FM (908-8649). Student-run station, affiliated with Northwestern University. Jazz weekday mornings, Su afternoons. Blues Su afternoon and evening.

WNIB/97.1 FM (633-9700). Blues weekdays, early morning.

WHPK/88.5 FM (702-1234). Affiliated with the University of Chicago. Jazz/blues some weekday evenings.

Some jazz and blues can also be heard on **WVON/1450 AM, WXRT/93.1 FM** and **WKKC/89.3 FM.**

Other Nearby Locations

DAVENPORT, IOWA

About three hours west of Chicago is the city of Davenport, Iowa, where Bix Beiderbecke was born. Davenport is situated on the banks of the Mississippi in the corner of the state, right next to Moline and Rock Island, Illinois, and Bettendorf, Iowa (the whole area is called the Quad Cities). Downtown Davenport was severely affected by the 1993 floods, but the other cities were more or less untouched, and none of the sites mentioned here were damaged.

In the 1920's, Davenport was the turnaround and mooring point for the Streckfus riverboats coming up from New Orleans. Louis Armstrong was a player on one of those boats, and for decades Bix Beiderbecke fans have speculated about whether or not the two horn players met at that time.

Bix is not the only musician associated with the Quad Cities. Louie Bellson, born in Rock Falls, Illinois, was raised in Moline, at number 2515 Fifth Ave., a solid, two-story home. Bellson, the son of a music store owner, won a national Gene Krupa contest while still in high school, and later played drums with the Benny Goodman, Tommy Dorsey, and Duke Ellington bands. He was married to the late jazz singer, Pearl Bailey.

Davenport has done more to honor its most famous son than most cities. Several memorials are located throughout the town, and the Davenport Public Library (Fourth and Main streets) has a small Beiderbecke exhibit that includes his piano. Live jazz and blues hasn't entirely left the area either. The **Rock Island Brewing Company** (1815 Second Ave., Rock Island, 309-793-1999) regularly books national blues acts, and jazz and blues can also be heard at **Hunters Club** in Rock Island (2107 Fourth Ave., 309-786-9880) and the **11th Street Precinct** in Davenport (2108 E. 11th St.; 319-322-9047).

Landmarks and Legends

Beiderbecke's home, *1934 Grand Ave.*

Leon "Bix" Beiderbecke was born in 1903 in this large white Victorian house set back from the road, and he went to school across the street at the Tyler Elementary School. He began playing the piano at about the age of 4 (a local paper called him a "boy music wonder"), and bought a cornet at 14, much to the consternation of his middle-class parents, who would never understand their son's attraction to jazz. On one dispiriting visit home, made years later when Beiderbecke was a renowned name in music circles, Bix found all the records he had proudly sent home to his parents in a closet, unopened.

Bix returned to his boyhood home periodically throughout his career, both to visit his family and to escape from an increasingly severe addiction to alcohol. It was during a 1924–25 visit that he wrote "Davenport Blues."

Bix Beiderbecke's grave, *Oakdale Memorial Park, 2501 Eastern Ave., 319-324-5121.*

Bix is buried in a large family plot in the cemetery where his brother worked up until the time of his own death at age 72. Near the gravesite is a garden dedicated to the musician. Once a small but lovely dancing figure playing a cornet stood here, but it was stolen several years ago.

Open: M–F, 8:30 a.m.–4:30 p.m.; Sa, 9 a.m.–noon.

Coliseum Ballroom, *1012 W. Fourth St.*

A wonderful red-brick building with a rounded roof facade and white highlights , the Coliseum dates back to the 1920's. Some of the biggest names in jazz and blues, from Louis Armstrong to Jimi Hendrix, have played there, and national touring artists continue to be booked through. The Bix Beiderbecke festival hosts events on its second floor every year.

Bix played the Coliseum on numerous occasions. He also appeared at Danceland, once located on the second story of 501 W. Fourth St. in downtown Davenport.

LeClaire Park, *Beiderbecke Drive (near the Mississippi River).*

Every year, during the last week of July, the four-day Bix Beiderbecke Festival is held in this charming, idyllic park by the riverside. A vintage bandshell stands at one end, next to a memorial honoring the cornet player. "He was a born genius, but they crowded him too much, with love," reads an inscription from Louis Armstrong.

The three-day Mississippi Valley Blues Festival with national and international talent is also held in the park every summer (see "Major Festivals," page 403).

Kan sas City, Missouri

Today, Kansas City may look like just another low-key middle-American city, but during the late '20's and '30's, K.C., known for its blues-based, riff-oriented sound, was at the top of the jazz world. A wide-open, 24-hour town controlled by gangsters, it attracted musicians from all over the Mid- and Southwest. More than 160 nightclubs, dance halls, and vaudeville houses rocked the city from dusk until dawn, with jam sessions, a Kansas City specialty, lasting for hours upon hours as musicians came and went.

"Jam sessions in Kansas City?" says piano player Sam Price in *Hear Me Talkin' to Ya.* "I remember once at the Subway Club, on Eighteenth Street, I came by a session at about ten o'clock and then went home to clean up and change my clothes. I came back a little after one o'clock and they were still playing the same song."

Count Basie, originally known as Bill Basie, from Red Bank, N.J., got his start in K.C. So did Mary Lou Williams, Lester Young, Andy Kirk, Jay McShann, Joe Turner, Jimmy Rushing, Bennie Moten, George Lee, Julia Lee, Ben Webster, and Charlie Parker.

Kansas City has a strong blues tradition as well, to be heard not only in its blues-influenced jazz but also in the early sounds of such singers as Lottie Beaman ("the Kansas City Butterball") and Laura Rucker. As the westernmost stop on the TOBA circuit (Theatre Owners Booking Association, a string of black vaudeville theaters across the country) the city was always filled with blues talent, groups disbanding and then reforming in the city's many vaudeville houses.

The man who unwittingly spurred all this activity was Tom Pendergast, a corrupt political boss who allowed mobster Johnny Lazia to control the city. Throughout the Depression, Prohibition and closing hours were virtually ignored in K.C., and everything imaginable went down.

One of Kansas City's earliest jazz bands was the Bennie Moten orchestra, first formed in 1921. By 1929, Moten's group had grown to 12 pieces, and by 1932, it had acquired numerous members of Walter Page's Blue Devils, based in Oklahoma City, including Bill Basie, Jimmy Rushing, Oran "Hot Lips" Page, Eddie Durham, and finally, Walter Page, himself.

Most of K.C.'s clubs were located in and around 18th and Vine Streets (see "Landmarks and Legends," page 240). Preeminent among them was the Reno Club (12th Street, near Cherry, no longer standing), a long narrow place that attracted both blacks and whites, but kept them apart with a divider running down the middle. Bill Basie and his nine-piece band began playing at the Reno in 1935, broadcasting live on an experimental shortwave radio station, whose announcer, calling Bill a rather ordinary name, gave Basie his nickname. The Reno was also the band's ticket out of obscurity: record producer/music critic John Hammond, hearing the Reno broadcast one early morning in a parking lot in Chicago, drove all the way to K.C. to witness the band live, and then convinced the Music Corporation of America to sign them up.

Other well-known K.C. bands were Andy Kirk and his Clouds of Joy, featuring pianist Mary Lou Williams, one of the first women to penetrate the male-dominated jazz world, and the Jay McShann Orchestra, whose best-known musician was Charlie Parker. Parker, who grew up in Kansas City, hung around all the local clubs, and it was at the Reno that the legendary incident involving Jo Jones, who threw a cymbal at the then-too-cocky 15-year-old, occurred.

In 1938, Tom Pendergast was indicted for income-tax evasion and sentenced to 15 months in Leavenworth. In the same year, a reform movement swept the city and nightclubs everywhere were shut down. Many musicians left K.C. An era had ended.

Sources

Listings can be found in *Pitch Weekly* (561-6061), a free news-paper, and the Friday edition of the *Kansas City Star* (234-4141). The *Kansas City Blues Society Newsletter,* which can be picked up at the Grand Emporium (see "Clubs, etc." page 249) is the best source for blues clubs listings. *Jam,* the free monthly publication of the Kansas City Jazz Ambassadors (913-967-6767), has good basic club information but no updated listings.

For recorded information, call the Jazz Hotline at 753-JASS, the JAMZ Jazz Brunch Line (more than just brunch) at 763-1052, and the Blues Hotline at 913-432-KCBS.

The Kansas City Visitor Information Center is located at 20 E. Fifth St., No. 4, 842-4386 or (800) 767-7700.

The area code for Kansas City is (816).

A Note on Neighborhoods

Kansas City, Missouri, not to be confused with Kansas City, Kansas, is bigger than it looks at first, with a downtown, located near the river, that then spreads south to Crown Center, midtown, and Country Club Plaza. Westport, located 10 minutes south of downtown, is a shopping district by day and a party district by night. On any given weekend, 15,000–18,000 revelers flood the four-block area, where 28 establishments have liquor licenses, many of them being allowed to serve until 3 a.m. Traditionally, Troost Avenue has been the dividing line between white and black Kansas City, and much of east K.C. is still predominantly black.

Driving in the city is a delight, as the traffic's usually light and free parking, plentiful.

Landmarks and Legends

18TH AND VINE HISTORIC DISTRICT

> Yes, I dreamed last night I was standing on the corner of Eighteenth and Vine,
>
> Yes, I dreamed last night I was standing on the corner of Eighteenth and Vine,
>
> I shook hands with Piney Brown and I could hardly keep from crying.
>
> *—Joe Turner, "Piney Brown Blues"*

The neighborhood centered on 18th and Vine streets was once the premier African-American district in Kansas City. Numerous affluent black businesses, including the Winston Holmes Music Company, the Peoples Finance Corporation, and the Williams Photo Studio, had offices here.

During the peak of the Pendergast era, 18th and Vine, encompassing just six blocks, was home to an astounding 50 jazz clubs. Among the best-known of these were the aforementioned Reno, the Sunset, the Subway, the Cherry Blossom, Lucille's Band Box, the Hey Hay Club, the Hi Hat, and the Hole in the Wall. Except

The ghosts of Basie, Joe Turner, and Bird still haunt the streets of 18th and Vine.

for a few core jazzmen hired by each club, musicians moved freely from joint to joint as the spirit moved them.

In addition to the Reno, one especially legendary club was the Sunset. Owned by a white man, Felix Payne, it was managed by a black man, Piney Brown, who was known throughout the city as the jazz musician's friend. The Subway also had a most unusual bartender, singer Joe Turner, who would turn the club's loudspeaker toward the main 12th Street–Highland Street intersection and begin to sing. His big blues voice attracted hundreds of patrons to the club.

Today, the 18th and Vine District is quiet and empty, yet the streets are clean and buildings that are left are in good shape. The 18th and Vine Planning Center (1501 E. 18th St., 421-5254) puts out an excellent free walking-tour map of the area that lists its historic sites. Each site is marked on the sidewalk with a small plaque, and those relating to jazz are listed below.

Count Basie residence, *1424½ E. 18th St.*
Basie lived at this address (no longer standing) for a short period after arriving in Kansas City in 1927. While here, he played the organ at the Eblon Theater (see page 243).

Subway Club, *1516 E. 18th St.*
The Subway Club, like the Sunset, was operated by Felix Payne and Piney Brown, and it was especially popular during the mid thirties, when it attracted more out-of-town jazzmen than any other K.C. club. Some of the many who were drawn to its all-night jam sessions were Benny Goodman, Gene Krupa, Chuck Berry, Coleman Hawkins, Roy Eldridge, and the Dorsey brothers.

Drummer Jesse Price performed a record feat at the Subway, now demolished, one morning. Challenged in a cutting contest by two drummers from out of town, he played 111 choruses of "Nagasaki." The solo went on for an incredible one hour and 15 minutes.

El Capitan Club, *1610 E. 18th St.*
Named after the Santa Fe passenger train, El Capitan was best known during the early 1940's. Charlie Parker, Dizzy Gillespie, and others passed through its doors.

Today, El Capitan still operates as a neighborhood bar and nightclub, with live music featured for special events about four times a year. It's a long, narrow, nice-looking place, with seating in the back and a long polished bar in the front.

Gem Theater, *1615 E. 18th St.*
A small, beautiful building with terra-cotta details from the past and jazz murals from the present, the Gem, originally called the Star, was opened by the Shriner Amusement Company in 1912. Back then, it had "the most modern heating, ventilating, and projection systems" in the area and featured many major

performers of the day. The theater is currently being refurbished and should be reopening soon. The original marquee still stands.

Bennie Moten residence, *1616 E. 18th St.*

In 1923, Bennie Moten and his orchestra made their first records, becoming only the third group in jazz history to do so. By 1929, Moten was known as "the most famous of the Kansas City bandleaders."

Nonetheless, times were often lean. In 1932, with the country in the midst of the Depression, the band, which by then included members of the Blue Devils band, traveled to Camden, N.J., for a long-awaited recording session. Recalls sideman Eddie Barefield: "We had to get to Camden to record, and along comes this little guy Archie with a raggedy old bus, and he took us there. He got us a rabbit and four loaves of bread, and we cooked rabbit stew right on a pool table. That kept us from starving, and then we went on to make the records."[1]

Moten once lived at this site; his home is no longer standing.

Highland Garden Theater, *701 E. 18th St.*

When it opened in 1922, the Highland was billed as "Kansas City's finest outdoor theater for colored people." In the late 1930's and early 1940's, it became the Boone theater, named after jazz pianist Blind Boone.

Lucille's Paradise Band Box, *1713 E. 18th St.*

One address in a long, narrow building with a balcony, just west of *The Kansas City Call* (an African-American newspaper, over 70 years old, at 1715 E. 18th), number 1713 was once a club owned by a woman named Miss Lucille. Charles "Crook" Goodwin's band did radio broadcasts from here, Moten's "Band Box Shuffle" was named after the place, and Buster Smith's band played the club for a while. Smith was by that time a veteran alto player, and at his side was a 17-year old neophyte, Charlie Parker.

"He used to call me his dad, and I called him my boy," Smith once said. "I couldn't get rid of him. He was always up under me. In my band, we'd split solos. If I took two, he'd take two; if I took three, he'd take three, and so forth. He always wanted me to take the first solo. I guess he thought he'd learn something that way. . . . But after a while, anything I could make on my horn, he could make, too—and make something better of it."[2]

Mutual Musicians Foundation, *1823 Highland Ave.,* *421-9297.*

A pink-and-white duplex with musical notes on its facade, the Mutual Musicians Foundation, now a National Historic Landmark, was the African-American musicians' union hall during the '30's and '40's, when Kansas City jazz was at its height. All the legends—Basie, Moten, Bird, McShann, George and Julia Lee, Andy Kirk, Mary Lou Williams—congregated here back then, and it was the first place where Charlie Parker and Dizzy Gillespie played together, when Dizzy came through town in 1940 with Cab Calloway.

"Yes, I introduced them. . . ." trumpet player Buddy Anderson says in Dizzy Gillespie's *To Be or Not to Bop,* "[Dizzy and I] were talking and Charlie showed up, just outta the clear, showed up with his horn. . . . Dizzy wanted to hear us play. So we went over to the Musicians Local, 627. We went upstairs to the piano and Dizzy sat down at the piano; he played. He wanted to hear me play trumpet and Charlie play saxophone. So we went through several numbers. . . . [Dizzy] really didn't dig Bird, or me either, at that time. But it was a fine meeting."

Local 627 disbanded in 1958, when the city's white and black musicians' unions merged to form one integrated entity. The Mutual Musicians Foundation lived on, however, as a private organization for the perpetuation of Kansas City jazz, and today, the building is still a hangout for local jazzmen, who come here to rehearse or pass the time of day. Downstairs, there's a small clubroom with a big white piano, lots of old pictures, and a simple bar. Upstairs, there's a big, well-lit rehearsal hall equipped with two pianos, one out in the open, the other in a closet. The one in the closet—old and worn and painted blue, with no ivory on the keys—is the piano that all the greats, from Joplin to Basie, once played.

Visitors are welcome at the Foundation on the weekends, when jam sessions are held in the clubroom (see "Clubs, etc.," page 247). If the place looks familiar, it's because parts of the film *The Last of the Blue Devils* were filmed here.

Eblon Theatre/Cherry Blossom, *1822 Vine St.*

Today just a facade standing exposed on all sides, the Eblon was once a movie theater where Count Basie, who traveled here from New Jersey with a vaudeville show, played accompaniment to silent films. Later, in 1933, the Eblon housed the Cherry Blossom, where what was probably the most famous cutting contest in all of jazz history took place on Dec. 18, 1933, between Coleman Hawkins, Ben Webster, Herschel Evans, and Lester Young.

Hawkins, then an established saxophonist playing with the Fletcher Henderson band, had heard about the prowess of the Kansas City saxmen in St. Louis and decided to stop by the Cherry Blossom to put them in their place. One half hour after his arrival, word of his presence had spread all over town, and sax players began arriving by the dozens, ready for a fight. By dawn, only Hawkins, Webster, Evans, and Young were left. Says Mary Lou Williams in *Hear Me Talkin' to Ya:*

> Around four a.m., I awoke to hear someone pecking on my screen. Opened the window on Ben Webster. He was saying, "Get up, pussycat, we're jamming and all the pianists are tired out now. . . ."

"Mac's" rocks with the blues every Friday and Saturday.

Lester's style was light and . . . it took him maybe five choruses to warm up. But then he would really blow, then you couldn't handle him at a cutting session.

That was how Hawkins got hung up. . . . When at last he gave up, he got straight in his car and drove to St. Louis. I heard he'd just bought a new Cadillac and that he burnt it out [getting there] . . . Yes, Hawkins was king until he met those crazy Kansas City tenor men.

Not only was the battle talked about by sidemen around country for weeks, but it also led to a change in jazz style. The heavy vibrato sound of Hawkins was now "out"; the lighter, more melodic sound of Young, "in."

Ol' Kentucky Barbeque, *1516–18 E. 19th St.*

A favorite hangout for young, aspiring musicians in the '30's, the Ol' Kentucky served a cheap menu (barbecue soup for 10 cents) and featured a piano and set of drums that patrons were invited to play. The Deans of Swing, a Lincoln High School dance band led by Lawrence 88 Keyes, often hung out here, as did Charlie Parker, who was a Lincoln High School student and a sometime member of the band. (Lincoln High School was known to have one of the Midwest's toughest and most respected music programs, directed by instructor Major N. Clark Smith.)

Later, the Ol' Kentucky—now closed—became Gates Ol' Kentuck (Gates is still a well-known name in K.C. barbecue) and then Dixie-Lan Bar-B-Cue, which was a favorite eating place of Doc Severinsen and his band whenever they were in town.

ELSEWHERE IN THE CITY

Kansas City Marriott Downtown 200 W. 12th St. (downtown), 421-6800.

The hotel's premier lounge, located on the main floor, right off the lobby, is a beautiful affair, with a huge mural around the tops of the walls depicting K.C.'s most famous jazz artists. Count Basie, Mary Lou Williams, Lester Young, and Charlie Parker—they're all here. The room, called the "12th Street Rag," was named after 12th Street, which it faces, and after the song of the same name written by Euday L. Bowman circa 1914.

Many of the hotel's meeting rooms are also named after K.C. jazzmen ("Yardbird Suite" seems particularly appropriate) and the sidewalk out front plays homage to the city's heritage, with stars embedded in the pavement honoring nine jazz artists.

Tom Pendergast's home, 200 W. 54th St. (20 min. from downtown).

Thomas J. Pendergast, the man who couldn't care less about jazz but nonetheless made it all happen, once lived in this large, attractive home on the north side of town. Pendergast, born in St. Joseph, Missouri, in 1872, started his Kansas City career working as a cashier in his brother's saloon; later, he was always in bed by 9 p.m. First elected to public office in 1896, he had a quick temper and a trademark derby that he wore cocked over one ear.

Charlie Parker's grave, Lincoln Cemetery, 8604 E. Truman Rd., near Blue Ridge Rd., 25 min. E of downtown. On I-435 going north, exit on Truman Road and go right (east) about $^2/_{10}$ mile. Take steep road on right to top of hill, bearing to the left.

Getting here is a bit tricky, but the setting, on top of a secluded hill framed with trees, is beautiful. Far in the distance shimmers the Kansas City skyline, while overhead, wildlife chatters quietly to itself. Parker's grave is located near the front of the cemetery, on the right-hand side of the drive. Bird never wanted to be buried in Kansas City, but he lies near his mother, Addie, and their grave stones lie flat and enclosed by a four-inch-high wall. Half disintegrating reeds and tapes, left by fans, are often laid respectfully on the plot.

One of Bird's honorary pallbearers was the great blind piano player and teacher, Lennie Tristano. At one point in the ceremony, the actual pallbearers almost dropped the casket, but through some mysterious, intuitive knowledge, Tristano reached out and caught it.

On March 13, 1993, one day after the thirty-eighth anniversary of Charlie Parker's death, the *Kansas City Star,* in a front-page story, reported that the nameplate from his and his mother's grave had been stolen. Since then, several Kansas City jazz organizations have been raising funds for new grave markers, and they should be in place by the spring of 1994.

Clubs, etc.

Kansas City has two major clubs that feature much first-rate local talent: the **Phoenix Bar & Grill** and **City Light.** Occasional national jazz acts and many national blues acts are brought in by the **Grand Emporium,** which was twice named the Number One Blues Club in America by the Blues Foundation. K.C. also boasts a large number of neighborhood blues joints, and a blues jam can be heard somewhere every night of the week.

Some of the jazz artists to watch out for in K.C. include veteran Jay McShann, who still plays around on occasion; violinist Claude "Fiddler" Williams; longtime drummer Speedy Huggins; bassist Milt Abel; legendary vocalist Queen Bey; keyboard players Steve Miller, Russ Long, and Joe Cartwright; saxophonists-reedmen Kim Park, Bill Caldwell, and Jim Mair; trumpet players Carmell Jones, Mike Metheny, and Stan Kessler; pianist Tim Whitmer and his band, the K.C. Express; vocalists Karrin Allyson, Kevin Mahogany, and Angela Hagenbach; bassist-vocalist David Basse; the Deans of Swing; the McFadden Brothers; the Scamps (a 45-year-old band); and the loosely knit Mutual Musicians Foundation group.

Among blues artists, there's Provine Little Hatch, a legendary harmonica player, the 360 Degree Band, the Dan Doran Band, the Full Blast band, jazz-blues vocalist Ida McBeth, blues-jazz guitarist Sonny Kenner, pianist Rory Searcy, guitarist-vocalist Mileage Gilbert, Big John & the 39th St. Blues Band, the B.W.B. Band, and John Paul & the Hellhounds.

In general, bars in K.C. remain open until 1 a.m., although some, especially those in Westport, serve liquor until 3 a.m.

Personal Choices

Best jazz club: *Phoenix*
Best jazz restaurant-club: *City Light*
Best jazz jams: *Epicurean Lounge, the Levee*
Best blues club: *Grand Emporium*
Best neighborhood blues clubs: *B.B.'s Lawnside, The Tuba* (*also jazz*)
Best after-hours blues: *H&M Bar-B-Q.*

F O R   J A Z Z

Phoenix Piano Bar & Grill, *302 W. 8th St. (downtown),*
472-0001.

Currently the hottest jazz spot in town, the Phoenix presents jazz every day from 5 p.m. 'till closing. Tim Whitmer and the K.C. Express play most regularly, often during the early part of the evening, followed by the many other top names in K.C. jazz, all of whom have appeared here at one time or another: the Scamps, Jay McShann, Karrin Allyson, Joe Cartwright, David Basse, Queen Bey, Stan Kessler.

Housed in a 100-year-old building in one of the city's older neighborhoods, the Phoenix has big picture windows, lots of dark wood, and dark green walls. There's just a handful of tables and chairs; the place only holds about 85.

Music: nightly, 5 p.m. on. *No cover. Food:* soups, sandwiches.

City Light, *4749 Penn Ave. (Country Club Plaza), 444-6969.*

Upscale and sophisticated and known for its food, City Light is painted light gray, and framed photographs of musicians are hung discreetly on the walls. A stained-glass window adorns the front door and elegant tables with flickering candles ring the room.

For years, City Light was Kansas City's only full-time jazz club, and it's still one of the best spots in town. The City Light Trio, with Joe Cartwright on piano, often plays with soloists such as Karrin Allyson, Queen Bey, Kevin Mahogany, or Claude "Fiddler" Williams, while other nights are devoted to groups such as David Basse and his Orchestra or the Jim Mair Quintet. On Saturdays there's often an after-hours jam.

Music: Tu–Su. *Cover:* $–$$. *Food:* contemporary American. CC.

Mutual Musicians Foundation, *1823 Highland Ave. (18th and Vine District), 421-9297.*

This small, historic clubroom (see "Landmarks and Legends," page 242) is simply laid out with a few tables, wooden chairs, and a makeshift stage, but on the weekend, the place is often filled with musicians from all over the city. Sometimes the music is great, sometimes it isn't, but there's always much potential here.

Music: F–Sa. *Cover:* donation at the door.

The Ritz-Carlton Rooftop Bar, *401 Ward Pkwy. (Country Club Plaza), 756-1500.*

A serious jazz spot, the Rooftop usually features the Russ Long Trio, playing with a guest soloist such as Angela Hagenbach or Stan Kessler. Located on the hotel's twelfth floor, the bar has the feel of a traditional English club, complete with rich woods, deep blues and golds, and paintings of sporting scenes.

Music: W–Sa. *No cover. Food:* appetizers, desserts.

The Levee, *16 W. 43rd St. (midtown), 561-2821.*

For years, the Levee has been hosting Saturday-afternoon jazz jams, and the place is usually packed with loyal fans. Run by drummer Tommy Ruskin, the sessions attract many of the city's most venerable players.

A multilevel place with an upstairs deck looking out over a yardful of trees, the Levee also presents jazz, blues, and Motown at night. Sonny Kenner, Little Hatch, and Kevin Mahogany are among the many who have appeared here. The music room is located on the club's lower level, and it's a dark, comfortable place with walls of deep green.

Music: nightly, Sa afternoons, much jazz and blues. *Cover:* $.
Food: American.

Epicurean Lounge, *7502 Troost Ave. (east K.C.), 333-8383.*

An institution in east Kansas City, the Epicurean has been featuring jazz jams on weekend late afternoons for over 12 years. Tenor saxophonist Horace Washington usually leads the sessions, and sometimes plays on Friday nights as well. The place is also known for its red beans and rice, and there's good parking security.

Music: Sa and Su late afternoons. *No cover. Food:* home-style.

Birdland, *1600 E. 18th St. (18th and Vine District), 842-8463.*

In the 1950's, Birdland was the Mardi Gras, a well-known club where everyone from John Coltrane to Dexter Gordon once played. The Mardi Gras shut down in the '60's, reopened for a period in the '80's, and then shut down again. Its present incarnation, complete with white grillwork and big picture windows, is only a few years old, but the superb mural on the wall, depicting a carousel, a fiery dragon, luscious ladies, and men in top hats, dates back to the club's earliest days. Some of the musicians from the Mutual Musicians Foundation play here.

Music: sporadic. *No cover.*

Also

Housed in a 1910 building that's on the National Register of Historic Places, the **Majestic Steak House** (931 Broadway, downtown, 471-8484) has high, pressed-tin ceilings, much fine food, and straight-ahead jazz. Trios and quartets such as the Billy Meynier Trio play here Thursdays through Sundays.

The **Bristol Bar & Grill** (4740 Jefferson, 756-0606) is the place to hear Dixieland and traditional jazz, Saturdays and Sundays; the New Red Onion Jazz Babies have played here for years and years. The **Boulevard Café** (703 Southwest Blvd., 842-6984) features a jazz brunch on Sundays.

Jazz can also be heard at **The Point,** the **Tuba** (their house band, KC Bottoms, is much jazz influenced, and jazz acts such as

Paul McCandless are occasionally booked) and **B.B.'s Lawnside Bar-B-Q** (hosting a jazz jam on Saturday afternoons). See "For Blues," below.

FOR BLUES

The Grand Emporium, *3832 Main St. (midtown), 531-1504.*

Now over 13 years old, the Grand Emporium is the premier blues and R&B club in Kansas City. A long, big room with tin ceilings, revolving fans, and posters all around, it also brings in a fair amount of rock and reggae, and is home to the Kansas City Blues Society, one of the most active blues societies in the United States.

The club's sound system is one of the best in town, and *everyone* has played here, including the late Albert Collins, John Lee Hooker, Junior Wells, and Dr. John. Robert Cray and Stevie Ray Vaughan played here before they hit it big, and local harmonica genius Little Hatch performs every Friday evening.

The club is also known for its prize-winning barbecue sauce and Creole food. Ms. Grace Harris is the woman responsible for that, and she can usually be found cooking away near the front of the bar. When the evenings end, Grace moves on to run her own after-hours place called H&M Bar-B-Q in Kansas City, Kansas (see page 250).

The Grand Emporium has a lot of atmosphere, partly because the building has housed a bar since 1912. A hotel, now abandoned, was once located up above, and its patrons would come down here to drink and socialize.

Music: M–Sa, mostly blues, some jazz. *Cover:* $–$$. *Food:* barbecue and Creole.

B.B.'s Lawnside Bar-B-Q, *1205 E. 85th St. (20 min. from downtown; one block E of Stroud's), 822-7427.*

Run by Lindsay Shannon, who hosts a blues show Sunday evenings on KCFX/101 FM, and his family, B.B.'s is a roadside barbecue restaurant, complete with a brick and wood front, beat-up wooden floors, and an old-time smoker out back. The walls are hung with lots of blues and jazz posters, except for one wall in the dining room that's painted to look like the inside of an old blues joint.

Many first-rate Kansas City bluesmen and -women play here, including Little Hatch, the Lonnie Ray Blues Band, and John Paul & the Hellhounds. Regional acts such as Catfish Keith from Iowa and the Barbecue Bob Trio from Colorado are also occasionally featured, and on Saturday afternoons there a "Rib Joint Jazz Jam."

Music: W–Su. *Cover:* $. *Food:* barbecue.

The Point, *917 W. 44th St. (midtown), 531-9800.*

A three-story club with exposed brick walls, pool tables and a comfortable feel, the Point has been featuring blues, some jazz, and a weekly open mike for the past 18 years. Most of the bigger acts play upstairs, where food is also served, while acoustic blues guitarists play in the basement on weekends. The Point is also home base for jazz-blues singer Ida McBeth.
Music: Tu–Su. *Cover:* $. *Food:* deli food.

Harling's Upstairs, *3941-A Main St. (midtown), 531-0303.*

A sprawling second-floor space with rooms and halls without doors, Harling's, located in an elegant-looking building with a white curlicue facade, has live music (rock, R&B, blues) most nights of the week. The best time to come, however, is on Saturday afternoons, when a huge blues jam attracts musicians from all over the city. The tradition, now seven years old, always packs the place.
Music: W–Sa, Sa afternoons. *Cover:* $, none for the jam.

Kiki's Bon Ton Maison, *1515 Westport Rd. (midtown), 931-9417.*

Louisiana cooking is the main attraction at this cozy restaurant with flickering candles and huge red crawfish stenciled on pale green walls, but music also plays an important and curious role. It all started about seven years ago, when graphic designer Richard Lucente, husband of Kiki Lucente, who runs the place, decided to take the singing he did every morning in the shower out in front of a live audience. A more direct route to surefire embarrassment seems hard to imagine, but amazingly enough, the man had talent and was an instant success. Since then, he's picked up the accordion and fronts the Bon Ton Soul Accordion Band, one of the most popular groups in town.
Music: W, Sa, zydeco-blues. *Cover:* none with dinner, $ at bar.
Food: Creole and Cajun.

The Tuba, *333 Southwest Blvd. (near downtown), 471-6510.*

A neighborhood bar with a laid-back young professional crowd, the Tuba is all blues, R&B, and jazz, no rock-and-roll. The bands play on a center stage, and the audience are serious listeners. A blues-jazz house band, KC Bottoms, plays most nights and national acts are brought in on occasion. The decor is deep forest green, and there's a shiny tuba hanging over the bar.
Music: M–Sa. *Cover:* $.

H&M Bar-B-Q, *1715 N. 13th St., Kansas City, Kan. (10 min. from downtown Kansas City, Mo.), (913) 371-9524.*

An after-hours joint that's one of the hottest blues spots in town, the H&M doesn't get going till well after midnight on Friday and Saturday nights, but then the music lasts until the wee hours, or about 5:30 a.m. Run by Grace Harris, the barbecue cook at the

Grand Emporium earlier in the evening, the joint is old and run-down and located in one of the city's rougher neighborhoods, but the trip is well worth the effort. The great saxman Abb Locke can usually be found behind the bar, blowing, serving drinks, and watching the door all at the same time, and there's never any telling who might show up.

Music: F, Sa, midnight till dawn. *No cover. Food:* barbecue.

MC's Bar and Grill, *5709 Troost Ave. (east K.C.), 363-9376.*

The "House of the Blues," better known as MC's (pronounced "Mac's," for the owners, Charles and Emma Jean McDaniel) has been featuring the blues every Thursday through Sunday night, including a Saturday matinee, for the past eight years. Bass player King Alex and his group, the Untouchables, are the current house band. Other attractions at MC's, a small, simple place with long tables and chairs, include chicken wings, catfish, and "foot longs" (those are overgrown hotdogs, for all you out-of-towners).

Music: F–Sa. *Cover:* $.*Food:* snacks.

Inferno, *4038 Troost Ave. (east K.C.), 931-4000.*

One of the top R&B clubs in town, the Inferno features local groups on the weekends and big acts such as Denise LaSalle and Little Milton about once a month. Open since 1952, the place is decorated to look like hell in its better moments. Everything is plush red and black, dusted over with gold highlights, and there's a huge seductive face with glittering eyes and lips on one wall. The face once depicted a devil with horns, but some patrons found it so frightening that the owners toned it down. Still, folks aren't happy. "They complained when we had it up," says owner Ella Vample, "and now they're complaining 'cause we took it down."

Music: intermittent. *Cover:* $–$$.

Blayney's, *415 Westport Rd. (Westport), 561-3747.*

Located in a low-ceilinged basement, Blayney's is an informal Kansas City institution. With exposed rock walls, and a crowd that includes both young locals and convention-business clientele (lots of hotels are nearby), it has a strange mix of elements that give it an almost carnival feel. Most of the music is local R&B and rock. The club also started the first weekly R&B jam session in K.C. 15 years ago; today, it's hosted by the 39th St. Blues Band.

Music: M–Sa. *Cover:* $.

The Hurricane, *4048 Broadway (Westport), 753-0884*

Just across the way from Blayney's is one of the oldest bars in K.C., The Hurricane. A dark green octagonal room with murky mirrors, hurricane lamps, and an almost nineteenth-century feel, it features a rotating roster of blues bands and is packed to the gills on weekends.

Music: M–Sa. *Cover:* $.

Nightmoves, *5110 N.E. Vivion Rd. (5 min. N of downtown),* *452-4393.*

Located across the river in an historic old house that dates back to 1937, Nightmoves bills itself as the "fanciest" blues room in the city. The ladies room especially is *très* elegant. Local acts such as the Dan Doran Band are usually featured, with national acts such as Johnny Copeland and Chick Willis brought in about once a month. Several nights every week and Saturday afternoons are devoted to jams, sometimes hosted by Little Hatch.
Music: M, W–Sa, Sa afternoons. *Cover:* $–$$.

Other Venues and Special Events

The historic **Folly Theater** (300 W. 12th St., 474-4444) in downtown Kansas City has a regular jazz concert series. The **University of Missouri–Kansas City Conservatory of Music** (4949 Cherry St., 276-2949), the **Music Hall** (13th & Wyandotte Streets, 931-3330) and the **Lyric Theatre** (10th and Central Streets, 471-7344) also feature jazz and blues talent on occasion.

The **Bird's Nest** (4615 Paseo, 924-2200), housed in the offices of the Charlie Parker Memorial Foundation, hosts touring and local artists about twice a month. The Foundation's main mission is educational, and it runs numerous jazz classes for all ages out of its Academy for the Arts.

The **Kansas City Blues & Jazz Festival** (800-530-KCMO; seasonal) has become a big affair, attracting crowds of over 100,000; it's usually held the last weekend of July. The Kansas City Blues Society (531-7557) puts on the four-day **Spirit Festival** over Labor Day weekend, and the **Blues Society Mardi Gras Pub Crawl** on Fat Tuesday. The Kansas City Jazz Commission (444-4414) puts on the **Jazz Pub Crawl** in June.

A free **Music in the Parks Concert Series,** featuring some jazz and blues, is sponsored by the Kansas City Parks and Recreation Commission every summer.

Every Thanksgiving since 1959, blues promoter Wylie Cyrus has produced a **Thanksgiving Day Breakfast Dance** from 10 a.m. to 2 p.m., featuring stars such as Little Milton and Tyrone Davis. The event is held in the Missouri National Guard Armory (889-3200) and is usually sold out months in advance.

Radio

KCUR/89.3 FM (235-1551). An NPR affiliate. Jazz weekday evenings, Sa afternoons. Of special note: "Fish Fry," F, Sa evenings with Chuck Haddix.

KKFI/90.1 FM (931-3122). Jazz mornings and afternoons. Of special note: "Traffic Jam" (blues) with Shirley Mae, Wendy and Groovy, weekday afternoons.

Jazz and blues can also be heard on **KANU/91.5 FM,** reception permitting, and occasionally on **KPRS/103.3 FM, KCFX/ 101 FM,** and **KBEA/1480 AM.**

Record Stores

Three top stores in town for jazz and blues are the **Music Exchange** (207-A Westport Rd., 931-7560), **PennyLane Records** (4128 Broadway, 561-1580) and **Classical Westport** (4130 Pennsylvania, 753-0433).

St. Louis

I hate to see the evening sun go down,
Hate to see the evening sun go down,
'Cause my baby, he done left this town . . .

—*W. C. Handy, "St. Louis Blues"*

The St. Louis blues go back to the beginning of the century. African-American music in general was a quintessential element in the city's nightlife as early as the late nineteenth century; the famous ballad "Frankie and Johnny" is said to be about the murder and violence that were once an everyday occurrence in this then raw riverport town.

St. Louis is the city most frequently referred to as the birthplace of ragtime. Scott Joplin lived here for a number of years at the turn of the century, as did pioneer piano players Tom Turpin and Louis Chauvin. The city's music was also strongly influenced by the New Orleans riverboat steamers bringing with them the sound of jazz.

From the 1910's through the 1930's, many jazz and bluesmen arriving from the South settled in "Deep Morgan" in St. Louis (now Delmar Blvd., between Tenth and 20th streets) or in the "Valley" in East St. Louis. Both neighborhoods have since been nearly completely torn down and rebuilt, but at one time, they were filled with drifters, hustlers, musicians, and the poor. East St. Louis in particular, located just across the river from St. Louis, in Illinois, was a notorious, ugly slum, and in 1917 it was the target of the most violent antiblack riots in U.S. history, from which some say it still has not recovered. Six thousand African-American workers who had been brought into the city by industrialists hoping to destroy a growing white unionization movement were burned out of their homes, and nearly two hundred died.

Big "Bad" Smitty, known for his big rough voice, can sometimes be heard at Spraggin's Hacienda.
Bill Greensmith

During the 1920's, St. Louis's largest jazz venue was the Arcadia Ballroom (first known as the Dreamland, and later called the Tune Town, after which Basie wrote the "Tune Town Shuffle"). Frank Trumbauer, Bix Beiderbecke, and Pee Wee Russell all played the Arcadia, once located at 3517 Olive St. Later, there was the Elks Club, where Clark Terry and Miles Davis struck up a friendship, and the Rhumboogie, where Tiny Bradshaw's orchestra, featuring Sonny Stitt, often played. All these venues have since been torn down.

Some of the early blues artists associated with St. Louis were the mythic Peetie Wheatstraw, (a.k.a. "Devil's Son-in-Law," upon whom Ralph Ellison based a character in his novel *Invisible Man*), Lonnie Johnson, Roosevelt Sykes, James "Stump" Johnson, and Charlie "Specks" McFadden. The city has also been home to a long line of trumpet players, the best-known of which are Harold Baker, Clark Terry, Miles Davis, and Lester Bowie.

Other jazz/blues/R&B artists associated with St. Louis include Josephine Baker, who was living in East St. Louis at the time of the riots; Tina Turner, a native of the city, born Annie Mae Bullock; Ike Turner, who moved to St. Louis from Mississippi, married Annie Mae, and gave her her new name; Chuck Berry, who grew up in and still lives in the city; Oliver Sain, a saxophonist and music producer also still in the city; saxman David Sanborn, and vocalist Bobby McFerrin. As a jazz town, the city was particularly alive in the late '60's–early '70's, when Oliver Lake, Julius Hemphill, Hamiet Bluiett, Charles "Bobo" Shaw, and various other artists of various mediums formed the Black Artists Group, a collective modeled after the Association for the Advancement of Creative Musicians in Chicago.

Sources

The best music source is *The Riverfront Times* (231-6666), a free weekly with excellent listings. Other sources include the Thursday entertainment section of the *St. Louis Post-Dispatch* (340-8000) and *The Blues Letter,* published bimonthly by the St. Louis Blues Society and available at 70 dropoff points (clubs, record stores, etc.).

For general information, contact the St. Louis Convention and Visitors Commission, 10 S. Broadway, Suite 1000, 800-916-0040 or 421-1023.

The area code for St. Louis is (314).

A Note on Neighborhoods

St. Louis, located on the western bank of the Mississippi River, is a flat sprawling city with a small downtown and lots of neighborhoods that merge into suburbs. East St. Louis, on the eastern bank of the Mississippi, also seems to stretch on for miles, but here, much of the cityscape is devastated and deserted.

In St. Louis, Laclede's Landing is a restored riverboat warehouse district located downtown and filled with cobblestone streets and wrought-iron street lamps. Soulard is another restored historic district, on the south side of town. Both are known for their nightlife. University City is located on Delmar Avenue, about 15 minutes west of St. Louis proper. The Central West End, another entertainment district, is also west of downtown. North St. Louis and East St. Louis, both about 15 minutes from downtown, are home to large African-American communities.

Driving in St. Louis is straightforward, as traffic is usually light, and free parking is plentiful.

Landmarks and Legends

(The first four sites are in St. Louis, the last three in East St. Louis. A car is necessary.)

The Scott Joplin House, *2658 Delmar Blvd. (5 min. NW of downtown).*
Scott Joplin left his home in Texarkana, Texas, in 1882 at age 14 and spent years traveling around the Midwest, playing in small bands and nightspots here and there. Then, around the turn of the century, his composition "Maple Leaf Rag" was published and sold approximately 75,000 copies in six months; with his newfound "wealth" he gave up the itinerant life to settle down with his

new bride. The Joplins lived on Delmar for less than three years (1900–1903), but the musician wrote some of his most famous compositions here, including "Elite Syncopations," "March Majestic," "The Ragtime Dance," and "The Entertainer."

The Joplins' former home, a Victorian row house where they occupied the upper east apartment, was declared a National Historic Landmark in 1976. Since then, the place has been renovated and part of it turned into a small museum. Items on display include sheet music, artifacts from the 1904 World's Fair (where Joplin was inspired to write "Cascade Blues," after viewing the fair's fountains and pools), and a player piano with rolls cut by Joplin. *Open:* M–Sa, 10 a.m.–4 p.m.; Su, noon–5 p.m. *Free admission.*

St. Louis Walk of Fame, *6504 Delmar Ave. (University City).*

Modeled after the Hollywood Walk of Fame, this stretch of sidewalk outside Blueberry Hill (see "For Blues," page 264) has approximately 40 stars embedded in it, complete with short bios. Scott Joplin, Tina Turner, and Chuck Berry are all honored.

Chuck Berry's home, *4319 Labadie (10 min. NW of downtown).*

Chuck Berry's family moved to this white wooden duplex when he was in the fourth grade. With the country in the midst of the Depression, Berry's father was working only three days a week, and young Chuck helped him deliver vegetables in the early morning for extra income.

In high school, Berry made his first public musical appearance by singing a popular hit, "Confessin' the Blues," at a class show. "Without thought of how bold it would be, singing such a lowly blues in the rather sophisticated affair," he writes in his autobiography *Chuck Berry,* "I belted out the purple pleading tune with crooning cries. . . . 'How dare you?' showed on the faces of a couple of faculty members, [but] at the completion of my selection I was complimented with a tremendous ovation. . . . I bowed away and exited the stage backwards, watching my pathway through my legs. I feel satisfied that stage fright, if it ever lived within me, was murdered during that applause."

Oliver Sain's studio, *4521 Natural Bridge (10 min NW of downtown).*

Oliver Sain, one of St. Louis's finest saxophonists as well as a songwriter and record producer, has recorded many an artist in this little windowless studio standing by itself on the side of a wide road. Fontella Bass, Barbara Carr, Bobby McClure, and Shirley Brown are among his most successful artists.

Lincoln High School, *1200 block of Bond Ave. (central East St. Louis).*

A one-story red-brick building built in the 1950's, Lincoln High School has produced some of our country's finest musicians, in-

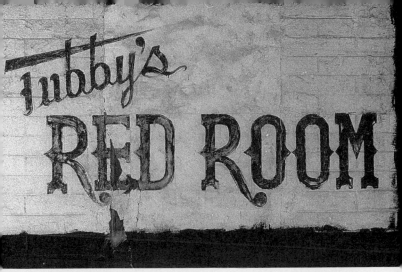

At Tubby's, the blues get down and dirty, low and mean, starting about 2 a.m.

cluding Miles Davis. Even today, the Lincoln High School Band, under the directorship of Ron Carter (who, like other teachers in economically devastated East St. Louis, is in constant danger of being laid off), wins repeatedly at festivals throughout the Midwest and is invited regularly to perform in Europe.

While at Lincoln High, Davis studied with trumpet player Elwood Buchanan, who had a tremendous influence both on his life and on his music. "One of the hippest things Mr. Buchanan taught me was not to play with vibrato in my tone. . . ." Davis says in his autobiography *Miles*, "One day while I was playing in that style, with all this vibrato, Mr. Buchanan stopped the band and told me, 'Look here, Miles. . . . stop shaking all those notes and trembling them, because you gonna be shaking enough when you get old. Play straight, develop your *own* style, because you can do it. You got enough talent to be your own trumpet man.' "

Also at Lincoln, Davis met Irene Birth, who bore his first child, Cheryl, the year he graduated. Irene was the one who dared him—at age 17—to call up Eddie Randle of the Blue Devils band and ask for a job. Miles rose to the challenge and was hired.

Cosmopolitan Club, *corner 17th St. and Bond Ave. (central East St. Louis).*
It was at the Cosmopolitan Club, then a renovated supermarket, that Chuck Berry's career took "its first firm step" in 1953. Initially Berry was playing in a group called Johnnie Johnson's Sir

John's Trio, but Berry proved to be so popular that the group soon renamed itself the Chuck Berryn Combo (an "n" was added to spare Berry Sr. any unnecessary embarrassment). Even so, Berry only earned about $21 for a weekend's worth of work, and so he volunteered to paint the place—in an elaborate design that included snow-capped mountains all around—for which he got paid $450.

Throughout the '50's and early '60's, the Cosmopolitan Club was one of the most important blues and R&B venues in the St. Louis area. Oliver Sain, Fontella Bass, Ike Turner, and Benny Sharp all played here. Today, alas, the club, though sturdy physically, is run-down and dispirited. There's no live music, and even in the middle of the afternoon, the place is filled with people down on their luck, drinking wordlessly at long thin tables while staring at the walls. Chuck Berry's snow-capped mountains are long gone.

Ike and Tina Turner's home, *3128 Virginia Pl. (south East St. Louis).*

Ike and Tina Turner lived in this red-brick house with the large front porch from 1957 until 1961–1962. Their whole band lived with them, too. Ike was a dictatorial sort who liked to have the group nearby so he could rehearse whenever he wanted.

Virginia Place was once a prestigious East St. Louis address, with a grass median running down its center and gates at either end. The street still has a touch of grandeur, but it's seen better days.

Clubs, etc.

St. Louis has an enormous number of atmospheric bars and restaurants housed in historic buildings. Most of these are located in the Soulard or Laclede's Landing districts, and they're filled with heavy wooden bars, big mirrors, old gaslight fixtures, exposed brick walls, and revolving fans.

St. Louis also has an enormous number of blues artists, black and white. The blues, so long a part of the city's subterranean current, are suddenly exploding into public view. National blues acts are often booked into **Mississippi Nights** and sometimes into **Off Broadway**. The top jazz spot in town, booking both national and local talent, is **Just Jazz.**

Some of the many blues and R&B artists to watch out for in St. Louis include the legendary Henry Townsend, who has been playing in St. Louis since the 1920's; sax veteran Oliver Sain; vocalist Barbara Carr; piano player Silvercloud; guitarists Big "Bad" Smitty, Bennie Smith and Big George; vocalist-pianist Screaming Joe Neal; the Leroy Pierson Band; Doc Terry and the Pirates; the Davis Brothers Band; Little Eddie and the All Stars; Johnnie Johnson; Tommy Bankhead and the Blues Eldorados; the Soulard Blues Band; Billy Peek; the James Family; and David Dee & the Hot Tracks Band.

Among the top jazz artists in town are the horn-playing Bosman Twins; saxophonists Peanuts Whalum, Willie Akins, Freddie Washington, and Roland Clark; trumpet player Sue Beshears; bass player Tommy Kennedy; piano players Ptah Williams, Kim Portnoy, Reggie Thomas, and Charles Fox; drummer Gary Sykes; guitar players Rob Block and Tom Byrne; keyboard player Pauline Stark; and the Lincoln High School Jazz Band.

Generally speaking, bars in St. Louis remain open until 1 a.m., but some districts, most notably Laclede's Landing, have a 3 a.m. license.

Personal Choices

Best national jazz club: *Just Jazz*
Best neighborhood jazz joint: *Moose Lounge*
Best blues bars: *Broadway Oyster Bar, the Soulard bars*
Best blues with barbecue: *Bob's Bar-B-Que*
Best neighborhood blues joint: *Tubby's*

FOR JAZZ

Just Jazz, *Hotel Majestic, 1019 Pine St. (downtown), 436-2355.*

Opened only a few years, Just Jazz has already acquired a national reputation for presenting first-class jazz. This is the club where many musicians stop to perform when traveling between Chicago and the West Coast. Some of the many who have done so include Ray Brown, Benny Green, Roy Hargrove, and Mulgrew Miller. PBS broadcast its 1993 New Year's Eve celebration from here, and WSIE/88.7 FM radio produces a radio show from the club called "Just Jazz," which has recently been picked up by NPR.

Located on the ground level of the venerable Hotel Majestic, which was built in 1914, Just Jazz is a stately affair filled with antique oak, cream-colored walls, exposed beams, and a big picture window looking out onto the street. An L-shaped place, it offers fine dining on one side, a lounge on the other, and the stage in between. Incredibly, especially given the talent that performs here, there is no cover.

Music: M–Sa; Su, late afternoons. *No cover. Minimum: $$. Food:* contemporary American. CC.

West End Wines, *309 Belt St. (Central West End), 367-3049.*

What started out as a retail wine shop has since opened up a wine bar that offers acoustic mainstream jazz on Friday nights. Top St. Louis–based players Ptah Williams, Steve Kirby, Tim Portnoy, and Steve Shenkel play here.

The wine bar was designed by some of the store's customers, who also happen to be architects, and it's been described as a "sleek and cool contemporary place" with "European atmosphere." Local artwork hangs on the walls.
Music: F. *Cover/minimum:* $–$$. *Food:* light fare.

Moose Lounge, *4571 Pope (north St. Louis), 385-5700.*

Small and comfortable with a high stage surrounded by shimmering, shining walls, the Moose Lounge is a 20-plus-year-old club run by firefighter and jazz lover Tommy Gooch. "I've always loved the music," he says. "My brother is a jazz musician, it runs in the family." All the top local talent has played here at one time or another and big names just passing through—Sonny Stitt, David Sanborn (who grew up in St. Louis and played here when he was just starting out)—still put in surprise appearances. The neighborhood is not the best, which is why Gooch hires a security guard to stand watch over the streets and patrons' cars.
Music: F–Sa. *No cover.*

Gene Lynn's Cocktail Lounge, *348 N. Sarah St. (Central West End; in small shopping mall), 652-6242*

A glitzy, upscale cocktail lounge with shiny chandeliers, three prominent TV's and jazz that even the owner Gene Lynn admits is frankly commercial, this place nonetheless attracts an interesting, racially and culturally diverse crowd. Bohemian types in exotic regalia sit cheek-by-jowl with stiff businessmen in dark suits.

Lynn, a large elegant man usually wearing a tux, is a veteran St. Louis jazz figure who once worked the Las Vegas–L.A. circuit. He and his band, the Trio Tres Bien, play on Fridays and Saturdays.
Music: W–Sa. *No cover.*

The Uptown, *3524 Washington Ave. (Central West End), 533-5540.*

A large, upscale African-American club, the Uptown presents jazz in the early part of the week. The Bosman Twins and trumpet player Russell Gunn perform here regularly, while Jim Rendall often hosts a jazz jam on Monday and/or Wednesday nights. The club features large picture windows and bar stools in the front room and a music room in back, complete with comfortable red booths, soft lighting, a stage, and a dance floor.
Music: Su–W. *Cover:* $. *Food:* appetizers.

Also

St. Louis Nites (2315 Olive, 421-2770), another upscale club run by the same company that runs The Uptown, presents jazz on Friday and Saturday nights. A jazz-blues-Motown band called The Coalition plays two nights a week at the **Parc Front Grill** (255 Union St., 367-6656), a casual restaurant serving Southwestern cuisine. Bigger names such as Oliver Sain also occasionally appear here. Scheduled to open: **The A-Train** in Webster Groves, to be run by percussionist Ken "Blue" Campbell.

F O R　B L U E S

Broadway Oyster Bar, 736 S. Broadway (downtown), 621-8811.

The Broadway is packed most nights, but fighting the crowds is worth the effort. In a city filled with unusual historic bars, this is one of the best. A narrow, crooked red-brick building standing by itself at the edge of town, the Broadway dates back to the nineteenth century. Inside, all is dark wood with a marble bar, stained-glass windows, a fireplace, and all sorts of paraphernalia (bottles, hurricane lights, piñatas) hanging from the ceiling and walls.

Among the blues bands who play here are the Soulard Blues Band, and Irma Whiteside & the Blues Deluxe. The musicians crowd onto a stage near the front, a stage so small that it scarcely seems capable of holding three musicians, let alone the five or six who are usually there.

Music: M–Sa. *Cover:* $. *Food:* Cajun, Creole. CC.

Molly's, 816 Geyer St. (Soulard), 436-0921.

Named after a dog who's "real old and kind of looks like a pig," Molly's is one of the most popular blues bars in Soulard. Housed in a brick building that's all dark wood, with lots of antiques, and old pictures and brass instruments on the walls, it features a mix of young blues bands (such as Buffalo Bob & the Bedroom Blues) and older masters (James Crutchfield, Doc Terry). Solo blues artists are usually presented early in the week, and there's often an open jam at midweek. On one side of the club are three doors that open out onto a New Orleans–style courtyard.

Music: M–Sa. *Cover:* $.

Mike & Min's, Tenth and Geyer (Soulard), 421-1655.

Mike & Min's, an all-blues bar-restaurant, is a cheerful two-level affair with dining on the upper level, music on the lower. A comfortable, old-fashioned place with a boisterous crowd, the decor is pressed tin ceilings, revolving fans, huge mirrors, big wooden doors with lace curtains, and a semi-enclosed garden out back. Regulars include the Soulard Blues Band, Tommy Bankhead, and Buffalo Bob.

Music: W–Sa. *Cover:* $. *Food:* American. MC/Visa.

Great Grizzly Bear, 1027 Geyer (Soulard), 231-0444.

Another historic Soulard bar with lots of character, the Great Grizzly features blues and R&B. Billy Peek, a guitar player who once played with Chuck Berry and Rod Stewart, is a regular here,

as is the Soulard Blues Band. The place itself is owned by two brothers with a passion for bears (check out the collection behind the bar) and feels more like someone's casual living room than a bar. There's wood paneling all around, a huge mirror behind a heavy oak bar, and old-fashioned engraved light fixtures. Outside is a, ahem, bear garden, with its own giant bear.
Music: Th–Sa. *Cover:* $.

1860 Saloon, *1860 S. Ninth St. at Geyer (Soulard), 231-1860.*

The 1860 Saloon, also located in the Soulard District, is more raucous than either Mike & Min's or the Great Grizzly. No one's afraid to dance or drink here, where the young-professional quotient is down, and the blue-collar quotient is up. Regulars include Patti & the Hit Men, Soul Reunion, and the Rhythm Imperials, and out back there's a courtyard and a new "Hard Shell Cafe," with brick walls, a brick fireplace and big picture windows.
Music: W–Su. *Cover:* $. *Food:* American, Cajun.

Off Broadway, *3509 Lemp (near Soulard), 773-3363.*

Run by a father-mother-and-son team, the Off Broadway has a different band almost every night of the week, some of which are local, some of which are from out of town (mostly Austin, California, and Chicago). About half of each month is devoted to roots rock, the other half to blues. Son Seals, Charmaine Neville, the Mannish Boys, A. C. Reed, Champion Jack Dupree, and James Harmon have all played here.

Unlike most clubs in town, the Off Broadway is large and spacious with a high ceiling, balcony area, carpeting, and exposed brick walls.
Music: M–Sa. *Cover:* $–$$.

Mississippi Nights, *914 N. First St. (Laclede's Landing), 421-3853.*

A low red-brick building with an unassuming awning, Mississippi Nights brings in some of St. Louis's larger acts and is bigger inside than it looks. Up to 1,000 people can be accommodated at this comfortable nightclub which features everything from heavy metal to reggae. Jazz and blues names from the past include Pat Metheny, Albert Collins, and Sonny Rollins, and every year Oliver Sain puts on a seven-hour "Soul Reunion," featuring some of the best musicians around.
Music: most nights. *Cover:* $–$$$.

Bob's Bar-B-Que & Cabaret, *412 N. Tucker Blvd. (downtown), 436-8811.*

A spiffy downtown club with "California atmosphere," Bob's is a small place with wide wooden beams, pink-green-blue decor, and big pillars separating the tables from the walkways. David Dee & the Hot Track Band usually play here on Friday and Sunday nights, while weekend afternoons are often devoted to jazz jams.

Music: F–Su. *No cover. Food:* barbecue.

Tubby's Red Room, *4107 Piggott (SE end of East St. Louis), 618-875-6128.*

The room is dark, the air smoky, and the music pounds, filling the senses until it seems as if the whole world will burst. Dozens of bodies are pushing and pulling, thrusting and turning on a crowded dance floor that quakes with every beat. Overhead burn dusky red lights casting shadows on sweat-streaked faces.

Tubby's, located on a deserted street in an often rough neighborhood, is as close to the blues as you can get. As the music swells out from the guitars, the bass, the drums, modern-day America is completely erased. Everyone—the dancers, the listeners, the players—is caught up in sound.

From the outside, during the day, Tubby's looks like a temporary will-'o-the-wisp shack. Yet the place has been here for over 18 years now, and if owner Margaret "Tubby" Stepp has her way, it will be here for 18 more, serving up barbecue chicken, pig-ear sandwiches, and the blues. The music starts late, 1 or 2 a.m., and goes until dawn; the hot, tight Davis Brothers Band are the men usually responsible for the madness.

Music: F–Sa. *No cover.*

Po' Bob's, *113 Allen St., Eagle Park, Ill. (10 min. N of East St. Louis), 618-876-9408; phone intermittent.*

A large man in a black leather jacket is prowling the floor. Two other large men in black leather jackets are having drinks at the bar. "EAST ST. LOUIS COBRAS," "POWER PIPES," "CROWN ROYALS," "SHE-DEVILS" read the fading posters on the wall.

Po' Bob's has been the headquarters for African-American motorcycle clubs in the Midwest for nearly four decades now (the annual Big Wheel dance draws people from as far away as Kentucky) and contrary to image, most of them are peaceful folk. "We used to have trouble sometimes," says Yellowjacket, a member of the Power Pipes, "but now we got a lot of professionals—doctors, lawyers, nurses."

The club is also known for its "low-down dirty Beale Street blues," which it's been showcasing for the past 25 years. Club legend has it that Little Walter used to play here before he went to Europe. Nowadays, however, live music at Po' Bob's is sporadic. Call or go by first.

Climmie's Western Inn, *6754 Page (near Ferguson, 10 min. NE of downtown), 727-3370.*

Located in a canopied brick building standing by itself by the side of the road, Climmie's is a neighborhood joint that has been offering blues for the past 10 years. A large-ish lounge equipped with lots of red tablecloths, dart boards, and mirrors, it usually fea-

A young Miles Davis (far right, back row) plays the Rhumboogie in 1944.

Frank Driggs Collection

tures Big George & the Houserockers or the Inner City Blues Band.
Music: Th–Sa. *No cover.*

Beulah's Red Velvet Lounge, *4769 Martin Luther King, Jr., Dr., near Walton (North St. Louis), 652-6154.*

Most Saturday afternoons, the barbecue pit is lit up outside and the blues are turned on inside at this small, well-kept neighborhood club done up in red and white. Screaming Joe Neal plays here on occasion, and as the hot sound of his piano drifts out the window, the sweet smell of the barbecue drifts in.
Music: Sa afternoons. *No cover.*

Blueberry Hill, *6504 Delmar Ave. (University City), 727-0880.*

A trendy music club, restaurant, funhouse, and museum all rolled into one, Blueberry Hill is a sort of Disneyland for vintage rock/blues fans. There are a lot of music memorabilia behind glass—a Chuck Berry guitar, a Chubby Checker album cover, Beatle dolls, a toothbrush adorned with Elvis's smiling face—to say nothing of a Pee Wee Herman collection, a comic-book collection, and a large assortment of baseball cards and beer bottles.

Blueberry's big, sprawling well-lit upstairs contains a restaurant, a dart room, a pinball corner, and more. Downstairs, there's the low-ceilinged Elvis room (filled with memorabilia of the King), where local blues can occasionally be heard.

Music: Th–Sa, some blues. *Cover:* $. *Food:* burgers, etc. CC.

Missouri Bar & Grill, *701 N. Tucker St. (downtown), 231-2234.*

The main advantage of the Missouri is that it closes at 3 a.m., an hour after most other St. Louis bars, and serves food until 2:30 a.m. The main disadvantages are that the atmosphere is bland, especially compared to that of other clubs in town, and the full cover price is charged even at the end of the evening.

The bands, who play in a large, cold rec-room-like space off the bar, tend to be many in number, and they often slip in a little rock with their blues.

Music: F–Su. *Cover:* $. *Food:* American.

Also

The list of blues clubs in St. Louis goes on and on. Other clubs worth visiting include **Gino's Lounge** (6161 Natural Bridge, 385-4546), a north St. Louis Saturday-afternoon blues spot similar to Beulah's; **Club Imperial** (W. Florissan and Goodfellow, 381-2288), where Ike and Tina once had a regular gig; and **Club 54** (2543 N. Grand Blvd., 533-0202), a large African-American showclub.

Vocalist Marcell Strong performs with a house band called the Apostles at **Marcell's Restaurant** (3624 S. Broadway, 772-5227), located downtown, most weekends. Steak, fish, hamburgers, and various appetizers are on the menu. The **St. Louis Brewery & Tap Room** (2100 Locust, 241-2337) is a large downtown microbrewery, restaurant, and beer garden that has blues on the weekends.

Spraggin's Hacianda (5700 Martin Luther King, Jr., Dr.), located in one of the city's rougher neighborhoods, features blues on Friday and Saturday nights, sometimes compliments of Big Smitty.

Other Venues and Special Events

The **Jefferson Arms Boulevard Room** at the Jefferson Arms Apartments (415 N. Tucker, 436-3307) presents several annual jazz series featuring both heavyweight local and national players. Back in the '40s and '50s, when the Jefferson Arms (built in 1904) was still a hotel, it presented many of the era's big bands, and its ballroom is a beautiful place, complete with chandeliers and vaulted ceilings.

National jazz and blues artists occasionally appear at the historic **Fox Theatre** (527 N. Grand Blvd., 534-1111), the **Westport Playhouse** (600 Westport Plaza, 275-8787), and the **Sheldon Concert Hall** (3648 Washington Ave., 533-9900).

The three-day **Mid—America Jazz Festival** is held every October at the Stouffer Concourse Hotel, 9801 Natural Bridge (429-1100). The **Soulard Mardi Gras,** now over 10 years old, is a celebration in the historic district that features music in all the clubs and a "Jazz Dollar Parade," in which up to 50 musicians parade the street and collect dollars for charity.

The St. Louis Blues Society (241-BLUE) sponsors the five-day **St. Louis Blues Heritage Festival,** featuring both local and national talent, over Labor Day weekend.

Radio

WSIE/88.7 FM (531-8870). A 24-hour jazz station affiliated with South Illinois University.

KWMU/90.7 FM (553-5968). Affiliated with NPR and the University of Missouri–St. Louis. Jazz Sa, Su evenings.

KDHX/88.1 FM (361-8870). Jazz and blues late afternoon weekdays and Su.

KATZ/1600 AM (361-1108). Blues. Of special note: Lou "Fatha" Thimes, weekday afternoons.

Record Stores

The best spot for local jazz/blues is **Vintage Vinyl** (6362 Delmar Blvd., 721-4096). **Streetside Records** (a chain throughout the city) and **Euclid Records** (4906 Laclede, 361-7353) also have good jazz selections.

 **Det**roit

Detroit is best known for its Motown sound, but the city has also produced an enormous number of jazz musicians, many of whom later moved on to New York. During the bebop era, especially, the city was churning with talent: Betty Carter, Yusef Lateef, the Jones brothers (Thad, Hank, Elvin), Kenny Burrell, Donald Byrd, Alice Coltrane, Dorothy Ashby, Barry Harris, Tommy Flanagan, Sir Roland Hanna, Pepper Adams, Paul Chambers, Hugh Lawson, Billy Mitchell, Roy Brooks, and Charles McPherson.

From the late 1800's on, African-American musicians played an important role in the city's entertainment scene (dominating it almost completely to the exclusion of white performers in the

1920's), which perhaps helps account for the fact that Detroit's musicians' union has long been integrated. Most other cities maintained segregated locals until well into the '50's.

During the 1920's and '30's, Detroit was famous for first its society bands and then its big bands, the most important of which were Jean Goldkette's Victor Recording Orchestra and McKinney's Cotton Pickers. Don Redman, the chief arranger for the Fletcher Henderson orchestra, directed the McKinney band for four years, and under his leadership it became the foremost big jazz band in the Midwest.

Both the Goldkette and McKinney bands played at Detroit's most famous ballroom, the Graystone, a place of much legend and lore. One such tale has it that jazz violinist Joe Venuti, then with the Detroit Orchestra, was passing by the Graystone one day when he heard jazz for the first time and decided to throw over his classical career forever.

After-hours, the jazz musicians often went down to Paradise Valley, which was known both for its fancy black-and-tan clubs and its juke joints. The Valley was also home base for numerous blues artists such as Big Maceo, Bobo Jenkins, Tampa Red, and John Lee Hooker, and R&B artists such as Jackie Wilson and Hank Ballard and the Midnighters.

In the '50's, Detroit's jazz scene shifted to private sessions and music societies. Barry Harris held regular jams in his home, and after-hours sessions were held at the Rappa House in Paradise Valley and the West End Hotel in Delray. Then there was the New Music Society, the World Stage and the Bluebird Inn, all of which helped give birth to the golden era of bebop in Detroit.

Sources

Excellent listings can be found in the Friday section of the *Detroit News* (222-2300) and in the *Metro Times* (961-4060), a free weekly. The Friday section of the *Detroit Free Press* (222-6400) also has some listings.

The Blues Factory, a blues management and record company, prints up a monthly calendar with club listings that can be picked up at music spots. Or call their hotline at 280-0363. *Blues Review* (582-5837) is a free monthly publication that can also be picked up at many of the clubs.

Funk and jazz radio station WJZZ-FM runs a hotline at 871-5267.

For maps and other information, contact the Metropolitan Detroit Visitor Information Center, 100 Renaissance Center, Suite 1900, 567-1170 or 800-DETROIT.

The area code for Detroit is (313).

A Note on Neighborhoods

Of all the problem-ridden cities in the United States, Detroit has one of the worst reputations for crime, drugs, violence, and general decay. That's what makes visiting here such a surprise. The city is just a city after all—albeit a run-down one—and not some terrifying hellhole rotting away at the earth.

The downtown is dominated by the Renaissance Center, six immense circular towers of dark glass surrounding the 73-floor Westin hotel. Small, revitalized historic neighborhoods—Bricktown, Greektown, Trappers Alley—surround the Renaissance and are connected by an elevated train called the "People Mover." Nearby are Rivertown, another historic neighborhood filled with cobblestone streets and renovated warehouses, and Eastern Market, the city's 11-acre farmers' market, also known for its restaurants and cafes.

Once outside the immediate downtown, the effects of Detroit's economic problems become more evident. Many streets and buildings are deserted; businesses are heavily guarded. Woodward Avenue is the city's main street, running north and south. Many theaters, clubs, and cultural institutions are located along this wide avenue. The New Center is situated around the Fisher Building, about 15 minutes from the downtown; Hamtramck is a Polish neighborhood 20 minutes to the northwest; Dearborn is an exclusive white suburb, located yet farther to the northwest.

Billie Holiday once played the Fox in "black-face."

Ann Arbor, home to the University of Michigan, is about 45 minutes west of Detroit.

Traffic in Detroit is generally light and parking plentiful.

Landmarks and Legends

(The following route begins downtown, takes a brief detour east to St. Antoine Street, and then proceeds north up Woodward Avenue to Grand Avenue before heading to the west side. A car is necessary.)

Fox Theatre, *2211 Woodward Ave., 396-7600.*
Once the largest movie theater in the nation, the 1928 Fox was recently restored to all of its sumptuous "Siamese Byzantine" splendour. Now, once again, its brilliant marquee illuminates Woodward Avenue at night.

Billie Holiday performed at the Fox while with the Count Basie Orchestra. "Detroit was between race riots then," she writes in *Lady Sings the Blues,* "and after three performances the first day, the theater management went crazy." First, they made the white chorus girls dress in "blackface" and "mammy getups" because there'd been too many complaints about "all those Negro men up there on the stage with those bare-legged white girls." Then, they made Billie wear dark greasepaint because they thought she "was too yellow to sing with all the black men in [the] band."

Paradise Valley/Black Bottom/Hastings Street
Today, the area has been completely torn up by interstates, but the east side, centering around St. Antoine and Adams streets, was once the heart of Detroit's African-American entertainment district. Known as Paradise Valley or Black Bottom, it was home to countless clubs, including the Melody Club, the Club Harlem, the B&C Club, the Rhythm Club, the Band Box, El Sino, Club 666, and Henry's Swing Club. As in Harlem, the most exclusive spots, such as the Plantation and the Chocolate Bar, were black-and-tan clubs attracting primarily an upper-class white audience looking for "exotic" entertainment.

At the heart of Paradise Valley was Hastings Street, where Big Maceo had a regular gig at a place called Brown's Bar, and where John Lee Hooker, probably Detroit's best-known bluesman, played upon arriving in the city in 1943. Hooker performed along Hastings for five years while working a day job in a steel mill before he was "discovered," and his first hit song, "Boogie Chillen," describes walking down Hastings Street and dropping into Henry's Swing Club.

Today, the only blocks in Paradise Valley that look as they once did lie along St. Antoine Street between Gratiot and Adams. The 606 Horseshoe Lounge located here is a descendant of an old club that was known for its fine piano players.

Orchestra Hall/Paradise Theater, *3711 Woodward Ave., 833-3700.*

Originally built for the Detroit Symphony in 1919, Orchestra Hall, later renamed Paradise Theater, became the Detroit venue of choice for many touring African-American big bands during the 1940's and '50's. The hall closed down in the early '70's, but was renovated two years ago, and is now once again called Orchestra Hall. The Symphony is also back, after leaving the auditorium in 1939, some say for racist reasons: the white symphony didn't want to share its hall with black bands.

Charlie Parker, then with the Earl Hines band and renowned for missing shows, played one concert at the Paradise in his stocking feet and slept completely through another. Says Billy Eckstine in *Hear Me Talkin' to Ya:*

> One time . . . Bird says, "I ain't gonna miss no more. I'm going to stay in the theater all night to make sure I'm here."
>
> We answered, "Okay. That's your business. Just make the show, huh?"
>
> Sure enough we come to work the next morning, we get on the stand—no Bird. As usual. We think, So, he said he was going to make the show and he didn't make it.
>
> This is the gospel truth. We played the whole show, the curtains closed, and we're coming off the band cart, when all of a sudden we hear a noise. We look under the stand, and here come Bird out from underneath. He had been under there asleep through the entire show!

Graystone Ballroom, *4237 Woodward Ave.*

Demolished in 1980 (look for a big empty lot), the Graystone was once Detroit's most famous ballroom, built by the bandleader Jean Goldkette in the 1920's. Goldkette also managed the place and directed the resident band, the Jean Goldkette Victor Recording Orchestra. Among his sidemen was Bix Beiderbecke, who often stayed around the corner from the ballroom at the still-standing Billinghurst Hotel (71 W. Willis).

In the 1930's, the Graystone was the only major ballroom in Detroit to employ black jazz bands, most notably the McKinney Synco Septet (better known as McKinney's Cotton Pickers, a name that Goldkette insisted the band adopt against their wishes). Racist attitudes prevailed in other ways as well, as African Americans were allowed to attend the ballroom on Monday nights only.

The 10-story Graystone was a grandiose terra-cotta affair, whose top three floors were never completed, owing to a lack of funds. The front hall was built of marble, while the second floor, reached via a magnificent red-carpeted staircase, was dominated by a tiled fountain lit with multicolored lights. No liquor was ever served at the Graystone.

Just before the Graystone was demolished, one James Jenkins, a retired bus driver and intensely devoted jazz lover, made a last-ditch effort to save it. His plan, which ultimately failed, was to transform the ballroom into a museum and entertainment center. "The Graystone was an enchanted place," he says. "It gave Detroit so much. It should still be here today."

Graystone International Jazz Museum, *1521 Broadway, 963-3813.*

James Jenkins was not only the last-minute protector of the Graystone Ballroom, but is also the founder of the Graystone International Jazz Museum, one of the only museums devoted to jazz in this country. The museum really has nothing to do with the Graystone, but was named after the ballroom in remembrance of good times.

Jenkins, a kindly man in his sixties who in addition to his work as a bus driver also once booked jazz talent for a local club, founded the museum in 1974, the year of Duke Ellington's death. He was driving down the highway, listening to the radio, when he learned that the great composer had died, and decided he just *had* to do something to honor the music he loved.

All of Jenkins's savings and much of his pension have gone into the museum, a simple but moving affair, recently relocated into an airy two-floored space, that's filled with photographs, instruments, posters, records, and other memorabilia. Some of the highlights include an excellent 15-minute video on the Graystone; pictures of Eubie Blake, Fats Waller, and an 11-year-old Bobby Short; a McKinney Cotton Picker guitar; and memorabilia from the Graystone.

Jenkins, who never stops dreaming, has plenty of plans for the future, including a Duke Ellington Room and a Count Basie Room. The museum also sponsors a variety of community outreach programs, a jazz hall of fame that honors living musicians, and a weekly concert series (see "Other Venues and Special Events," page 278). Last year, the Montreux Detroit Jazz Fest kicked off its festivities here.

Open: Tu–F, 11 a.m.–4 p.m.; M, by appointment. *Admission:* $.

Motown Museum, *2648 W. Grand Blvd., 875-2264.*

HITSVILLE U.S.A. reads the sign on the roof. YESTERDAY—TODAY—FOREVER reads the sign on the door.

Back in 1959, Berry Gordy, Jr., was an aspiring songwriter who had just quit his $85-a-week job with General Motors to pursue a writing and music management career. He bought this small, cheerful, turquoise abode as a base for his new operations, but before many years were up, he had become so successful that he also owned six other houses on the block.

From the very beginning, Motown (for "Motor City") functioned as a surrogate home for inner-city kids with musical ambitions—kids like an 11-year-old Stevie Wonder and the teenage Supremes. It was a place for them to play football, grab a sand-

The Graystone Ball-
room was once
home base for Jean
Goldkette's band.

*Graystone Interna-
tional Jazz Museum*

wich, or simply hang out, while at the same time working on their
music.

Today, a visit to the museum, which maintains a wonderfully
simple, homespun feel, begins with a nine-minute video on the history of Motown. Next comes an escorted tour through the original
recording studio, a small, wood-floored affair where everyone
from the Four Tops to the Jackson Five once recorded. One of the
highlights here is the toy piano that Diana Ross and the Supremes
used in "I Hear a Symphony."

The rest of the museum is filled with photographs, album covers, sheet music, newspaper clippings, and gold and platinum records divided up into the Gordy Room, the International Room, the
Black Forum Room, and others. The Michael Jackson Room contains a black hat and sequined glove, donated by the artist, who
also contributed $125,000 to the museum.
Open: Tu–Sa, 10 a.m.–5 p.m; M, noon–5 p.m., Su, 2 p.m.–5 p.m.
Admission: $.

Baker's Keyboard Lounge, *20510 Livernois Ave. at Eight
Mile Rd. (30 min. N of downtown).*
Recently closed down for what seems like good, Baker's dates
back to 1934; for years, it was "the longest-running jazz club in the

world." Art Tatum picked out its seven-foot-long piano just before he died, and many greats from Sippie Wallace to John Coltrane, Charlie Parker to Yusef Lateef passed through its doors.

The 99-seat club was Art Deco inside and out and was fitted with a keyboard-shaped bar (which inspired Liberace to install a piano-shaped pool in his Beverly Hills mansion), hand-painted murals, and tilted mirrors that allowed the audience to see the pianist's hands. Founded by Chris Baker and later run by his son, Clarence, the club offered a mix of straight-ahead and fusion.

Eddie Jefferson, the musician credited with inventing vocalese, was killed outside Baker's on May 9, 1979. He had just come out of the club following a performance and was about to enter a taxi when he was blown away by four blasts from a slowly passing Lincoln Continental. William Perryman, an unemployed factory worker whom Jefferson had allegedly discouraged from becoming a professional dancer, was charged with the murder. (Jefferson himself had begun his career as a dancer).

Bluebird Inn, 5021 Tireman Ave., 894-9539.

"I practically raised Tommy Flanagan and Barry Harris," said the late Clarence Eddins in 1989, owner of the Bluebird from 1953 to 1993, "I used to let them in through the backdoor and then when the music stopped, I put them back out."

During the '40's and '50's, all of the top names in jazz played the Bluebird, now a neat smallish bar done up in muted blues and reds. Some of the regulars back then included Billy Mitchell, Pepper Adams, Sonny Stitt, Donald Walden, Miles Davis (whom Eddins took under his wing while he was recovering from a long bout with drug addiction), Jimmy Smith ("He drove up here in a hearse," said Eddins, "And I thought, I done really made a mistake now"), and Gene Ammons ("He went to feeling the walls, I thought he was crazy. I didn't think nothing about acoustics back then").

The Bluebird, which opened shortly after Prohibition was repealed, was first known for its swing music, dining, and dancing, which drew customers from all over the city's African-American community. During World War II, a soldier in France even called the club to remind himself of home.

Ahmad Jamal was the last musician to play at the Bluebird, which is now open for drinking only, in a gig that took place about 13 years ago. "I usually rebooked a musician right away," said Eddins, "but when I went to rebook Jamal, the agent raised the price $5,000. That was it for me. I couldn't afford it. [Later] I ran into Ahmad. He said, 'I'd play here for nothing.' . . . I never did take him up on it."

The Bluebird is now a bar run by Eddins' wife.

Clubs, etc.

Even more than most cities, Detroit has very few jazz clubs but very much jazz talent. Often the only way to hear the best players in town is through a concert series or festival (of which luckily, there are many; see "Other Venues and Special Events," page 278). Summers are far and away the best time for jazz in Detroit.

Among area clubs, only two offer live jazz six or seven nights a week: **Bert's Marketplace** and the **Bird of Paradise** in Ann Arbor. **Bo-Mac's** and **Cafe Ricardo** are also good spots in which to hear local jazz.

Blues clubs are in a healthier state, even though, comparatively speaking, the city's blues talent does not equal its jazz. Longtime deejay Famous Coachman and blues veteran Bobo Jenkins helped bring the music back to Detroit in the mid-1970's, and today the area boasts a number of steady blues clubs, including the **Soup Kitchen,** which brings in primarily Chicago acts; **Sully's,** in Dearborn, which features much Texas and West Coast blues and R&B; and **Moby Dick's,** also in Dearborn, which concentrates on local blues.

Preeminent among the area's jazz musicians are trumpet player Marcus Belgrave; drummer Roy Brooks; sax player James Carter; pianists Kenny Cox, Harold McKinney, and Bess Bonier; saxophonists Donald Walden, Charlie Gabriel, and Phil Lasley; the all-woman band Straight Ahead; Francisco Mora and his Latin band; the Sun Sounds Orchestra; guitar player Ron English; and vocalist Patti Richards. There are also 10 to 12 very fine big bands, the best of which are the Jimmy Wilkins Orchestra, the New Breed Bebop Society (led by Teddy Harris) and the Graystone Big Band.

Top blues-R&B artists include veteran piano player Jesse White; saxophonist Norma Jean Bell; guitarists-singers the Butler Twins, Willie D. Warren, Rob Noll, and Eddie Burns; Harmonica Shah; vocalists Juanita McCray, Alberta Adams, and Ortheia Barnes; and the Detroit Blues Band, a rock-blues band.

Most clubs in Detroit close at 2 a.m.

Personal Choices

Best late-night jazz: *Bert's Marketplace*
Best club for bebop and big bands: *Bo-Mac's*
Best sophisticated soul-jazz club: *Club Penta*
Best neighborhood club: *Alvin's*
Best national blues club: *Soup Kitchen*
Best local blues club: *Moby Dick's*
Best area jazz club: *Bird of Paradise* (Ann Arbor)

FOR JAZZ

Bert's Marketplace, *2027 Russell St. (Eastern Market), 567-2030.*
Detroit's premier late-night and after-hours spot, Bert's is an especially fine place to visit on Saturday and Sunday mornings be-

tween 2 a.m. and 6 a.m. That is when all the top musicians in town come to jam after their gigs elsewhere are done. Earlier in the evening and on weekday nights, scheduled bands such as the New World Order with Dwight Adams or Harold McKinney & Friends take to the stage.

Bert's is located in Eastern Market, an enormous farmer's market lined with Victorian-style sheds. Intimate and upscale, the restaurant-club is housed in an old refurbished building and is filled with black Formica tables, white tablecloths, fresh flowers, and a staff dressed in tuxedos. Food (everything from steak and lobster to hamburgers) is served at all hours.

Music: Tu–Su; F, Sa, after-hours. *Cover:* $. *Food:* American. CC.

Bo-Mac's, *281 Gratiot Ave. (downtown), 961-5152.*

What started out as a "traditional organ jazz joint" is now a jumpin' hot spot where bebop and big-band sounds can be heard. Piano player Teddy Harris is the man of the hour here, leading his quartet three nights a week and the New Breed Bebop Society Big Band on Sunday nights. Once a week, there's usually a jam.

Bo-Mac's was opened five years ago by a barber and a clothing salesman whose respective businesses had just closed down. The club, now twice its original size, is a warm and cozy place set up with flowers and tall candles gracing the tables. Everyone knows everyone at Bo-Mac's, where the bartender heartily welcomes strangers, and the owners, one or the other of whom is always on duty, double as security guards.

Music: W–Su. *No cover. Food:* soul food.

Café Ricardo's, *15103 E. Warren (at Alter, 5 min. NE of downtown), 881-8610.*

One of the newest jazz spots in town, Ricardo's presents a mix of straight-ahead jazz, blues, and fusion. During a typical week, the James O'Donnell Quartet will host a jazz jam on Wednesday, the Blues Insurgents will play on Thursday, and a contemporary group such as Za Bop or the Janet Tenaj Trio will perform on the weekend.

Lined with wood and giant pictures of old jazz greats (Miles, Dizzy, Ella, Louis), Ricardo's is a smallish, modern place all done up in green and gold, with a marble bar, black blinds, and candles on the tables. A jukebox contains everything from old torch songs to pop.

Music: W–Su. *No cover.*

Club Penta, *Fisher Building, 3011 W. Grand Blvd. (New Center), 972-3760.*

Located in the basement of the historic Fisher Building, designed by architect Albert Kahn in 1928, the Club Penta is a small, elegant affair usually featuring local soul/jazz/blues vocal groups.

Run by five businessmen friends, the club has a sophisticated yet friendly feel, with a black-and-white Art Deco decor punc-

tuated with big red flowers. Located near Detroit's theater district (the Fisher Theater is in the same building), it often attracts a late-night crowd. Singles, couples, young, old, black, white—the place has a nice mix.
Music: Tu–Sa. *Cover:* $.

Alvin's Detroit Bar, *5756 Cass (near downtown), 832-2355.*

A spacious old neighborhood bar and club with brick walls, a cement floor and a comfortable feel, Alvin's mixes up both its music and its people. Everything from alternative rock to jug bands can be found here, along with everyone from college students to 70-year-old habitués.

For jazz fans, Monday nights are *the* nights. That's when the Pam Wise Quartet runs a hot jazz jam. An R&B jam is usually featured on Tuesday, compliments of Thornetta Davis and the Chisel Brothers. R&B is also often presented on the weekends.
Music: nightly, some jazz and blues. *Cover:* $. *Food:* deli style, burgers.

Magic Bag Theatre Café, *22918 Woodward (Ferndale, just N of Nine Mile Rd., 20 min. N of downtown), 544-3030.*

A wonderful revamped 1925 theater with cabaret seating, a good sound system, and a lobby bar, the Magic Bag presents a little bit of everything: film, rock, alternative, jazz. The record store Sam's Jams often presents free jazz concerts here on Friday nights, and other jazz series are sometimes scheduled as well. Touring talent also performs here regularly.
Music: most nights, jazz most F (call ahead). *Cover:* $–$$$.

Rattlesnake Club, *300 River Pl. (Rivertown), 567-4400.*

An airy and sophisticated blond-wood restaurant with modern artwork on the walls and a view of the river, the upscale Rattlesnake Club has a reputation for some of the finest food in town. The chef is the acclaimed Jimmy Schmidt, and *Esquire* magazine voted the Rattlesnake one of the nation's best new restaurants when it opened in 1988. Two years ago, the eatery also started presenting jazz—out on the patio during the summer, in the casual grill room during the winter. Among the regular performers are Donald Walden, Marcus Belgrave, and the group Straight Ahead.
Music: F–Sa. *No cover.* *Food:* contemporary American. CC. Reservations recommended.

Also

R.I.K.'s, The Restaurant (6303 Orchard Lake Rd., 855-9889) is a contemporary Italian eatery, located in West Bloomfield, 30 miles northwest of downtown, that has much jazz. **Flood's Bar & Grill** *(731 St. Antoine St., 963-1090)* is a sophisticated downtown club-restaurant that offers much fusion and a weekly jazz jam. **Dummy George's Jazz Lounge** (10320 W. McNichols, 341-2700), a modern neighborhood club in northwest Detroit, is known for its jazz but is presently operating on a sporadic basis. Jazz can also be heard at **Mr. Lou's** (see page 278).

F O R   B L U E S

Soup Kitchen Saloon, *1585 Franklin St. (Rivertown) 259-2643.*

The oldest saloon in the city, the Soup Kitchen was once a bar and restaurant frequented by sailors from vessels on the nearby Detroit River who paid a mere five cents for a full dinner. Later, during Prohibition, the nineteenth-century brick building was used by the "Purple Gang" and other bootleggers.

More recently—18 years ago, to be exact— the Soup Kitchen became the first commercial blues bar in Detroit and since then a long list of performers have come through its doors, including John Lee Hooker, James Cotton, Koko Taylor, and Sunnyland Slim. In the club's early days, according to local fans, it was a get-down funky kind of place, but since then it's become "prettified," with nice wooden furniture, matching tablecloths, and quaint light fixtures. Still, the place has character. Dining takes place in one room, music in the other, and outside, there's a patio that's open during the summer.

Music: Th–Su. *Cover:* $–$$. *Food:* American. CC.

Sully's, *4758 Greenfield (Dearborn), 846-5377.*

One part long bar, the other part listening room, Sully's is a friendly high-ceilinged place featuring an eclectic mix of blues and R&B acts, including the Kinsey Report, Kim Wilson, Marcia Ball, Asleep at the Wheel, and Commander Cody. The club, which has been a bar for the past 50 years, is located next to a supermarket, and it attracts a varied suburban clientele that ranges from college students to auto workers. The listening room, filled with rickety tables and chairs, is separated from the bar by an informal curtain.

Music: F–Sa. *Cover:* $–$$.

Moby Dick's, *5452 Schaefer Rd. (Dearborn), 581-3650.*

A top spot for local blues, Moby Dick's has a regular lineup of Detroit acts: the Butler Twins, Robert Penn, Robert Noll, the Chisel Brothers, and the James Wailin Blues Band. Special events, such as a "M. L. King Jubilee" and a "Fall Blues Jubilee," are also presented regularly.

As befits its name, Moby Dick's is equipped with things nautical—model ships, lifejackets, a blue neon whale logo, and a back bar that was once part of a ship. The large, squarish room, also

features a sizeable collection of tarnished musical instruments hanging from the walls and ceiling.
Music: F–Sa. *Cover:* $. *Food:* Cajun, etc.

Attic Bar, *11667 Joseph Campau (Hamtramck), 365-4194*
Creaky and cavernous, with a bar on one side and seating on the other, the Attic is home base for the superb veteran bluesman Jesse White. White, who plays both piano and harp, hosts an open jam once a week. On other nights, the neighborhood spot, with its pressed tin ceilings, "antique" collection (milk urns to beer ads), and bare bones feel, offers up a combination of blues and rock.
Music: Th–M. *Cover:* $.

Mr. Lou's Rhythm & Blues, *16117 Mack Ave. (20 min. NW of downtown, near Grosse Point), 882-1700.*
Housed in a building that's been a bar for close to 40 years, Mr. Lou's presents mostly R&B and blues and some jazz. Among the top local bands that have appeared here are the Three of Us, the Chisel Brothers, the Sun Messengers, and harpman James Wailin. Recently remodeled with mirrors all around, the club boasts a dance floor, a game room, and a long delightful mural depicting jazz musicians.
Music: W–Sa. *Cover:* $. *Food:* pizza, sandwiches.

Also

Blues can be heard at **Alvin's Detroit Bar** (see "For Jazz," page 276) and at a number of local bars that feature the music on a rotating one-night-a-week basis. Check the Blues Factory calendar (see "Sources" page 267).

Other Venues and Special Events

The **Creative Arts Collective,** run by Spencer Barefield, presents a superb series of avant-garde jazz concerts, currently at the Magic Bag Theatre Café. Both area artists (Spencer Barefield, Jaribu Shahid) and national talent (Oliver Lake, Richard Davis) are featured.

The **Graystone International Museum of Jazz** (963-3813) has an annual jazz concert series, usually held October through May, that changes its venue and focus from year to year. For the past two years, the program has been called "Blue Monday" and has been presented on Mondays, 6–9 p.m., at the Press Club (393-3090) in the Renaissance Center.

In addition to the city's largest jazz fest, **Montreux Detroit Jazz** (see "Major Festivals," page 403), the three-day **Frog Island Festival** (487-2229), featuring jazz, blues, gospel, and zydeco, takes place every late June in an idyllic riverside setting. The **Ann Arbor Blues & Jazz Festival** (665-4755) is held in mid-September, and the **Hart Plaza Blues Festival** is held over

Memorial Day weekend. Deejay Famous Coachman emcees a **Detroit Indoor Blues Festival** (571-2222) in the spring, **Flint's King Cobra Jazz Festival** takes place the last weekend of August, and the **Pontiac Jazz Festival** also takes place in August. During the summer, the city of Detroit presents free outdoor concerts in **Chene Park** that include some jazz and blues.

Orchestra Hall (3711 Woodward Ave., 833-3700) has a jazz concert series, while the posh, recently restored **State Theatre** (2111 Woodward Ave., 961-5450) presents big-band dancing and nationally known artists on occasion. Touring acts can also be heard at the **Fox Theatre** (2211 Woodward Ave., 936-7600), the **Majestic Theatre** (4140 Woodward Ave., 833-9700), the **Royal Oak Music Theater** (318 W. Fourth St., Royal Oak, 546-7610), and the **Whittier Crystal Ballroom** (415 Burns, 822-9000).

Radio

WEMU/89.1 FM (487-2229). A 24-hour news and jazz station. Affiliated with NPR and Eastern Michigan University, Ann Arbor.

WDET/101.9 FM (577-4146). Affiliated with Wayne State University. Some jazz and blues daily. Of special note: blues with Famous Coachman, Su 2 a.m.–6 a.m.

WCBN/88.3 FM (763-3501). Student-run station affiliated with University of Michigan, Ann Arbor. Jazz weekday mornings, some evenings. Blues, Sa afternoons and M evenings.

WJZZ/105.9 FM (871-0590). A 24-hour funk and jazz station.
WQBH/1400 AM. Blues weekday evenings.

Record Stores

Sam's Jams in Ferndale (279 W. 9 Mile Rd., 547-SAMS); **Street Corner Music** in Birmingham (17620 W. 13 Mile Rd., 644-4777); and **Coachman's Records** (6340 Charlevoix, near Mt. Elliot, 571-2222), a funky neighborhood place run by deejay Famous Coachman, are top area stores.

Other Nearby Locations

Bird of Paradise, *207 S. Ashley, Ann Arbor (45 min. from Detroit), 662-8310.*
Dubbed the "best jazz club in Southeast Michigan" by *Monthly Detroit,* the Bird has been presenting jazz seven nights a week for years. Regulars include the Ron Brooks Trio (Ron Brooks owns the joint) and the Keller Kocher Quartet, while Monday nights are devoted to big-band sounds, usually provided by the Bird of Paradise Orchestra. Sunday night is open jam night, and national acts—Ray Brown, Betty Carter—come through about once a month.

The club is located in an old brick building that has been remodeled with walls designed to absorb sound. Long and narrow, it has a black raftered ceiling and lots of tables and chairs; sight lines are excellent.

Music: nightly. *Cover:* $–$$. *Food:* international.

Schoolkids' Records, said by some to have the best jazz and blues selection in the state, is also located in Ann Arbor (523 E. Liberty, 994-8031).

Indianapolis

Indianapolis has had a long and proud jazz and blues history. One of the earliest jazz musicians, Noble Sissle, was born here in 1889, and others who have come out of the city include Freddie Hubbard, J. J. Johnson, Dave Baker, Leroy Vinnegar, and Wes and Buddy Montgomery. Blues artists Leroy Carr and Francis "Scrapper" Blackwell also had a long association with the city, as has the Hampton family, several members of which (the Hampton Sisters and Pharez Whitted, the son of one of the sisters) still perform regularly around town.

Like other Midwestern cities, Indianapolis's African-American population grew enormously in the first part of the century—by 59 percent between 1910 and 1920 alone. Many of the new arrivals settled on Indiana Avenue, where most of the early jazz and blues clubs were also located (see "Landmarks and Legends," page 282).

During the 1930's and '40's, Indianapolis's reputation as a music center grew, and it attracted musicians from all over the Midwest, many of whom came to the Avenue to prove themselves. "You'd go from one jam session to another and stay out all night," said the late Thomas Parker, a former clarinet player and city government official who once played the street. "And when you were out West and said you were from Indiana Avenue, you were respected."

Indianapolis was also the sort of place where musicians waited out the low periods in between gigs. Known as an inexpensive and hassle-free city, numerous groups disbanded and reformed themselves here.

Sources

The best source for listings is *Nuvo News Weekly* (254-2400), a free publication. *BlueS Indy,* the newsletter of the Blues Society of Indiana and an excellent source for blues information, is available at the City Center, 201 S. Capital Ave. The Sunday section of the *Indianapolis Star* (633-1240) and the Thursday section of the *Indianapolis News* (633-1240) also contains listings. The *Indianapolis Recorder* (924-5143), one of the oldest African-American newspapers in the country, runs a regular music column by drummer Clem Tiggs.

For maps and other information, contact the Indianapolis City Center, Pan American Plaza, 201 S. Capital Ave., 237-5200.

The area code for Indianapolis is (317).

A Note on Neighborhoods

Once sneered at as a placid cow-town, Indianapolis has recently earned the epithet, "Cinderella of the Rust Belt." A $1.8 billion downtown renaissance has resulted in a whole host of new hotels, restaurants, and office buildings.

What's most striking to the visitor, however, is how safe the city seems. Indianapolis has the lowest crime rate of the 50 largest cities in the United States, and it's possible to venture absolutely anywhere without feeling threatened.

The city has a small blossoming downtown that's home to the

C.T. Peppers may
be mostly chrome
and glass, but it's
still got the blues.

vast Hoosier Dome and historic Indiana Avenue. Broad Ripple is a half Bohemian, half gentrified area filled with clapboard houses that have been turned into restaurants, boutiques, and clubs. It's located 20 minutes north of downtown.

Traffic in Indianapolis is light, and there's plenty of free parking available.

Landmarks and Legends

(The locations below are located in or near the downtown area.)

Indiana Avenue

Before Indiana Avenue was Indiana Avenue, it was Front Street, an important thoroughfare in the then fledgling city of Indianapolis. Many of the town's most powerful early families had homes here, just north of White River.

Then came the malaria epidemic of 1821. It decimated the city's population, and the white settlers, suspecting the river as the source of the plague, fled in terror, leaving their homes behind. That left the Avenue open for newer immigrants coming in from Europe and for African Americans from the South, who began arriving in the city in the late nineteenth century. Doctors and lawyers, gardeners and laborers, all made their homes along the Avenue, which was also lined with restaurants, businesses, bars, and nightclubs. The Madame C. J. Walker Company opened up, as did the nearby Crispus Attucks High School, both now on the National Register of Historic Places.

But it was jazz that drew musicians from all over the country to the Avenue. By the '30's and on through the '40's and '50's, the street, especially the 400 block, was bursting with dozens of clubs, including the Sunset Terrace, Henri's, the Mitchell Inn, the British Lounge, the Place To Play, George's Bar, the Red Keg, and the Cotton Club.

No one club was predominant, but the Sunset Terrace, now a parking lot behind the Madame Walker Center, was especially popular. "It was a big dance hall with a balcony," said Thomas Parker. "I can remember hearing Billy Eckstine, Charlie Parker, Count Basie, Ella Fitzgerald. . . . Lots of white musicians came there for their education."

Local names who started out on the Avenue included Wes Montgomery, Earl Walker, Dave Baker, J. J. Johnson, The Inkspots, and Jimmy Coe. Members of big-name bands coming to perform at the Indiana Roof Ballroom or Circle Theater also often stopped in on the Avenue after the show.

Indiana Avenue began to decline in the late '50's with the advent of rock, the breakdown of color barriers, and the building of Interstate I-65, which cut the neighborhood in half. By the 1970's, except for a few liquor stores and pawnshops, the neighborhood was virtually dead. All the old jazz clubs were torn down.

Today, the area is being revitalized, with small businesses, restaurants and shops gradually opening up.

Madame Walker Urban Life Center, *617 Indiana Ave., 236-2099 or 2088 (box office).*

This triangular four-story building is a memorial to Madame C. J. Walker, America's first self-made African-American female millionaire. It is also the site of a lavish theater, where everyone from Noble Sissle to Dinah Washington once played.

Madame Walker, the daughter of impoverished ex-slaves, made her fortune by manufacturing hair-care products. Raised in Louisiana, she began by selling her products door to door, but when she moved to Indianapolis in 1910 she was already a wealthy businesswoman. Upon her arrival, she not only set up her company but also established a beauty school, became close friends with the leading artists and musicians of the day, and contributed generously to a wide variety of community projects.

The building itself was erected by Madame Walker's daughter in 1927 as both a tribute to her mother and a headquarters for the Madame C. J. Walker Manufacturing Co. Also in the center was a College of Beauty Culture; a salon, barber shop, and grocery store; the Coffee Pot Restaurant, a meeting place for African-American intellectuals; and a magnificent theater decorated with elaborate stucco sculptures and masks, elephant heads, spears, and brass fixtures.

Today, the building—one of the few surviving examples of the once popular Afro-Egyptian Art Deco architectural style—houses offices and community organizations, while its recently renovated theater puts on a variety of cultural events, including jazz and blues concerts. On the center's fourth floor is a small historical exhibit on Madame Walker, and the Casino Ballroom (see "Other Venues and Special Events," page 288), where jazz is presented on Friday nights.

Tours of the Center are available. Call for an appointment.

Indiana Roof Ballroom, *140 W. Washington St., 236-1870.*

For nearly 50 years, the "Indiana Roof," built in 1927, was the center of elegant nightlife in Indianapolis. Women in ballgowns and men in tuxedos danced across its polished wooden floors—made up of one-inch pieces of wood laid out in an ever-widening spiral—while wispy clouds and stars drifted across the domed ceiling overhead.

Back then, it only cost 25 cents to get in, though once, a man who had been thrown out for misbehavior tried to offer an employee a $5,000 bribe. The employee turned him down; the ballroom had rules, lots of rules, including those that banned liquor on the premises and blacks from the audience.

The ballroom, situated on the sixth floor, was closed for renovation during the '70's and '80's, but today, it's much the same as it ever was. The machine capable of creating clouds, bubbles, and

Indianapolis-born Noble Sissle (right) confers with Russell Smith.

Courtesy Indiana Historical Society.

fog is still here, and so are the strange, mock-villa facades that line the balconies. The dancing still exists too, with local big bands putting on nostalgic dance concerts about once a month (see "Other Venues and Special Events," page 288).

Of special interest is the room's "jazz door," preserved behind glass. It seems that during the '30's, two of the ballroom's lowlier employees, porter John M. Young and elevator operator Thomas Kelley, took it upon themselves to rate the bands coming through town. Cab Calloway got four stars, as did Noble Sissle, while Benny Goodman scored three. Though the twosome rated over 100 performers, they only gave out two five-star ratings—to themselves.

Clubs, etc.

Indianapolis has no club that presents national-level jazz or blues artists on a regular basis, but the city has plenty of local talent and a number of small bars and restaurants that have music. Preeminent among these are the **Chatterbox Tavern** and **Rick's Café Américain,** both of which present jazz six or seven nights a week, and the **Slippery Noodle Inn** and the **Barrel House Blues Supper Club,** which feature local and regional blues.

Among the many jazz musicians to watch out for in Indianapolis are veteran saxophonist Jimmy Coe; trombonist J. J. Johnson, who recently moved back to his hometown; cellist David Baker; the Hampton Sisters; trumpet player Pharez Whitted and his band, Decoy; piano players Claude Sifferlen, Steve Allee, Carl Hines, and Al Walton (also on organ); saxophonists Pookie Johnson, Mike Brown, and Kenny Washington; drummers Clem Tiggs, Dick Dickinson, "Mad" Harold Cardwell, Don Auston, and Larry

Clark; trumpet players Clifford Ratliff and Michael Rodman; guitarist Steve Weakley; the contemporary group Affinity; and vocalists Everette Green, Cherryl Hayes, Sam Gibson, and Vickie Daniel.

Among blues artists are the legendary mandolin player James "Yank" Rachell, and Duke Tumatoe, one of the city's best-known bluesmen. Others include vocalist-guitarist Charlie Edmonds, vocalist James Bell, David Morgan (guitar) and Allen Stratyner (harmonica), Margaret Floyd, Chubby Massey, Big Daddy Graham, Chico Crawford, Harvey Cook, the Allnighters, the Rebirth Blues Band, Harvey & the Bluetones, the Blues Ambassadors, Savoy Slim & the Sheiks, Gene Deer & the Groove Merchants, Gordon Bonham & the Cooler Kings, the Wolf Pack, Bangkok Rooster, Blues Crew, and Red Beans & Rice.

Generally speaking, bars and clubs close at 2 or 3 a.m.

Personal Choices

Best jazz bar: *Chatterbox Tavern*
Best jazz series: *Madame Walker*
Best blues club: *Slippery Noodle*
Best upscale blues club: *Barrel House Blues*

F O R J A Z Z

Chatterbox Tavern, *435 Massachusetts Ave. (midtown), 636-0584.*
Surely this is the only place in the world where you'll find an autographed refrigerator—famous (Lou Rawls, John Hiatt) names only please—standing right next to the bar. Not that that's the best of what the Chatterbox, a small friendly neighborhood bar located in a 100-year-old building, has to offer. Some of the top jazz musicians in the city, playing everything from straight-ahead to progressive, can be found here. Regulars include Dick Dickinson, Claude Sifferlen, and Frank Glover. The club, which is done up with Christmas-tree lights and crazy sculptures created by area artists, is also one of the few places in town where musicians are welcome to sit in informally, anytime.
Music: M–Sa. *Cover:* $. *Food:* snacks.

Rick's Café Américain, *Union Station, 39 Jackson Place (downtown), 634-6666.*
*T*he jazz place for young urban professionals in Indianapolis, Rick's is nonetheless very attractive and worth a visit. Big and long, with one side overlooking downtown, the other facing the newly restored Union Station (now a sophisticated mall), it's filled with small, round, black and pink tables, plants, and slowly revolving fans. Over 100 items are on the menu.

Mainstream tuxedoed quartets are usually on tap here, and the musicians are among the city's best. Unfortunately, however, they play in a small enclosed stage area that looks uncomfortably crowded. Sometimes, too, they're hard to hear over the noise of the crowd.

Music: nightly. *No cover. Food:* American. CC.

Faces Midtown Night Club, *2145 N. Talbott St. (midtown), 923-9886.*

The only African-American-owned nightclub in the city, Faces is a large multileveled place with a disco on one side and a listening room on the other. The jazz room, small and intimate, features a little of everything, from fusion to traditional, and African-American VIPs visiting the city—Isaac Hayes, Alex Haley when he was alive, Spike Lee and his entourage—have been known to drop by.

Music: Su, occasionally F, Sa. *Cover:* $.

Jazz Cooker, *925 E. Westfield Blvd. (Broad Ripple), 253-2883.*

A Southern-style restaurant with as much seating outdoors as in, the Jazz Cooker has presented the traditional Dick Laswell Trio for the past eight years, and blues acts and ragtime piano players also take to the stage from time to time. The decor is pure New Orleans, with lots of posters and old instruments hanging from the walls.

Music: W–Su, Su brunch. *No cover. Food:* Creole, Cajun. CC.

Also

Jazz can be heard, usually on the weekends only, at the **Melody Inn** (3826 N. Illinois, 923-4707) and the **Midtown Café** (814 Broad Ripple Ave., 255-0466). The **City Taproom** (28 S. Pennsylvania, 637-1334), a wood-paneled restaurant-bar in the heart of the financial district, features both jazz and blues, while the **Keystone Grill** (8650 Keystone at the Crossing, 848-5202) has a jazz brunch on Sundays.

Several Indianapolis hotels, including the **Ramada Indianapolis Downtown** (31 W. Ohio St., 635-2000), the **Hyatt Regency** (1 S. Capital Ave., 632-1234), and the **Days Inn Hotel** (401 E. Washington, 637-6464) also present jazz on a regular basis.

FOR BLUES

Slippery Noodle Inn, *372 S. Meridian St. (downtown), 631-6968.*

The oldest bar in Indiana is also the best blues bar in Indianapolis, featuring local and regional acts most nights of the week, national acts on occasion. Blues Crew and Red Beans & Rice are among the regular locals; Lonnie Mack and Clarence Gatemouth Brown among the occasional nationals.

The Slippery Noodle, built in 1850, is on the National Register of Historic Places. Run by the Hal Yeagy family for about 30 years, it's a small funky place with a pressed-tin ceiling, hanging gaslight fixtures, and a beautiful wooden bar dating back to 1890. One side of the Noodle is for drinking and eating, the other side is for music. Next door is a second stage, housed in a building (adjacent to the first) that was once a stable. Most nights, two bands perform.

The Noodle's basement once was a haven for runaway slaves on the Underground Railroad; later, the inn's 16 upstairs rooms were converted into "a house of ill repute," where at least one murder took place. During the '30's and '40's, the bar was a haunt of gangsters "Diamond" Jim Brady and John Dillinger, and bullet holes can still be found in the walls.
Music: W–Sa. *Cover:* $–$$. *Food:* American. CC.

Barrel House Blues Supper Club, *8702 Keystone at the Crossing (15 min. N of downtown), 846-6500.*

The newest blues club in town, the Barrel House is at the opposite end of the spectrum, atmospherically speaking, from the Slippery Noodle. An upscale two-tiered place with dining tables on one level and cocktail tables on the other, it features a glass ceiling, exposed brick walls, lots of grays and pinks, and posters and artwork everywhere. Live blues can be heard every night, usually by local, regional, and Chicago-based bands. Among those who have played here recently are Sugar Blue, Big Shoulders, and the Chicago Rhythm & Blues Kings.
Music: nightly. *Cover:* $–$$. *Food:* Cajun.

Chubby's Club LaSalle, *3219 E. Michigan St. (near downtown), 632-6011.*

A small neighborhood tavern with lots of atmosphere, Chubby's serves up simple food and acoustic music most nights of the week, but on Mondays, a popular blues jam is featured. Many of the city's top blues musicians come by here then.
Music: nightly; blues, M. *No cover. Food:* American.

C. T. Peppers, *6283 N. College Ave. (Broad Ripple), 257-6277.*

A large and modern glass and chrome club with a huge central bar, frosted-glass windows, and tall tiny tables, C.T.'s has a rotating roster of blues talent, most of whom play for a week at a time. Paul Orta & the Kingpins and Bangkok Rooster are regulars, and regional acts such as Albert Washington are also brought in from time to time.
Music: W–Su. *Cover:* $. *Food:* American. CC.

Also

BowSprit (7402 N. Michigan Rd., 20 min. N of downtown, 297-4652), a favorite hangout among the city's amateur sailors, usually presents blues once or twice a week. The **Patio** (6308 N. Guilford Ave., 255-2828) has acoustic blues early Monday nights, often led by Yuni and Robert Coleman. National blues and R&B acts can sometimes be heard at **The Vogue** (6259 N. College Ave., 255-2828), a large predominantly rock venue where the Blues Society of Indiana books regular concerts.

Other Venues and Special Events

A "Jazz on the Avenue" concert series, complete with a buffet, is held at the **Walker Center's** Casino Ballroom (617 Indiana Ave., 236-2099) every Friday evening. Every August the multi-day **Indiana Avenue Jazz Festival** is also held here, as is the July "Women in Jazz Series."

The Blues Society of Indiana (470-8795), a statewide organization, hosts a **Blues, Brew & Bar-be-que** picnic in the late summer. Big-band dance concerts are held monthly at the **Indiana Roof Ballroom** (140 W. Washington St., 236-1870). The **Indianapolis Museum of Art** (1200 W. 38th St., 923-1331) has a jazz series featuring local artists, and the Indianapolis Parks and Recreation Commission, together with the Music Performance Trust Funds, puts on a free **Downtown Summer Concert Series** every year at various locations throughout the city. A **Blue Monday Jazz Series** is sponsored annually by the Athenaeum (401 E. Michigan St., 630-4569).

Record Stores

Rick's Records (5605 N. Keystone Ave., 259-4087) and **Tracks** (3748 Commercial Dr., 293-6886; 5485 E. 82nd St., 576-0404) have good selections of both jazz and blues.

Radio

WFYI/90 FM (636-2020). Affiliated with NPR. Jazz most afternoons and late nights. Blues Sa afternoons.

WICR/88.7 FM (788-3280). Affiliated with University of Indianapolis. Jazz and some blues weekday afternoons and weekends.

WTPI/107.9 FM (925-1079). Jazz evenings and nights.

WTLC/1310 AM (923-1456). Longtime deejay King Ro hosts a blues program late weekday afternoons.

WXLW/950 AM (293-9600). Blues M–F nights.

Blues can also be heard Sunday nights on **WTTS/92.3 AM** out of Bloomington.

Cincinnati

This may be a square ofay town in general but there's shit happening here.

—Ed Moss, piano player

In jazz history, Cincinnati has occupied a sort of mainstream of the mainstream position. Only a few nationally known figures (George Russell, Frank Foster, Fred Hersch, Dave Matthews, Michael Moore, Cal Collins) have come out of here, and although the city has had a fair number of clubs over the years, its scene—historically speaking, at least—was never anything to compare with that of nearby Indianapolis. Some of the area's best nightspots were, in fact, actually located over the river in Newport and Covington, Kentucky, which have traditionally served as something of vice centers for Cincinnati.

Nonetheless, within the mainstream framework, Cincinnati has always provided musicians with plenty of work. During the '40's and early '50's there was the Cotton Club in the Hotel Sterling, and during the '50's there was downtown Walnut Street, lined with such clubs as the Living Room, the Blue Angel, the Wine Bar, and the Gibson Girl Lounge. Later, there was Babe Baker's and "the Strip," seven or eight bars located along Reading Road.

Blues, especially R&B, has always been part of Cincinnati as well. King Records, James Brown's label, was once based here, and it drew musicians from all over the country, who came looking for studio work. Then there was Mamie Smith, who was born here in 1883; John Lee Hooker, who lived here in the '30's and '40's; and Lonnie Johnson, who lived at 828 Rockdale Rd. (still standing) in the early '50's. Other blues and R&B figures connected with the city include Amos Milburn; Charles Brown; Roosevelt Lee, who still lives here; Tiny Bradshaw, who is buried in the Union Baptist Cemetery; and the tap dancer Marie Reynolds, who claimed that Louis Jordan wrote the song "Caldonia" about her.

Also not to be forgotten is the dean of jazz deejays, Oscar Treadwell. Treadwell, for whom Bird wrote "An Oscar for Treadwell" and Monk wrote "Oska T.," was a young deejay at WDAS in Philadelphia when he first played Monk's "Misterioso" on the air. The station manager, listening, said that if the deejay ever played that work again, he'd be fired. Treadwell played it five more times and was thrown off. He now hosts a late-night jazz show on the University of Cincinnati's WGUC, where he is given carte blanche to play whatever he likes.

Sources

Radio station WVXU-FM runs a 24-hour Jazz Calendar Hotline that's updated daily: 745-1948.

Listings can be found in two free bimonthlies, *EveryBody's*

News (651-2606) and the *Entertainer* magazine (606-581-6585), as well as in the Thursday section of the *Cincinnati Post* (352-2000) and the Thursday and Sunday sections of the *Cincinnati Enquirer* (721-2700).

For maps and other general information, contact the Greater Cincinnati Convention and Visitors Bureau, 300 W. Sixth St., 621-2142 or 800-344-3445.

The area code for Cincinnati is (513).

A Note on Neighborhoods

Cincinnati, sitting on the north bank of the Ohio River across from Kentucky, is an old Midwestern city with a solid Northeastern feel. Skyscraping hotels and office buildings dominate its small downtown, while its sidewalks are usually bustling with activity.

Historic Mt. Adams, located on a hill overlooking the city, is celebrated for its nightlife, but there are few jazz or blues clubs here. Corryville is a residential area that's also home to the University of Cincinnati; Over-the-Rhine is a partially gentrified area on the Western edge of downtown. Walnut Hills and Bond Hill are districts with large African-American populations, while Roselawn is known as a "black-Jewish neighborhood." All of these areas are located within 20 minutes of downtown.

The Blue Wisp is Cincinnati's oldest and most beloved jazz club.

Cincinnatians pass over to Covington and Newport, Kentucky, located just a five-minute bridge-ride away, without giving it a second thought. Numerous clubs and restaurants are located here.

Traffic in Cincinnati is usually light and parking spaces are plentiful, except in the downtown during the day and in Mt. Adams at night.

Landmarks and Legends

Moonlight Gardens Ballroom, *Coney Island, 6201 Kellogg Ave. (at I-275), 232-8230.*

A big white beautiful building lined with white wrought-iron balconies and sturdy green shutters, the Moonlight is located in an idyllic park on the banks of the Ohio River. At one time all the big bands played here, and in 1936, Noble Sissle and his group, which then included Sidney Bechet and Lena Horne, were scheduled to appear. They were the first African-American band to do so, but en route to the event, Sissle was injured in an automobile accident, and Lena Horne, then only 19 years old, had to front the band.

Today, the Moonlight is part of Coney Island, a low-key amusement park complete with a large pool, water rides, miniature golf, restaurants, and gardens. Outdoor concerts are occasionally presented.

Open: Memorial Day weekend through Labor Day, 10 a.m.–10 p.m.

King Records, *1540 Brewster St.*

Founded by Syd Nathan, formerly of the furniture business, in 1945, King Records was known for its country-and-western singers on the one hand and its R&B artists on the other. Most famous among them all was R&B-soulman James Brown.

Brown was signed to King on January 23, 1956, against the fierce objections of Nathan, who nonetheless let an employee talk him into it. At first, the public seemed to prove Nathan right, for Brown's records sold very poorly. Nathan was on the verge of letting him go when, in 1958, "Try Me" was released. It made No. 1 in R&B and the Top 50 in pop, and by the '60's, Brown was a legend. A publicity release from the time stated: "In an average month, he will give away some 5,000 autographed photos and 1,000 pairs of cuff links, will wear 120 freshly laundered shirts and more than 80 pairs of shoes, will change his performing costume 150 times, and will perform over 80 hours on the stage—singing, dancing, and also playing at least 960 songs on one or more of eight instruments."[1]

Today, all that's left of the record company, which once included a pressing plant and a warehouse, is a complex of brown buildings located near I-71. A dairy company now occupies the premises.

Babe Baker's, *3128 Reading Rd., 751-9272.*

Run by black real estate entrepreneur Babe Baker, this club, now a bar and restaurant called Babe's, was important from the mid-1950s through the 1960s. A long and narrow room, it brought in lots of name talent such as John Coltrane, Miles Davis, and McCoy Tyner, and featured a house band called the Jazz Disciples. "There'd be fast tempos all night long," recalls guitarist Cal Collins, "Lots of bebop, straight-ahead, Clifford Brown–type stuff."

Clubs, etc.

The mainstream tradition is still going strong in Cincinnati today. "Musicians here say that you can't play music in Cincinnati unless you own a tuxedo," says Ron Esposito, former music director for Xavier University's WVXU-FM radio.

Cincinnati's most important jazz spots are the **Blue Wisp, JP's Place,** and the **Greenwich Tavern,** all of which present local and national talent. **Dee Felice's** is an upscale restaurant known for its traditional jazz. Meanwhile, the blues scene in the Cincinnati area is exploding: Whereas three years ago there were only two consistent blues clubs in town (most notably **Cory's,** still a top spot), there are now about half a dozen, including **Local 1207,** the **Mansion Hill Tavern,** and **Miss Catie's.** The preeminent venue in the area for large touring acts is **Gilly's,** located in Dayton, one hour away.

Some of the top jazz artists now working in Cincinnati include guitarist Cal Collins; saxophonist Paul Plummer; pianists Steve Schmidt, Ed Moss, Phil DeGreg, and Frank Vincent; drummers Art Gore, Bobby Scott, and John Von Ohlen; bass players Mike Sharfe and Jim Anderson; and vocalist Ann Chamberlain. Blues artists include John "Pigmeat" Jarrett, Albert Washington, Big Joe Duskin, H-Bomb Ferguson, Cincinnati Slim & the Headhunters, Sweet Alice & the Unfinished Business Blues Band, the High Street Rhythm Rockers, the Cincinnati Blues All-Stars, and Blue Lou & the Accusation, a blues-rock group.

Most clubs in Cincinnati close at 2 a.m.

Personal Choices

Best jazz clubs: *Blue Wisp, Greenwich Tavern*
Best contemporary jazz club: *JP's Place*
Best traditional jazz restaurant-club: *Dee Felice's*
Best blues clubs: *Cory's, Mansion Hill*
Trendiest blues club: *Local 1207*
Best area club for large national acts: *Gilly's (in Dayton)*

FOR JAZZ

Blue Wisp, *19 Garfield Pl. (downtown), 721-9801*.

For 16 years, Marjean and Paul Wisby ran a jazz club in the O'Bryonville section of Cincinnati. It started as a whim—the couple had just bought a neighborhood bar and wanted to add entertainment—and ended up as a legend. The Blue Wisp is now Cincinnati's oldest and most beloved jazz club.

The Wisp, recently relocated to the downtown, has old neighborhood stories galore. Numerous local musicians got their starts there; numerous local artists donated their work to the club. Jazz only came to the old venue, a dusty, hodgepodge place, because a neighbor who ran a piano store business told the Wisbys that jazz would go over better in Cincinnati than country-and-western, their first choice.

So far, the Wisp's move from its old location to its new has not seemed to hurt it. All of the best local talent still plays here, and national talent usually comes through on the weekends. The new club, though larger and much more sophisticated than the old, still has an intimate feel. Located in the cellar of an upscale office building, it's filled with comfortable tables and chairs and bathed in a dark blue light. The original Blue Wisp sign still flaunts its black magic above the stairs.
Music: nightly. *Cover:* $–$$.

JP's Place, *513 Race St. (downtown), 241-8818*.

A large and contemporary club with two bars, teakwood walls, a state-of-the-art sound system, and jazz-theme prints hanging here and there, JP's is one of the newest music spots in town. A lot of top locally based talent plays here, including Tony Riley, Art Gore, the fusion band Ekimi, and Miss P. Ann Everson. On the national level, mostly contemporary acts (Pieces of a Dream, Larry Carlton, Angela Bofill) are booked about once a month, and blues are also featured weekly. On off-music nights, the stage doubles as a dance floor and a deejay spins records.
Music: Th–M. *Cover:* $–$$$ (national acts). *Food:* appetizers.

Greenwich Tavern, *2440 Gilbert Ave. (Walnut Hills), 221-6764*.

The Greenwich is a surprising, eclectic mix of mostly straight-ahead jazz, simple Italian-American food, and friendly, homey atmosphere. Easily the most integrated club in town, it features both national players (Mark Murphy, Jack McDuff) and local stars (Jim Anderson, Art Gore). National blues artists such as "Gatemouth" Brown are also here from time to time.

The 80-plus-year-old restaurant-club is old and creaky, with low ceilings, green curtains, and plastic tablecloths that somehow add up to a lot of atmosphere. The dining takes place in a well-lit room with olive green booths adjacent to the bar, while the music

room, dark and womblike, is off to one side, through a curtained door.
Music: F–Sa. *Cover:* $–$$. *Food:* Italian-American. CC.

Dee Felice Café, *529 Main St., Covington (downtown), 606-261-2365.*

A sedate, well-heeled restaurant heralded for its elegant dining, Dee's, as it's locally known, also offers up some fine Dixieland and traditional jazz. The six-piece Sleep Cat Dixieland Band plays the weekends, and piano players and trios perform during the rest of the week.

The restaurant is nicely laid out in two large rooms with a rose-and-gray color scheme, frosted-glass windows, and pressed-tin ceilings. The stage, very long and narrow, is set up just above and behind a gleaming wooden bar.
Music: nightly. *No cover. Food:* Cajun. CC.

Coco's, *322 Greenup St., Covington (downtown), 606-491-1369.*

Owned by a painter named Bonnie Coe, Coco's is a restaurant-club that features jazz, reggae, and some blues. Veteran blues piano player Pigmeat Jarrett is a regular here; now near 90, he started performing in his seventies, and acquired his nickname because of his passion for pork sandwiches.

Coco's is located in a 100-year-old building that was once a women's trade union and then a neighborhood bar riddled with bookies' wires. Long and narrow with exposed brick walls, wooden beams, and a low-slung balcony, the club is decorated with brightly colored rugs and sun-bleached skulls from the Southwest.
Music: W–Su. *No cover. Food:* American. CC.

Kaldi's Coffeehouse & Bookstore, *1204 Main St. (Over-the-Rhine), 241-3070.*

A second-hand bookstore that's set up with tables among the bookcases, Kaldi's presents jazz four nights a week, usually compliments of the Ron Enyard Trio or the Steve Schmidt Trio. Guitarist Cal Collins and Joshua Breakstone also play here.

Kaldi's is housed in an atmospheric nineteenth-century building, complete with tin ceilings and wood floors. A simple menu is served, and some nights are devoted to combination jazz concerts–poetry readings.
Music: Th–Su. *No cover. Food:* sandwiches, soups, etc.

Also

Sonny's Café & Lounge (1227 California Ave., 242-4579) in Bond Hill is a small and modern neighborhood club that has one of the liveliest jazz jams in the city on Thursday nights. **Joannie's Harmony Club** (7532 Reading Rd., 761-5729), a small neighborhood bar in Roselawn, can be a good spot to hear up-and-coming talent.

Superb vocalist Mary Ellen Tanner, singing a mix of Gershwin and Tin Pan Alley tunes, can often be heard at **The Celestial** (1071 Celestial St., 241-4455), a restaurant in Mt. Adams known for its continental cuisine. Some of the blues clubs listed below, most notably **Local 1207,** also present jazz.

F O R   B L U E S

Cory's, *1 E. McMillan St. (Corryville), 721-6339.*
The oldest blues bar in town, Cory's is primarily housed in a sturdy historic building with pressed-tin ceilings, wooden paneling, and an old-fashioned pendulum clock. Out back is a large new showroom where regional and national acts perform, while downstairs is a bar equipped with a jukebox.

Intimate and friendly, Cory's has a lot of atmosphere. All the top local talent plays here—Pigmeat Jarrett, Sweet Alice, H-Bomb Ferguson—and the place is always packed with both students and residents from the surrounding working-class neighborhood.
Music: nightly. *Cover:* $.

Local 1207, *1207 Main St. (Over-the-Rhine), 651-1207.*
Currently the trendiest blues spot in town, the Local presents many Cincinnati acts (Blue Lou & the Accusations, Staci, the Blues Doctor) as well as occasional regional (Duke Tumatoe) and Chicago-based talent (Buddy Guy, Junior Wells). Jazz, usually of the contemporary sort, is also featured weekly.

Housed in a 100-year-old building that's about 20 feet wide and 100 feet long, the Local has a tin ceiling painted purple with silver sparkles, some exposed brick walls, and wooden floors. Celebrities passing through town often stop by here, as do young professionals hanging out after work.
Music: Tu–Su. *Cover:* $.

Mansion Hill Tavern, *502 Washington St., Newport, Ky., 606-431-3538.*
A neighborhood saloon that's been a bar for over 75 years, the Mansion is a dark and laid-back place with exposed brick walls, wood wainscot, lots of neon, boat paraphernalia, plants, and artwork. Blues come to the Mansion on weekend nights, and it's a favorite spot among the *cognoscenti,* drawing everyone, says one habitué, from "strippers to yuppies, blues aficionados to neighborhood people." Blue Lou & the Accusations is the bar's house band, and the Greater Cincinnati Blues Society meets here the first Sunday of every month. Every other Sunday there's a blues jam.
Music: F, Sa, every other Su. *Cover:* $. *Food:* burgers, etc.

Miss Catie's, *201 E. Second (at Saratoga), Newport, Ky.,*
606-291-6651.

Housed in a 120-year-old brick building that's always been in
the same family, Miss Catie's was once a meat market and a bar-
bershop. A rustic place with hand-hewn wooden tables that were
made by its present owners, it features a big bar in the front, a
small game room to one side, and a beautiful garden out back,
complete with pits for horseshoe throwing and a stage where the
bands play, weather permitting. During the day and much of the
week, Miss Catie's is a neighborhood hangout, but on the weekends, its blues attract a big crowd. Sweet Alice & the Unfinished
Blues Band, the High Street Rhythm Rockers, and the Blues All-
Stars are regulars here.
Music: F, Sa. *Cover:* $. *Food:* sandwiches, etc.

Allyn's Café, *3538 Columbia Parkway (5 min. N of*
downtown), 871-5779.

There's no dearth of odd memorabilia is this eclectic Cajun and
Mexican restaurant, including more than 50 antique radios, a
large collection of cuckoo clocks, and dozens of posters from Cincinnati's yearly Oktoberfest. The booths are all done up in Mexican pastels, and there's a patio out back.

Blues is also part of the scene, and it ranges from the unknown
("we encourage musicians starting up to come down here," says
owner Allyn Raifstanger) to regional acts. Some of the bands who
have played here include the Bluebirds, Out of the Blue, and Liz
Pennock & Dr. Blues (from northern Ohio).
Music: F–Su. *Cover:* $. *Food:* Mexican, Cajun.

Burbank's Real Bar-B-Que Sharonville, *11167 Dowlin*
Dr. (12 min. N of downtown), 771-1440.
Burbank's Real Bar-B-Que Eastgate, *4389 Eastgate Sq.*
Dr. (in Bigg's Shopping Center on Rt. 32, 5 min. E of
downtown), 753-3313.
Burbank's Real Bar-B-Que Florence, *7908 Dream St. (in*
Ky., corner of U.S. 42), 606-371-7373.
Burbank's Real Bar-B-Que Forest Fair, *211 Forest Fair*
Dr. (Forest Park area, 10 min. NW of downtown), 671-6330.

A chain of modern rib joints that must be the largest employer
of blues musicians in the Cincinnati area, Burbank's presents
blues six nights a week at all four of its locations. Many of the top
bands in town play for them, including the Blues All-Stars, Cincinnati Slim & the Headhunters, and H-Bomb Ferguson, and regional talent such as Duke Tumatoe and Luther "Guitar Junior"
Johnson are also booked regularly.

All of the Burbank's (all located just off I-275) look more or less
the same, with lots of aged wood, gray-and-blue booths, and two
large dining rooms with a circular bar in the middle.
Music: M–Sa. *No cover. Food:* barbecue.

Also

Acoustic blues can be heard weekly at **Arnold's Bar & Grill** (210 E. Eighth St., 421-6234), a well-lit checkered-tablecloth affair that's the oldest bar in Cincinnati.

Other Venues and Special Events

Jazz Live at the Hyatt (Hyatt Regency Hotel, 151 W. Fifth St., 579-1234) is a free monthly series held during the fall and winter that features both local and national jazz acts. The music is presented in the Sungarden Lounge, located on the second floor of an airy four-story atrium.

A free **Riverboat Row Jazz Festival,** featuring both local and national artists, is held over Labor Day weekend. The **Queen City Blues Festival,** put on by the Greater Cincinnati Blues Society (684-GCBS or 721-0314), usually takes place in October. The **Cincinnati Recreation Commission** (352-4000) puts on a multitude of free summer concerts in the city's parks.

Touring blues and jazz talent sometimes appears at **Bogart's** (2621 Vine St., 281-8400), a large predominantly rock venue in Corryville, and **Music Hall** (1243 Elm St., 721-8222).

Record Stores

The best stores for new and used jazz and blues records are **Everybody's Records** (6106 Montgomery Rd. at Ridge, 531-4500), and **Record Theater** (4590 Montgomery Rd., 531-8877).

Radio

WVXU/91.7 FM (745-3738). Affiliated with NPR and Xavier University. Jazz afternoons, nights; blues Th, Su evenings.

WGUC/90.9 FM (556-4444). Affiliated with the University of Cincinatti. Of special note, "Jazz with O.T.," M–F, late nights.

WAIF/88.3 FM (961-8900). Jazz, Su midday and evening; blues, Th evening, Su night. Of special note: "Kitty's Blues Live" with Kitty Carson, Th evening.

Other Nearby Locations

Gilly's, *Fifth and Jefferson Streets, Dayton (downtown), 228-8414.*

Adjoining a bus station, just over an hour north of Cincinnati, is the premier club in the area. Gilly's, which seats about 250, has been presenting top talent for 20 years, and it's a beautiful place, with an excellent sound system and superb sight lines. The music runs the jazz-blues gamut: Wynton Marsalis, Woody Herman, and Stanley Jordan; B. B. King, Lonnie Mack, and Denise LaSalle.

Rock is also sometimes featured, and the place is closed if there's no talent booked.

Music: most nights. *Cover:* $$–$$$.

▮Min▮neapolis/St. Paul

The Twin Cities have played only a small role in jazz and blues history, but several major figures are connected with the area. Oscar Pettiford, the bassist of mixed black and Native American extraction who pioneered the use of the jazz cello, moved here from Oklahoma with his family's band during the 1930's and spent his youth in the cities. Lester Young also moved to Minneapolis with his family's band for a brief period in the 1920's and then returned as a young man in 1930. During his second stay, he played at the Nest Club with Frank Hines, Leroy White and Eddie Barefield, and at the Cotton Club in the suburb of St. Louis Park.

According to Eddie Barefield, Minneapolis did have its share of jazz life in the late '20's and '30's, to be found mostly in speakeasies and back-street bars. The local radio stations also had their staff orchestras, and the hotels, their touring big bands. Peggy Lee, originally from North Dakota, took a big step in her career when she appeared at the Radisson Hotel with Sev Olson's band.

Later, there were the Prom Center ballroom in St. Paul and the Merigold ballroom in Minneapolis, along with a club called Freddie's, which had an NBC wire and featured major players such as Ella Fitzgerald and Teddy Wilson. Duke Ellington presented one of his rare sacred concerts at Minneapolis's Hennepin Avenue Baptist Church, and cornet player Paul "Doc" Evans was a regular at a traditional jazz joint called Mitch's.

Two major blues figures, Baby Doo Caston from Mississippi and Lazy Bill Lucas from Arkansas, also settled down in the Twin Cities area, while the '60's brought with them several significant white blues artists. Among these were the group Koerner, Ray, and Glover, an early John Lennon favorite, and the piano player Willie Murphy. Back then, the center of the Cities' music scene was the Triangle Bar at 1822 Riverside (still standing but no longer in use), where Bonnie Raitt and Bob Dylan also played. The Triangle was located on Minneapolis's rebellious West Bank near Cedar and Riverside, then called "the biomagnetic center of the universe."

The West Bank is also one of the oldest districts in the Twin Cities; its bars date back to the early 1900's and were once watering holes for riverboat captains.

Sources

The *Twin Cities Reader* (591-2500) and *City Pages* (375-1015), both free weeklies, are excellent sources. The Friday sections of the *St. Paul Pioneer Press Dispatch* (222-5011) and the *Minneapolis Star-Tribune* (673-4000) also contain listings.

The Twin Cities Jazz Society runs a hotline at 633-0329.

For maps and other information, contact the Greater Minneapolis Convention and Visitors Association at 4000 Multifoods Tower, 33 S. Sixth St., 661-4700, and the St. Paul Area Chamber of Commerce/St. Paul Convention & Visitor's Bureau at 55 East Fifth St., 223-5000/297-6985.

The area code for Minneapolis/St. Paul is (612).

A Note on Neighborhoods

The Twin Cities, located about 10 minutes apart, like to enumerate their differences. Minneapolis is the newer, bigger, brasher of the two. St. Paul is older—more cultured but also somewhat stodgy.

To an outsider, however, the cities have much in common: lots of clean streets and city parks and big bearded men in winter parkas, numerous cultural institutions, little street crime, and relatively small ethnic populations. The restored Warehouse District, now filled with shops and restaurants, is in downtown Minneapolis; the West Bank, located near the University of Minnesota, is still a sort of "ex-hippie" district in east Minneapolis, and Seven Corners is a restaurant and theater district also in east Minneapolis.

Traffic in the Twin Cities is light and street parking is available almost everywhere.

Clubs, etc.

The Twin Cities has no full-time jazz club, but national artists are brought in frequently through the **Dakota** restaurant and several active concert series (see "Other Venues and Special Events," page 306). Local jazz can best be heard at the Dakota and a number of other restaurants.

The top blues club in town, bringing in many national acts, is the **Blues Saloon**. The **Cabooze** also brings in national blues acts on occasion. For local blues and R&B of varying quality, there are a handful of very lively historic bars along the West Bank, most of which offer music nightly for little or no cover.

Area jazz artists to watch for include organ player Brother Jack McDuff, bassist Anthony Cox, stride piano player Butch Thompson, tenor saxophonist Irv Williams, woodwind artists Eddie Berger and John Devine, vocalist Debbie Duncan, the Bobby Peterson Trio, reedman Dave Karr, saxman Morris Wilson, multi-

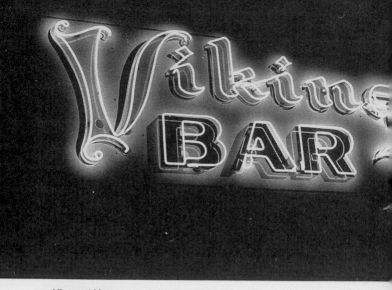

Like most blues bars on the West Bank, the Viking once catered to Mississippi riverboat captains.

instrumentalist Milo Fine, the Terrence Hughes Trio, string instrumentalist Richard Paske, the Cedar Avenue Big Band, the Dey Big Band, the Illicit Sextet, the Hall Brothers New Orleans Jazz Band, and drummers Eric Kamal Gravatt, Kenny Horst, and Wallace Hill.

Blues artists include Big Walter Smith & the Groove Merchants, Dave Ray and Tony Glover, piano player Willie Murphy, the Hoopsnakes, the Butanes and the Butanes Soul Revue (a larger, more soul-oriented version of the same band), harmonica player Lamont Cranston, Rockin' Daddy & the Rough Cuts, True Blue, Dr. Mambo's Combo, the Joel Johnson Band, Out All Night, Downright Tight, Percy Strother, and 3 Bedroom Rambler.

Personal Choices

Best jazz restaurant: *Dakota*
Most atmospheric jazz spots: *Nostalgia, The Times*
Best progressive jazz: *Loring Café*
Best club for big bands: *O'Gara's*
Best blues club: *Blues Saloon*
Best hole-in-the-wall blues clubs: *Viking Bar, Blues Alley*

F O R   J A Z Z

Dakota Bar & Grill, *Bandana Sq., 1021 Bandana Blvd., St. Paul (near downtown), 642-1442.*

One of the best restaurants in town (critically acclaimed by all the local papers and the *New York Times*), the Dakota is large and sprawling, filled with mauves, maroons, and blond wood. Music is most definitely a sideline here, but it's a very fine sideline. National artists such as McCoy Tyner, Ahmad Jamal, Betty Carter, Max Roach, and Roy Hargrove come through a few times a month, while the rest of the week is devoted to top local artists. Vocalists, especially, are well represented: Moore By Four, Debbie Duncan, and Connie Evingson.

The Dakota is housed in what used to be a repair garage for the National Pacific Railroad, and it's part of a renovated warehouse district known as Bandana Square.

Music: nightly. *Cover :* $–$$$. *Food:* American. CC. Reservations recommended.

Nostalgia, *247 Cedar Ave. S. (Seven Corners), M'polis, 330-0926.*

An atmospheric three-story building complete with exposed brick walls, thick wooden beams, and an outdoor patio, Nostalgia features dining on the first and second floors, jazz on the third. The jazz bar is a small and cozy place with instruments hanging from the walls and candles lighting the tables. Local artists, especially vocalists, are usually on hand; regulars include Debbie Duncan and Dennis Spears, and Gwen and Kandii Matthews. National artists also come through on rare occasion, and on Sundays a jazz or gospel brunch is served.

Music: nightly *Cover:* $–$$. *Food:* American. CC.

The Times, *1036 Nicollet Mall (downtown, near Orchestra Hall), M'polis, 333-2762.*

A tiny wood-paneled restaurant-club that's a favorite among young professionals, the Times offers live music every night of the week, usually compliments of a steady, rotating roster of bands. Jazz vocalists are usually featured on Mondays and Tuesdays, while bluesmen Dave Ray and Tony Glover play Thursdays, and the Wolverines Jazz Trio, often accompanied by a guest artist, play the weekends. Sundays are usually devoted to a jazz brunch.

Music: nightly. *No cover. Food:* American. Reservations recommended.

Café Luxeford, *Luxeford Suites, 1101 LaSalle (near Orchestra Hall), M'polis, 332-6800.*

Located on the lobby level of the Luxeford Suites hotel, the Luxeford is a small "European-style" restaurant serving up breakfast, lunch, dinner, and jazz. Local artists, especially vocalists, are usually presented, although big-name musicians do come through from time to time. The Luxeford, known locally for its good acoustics and fine piano, is abutted by Crowley's Lounge, a larger room from which the music can also be heard. Big picture windows face onto the street.

Music: F, Sa. *Cover:* $. *Food:* Continental. CC.

Arnella's, *1183 University Ave. (10 min. W of downtown, near M'polis), St. Paul, 642-5975.*

One of the few black-owned jazz venues in the Twin Cities, Arnella's (named after its owner, Arnella Alles) usually features music about three nights a week. A large place with a bar to one side, tables and chairs to the other, the club is also a restaurant serving up good, old-fashioned American food such as meatloaf, roast chicken, and pork chops. Chandeliers hang from the ceiling and candles light the tables. Jam sessions are usually held on Sunday nights, while special events such as a "Battle of the Saxophones" are sometimes featured.

Music: Su, M, W. *Cover:* $. *Food:* American.

Loring Café & Playhouse, *1624 Harmon Pl. (downtown), M'polis, 332-1617.*

Housed in an atmospheric old building with a lot of mismatched furniture, the Loring is an eclectic restaurant-club that attracts a youngish, arts-oriented crowd. "More European than American," as one local fan describes it, it's located in a park overlooking a pond and offers both indoor and outdoor dining.

Music at the Loring runs the gamut, but it's always somewhat removed from the mainstream, and jazz is a regular feature. Top area names such as John Devine and the illicit sextet are regulars.

Music: nightly, jazz about twice weekly. *No cover. Food:* American.

Also

O'Gara's (see "For Blues," page 305) has been presenting big bands on Monday nights for years and years. Other restaurants that have jazz on occasion include the **Fine Line Music Café** and the **New Riverside Café** (see "For Blues," page 304); and the **Kuppernicus Coffee House** (308 Prince St., St. Paul, 290-2718), which is similar in atmosphere to the New Riverside, but presents more jazz.

Two riverboat companies offer Dixieland and traditional jazz cruises during the summer months: the **Andiamo Showboat** (430-1234) and the **Padelford Packet Boat Co.** (227-1100). Jazz brunches, also featuring Dixieland and traditional jazz, are served on Sundays by the **Carousel Room** at the Radisson Hotel St. Paul (11 E. Kellogg Blvd., 292-1900) and **Koziak's Royal Oak** (4785 Hodgson Rd., Shoreview, 484-8484).

FOR BLUES

The Blues Saloon, *601 N. Western Ave., St. Paul (5 min. N of downtown), 228-9959.*

The best blues bar in the area, the Saloon is tucked away in what used to be a ballroom above a neighborhood bar. Crazy Aztec-like orange and blue animal figures cover its walls, and there's a wrought-iron balcony and big dance floor. Meanwhile, up on a small, elevated stage, the blues bands smoke away.

Many of the Alligator recording acts come through here, as do numerous national groups on their way to Canada. Little Milton, Bobby Rush, Johnny Copeland, and Etta James have all played the Saloon, which is also one of the few commercial clubs in the country owned and largely run by women.

Music: Th–M. *Cover:* $–$$.

The Cabooze, *917 Cedar Ave. S., M'polis (West Bank), 338-6425.*

From the outside the Cabooze looks small and narrow, like its namesake, but inside, it's a long and friendly atmospheric hall with crowds of people and a bandstand located way down at the other end. A large wooden bar dominates the place, along with neon strips of blue and red and larger-than-life posters of artists such as Little Richard and Dr. John.

The original Cabooze, founded in the early '70's, was a small locally renowned club that featured almost exclusively blues (Albert King, Junior Walker, Willie Dixon). Since then, it's become primarily a rock-and-roll club presenting national acts, but blues, both local and national, still play an occasional role.

Music: nightly, occasional blues. *Cover:* $–$$.

Viking Bar, *1829 Riverside Ave. S., M'polis (West Bank), 332-4259.*

A West Bank bar that's been here since the 1920's, the Viking, long and narrow, is friendly and laid-back, soaked in the alcohol of time. Booths line one wall while a stained-glass sun pattern is splashed behind the bar. The Joel Johnson Band is the mainstay here; Johnson also books the place.

Music: Th–Su. *Cover:* Occasional, $.

Whiskey Junction, *901 Cedar Ave. S., M'polis (West Bank), 338-9550.*

Though lacking the dark and cozy character of the other, older West Bank bars, the Junction offers a steady diet of local blues talent with Blues Deluxe hosting a popular jam on Monday nights. A large, two-roomed place with a long, long bar, it has walls of exposed brick and a floor of black-and-white tile. The musicians crowd onto a small stage located at the far end, leaving plenty of room for dancing and drinking.

Music: nightly. *No cover.*

New Riverside Café, *329 S. Cedar Ave. S., M'polis (West Bank), 333-4814.*

Stepping in here is like stepping into a time warp. Long-haired men in vests sit next to soft-spoken women in peasant blouses. Meanwhile, behind a cafeteria-style food counter, friendly folk serve up immense plates of black-eyed peas, wild rice, lentil loaf, and the like.

Music at the New Riverside, which is now over 20 years old, runs the gamut, but acoustic blues and occasional jazz is sometimes on the menu. The place, small and well lit, is usually quite crowded, yet there always seems to be room for one more.

Music: Tu–Sa, some jazz/blues. *No cover. Food:* vegetarian.

Blues Alley, *15 Glenwood Ave. N., M'polis (10 min. N of downtown), 333-1327.*

One of the oldest blues clubs in the city, Blues Alley is home to True Blue, a band that has played here in various incarnations for over a decade. The club was also one of the first in the city to present a weekly blues jam (now usually held on Sunday nights).

Housed in an old building with exposed brick walls and ceiling fans, Blues Alley is divided into three small rooms. The stage is in the center room, and there's a wonderful big old bar up front. Until recently, the neighborhood around the club was considered to be somewhat rough, but since the construction of the Target Center Arena (home to the Timberwolves) across the street, the club and its neighborhood are prospering.

Music: F–Su. *Cover: $. Food:* burgers, etc.

The Fine Line Music Café, *318 First Ave. N., M'polis (Warehouse District), 338-8100.*

A spacious restaurant-club with exposed brick walls, a low-slung balcony, and a refined feel, the Fine Line presents blues and R&B and occasional jazz once or twice a week. Other nights are devoted to folk and light rock, while national artists (Al di Meola, John Scofield) are presented from time to time. Local regulars include Dr. Mambo's Combo and the Steeles, and Sundays often feature a gospel brunch.

Music: nightly, some blues and jazz. *Cover:* $–$$. *Food:* American. CC.

First Avenue/Seventh Street Entry, *701 First Ave. N., M'polis (Warehouse District) 332-1775.*

Though mostly known as a rock, funk, and new music club made famous through Prince's 1984 movie *Purple Rain,* First Avenue, a rounded cinderblock building painted flat black, prides itself on offering all kinds of music, including jazz, blues, and R&B. National acts who have played here include everyone from the Dead Milkmen and Burning Spear to Lonnie Mack and Dr. John.

First Avenue, which can accommodate 1,200, is actually

housed in an old Greyhound bus terminal. There's a sunken dance floor flanked by large video screens, a game room, and a glassed-in mezzanine with another bar (this is where Prince used to sit, surrounded by bodyguards).

Ever since *Purple Rain*'s release, First Avenue has also become a tourist attraction. Never mind the fact that the movie is now nearly 10 years old—out-of-towners still come by all the time, clicking their cameras.

Adjacent to First Avenue is the small, dark Seventh Street-Entry, which is still a good place to catch local bands and up-and-coming talent. Tracy Chapman, Public Enemy, and Living Colour all played here before making it big.

Music: nightly, occasional blues and jazz. *Cover:* $–$$$.

Bunker's Music Bar & Grill, *761 Washington Ave. N., M'polis. (Warehouse District) 338-8188.*

Once a dingy neighborhood bar with nothing but a widescreen TV and a corny name (Archie's Bunker), Bunker's metamorphosed a few years ago into a hot spot drawing both its old steady biker's crowd and a newer young, professional set, all of whom, curiously enough, seem to coexist peacefully. Acts in this big square-shaped club, newly decorated to fit its new image, are mostly local (Dr. Mambo's Combo, the Stud Brothers), but national artists (Koko Taylor, Clarence "Gatemouth" Brown) come through from time to time.

Music: nightly. *Cover:* $, except for national acts. *Food:* burgers, etc.

O'Gara's Bar and Grill/O'Gara's Garage, *164 N. Snelling Ave., St. Paul (5 min. W of downtown), 644-3333.*

Basically an old-time Irish bar and restaurant filled with green booths and frosted glass, O'Gara's presents a a big band on Monday nights and occasional jazz during the rest of the month. Meanwhile, out back in O'Gara's Garage, a big spiffy place with lime-green lights and a black-and-chrome bar, blues bands such as the Hoopsnakes perform most weekends.

O'Gara's, which dates back to 1941, began as a restaurant that served food and liquor to factory workers who helped manufacture World War II munitions. Another historical tidbit: today's game room is housed in what used to be a barbershop that was run by Charles "Peanuts" Schulz's father.

Music: S–M, Th–Sa. *Cover:* $. *Food:* American.

Also

Blues jams can be heard in many of the above clubs on Monday nights. **The Times** and several other jazz clubs also have blues on occasion (see "For Jazz," page 301).

The popular blues-funk piano player Willie Murphy plays twice a month or so at the **400 Bar** (400 Cedar Ave. S., M'polis,

332-2903), one of the most atmospheric of the West Bank bars. The **Five Corners Saloon** (501 Cedar Ave. S., M'polis; 338-6424), another West Bank club, once presented almost exclusively blues and R&B and still features blues from time to time.

Other Venues and Special Events

Both the **World Theater** (10 E. Exchange St., St. Paul, 290-1221) and the **Ordway Music Theatre** (345 Washington St., St. Paul, 224-4222) present a regular jazz series. **Northrop Auditorium** at the University of Minnesota (348-2226) has a summer series featuring more avant-garde sounds. Other auditoriums sponsoring jazz and blues events on occasion include the **Walker Art Centre** (725 Vineland Pl., M'polis, 375-7577), the **Cedar Cultural Center** (416 Cedar Ave. S., M'polis, 338-2674), the **Minnesota Composers Forum** (26 E. Exchange St., St. Paul, 228–1407) and **Orchestra Hall** (1111 Nicollet Mall, M'polis, 371-5656).

The **Twin Cities Jazz Society** (633-0329), one of the largest jazz societies in the U.S., runs a concert series October through March. Sessions are held in rotating clubs, and nonmembers are welcome.

Numerous free concerts sponsored by the Twin Cities' Parks and Recreation Commissions are held throughout the summer months; watch the papers. The largest blues festival in the area is the **Bayfront Blues Festival** (800-4-DULUTH), a free three-day event held in August in Duluth, Minn., approximately three hours away.

Radio

KBEM/88.5 FM (627-2833). A 24-hour jazz station. Licensed to the Minneapolis Public Schools.

KFAI/90.3 FM (341-3144). Jazz weekday early afternoons. Blues Th, F, Su afternoons; Tu midday and night; Th early morning.

KSJN/99.5 FM. Some jazz. Of special note: "The Jazz Image" with Leigh Kamman, Sa nights.

Some jazz and blues can also be heard on **KMOJ/89.9 FM**, **WCAL/89.4 FM**, and **KLBB/1450 AM**.

Record Stores

Electric Fetus (2010 Fourth Ave. S., M'polis, 870-9300), a longtime head shop and a major record distributor for the seven-state area, has a good jazz-blues selection. Cold Wind Records, which records local blues artists such as Lamont Cranston, are sold here. Other good choices are **Oar Folkjokeopus** (2557 Lyndale Ave. S., M'polis, 872-7400); **Hymie's Vintage Records** (3318 E. Lake St., M'polis, 729-8890), a top place for imports; and **Hazen's Books & Records** (3318 E. Lake St., downstairs; 721-3854), which has a large used-records section.

**Deep Ellum once
teemed with night-
clubs, theaters, and
dance halls that
rocked until dawn.**

*Texas/Dallas History
and Archives Division,
Dallas Public Library*

Texas

"The Texas sound has more feeling, melodic syncopation and a different beat. . . . Anytime there's a Texan band, blues and jazz fit together."

So says Milton Larkin, speaking to Alan Govenar in *Meeting the Blues*. Larkin, a trumpet/trombone player and vocalist still active in Houston today, was a territorial bandleader back in the 1930's when the Texas sound was first exploding into view. Some of the greatest of the Texas saxmen came up under his leadership: Arnett Cobb, Illinois Jacquet, Eddie "Cleanhead" Vinson.

Texas has made an enormous, yet often understated, contribution to jazz and blues. Scott Joplin was born in Texarkana in 1868 and two of the most seminal of bluesmen, Huddie Ledbetter (better known as Leadbelly) and Blind Lemon Jefferson, were playing the streets of Dallas as early as 1912. In the 1920's and 1930's, the state was teeming not only with territorial jazz bands such as the one led by Larkin, but also with blues singers, small combos, and boogie-woogie piano players. Later, there was Charlie Christian, bringing the electric guitar to jazz, and the big, blow-away sound of the sax, the instrument most frequently associated with Texas jazz and blues.

Texas has never had one dominant metropolis, and so many of its early jazz- and bluesmen moved freely between its cities. San Antonio, Houston, and Dallas were especially important. San Antonio was the city where Jack Teagarden, one of the most important trombone players of all time, got his start. Houston was the site of numerous "battles of the bands" and home to Peck Kelley, a legendary piano player. Dallas was once the most important band town in Texas, launching the careers of innumerable first-rate musicians, including T-Bone Walker, Buster Smith, Charlie Christian, Oran Page, Herschel Evans, and Alphonso Trent.

Austin's primary contribution to the state's music took place a bit later. Gene Ramey and Teddy Wilson came out of the small tree-lined city in the 1940's, and in the '60s, '70's and '80's, there were Stevie Ray Vaughan, Kim Wilson, Angela Strehli, and others.

Houston

One of the most famous of Houston's bluesmen is Lightnin' Hopkins; one of the most famous of its jazzmen is big-band leader Illinois Jacquet. Others associated with the sprawling coastal city include Beulah "Sippie" Wallace, who spent her childhood playing the organ in a local church; Willie Mae "Big Mama" Thornton, who moved here from Alabama in the hopes of furthering her career; Johnny Copeland, originally from Haynesville, Louisiana;

saxophonists Arnett Cobb and Harold Land; saxophonist-vocalist Eddie "Cleanhead" Vinson; and bandleader Milton Larkin, whose band led many of the "battles of the bands" at the Harlem Square Club.

Then, too, there was the legendary Peck Kelley, who, despite many offers to join large prestigious bands on both coasts, spent most of his life playing in a Houston supper club and never recorded an album. Jack Teagarden often compared Peck to Art Tatum and once said of him, "If you didn't look at him, Peck would play ten choruses in a row. But it would get so great, you'd just have to look; then he'd get self-conscious and stop."[1]

Houston was once also home to the legendary Bronze Peacock Club and Peacock Records, both owned by African-American businessman Don Robey. During the 1950's, Robey recorded everyone from Clarence "Gatemouth" Brown and Junior Parker to the Dixie Hummingbirds and the Five Blind Boys of Mississippi. Robey also recorded Johnny Ace, who met his untimely end in Houston's City Auditorium on Christmas Eve, 1954, (see "Landmarks and Legends," page 313).

Sources

Excellent listings can be found in the *Houston Press* (961-0300), a free weekly. The Sunday edition of the *Houston Post* (840-5600), the Friday edition of the *Houston Chronicle* (220-7171), and the *Public News* (520-1520) also carry listings.

Maps and other information can be obtained from the Greater Houston Convention and Visitors Bureau, 801 Congress, 227-3100 or (800) 231-7799.

The area code for Houston is (713).

A Note on Neighborhoods

Houston is the fourth-largest city in the U.S., surrounded by immense expressways that are always teeming with traffic. Somehow, however, the downtown, modern and glass-sheathed though it is, often feels empty, almost sleepy, as if it were remembering quieter days.

Houston was originally laid out in a ward system of political boundaries arranged around the quadrants formed by Congress Avenue and Main Street. The northwest corner of the Congress-Main intersection was the First Ward, the northeast corner the Second, the southeast corner the Third, and the southwest corner the Fourth. As the city grew, more wards, eventually totaling nine, were added, with the African-American population settling into the Third, Fourth and Fifth wards.

By the '20's and '30's, the ward system had lost its rigidity, and today the city is officially divided into council districts. People still refer to addresses by the old ward system, however. Other neighborhood names are also used. The Heights is an upper-middle-class area just northwest of downtown; Montrose is a young, somewhat Bohemian arts and theater area just west of downtown; the Galleria is an upscale district filled with shopping malls to the south of the city.

Despite the many intimidating highways surrounding the city, driving in Houston is relatively easy. Streets are well marked and parking is usually plentiful.

Landmarks and Legends

(The sites below are all located in or near the downtown, but are relatively far apart and should be viewed by car.)

The Third and Fourth wards, *south of Congress Ave. (centering on Dowling St. between Gray and Elgin, and around West Dallas St. between downtown and Taft).*

Most of Houston's African-American population once lived in the Third, Fourth, and Fifth wards, and the Third and Fourth wards were especially well known for their nightlife. The Eldorado Ballroom, along with the Lincoln Dance Hall, the Emancipation Park Dance Pavilion, the Lincoln Theater, and the Key Theater were all located here. Today, only the Eldorado remains standing, although Emancipation Park—*sans* dance pavilion—is still located across the street.

Dowling and West Dallas streets ran through the hearts of the Third and Fourth wards, respectively, and were home base for many bluesmen. Lightnin' Hopkins used to play for change along the sidewalks of Dowling, while the Santa Fe group of barrelhouse piano players (a loose group of traveling men who once played the jukes along the Santa Fe railroad) played along West Dallas.

Eldorado Ballroom, *corner of Elgin and Dowling streets.*

Looking much the same on the outside today as it did back in the '50's, this large curved white building once housed one of the most famous dance halls in Texas. Nat "King" Cole and Ray Charles sang here, and Big Mama Thornton was discovered here by Don Robey, who immediately signed her up to an exclusive five-year contract. Two of Big Mama's most popular songs were "Hound Dog" and "Ball and Chain," which were later made into hits by Elvis Presley and Janis Joplin respectively. Presley and Joplin received much money and acclaim for their efforts, while Thornton's original versions went virtually unacknowledged.

The Eldorado, located on the building's second floor, was nicknamed "the house of happy feet." With a stage that could be pushed in and out of the wall as the occasion demanded, it attracted crowds of all ages. "In the afternoons," says Houston drummer George Haynes, "The young teenagers would come in. Admission was thirty-five or fifty cents, and then they'd go to the ice cream parlor for a triple dip. The older crowd would

Milton Larkin, an early territorial bandleader, still plays around town on occasion.

come in from eight to twelve, and then it was a brown-bag sort of situation."

Club La Veek, *1511 Blodgett (Third Ward), 528-8267.*

For nearly two decades, the La Veek, situated in a small run-down shopping strip, with cars pulled close to its brilliant graffiti'd facade, was the mainstay of Houston's jazz community. Arnett Cobb once led a house band here, and many jazz and blues greats—Little Milton, Buddy Rich, Jimmy Smith—passed through its doors. Today, the club operates as a neighborhood bar and social center only; there is no live music.

Old City Auditorium, *since replaced by Jones Hall for the Performing Arts, 615 Louisiana St.*

While sitting in his dressing room at the Old City waiting to go back on stage, blues singer Johnny Ace, who had once played piano in B. B. King's band, started fooling around with a gun. He liked to play with guns, and, feeling daring, dropped a bullet into the chamber. Then he spun the barrel and pointed the gun to his head—some say to impress a girl. He pulled the trigger and "his hair stood on end like horror movies. His brain oozed out of that little hole. . . ."[2] He was 26 years old.

Music Hall, *810 Bagby St.*

Built in the late 1940's, the still operating Music Hall was the site of a Jazz at the Philharmonic (JATP) concert produced by Norman Granz in 1955. JATP was a milestone in jazz history in that it gave first-class treatment to jazz musicians for the first time (see "Los Angeles," page 354). The musicians traveled first class all the way, and no segregation in the audience was allowed.

"The first thing I'd do," says Norman Granz in Gillespie's *To Be or Not To Bop*, "was rent the auditorium myself. Then I'd hire the ticket seller to sell tickets to my concert and tell him that there was to be no segregation whatsoever. . . . I removed the signs that said 'White toilets' and 'Negro toilets.' That was new. . . . The whole idea was to break all that shit open."

When JATP arrived in Houston, it was business as usual as far as Granz was concerned. But Houston had never had an integrated concert before, and the authorities were going to cause trouble one way or another. Dizzy Gillespie relates the story in his autobiography: "Between sets, we'd be in the back, shooting dice, playing cards, or whatever, and this time in Texas . . . the dressing room door burst open. The police came in and took us all to jail, including Ella Fitzgerald. They took us down, finger-printed us, and put us in jail. Norman put up a bond and got us out. He just wouldn't be intimidated by these people."

Clubs, etc.

Although Houston is home to a large number of first-class jazz musicians, it has no full-time jazz club and no room that brings in national artists on a regular basis. The best place to hear top local jazz talent is **Cezanne.** The **Bonton Room** brings in national blues acts weekly, while **Rockefeller's** and **Rockefeller's West** book national acts of all types, including some jazz and blues.

The city's real treasures, however, are its many small neighborhood clubs, a few of which feature jazz, many of which feature blues, some of which feature both. The steadier of these small clubs are listed below.

Some of the jazz artists to look out for in Houston today include Milton Larkin, now in his eighties, who still plays for special events, vibraphonist Harry Sheppard, keyboard player Joe Lo-Cascio, pianist Dave Catney, saxman Horace Young, trumpet player Dennis Dotson, bassist David Craig, flugelhorn player George Thomas, Jr., Norma Zenteno, who, according to *Houston Chronicle* music critic Rick Mitchell, leads the top Latin jazz band in the city, and drummers Malcolm Pinson, Carl Lote, and G.T. Hogan (who once played with Bud Powell). Some of the blues artists include saxophonist Grady Gaines; guitarists Joe Hughes, Clarence Green, Guitar Slim, James Bolden, Milton Hopkins, Clarence Holliman, Pete Mayes, and Texas Johnny Brown; piano player Teddy Reynolds; and vocalist Carol Fran.

Most bars and clubs in Houston close at 2 a.m.

Personal Choices

Best jazz club: *Cezanne*
Best neighborhood jazz club: *Mingo's*

Best national blues club: *Bonton Room*
Best regional blues club: *Billy Blues*
Best hole-in-the-wall blues clubs: *Reddi Room, Mardi Gras*
Best eclectic club: *Fabulous Satellite Lounge*
Best jam sessions: *Etta's Lounge, Pick's Place*

F O R   J A Z Z

Cezanne, *4100 Montrose Blvd. (at West Main), 867-7992.*
A cozy yet elegant club located upstairs from the Black Labrador Restaurant (529-1199), Cezanne's is currently the steadiest place in town to hear straight-ahead jazz. A small room with a fine piano, the club features local artists most nights, touring guest soloists on occasion. Piano player Dave Catney books the place and performs regularly; others who have appeared here include Joe LoCasio, Harry Sheppard, David Craig, and Dennis Dotson.
Music: Th–Sa. *Cover:* $–$$. Seating is limited; early arrival recommended.

Ovations, *Times Blvd. at Kirby St. in the Rice University Village (near the Texas Medical Center), 522-9801.*
Located in Houston's oldest shopping center, Ovations is an upscale three-tiered club with dramatic 25-foot-high ceilings that presents a mix of jazz, classical, and cabaret. Jazz vocalists usually perform on the weekends. Seating for about 125 is arranged around its stage, and many of the music majors and faculty from nearby Rice University and the University of Houston frequent the place.
Music: M–Sa, much jazz. *Cover:* $–$$.

Rockefeller's, *3620 Washington Ave. (near The Heights), 861-9365.*
The premier nightclub in Houston for large touring acts, Rockefeller's is housed in the old Citizens State Bank, an imposing 1812 building with Greek columns, marble floors, and a chiseled sign over the stage reading "Devoted . . . to the encouragement of thrift, the molding of character and the upbuilding of Americanism." Once *the* bank for Houston's oil wildcatters, the place is rumored to have been robbed first by Bonnie and Clyde, and then, having proved itself an easy target, by Bonnie alone.
Opened as a club in 1979, Rockefeller's has featured all kinds of talent, with about a third of its schedule devoted to jazz, blues, or R&B artists. Past performers include everyone from Stephane Grappelli to B. B. King, who does a five-night stint here every year.
A second **Rockefeller's West** (6400 Richmond Ave., 977-5495) was opened several years ago. More a small theater than a

club (capacity: 1,500), it's a two-story affair presenting touring acts that are too large for the original Rockefeller's.

True to their origins, both Rockefeller's are plush, classy places, with pretty balconies, pretty tables, and a well-dressed crowd.

Music: most nights. *Cover:* $$–$$$$. CC.

Cody's Jazz Bar & Grill, *3400 Montrose Blvd., 10th Fl. (the Galleria), 522-9747.*
Cody's Jazz Bar & Grill, *2540 University Blvd., 520-5660*

A jazz bar in name only, Cody's offers up pop and pop funk most nights of the week, and contemporary jazz on occasion. The club's original rooftop location on Montrose has outdoor patios and a panoramic view of the city. The second Cody's serves food on Friday and Saturday nights only.

Music: Tu–Sa, occasional jazz. *Cover:* $. *Food:* Continental. CC.

Club Mingo's, *2541 N. McGregory Way (Third Ward), 520-6750.*

Joyce Mingo, an elegant middle-aged woman, had been working in clubs all her life when, six years ago, she decided to open a place of her own. The result: Mingo's, a small modern neighborhood place with mirrors all around, a clock made of red dice, clefs on the walls, and plenty of simple but comfortable tables and chairs. The bands are local and hot, and the place is usually packed with a well-dressed, over-30 crowd.

Music: F, some Sa, M. *Cover:* $.

Gallant Knight, *2337 W. Holcombe (15 min. SE of downtown), 665-9762.*

Named after the English liqueur, this small, dark club, filled with nooks and crannies, has been offering jazz since the early 1980s. Located near Rice University, it attracts a well-integrated crowd that includes many students and academics. Candles flicker in wrought-iron chandeliers as owner Monroe Wilkins greets his guests, many of whom have been coming here for years, at the door.

At one time, the music at the Gallant Knight was strictly jazz; now it tends more toward the "up-tempo and progressive."

Music: Th–Sa. *Cover:* $.

Also

A jazz jam, usually led by the Gerald Stewart Quartet, can be heard on Sunday nights at **Pick's Place** (2315 Truxillo at Dowling, 522-4822), a cozy neighborhood bar with a BYO liquor policy.

FOR BLUES

Pat and Pete's Bonton Room, *4216 Washington Ave., 863-PETE.*

One of the best clubs in the city for live music, the Bonton presents both top local blues and roots rock bands, and touring acts. R&B, Cajun, and zydeco are also often on offer. Some of the many who have appeared here include Marcia Ball, Lou Ann Barton, Clinton Chenier, and the Delta Rhythm Kings.

A moderately large place with an exterior that one of the owners describes as painted "wing ding green with red-tassel Chinese trim," Bonton's is equipped with a raised stage, black-and-blue booths, hundreds of Christmas-tree lights, and stuffed animal heads (including a buffalo and caribou). Out back is a large wooden deck with a tree growing through it.

The club serves no food, but not too far away is **Pat and Pete's Blues Burgers** (311 Travis St., 222-7337), housed in a narrow, historic brick building with a courtyard. The menu includes burgers named after B. B. King, Lightnin' Hopkins, and others, and then there's the "Mighty Flyer" (chicken) and the "Muddy Waters" (a milkshake).

Music: Tu–Sa, much blues. *Cover:* $–$$.

Mickey's Mardi Gras, *4219 Washington Ave., 862-0628.*

Located right across the street from the Bonton, the atmospheric Mardi Gras is known for its blues, zydeco, and rock. Sandy Hickey & the Blue Coyote Band host a blues jam here every Thursday, and Rick Lee & the Night Owls are regulars as well. Housed in a small and dark hole-in-the-wall that's been a cantina since the 1940's, the club serves beer and wine only; the harder stuff is BYO. The walls are covered with Mardi Gras posters and memorabilia, and a pool table and jukebox are situated in back.

Music: W–Su, much blues. *Cover:* $.

Billy Blues, *6025 Richmond Ave., 266-9294.*

It's hard to miss this club, thanks to the 62-foot-long blue saxophone lying at its entrance made up of Volkswagon parts, washtubs, empty kegs of beer, surfboards, and anything else that happened to be lying around at the time of its creation. Fact is, the saxophone was the subject of local controversy not long ago, with some arguing that it violated advertising codes, others arguing that it was art. Luckily for fans of the offbeat, the city council came down on the side of art.

One of a growing chain (the flagship location is in San Antonio), Billy Blues is a barbecue restaurant-club that, as one local critic puts it, has a "touristy yuppie vibe but also tries to do right by the music." Some of the regulars who appear here include Clarence Green and Guitar Slim, Joe Hughes, and the Adams Boys (all under the age of 18).

Music: W–M. *Cover:* $–$$. *Food:* barbecue, some grilled items.

Reddi Room, *2626 White Oak Dr. (near The Heights), 868-6188.*

Housed in a cement-block building, the tiny Reddi Room is one of the most comfortable blues clubs in town. With an integrated clientele that ranges from down-and-out to young professional and music that's usually more R&B than pure blues, it's rather incongruously run by a former nurse who seems to know everyone.

Some of the regulars at the Reddi include Milton Hopkins, who once played lead guitar for B. B. King, and Joe James, a soft-spoken man off-stage who does everything from standing on his head to playing the guitar with his teeth on-stage. B. B. King and Freddie Fender have been known to stop by, and the place is always packed on weekends.
Music: nightly. *Cover:* $

Etta's Lounge & Restaurant, *5120 Scott St. (Third Ward) 528-2611.*

Grady Gaines is one of the best sax players you'll find in this city, and he blows what one local critic calls the "hottest, baddest blues to be found in Houston" every Sunday night at this small diner-type place with run-down booths and red gauze curtains. Owner Etta Coby, a nurse by day, started the place up about 12 years ago, and her jam sessions have since become legendary, attracting musicians from all over the city. "It's a home place," she says proudly. "We get people from all over. Yellow, purple, white—they're all welcome."
Music: Su. *Cover:* $.

Shakespeare Pub, *14129 Memorial Dr. (West Houston, between Kirkwood and Dairy-Ashford), 497-4625.*

A comfortable neighborhood joint patterned after an English pub, with lots of wood and imported beer, Shakespeare's presents top local blues and zydeco acts most nights of the week. A horseshoe-shaped bar dominates the place, and there's a nook with two pool tables and a dart board in the back.
Music: Tu–Sa, much blues. *No cover.*

Local Charm, *1501 Telephone Rd., 926-0329.*

The oldest bar in Houston, stuffed full of beer memorabilia and aging photographs, Local Charm is known for its quality local blues, zydeco, and rockabilly acts. Regulars include Pete Mayes, Joe Hughes, and Texas Johnny Brown.

The bar is long and rectangular, with red-brick walls and a patio in front and back. Seating comes in three forms: chairs, bar stools, and school desks. The school desks were there when the present owners took over nearly a decade ago, and they saw no reason to clear them out.
Music: Th–Sa. *Cover:* $. *Food:* Cajun.

Fabulous Satellite Lounge, *3616 Washington Ave. (near Heights Blvd.), 869-COOL.*

Located right next door to Rockefeller's and started up by the same people, the Satellite won the *Houston Press*'s "best rock club" of the year award in 1993. But rock isn't the only kind of music featured here—T.D. Bell and Erbie Bowser, two veteran bluesmen from Austin, play the club from time to time, as do lots of zydeco, rockabilly, and Blacktop recording artists (including Joe Hughes and Grady Gaines).

Stepping into the club is like stepping onto the set of the movie *Blade Runner.* The lounge's floors and walls are made of concrete, while futuristic artwork hangs on the walls. Lights projecting kaleidoscopic images brush across the room and lava lamps illuminate the corners. Tables and chairs are cut into weird, asymmetrical shapes.

Music: Th–Sa. *Cover:* $–$$.

Davis's Bar-B-Q, *4833 Reed Rd. (20 min. S of downtown), 734-9051.*

The parking lot is filled with pickup trucks; the club is filled with cowboy hats. Everywhere, inside and out, are people dining on fried chicken.

Davis's, almost 20 years old, is a neighborhood place that's home to both blues and R&B, and it has a raw, rough, cowboy feel. Located in a working-class African-American community, its two small rooms—the bar in the front, the music in the back—are run by a father-and-son team who do the cooking as well as the serving.

Music: Tu, Su. *No cover.*

Also

Blues can sometimes be found at a number of small African-American neighborhood joints, including **Super Star** (8128 Scott St., Third Ward, 733-4567) and the **Doll House** (2834 Holmes Rd., 733-1640). Out-of-town blues or R&B acts often come through **Rockefeller's. Fitzgerald's** (2706 White Oak Dr., 862-7625) a large, predominantly-rock venue housed in a rambling white house also features occasional blues and R&B.

Although not, strictly speaking, a blues venue, the **Continental Ballroom Zydeco Lounge** (3101 Collingsworth St., 229-8624) is a Houston institution, a little bit of backwoods Louisiana in the heart of the big city. The **J. B. Entertainment Center** (5901 Long Dr., 649-0000) presents major touring blues and R&B artists such as Little Milton, Bobby Bland, and Denise LaSalle.

Other Venues and Special Events

August-Is-Jazz-Month in Houston and the celebration involves exhibits, films, concerts and music at clubs all over the city, as well as an intensive four-day **Houston International Jazz Festival.** For information, call Jazz Education, Inc., at 227-8706. The **Houston International Festival** happens in late March and features everything from jazz and blues to arts and crafts. The **Juneteenth Blues Festival** is held on June 19 to commemorate the 1865 day when Texan African Americans first learned of the Emancipation Proclamation (it had been signed two years earlier). SumArts (626-8000) sponsors occasional jazz concerts around town featuring national artists.

Jazz concerts can sometimes be heard at **Music Hall** (810 Bagby St., 247-2592), **Jones Hall for the Performing Arts** (615 Louisiana St., 227-3974), and the **Wortham Theater Center** (510 Preston Blvd., 237-1439).

Radio

KTSU/90.9 FM (527-7591). Student-run station affiliated with Texas Southern University. Jazz all day, M–Th; blues M nights.

Jazz and blues can sometimes be heard on **KPFT/90.1 FM** and **KTRU/91.7 FM**.

Record Stores

Infinite Records (528 Westheimer, 521-0187) has a large collection of new and used jazz records. **All Records** (1960 W. Gray, 524-4900) also carries jazz.

Elsewhere in Southeast Texas

American Pop Culture Exhibit, Museum of the Gulf Coast, 700 Proctor St., Port Arthur (90 miles east of Houston), 409-982-7000.

Numerous musicians have come out of the southeast Texas–southwest Louisiana area, including Janis Joplin, Clarence "Gatemouth" Moore, Ivory Joe Hunter, Buddy Holly, and the Big Bopper; and the Museum of the Gulf Coast has set up an exhibit in their honor. Among the items on display are life-sized statues of Janis Joplin, Buddy Holly, Ritchie Valens, and the Big Bopper, and memorabilia from over 30 artists. Janis's corner includes pictures from her early childhood, a purple pantsuit with rhinestones, a slide-rule that she used in high school, "her personal Bible," and a reproduction of her psychedelic Porsche automobile, painted by the same artist who did the original back then.
Open: M–F, 9 a.m.–5 p.m. *Admission:* $.

las

In the 1920's, Dallas was a hotbed of both jazz and blues. The polished Alphonso Trent Orchestra was then playing to packed houses at the elegant Adolphus Hotel downtown, while out in Deep Ellum, along the abandoned railroad tracks, boogie-woogie piano players, blues singers, and small combos were rocking away until dawn and beyond.

One of the best-known musicians to come out of Deep Ellum was Blind Lemon Jefferson, who would walk the streets with a cane in one hand, a tin cup in another, and a guitar slung over his back. For a period, beginning in 1912, Blind Lemon was accompanied by Leadbelly, the singer later jailed for murder who eventually became the darling of New York City's folk-music scene. Leadbelly once said that when he and Lemon began to play, "The women would come running, Lawd have mercy! They'd hug and kiss us so much we could hardly play."[1]

Another important musician to come out of Dallas in the '20's was Buster Smith, born just south of the city. Smith—who would later join the Blue Devils, take Charlie Parker under his wing, and write Count Basie's signature song, "One O'Clock Jump," which he failed to copyright—began frequenting Deep Ellum as a young, serious student of music. He would watch the other clarinet players at work and pick up techniques from them.

Some of Dallas's most legendary nightspots—the Tip Top Club, Ella B. Moore's Park Theater, Fat Jack's Theater, the Green Parrot, and the Pythian Temple—were located in Deep Ellum. Later, in the 1940's, much of the area was destroyed by an expressway, and the jazz and blues scene moved elsewhere. The Rose Ballroom, later known as the Rose Room and then the Empire Room, was especially important, presenting everyone from T-Bone Walker, who later moved to the West Coast, to Zuzu Bollin, who, until his death in 1990, was one of the last surviving jump blues musicians.

Other musicians associated with the Dallas/Fort Worth area include Charlie Christian, who brought the electric guitar to jazz; boogie-woogie piano players Alex Moore and Sam Price; jazz pianists Red Garland and Cedar Walton; trumpeter-vocalist Oran "Hot Lips" Page; R&B singers Freddie King, Al Braggs, and Z. Z. Hill; white R&B band Anson Funderburgh and the Rockets; singer-songwriter Cal Valentine; saxophonist-composer Ornette Coleman; saxophonists James Clay, David "Fathead" Newman, and Julius Hemphill; and, most recently, trumpet player Roy Hargrove.

Sources

The *Dallas Observer* (637-2027), a free weekly, has excellent listings. Other good sources are the Friday sections of the *Dallas*

Morning News (977-8222) and the *Fort Worth Star Telegram* (817-390-7400).

The Dallas Jazz Society runs an intermittent Jazz Hotline at 744-BBOP. The Dallas Blues Society runs a Blues Hotline at 521-BLUE.

For maps and other information, visit the Dallas Visitors Center, 1303 Commerce St., or the Dallas Convention and Visitors Bureau, 1201 Elm St., Suite 2000, 746-6600.

The area code for Dallas is (214).

A Note on Neighborhoods

Filled with enormous, futuristic glass buildings and surrounded by superhighways, Dallas seems to have forgotten that it ever had a past. The city stretches out forever with trendy nightspots, expensive restaurants, and exclusive boutiques.

Greenville Avenue Strip, stretching from downtown to I-635, is where much of the city's nightlife is located. Lower Greenville is known for its small cafés and restaurants, Upper Greenville for its chrome, singles bars, and $50,000 cars. The West End, situated downtown, is a former factory and warehouse district now filled with restaurants, clubs, and shops. South Dallas is home to the city's largest African-American community.

Fort Worth is located approximately 40 minutes west of Dallas.

Landmarks and Legends

(The first four sites are located in or near the downtown and can be viewed on foot; the last three are in South Dallas and are best reached by car.)

Deep Ellum, *Centering on Elm Street, between Preston and Good streets.*

Located just east of the Central Expressway, Deep Ellum was first settled by free slaves after the Civil War; it was then called Freedman's Town. Elm Street was its main drag, and by the turn of the century, it was lined with shops and amusements of all kinds, including speakeasies, dance halls, nightclubs, and whorehouses. Medicine men staged shows on the corners, while bands and dancers performed for pennies in the streets. Love potions were for sale in back alleys, and there were stabbings and shootings almost every Saturday night.

In addition to Blind Lemon Jefferson, Leadbelly, and Buster Smith, some of the many musicians playing along the Central Tracks included Lonnie Johnson, Eddie Durham, Charlie Christian, Hot Lips Page, Herschel Evans, Alex Moore, and Sam Price. National stars such as Bessie Smith and Ma Rainey also played the area whenever they were in town.

After World War II and the construction of the Central Ex-

pressway, businesses moved out of Deep Ellum. Today, however, the once gray, abandoned area is going through a revival, with art galleries, alternative music clubs, and small restaurants opening up left and right.

The Pythian Temple/Union Bankers Building, *2551 Elm St. (Deep Ellum).*

A big gray stone building in the "eclectic Beaux Arts style," the 1915 Pythian was designed by William Sidney Pittman, the first black architect to practice in Dallas. The building, commissioned by a fraternal organization, the Knights of Pythian, had a big dance hall where musical events featuring the likes of Cab Calloway were presented. After the Depression, the imposing edifice was taken over by the Union Bankers Insurance Company.

Majestic Theatre, *1925 Elm St., 373-8000.*

Looking as if it was sculpted out of candy, the newly restored five-story Beaux Arts Majestic was once one of the finest vaudeville/movie houses in town. During the '20's and '30's, the plush theater, decorated in mirrors, gilt, and marble, hosted everyone from Harry Houdini to Mae West. Billing itself "a place where a man could bring his family without question," it featured the unusual "Land of Nod," a complete nursery with beds, trained nurses, and free milk and crackers, where patrons could leave their children during the show. The theater was renovated in 1979 and today is home to the Dallas Opera, the Dallas Black Dance Theatre, and others.

T-Bone Walker got one of his early breaks at the Majestic. He had just won first prize in an amateur concert sponsored there when Cab Calloway, also playing the theater, came through town. Cab invited T-Bone to join him in Houston and while there, T-Bone was approached by a Columbia Records representative. Shortly thereafter, he made his first recordings—recordings that he did not hear until the 1980's (many early bluesmen had similar experiences; they were seldom notified when their records were released).

The Adolphus Hotel, *1321 Commerce St., 742-8200.*

Built by beer baron Adolphus Busch in 1912, the Adolphus Hotel is an opulent Dallas landmark, once called "the most beautiful building west of Venice." Completely restored in 1981 to the tune of $60 million, the 21-story neobaroque edifice featured jazz from the mid-1920's through the '50's. Alphonso Trent's orchestra played a long residency here in 1924, during which time shows were broadcast from the hotel on radio station WFAA.

The Alphonso Trent Orchestra was one of the most polished and successful of the Texas territorial bands. Trent—a "small, wiry, durable, even-tempered"[2] African American originally from Arkansas—first brought his then six-piece band, the Synco Six, to the hotel for what was to be a two-week stand. Their shows proved to be so popular, however, that they were held over 18 months. They became the foremost music draw in Dallas and began touring the state, eventually earning so much money that the sidemen (making $150 per week, an enormous sum at that time), wore silk shirts, drove Cadillacs, and played gold-plated instruments.

Later, during the Swing Era, Artie Shaw, Benny Goodman, Harry James, Tommy and Jimmy Dorsey, and Glenn Miller all played the Adolphus.

American Woodmen's Hall, *SW corner Oakland Ave. and Carpenter.*

A solid yellow-brick building with maroon highlights, the Hall was once famous for its weekend jam sessions. "Everyone played there," says Dallas piano player Robert Clayton Sanders. "There were long picnic-type tables and you'd get your setups and sit down and groove to the music. There wasn't any noise—you just sat your ass down and listened, that was the jazz attitude."

Some of the many musicians who played the Hall during its heydey in the late '50's were David Newman, Marchel Ivery, and Red Garland. The jam sessions were often led by saxophonist James Clay and keyboardist-saxophonist Claude Johnson.

Lincoln High School, *2826 Hatcher St. near Oakland Ave.*

Many well-known Dallas jazz musicians once attended the old Lincoln (located in back of the newer building). Among them were Cedar Walton, Marchel Ivery, and David "Fathead" Newman, who got his nickname here from a temperamental teacher who blew up at him after he'd flubbed an arpeggio.

Clubs, etc.

Dallas has no full-time jazz club, but a number of restaurants, most notably **Sambuca** and, to a lesser degree, **Strictly Tabu**, feature first-class local artists on a regular basis, and the **Sammon Center for the Arts** hosts a unique and frequent jazz series. The largest club for national talent in the area is **Caravan of Dreams** in Fort Worth, which once presented almost exclusively jazz and now features a little bit of everything. National blues acts are sometimes booked into **Blue Cat Blues** and **Poor David's Pub**, while the premier blues club in South Dallas is **Blues Palace**.

Some of the best jazz musicians playing in Dallas today include the fine Texas tenors Marchel Ivery and James Clay, drummer Herbie Cowens, Latin sax-flute player Vicho Vicencio, piano players Robert Clayton Sanders and Claude Johnson, vocalist Martha Burks, contemporary artist Tom Braxton, Peter Petersen and the Collection Jazz Orchestra, and the Dallas Jazz Orchestra. Among the top blues artists are Sam Myers, Big Al Dupree, Roger Boykin, Robert Ealey, Joe Jonas, Hash Brown, Smokin' Joe Kubek, Cookie McGee, Curly Barefoot Miller, Mike Morgan, R. L. Griffin, and Ernie Johnson.

Generally speaking, clubs in Dallas close at 2 a.m.

Personal Choices

Best jazz spot: *Sambuca*
Best after-hours jazz: *Not Just Jazz*
Best Deep Ellum blues: *Blue Cat Blues, Bone*
Best South Dallas blues: *Blues Palace*
Best listening club: *Poor David's Pub*
Best historic spot: *Longhorn Ballroom*

F O R   J A Z Z

Caravan of Dreams, *312 Houston (downtown), Fort Worth, 817-877-3000.*

The premier music club in the area, Caravan, which is financed by Edward Bass of the old Fort Worth Bass family, brings in a whole host of national talent. At one time, much of it was jazz. Ornette Coleman, a Fort Worth native, opened the place up 10 years ago, and Dizzy Gillespie, Herbie Hancock, Stanley Turrentine, Carmen McRae, and Billy Eckstine were among the many who played here.

Today the club's booking policy is much more eclectic. Everything from rock to Irish music can be heard, and the jazz that is presented tends toward the contemporary—Kirk Whalum, Grover Washington, Jr., and the like.

The club is a large sumptuous affair, made up to look like a plush sultan's tent, with a ceiling of silky fabric and a floor of red carpeting. Huge murals tracing the history of jazz cover one wall and the sound system is state of the art.

On the second floor of the Caravan is a theater, and on the roof is the Grotto Bar, built to look like a cave. The view from up here is spectacular. And then there's the odd rooftop "Desert Dome," housing the "largest collection of cacti and succulents in Texas." So what if it's strange; this is Texas. Downstairs in the gift shop, cacti are for sale right next to record albums.

Music: W–Su. *Cover:* $–$$$. *Food:* American. CC.

Sambuca Mediterranean Café & Jazz Bah, *2618 Elm St. (Deep Ellum), 744-0820.*

The best place in Dallas to hear straight-ahead jazz, Sambuca is a stylish restaurant that presents many of the top musicians residing in the area, including Marchel Ivory, James Clay, Claude Johnson, Robert Sanders, and Smokin' Joe McBride. Latin jazz is also featured on occasion, and Roy Hargrove jams here whenever he's back in his hometown.

Located in an historic building, Sambuca's boasts exposed brick walls and leopard-skin booths. One room is enclosed glass, with a skylight; the other contains a long bar and the stage.

Music: nightly. *Cover:* none, if having dinner (the only way to get a table between 7 and 11 p.m.). *Minimum (at bar):* $$. *Food:* Mediterranean. CC. *Reservations taken Su–W only.*

Strictly Tabu, *4111 Lomo Alto Dr. (15 min N of downtown), 528-5200.*

This Art Deco–style restaurant has been offering jazz since the 1940s', but it's had an on-again, off-again history, with a couple of closings. Reopened under its present ownership about six years ago, it's now known for its contemporary and fusion, although bebop is thrown in from time to time and Tuesdays are usually reserved for the big-band sound of Peter Petersen and the Collection Jazz Orchestra.

Filled with pink tablecloths and silver metal-backed chairs, the smallish Tabu has two levels, with a balcony overlooking the stage. Flamingos strut in the stained-glass windows near the door, while waiters dress in formal black. The place even has a resident ghost, a waitress who killed herself, that the staff sometimes hears creeping around out back.

Music: Tu–Su. *Cover:* $. *Food:* Italian. CC.

New York, New York *3100 W. Northwest Highway (20 min. NW of downtown, near Webb Chapel Rd.), 904-1770.*

Known primarily for its large upscale disco catering to a professional African-American crowd, New York, New York also offers

jazz and R&B in an intimate downstairs lounge called the **Dallas Café Society** that overlooks Bachman Lake. The atmosphere down here is warm yet elegant, with small round tables and dark red lights; and the regular acts (especially Martha Burks) are among the best in town.
Music: Th–Su. *Cover:* $.

Terilli's Restaurant, *2815 Greenville Ave., 827-3993.*

Located in the heart of trendy Lower Greenville Avenue, Terilli's, with large arched doorways, wood-framed booths and a lively outdoor patio, has a good dose of yuppie atmosphere. Nonetheless, decent jazz, ranging from straight-ahead to contemporary, is offered up six nights a week. Unfortunately, the stage is located near the bar, where it's often crowded and noisy, and the sound system is mediocre at best.
Music: Tu–Su. *No cover. Food:* Italian. CC.

Not Just Jazz, *2914 Greenville Ave., 824-8644.*

Just up the street from Terilli's is another midsized restaurant serving up straight-ahead and contemporary jazz, but here the music alternates with R&B and Top 40. The restaurant's biggest musical attraction, however, is its late-late-night jazz brunches on Fridays and Saturdays, when a jazz combo plays from 1:30 to 3:30 a.m. Lots of other musicians who've just finished gigs elsewhere come by to sit in, and a brunch menu is served.

Not Just Jazz is an upscale two-story affair with a balcony, cocktail tables, and gray-and-black booths. The patio outside is equipped with a bar.
Music: Tu–Su, much jazz. *Cover:* $–$$. *Food:* New Orleans. CC.

Martini's, *2013 Greenville Ave., 821-3660.*

Also located on Lower Greenville, Martini's presents straight-ahead jazz one half the week, and contemporary jazz the other. Primarily a restaurant known for its "casual New American" cuisine, it's a mid-sized place with a lot of dark wood, housed in what were once three separate storefronts. Mauve and burgundy banquettes line the walls, and white tablecloths drape the tables.
Music: nightly. *No cover. Food:* American. CC.

Dick's Last Resort, *1701 N. Market St., facing Ross (West End), 747-0001.*

"You can go to a fine French restaurant and get treated like dirt. We do the same for a lot cheaper."

So speaks the management of Dick's Last Resort, which may be the best place in town for Dixieland but is definitely not the best place in town for a relaxing night out. One of a chain, the club is loud, boisterous, and brightly lit, but the musicians are often first class. Rodney and the Reporters and Crawfish are among the most popular of the regulars.
Music: nightly. *No cover. Food:* catfish, burgers, etc.

Also

Dallas Alley (Market St. at Munger, 988-WEST) is a place to be avoided. With eight clubs under one roof (some of which claim to offer jazz and blues), it's a sort of horror show, complete with lots of neon and blow-dried hair.

F O R   B L U E S

Blue Cat Blues, *2617 Commerce St. (Deep Ellum), 744-2287.*

Housed in the back half of a former warehouse, complete with exposed brick walls and large, blackened beams, the Blue Cat offers up a solid mix of local, regional, and national blues. Smokin' Joe Kubek is a regular, and others who have played here include Lonnie Brooks, William Clark, Lucky Peterson, and the Kinsey Report.

The club's walls are lined with photos of blues greats, and most of the light in the place comes from the neon beer signs on the walls. Outside, there's a patio.

Music: W–Su; happy hour with blues recordings, M–F, 4:30–7 p.m. *Cover:* $–$$. *Food:* snacks.

Bone, *2724 Elm St. (Deep Ellum), 744-2663.*

Also housed in an atmospheric old building with exposed brick walls, high ceilings, and lazy ceiling fans, the Bone feels like a little bit of New Orleans set down in Dallas. A big wooden bar sits off to one side, while one room is filled with tables and chairs, another with three pool tables. Blues guitarist Hash Brown is a regular and he usually hosts a jam on Tuesday nights that attracts musicians from all over the city.

Music: Tu–Th. *No cover. Food:* New Orleans Cajun.

Schooner's, *1212 Skillman at Live Oak (near Lower Greenville), 821-1934.*

A former neighborhood bar (these are rare in Dallas) just off the trendy beaten track, Schooner's is a small and friendly odd-shaped room with a fireplace and nautical decor. Many of its bigger weekend acts come up from Austin, while two nights a week are reserved for blues jams. Sam Myers is a regular along with local favorites Mike Morgan, Jim Suhler, and Bugs Henderson.

Music: Th–Su. *Cover:* $.

Poor David's Pub, *1924 Greenville Ave., 821-9891.*

Started up in the mid-1970's, Poor David's is the oldest continuously running club in town, and the second oldest continuously operating club in the state (Antone's in Austin is eight or nine months older). Long and thin and friendly with chairs and tables

set in a semicircle, this is an eclectic club that's also a serious listening place. Everything from zydeco to R&B to folk to blues is featured, and blues regulars include John Lee Hooker, Buddy Guy, Junior Walker, and Delbert McClinton. Anson Funderburgh and the Rockets got their start here, playing every Monday night for 10 years, and they still perform on occasion.
Music: Tu–Sa, much blues and jazz. *Cover:* $–$$.

Billy Blues, *Hillside Shopping Center, Mockingbird and Abrams, 578-6903.*
A new Billy Blues (see also San Antonio, page 337) opened at this location in the fall of 1993. Modern and clean-lined, the club serves up barbecue buffet style during the day and blues at night. The walls are hung with lots of blues memorabilia, and most of the acts are local, although touring names such as Johnny Copeland and the Fabulous Thunderbirds come through on occasion.
Music: Th–Sa. *Cover:* $. *Food:* barbecue.

Blues Palace, *2715 Meadow St. (South Dallas, at Grand Ave.), 421-9867.*
Owned and operated by blues singer R. L. Griffin, the Blues Palace is a large, 300-seat club located in the heart of South Dallas that sometimes presents top touring blues and R&B artists such as Bobby "Blue" Bland, Denise LaSalle, and Tyrone Davis. Lots of local artists perform here as well, including Ernie Johnson, Charlie Roberson, and Griffin, and name talent touring the area often stop by here after their gigs elsewhere are done.

The inside of the Blues Palace is all done up in red, with red walls, red tables, and red chairs. KKDA/730 AM radio broadcasts a live show from here every Saturday night (10 p.m.–midnight) with Babyface Gary.
Music: Th–Su. *Cover:* $.

Longhorn Ballroom, *216 Corinth (near downtown), 421-6262.*
Outside, the red-barn compound is lit up like a Christmas tree, with a huge painted cowboy, a mural of the gunfight at the O.K. Corral, and a blinding marquee below which stands an immense mock steer. Wind gusts through the place, leaving dust in its wake. A tall man in a cowboy hat walks slowly by.

The Longhorn Ballroom, which can seat 2,300, was built in 1949 for country-and-western swingman Bob Wills. Wills would play here five or six nights a week, leaving one night free for local African-American promoters, and soon the place became legendary for its Monday-night blues and R&B. Big Joe Turner, Nat King Cole, Lionel Hampton, Al Green, Bobby "Blue" Bland, B. B. King, Tyrone Davis, Millie Jackson, Little Johnny Taylor— everyone who was anyone played the Longhorn.

During the early 1950's the Longhorn was managed by Jack Ruby, who went on to murder JFK's assassin, Lee Harvey Oswald.

Today's manager, Willie Wren, has been here since 1964. "Back when I started," he says, "They had a rope down the middle with whites on one side, blacks on the other . . . People came from all over, and all the girls in the telephone company used to ask for Tuesdays off so they could stay out late."

Alas, blue Mondays at the Longhorn are no longer, but the hall does present big-name acts—rock, Latino, occasional blues—on the weekends. The hall—smelling of dust and time—stretches out forever, with lots of wooden folding chairs, checkered tablecloths, and revolving fans. A Texas flag hangs from the ceiling.
Music: F, Sa, some blues. *Cover:* $$–$$$.

Also

Robert Ealey's Underground, beneath the Deep Ellum Café (400 Main St., downtown Fort Worth, 817-332-2232), is home to the "King of the Blues" in Fort Worth. The club is smallish and dark, lit by candles and neon signs, and Ealey usually plays at least one weekend night.

J&J Blues Bar (937 Woodward, 817-870-2337), also in Fort Worth, is a fine, eclectic club, housed in a former machine shop, that brings in name blues players.

Other Venues and Special Events

The **Sammon Center for the Arts** (3630 Harry Hines Blvd. at Oak Lawn, 520-ARTS) sponsors a unique jazz series featuring the best of local talent at an historic three-storied water pumping station known as Turtle Creek. A low cover charge includes hors d'oeuvres, beer, and wine; valet parking is available.

The **Dallas Museum of Art** (1717 N. Harwood, 922-1200) hosts a "Jazz Under the Stars" series every summer featuring internationally recognized artists. The Dallas Jazz Orchestra plays regularly around town and sometimes brings in national artists (hotline: 644-8833).

Jazz and blues concerts can occasionally be heard at **Starplex Amphitheater** (I-30 at Second, 373-8000) and the **Dallas Convention Center** (650 S. Griffin St., 939-2700).

Radio

KNTU/88.1 FM (817-565-3688). Jazz, 6 a.m.-midnight. Affiliated with the University of North Texas in Denton.
KNON/89.3 FM (828-9500). Blues M, Th and F nights.
Blues can also be heard occasionally on **KKDA/730 AM**.

Record Stores

Three top jazz and blues stores in the area are **Collectors Records** (10616 Garland Rd., Dallas, 327-3313), **Record Town**

(3025 S. University, Fort Worth, 817-926-1331) and **Borders Books & Music** (10720 Preston Rd., Dallas, 363-1977).

Elsewhere in North Central Texas

Blind Lemon Jefferson's grave, *off Highway 14, Wortham (45 miles S of Dallas).*

Blind Lemon Jefferson, who died tragically in a snowstorm in Chicago just after an important recording session, is buried here, the town of his birth, at the back of a small African-American cemetery next to the spiffier, easier-to-find white Wortham Cemetery. The grounds, though modest, are well kept, and Blind Lemon's grave, an unmarked concrete slab, is identified with a Texas State Historical Society plaque. Just behind the grave, behind a barbed-wire fence, cows placidly chew their cuds.

During the 1910's, when Lemon was living in Texas, Wortham was a booming oil town, with hotels, bars, and restaurants lining its railroad tracks. Now, it's a quiet, windswept place, population 1,187. "We're not all convalescents," says one of today's residents, a large elderly black man dressed in overalls and a big straw hat. "But we're all older. We baby them baby boomers on up and ship them out of here."

Jack Teagarden exhibit, *Red River Valley Museum, 4600 College Dr., Vernon (180 miles NW of Dallas), 817-553-1848.*

The musical Teagarden family, which included Charles on trumpet, Clois on drums, Norma on piano, and Jack on trombone, originally came from Vernon, Texas. Their mother, Helen Teagarden, was a ragtime piano player and a remarkable woman who encouraged her four children to become professional jazz musicians.

The small Jack Teagarden exhibit includes his desk, his trombone, and his personal correspondence. There are also lots of books, records, and newspaper clippings. The rest of the museum is dedicated to local history (ranching, cattle drives, the 530,000-acre Wagner Ranch, sculptress Electra Wagner Biggs), and natural history.

Open: Tu–Su, 1–5 p.m. *Free admission.*

San Antonio

During the 1920's, San Antonio, then the largest city between New Orleans and Los Angeles, attracted musicians from all over Texas. Two major clubs were the Horn Palace Inn and the Shadowland Club. The Troy Floyd orchestra, a successful territorial band of the time, played a long residency at the Shadowland, while the Horn Palace was the site of Jack Teagarden's first professional gig.

Teagarden came to San Antonio from Vernon, Texas, in 1921, at the age of 16. At first his new job at the Shadowland delighted him, but then one night a gangland shooting occurred directly in front of the stage. The other, more experienced, musicians dove for cover, but Teagarden remained rooted to the spot—and when it came time for a trial, he was to be the prosecution's star witness.

That meant nothing but trouble. Gang members threatened to take his life. Then, providence intervened in the form of the great flood of 1921, which covered parts of San Antonio with 15 feet of water. Houses, businesses—and municipal records—were destroyed. All pending court cases were dismissed, and Teagarden lost no time in heading to Houston, where he joined Peck Kelley's band.

Another extraordinary musician associated with San Antonio is the enigmatic blues singer Robert Johnson, who recorded three of the only five sessions he ever did in a makeshift studio set up in the old Blue Bonnet Hotel (see "Landmarks and Legends," page 333). The three sessions took place in November 1936 and included some of his greatest songs, including "Terraplane Blues," "Walking Blues," and "Crossroad Blues."

Other jazz and blues musicians either from or associated with San Antonio include sax player Herschel Evans, who played with the Troy Floyd Orchestra; bandleader Don Albert, who came here from New Orleans; saxman Clifford Scott, who's played with Lionel Hampton and Ray Charles; Doug Sahm, who formed the city's first white R&B group; and keyboard player Augie Meyers.

The city also has a strong Mexican-American jazz-blues tradition dating back to the '30's that continues to this day. During the '40's and '50's especially, a number of Mexican-American groups came out of San Antonio and the surrounding Rio Grande Valley. Most of these were known only to Texans, but one popular singer, Freddy Fender, achieved national recognition.

Sources

The best listings can be found in the Friday section of the *San Antonio Express-News* (225-7411) and in *The Current* (828-7660), a free weekly.

For maps and other information, contact the San Antonio Convention and Visitors Bureau, 121 Alamo Plaza, 270-8700.

The area code for San Antonio is 210.

A Note on Neighborhoods

San Antonio is a small, friendly, quirky city, over half of whose population is Mexican-American. River Walk (Paseo Del Rio), located 20 feet below street level, is a pedestrian walkway that follows the course of the San Antonio River. Lined with tropical plants, shops, restaurants, and music clubs, it's usually teeming with tourists. St. Mary's Street, or "The Strip," located about ten minutes north of the downtown, is another entertainment district. Here, the crowd tends to be younger and trendier.

Though small and easy to explore, San Antonio has its share of traffic problems. Parking downtown is usually available in high-rise lots only.

Landmarks and Legends

Blue Bonnet Hotel, *St. Mary's and Pecan streets (downtown, now an open plaza).*

When Robert Johnson appeared one day in 1936 in the makeshift field studio of the American Record Corporation in the Blue Bonnet Hotel, he was a shy young man who had seldom been out of the Mississippi Delta. Slender and handsome, he only played for A&R man Don Law with his face turned toward the wall.

Later that night there was trouble. Law, who had found Johnson a room at the boarding house, was having dinner with his wife and friends when he was called to the phone. A policeman had picked Johnson up on a vagrancy charge. Law hurried down to the

At the Landing, the Jim Cullum band plays some of the finest traditional jazz in the country.

jail, where with some difficulty he had Johnson released; he had been worked over by the cops. Law took him back to the boarding house, gave him 45 cents for breakfast and told him not to go out again. Then he returned to his dinner, only to have Johnson call him on the phone. "I'm lonesome," Johnson said. "Lonesome?" Law asked. Johnson replied, "I'm lonesome and there's a lady here. She wants fifty cents and I lacks a nickel. . . ."[1]

The Blue Bonnet was demolished in 1988.

(Some blues historians believe that it was the Gunter Hotel in which Johnson recorded, but more recent scholarship has pointed to the Blue Bonnet. The Gunter is still standing at 205 E. Houston St.)

Cameo Theater, *1123 E. Commerce St., St. Paul Sq.*

A pretty mustard-colored building in the Art Deco style, the renovated Cameo is located in the heart of St. Paul Square. During the '30's, '40's, and '50's, the square was the center of San Antonio's black entertainment district, jammed with nightclubs, restaurants, and the only hotels in town in which African Americans were allowed to stay overnight.

Most of the more famous clubs—the Avalon Grill and the Mona Lisa Club—are gone now, but the Cameo remains. Cab Calloway and Duke Ellington were among the greats who performed here.

St. Paul Square itself, which is lined with many other early twentieth-century buildings, has been declared a National Historic District and is in the process of restoration. The project is still in progress, however, and the streets tend to be deserted. The Cameo is opened up only for special events.

Keyhole Inn, *1619 W. Poplar.*

During the '50's and early '60's, this sturdy building, now a Spanish social club, was famous for blues and R&B. Clarence "Gatemouth" Brown got his start here just after being released from military service (San Antonio is the site of five military bases).

"The Keyhole could hold more than a thousand," says Nyolia Johnson, a blues singer born and bred in San Antonio who often plays with the Houserockers. "B.B., Big Joe Turner, Bobby 'Blue' Bland, they all played there. Miss Wiggles, the exotic dancer—she was there. It was a fancy and beautiful place."

Clubs, etc.

The Landing is the only club in town expressly designed for jazz, but there are a number of restaurants and unusual joints where some of the best music anywhere can be heard. San Antonians, especially those of Mexican-American heritage, carry on the Texas sax tradition in a big and serious way. **Billy Blues** is the most consistent club for national blues acts.

Some of the local jazz and blues players to watch out for include Jim Cullum's Jazz Band, one of the top traditional bands in the country, Randy Garibay and Cats Don't Sleep, the Regency Jazz Band, the Navarro Bridge Jazz Orchestra, trumpet players Al Gomez and Charlie McBirney, saxmen Rocky Morales and Louie Bustos, guitar players Steve James and Jackie King, Sylvia Salas & the Swingtet, and blues vocalist Little Neesie. The town also has a number of up-and-coming blues bands, including the House-rockers featuring Nyolia Johnson, Eddie and the All-niters, River City Slim and the Rhythm Kings, Toat Lee Bluz, the Smith Brothers, and Rodney Warner & the Bluz Express.

Most bars and clubs in San Antonio close at 1 or 2 a.m.

Personal Choices

Best jazz spots: *The Landing, La Louisiane*
Best acoustic jazz: *Boardwalk Bistro*
Best blues club: *Billy Blues*
Best jazz/blues jams: *Saluté*
Best area dance halls: *Gruene Hall, Cibolo Creek.*
Best area roadhouses: *Leon Springs Café, Bruno's Texas Star*

F O R   J A Z Z

The Landing, *Hyatt Regency Hotel, 123 Losoya (River Walk), 222-1234 or 223-7266.*
Jim Cullum's Jazz Band, a traditional group with dozens of albums to its credit, call the Landing home. Their superb sound, always precise and energetic, offers a welcome respite from the commercial hubbub of River Walk.

The original Landing was founded in 1963 in another location by Jim Cullum's father, who was also a musician, and about 20 other jazz enthusiasts. Each put up $1,000 and then contributed time and energy to painting and restoring an old atmospheric basement club.

The new Landing, as its Hyatt address suggests, is a very different sort of place. Two-tiered and modern-elegant, with lots of little black tables and waitresses in evening clothes, it's usually packed (too packed) with a well-dressed crowd. There's also a bit of a fishbowl feel: the club has large windows and is located at the edge of a mall.

Still, the music's worth it. Cullum's seven-piece band puts on a terrific performance, and on Sundays, when he isn't playing, Sylvia Salas fronts a top-caliber quintet. A public radio show, "River Walk," is taped here and broadcast to over 150 stations nationwide.
Music: nightly, also jazz duos on outside patio afternoons and F, Sa nights. *Cover:* $, none on the patio. *Food:* desserts; lunch served on the patio.

La Louisiane, *2632 Broadway (near downtown), 225-7984.*
Known for its fine and formal dining since 1935 (it was the first fine dining establishment in San Antonio), La Louisiane was taken over by a new owner in 1991, who opened a New Orleans—style courtyard out back serving lighter fare and jazz. It's all caught on quite successfully, and some of the city's top bands play here now, including Randy Garibay and the Regency Jazz Band.

The red-brick courtyard is a delightful place, filled with tropical plants, gas lanterns, and pools stocked with fish. Meanwhile, inside, the formal dining tradition continues.
Music: nightly. *No cover. Food:* Louisiana-style. CC.

Boardwalk Bistro, *4011 Broadway (10 min. N of downtown), 824-0100.*
A casual indoor/outdoor restaurant that won five awards in *The Current's* 1993 Reader's Poll (including "Best Place to Eat Paella" and "Best Place to Hear Acoustic Music"), the Boardwalk Bistro features jazz about three nights a week, and Celtic and folk music the rest of the time. Small World, a popular drum-bass jazz duo, appears here regularly, along with duo guitarists Sergio Lara and Joe Reyes. The bistro-style restaurant also features a large beer and imported wine list, and there are lots of plants and artwork on the walls.
Music: M–Sa; much jazz. *No cover. Food:* international.

Nona's, *3000 N. St. Mary's St., 732-6662.*
Primarily a restaurant, Nona's also offers up jazz, blues, and Latin music most nights of the week. Mariachi guitar player and jazz percussionist David Chapa is a regular, and so are the Infidels, a jazz-blues band. Austin acts are also featured from time to time. The restaurant, lined with big glass windows facing the street, is large and airy, made up to look like an Italian villa complete with hanging plants and pastel-colored murals.
Music: Tu–Sa. *No cover,* except for big acts. *Food:* northern Italian. CC.

Saluté, *2801 St. Mary's St., 732-5307.*
A narrow, triangular-shaped room dominated by a large bar, Saluté is a casual neighborhood joint, popular among both Anglos and Hispanics, where some of the best music in the city can be heard. With concrete walls painted bright colors and a small dance floor, the club features a mix of jazz, blues, and *conjunto* music.

On Sundays there's usually a jazz jam led by Randy Garibay and Cats Don't Sleep. And that's when some extraordinary musicians take to the stage: Al Gomez, a slight man with a silver trumpet and mellifluous sound; Little Robert, an Hispanic blues and soul singer whom Bobby "Blue" Bland once called backstage because he couldn't believe he wasn't black; saxman Rocky Morales, looking like a beatnik in a black beret; and Augie Meyers, home from touring with Doug Sahm.

Music: Th–Su, much jazz, some blues. *No cover.*

Dick's Last Resort, *406 Navarro St. (River Walk), 224-0026.*

The place is a dump, filled with young beefy tourists downing "Love Cocktails" served with blown-up condoms, but the musicians are among the best in town. If you can stand the bright lights and the constant frat-house chatter, it's worth a short visit, but sit near the front, near the music. Some of the regulars include the Navarro Bridge Jazz Orchestra, the Regency Jazz Band with George Prado, and blues singer Bette Butler.

This Dick's is one of a chain of six.

Music: nightly. *No cover. Food:* burgers, catfish, etc.

Also

Top-caliber jazz can be heard once a week or so at **The Clubhouse** (2218 Broadway, 229-9945), a barbecue joint not far from downtown. "Not too many people know about this place," says one of the owners, "and this may sound conceited, but we're serious about what we do and we don't want people to come if they're not into the music."

F O R   B L U E S

Billy Blues, *330 E. Grayson St. (at Broadway, 5 min. from downtown), 824-9414.*

The flagship location of a burgeoning chain (others are located in Houston, Dallas, Austin, Denver, Phoenix, and Heidelberg, Germany), this sprawling club is housed in a 25-year-old Dairy Queen, an old ice house, and the "Billy Dome"—a tin barn of a place reminiscent of a West Texas grain elevator. Somehow, it all adds up to atmosphere.

The bands play in the Billy Dome, which is equipped with garage-size doors, ceiling fans, a dance floor, and plenty of tables and chairs. Talent ranges from local to regional to national— Johnny Copeland, Junior Wells, Grady Gaines, Toat Lee Bluz. Zydeco is also often on tap, while Monday nights are devoted to blues jams. Meanwhile, the old Dairy Queen has been converted into a restaurant and the ice house into a back bar.

Music: nightly. *Cover:* $–$$. *Food:* barbecue.

Cibolo Creek Country Club, *8640 E. Evans Rd. (20 min. NE of downtown), 651-6652.*

A 100-plus-year-old dance hall located on the outskirts of town and surrounded by fields, the Cibolo was once the gathering place for San Antonio's rural German-American community. Polka dances were held here and at times the place was also a feed store, church, school, train depot, and post office.

Today, the Cibolo presents an eclectic mix of music, including zydeco, R&B, some country, a little rock, and blues. Bo Didley, Johnny Winter, and Omar and the Howlers are among the groups that have appeared here. Built in an old shotgun style with a tin roof and concrete dance floor, the club also serves barbecue, and children are welcome at all times. "It's just an old hippie place," says one of the owners.

Music: F–Su, some blues. *Cover:* $–$$. *Food:* barbecue.

Taco Land, *103 W. Grayson (10 min. N of downtown),* *223-8406.*

Made "famous" through a song recorded by the Dead Milkmen, Taco Land, located on a wooded lane somewhat off the beaten track, has been home to hundreds of young San Antonio musicians. Anyone, absolutely anyone, can play here, and lots of new groups, especially alternative music groups (as well as some blues), do. "Some of the bands are great, some of them run my customers away," says owner Ram Ayala, now in his fifties. "But I don't care. As long as they get a chance to play."

Taco Land used to serve food, but that ended years ago. Now the tiny building with its suspended ceiling, and sparkling red vinyl booths is mostly a bar and pool room. The crowd, depending on the night, is usually either young and white, or middle-aged and Hispanic. Of special note: a wonderful bluesy tune on the jukebox called "Stop It, You're Killing Me" by local singer Little Neesie.

Music: W–Su. *Cover:* $.

Other Venues and Special Events

The **Carver Community Cultural Center** (226 N. Hackberry, 299-7211) has a concert series featuring national jazz talent. Jazz and blues can also sometimes be heard at the newly renovated **Majestic Theater** (230 E. Houston St., 226-3333), the **Laurie Auditorium** at Trinity University (736-8117), and the **Cockrell Theatre for the Performing Arts** (Convention Center at Market near Bowie, 299-8500).

Jazz'SAlive is a free weekend festival held in Travis Park in September featuring primarily local artists (299-8486). The 17-year-old **Carver Jazz Festival** (299-7211) is a four-day festival that takes place every August and brings in much national talent. The four-day **Texas Folklife Festival** (558-2235), held every late summer since 1971, features 10 stages of live entertainment showcasing everything from Texas jazz to Celtic music.

Radio

KRTU/91.7 FM (736-8313) has jazz nightly. Jazz and blues can also be heard occasionally on **KSTX/89.1 FM**, **KZEP/104.5 FM** and **KFAN/107.9 FM**.

Record Stores

Three good sources for blues and Texas music are **Hogwild Records and Tapes** (1824 N. Main St., 733-5354), **JR's Record Exchange** (5301 McCullough, 829-8663) and **Good Vibrations** (6722 San Pedro, 828-3472).

Other Nearby Locations

Gruene Hall, *1281 Gruene Rd., New Braunfels, 625-0142.*

Gruene Hall, located half-way between San Antonio and Austin, is the oldest dance hall in Texas. A huge wooden building, half as long as a football field, with sawdust on the floor, chicken wire across the windows, and hundreds of burlap sacks hanging from the ceiling (for acoustical purposes), it opened in 1878 as a saloon and social hall for the area cotton farmers. Back then, the local residents, mostly Germans, used the hall for polkas and waltzes.

When the present owners took the place over in 1974, however, the dance floor hadn't been used in years. Only the bar up front was open, and, even worse, the tiny town of Gruene (pronounced "green") itself was a virtual ghost town.

Since then, Gruene Hall has been lovingly restored with the help of a longtime local resident and is back in full operation. Seven other buildings in town have also been restored, but although tourists now come to lunch in an old gristmill out back, the place has thus far escaped full-scale commercialization.

The hall, lined with advertisements from the turn of the century ("FEDERAL BANK LOANS, 4%", "FOR GOOD EATS AND DRINKS, BLUES SUGAR BOWL"), is open daily, but music is only featured at the end of the week. Most of the entertainment is progressive country, but blues come through regularly. Past performers include Bo Diddley, Marcia Ball, Omar and the Howlers, and Roomful of Blues.

Music: Th–Su, some blues. *Cover:* $–$$$.

Leon Springs Café, *I-10 West at Boerne Stage Dr. (25 min. NW of downtown San Antonio), 698-3338.*

Once a stagecoach stop, Leon Springs is now known for its acoustic music: folk, bluegrass, and blues. Lots of Texas greats have played here, along with touring talent such as John Hammond and Snooky Pryor.

The café, which is also a full-service restaurant, overlooks the Texas hill country, and it's equipped with an outdoor patio and a

beer garden, where the music acts are presented. Inside, the late 1880's building is filled with pressed-tin ceilings, old wooden beams, slowly rotating fans, and lots of antiques.
Music: F–Su. *Cover:* $–$$. *Food:* American.

Bruno's Texas Star, *I-10 West at Comfort (40 min. NW of downtown San Antonio), 995-4000.*

Farther west on Interstate 10 is an old roadhouse and dance hall overlooking the Guadalupe River, whose banks are lined with cypress trees. Blues, rock, reggae (now very popular in this out-of-the-way part of the world), *conjunto,* and occasionally bluegrass are presented here, with blues acts appearing once or twice a week. The Smith Brothers, W. C. Clark, and Floyd Moore (filmed in Bruno's last year by a Swedish television crew) are among those who've played the club-restaurant.

Built in 1937, when it was used for country-and-western dancing, Bruno's has pecan-wood floors and a stage area equipped with floor lighting. Out front are flowering cacti and a grove of oak trees, while out back are two smoking barbecue pits.
Music: F–Su. *Cover:* $–$$. *Food:* barbecue, etc.

Austin

Largely because Austin did not have much of an African-American population, it was slower to develop a jazz-blues tradition than other Texas cities. The music could still be heard, however, along East 11th Street, the heart of the city's black community, as early as the 1920's, while the 1940's brought with them the founding of an important African-American music venue, the Victory Grill (see "Landmarks and Legends," page 342).

Also in the 1940's, Austin produced one of its most famous native sons, bassist Gene Ramey, who began his career at the age of 16 by playing the tuba in a local band. Ramey had a hard time getting anywhere in Austin, however, and soon moved on to Kansas City where he took up with Jay McShann's band. Austin's other 1940's star, pianist Teddy Wilson, moved as well, eventually landing in New York City, where he joined Benny Goodman.

Austin made its biggest contribution to music history in the 1960's and '70's, when the city's liberal reputation drew to it creative souls from all over the state. In the mid-1960's, there was Threadgill's, featuring a young new singer named Janis Joplin, and in the late '60's–early '70's, the Vulcan Gas Company and the Armadillo World Headquarters opened up. Both clubs presented

Austin is home to over 100 live music venues.

white rock bands creating a new "Austin sound" and black blues-men who had seldom performed before white audiences before.

Nineteen-seventy-five marked the opening of Antone's, Austin's most famous club, which has since become virtually a god-father of blues bars everywhere. In addition to featuring legends from all over the country, Antone's (now Antone's Billy Blues) has been instrumental in launching the careers of innumerable Texas bluesmen, including the late Stevie Ray Vaughan, Jimmie Vaughan, Angela Strehli, Marcia Ball, and Kim Wilson.

Other jazz and blues artists associated with Austin include trumpet player Kenny Dorham; blues guitarists Pee Wee Crayton and Mance Lipscomb; barrelhouse piano players Robert Shaw, Lavada Durst, and Grey Ghost; saxophonist Tomas Ramirez; and singer-songwriter Bill Neely.

Sources

The Austin Chronicle (454-5766), a free weekly, has excellent listings. Other sources include the Thursday and Saturday sections of the *Austin American-Statesman* (445-3500), and *Music City Texas* (444-0693), a free monthly.

For maps, a general guide to music venues (called *Austin Music Live*) and other information, contact the Austin Visitor Information Center, 201 E. Second St., 478-0098 or 800-888-8AUS.

KLBJ radio runs "The KLBJ Austintatious Entertainment Hotline," which includes information on music, at 832-4094.

The area code for Austin is (512).

A Note on Neighborhoods

Though small, Austin, the state capital, is quite spread out, sprawled over hills along the Colorado River. The city is filled with fine old homes and buildings, and is the site of the University of Texas, which with 50,000 students is one of the largest universities in the United States.

East Austin is the city's oldest African-American neighborhood. Sixth Street (Old Pecan Street) is an historic district that's recently been restored. Now squeaky-clean and lined with restaurants and second-rate music clubs (although there are exceptions, some of which are noted below), it attracts an estimated 40,000 to 50,000 people on the weekends, many of whom traipse up and down the street, drinks in hand, in a never-ending quest for that elusive goal—fun.

Despite this, Austin still has a decidedly rebel feel. "Ex-hippies" and Texan freethinkers apparently gone straight pop up in the most unexpected of places with the most unexpected of opinions.

Landmarks and Legends

(The following route starts in East Austin, and proceeds west to the downtown and north to Manor Road and North Lamar. A car is necessary.)

East 11th Street, *from I-35 to Rosewood Ave.*

For 40 years, East 11th Street was the main thoroughfare for jazz and blues in Austin. During the '20's and '30's, there was the Cotton Club and the Paradise Club; during the '40's and '50's, the Victory Grill, Slim's, the Derby Lounge, and the Clock Lounge; during the '60's, Charlie's Playhouse and the IL Club.

Victory Grill, *1104 E. 11th St.*

"I was responsible for booking B. B. King's first time in Texas," says Johnny Holmes, a tall man dressed in a light blue embroidered shirt, shiny patent leather shoes, and a big Stetson hat. "He came all the way out here from Tennessee for that show, and now look how big he is. We ate cheese and crackers in the car many times. We were just little country boys then. . . ."

Johnny Holmes and his Victory Grill are legendary names in Austin's music community. Holmes, now in his seventies, brought them all to Austin—Clarence "Gatemouth" Brown, Little Johnny Taylor, James Brown, and many, many more. He also booked talent into other venues all over the state.

The Grill, which can hold about 300 people, opened in 1945. In 1947, Bobby "Blue" Bland, then just an unknown soldier stationed at nearby Fort Hood, started playing at the club every weekend, dependably winning the weekly prize that the Grill offered to the best performer until Holmes made him stop.

Back then, 11th Street was teeming with clubs. "This whole street was like Little Harlem," says Holmes, "Business was bull. Some of the other clubs had trios or singers, but many didn't, because I had my place and it wasn't necessary."

The Grill's heydey lasted until the mid-1960's, when Holmes left for West Texas, leaving the club in the hands of his uncles. When he returned 13 years later, he continued to run the place, which still functioned as a bar until a fire broke out two years ago. Today, Holmes is in the process of rebuilding, and the club is slated to reopen with live music in 1994 or 1995.

Charlie's Playhouse and IL Club, *1206 and 1124 E. 11 St.*

When Holmes left for West Texas, business at the Grill died down and Charlie's Playhouse and the IL Club (both located on the north side of East 11th Street with a street running between them but both now deserted), stepped in to fill the void. Bobby "Blue" Bland, Freddie King, and Joe Tex all performed at Charlie's, along with the house band, Blues Boy Hubbard and the Jets, who were the city's premier local group in the '60's.

"Charlie's was always packed," says Clifford Antone of Antone's. "The crowd was half black, half college students. It was a beautiful scene."

Doris Miller Auditorium, *corner of Rosewood and Chestnut avenues, near Rosewood Park.*

Dr. Hepcat, a barrelhouse piano player and the first African-American deejay in Texas, once booked talent with Johnny Holmes into this small auditorium. The two brought in everyone from Louis Armstrong to Aretha Franklin, and always hired local talent for backup.

Since then, Dr. Hepcat has found religion. Now known as the Reverend Lavada Durst, he refuses to play in clubs, but does put in occasional appearances at festivals.

Huston Tillotson College, *1820 E. Eighth St.*

During the '50's and '60's, this African-American college, known for its jazz program, and Austin, known as the only liberal city in Texas, drew black musicians from all over the state. James Polk, Bobby Bradford, and Fred Smith all went to school at Huston Tillotson, and their Sunday-afternoon jam sessions, played at various venues throughout the city, became legendary.

Grey Ghost's home, *1914 E. 8th St.*

A few years ago, most people had given Grey Ghost up for dead. A mythic barrelhouse piano player who had played the circuit from the '20's to the '60's, he hadn't performed in public since 1965. Then, in 1986, the Barker Texas History Center put on an exhibit called "From Lemon to Lightnin'," in which they featured Ghost's music and his photograph. Local blues fan Tary Owens, once a good friend of Janis Joplin's and founder of Catfish Records, recognized Ghost's face from the community work he did on 11th Street, and went to seek him out. At first, the older man was suspicious and surly, and refused to leave his house. Owens kept going back, however, and back, and back, until finally Ghost agreed to accompany him to the exhibit.

Once there, he was astounded. He had no idea anyone remembered him, and never before had he heard his recordings, not even "The Hitler Blues," a song that Alistair Cooke had used to rally the troops during World War II. The exhibit woke Ghost up, and when he was asked to perform at the local Carver Museum, he did. That gig led to another and another until Ghost—real name: Roosevelt T. Williams—was playing as well as or better than ever.

Since then, Ghost, who still lives in the same small wooden house he's inhabited for years, has become nationally renowned. Now near 90, he's recorded on Owen's Catfish label and traveled to festivals around the country. He also plays regularly at La Zona Rosa and the Continental Club (see "For Blues," page 350).

"It's good to be recognized at my late date," he says. "I like to play. I don't like to play with no trumpet or singer. It's just me, myself, and I."

Walk of the Stars, *Sixth and Brazos streets.*

Outside the elegant Driskill Hotel, an old cattlemen's establishment that is the second oldest hotel in Texas, there are stars embedded in the sidewalk. Willie Nelson was the first Austin musician to be so honored, and Janis Joplin and Kenneth Threadgill (see Threadgill's, page 345) among others, have since followed.

Vulcan Gas Company, *316 Congress Ave.*

The W. B. Smith Building, now a sedate-looking office building, was once home to the Vulcan Gas Company, a locally infamous club that was more or less credited with starting the music scene in Austin. Opened in 1967—and named after an advertising sign found in an antique store—it was a sort of flagship rock club for local talent such as Shiva's Headband, Conqueroo, and Johnny Winter, as well as touring talent such as Moby Grape, Canned Heat, and the Velvet Underground. Once the club got off the ground, it also started booking blues acts—Sleepy John Estes, Lightnin' Hopkins, Muddy Waters, Big Mama Thornton—who had been touring through East Austin for years but had seldom crossed over into the white part of town.

Stephen F. Austin Hotel, *701 Congress Ave.*

Though now abandoned, the Stephen F. Austin was once a grand old hotel that started featuring swing bands in the early 1930's. Back then, white Austin really wasn't ready for jazz yet, as Charlie Barnet, a popular bandleader of that time, relates in *Those Swinging Years*: "On arrival, I found we were all living in one big room, an unused banquet room, and that we played in the lobby of the hotel at noon every day and on Saturdays in the ballroom on the roof. We got twenty-five dollars a week besides our accommodations in the banquet room.

"It was a weird scene. The people would sit around the lobby and stare at us as we played. . . ."

Robert Shaw's store and home, *1917 Manor Rd.*

Robert Shaw, the great barrelhouse piano player, started out as an itinerant musician riding the Santa Fe rails like many others of his time. He saw no future in it, however, and so moved back home where he opened up a small store and barbecue place, got married, and became involved in the church. He stopped playing the piano altogether and devoted himself to his business so completely that in 1964 he was voted the outstanding black businessman of the year.

Then along came Mack McCormick, a Houston music historian who cofounded Arhoolie Records with Chris Strachwitz. McCormick found Shaw through Dr. Hepcat (Shaw had been Hepcat's piano teacher), and persuaded him to return to music. Soon thereafter, Shaw was on the circuit once again, this time touring the United States and Europe.

Shaw died in 1985, and his long, low-slung store is now closed. His former home, a small white building, stands just behind the market.

Threadgill's, *6416 N. Lamar Blvd. (20 min. N of downtown), 451-5440.*

Though never a true blues or jazz spot, Threadgill's was the club where Janis Joplin got her start. A picture of the star hangs on

Buddy Guy gets down at Antone's.

Susan Antone

one side of the stage, a picture of onetime owner Kenneth Threadgill on the other, and there's a "History Room," lined with Joplin memorabilia in the center of the restaurant.

Threadgill was a former bootlegger and blues yodeler in the Jimmie Rodgers tradition. He opened his joint up in 1933, but for years, it wasn't a club at all, just a gas station and beer café. Then, in the late '40's, Threadgill started holding informal Wednesday-night jam sessions for local musicians.

The sessions were still a going concern by the time Joplin entered the University of Texas in 1962, the same year she was humiliated by being nominated for the university's "Ugly Man" contest. The first few times she performed at Threadgill's, she sang in a pure clear voice, but that soon changed.

Threadgill first recognized Joplin's talent when he heard her sing "Silver Thread and Golden Needles," and was extremely supportive of her throughout her career. She reciprocated his affection and when, in 1971, a birthday party was held in his honor, she canceled a concert in Hawaii to attend.

After Threadgill's death, the club was taken over by Eddie Wilson, who once ran the Armadillo World Headquarters. Today the multiroom place, filled with checkered tablecloths, is a restaurant serving great heaping plates of soul food. The Wednesday-night music tradition continues, usually through the folk music of Champ Hood & His Troubadours.

Music: W. *No cover. Food:* Southern.

Clubs, etc.

Home to over 100 live music venues, Austin has a very eclectic music scene, with many clubs presenting blues, and sometimes jazz, once a week or so, along with other kinds of Texas music. The top full-time blues clubs in town are **Antone's Billy Blues** (formerly Antone's but now part of the Billy Blues network), a world-famous club that books both national and heavyweight local acts, and **Pearl's,** known for its Texas blues. The city's only real full-time jazz venue is the **Elephant Room.**

Legendary blues artists still playing around town include barrelhouse piano player Grey Ghost (sometimes with the Grey Ghost Orchestra), boogie-woogie pianoman Erbie Bowser, guitarist T. D. Bell, the Reverend Lavada Durst, Hosea Hargrove, and Snuff Johnson. Other top blues musicans include Kim Wilson, Blues Boy Hubbard, W. C. Clark, Alan Haynes, Lou Ann Barton, Marcia Ball, Jimmie Vaughan, Long John Hunter, the Mannish Boys, the LeRoi Brothers, Omar and the Howlers, and the teenage Jake "Guitar" Andrews.

Jazz talent to watch for includes piano players James Polk, Floyd Domino, Rich Harney, and Bobby Doyle; trumpet player Martin Banks; saxman Tony Campise; vocalists Marian Price, Carmen Bradford and Chris O'Connell; mandolin player Paul Glass; viola and guitar player Will Taylor; piano and violin player

Danny Levin; drummer A. D. Manion; guitarist Mitch Watkins;
Beto y Los Fairlanes; the Creative Opportunity Orchestra (CO2);
the Jazz Pharaohs; and Tomas Ramirez's fusion band.

Personal Choices

Best jazz clubs: *Elephant Room, Catfish Station (also blues)*
Best blues clubs: *Antone's Billy Blues, Pearl's*
Best acoustic jazz and blues: *Waterloo Ice House*
Best neighborhood blues joint: *Eastside Lounge*

F O R   J A Z Z

Elephant Room, *315 Congress (downtown), 473-2279.*
An old brick basement with a smattering of tables, one token
neon sign (a Martini glass), and lots of old beer advertisements, the
Elephant presents jazz seven nights a week and a jazz happy hour
on the weekdays. Regulars include many of the top jazz musicians
in town—Tony Campise, Tomas Ramirez, Bobby Doyle, the Jazz
Pharaohs, and others. Touring acts are also brought through from
time to time, and celebrities such as Clint Eastwood and Kevin
Costner have occasionally stopped by.

The Elephant was once a storage room, used to keep wine and,
some say, old elephant bones (hence the name) warehoused here
by the University of Texas.
Music: nightly. *Cover:* $.

Catfish Station, *418 E. Sixth St., 477-8875.*
The only black-owned club on Sixth Street, the Catfish pre-
sents jazz, blues, and R&B, as well as a little reggae and funk.
Some of the jazz and blues regulars include the Dynamic Duo
(Blues Boy Hubbard and Matthew Robinson), T. D. Bell and
Erbie Bowser, and Kyle Turner & Standing Room Only. National
acts such as Kirk Whalum are featured about once a month.

The club is set up on two levels, with the stage downstairs and a
balcony around the top. The walls are covered with artwork, including a large mural by The Body Man, an Austin-based artist
originally from Trinidad.
Music: Tu–Sa, mostly jazz, blues. *Cover:* $. *Food:* Cajun, soul
food.

Waterloo Ice House/Lamar, *600 N. Lamar, 472-5400.*
Waterloo Ice House/38th, *1106 W. 38th St., 451-5245.*
Two restaurants, devoted to acoustic music, the Waterloos
present such unusual top-ranked artists as blues guitarist Steve
James, jazz mandolin player Paul Glass, and jazz viola player Will
Taylor. Taylor and Glass usually play the Lamar location, while
James plays both. Other nights are devoted to bluegrass, singer-
songwriters, and other original music.

"Waterloo" was once the name of Austin; an "ice house" is Texanese for a beer joint or convenience store (from back in the days when the only place to get cold beer was an ice house). The Waterloos are considerably more upscale than that, with comfortable booths, pine and cypress bars, and artwork on the walls.
Music: Th–Sa, much jazz, blues. *Cover:* $–$$. *Food:* homemade American.

Jazz: A Louisiana Kitchen, *212 E. 12th St. 479-0474.*

Mostly a large, noisy, too-well-lit restaurant that presents much fusion, Jazz is well worth a visit when the Jazz Pharoahs play. Their music is late '30's and '40's swing. W. C. Clark and other blues artists also appear here from time to time. The theme throughout the restaurant is Louisiana, and there are lots of Mardi Gras masks, Mardi Gras beads, crocodiles, etc., everywhere.
Music: W–Sa, some jazz. *No cover. Food:* Cajun.

Also

Manuel's (310 Congress Ave., 472-7555) is a Mexican restaurant that has been presenting a first-class jazz brunch on Sundays for years and years. **Top of the Marc** (618 W. Sixth St., 472-9849) is a modern, second-story club with a dance floor that occasionally books contemporary jazz. **Chez Fred Crossroads** (9070 Research Blvd., 451-6494) and **Chez Fred West Lake** (1014 Walsh Tarlton La., 328-9187), well-lit restaurants serving American cuisine, feature jazz on the weekends. An upscale wine and champagne bar, **Picasso's** (501 E. Sixth St., 472-8922), often books jazz on the weekends as well.

Jazz can also be heard at some of the blues clubs listed below.

FOR BLUES

Antone's Billy Blues, *corner of Second and Colorado Streets (downtown), 474-5314.*

For nearly 20 years, the old Antone's was a mecca for blues fans, a mythic place that people in other parts of the country talked about with awe. With any luck, the new Antone's, which merged with the San Antonio-based Billy Blues club network (see page 337) in the fall of 1993, will carry on in that tradition.

Antone himself says that the new club hybrid will allow him to book bigger acts, and also save him from worrying about the high property taxes that have threatened to close him down over the past few years. "The reality is that a city supposedly so behind live music raises my property taxes every year. . . ." he told the *Austin Chronicle* shortly after the merger was announced. "[They don't] care how many great people have played in that club."

A native of Port Arthur, Texas, Antone started up his club

when he was just 25 years old. Clifton Chenier (also from Port Arthur and a friend from way back) was the opening act, and for many years the Fabulous Thunderbirds were the house band. Little Walter was in the club logo and Antone had a habit of honoring other departed blues musicians by staging festivals in their honor.

Over time, Antone's featured almost all the blues legends, while also presenting as many unknown Texas musicians as possible. Some, including Angela Strehli, Kim Wilson, and Stevie Ray Vaughan, went on to win international fame.

Blues is Clifford Antone's entire life. "I'm not anything," he says. "I'm just a guy who likes the blues. The musicians are the people. They're the ones who get out on stage."

The new Antone's Billy Blues is located in a warehouse downtown, directly across from Antone's original location. An enormous club, it features three music rooms with retractable walls, a patio, and a restaurant.

Music: nightly. *Cover:* $–$$$. *Food:* barbecue.

Pearl's Oyster Bar, *9033 Research Blvd. (at Anderson La., 15 min. N of downtown), 339-7444.*

One of the best spots in the city to hear blues, Pearl's is a restaurant that presents mostly Texas blues, with a little bit of jazz and classic rock mixed in. Some of the many who've played here include Joe Ely, Marcia Ball, and Smokin' Joe Kubek, and touring acts such as Deanna Bogart are brought through about once a month.

All done up in black and white, with lots of tile and Formica, Pearl's looks like a " '50s shake shop," complete with lots of music memorabilia. It's housed in one large room with partitions that are moved once the music begins.

Music: Tu–Sa. *Cover:* $–$$. *Food:* oysters, seafood, Cajun, Creole.

Joe's Generic Bar, *315 E. Sixth St., 480-0171.*

"The Austin blues scene would collapse without Joe's," says John Conquest, editor of *Music City Texas*. This hole-in-the-wall joint—"the only dive on Sixth Street"—is the place to go to hear young musicians and up-and-coming bands. Some are genuine talent who go on to play much larger clubs, others are . . . well . . . umm . . . no comment.

Joe's has live music every night, often in the beer garden outside, where a chicken wire separates the audience from the band. Inside are Elvis tapestries, old advertising signs, and a hodgepodge of mismatched tables and chairs. No hard liquor is served; only beer and wine coolers.

Music: nightly. *No cover.*

Babe's on Sixth, *208 E. Sixth St., 473-2262.*

Home of Babe's Old Fashioned Burgers, this restaurant-club is often a local band's next step after building up a following at Joe's.

Most of the music here is blues or blues-rock, but Monday nights are usually devoted to a popular bluegrass-C&W slide guitarist, Don Walser, and national acts come through on occasion.

Housed in an old brick building with lots of dark stained wood, Babe's is divided into two rooms. One room contains the restaurant and a small and a big stage, the other a big stage and lots of pics of Marilyn Monroe. Three bands usually play on any given night, and there are also plenty of TV's to satisfy the club's many football fans.

Music: nightly. *Cover:* $. *Food:* burgers, chicken fried steak, etc.

La Zona Rosa, *612 W. Fourth St., 482-0662.*

Currently considered by many to be the hottest club in town, La Zona bills itself as Austin's "Ice House for the Arts." Marcia Ball's husband is one of the owners, and the club features all types of Texas music, from singer-songwriters to *conjunto,* zydeco to blues-R&B.

The inside of the club has been decorated by Austin artists, and each table is painted with a one-of-a-kind design. The musicians perform in the "Marcia Ballroom."

Music: nightly, some blues. *Cover:* $–$$. *Food:* "nuevo Tex-Mex."

Liberty Lunch, *405 W. Second St., 477-0461.*

An Austin institution that's now over 15 years old, Liberty Lunch presents a wide variety of touring acts, from Nirvana to Johnny Winters, Robben Ford to Bad Religion. Once a drive-through lumber yard, it is now a large, covered patio area capable of accommodating up to 1,000 people. "Liberty Lunch" comes from the name of a restaurant that was located here in the 1940's, and back in the 1820's, the lot was a wagon yard adjacent to the town's first dry goods store.

Music: Th–Su, some blues, very occasional jazz. *Cover:* $–$$$.

Continental Club, *1315 S. Congress Ave. (15 min. S of downtown), 441-2444.*

A dark square room, with vintage murals on the walls, the Continental dates back to the 1950's. Tommy Dorsey is said to have stopped by in his day, and the place has also played host to a topless bar and a red-neck hangout. Nowadays, the Continental presents mostly roots rock and rockabilly.

What makes the club interesting for blues fans, though, are its late weekday afternoons. That's when old-time piano players such as Erbie Bowser, and sometimes Grey Ghost, take to the stage. Grey Ghost is very serious about his music; once he sits down at his piano, he doesn't get up to take a single break. Bowser's a bit more upbeat, playing in the boogie-woogie style.

Music: rock and roll nightly, blues, weekdays 5–8pm. *Cover:* $ nights, none in the afternoons.

Eastside Lounge, *E. 12th St., just east of Comal St., (East Austin). No phone.*

A small cinderblock building set back from the street, the Eastside is a neighborhood joint that features some of the best veteran blues talent around, including T. D. Bell and Hosea Hargrove, often playing with the Eastside Band. The musicians usually set up in a space behind the pool tables, and on weekends the place is packed, mostly with a middle-aged crowd. The music usually runs Thursdays through Saturdays, but it's a good idea to drive by and doublecheck during the afternoon to make sure.

Also

Small and dark, the **Hole in the Wall** (2538 Guadalupe St., 472-5599) is one of Austin's oldest live music clubs. The late Stevie Ray Vaughan and Omar and the Howlers played here before making it big, but nowadays the club presents only occasional blues.

Touring blues-R&B and Malaco artists are often booked into **The C-U-Later Club** (389-0002), a showcase venue in the Montopolis section of East Austin. **The Shack** (1167 Webberville Rd., 926-9045), also in East Austin, is a long, well-kept restaurant that was once Ernie's Chicken Shack, a legendary after-hours joint run by the same man who owned Charlie's Playhouse (see "Landmarks and Legends," page 343). The Shack is currently in a dry spell, musically speaking, but it still features blues on occasion.

Blues can also be heard at a number of the jazz clubs listed above, most notably the **Waterloo Ice House** and **Catfish Station.**

Other Venues and Special Events

The nationally syndicated TV show "Austin City Limits" is taped August–January at the University of Texas by public television station KLRU. Tickets are free, but getting them is tricky: local radio stations KUT and KVET announce ticket availability at about 8 a.m. the morning of the event. For more information, call the KLRU hotline at 471-4812.

National jazz and blues acts can sometimes be heard at the **Paramount Theatre** (713 Congress Ave., 472-5411), and the **University of Texas Performing Arts Center** (E. 23rd St. at E. Campus Dr., 471-1444).

The weekend-long **Longhorn Jazz Festival** is held at the University of Texas every summer, while the **Austin Aqua Festival** (472-5664), held over three weekends in July–August, features jazz and blues along with other events. The **Clarksville–West End Jazz & Arts Festival** is held in June, and the **Zilker Park Fall Jazz Festival** takes place in September.

Radio

KAZI/88.7 FM (836-9544). 20 hours of jazz/blues weekly.

KUT/90.5 FM (471-1631). Affiliated with the University of Texas. Very occasional jazz. Blues M nights.

KGSR/107 FM (390-5477). Some contemporary jazz.

Record Stores

The most comprehensive store in town is **Antone's Record Store** (2928 Guadalupe St., across the street from the club's former location, 322-0660), which carries many local labels, including Catfish Records, Watermelon Records, and Antone's Records. Other stores are **Waterloo Records** (600-A N. Lamar Blvd., 474-2500), and **Music Mania** (3909 N. Interstate 35, Suite One, 451-3361), a good spot for imports.

At L.A.'s Grand Avenue Bar, Tom Scott and friends play for a surprisingly hip afternoon crowd.

Courtesy Biltmore Hotel

"West Coast" jazz has come to connote a sort of light, airy sound originated by a group of mostly white musicians working in the 1950's, but the term is misleading, because the West Coast's contribution to the music is considerably older and more complex than that. Jazz and blues in L.A. was already well established by the 1940's at the latest, when Central Avenue, a long straight street that runs from the downtown to Watts, was filled with African-American clubs and theaters of all kinds. Among the most famous of these were the Club Alabam, an extravagant dance hall; the Down Beat, where Charles Mingus and Buddy Collette led a septet; the Brown Bomber, named after Joe Louis, the heavyweight boxing champion; and the 331 Club, where Nat "King" Cole got his start.

Somehow, though, Los Angeles' early contribution to jazz and blues is often downplayed, perhaps because, like San Francisco, it got a late start. The city had no sizable African-American population until World War II, when the war industries and the Southern Pacific Railroad brought hundreds of workers to the Coast from the Southern states.

Some of the many Los Angeles musicians who came of age on Central Avenue included Dexter Gordon, Art Pepper, Hampton Hawes, Charles Mingus, Chico Hamilton, Ernie Andrews, Art Farmer, Teddy Edwards, Sonny Criss, and Harold Land. Bluesmen Percy Mayfield, Jimmy Witherspoon, T-Bone Walker, and Big Jay McNeely were also Avenue fixtures, as was blind pianist Art Tatum, who played through the wee morning hours at a breakfast club called Lovejoy's, and Oakland artist Johnny Otis, whose big band swung away at the Club Alabam.

At the other end of town, Hollywood was also happening during the '40's, with the famous Billy Berg's on Vine Street presenting Lee and Lester Young in 1941 and Benny Carter in 1943. Charlie Parker (with Dizzy Gillespie) played Billy Berg's in 1945, igniting the local bebop scene while procuring heroin from one Emry Byrd, a.k.a. "Moose the Mooche." Moose, a former honor student and athletic star at Jefferson High, who became paralyzed through polio, ran a shoeshine stand on Central Avenue that featured racks of records but actually sold dope.

Another significant 1940's development was Jazz at the Philharmonic (JATP). Started up in 1944 at the downtown Philharmonic Auditorium (since torn down) on Pershing Square by Norman Granz, a young film producer and jazz fan, it was the first concert series ever to give first-class treatment to jazz musicians. By the 1950's, JATP concerts, many featuring outstanding performances that are preserved on vinyl, were being produced at concert halls around the world, including Europe, Australia, and Japan. (The series was discontinued at the conservative L.A. Philharmonic in 1946 owing to "audience disturbances.)

Diz and Bird ignited
the West Coast
bebop scene at Billy
Berg's in 1945.

*Frank Driggs
Collection*

"Cool" or "West Coast" jazz came to Los Angeles in the early 1950's, following the release of Miles Davis's influential *Birth of the Cool* album. Among its top L.A. proponents were Shelly Manne, Gerry Mulligan, Shorty Rogers, Lee Konitz, and Bud Shank, most of whom had actually come to the West Coast from elsewhere. Howard Rumsey's Lighthouse Café in Hermosa Beach was the center of the new 1950's sound, although The Haig on Wilshire Boulevard and later Shelly's Manne-Hole in Hollywood were also important.

Some of the many other musicians associated with Los Angeles over the years include multi-instrumentalist Eric Dolphy, drummer Billy Higgins, trumpet players Chet Baker and Don Cherry, saxophonists Arthur Blythe and David Murray, and pianist Joanne Brackeen.

Sources

The *L.A. Weekly* (667-2620) has superb listings, with the "Blues" section including everything from commercial spots to small African-American neighborhood bars. The *Los Angeles Times* (237-5000) carries its most complete listings on Sundays, and some on Fridays, while the *Los Angeles Daily News* (818-713-

3000) has listings on Fridays. The *Reader* (933-0161), a free weekly, also has listings.

KLON-FM runs a jazz hotline at 310-597-LIVE. JAZZ-FM runs a concert line at 800-426-7779. For 24-hour blues information, call the Blues Information Hotline at 465-9880, or the KLON-FM blues hotline at 310-498-8052.

For maps and other information, contact the Los Angeles Visitors and Convention Bureau, 633 W. Fifth St., Suite 6000, 624-7300.

The area code for downtown Los Angeles is (213), surrounding areas, (310) or (818). All numbers below are (213) unless otherwise noted.

A Note on Neighborhoods

Los Angeles, population 8 million, is intimidating at first: all that sprawl, all that highway, all those districts (Hollywood, Santa Monica, Beverly Hills), or are they separate cities? Except during rush hour, however, the city is surprisingly painless to navigate, and addresses relatively easy to find as long as you're equipped with a detailed map. Parking downtown during the day and in Hollywood, day or night, is generally available only in paying lots; otherwise, street parking is plentiful.

Los Angeles' downtown is small and compact, and though it was once next to deserted after 5 p.m., it's now just beginning to exhibit a nightlife. Hollywood, to the north, has always had a reputation as an entertainment center, and Westwood, to the northwest, is home to UCLA. Venice and Santa Monica, about 20 minutes west of downtown, are on the beach: Venice is known as an arts community, Santa Monica as a retirement one that's now being gentrified. South Central L.A. is located to the immediate west of downtown, just below the Santa Monica Freeway, and many of the "Landmarks and Legends" situated there were untouched by the 1992 riots. The Leimert Park–Crenshaw District in South Central, also untouched by the riots, is a burgeoning artistic community complete with inexpensive shops, boutiques, and sidewalk vendors. (It could be located anywhere in the world, and one can't help but wonder why it was so rarely mentioned in all the media coverage of South Central following the riots.) Sherman Oaks and North Hollywood are in the San Fernando Valley, 40 minutes north of downtown; Compton is an African-American suburb, 20 minutes to the southwest.

Long Beach, a big, completely separate city, lies 40 minutes southwest of L.A.

Landmarks and Legends

(With the exception of the Lighthouse Café, all of the sites below are in or relatively near South Central L.A. and can easily be toured in an hour or two by car.)

Central Avenue, *downtown to 103rd St.*

"There was always something happening on Central Avenue," says flugelhorn and trumpet player Art Farmer. "One time, I was at the Down Beat, and Big Jay McNeely was playing across the street. He marched up and down the street playing his horn, he lay down on his back playing his horn, he came into the Down Beat playing his horn. Then the owner started shouting at us, 'Get a horn!, Get a horn!,' like it was some kind of duel, like his sax was a gun. [Central Avenue] was like a wild, wild Western show."

During its 1940's heyday, Central Avenue was somewhat of a mix between New York's 52nd Street and Harlem. Like 52nd Street, it was filled with dozens of small clubs and hundreds of musicians making the rounds from one spot to another (unlike 52nd Street, though, things were very spread out, stretching as they did for over 100 blocks). Like Harlem, it also had its share of classy theaters and dance halls that attracted not only African-Americans of varying economic classes but also middle-class whites and Hollywood entertainers.

Central Avenue went into decline in the early 1950's when the economic boom of the war years was over, and the city's electric Red Car trolley system, the street's main form of public transportation, was disbanded. Today, much of Avenue is delapidated, boarded up, or torn down. Only a few reminders—the Hotel Dunbar, the Lincoln Theater—remain, and only one club, Babe & Ricky's, is still in operation (see "For Blues," page 368).

Hotel Dunbar, *4225 Central Ave., corner 42nd St.*

From the 1920's through the 1940's, most of the top African-American entertainers passing through Los Angeles stayed at the Dunbar, which was the first hotel in the U.S. built specifically for blacks. A large solid brick building with arched doorways on the ground floor, it later stood unoccupied for many years except for one longtime resident, comedian Rudy Ray Moore. Moore did finally move out, in 1988, and the building is now an apartment house for senior citizens. A small museum with black entertainment memorabilia is on the ground floor.

Duke Ellington and his band sometimes stayed at the Dunbar, as Buck Clayton, who had an apartment there at one time, recalls in *Buck Clayton's Jazz World*:

I'll never forget one day when I happened to be in a restaurant in the Dunbar and most of Duke's guys were in there too and they were all listening to the jukebox. It was the first time since leaving the East that they had heard their recording of *It don't mean a thing if it ain't got that swing,* and that restaurant was swinging like crazy. So much rhythm I'd never heard, as guys were beating on tables, instrument cases or anything else that they could beat on with knives, forks, rolled-up newspapers. . . . It was absolutely crazy. I found out one more thing about Duke's band being in a restaurant. If there is fifteen musicians that enter a restaurant they take up fifteen tables as everybody takes a table for himself. I never knew why, but everyone wanted and got his own table.

Club Alabam, *Central Ave. near 42nd St.*

Now a big vacant lot next door to the Hotel Dunbar, the opulent Club Alabam with its silk drapes, colored lights, and waitresses in scanty dress, was once the focal point of jazz on the Avenue. Founded in the '20's by drummer and bandleader Curtis Mosby (whose brother, Esvan, was elected mayor of Central Avenue), it featured dancing and entertainment nightly.

Among the many who showed up at the Club at one time or another were Andy Kirk, Fats Waller, Lena Horne, and Frank Sinatra, who came as a listener only but then sang a spontaneous number after the scheduled performers were done. Eddie Barefield's band played here in the '30's and Lee Young's (Lester Young's brother) during the war years. Among those who played with Young were Dexter Gordon, Art Pepper, and Charles Mingus.

Lincoln Theater, *Central Ave. and 23rd St.*

Now a somewhat run-down temple, the Lincoln Theater was popular during the '20's and '30's, when many of the local big bands and musicians performed here. Vocalist Ernie Andrews was once an usher at the Lincoln, and—rather ironically, given Central Avenue's current condition—the theater was once known for the benefits it sponsored for the poor.

5-4 Ballroom, *308 W. 54th St. at Broadway (South Central), 752-4933 or 291-3102.*

First built in 1922 for whites who resided in South Central, the 5-4 became a cultural mecca for the city's black population around World War II, by which time the neighborhood's racial makeup had changed. All sorts of top African-American entertainers could be heard here back then, including Nat "King" Cole, B. B. King, Fats Domino, Dizzy Gillespie, and, later, Ornette Coleman. Ray Charles broadcast a TV program from here in the early 1960's, and the ballroom was still in operation as late as 1968.

Located on the second floor, with sparkling picture windows all around, the 5-4 is currently in the process of being restored. Dr. O. W. Wilson, who has worked as both a high school principal and a professor of political science at Cal State, bought the place a few years ago with the hopes of bringing a first-class restaurant and club back to South Central. Thus far he has succeeded in getting the place about three quarters finished, but is still seeking further funding. He's even gone so far as to refinance his home. "I have to get it open," he says. "It's a compulsion."

Western Avenue, *30th to 40th streets.*

Following the demise of Central Avenue, much of the city's jazz activity moved westward, to clubs such as the **Tiki Room** (still standing at Western Ave. and 37th St.), the **Club Oasis** (also at 37th St. near Western), the **It Club**, and the **California Club** (at St. Andrew and Martin Luther King, near Western, now a lounge). Western Avenue was never able to recreate Central's old magic, however.

Thomas Jefferson High School, *1319 E. 41st St.*

Many now well-known Los Angeles musicians once attended this stolid old high school, located just off Central Avenue. Among them were Dexter Gordon, Chico Hamilton, Big Jay McNeely, Sonny Criss, Ed Thigpen, Ernie Andrews, Horace Tapscott, Frank Morgan, Art and Addison Farmer, and Roy Ayers. All studied under one extraordinary teacher, Samuel Browne, who was the first African-American high school teacher hired by the Los Angeles school system. ("The oral exam committee," Browne said to Clint Rosemond of L.A.'s Jazz Heritage Foundation in 1983 "was concerned about what I would do if I had white students in my class; how would I handle it? I said, 'I'll just try to teach them, that's all; nothing special.' ")

Browne, who was also known as the Count, was responsible for three school orchestras that performed around town for both public and private events. In addition to teaching music classes and running rehearsals, he also brought in many top musicians—Jimmie Lunceford, Nat "King" Cole, and Lionel Hampton—to perform and talk to his students.

Lighthouse Café, *30 Pier Ave., Hermosa Beach, 310-372-6911.*

Still a handsome music club, now featuring a mix of rock-and-roll, blues, and some jazz, the legendary Lighthouse is in the laid-back beach community of Hermosa Beach. Started up by band-leader Howard Rumsey in 1949, the Lighthouse was a jazz club for over 20 years. During the 1950's it was home base for Shorty Rogers, Shelly Manne, Teddy Edwards, Art Pepper, Sonny Criss, and Hampton Hawes, some of whom formed a recording group called the Lighthouse All Stars.

The Lighthouse was especially famous for its Sunday jam sessions, which began at two in the afternoon and lasted until two the following morning. "All those hours!" Shorty Rogers says in *Jazz West Coast* by Robert Gordon. "We'd start at two and I'd look out and there'd be people sitting in bathing suits, listening to the music. And then, just as I'd be about ready to collapse at two in the morning, I'd look again and they were still there—two in the morning in their bathing suits!"

Also

Ethel Waters once lived in a large Victorian home (1910 Harvard Blvd., near Washington Blvd.), now painted white with light green trim, in what was then known as the "Sugar Hill" district of

Los Angeles. **Nat "King" Cole** once lived in a beautiful brick house (401 Muirfield Rd. at Fourth St.), now draped with ivy and surrounded by landscaped gardens, in exclusive Hancock Park. When he died of lung cancer in 1965 at the age of 45, he was buried in the Forest Lawn Cemetery (1712 S. Glendale Ave., Glendale, 818-241-4151).

Clubs, etc.

Perhaps because of the "Tonight Show" band, jazz activity in Los Angeles seems to be on the upswing. Touring national talent can be heard regularly at **Catalina's, The Jazz Bakery, Birdland West,** and, to a lesser extent, **Vine Street;** while top L.A.-based talent appear almost nightly at the **Club Brasserie,** the **Grand Avenue Bar,** and **Lunaria.** One of the best places to catch up-and-coming artists is the **World Stage.**

Blues is experiencing even more of a renaissance. Whereas three and a half years ago, there were only two or three clubs in town offering live blues most nights of the week, there are now a good half dozen, with several others featuring blues about half the time. Two of the best of these new clubs are **The Mint** and **Fais Do Do,** while **House of Blues** promises to be a top spot for national talent.

Some of the many fine L.A.-based jazz musicians who play around town regularly include veteran saxophonists Teddy Edwards and Harold Land, Bulgarian pianist Milcho Leviev, trumpet players Jack Sheldon and Bobby Bradford, pianists Horace Tapscott and Alan Broadbent, bassists Larry Gales, Jimmy and Stacy Rowles, the Black-Note Quartet, and the members of the "Tonight Show" band, including Branford Marsalis, Kenny Kirkland, and Jeff Watts. Two big bands, Bob Florence's band and Capp-Pierce Juggernaut, are also worth catching.

Among blues and R&B talent, there are the legends: Lowell Fulson, Harmonica Fats, Jimmy Witherspoon, Guitar Shorty, Johnny Dyer, and Blind Joe Hill. Other top blues acts include J. J. "Bad Boy" Jones and His Bad Boys, the Bernie Pearl Blues Band, and William Clarke.

Generally speaking, music in L.A. stops at 2 a.m.

Personal Choices

Hottest L.A. jazz club: *Club Brasserie*
Best national jazz club: *Catalina's*
Best listening room: *Jazz Bakery*
Best jazz surprise: *Grand Avenue Bar*
Best neighborhood jazz spots: *World Stage, Legends*
Best blues club: *The Mint Lounge*
Best historic blues joint: *Babe & Ricky's*
Best eclectic club: *Fais Do Do*

Babe and Ricky's, the last of the Central Avenue clubs, still smokes with the blues.

FOR JAZZ

Catalina Bar & Grill, *1640 N. Cahuenga Blvd., Hollywood, 466-2210.*

A friendly, intimate place with rose stucco walls, pretty gold lights, and tables that all face forward, Catalina's roster of performers is impressive, ranging from traditional to avant garde, with fusion thrown in every once in a great while. Max Roach and Ahmad Jamal have played here, as have Steve Lacy and Andrew Hill, and then there are the local greats such as Horace Tapscott and Bobby Bradford. If you don't want to sit at a table, there's a comfortable bar off to one side.
Music: Tu–Su. *Cover:* $$–$$$. *Food:* Continental. CC. Reservations recommended.

Vine Street Bar & Grill, *1610 N. Vine St., Hollywood, 463-4375.*

Just around the corner from Catalina's, marked with a pink-and-white marquee and yellow COCKTAILS sign, is the Vine Street Bar & Grill. The tiny place (it only seats 80) has an old-fashioned Hollywood feel, with red booths and a bandstand, a serpentine bar, and a big shiny mirror. A variety of nationally known artists, especially vocalists, appear here, Mose Allison, Johnny Otis, Joe Williams, and Nina Simone among them.

Music: Tu–Su. *Cover:* $$. *Food:* northern Italian. MC/Visa only. Reservations recommended.

Jazz Bakery, *3233 Helms Ave., Culver City, 310-271-9039.*

More a small concert hall than a club, the Jazz Bakery is one of the best places in town to hear jazz. Located in a clean, well-lit, high-ceilinged space that was once part of the Helms Bakery garage, it's set up with rows of folding chairs (seating 180), and there's no talking, smoking, or drinking allowed. A small counter in back serves coffee, fruit juices, and baked goods, which come free with the price of admission.

The Bakery is the brainchild of singer Ruth Price. Some of the many who have played here include Tommy Flanagan, Chico Hamilton, Annie Ross, and Harold Land.

Music: F–Su. *Cover:* $–$$$. *Free parking out front.*

Birdland West, *105 W. Broadway, Long Beach (downtown), 310-436-9341.*

Located on the second story of a large corner building, Birdland West is lined with windows overlooking a deserted downtown street. Nationally known artists playing everything from Latin and straight–ahead to fusion and cabaret appear here; the sight lines and acoustics are excellent.

The neo–Art Deco club, filled with black tables and chairs, is spacious but somewhat cold in atmosphere. It's owned by drummer Al Williams, who fronts his own band most Thursday nights. Williams is also the producer of the Long Beach Jazz Festival.

Music: W–Sa. *Cover/minimum:* $$$–$$$$. *Food:* Cajun/Creole. CC. Reservations recommended.

Club Brasserie, *Bel Age Hotel, 1020 N. San Vicente Blvd., West Hollywood, 310-854-1111.*

Situated on a hill overlooking the city, the Club Brasserie, with its wide picture windows, spacious dining tables, and long polished bar, is a first-class place from which to view Los Angeles at night. It's also a first-class place in which to hear jazz. The club is currently the hottest spot in town, attracting large numbers of well-known musicians and an enthusiastic crowd who can't believe they're hearing players they usually pay big bucks for—Teddy Edwards, Harold Land, Delfeayo Marsalis—for no cover. Piano player Kenny Kirkland of the "Tonight Show" band plays here weekly.

The club is booked by guitarist Sid Jacobs, who is friends with most of the other musicians in town and simply picks up the phone whenever he wants someone to play. "It's not like a concert scene here," he says, "and lots of players like that. They have complete artistic freedom."

Music: Tu–Sa. *No cover. Food:* Californian. CC. Dinner reservations recommended.

Grand Avenue Bar, *Biltmore Hotel, 506 S. Grand Ave. (downtown), 612-1532; jazz line, 612-1595.*

One of L.A.'s greatest jazz surprises is the Grand Avenue Bar, which *L.A. Times* critic Leonard Feather calls "the hippest corner downtown." All sorts of jazz greats—Harold Land, Teddy Edwards, Ernie Andrews—appear here in the late afternoon, often for no cover.

The Grand Avenue itself is a large, very elegant affair (solid black tables, fresh flowers, jazz photos on the walls), and while the music is happening, a lavish free buffet is served with pasta, Mexican nachos, cheese, fruit, and crudités. The after-work crowd is equally delightful: It's well mixed, racially, economically, and generationally.

Music: weekday afternoons, 5:30–9:30 pm. *No cover,* except for special events.

Lunaria, *10351 Santa Monica Blvd. (between Beverly Hills and Venice), 310-282-8870.*

A large and sophisticated restaurant filled with men in expensive white suits and women in designer cocktail dresses, Lunaria is best known for its gastronomic delights. But jazz is also a serious matter here, where straight-ahead artists are presented during the week and vocalists on the weekends. Some of the musicians who have appeared here include Branford Marsalis, Alan Broadbent, Barbara Morrison, and John Wood, who also books the club. Sunday nights, when no food is served, are devoted to the blues.

Lunaria is a low-ceilinged, low-lit place painted a peachy cream. The walls are hung with impressive watercolors, and a lively bar is situated near the entrance by big picture windows.

Music: Tu–Su. *Cover:* $–$$$. *Food:* Californian-Continental. CC. Dinner reservations recommended.

World Stage, *4344 Degnan Blvd., Leimert Park–Crenshaw District, South Central, 293-2451.*

A no-frills, community-based musicians' and poets' collective, the World Stage was started up in 1989 by drummer Billy Higgins, poet-writer Kamau Daa'ood, and organizer Dawan Muhammad. Since then, it has presented music workshops and performances by many jazz legends, including Horace Tapscott, Harold Land, Cedar Walton, and Max Roach, all of whom have donated their time to talk to the community and instruct its youth.

All workshops and concerts, usually held on the weekends, are open to the public for a nominal fee, and they're great opportunities to hear both big names and up-and-coming talent. The stage is a small, friendly, and informal place, simply equipped with rows of yellow chairs and a raised stage. No food or drinks are served, and there's plenty of free and secure parking outside.

Billy Higgins has also established a record label connected with the stage (World Stage Records), on which he's recorded several of the young jazz bands that have started up here. One of these,

Black/Note, has since been signed by Columbia Records and played the Montreal Jazz Festival. "All that happened because of Billy Higgins," says Black/Note's leader Mark Shelby. "He's one of the few cats who puts his money where his mouth is."
Music: F and Sa nights, Sa afternoons; call for other times. *Donation:* $.

5th Street Dick's Coffee Company, *3347½ W. 43rd Pl., Leimert Park—Crenshaw District, South Central, 296-3970.*

Right around the corner from Billy Higgins's place is a jazz coffeehouse serving espresso and iced drinks, but no alcohol, that also presents many of the bands that appear at the World Stage. Name musicians have been known to stop by as well, especially on Saturday mornings when an after-hours jam session rocks the joint from 1 to 6 a.m.

This is a long, neat, and narrow club, with stools, paintings, and posters. Upstairs is a small balcony and sitting area, while outside is a patio perfect for people watching. Sharing the building with the coffeehouse is **Final Vinyl** (3347 W. 43rd Pl., 296-1372), which specializes in used records.
Music: F—W. *Cover:* $. *Food:* pastries, snacks.

Marla's Memory Lane, *2323 Martin Luther King, Jr., Blvd. (South Central L.A.), 294-8430.*

A long low-ceilinged room with lots of small green tables, booths, and a large dance floor, this club has been around since the '40's. Now owned by singer-actress Marla Gibbs, it's known for presenting L.A.-based greats: Harold Land, Billy Higgins, Teddy Edwards. Mirrors line one wall, black-and-white photos another, while the bar is strewn with tiny lights. Comedians are often on tap early in the evenings.
Music: Th—Su. *Cover:* $$. *Food:* American. CC.

Legends of Hollywood, *6555 Hollywood Blvd., Hollywood (at Whitley Ave.), 464-7780.*

A big old wonderful hall of a place with enormous red booths, a meandering lunch counter, and murals of Old California lining its walls, Legends was built in the 1920's as a silent-movie theater. After going through several incarnations, it's now a New York–style deli that offers a bird's-eye view of the unpredictable Hollywood street life passing by outside while at the same time serving up large portions of mainstream and straight-ahead jazz.

Legends is owned and operated by vocalist Bob Marks, who once worked the Vegas clubs and still takes to the stage, for at least a song or two, most nights. Marks is also the deli's cook and he specializes in "old family recipes," Russian Jewish style.

The murals on the walls were painted by Russian artist George Ivans in 1952. The project took two years to complete and the then 70-year-old Ivans always came to work accompanied by his 8-year-old son, who carried his paint cans. His son is now a street

person who plays the fiddle on Hollywood Boulevard from time to time.
Music: Tu–Su. *No cover. Food:* New York deli. Free parking in back.

Atlas Bar & Grill, *3760 Wilshire Blvd., Mid City (at Western Ave.), 380-8400.*

A cavernous and dark, high-ceilinged place with bright stars, crazy iron sculptures, and sparkling zigzags on the walls, the Atlas is a theatrical restaurant-club offering up a little salsa, a little cabaret, a little swing, and a lot of jazz. Attracting a well-mixed crowd that's equal parts Latino, black, and Anglo, it's also well known as a dance spot.

Mario Tamayo, who owns the Atlas, wants to "give jazz a young face again" by running a club where "kids in dreadlocks who wouldn't be caught dead in a place like Catalina's can be exposed to jazz." Black/Note and Boptet perform here regularly, and there's usually a jazz jam on Tuesday nights.
Music: Tu–Su. *Cover:* $–$$. *Food:* international. CC.

Le Café, *14633 Ventura Blvd., Sherman Oaks, 818-986-2662.*

A hip and modern club showcasing much contemporary and fusion, Le Café started out as just another pretty, high-ceilinged restaurant filled with plants, pillars, exposed black pipes, and revolving artwork. A few years ago, however, it started presenting quality jazz in a small glassed-in room upstairs (seating only 66), and today it's known as a hot spot to catch top session musicians. Artists who've played with everyone from Miles to Madonna play here.
Music: nightly. *Cover:* $$. *Food:* Californian, international. CC. Reservations for the music room taken for dinner patrons only.

Baked Potato, *3787 Cahuenga Blvd, N. Hollywood, 818-980-1615.*

This may have been a famous contemporary jazz joint at one time (Lee Ritenour and Larry Carlton got their starts here), but nowadays, the North Hollywood club—almost pitch-black except for the stage lights and a few flickering candles—has a decidedly sleazy feel. Japanese and European tourists arrive by the busloads, and the doorman counts his money by flashlight beam.

Multikeyboardist Dan Randi owns the club, and he and his band, Quest, play Thursdays through Saturdays. The specialty of the house is baked potato with toppings.

A second **Baked Potato** (26 E. Colorado Blvd., Pasadena, 818-564-1122) was recently opened in Pasadena, and it's nearly identical to the first.
Music: nightly. *Cover:* $$. *Food:* potatoes.

Indigo Jazz Lounge, *91 Freeway and Alameda, 111 E. Artesia Blvd., Compton (in the Ramada Hotel and Convention Center), 310-632-1234.*

Located at the far end of a new high-rise hotel, the Indigo was specifically designed for jazz. A small, intimate, comfortable place with a dark blue decor and flickering candles, it's fitted with staggered walls, lots of black tables, and a fine Baldwin concert grand. Sight lines and acoustics are excellent.

Musically, the emphasis is on local jazz, blues, and R&B artists. *Music:* Th–Sa. *Cover:* $. *Food:* appetizers. CC.

The Living Room, *2636 Crenshaw Blvd. (South Central L.A.), 735-8748.*

A cozy red room with red lights, a modern bar, and a small step-up stage, the Living Room is the kind of place that from the outside looks like just a place, but inside . . . ah, inside! Cornets and saxes overwhelm you with blasts of crazy notes circling through the air. An ultracool cat in a hat and dark gray suit wails away on alto sax, while a man with a wired flute blows in from far back near the bar. Everyone knows everyone at the Living Room, a 30-plus-year-old neighborhood institution owned by Barbie Bostick.
Music: Su. *No cover.*

The Townhouse, *6835 La Tijera Blvd., Ladera Heights, 310-649-0091.*

An upscale restaurant-club in a middle-class African-American neighborhood, the Townhouse is large, friendly, and multi-roomed, with live music every night of the week. Vocalist Barbara Morrison is a regular, along with bluesman King Ernest. A jazz champagne brunch, followed by a jam session, is served on Sunday afternoons. Located only five minutes from LAX, the Townhouse is a favorite stopping-off spot among celebrities passing through town; Stevie Wonder, Chaka Kahn, Don King, Daryl Strawberry, Nancy Wilson, and Dionne Warwick are among the many who have done so.
Music: nightly. *Cover:* $. *Food:* American. CC.

Also

The **Cat & Fiddle Pub** (6530 Sunset Blvd., Hollywood, 213-468-3800) is a lively, rambling joint with an outside garden that features mainstream jazz on Sunday nights. **Nightwinds** (1026 Wilshire Blvd., Santa Monica, 310-917-9111) is a large, dark, and cavernous place that often presents fusion artists. The **Loew's Santa Monica Beach Hotel** (1700 Ocean Ave., 310-458-6700) features first-class musicians in its lobby lounge, while the **Cinegrill** in the grand Art Deco Hollywood Roosevelt Hotel (7000 Hollywood Blvd., 466-7000) also offers jazz on occasion. **La Louisanne** (5812 Overhill Dr., Ladera Heights, 293-5073) is an upscale African-American restaurant that presents jazz most weekends.

Other decent jazz spots north of the city include **Chadney's** (3000 W. Olive Ave., Burbank, 818-843-5333), adjacent to the NBC studios, which features mostly mainstream and straight-ahead jazz Tuesdays through Saturdays; the **Dodsworth Bar & Grill** (2 W. Colorado Blvd., Pasadena, 818-578-1344), a crowded spot with live local jazz nightly; and **Jax** (399 N. Brand Blvd., Glendale, 818-500-1604), an often noisy restaurant with straight-ahead jazz.

F O R   B L U E S

House of Blues, *8434 Sunset Strip, West Hollywood.*
The third House of Blues (see Boston, page 158) is slated to open in Los Angeles in the spring of 1994. Like its predecessors in Cambridge and New Orleans, it will be a three-story "juke joint mansion" filled with blues memorabilia and Southern folk art. The L.A. location will also serve as the company's headquarters.

The Mint Lounge, *6010 W. Pico Blvd., Mid City, 937-9630.*
What started out as an underground blues party in the mid-1980s has since evolved into one of the best blues clubs in town, pleasing both purists and nonpurists alike. Lots of Alligator recording artists and local favorites, such as William Clarke and Arthur Adams, play in this easy-to-miss hole-in-the-wall with grills over its windows.

The Mint has been the Mint since 1937, and although it was just a local watering hole for most of those years, some oldtime blues artists can remember playing here way back when. Atmospheric, intimate, and dark, with a few red booths and red lights over the bar, it's a tiny place that accommodates only about 100 people.

Lots of celebs have stopped by and sat in at the club, including Bonnie Raitt, Ron Wood, Lou Rawls, Natalie Cole, Stevie Wonder, and Mick Jagger (who didn't sit in).
Music: nightly. *Cover:* $–$$. *Food:* American.

Jack's Sugar Shack, *8751 W. Pico Blvd., Mid City, 310-271-7887.*
Just down the street from the Mint Lounge is another solid L.A. blues club, this one a big sprawling well-lit place housed in what was once a tropical restaurant, complete with palm trees, bamboo, painted fish, and running fountains. A large square bar with 32 beers on tap dominates the main room, and there are plenty of pool tables and an outdoor patio in back.

Many Alligator recording artists have played Jack's as well, and the club has its own share of celebrity stories to tell, including

the one about the time Van Morrison sat in with club regulars Ray Bailey & the Camarillo All-Stars. This Jack's is owned by the same people who run Jack's in San Francisco (see page 380).
Music: nightly. *Cover:* $. *Food:* sandwiches, etc.

Fais Do Do, *5257 W. Adams Blvd., Mid City, 310-842-6171.*

Named after the Cajun expression for "put the kids to sleep, the grown-ups are going to party," Fais Do Do (pronounced "fay dough-dough") is a hip and friendly, no-frills club that offers a mix of much blues, New Orleans, and Brazilian music, and some world beat. Attracting a somewhat more racially mixed audience than most of the blues clubs in town, it's housed in a marvelous, worn-around-the-edges Art Deco building that was once a bank. High windows line the walls; high ceilings loom over a scuffed black-and-white-tiled floor. The blue bar along the far wall serves espresso and capuccino, along with the standard alcoholic fare.

The club is located on the edge of a somewhat marginal neighborhood, and owner Steven Yablok has made a conscious effort to reach out to the surrounding community. "The point is to mix people together and give the club roots," he says. "Create something real."
Music: nightly, much blues. *Cover:* $. *Food:* Cajun.

Babe & Ricky's Inn, *5259 S. Central Ave. (South Central L.A.), 235-4866.*

Laura Mae Gross, the owner of Babe & Ricky's, sits beside a big lace-cloth-covered table marked RESERVED. A grandmotherly woman in a blue sequined dress with a white crocheted hat, she remembers the old Central Avenue well. "It was a dazzling scene," she says, her gold tooth flashing. "Blues, bebop, and swing from one end to the other."

Untouched by the 1992 riots, Babe & Ricky's, with its cement floors and iron-grille front, is the last of the Central Avenue clubs, and largely because of Laura Mae Gross, it's a beautiful place with a beautiful feel. She greets most of her guests at the door with a smile and a hug, and the band (usually The Mighty Balls of Fire or J. J. "Bad Boy" Jones & His Bad Boys) blows so hard and so fierce that the room's old walls seem to shake. Up front, there's a big old bar lined with lights; out back stands a pool table. The clientele is a mix of older, neighborhood folk, and young college students.
Music: Th–M. *No cover.*

Sunset Social Club, *8210 Sunset Blvd., West Hollywood, 654-1001.*

A blues club with valet parking, the Sunset is a trendy late-night spot that one of its managers calls a hangout for young Hollywood. Housed in an old and atmospheric wooden house with lots of small rooms painted dark green, it's lit by muted red lights and

draped with red velveteen curtains. Hook & the Hitchhikers are
regulars; food is served until 3:30 a.m.
Music: nightly. *Cover:* $. *Food:* American.

Harvelle's, *1432 Fourth St., Santa Monica, 395-1676.*
The oldest bar in Santa Monica (established in 1931) is now a
popular blues club that's often packed to the bursting point, especially on the weekends. A longish room fitted with a heavy wooden
bar, engraved mirrors, and high ceiling fans, it usually features
local blues and R&B bands such as Larry Johnson & the New
Breed or The Sugardaddys. Mondays are devoted to jam sessions.
Music: nightly. *Cover:* $–$$.

St. Mark's, *23 Windward Ave., Venice, 310-452-2222.*
Located less than a block from Venice Beach, St. Mark's is an
upscale supper club that presents much R&B and Motown, some
blues, and occasional jazz. Done up in two-tiered "modern Italian"
elegance with a dance floor and sophisticated sound system, it's
better known for its food and wine than for its music. Out in front of
the 1907 building are large white columns topped with eleborate
cornices; at one time, these columns ran the length of the street
down to the beach.
Music: Tu–Su, some blues. *Cover:* $–$$. *Food:* California. CC.
Dinner reservations recommended.

Village Bar & Grill, *4201 W. Olive Ave., Burbank, 818-846-
2342.*
A pretty club decorated in pastels, with hanging plants, canvas
chairs and striking oil paintings of musicians, the Village Bar features a lot of guitar-based, Texas-style blues. Once a hangout for
stuntmen, the place now caters to the people behind the movie
scenes: laborers, riggers, grips, makeup artists. (Warner Brothers
is located directly across the street and owns almost everything in
the immediate area.) Most of the bands are local, though national
acts are often featured on the weekends. The Bruno Brothers host
an open jam on Tuesday nights that's sometimes attended by a
harmonica-playing Bruce Willis.
Music: nightly. *Cover:* $. *Food:* sandwiches, etc.

Also

The Blue Café in Long Beach (210 The Promenade, 310-983-
7111) features blues, R&B, and roots rock-and-roll most nights of
the week. **Alligator Lounge** (3321 Pico Blvd., 310-449-1844)
has blues on a regular basis, as does **Bogart's** (6288 Pacific Coast
Hwy., 594-8975), a large venue in Long Beach. **The Townhouse**
(see "For Jazz," page 366) has a blues jam on Monday nights.

Other Venues and Special Events

In addition to **Playboy Jazz Festival**, which is the biggest jazz fest in town (see "Major Festivals" page 403), there's the two-day **John Coltrane Festival**, held in late September; the two-day **Simon Rodeo Music and Arts Festival**, held near Watts Towers at the end of July; the **Day of the Drum** festival, held in late September; the three-day **Long Beach Jazz Festival** (310-436-7794), held in August; the **Jazz Trax** fest held on Catalina Island in October (619-233-3722 or 800-866-TRAX) and the two-day **Long Beach Blues Festival** (985-5566), held in September. **Blues cruises** leave from Long Beach several times a year. For details on these and other special events, check the local papers.

The outdoor **Hollywood Bowl** (2301 N. Highland Ave., 850-2000), where the Playboy Jazz Festival takes place and where Art Tatum gave his last major performance, hosts a jazz series in the summer. Nationally known jazz and blues figures also occasionally appear at the **Greek Theater** in North Hollywood (2700 N. Vermont Ave., 665-1927); the historic **Palace** in Hollywood (1735 N. Vine, 467-4571), formerly the Hollywood Palace, built in 1927; and the **Strand**, a showcase-nightclub in Redondo Beach, (1700 S. Pacific Coast Highway, 310-316-1700).

Radio

KLON/88.1 FM (310-985-5566). A 24-hour jazz station. Affiliated with California State University, Long Beach. Blues weekend afternoons.

JAZZ-FM/103.1 FM (310-450-1031). A 24-hour contemporary jazz station.

KPCC/89.3 FM (818-578-7231). Affiliated with NPR and Pasadena City College. Jazz daily, some evenings. Blues, F afternoons.

Some jazz and blues can also be heard on **KPFK/90.7 FM** and **KCRW/89.9 FM**.

Record Stores

The Sunset Strip branch of **Tower Records** (8801 W. Sunset Blvd., 310-657-7300) has a good jazz CD collection, and **Lamar's Records** in Long Beach (1150 Wardlow, 310-426-2254) carries nothing but the blues. **Rhino Records** (1720 Westwood Blvd., 310-474-8685) and **Poo Bah Records** (1101 E. Walnut, Pasadena, 818-449-3359) also carry blues, while **Aron's Record Shop** (1150 N. Highland, 469-4700) is a good spot for jazz.

Prior to World War II, few people thought of San Francisco as either a jazz or blues town. Touring swing bands passed through the city's big hotels, major African-American entertainers appeared at Slim Jenkins's place in Oakland, and the Fillmore District boasted a few jazz-blues clubs (including what is now Jack's, see "for Blues," page 380) but there was little home-grown talent, largely because San Francisco had virtually no black population.

Then came World War II, and the growth of the shipyards, and suddenly a tremendous influx of African-American workers arrived from Texas and the rural South. Many settled across the Bay in Oakland and Richmond (East Bay), and soon a black entertainment strip developed down the street from Slim Jenkins's Place. Jenkins continued to run the premier nightclub in town, attracting both blacks and whites to hear such stars as Dinah Washington, Earl Hines, and Ivory Joe Hunter (who wrote "Seventh Street Boogie" in its tribute), but now there were also smaller, rougher places offering a more raw, more mournful blues.

Lowell Fulson, Pee Wee Crayton, Jimmy McCracklin, and Jimmy Wilson were among the new arrivals, many of whom were eventually recorded by Bob Geddins, an African American also from Texas, who had started up a record company in Oakland in 1945. Geddins, who had called his business Big Town Recordings, would scour the local clubs and churches looking for talent, and then record them on acetate disc in his garage-like shop at Eighth and Chestnut streets.

The Oakland blues scene peaked in the mid- to late-1960's. In the late '70's, however, according to East Bay blues writer Lee Hildebrand, the music again came to life through a new generation of artists: Sonny Rhodes, J. J. Malone, Troyce Key (see Eli's Mile High Club & Restaurant, page 381), Frankie Lee, and Bobby Murray. Clubs were packed once more, this time with young middle-class whites and blacks, as well as with the older black working class.

Jazz in the Bay Area took a somewhat different route. "San Francisco's biggest contribution to jazz is traditional jazz," says Philip Elwood, longtime critic for the *San Francisco Examiner*. He goes on to point to trombonist Turk Murphy and Lu Watters and his Yerba Buena Jazz Band, both of whom brought about the revival of the New Orleans sound in the 1940's. Traditional jazz continues to play a role in the Bay Area today: every Memorial Day, the world's largest Dixieland and swing festival, the Sacramento Dixieland Jubilee, takes place near here, drawing over 100 bands (see "Major Festivals," page 403).

The '50's and '60's were also particularly fertile times for jazz in San Francisco. Small clubs were flourishing all over the city, including the Blackhawk, where Art Tatum played one of his last residencies; the Jazz Workshop, where Cannonball Adderley re-

A mural commemorates the jazz clubs that once packed San Francisco's North Beach.

corded with his quintet; the Club Hangover, where Earl Hines performed; and Bop City, where Dexter Gordon and Sonny Criss once played. Cool jazz proponents Dave Brubeck and Paul Desmond, and jazz/Latin/rock musician Carlos Santana were three of the best-known artists to emerge during this period, along with vibraphonist Cal Tjader, who was later known for his Latin jazz, and pianist-composer Vince Guaraldi.

The last of the legendary San Francisco jazz clubs was the Keystone Korner, which opened in 1972 and closed in the early '80's. Bay Area jazz fans still mention it with a sigh.

Sources

Excellent listings and music coverage can be found in most local publications, including the *San Francisco Bay Guardian* (255-3100), the Sunday "pink section" of the jointly printed *San Francisco Chronicle-Examiner* (777-1111/2424), the *East Bay Express* (510-540-7400), a free weekly, and the *SF Weekly* (541-0700).

Radio station KJAZ runs a Jazzline at 769-4818.

For maps and other information, contact the San Francisco Visitor Information Center on the lower level of Hallidie Plaza, 900 Market St. at Powell St., 391-2000 or 974-6900.

The area code for San Francisco is (415). For most of Oakland

and other East Bay communities, (510). All numbers listed here are (415) unless otherwise noted.

A Note on Neighborhoods

Built on the hills of San Francisco Bay, San Francisco is a compact city of neighborhoods. Fisherman's Wharf is the famous tourist area on the waterfront to the north; North Beach is a former Italian neighborhood filled with cafés, restaurants, art galleries, and music clubs.

Across the Bay from San Francisco, connected by the Bay Bridge, are the East Bay communities, including Oakland, Richmond, Berkeley, and Emeryville. Oakland is the farthest south of the four; Richmond, the farthest north. Berkeley is the liberal community that's home to the University of California; Emeryville is a commercial district along the freeway. West Oakland and Richmond are home to large African-American communities.

Traveling across the bay, unless you're driving during rush hour, takes about 15 minutes. Driving in San Francisco can be tricky for those not accustomed to stopping on steep hills, and parking downtown is often difficult. The city's BART (Bay Area Rapid Transit) transportation system, which extends to the East Bay, is excellent.

Landmarks and Legends

SAN FRANCISCO

(With the exception of St. John's, the following sites can be toured on foot. The route starts downtown near Market Street and proceeds north, past Nob Hill to North Beach.)

Dawn Club, *20 Annie St.*

During the 1920's, 20 Annie St. was a notorious speakeasy, where ladies of the night picked their customers' pockets and hid their empty wallets in niches in the walls. When the building was renovated a few years ago, workmen came across numerous samples of the ladies' spoils.

During the 1940's, number 20 became home base for Lu Watters and his Yerba Buena Jazz Band. Watters, who was also a professional chef, would cook out back and play his trumpet up front. As the music changed in the late '40's, however, he retired from performing for good and went to work as a cook for the Sonoma State Hospital.

Turk Murphy was another name associated with the Dawn Club; he also played the room in the 1980's when it was known as the Front Page.

Club Hangover, *729 Bush St. (downtown).*

Now a gay moviehouse with a facade of mock gray stone, No. 729 once housed the Club Hangover, owned by Doc Dougherty. During the late '40's and early '50's, Kid Ory and George Lewis led bands here, and in 1952, Earl Hines was hired to front an all-star Dixieland band.

"When I got there," he says in *The World of Earl Hines,* "I saw all these elderly guys sitting around, and I said to the owner, 'Doc, when're you going to have the rehearsal? Where are the musicians?'

" 'They're all here,' he said.

" 'My goodness, what is this?' I thought as I looked at them."

Nonetheless, the arrangement worked out well, and Hines's initial eight-week engagement was extended first to three months and then to six. He moved his family out to San Francisco, bought a home in Oakland, and eventually ended up staying with the Hangover for five years.

Grace Cathedral, *1051 Taylor St., near California St. (Nob Hill), 776-6611.*

Duke Ellington presented his first concert of sacred music in the impressive Episcopal Grace Cathedral atop Nob Hill on September 16, 1965. Though he was filled with trepidation beforehand, the event met with widespread critical acclaim.

Jazz Workshop, *473 Broadway (North Beach).*

During the 1950s and '60's, many bop and free-jazz musicians, including John Coltrane and Ornette Coleman, worked in this now abandoned building whose marquee reads "VIP Cocktails" in both English and Chinese. Cannonball Adderley and Charles Mingus both recorded albums here.

Keystone Korner, *NW corner of Vallejo and Stockton Streets (North Beach).*

Now a Chinese mom-and-pop store, the Keystone was one of the most important jazz clubs around during the 1970's and early '80's, when it was known for its fine acoustics and appreciative audiences. A number of recordings were made here, including *In This Korner* by Art Blakey and his Jazz Messengers, and NPR broadcast a show from the club every New Year's Eve as part of its coast-to-coast celebration.

St. John's African Orthodox Church, *351 Divisadero St. (near Oak), 621-4054.*

A small, storefront orthodox Catholic church, St. John's canonized John Coltrane about ten years ago. "Every Sunday, we take his music and put the liturgy on top of it," says Bishop F. W. King. "It's a beautiful, beautiful thing." One of St. John's priests, Father James Haven, is also a reedman, and the church has a small memorial band called Ohnedaruth that plays both during the services and at jam sessions around the city.

Services: Su, 11:45 a.m.

WEST OAKLAND

Seventh Street, *from Wood to Broadway*.

During the 1940's, Seventh Street was the center of African-American music in the Bay Area. Today, however, it is a sad and empty place, lined with nothing more than boarded-up storefronts and empty lots.

Esther's Breakfast Club, *1724 Seventh St., 451-5069*.

One of the only remaining Seventh Street establishments is Esther's Breakfast Club, once located across the street from its present site and called at first Esther's Cocktail Lounge and then Esther's Orbit Room. Opened by Texan Esther Mabry in 1950, the lounge presented many of the greatest R&B and soul stars of the day: Lou Rawls, Joe Turner, Pee Wee Crayton, Lowell Fulson, Etta James, and Al Green.

Today Esther's no longer offers live music, but a deejay does sometimes spin records at the large, neat club on the weekends. Esther and/or her husband Bill are usually somewhere on the premises.

Clubs, etc.

San Francisco has a reputation for a lively music scene, but reality does not measure up to hearsay. As usual, jazz and blues must be sought out.

The area has three major clubs bringing in national acts: **Kimball's**, **Kimball's East**, and **Yoshi's**. These last two are located in the East Bay, where the unique **Maybeck Recital Hall** is also situated. Another top spot for national acts is the **New Orleans Room** of the Fairmont Hotel.

The heydey of Oakland's revived '70's blues scene is over, but several historic spots, most notably **Eli's Mile High Club**, are still going strong. National blues acts are brought in by **Slim's**, **Jack's**, and some of the jazz clubs.

Jazz talent to watch for in the Bay Area include veteran multi-instrumentalist John Handy; veteran saxophonist Joe Henderson; sax and clarinet player Anthony Braxton; vocalists Kitty Margolis, Ann Dyer, Madeline Eastman, and Faye Carrol; guitarist Bruce Forman; pianist George Cables; drummer Eddie Moore; saxophonists Harvey Wainapel and Frances Wong; Peter Apfelbaum and his big band; and pianist/big band leader Jon Jang.

Blues talent includes veteran vocalist–piano player Charles Brown; piano player–songwriter Jimmy McCracklin; singer-guitarists Joe Louis Walker (in the Robert Cray style), Ron Thompson, Paris Slim, and Mark Hummel; vocalist Brenda Boykin; the Troyce Key Blues Band; Bobby Reed & Surprize; Maurice McKinnies & the Galaxy Band; Mark Naftalin; Johnny Nitro & the Doorslammers; Ron Hacker & the Hacksaws; Larry Holmes & Blues Express; and the Johnny Nocturne Band (with four saxes).

Generally speaking, clubs close at 2 a.m.

Personal Choices

Best jazz clubs: *Yoshi's, New Orleans Room*
Best one-of-a-kind spot: *Bach's Dancing and Dynamite Society*
Best eclectic jazz club: *Cafe Du Nord*
Best Oakland blues joint: *Eli's Mile High*
Best San Francisco blues clubs: *Jack's, Blues*
Best soul-blues club: *Fifth Amendment*
Best R&B nightclub: *Jimmie's Cocktail Lounge*

F O R   J A Z Z

SAN FRANCISCO

Kimball's, *300 Grove St. (downtown), 861-5555.*

A restaurant and club located in the heart of the city's performing arts district, Kimball's is all blond wood, white tablecloths, and exposed brick walls, with fine dining on the first floor, fine dining and music on the second. The artists are top drawer—Freddie Hubbard, Bobby Hutcherson, Peter Apfelbaum—but the sight lines are mediocre, and the atmosphere, somewhat stiff.

Kimball's is owned by Kimball Allen, a wealthy businessman who made his fortune first by inventing the coin box for laundromats and then by starting up the Real Food Company, now the biggest health-food chain in the city. When he and his wife, Jane, began booking jazz in the early '80's, they knew little about it, but have since become so enamored of the music that they recently opened up a second club, the magnificent Kimball's East (see page 378).

Music: W–Sa. *Cover:* $$–$$$. *Food:* Californian. CC. Reservations recommended weekends.

New Orleans Room, Fairmont Hotel *California and Mason streets (atop Nob Hill), 772-5259.*

An intimate room with colorful murals swirling about its walls, the New Orleans Room began featuring top-quality jazz about a year ago, and has already built up a solid musical reputation for itself. Some of the greats who have performed here include Art Farmer, Jimmy McGriff, Harold Land, and Ruth Brown.

The room abuts the hotel's magnificent marbled lobby, and offers a light appetizer menu featuring such delicacies as Creole duck gumbo, black-eyed-pea cakes with crème fraîche, and champagne by the glass. Local piano soloists and trios usually play dur-

ing the early part of the week, while Wednesdays through Saturdays are reserved for the headliners.
Music: nightly. *Cover:* $–$$$. *Food:* Southern. CC. Reservations recommended; parking available in hotel garage, bring ticket for validation.

Jazz at Pearl's, *256 Columbus Ave. (North Beach), 291-8255.*

Pearl Wong used to run a restaurant in Chinatown where musicians came to eat and jam after-hours after the famous Keystone Korner closed down. She sold that place about seven years ago but got bored with retired life and a few years thereafter opened up this small, informal place serving ribs, pizza, burgers and the like.

The new Pearl's is a wedge-shaped bricked-walled club that's better visited for its jazz than its food. Most nights feature solid mainstream trios, though vocalists and Latin jazz groups also perform on occasion. Pearl's is still a moderately late-night place serving food until 2 a.m.
Music: nightly. *No cover,* $$ minimum. CC.

Rasselas, *2801 Calfornia (at Divisadero), 567-5010.*

A large and high-ceilinged Ethiopian restaurant with one room devoted to music, the other to dining, Rasselas is a good spot to catch some of the city's younger musicians. Fusion is often on tap, but the room—painted dark blue, with clouds—is also a favorite of veteran multi-instrumentalist John Handy.
Music: nightly. *Cover:* $–$$. *Food:* Ethiopian. CC.

Café du Nord, *2170 Market St. (at Sanchez), 861-5016.*

A hip cellar lounge that's somehow reminiscent of a fraying-around-the-edges Victorian sitting room, the Café du Nord attracts a youngish, arts-oriented crowd. Jazz, very loosely defined, is featured nightly, with each night of the week devoted to a different style of music. Two of the bands who play here regularly are Alphabet Soup, playing hip-hop bebop, and Ohnedaruth playing Coltrane.
Music: nightly. *Cover:* $.

Also

Music of the ho-hum "jazz, blues, pop" variety has been a mainstay at the **Pasand Lounge** (1875 Union St., 922-4498), a pleasant but unexciting Indian restaurant, for nearly 10 years. **Pier 23** (at Embarcadero, 362-5125) is a friendly ramshackle joint that's right on the water. Though best known for its Sunday brunches, zydeco, and Motown, it also features jazz on occasion.

EAST BAY COMMUNITIES

Kimball's East, *5800 Shellmound, EmeryBay Marketplace, Emeryville, 510-658-2555.*
What a room this is, surely a most impressive venue for jazz. Built exclusively for the music, it's a new kind of animal, a sort-of club-auditorium hybrid with high ceilings, tiered seating for nearly 400, a dance floor, and a big concert stage, where a Steinway concert grand stands that was picked out by Tommy Flanagan. Everything is state of the art, including the Meyer sound system (the kind they use at Carnegie Hall).

The hall features national talent ranging from traditional to quasi-pop, with straight-ahead being the music of choice whenever possible. Past performers include Joe Henderson, Wayne Shorter, Dizzy Gillespie, Herbie Hancock (who opened the place), and Willie Colon. A full dinner menu is available, and there's a simple café in the lobby.
Music: W–Su. *Cover:* $$–$$$. *Food:* California grill. CC.

Yoshi's Nite Spot, *6030 Claremont Ave., Oakland (5 min N of downtown), 510-652-9200.*
Originally just another big Japanese restaurant, Yoshi's added a club to its premises about 11 years ago, and soon thereafter, developed a fine reputation for jazz. Stan Getz, Carmen McCrae, Betty Carter, Horace Silver, Jack McDuff, and McCoy Tyner are among the many who've played here, in a low, intimate room equipped with rattan chairs, and a long, stained-glass window.

The club usually presents national acts during most of the week, and lesser-known talent on Mondays and Tuesdays (often compliments of Jazz in Flight, a nonprofit group that promotes Bay Area musicians). The Christmas–New Year's week is reserved for an all-star band that can include almost anyone.
Music: nightly. *Cover:* $$–$$ (hotel packages available with the nearby Art Deco Lake Merit Hotel). *Food:* sushi snacks. CC. Reservations recommended.

Maybeck Recital Hall, *1537 Euclid, Berkeley, 510-848-3228.*
Almost every Sunday, jazz comes to this small, high-ceilinged redwood-lined hall with seats for only 50 guests. Impeccably designed, with fine acoustics, the 1914 hall was built by Bernard Maybeck (who also designed San Francisco's rococo Palace of Fine Arts) for a classical piano teacher who used it for her students' recitals. Now owned by a jazz pianist and his wife, the Maybeck showcases the internationally famous: Kenny Barron, Dave Frishberg, Dick Hyman, Joe Henderson. Concord Jazz Records has a "Live at Maybeck Hall" series.
Music: Su afternoons. *Cover:* $$$. Reservations recommended.

Lowell Fulson (with his wife, Sadie) plays Eli's in 1982.

Pat Monaco

Bach Dancing and Dynamite Society, *Douglas Beach House, Half Moon Bay, 726-4143 (22 miles south of San Francisco on Miramar Beach, in Half Moon Bay, off Highway 1).*

"The best-kept secret in the world" is what Pete Douglas calls his Bach Dancing and Dynamite Society, and he could be right. Most Sunday afternoons for the past 28 years (though he's recently cut back considerably), Douglas has been presenting the best of jazzmen—Roach, Dexter, the World Saxophone Quartet—in the best of settings—a high-ceilinged wood-paneled beach house overlooking the sea. As the musicians play on a stage up front surrounded by small stained glass windows, a fire crackles in the fireplace and waves lap the shore. No liquor is served, but there's always a buffet with wine before the show, and guests are welcome to bring their own picnics.

Douglas—a rugged white-haired man usually dressed in Levi's—lives in the dark wood beachhouse where he works, and he's put a lot of time and thought into his operation. On Friday evenings, he presents classical music in his 95-seat Douglas concert hall.

Music: some Su afternoons. *Cover:* $$. *Food:* simple buffet.

Also

Jazz can be heard regularly at **Jimmie's** (see "For Blues," page 382) and occasionally at the Terrace Bar in the **Claremont Resort, Spa and Tennis Club** (formerly the Claremont Hotel) at the Oakland/Berkeley city limits (Ashby and Domingo avenues, near Tunnel Rd., 510-843-3000). Once known for its swing dance bands, the hotel now offers everything from World and Latin to jazz and R&B.

FOR BLUES

SAN FRANCISCO

Slim's, *333 11th St. (near downtown), 621-3330.*
Ask the average person on the street where to hear blues in San Francisco and he'll direct you to Slim's, a big brick building with a blue awning and shutters. Alas, the place is not all it's cracked up to be—it's cavernous, with little atmosphere—but it does present some of the biggest blues acts that come through town (Kim Wilson, Delbert McClinton, Pinetop Perkins).
Music: most nights, much blues. *Cover:* $–$$$.

Jack's Bar, *1601 Fillmore St. (near Japanese Cultural Center), 567-3227.*
Located not far from the site of the old Fillmore, Jack's, a long, dark bar that dates back to 1932, when it was a mainstay of the black community, was also a happening place in the '60's and '70's. It fell on sleazy, hard times in the '80's but has recently been revamped to become one of the best blues clubs in town. A big, comfortable place with swirling lights, and a makeshift stage, Jack's attracts an extremely diverse crowd—aging hipsters, young Europeans, whites, blacks. The house band, Oscar Myer's Blues Beat, often packs the place during the week, while national acts sometimes play the weekends.
Music: nightly. *Cover:* $–$$.

Blues, *2125 Lombard St. (near Fillmore St.), 771-BLUE.*
The newest blues club in San Francisco is off to an enthusiastic start, with local bands playing every night of the week. The long black room, strewn with tiny red lights, has a comfortable get-down feel, perfect for the dance-happy crowd that fills the place on weekends. Johnny Nitro & the Doorslammers, the Bachelors, and singer Earl Thomas are among the regulars here, and R&B and reggae are sometimes mixed in with the regular blues fare. Every three months, the club sponsors a "Bartender Blues Benefit," during which time the city's bartenders show off their talents. "Some are great, others . . ." Co-owner Max Young lets his words trail off with a grin.
Music: nightly. *Cover:* $

The Saloon, *1232 Grant Ave. (North Beach), 989-7666.*

The oldest bar on record in San Francisco, the friendly, hole-in-the-wall Saloon features live music—mostly white R&B, with some blues, some rock—364 days of the year. It's closed on Christmas; everyone has to rest sometimes.

The original Saloon was called Wagner's Beer Hall and it was opened in 1861 by an Alsatian immigrant who also peddled beer in stone bottles on the street. Today, the Saloon, with its murky paintings, old wooden bar, and stained-glass windows, attracts an odd mix of long-haired ex-hipsters in leather and eager-faced tourists. The tiny dance floor is always densely packed, and there's usually a line out front on weekends waiting to get in.

Music: nightly; also Sa, Su, late afternoons. *Cover:* $.

Lou's Pier 47, *300 Jefferson St. (Fisherman's Wharf), 771-0377.*

Though mostly a tourist spot, Lou's does present legitimate blues and R&B acts such as J. J. Malone and Mark Naftalin. Located on the second story of a long building with big windows overlooking the street, the room is filled with spiffy tables, chrome railings, and a sort of whitebread crowd. Downstairs is a restaurant serving everything from seafood to steak. Upstairs, appetizers are served.

Music: nightly, F–Su afternoons. *Cover:* $. *Food:* American. CC.

EAST BAY COMMUNITIES

Eli's Mile High Club & Restaurant, *3629 Martin Luther King, Jr., Way, (near 36th St.), West Oakland, 510-655-6661.*

A dark and creaky L-shaped place that was once just a neighborhood joint, Eli's now attracts visitors from around the world. Nonetheless, it's still the funkiest blues club in town, with a warm down-home feel and lots of great sounds. A SUBJECT TO SEARCH sign hangs on the wall; a pool table beckons up front.

Many greats have played Eli's, including Lowell Fulson, Jimmy McCracklin, and Charlie Musselwhite, and many "names" have stopped by, including Bruce Springsteen, Chuck Berry, and Angela Davis. Up until his death two years ago, the owner, Troyce Key, a slim Southern gentleman usually given to wearing cream-colored suits, played most weekends, and his band full of brass, the Troyce Key Blues Band, still carries on. Beverly Stovall, a blues piano player, is a regular during the week while Sundays are devoted to jam sessions attracting up to 30 musicians.

Eli's original owner was Eli Thornton, who was killed at the club (notorious back then as a gambling den) by a jealous mistress, a blues singer named Frankie Williams. Those rough days are long gone; nowadays, there's even a security guard out front keeping an eye on patrons' cars.

Music: W–Su. *Cover:* $. *Food:* soul and health food.

Your Place Too, *5319 Martin Luther King, Jr., Way, West Oakland, 510-652-5837.*

For years, people called Mr. Louis KeeSee the godfather of the blues. Need a break, a place to play? Go see Mr. Louis. Need a meal, a place to sleep? Go see Mr. Louis. Need a Thanksgiving dinner? One year Mr. Louis prepared 350 turkeys in his small, homey club with its pool tables and baby-blue walls, and fed them to the homeless.

Last year, however, Mr. KeeSee decided to call it quits. His poor health and his co-owner's new baby made running a full-time club difficult. At first, they tried to sell the place through the traditional routes, but when that didn't work, they came up with an unusual solution: they would hold an essay contest. Contestants were asked to plunk down a $100 entry fee and write a two-page essay beginning with the words, "I would be the best new owner for the blues club because. . . ."

As of this writing, results are still up in the air; check the local papers to see if a new blues club has opened at this spot.

Fifth Amendment, *3255 Lakeshore Ave., Oakland (near downtown), 510-832-3242.*

Packed almost every night with an upscale African-American crowd, the friendly Fifth Amendment won the Bay Area Blues Society's Blues Club of the Year Award several years ago. Done up in muted orange and black, the place is really much more sophisticated than your average blues club, however, and it's music is usually a jazz-blues-R&B mix. There's a long polished bar to one side, and a crowded dance floor to the front. The musicians, all local, put on a tight, hot show, and names such as B. B. King and Bobby "Blue" Bland have been known to stop by.
Music: nightly. *No cover.*

Jimmie's Cocktail Lounge & Nightclub, *1731 San Pablo Ave., Oakland, 510-268-8445.*

A complex of several buildings built around a small outdoor patio, Jimmie's—capacity 600—brings in some of the biggest blues and R&B acts in the Bay Area. Many top names have appeared here, including Solomon Burke, Ike Turner (he made his first appearance here after his recent release from prison), Denise LaSalle, and Frankie Lee. Unlike most venues, the club usually presents its live acts (including soul, big bands, and a weekly amateur night) during the week, reserving the weekends for a popular "Battle of the Deejays." Sunday late afternoons are devoted to jazz, usually compliments of the Hubert Gibson Trio, and well-known jazz artists touring the area, such as Pharaoh Sanders and Milt Jackson, occasionally stop by.

Owned by a trio of old friends—"Sweet" Jimmie Ward, Irvin "Dusty" Williams, and Beret "Chief" Armstrong—Jimmie's is a modern, sophisticated club that attracts many of the city's top African-American professionals. Don't be put off by the strong-

armed men in red satin jackets frisking people at the door—this is one safe club. It's frequented by a large number of off-duty cops, and security guards with walkie-talkies keep the parking lots under surveillance.
Music: Su–Th; deejays, F–Sa; much blues, some jazz. *Cover:* $– $$$.

T-Bone, *2021 Fruitvale Ave. at Foothill, Oakland, 510-533-1325.*

A large and friendly club located in a somewhat rough neighborhood, T-Bone's boasts a game room (pool and pinball), a party room, a music room, and a "love nest," which is just what its name implies—a dark room lined with soft sofas and big cushions. Dozens of black-and-white photographs of blues legends such as Jimmy Witherspoon and Johnny Otis line the walls; Beverly Stovall and Lady Margaret often play the weekends. NO BASEBALL HATS, NO TENNIS SHOES reads a stern sign at the front door, but it goes completely ignored.
Music: F–Sa. *Cover/minimum:* $–$$.

Larry Blake's R&B Café, *2367 Telegraph Ave., Berkeley, 510-848-0888 (concert line) or 0886 (club).*

A laid-back basement club in the heart of Berkeley, Larry Blake's caters to a mixed clientele of students, neighborhood folk, and blues aficionados. Equipped with rough thick pillars, heavy wooden tables, and black cement walls, the room features top local blues and R&B bands most nights of the week. National artists are also booked from time to time and well-known musicians such as John Lee Hooker, Gregg Allman, and Robert Cray have been known to drop by unexpectedly. On Mondays, the club hosts a blues jam that has long been a favorite among Bay Area musicians.

Upstairs from the music club is a two-tiered dining area with a mezzanine and bar. The restaurant dates back to the 1940's.
Music: M–Sa. *Cover:* $ ($$ for special events). *Food:* American. CC.

Also

Blues can be heard at **The Serenader** (504 Lake Park Ave., 510-832-2644), which is similar to (and near) the Fifth Amendment; and at **Sweetwater** (153 Throckmorton, Mill Valley, 388-2820), an eclectic club that features occasional national blues acts. James Anthony Cotton plays nightly at the **Berkeley Marina Marriott** (200 Marina Blvd., near University Ave., 510-548-7920.)

Other Venues and Special Events

Koncepts Cultural Gallery (510-763-0682), once housed in the old Union Pacific Railroad Station in Oakland's downtown, no longer has a music space of its own, but it does continue to sponsor monthly concerts around town. A nonprofit African-American organization best known for presenting avant-garde jazz (Sun Ra, Muhal Richards Abrams, Oliver Lake), Koncepts was also the first organization in the Bay Area to present blueswoman Katie Webster and the then reemerging pianist Dorothy Donegan.

The grand, old-world **Great American Music Hall** (859 O'Farrell St., 885-0750) often presents big-name jazz and blues artists. The **Herbst Theatre** at the Performing Arts Center (401 Van Ness Ave.), the setting for the city's first jazz festival in 1983, also presents occasional jazz concerts, as do the **Calvin Simmons Theater** in Oakland (Oak and Tenth Streets, 893-2082), **Davies Symphony Hall** in the San Francisco Civic Center (Grove and Van Ness Ave. 431-5400), and **Bimbo's 365 Club** (1025 Columbus Ave., 474-0365), a San Francisco hall that's open for public lease.

Two large music festivals, the **San Francisco Jazz Festival** and the **San Francisco Blues Festival** (see "Major Festivals," page 403) are held every fall. A two-day **Jazz and All That Art on Fillmore Fair** takes place on Fillmore Street every July; a two-day **Blues and Art on Polk** is held on Polk Street every June; and a two-day **Concord Jazz Festival** has been held at the Concord Pavilion (800-7CONCORD or 510-676-8742) in Concord, Calif., every summer for over 20 years. The Bay Area Blues Society (510-836-2227) also presents a number of festivals during the summer and early fall, including the **Juneteenth Celebration** and the **Great Ladies of the Blues Festival.**

Several wineries in nearby Napa Valley and Sonoma County produce outdoor jazz concerts. Watch the papers. The **Robert Mondavi Winery** (7801 St. Helena Highway, Oakville, 707-963-9611) is especially active.

Radio

KCSM/91.1 FM (574-6427). A 24-hour jazz station.
KJAZ/92.7 FM (769-4800). A 24-hour jazz station.
KPOO/89.5 FM (346-5373). Some jazz and blues daily.
KPFA/94.1 FM (848-6767). Some jazz and blues most days.
Jazz and blues can also be heard occasionally on **KUSP/88.9 FM, KDIA/1310 AM, KALW/91.7 FM**, and **KKSF/103.7 FM**.

Record Stores

Numerous record stores in the San Francisco area have excellent jazz and blues selections, especially **Village Music** in Mill Valley (9 E. Blythedale Ave., 388-7400). **Down Home Music** in El Cerrito (10341 San Pablo Ave., 525-2129) is a gold mine for blues lovers; and then there's **The Jazz Quarter** in San Francisco (1267 20th Ave., 661-2331), **Jack's Record Cellar** (254 Scott

St., 431-3047), also in San Francisco, and **Leopold's** (2518 Durant, 848-2015) in Berkeley.

Portland

Portland's contribution to jazz and blues history may be small, but the city can claim several important sons and daughters. Two premier, though not particularly well-known, women bebop artists emerged from the city in the 1940's: piano player Lorraine Geller, who had studied with Gene Confer, an influential Portland jazz educator, and trumpet player Norma Carson, who later played with Charlie Parker and others. Also associated with the city are pianist-arranger-composer Tommy Todd, baritone saxophonist Bill Hood, and, more recently, bass player David Friesen. Max Gordon, founder of New York's Village Vanguard, once lived in Portland and attended Reed College, and Ralph Towner and Glen Moore formed the nucleus of the group Oregon while studying at the University of Oregon in Eugene.

Like other West Coast cities, Portland had no African-American population to speak of until World War II, when the city's shipyards began attracting workers from Texas and the South. Most settled near the Memorial Coliseum in Northeast Portland, and soon that area was thriving with hole-in-the wall music clubs and all-night jam sessions. Whenever major touring artists such as Nat "King" Cole or Duke Ellington passed through town, they always stopped by Northeast Portland after the show.

Portland's most legendary club of all time was Sidney's (now a blues club called the Candlelight, see "For Blues," page 389) run by a character named Sid Porter. At 6 feet 6 inches tall, Sid was both the club's host and its main performer, and during the '50's and '60's, everyone, from the mayor on down, hung out at the joint.

Sources

Willamette Week (243-2122), a free weekly, contains excellent listings. Another source is the Friday edition of *The Oregonian* (221-8327). *Blues Notes* is a free monthly publication put out by the Cascade Blues Association that can be found in many of the clubs.

For maps and other information, contact the Portland, Oregon, Visitors Association at 26 S.W. Salmon St., 222-2223.

The area code for Portland is (503).

A Note on Neighborhoods

Portland is a small and friendly city divided into east and west by the Willamette River (the two sections are connected by 11 bridges) and into north and south by Burnside Street. Streets are named according to the quadrant they are in (S.E., N.E., etc.), which makes finding places very easy, especially since, in Portland, nothing is located too far apart.

Clubs, etc.

For a small city, Portland has considerably more than its share of first-rate jazz musicians, many of whom play the clubs on a rotating basis and have an enthusiastic following. Only two spots, however, the **Brasserie Montmartre** and **Jazz de Opus,** present jazz more than three nights a week. There is also no regular venue for touring talent.

Portland also has a burgeoning blues and R&B scene. Numerous small clubs and restaurants feature local artists five or six nights a week, and national figures are brought in regularly through **Bojangles,** the **Dandelion,** and several other larger venues.

Top jazz talent in town includes legendary bassist Leroy Vinnegar, recently relocated here from Los Angeles; pianist-singer-songwriter Dave Frishberg; bass players David Friesen and Ed Bennett; drummers Mel Brown, Ron Steen, and Dick Berk; Russian piano player Andrei Kitaev; popular fusion pianist Tom Grant; up-and-coming pianist Randy Cannon; cornetist Jim Goodwin; trumpet player Thara Memory; vocalist/bassist Marianne Mayfield; and vocalists Nancy King, Shirley Nanette, and Rebecca Kilgore.

The most popular blues act in town, playing around frequently, is Curtis Salgado & the Stilettos. Curtis is a veteran blues shouter on whom John Belushi and Dan Aykroyd patterned their Blues Brothers act while filming *Animal House* at the University of Oregon in Eugene. Other top blues-R&B talent includes singer Ralph Black, the No Delay Band (now minus its former leader, Paul deLay, in jail for cocaine possession), Lloyd Jones's Struggle, Back Porch Blues (acoustic blues), the Terry Robb Band, keyboard player Janice Scroggins, the Jim Mesi Band, the Norman Sylvester Band, Paulette 'N' Power, the Margo Tufo Band, and Pin & the Horn-its.

Most clubs and bars in Portland close at 2 a.m.

Personal Choices

Best jazz restaurant-bars: *Brasserie, Jazz de Opus*
Best jazz lounges: *Atwater's, Heathman Hotel*
Best blues club: *Bojangles*
Best historic blues club: *Candelight*

FOR JAZZ

Brasserie Montmartre, *626 S.W. Park Ave. (downtown), 224-5552.*

An elegant French restaurant located in the historic 1908 Calumet Hotel, the Brasserie is filled with all those charming continental accoutrements: tassled silk curtains, chandeliers, green velvet banquettes. This being Portland, however, and not Paris or New York, the atmosphere is laid-back and relaxed, with items on the menu to suit every taste—burgers to escargot—and budget.

Jazz by the best area musicians happens every night on the Brasserie's large central stage. Sight lines are only fair but acoustics are good. There's also a resident magician (*that* accounts for all those playing cards on the ceiling) who performs table to table.

Just about every celebrity passing through Portland (Matt Dillon, Tom Berenger, Burt Reynolds) stops at the Brasserie, as do teenagers returning from prom night, children celebrating their birthdays, and musicians and party animals with late-night munchies. The kitchen remains open until 3 a.m. on Fridays and Saturdays, 2 a.m. the rest of the week.

Music: nightly. *No cover. Food:* French continental. CC.

Jazz de Opus, *33 N.W. Second Ave. (downtown), 222-6077.*

When Jazz de Opus first opened its doors in the early 1980's, it was a small beer and wine bar presenting such greats as Sonny Rollins, Nat Adderley, Roy Eldridge, and Oscar Peterson. Then, it added on a large restaurant with an open kitchen and for about six years stopped featuring music. Recently, however, to the delight of local jazz fans, the place has returned to its roots.

Leroy Vinnegar is now a regular here, along with Nancy King, Mary Kadderly, David Friesen, and Dick Berk. The musicians play in a small, dark, informal bar area near the door, while the dining takes place in the back.

Harry Connick, Jr., touring the area, came in to hear Vinnegar once, and the next night came back with his entire band. The place was so packed that some of the musicians had to play while standing behind the bar.

Music: Tu–Sa. *Cover:* none. *Food:* Continental, Northwest. CC.

Atwater's, *111 S.W. Fifth Ave. (downtown), 275-3600.*

Located high atop a downtown office building, Atwater's is one of the finest restaurants in Portland. Recently, too, it has earned a reputation for presenting top-quality jazz.

Leroy Vinnegar is here most weekend nights, along with drummer Mel Brown. Andrei Kitaev is a regular as well, and the music takes place in a hushed, thick-carpeted lounge with plush sofas, peach-colored walls, and big picture windows. A light menu—eggplant sandwiches, wild mushroom and brie raviolis—is available in the lounge, while the main restaurant is located next door.

Music: F, Sa. *Cover:* none. *Food:* American, Northwest. CC.

Heathman Hotel, *1001 S.W. Broadway (downtown), 241-4100.*

The Heathman may be a modern hotel, but its high-ceilinged lobby lounge has a luxurious Old World feel, thanks to rich wood paneling, balconies all around, Persian rugs, and chandeliers. Candles flicker discreetly on small, round tables while couples and friends relax on brocade chairs, sipping brandy and cognac. The delightful Rebecca Kilgore–Dave Frishberg Duo often appear here, performing a surprising mix of new and old.
Music: W–F. *Cover:* none.

Also

Traditional jazzmen Jim Goodwin and Gary Guenther can be heard most Fridays at the **Portland Brewing Company** (1339 N.W. Flanders St., 222-7150), a high-ceilinged pub that brews its own beer. The musicians play in a tiny balcony overlooking the well-lit room.

One of the best jazz jam sessions in the city, presided over by drummer Ron Steen, takes place on Monday nights at the **Produce Row Café** (204 S.E. Oak St., 232-8355), a ramshackle pub with a large beer-can collection and lots of dark booths. Steen also runs jam sessions at the **Brasserie** and the **Polo Restaurant** (718 N.E. 12th Ave., 232-1801), a large eatery all done up in plaid and Hunter green.

Two other restaurants featuring jazz on a regular basis are the **Rusty Pelican** (4630 S.W. Macadam Ave., 222-4630) and **Cal's** at John's Landing (5310 Macadam Ave., 241-2971), on the Willamette River. **Parchman Farm** (see "For Blues," page 389) often has jazz as well, while the **Benson Hotel Lobby Court** (309 S.W. Broadway, 228-2000) has been presenting piano-bass duos for years.

FOR BLUES

Bojangles, *2229 S.E. Hawthorne, 233-1201.*

Winner of Portland's 1992 Muddy Award for the best blues venue, Bojangles is a large, square, friendly place with a high stage and dance floor to one side, a polished blond-wood bar to the other. It's owned and run by drummer Randy Lilya, a tall man with a graying ponytail who got tired of life on the road and wanted to open a club where "the musicians got treated well and the audience had a good time."

Regulars at Bojangles—which was once a biker's bar called Ken's Afterglow—include the Jim Mesi band, Lloyd Jones's Struggle, the No Delay Band, and Linda Hornbuckle. Lots of national acts come through as well, including Charlie Musselwhite, Little Charlie & the Nightcats, and James Cotton.
Music: W–M. *Cover:* $–$$.

Dandelion Pub, *1033 N.W. 16th St., 223-0099.*

After being housed in an uptown shopping center for over 17 years, the Dandelion relocated last year to this old brick building with a dance floor, interior columns, and exposed wooden beams. Long a favorite club among Portlandites, the Dandelion is best known for its R&B. Duffy Bishop, Linda Hornbuckle, Lloyd Jones, and Curtis Salgado perform regularly, and the club has hosted a Monday-night jam session for years and years. Even the 6 foot 7 inch doorman, William Clarke, is a bit of an institution, as he was the first doorman the club ever hired and has been here for eight years.

During the day, the pub operates as a restaurant, and is open for breakfast, lunch, and dinner.

Music: nightly. *Cover:* $. *Food:* American.

Candlelight Room, *2032 S.W. Fifth Ave. (at Lincoln, near downtown), 222-3378.*

Though at first glance a too clean and neat spiffed-up club with hanging plants, blond-wood tables, and dark blue carpets, the Candlelight nonetheless has atmosphere. Once an old whisky bar and then a famous jazz joint (Sidney's), good times and sweet sounds seem to hover in the air. A large square-shaped bar dominates the inside, while outside, the club's cement walls are painted baby blue. Regulars here include the Norman Sylvester Band, the Margo Tufo Band, the Jim Mesi Band, and the No Delay Band.

Music: nightly. *Cover:* none. *Food:* sandwiches, etc.

M&M Lounge, *137 N. Main St., Gresham (15 min. W of downtown), 665-2626.*

A large and low-ceilinged lounge with mock-leather armchairs and an abundance of pool tables, the M&M caters to everyone from young construction workers to middle-aged office workers. It's been a favorite neighborhood hangout for decades, and was once known for its country-and-western music.

One half of the M&M is a diner dating back to the '50's, and the place still has a fine Edward Hopper—esque feel. Started up by two owners whose last names began with M, the diner gave away free packages of M&M's candies for years. Margo Tufo does the club's booking, and regulars include the Margo Tufo Band, the Hurricanes, and the Jim Mesi Band.

Music: W–Sa. *Cover:* none.

Parchman Farm, *1204 S.E. Clay St., 235-7831.*

A small, cozy restaurant and bar with low ceilings, hanging lights, a sunken bar, and a big screened-in fireplace, the 18-year-old Parchman's presents much local blues, some jazz. During the summer, a sidewalk café filled with tables, chairs, and flower boxes is opened up outside.

Music: W–Sa. *No cover. Food:* Italian. CC.

Also

Another major blues club in the Portland area, offering live music most nights of the week, is the **Cascade Tavern** (1500 S.E. Mill Plain Rd., 206-254-0749), located in nearby Vancouver, Washington. The **Produce Row Café** (see "For Jazz," page 388) presents blues acts on the weekends.

The **Dakota Café** (239 S.W. Broadway, 241-4151), a multiroom predominantly rock club with a dance floor and excellent sound system, sometimes features blues. So does **Belmont's Inn** (3357 S.E. Belmont St., 232-1998), a spacious restaurant and alternative rock club with a '59 Edsel Ford hanging from the ceiling, and the **White Eagle Café and Saloon** (836 N. Russell St., 282-6810), a long, dark, atmospheric bar that dates back to the early 1900's and once housed a brothel.

National blues acts are often booked into **Key Largo** (31 N.W. First Ave., 223-9919), a large restaurant-club that features a variety of different types of music; the **Melody Ballroom** (615 S.E. Alder, 232-2759), a former Masonic Hall; and the **Roseland Theater** (8 N.W. Sixth Ave., 227-0071), a large venue with a dance floor.

Other Venues and Special Events

The **Portland Arts Museum** (S.W. Park and Madison, 226-2811) sponsors a jazz concert series called "Museum After Hours" Wednesday evenings, October through May. The **Metro Washington Park Zoo** (4001 S.W. Canyon Rd., 226-7627) hosts a Wednesday-evening outdoor concert series in July and August that brings in national jazz and blues acts.

In addition to the top-caliber **Mt. Hood Festival of Jazz** (see "Major Festivals," page 403), the Portland area hosts the three-day **Otter Crest Jazz Festival** every May, and the four-day **Waterfront Blues Festival** (the largest blues fest in the Northwest) every July. The Governor Tom McCall Waterfront Park, just off S.W. Front Ave., also presents outdoor blues concerts on summer weekends.

For other special events, check the local paper.

Radio

KMHD/89.1 FM (661-8900). Student-run station affiliated with Mt. Hood Community College. Jazz 6 a.m.–midnight.

KBOO/90.7 FM (231-8032). Jazz and some blues most days.

KOPB/91.5 FM (293-1905). Jazz F–Su nights.

KINK/101.9 FM (226-5080). Contemporary jazz station.

Blues can also be heard occasionally on **KGON/92.3 FM** and **KMCQ/104.5 FM.**

Record Stores

For jazz, top stores are **Django Records** (1111 S.W. Stark St., 227-4381) and **Birdland** (1000 S.W. Taylor, 274-2738). Two stores with strong blues selections are **Music Millennium** (32nd Ave. and E. Burnside St., 231-8926, and 23rd Ave. and N.W. Johnson St., 248-0163) and **Crossroads** (3130-B S.E. Hawthorne, 232-1767), a cooperative of approximately 25 different music vendors (CD companies, poster companies, etc.)

Seattle

Although there were few African Americans living in Seattle in the first decades of this century, the city already had integrated jazz bands as early as 1926. Soon thereafter, clubs—eventually numbering about 30—started springing up along Jackson Street, which was to remain the heart of the city's jazz scene until the 1950's. The most famous of these joints, which were mostly owned by African Americans and Chinese Americans, were the Rocking Horse Club, the Black & Tan Club (still standing at 1201 Jackson), Basin Street, and Club Maynard. These last two were best known for their blues, which could be heard in Seattle beginning in the 1940's.

Much of the reason why Seattle responded so quickly to jazz and blues, according to jazz historian Paul de Barros, was that the city was "completely corrupt." "Seattle was a speakeasy town even before Prohibition," de Barros said in a recent interview with *The Seattle Times/Seattle Post-Intelligencer.* "There was all the entertainment required by single male loggers and the city supported it. So although the black population was small in the beginning, it was very active musically and we had an underworld that supported jazz speakeasies."

Two of the best-known musicians associated with Seattle are Jimi Hendrix and Ray Charles. Jimi Hendrix, who was born in Seattle and raised primarily by his father, taught himself to play the guitar and joined a high school band called the Rocking Kings. The other members of the band were jealous of his popularity with girls, and he left the band after an intrigue with another member's girlfriend. Shortly thereafter, he also left Seattle, to become a paratrooper in the U.S. Army.

Hendrix, who fused jazz and blues into rock-and-roll, is considered by many to be one of the greatest guitarists of our time. He died at the age of 27 and is buried just south of the city in Greenwood Memorial Park (Fourth and Monroe streets, 255-1511; open 8:30 a.m.–5 p.m. daily) in the suburb of Renton.

Jimi Hendrix is buried just south of Seattle.

Ray Charles is another major music figure connected with Seattle. Blind and alone in the world, he moved up to the city from Jacksonville, Florida, at the age of 17 with only one small suitcase and $600 to his name. "I had done as good in Florida as I was going to do . . . ," he writes in his autobiography, *Brother Ray: Ray Charles' Own Story*. "I didn't know anything about Seattle, I didn't know anyone living up there, and I hadn't heard a thing about the town. It just seemed like a reasonable place to go. All mystery and adventure."

Upon arrival, Charles, who had already gained much experience gigging around Florida, quickly picked up jobs along Jackson Street. He met Seattle resident Quincy Jones, who became a good friend; recorded his first record, "Confession Blues," and changed his named from Ray Charles Robinson to Ray Charles (to avoid confusion with Sugar Ray Robinson).

Other jazz and blues figures associated with Seattle included Ernestine Anderson, who now lives in the city; Larry Coryell, who grew up in Washington state and played some of his earliest gigs in Seattle; Robert Cray, who grew up in nearby Tacoma; Bing Crosby, who was born in Tacoma; Diane Schuur, who grew up in Seattle; and Floyd Standifer, who still plays around town regularly.

Sources

The *Seattle Weekly* (441-5555) has excellent listings, as do the Friday editions of the *Seattle Post-Intelligencer* (448-8000) and the *Seattle Times* (464-2111). *Earshot Jazz,* the monthly publication of the Earshot Jazz society (547-6763) and *BluesLetter,* the monthly publication of the Washington Blues Society (324-5491) also have extensive listings; both are free and can be picked up in most clubs. *The Rocket* (728-7625), a free monthly, is another source.

The Seattle–King County Convention and Visitors Bureau is located at 800 Convention Place, 461-5840.

The area code for Seattle is (206).

A Note on Neighborhoods

Pioneer Square is a National Register Historic District located near the downtown. Filled with restored brick buildings dating back to the 1890's, it is the city's most popular entertainment district and is often packed on the weekends. Ballard, founded by Scandinavian fishermen and loggers, is located about 10 minutes north of the downtown (just over the Lake Washington Ship Canal), and is also known for its nightlife.

Clubs, etc.

Seattle is home to one of the premier jazz clubs in the Northwest, **Dimitriou's Jazz Alley,** which brings in a wide variety of national artists. The **New Orleans Creole Restaurant,** which tends more toward mainstream acts, also presents some touring talent, along with top local musicians. More avant-garde sounds can be heard at the **OK Hotel.**

A number of clubs feature local blues six or seven nights a week. National blues artists are sometimes brought in by the **Ballard Firehouse,** the **Backstage,** Jazz Alley, or the New Orleans Creole Restaurant.

Jazz artists to look out for include veteran bass player Buddy Catlett; trombonist Julian Priester; trumpet player Floyd Standifer; vocalist Jay Clayton; guitarist Ralph Towner; recent ex–New Yorkers Bill Frisell and Wayne Horvitz; drummers Larry Jones and John Bishop; saxophone players Hadley Caliman and Bert Wilson; violinist Michael White; multi-instrumentalist Denney Goodhew; guitarist Brian Nova; and pianists Marc Seales and Jessica Williams.

Top blues-R&B talent in the city includes singer-songwriter Tom McFarland; local favorite Isaac Scott; the David Brewer Band; vocalists Duffy Bishop, Kathi McDonald, Patti Allen, and Nora Michaels; drummers Chris Leighton and Leslie "Star Drums" Milton; harpman–keyboard player Dick Powell; and keyboard player–vocalist Norm Ballas. Several times every year, blues singer Kathy Hart organizes shows featuring seven to 13 "Seattle Women in Rhythm and Blues."

Many of the clubs in Pioneer Square, including the ones listed below, have a joint cover charge ($–$$) during the week and/or on the weekends. Five clubs join in this program Mondays–Wednesdays, six on Thursdays, and nine on Friday and Saturdays.

Music can often be heard as late as 1:30 or 2 a.m.

Personal Choices

Best jazz restaurant-clubs: *Jazz Alley, New Orleans*
Best progressive jazz: *OK Hotel*
Best jazz jam: *Salute! in Citta*
Best blues-R&B: *Pioneer Square bars, Scarlet Tree*

F O R   J A Z Z

Dimitriou's Jazz Alley, *2033 Sixth Ave. (at Lenora; entrance is in the back, just off Lenora), 441-9729.*

A large and spacious club with excellent acoustics and sight lines, Jazz Alley presents virtually all the top touring jazz acts in the country. Max Roach, Eddie Palmieri, Charlie Byrd, and Ruth Brown are just a few of the many musicians who have appeared here recently. Meanwhile, on Sunday nights Earshot Jazz produces a series at the Alley featuring top regional artists, including Dave Frishberg, Jessica Williams, and the Roosevelt High Jazz Band.

Though usually quite full, the club never feels crowded, owing to its big, comfortable booths and tables. A wide balcony lines one wall, and large picture windows look out onto the street. Free parking is available in back.
Music: W–Su. *Cover:* $$. *Food:* Italian-Mediterranean. CC.

New Orleans Creole Restaurant, *114 First Ave. S. (Pioneer Sq.), 622-2563.*

Big, long, and high-ceilinged, the New Orleans is all atmosphere, thanks to exposed brick walls, old wooden balconies, scuffed floors, and turn-of-the-century light fixtures. Once a stagecoach hotel used by men on their way to the Alaskan gold rush (rooms cost a mere 75 cents per night back then, as the sign outside still reads), it now serves Creole-Cajun food and jazz. Music styles range from traditional to bebop to contemporary, with some blues and zydeco thrown in. The great trumpet player Floyd Standifer has been playing here once a week for over eight years, and large national acts—Ramsey Lewis, Mark Murphy, Katie Webster—come through about twice a month.
Music: nightly. *Cover:* $–$$. *Food:* Creole-Cajun. CC.

OK Hotel, *212 Alaskan Way S. (behind Pioneer Sq.),*
621-7903.

Under the viaduct behind Pioneer Square is Seattle's answer to
the Knitting Factory in New York. A large, square, no-frills room,
filled with rows of folding chairs, the OK presents everyone from
former downtown New Yorkers Bill Frisell and Wayne Horvitz to
the Baba Balkanettes ("eastern Euro-soul music") and Jeff
Greinke ("ambient-industrial ethereal salon"). This is the place to
go to hear the unexpected.

There's no drinking inside the OK's music room, but outside is a
long and high-ceilinged café, lined with modern art and enormous
dilapidated booths, where beer, wine, and food are served. To
one side is a rickety, boarded-up staircase; this 1917 building
was once a 300-room hotel and cat house, serving sailors and gold
prospectors.
Music: W–Su, some jazz. *Cover:* $$. *Food:* American.

Salute! in Citta, *West Coast Vance Hotel, 615 Stewart St. (at*
Sixth Ave., downtown), 728-1611.

A convivial Italian restaurant with red-and-white-checkered
tablecloths by day, Salute! in Citta (literally "Cheers in the City")
turns into a jazz joint by night. Candles flicker on the tabletops and
ceiling flags ripple in the breeze from the door as some of the city's
best musicians come out to play.

Guitarist Brian Nova and his trio are regulars, and they run a
jam on Sunday nights that attracts a wide variety of musicians.
Many of the nationally known artists appearing at Jazz Alley, lo-
cated just two blocks away, stop by here after their gigs are done.
Some of those who have done so include Herb Ellis, Joe Pass,
McCoy Tyner, Stanley Turrentine, and Ernestine Anderson.
Music: Th–Su. *Cover:* none. *Food:* Italian. CC.

Also

Serafina (2043 Eastlake Ave. E., 323-0807), which bills itself
as a "rustic Euro-Italian restaurant and bar," features vocalists on
the weekends, jazz jams on Monday nights. **Wild Ginger** (1400
Western Ave., 623-4450) is a sleek modern restaurant, known for
its fine Asian cuisine, that presents jazz trios on Monday nights.
Café Cielo (611 Broadway, 324-9084) showcases solo piano play-
ers and singers, while **Julia's Park Place** in Ballard (5410 Bal-
lard Ave., NW, 783-2033) often presents up-and-coming jazz
vocalists.

Traditional jazzmen take to the stage of **Latona's** (6423 La-
tona Ave., NE, 525-2238), a neighborhood café with aqua-blue
walls and big picture windows, most weekend nights. Cabaret
singer **Patti Summers** can often be found behind the piano of her
namesake club, a dark, red-curtained place on the fringe of the
city's adult entertainment district (94 Pike St., near First Ave.,
621-8555).

FOR BLUES

Larry's Greenfront, *209 First Ave. S. (Pioneer Sq.),* 624-7665.

An often crowded but comfortable and laid-back bar and grill with brick walls, exposed beams, and a wooden floor, Larry's books top local R&B-blues bands every night of the week. The Dick Powell Band plays here regularly, while bluesman Charles White leads a jam on Wednesday nights.

Larry's is owned and run by R&B fan and ex-musician Larry Culp and his brother, Charlie. The bar has been in their family for the past 30 years, but it wasn't until they took over in 1986 that it started offering live blues.

Music: nightly. *Cover:* $–$$. *Food:* burgers, salads, etc.

The Central, *207 First Ave. S. (Pioneer Sq.),* 622-0209.

The oldest saloon in Seattle, dating back to 1892, when it was also an employment office, post office, and gambling den for gold prospectors, the Central is a long, long, long room with a long, long, long bar (all dark wood, with enormous mirrors and old-fashioned light fixtures). Way down in the darkness at the end is a high stage where the musicians perform.

The lounge has had its share of history, new as well as old. In the late 1980's, the Central was the Central Tavern (what a difference a word makes), the spawning ground of Nirvana, Alice in Chains, and other grunge rock bands. Today, the Central's music is mostly R&B, and there's a barbecue smoker out back. The clientele ranges from biker types to preppies.

Music: nightly. *Cover:* $–$$. *Food:* smoked meats, chicken, ribs.

Fenix Café, 111 Yesler Way (Pioneer Sq.), 447-1514.

Once the "grungiest tavern in town," number 111 is now a spiffed-up club-restaurant often presenting Isaac Scott, possibly Seattle's most popular bluesman. Little Bill and the Bluenotes are also regulars.

The Fenix, done up with tile floors, brick walls, and a balcony, is a tiny place, seating only 120. Mexican food is served, and there's an espresso cart and tables out front for loitering.

Music: M–Sa. *Cover:* $–$$. *Food:* Mexican. CC.

Old Timers' Café, *620 First Ave. (Pioneer Sq.),* 623-9800.

Featuring mostly R&B, the atmospheric Old Timers' is a long, narrow, inviting place with heavy mirrored bars lining the walls and wrought-iron balconies all around. The patrons here often dance in the aisles and there's a patio area out front for the collective catching of breath. Regulars include saxmen Lonnie Williams and Fat James, and the Royals. The club also books national acts

such as Otis Rush (in one of his few Northwest appearances) on rare occasions.
Music: nightly. *Cover:* $–$$. *Food:* American.

Scarlet Tree, *6521 Roosevelt (10 min. N of downtown),*
523-7153.
A dark and intimate neighborhood lounge with cushiony black and red seats and a well-mixed crowd (Hawaiian, Filipino, black, white), the Scarlet Tree offers R&B, with some blues mixed in, every night of the week. A rotating roster of eight to ten bands perform; one is called B.I.G. because its six members add up to "two thousand pounds of blues."

One side of the Scarlet Tree is a restaurant known for its breakfasts, the other is the bar and lounge. Carved wooden animals and dusty instruments hang above the informal, makeshift stage.
Music: nightly. *Cover:* $. *Food:* American (until 8 p.m. only).

Also

The **Backstage,** a music club in Ballard (2208 N.W. Market St., 781-2805), sometimes features local and national blues acts, as does the **Ballard Firehouse** (5429 Russell Ave. N.W. at Market, Ballard, 784-3516), a converted firehouse that's primarily a rock club. Folk-blues can sometimes be heard at **Latona's** (see "For Jazz," page 395).

Other Venues and Special Events

Touring jazz and blues artists sometimes appear at the **Seattle Center's Opera House** (443-4747), the **Paramount Theater** (Ninth and Pine, 628-0888), and the University of Washington's **Meany Theater** (543-4880).

Earshot Jazz (547-6763) produces the **Earshot World Jazz Festival** in October. The two-week event, consisting of about 15 concerts in various venues around the city, concentrates on "ethnic interpretations of the jazz art form" (e.g., Randy Weston playing with drummers from Ghana). The city also hosts a number of other festivals that feature some jazz and blues, including **Bumbershoot, The Seattle Arts Festival** (622-5123), which takes place over Labor Day weekend, and the **Northwest Folklife Festival** (684-7300), which takes place over Memorial Day weekend. The West Seattle **Dixieland Jazz Festival** is held in June and the **Ballard Dixieland Jazz Festival** is held in August. Other area events include the four-day **Jazz Port Townsend,** usually in July, and the two-day **Port Townsend Blues Festival,** usually in June (800-733-3608 or 385-3102 for both).

Summer Nights at the Pier (Pier 62/63 on the waterfront) is an outdoor music series, held in July and August, that presents all types of music, including jazz and blues. A number of the wineries in the area also feature music in the summer. Check the local papers.

Record Stores

Bud's Jazz Records (102 S. Jackson, 628-0445) is the city's top store for jazz and blues. **Cherry Records** (706 N. 34th St., 632-0525) specializes in blues, jazz, and Cajun.

Radio

KPLU/88.5 FM (535-7758). A 24-hour jazz station. Blues Sa, Su nights.

KBCS/91.3 FM (641-2424). Associated with Bellevue Community College. Mostly jazz. Blues, Tu, Th, Sa nights.

K-LITE/95.7 FM (286-9536). Contemporary jazz station.

Jazz and blues can also be heard occasionally on **KCMU/90.3 FM**, **KSER/91.7 FM** and **KXRX/96.5 FM**.

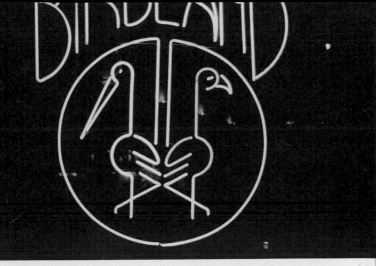

New York: *This* Birdland is not *that* Birdland but it's still got jazz.

Appendix

A Brief History of Jazz and Blues

Although many scholars now believe that jazz, created primarily by African Americans in the early twentieth century, may have started developing in many parts of the country at once, New Orleans is generally credited as being the birthplace of the new music. In this sultry Southern town, with its brass-band traditions, French and Spanish influences, and outdoor marketplaces where African drumming was allowed (it was banned in many parts of the country as slave owners felt it led to rioting), the complex rhythms and harmonies of African musics, ragtime, and blues merged with Western melodies to create a new sound. Among the earliest of the New Orleans musicians were cornet player Buddy Bolden, who may have been the first jazzman ever; bandleader and cornet player Joseph "King" Oliver, who was Louis Armstrong's mentor; composer–piano player Jelly Roll Morton, a Creole who wore a 24-carat diamond in his front tooth; and soprano saxophonist–clarinet player Sidney Bechet, another Creole who was the first to take jazz to Europe. Jazz could be heard in many parts of New Orleans, but Storyville, a notorious red-light district with a dance hall or honky tonk on every corner, was especially known for the new sound.

Part of the reason that jazz first evolved in New Orleans was the existence there of the blues, an even earlier form of African-American music that probably first developed in the Mississippi Delta in the late nineteenth century. At first, the blues were heard only in the cotton fields and railroad work gangs, but by the early 1910's, a number of bluesmen, Charlie Patton and Tommy Johnson in the Delta, and Blind Lemon Jefferson and Leadbelly in Texas, were playing "professionally," for meager tips. W. C. Handy published the first formal blues in 1912, and in the early 1920's, a blues craze, honoring "classic" blues singers such as Alberta Hunter, Ma Rainey, and Bessie Smith, swept African-American communities throughout the country.

New Orleans remained the center of jazz until World War I, when a combination of elements—Mississippi riverboats, the closing of Storyville, and, especially, the economic pull of the auto and munitions factories—led many musicians, along with other African Americans, to head North. This migration was to continue for decades, but already by the early 1920's, Chicago was the new jazz capital and was teeming with talent, including Jelly Roll Morton, Louis Armstrong, and King Oliver. Pittsburgh piano player Earl Hines was also there, along with pianist Lil Hardin, the first woman jazz instrumentalist and Armstrong's second wife; Bix Biederbecke, a young, white cornet player from Davenport, Iowa, who was to die of alcoholism at the age of 28; and the Austin High School Gang, a group of native white Chicagoans, Jimmy Mc-

Partland and Bud Freeman among them, who later came to epitomize the hard-edged sound of "Chicago jazz." The time was the
Roarin' Twenties, an era of drinking, dancing, and abandonment,
and there were constant clashes between the new jazz clubs, many
of which were controlled by gangsters, and the police.

Chicago's heydey as the capital of jazz was short-lived, however. In 1928, many of its illegal cabarets were shut down by a
reformist government, and by the 1930's, largely because of the
growing importance of the radio and recording industries, the center of jazz had shifted once again, this time to New York, where it
remains today.

The very first jazz recording ever had been made in New York
in 1917 by New Orleans's Original Dixieland Jazz Band. Throughout the 1920's, the city was home to many early stride piano players such as James P. Johnson, Willie "The Lion" Smith, and Fats
Waller (the stride style features a steady "striding" left hand and
an improvising right), and to numerous hot Harlem nightspots
such as the Cotton Club—then featuring the greatest of all jazz
composers and bandleaders, Duke Ellington—Connie's Inn, and
Smalls' Paradise. All this was nothing, however, compared to the
1930's, when New York, along with the rest of the country, witnessed an unprecedented rise in the popularity of jazz. As the big-
band era began in earnest, crowds black and white flocked to
dance halls and ballrooms all over the city to hear the then new
swing sounds of bands led by Fletcher Henderson, Chick Webb,
Lionel Hampton, Paul Whiteman, Benny Goodman, Tommy
Dorsey, and many others. "Battles of the bands," in which two
competitive big bands were pitted against each other on opposite
sides of a huge dance floor, became common.

Just prior to the big band era, Kansas City also played an important role in the history of jazz. Then under the control of a corrupt political boss, Tom Pendergast, K.C. was a wide-open 24-
hour town best known for its all-night jam sessions and "cutting
contests," in which musicians tried to outdo each other by playing
ever more complicated riffs and choruses. Out of Kansas City during this period came many future stars, including alto saxophonist
Charlie Parker, tenor saxophonist Lester Young, bandleaders
Count Basie, Jay McShann and Bennie Moten, piano player
Mary Lou Williams, and vocalist Joe Turner.

Meanwhile, the blues were flourishing throughout the South,
with many musicians living itinerant lives that were taking them
farther and farther from home. Bluesmen from the Delta tended to
head first to Memphis and then on to Chicago and other points
north, where they eventually settled, while bluesmen from Texas
often congregated first in Dallas or Houston and then moved on to
the West Coast. Among the many fine blues artists to emerge in
the 1930's were Sonny Boy Williamson (Rice Miller) who later
played harmonica on what was probably the most influential blues
radio program ever, the "King Biscuit Time" on KFFA radio in
Helena, Arkansas; Robert Johnson, the enigmatic singer-guitarist

who reputedly sold his soul to the devil; T-Bone Walker, known for his lean, biting guitar licks; and Lightnin' Hopkins, a poetic blues minstrel from Houston.

The 1940's brought with them a major revolution in jazz: the advent of bebop or modern jazz, which was largely created by Charlie Parker on alto sax, Dizzy Gillespie on trumpet, Kenny Clarke on drums, and Thelonious Monk on piano in a small club in Harlem called Minton's. The first real avant-garde movement in jazz, bebop musicians turned the music around by experimenting with new chord progressions, harmonies, and rhythms. The innovative sound spread quickly, especially in New York (where it centered around 52nd Street), Detroit, and Philadelphia; simultaneously, sit-down jazz clubs intended for listening rather than dancing emerged for the first time. Among the many other artists associated with the new modern sound were drummer Max Roach; trumpet player Miles Davis; vocalists Billie Holiday, Sarah Vaughan, and Eddie Jefferson; and pianist Bud Powell. Charlie Christian, who brought the electric guitar to jazz, also played a seminal role in bebop's development.

Blues had changed considerably by the 1940's as well. Chicago, and not the Delta, was now the cutting edge of the music, and it was churning with bluesmen playing a grittier, more urban sound than their rural counterparts. Most important among the new city players were Muddy Waters, who later headed the first major electric blues band; Howlin' Wolf, the wild and passionate player who was Muddy's chief rival; and Willie Dixon, who composed dozens of blues hits. Others included Tampa Red, John Lee "Sonny Boy" Williamson, Lonnie Johnson, Memphis Minnie, Big Bill Broonzy, and Big Maceo. Meanwhile, down in Memphis, a young B. B. King was hosting his first radio show, while out on the West Coast, a strong blues community nurturing such greats as Lowell Fulson was developing for the first time.

In the early 1950's, Miles Davis, who had started out in the bebop tradition, helped usher in the "cool school" of jazz through the release of his influential album, *The Birth of the Cool*. "Cool jazz," with its reflective, minimalist style, was soon heard in many parts of the United States, but it came to be especially closely associated with the West Coast, where Dave Brubeck and his quartet, which included Paul Desmond, were its most popular proponents. Other West Coast "cool" players, who were predominantly white, included drummer Shelly Manne, saxophonist Gerry Mulligan, and trumpet player Chet Baker. The Modern Jazz Quartet, pianist Lennie Tristano, and saxophonist Lee Konitz were also associated with the "cool" tradition.

After "cool jazz" came hard bop, which once again celebrated the more emotional roots of jazz. Drummer Art Blakey, bassist Charles Mingus, pianist Horace Silver, saxophonists Sonny Rollins and John Coltrane, and the Max Roach–Clifford Brown quintet came to the fore during this late-fifties period.

Yet other movements followed. The 1960's and early '70's saw the development of free jazz, which ignored the formal structures of more traditional jazz, and fusion, which combined elements of jazz and rock. Pianist-composer Cecil Taylor and saxophonists Ornette Coleman and John Coltrane were the names most frequently associated with early free jazz, while Miles Davis, Weather Report, and keyboard players Chick Corea and Herbie Hancock were those most frequently associated with early fusion. Later, whole new generations of players, including the Association for the Advancement of Creative Musicians, Sun Ra and his Arkestra, the Art Ensemble of Chicago, Anthony Braxton, and Lester Bowie brought yet more energy to the avant-garde sound.

Today's jazz and blues scene is extremely diverse. No longer does everyone seem to be searching for the "new." A hot group of "young traditionalists," led by trumpet player Wynton Marsalis, is being received with enormous respect, along with young, more experimental players such as saxophonist John Zorn. Meanwhile, the music's older masters like big band leader Illinois Jacquet and trumpet player Doc Cheatham continue to attract enthusiastic audiences, as do bluesmen and women (B. B. King, Koko Taylor, Ruth Brown, John Lee Hooker, and Jimmie Vaughan, to name but a few) playing everything from acoustic blues to soul blues to R&B to blues-rock.

Major Festivals

The most complete listing of jazz festivals can be found in *Jazz Times* every April or May. The most complete listings of blues festivals can be found in *Living Blues* magazine every May/June, or in the semiannual *Living Blues Directory* (see "National Sources" page 11). *Music Festival Directory* (P.O. Box 187, Washington, Ill. 61571; 309-745-8643; $$) is a guide to more than 1,000 music festivals in the United States and Canada, including blues, jazz, bluegrass, Cajun, country, folk, zydeco, and more. The directory is updated annually, and the same people also put out a festival newsletter.

The events listed below are a selected list of major festivals only; some smaller citywide fests are also included under the city headings.

APRIL

Sarasota Jazz Festival, Sarasota, Fla. Contact: Jazz Club of Sarasota, Jerry Roucher, 290 Cocoanut Ave., Bldg. 3, Sarasota, Fla. 34236; 813-366-1552.

Three to four days of indoor, ticketed events.

Pensacola Jazz Fest, Pensacola, Fla.
Contact: WUWF Radio, University of West Florida, 11000 University Parkway, Pensacola, Fla. 32514; 904-474-2327 or 800-239-WUWF.
   A two- or three-day outdoor festival.

New Orleans Jazz and Heritage Festival, New Orleans, La.
Contact: New Orleans Jazz and Heritage Foundation, P.O. Box 53407, New Orleans, La. 70153; 504-522-4786.
   The premier music festival in the U.S. (see page 25). Ten days of music, food, and crafts, both indoors and out. Some events are free; most are not.

M A Y

Sacramento Dixieland Jubilee, Sacramento, Calif.
Contact: Sacramento Traditional Jazz Society, 2787 Del Monte St., West Sacramento, Calif. 95691; 916-372-5277.
   The largest traditional jazz fest in the U.S.; four days of music featuring over 100 bands.

Chicago Blues Festival, Chicago, Ill.
Contact: City of Chicago, Mayor's Office of Special Events, City Hall, Room 703, 121 N. LaSalle St., Chicago, Ill. 60602; 312-744-3315 or 800-ITS-CHGO.
   One of the largest free blues festivals in the world. Three days of outdoor blues.

J U N E

Mellon Jazz Festival, Philadelphia, Penn.
Contact: Mellon Jazz Festival/Philadelphia, P.O. Box 1169, New York, N.Y. 10023, 215-236-1666.
   A 10-day festival featuring over 40 free and paid events, held indoors and out.

Mellon Jazz Festival, Pittsburgh, Penn.
Contact: Mellon Jazz Festival/Pittsburgh, P.O. Box 1169, New York, N.Y. 10023; 412-281-3881, after May 1.
   Ten days of festivities featuring national and local artists in over 40 concerts.

The late Lefty Dizz plays the 1989 Delta Blues Festival in Greenville, Miss.

Playboy Jazz Festival, Los Angeles, Calif.
Contact: Playboy Jazz Festival, 9242 Beverly Blvd., Los Angeles, Calif. 90210; 310-246-4000.

One of the best outdoor jazz festivals. Two days of top talent.

Boston Globe Jazz Festival, Boston, Mass.
Contact: Public Affairs Dept., P.O. Box 2378, Boston Globe, Boston, Mass. 02107.

Seven days of concerts held throughout Boston.

Newport Jazz Festival, Saratoga Springs, N.Y.
Contact: Saratoga Performing Arts Center, Saratoga Springs, N.Y. 12866; 518-584-9330.

Two days of outdoor jazz, held in conjunction with the JVC Jazz Festival in New York City.

JVC Jazz Festival, New York, N.Y.
Contact: JVC Jazz Festival, P.O. Box 1169, New York, N.Y. 10023; 212-787-2020.

A descendant of the Newport Jazz Festival, the oldest jazz festival in the U.S. Held in New York since 1972; 8 to 10 days of ticketed events.

J U L Y

Mississippi Valley Blues Festival, Davenport, Iowa.
Contact: P.O. Box 2014, Davenport, Iowa 52809-2014; 800-747-7800.
A three-day festival put on by the Mississippi Valley Blues Society.

Jazz and Rib Restival, Columbus, Ohio.
Contact: Karen Chervenak, Music in the Air, Columbus Recreation and Parks Dept., 549 Franklin Ave., Columbus, Ohio 43215; 614-645-7995.
Three days of free events.

RiverBlues, Philadelphia, Pa.
Contact: Philadelphia Convention & Visitors Bureau, 1525 JFK Blvd., Philadelphia, Pa. 19102; 215-636-1666.
The biggest blues festival on the East Coast; two days of events.

The Texas Jazz Festival, Corpus Christi, Texas
Contact: Texas Jazz Festival Society, P.O. Box 424, Corpus Christi, Texas 78403; 512-883-4500.
Five to seven days of music.

A U G U S T

W. C. Handy Music Festival, Florence, Ala.
Contact: Music Preservation Society, P.O. Box 1827, Florence, Ala. 35631; 205-766-7642.
A week-long fest featuring national and local artists (see page 57).

Mt. Hood Festival of Jazz, Gresham, Oregon
Contact: Mt. Hood Festival of Jazz Foundation, Inc., P.O. Box 2001, Gresham, Ore. 97030; 503-666-3810.
One of the best jazz festivals in the country; three days of music.

JVC Jazz Festival Newport, Newport, R.I.
Contact: JVC Jazz Festival Newport, P.O. Box 605, Newport, R.I. 02840; 401-847-3700, after June 1.
America's first jazz festival, begun in 1953. Three days of jazz in a glorious setting.

Chicago Jazz Festival, Chicago, Ill.
Contact: City of Chicago, Mayor's Office of Special Events, City Hall, Room 703, 121 N. LaSalle St., Chicago, Ill. 60602; 312-744-3315 or 800-ITS-CHGO.
Two to four days of outdoor jazz, and a jazz pub crawl.

River City/Bayou Blues Festival, Baton Rouge, La.
Contact: River City Festival Assn., 448 N. 11 St., Baton Rouge, La. 70802, or the Baton Rouge Visitors & Convention Bureau; 800-527-6843 or 504-383-1825.
Louisiana's *other* big festival. Two to three days of events.

SEPTEMBER

Montreux Detroit Jazz, Detroit, Mich.
Contact: Detroit Renaissance Foundation, 100 Renaissance Center, Suite 1760, Detroit, Mich. 48243; 313-259-5400.
Five days of over 90 free open-air concerts, as well as some paid club events. Features international, national, and Detroit artists.

Mississippi Delta Blues Festival, Greenville, Miss.
Contact: MACE, 119 S. Theobald St., Greenville, Miss. 38701; 601-335-3523.
Only a one-day festival, but one of the best.

Russian River Jazz Festival, Guerneville, Calif.
Contact: Russian River Jazz Festival, P.O. Box 1913, Guerneville, Calif. 95446; 707-869-3940.
Two days of jazz on the banks of the Russian River, surrounded by redwoods.

Monterey Jazz Festival, Monterey, Calif.
Contact: P.O. Box JAZZ, Monterey, Calif. 93940; 408-373-3366.
Three days of ticketed concerts; no single-performance tickets available.

San Francisco Blues Festival, San Francisco, Calif.
Contact: Tom Mazzolini, 573 Hill St., San Francisco, Calif. 94114; 415-826-6837.
The oldest blues festival in the U.S., begun in 1973. Two days of ticketed events that feature both Bay Area and national artists.

O C T O B E R

Jacksonville Jazz Festival, Jacksonville, Fla.
Contact: 100 Festival Park Ave., Jacksonville, Fla. 32202; 904-353-7770.
>One of the largest free festivals. Three days of jazz events.

San Francisco Jazz Festival, San Francisco, Calif.
Contact: Jazz in the City, 141 10th St., San Francisco, Calif. 94103; 415-864-5449.
>Eleven days of free and ticketed events.

King Biscuit Blues Festival, Helena, Ark.
Contact: Main Street Helena, P.O. Box 247, Helena, Ark. 72342; 501-338-9144.
>Two days of outdoor blues concerts featuring national and local talent.

Notes

New Orleans

1. Whitney Balliett, *Such Sweet Thunder* (New York: Bobbs-Merrill, 1966), p. 235.
2. Jason Berry, Jonathan Foose, and Tad Jones, *Up from the Cradle of Jazz* (Athens, Ga.: University of Georgia Press, 1986), p. 21.

Mississippi

1. Robert Palmer, *Deep Blues* (New York: Penguin Books, 1981), p. 55.
2. Peter Guralnick, "Searching for Robert Johnson," *Living Blues,* Summer–Autumn 1982, p. 30.
3. Chris Albertson, *Bessie* (New York: Stein and Day, 1972), p. 217.

Atlanta

1. Giles Oakley, *The Devil's Music: A History of the Blues* (New York: Taplinger, 1976), p. 136.
2. Albertson, *Bessie,* p. 27.

New York

1. Jim Haskins, *The Cotton Club* (New York: New American Library, 1977), p. 44.
2. Nat Shapiro and Nat Hentoff, eds., *Hear Me Talkin' to Ya* (New York: Dover, 1966), p. 354.
3. Samuel B. Charters and Leonard Kunstadt, *Jazz: A History of the New York Scene* (New York: Da Capo Press, 1981), p. 278.
4. Ellen Hopkins, "Where They Lived," *New York*, March 7, 1983, pp. 43–44.
5. Robert Reisner, *Bird: The Legend of Charlie Parker* (New York: Da Capo Press, 1975) p. 81.
6. John Chilton, *Billie's Blues: Billie Holiday's Story, 1933–59* (New York: Stein and Day, 1975), p. 57.
7. James Lincoln Collier, *Louis Armstrong: An American Genius* (New York: Oxford University Press, 1983), p. 331.
8. Hopkins, "Where They Lived," p. 50.

Chicago

1. Shapiro and Hentoff, *Hear Me Talkin',* p. 135.
2. Palmer, *Deep Blues,* p. 144.
3. Arnold Shaw, *Honkers and Shouters* (New York: Collier Books, 1978), p. 306.

Kansas City

1. Ross Russell, *Jazz Style in Kansas City and the Southwest* (Los Angeles: University of California Press, 1971), p. 107
2. *Ibid.,* p. 184.

Cincinnati

1. Peter Guralnick, *Sweet Soul Music: Rhythm and Blues and the Southern Dream of Freedom* (New York: Harper & Row, 1986), p. 234.

Houston

1. Russell, *Jazz Style,* p. 129.
2. Alan Govenar, *Meeting the Blues* (Dallas: Taylor, 1988), p. 99.

Dallas

1. Alan Govenar, *Meeting the Blues,* p. 9.
2. Russell, *Jazz Style,* p. 61.

San Antonio

1. Frank Driggs, liner notes for *Robert Johnson, King of the Delta Blues Singers,* Columbia Records, No. CL 1654.

Bibliography

BOOKS

Albertson, Chris. *Bessie*. New York: Stein and Day, 1972.

Alleman, Richard. *The Movie Lover's Guide to New York*. New York: Harper & Row, 1988.

Armstrong, Louis. *Satchmo: My Life in New Orleans*. New York: Prentice-Hall, 1954.

Balliett, Whitney. *American Musicians: 56 Portraits in Jazz*. New York: Oxford University Press, 1986.

———*Dinosaurs in the Morning*. New York: J. P. Lippincott, 1962.

———*Ecstasy at the Onion*. New York: Bobbs-Merrill, 1971.

———*Such Sweet Thunder*. New York: Bobbs-Merrill, 1966.

Barnet, Charlie, with Stanley Dance. *Those Swinging Years: The Autobiography of Charlie Barnet*. Baton Rouge: Louisiana State University Press, 1984.

Bechet, Sidney. *Treat It Gentle*. New York: Hill and Wang, 1960.

Berry, Chuck. *Chuck Berry: The Autobiography*. New York: Fireside Books, 1988.

Berry, Jason, Jonathan Foose, and Tad Jones. *Up from the Cradle of Jazz: New Orleans Music Since World War II*. Athens, Ga.: University of Georgia Press, 1986.

Bigard, Barney. *With Louis and the Duke: The Autobiography of a Jazz Clarinetist*. New York: Oxford University Press, 1986.

Britt, Stan. *Dexter Gordon: A Musical Biography*. New York: Da Capo Press, 1989.

Brown, Scott E. *James P. Johnson: A Case of Mistaken Identity*. Metuchen, N.J.: The Scarecrow Press and the Institute of Jazz Studies, Rutgers University, 1982.

Carr, Ian. *Miles Davis: A Biography*. New York: William Morrow, 1982.

Clayton, Buck, assisted by Nancy Miller Elliott. *Buck Clayton's Jazz World*. New York: Oxford University Press, 1987.

Center for Southern Folklore. *The Heritage of Black Music in Memphis*. Memphis: Center for Southern Folklore, 1986.

Charles, Ray, and David Ritz. *Brother Ray: Ray Charles' Own Story*. New York: Warner Books, 1979.

Charters, Samuel B., and Leonard Kunstadt. *Jazz: A History of the New York Scene*. New York: Da Capo Press, 1984.

Chilton, John. *Billie's Blues: Billie Holiday's Story, 1933–59*. New York: Stein and Day, 1975.

Collier, James Lincoln. *Louis Armstrong: An American Genius*. New York: Oxford University Press, 1983.

Dance, Helen Oakley. *Stormy Monday: The T-Bone Walker Story*. Baton Rouge: Louisiana State University Press, 1987.

Dance, Stanley. *The World of Earl Hines*. New York: Da Capo Press, 1983.

Davis, Miles, with Quincy Troupe. *Miles: The Autobiography*. New York: Simon & Schuster, 1989.

Ellington, Edward Kennedy. *Music Is My Mistress.* New York: Da Capo Press, 1976.

Feather, Leonard. *The Encyclopedia of Jazz.* New York: Horizon Press, 1960.

——. *The Encyclopedia of Jazz in the '60s.* New York: Da Capo Press, 1986.

Feather, Leonard, and Ira Gitler. *The Encyclopedia of Jazz in the '70s.* New York: Da Capo Press, 1987.

Fodor's 89. *New Orleans.* New York: Fodor's Travel Publications, 1988.

Giddons, Gary. *Celebrating Bird: The Triumph of Charlie Parker.* New York: Beech Tree Books, 1987.

Gillespie, Dizzy, with Al Fraser. *To Be or Not to Bop.* New York: Da Capo Press, 1985.

Goldberg, Joe. *Jazz Masters of the Fifties.* New York: Da Capo Press, 1983.

Gordon, Max. *Live at the Village Vanguard.* New York: Da Capo Press, 1982.

Gordon, Robert. *Jazz West Coast.* New York: Quartet Books, 1986.

Govenar, Alan. *Meeting the Blues.* Dallas: Taylor, 1988.

Guralnick, Peter. *Lost Highway: Journeys and Arrivals of American Musicians.* New York: Vintage Books, 1982.

——. *Sweet Soul Music: Rhythm and Blues and the Southern Dream of Freedom.* New York: Harper & Row, 1986.

Hammond, John, with Irving Townsend. *John Hammond on Record.* New York: Ridge Press, 1977.

Handy, W. C. *Father of the Blues: An Autobiography.* New York: Macmillan, 1941.

Harris, Sheldon. *Blues Who's Who.* New York: Da Capo Press, 1979.

Haskins, Jim. *The Cotton Club.* New York: New American Library, 1977.

Henderson, David. *'Scuse Me While I Kiss the Sky: The Life of Jimi Hendrix.* New York: Bantam Books, 1981.

Holiday, Billie, with William Dufty. *Lady Sings the Blues.* New York: Penguin Books, 1984.

Lewis, David Levering. *When Harlem Was in Vogue.* New York: Oxford University Press, 1979.

Lieb, Sandra. *Mother of the Blues: A Study of Ma Rainey.* Amherst, Mass.: University of Massachusetts Press, 1981.

Lomax, Alan. *Mister Jelly Roll.* London: Cassell & Co., 1952.

Marquis, Donald M. *In Search of Buddy Bolden: First Man of Jazz.* Baton Rouge: Louisiana State University Press, 1978.

McKee, Margaret, and Fred Chisenhall. *Beale Black and Blue: Life and Music on Black America's Main Street.* Baton Rouge: Louisiana State University Press, 1981.

Mezzrow, Milton, and Bernard Wolfe. *Really the Blues.* New York: Random House, 1946.

The New Grove Dictionary of Jazz. New York: Grove's Dictionaries of Music, 1988.

Oakley, Giles. *The Devil's Music: A History of the Blues.* New York: Taplinger, 1976.

Overbeck, Ruth Ann, et al. *D.C. "Blacks in the Arts."* 1987–1988 Completion Report of the Shaw School Urban Renewal Area, Washington, D.C.

Palmer, Robert. *Deep Blues*. New York: Penguin Books, 1982.

Pepper, Art, and Laurie Pepper. *Straight Life: The Story of Art Pepper*. New York: Schirmer Books, 1979.

Porter, Lewis. *Lester Young*. Boston: Twayne, 1985.

Priestley, Brian. *Mingus: A Critical Biography*. New York: Da Capo Press, 1983.

Reisner, Robert. *Bird: The Legend of Charlie Parker*. New York, Da Capo Press, 1977.

Rose, Al, and Eubie Blake. *Eubie Blake*. New York: Schirmer Books, 1979.

Rose, Al. *Storyville, New Orleans*. City University, Ala.: University of Alabama Press, 1974.

Rowe, Mike. *Chicago Blues: The City and the Music*. New York: Da Capo Press, 1981.

Russell, Ross. *Jazz Style in Kansas City and the Southwest*. Los Angeles: University of California Press, 1971.

Sales, Grover. *Jazz: America's Classical Music*. Englewood Cliffs, N.J.: Prentice-Hall, 1988.

Sawyer, Charles. *The Arrival of B. B. King: The Authorized Biography*. New York: Da Capo Press, 1980.

Shapiro, Nat, and Nat Hentoff, eds. *Hear Me Talkin' to Ya*. New York: Dover, 1966.

Shaw, Arnold. *52nd St.: The Street of Jazz*. New York: Da Capo Press, 1977.

———*Honkers and Shouters: The Golden Years of Rhythm and Blues*. New York: Collier Books, 1978.

———. *The Jazz Age*. New York: Oxford University Press, 1987.

Stearns, Marshall W. *The Story of Jazz*. New York: Oxford University Press, 1956.

Sudhalter, Richard M., Philip R. Evans, with William Dean-Myatt. *Bix: Man and Legend*. New Rochelle, N.Y.: Arlington House, 1974.

Taylor, Frank C, with Gerald Cook. *Alberta Hunter: A Celebration in Blues*. New York: McGraw-Hill, 1987.

Thomas, J. C. *Chasin' the Trane: The Music and Mystique of John Coltrane*. New York: Da Capo Press, 1976.

Titon, Jeff Todd. *Early Downhome Blues: A Musical and Cultural Analysis*. Chicago: University of Illinois Press, 1977.

Townley, Eric. *Tell Your Story*. Chigwell, England: Storyville Publications, 1976.

Travis, D. J. *An Autobiography of Black Jazz*. Chicago: Urban Research Institute, 1983.

Ulanov, Barry. *A History of Jazz in America*. New York: Viking Press, 1954.

Williams, Martin. *Jazz Masters in Transition, 1957–69*. New York: Da Capo Press, 1982.

ARTICLES

For background material, I referred to back issues of *Living Blues, Down Beat* and *Jazz Times* and to local newspapers and magazines. The following articles are of particular relevance.

Bjorn, Lars. "Black Men in a White World: The Development of the Black Jazz Community in Detroit, 1917–1940." *Detroit in Perspective: A Journal of Regional History* (Fall 1980): 1–18.

"From Hastings Street to the Bluebird: The Blues and Jazz Tradition in Detroit." *Michigan Quarterly Review* (Spring 1986): 257–268.

Comiskey, Nancy L. "On the Avenue." *Indianapolis Monthly*, Feb. 1984, pp. 75–79.

Guralnick, Peter. "Searching for Robert Johnson." *Living Blues 53* (Summer–Autumn 1982): 27–41.

Hildebrand, Lee. "Oakland Blues: The Thrill Goes On." *Museum of California*, Sept.–Oct. 1982, pp. 5–7.

Hopkins, Ellen. "Where They Lived." *New York*, March 7, 1983, pp. 42–53.

Joseph, Frank. "We Got Jazz," *Pittsburgh*, Oct. 1979, pp. 31–52.

Marmorstein, Gary. "Jazz: The Men Who Won the West." *Los Angeles Herald Examiner*, Nov. 18, 1984, pp. 6–18.

Schuller, Tim. "Rebirth of a Bluesman." *D Magazine*, July 1989, pp. 34–36.

Selected Index

Able, Emerson, 48

Abrams, Muhal Richard, 209, 384

Abyssinian Baptist Church, 108

Academy of Music, 165, 172

Ace, Johnny, 40, 41, 42, 311, 313

Ace Records, 81, 82

Adams, George, 83

Adams, Pepper, 266, 273

Adderley, Cannonball, 90, 125, 212, 371, 374

Adderley, Nat, 125, 387

Adderley brothers, 94

Adolphus Hotel, 5, 324

Aeolian Hall, 122

Akiyoshi, Toshiko, 131

Albert, Don, 332

Alexander, Mary, 166

Alexander's Steak House, 229

Alhambra Theater, 104, 111–112

Allen, Henry "Red," 19, 123

Allen, Woody, 25, 130, 141

Allison, Mose, 52, 180

Alvin's Detroit Bar, 276, 278

American Pop Culture Exhibit, 320

American Woodmen's Hall, 324

Ames, Abie "Boogaloo," 60, 80

Ammons, Albert, 117, 213

Ammons, Gene, 190, 217, 228, 273

Amram, David, 162

Anderson, Buddy, 243

Anderson, Ernestine, 392

Anderson, Ivie, 106

Anderson, Lew 140

Anderson, Marian, 165

Andrews, Ernie, 354, 358, 359, 363

Andy's, 221, 223

Anthony's South Side, 183

Antone, Clifford, 5, 343, 348–349

Antone's Billy Blues, 5, 341, 346, 348–349

APEX Museum, 86

Apollo Theatre, 104, 107, 112–113, 149, 164, 188

Aragon Ballroom, 217

Arcadia Ballroom, 254

Armstrong, Lil Hardin, 38, 112, 208, 212, 229
home of, 212

Armstrong, Louis (Satchmo), 6, 14, 17, 18, 19–20, 21, 22, 25, 38, 81, 94, 106, 111, 112, 119, 165, 207, 208, 211, 212, 218, 223, 236, 237, 343
home of, 126–127
last concert of, 123

Armstrong, Lucille, 127

Arnella's, 302

Art Ensemble of Chicago, 223

Arter, Carl, 175, 179, 180, 182

Arthur's Tavern, 129, 133

Artis's, 234

Ashby, Dorothy, 266

Association for the Advancement of Creative Musicians (AACM), 209, 221, 235, 255

Atlanta Jazz Festival, 92

Atlanta Renaissance Downtown Hotel, 88, 89

Atlas Bar & Grill, 365

"A Train," 110

At the Tracks, 224

Attic Bar, 278

Atwater's, 387

Auburn Avenue, 85

Augie's Pub, 143

Austin, James, 51

Austin Aqua Festival, 351

"Austin City Limits," 351

Austin High School, 213–214
Gang, 208, 214

Ayers, Roy, 181, 359

B. Smith's, 139

Babe & Ricky's Inn, 2, 361, 368

Babe Baker's, 292

Babe's on Sixth, 349–350

Baby Grand, 113

Bach Dancing and Dynamite Society, 9, 379

Bailey, Mildred, 125

Bailey, Pearl, 112, 165, 186, 196, 236

Baked Potato, 365

Baker, Chet, 355

Baker, Dave, 280, 282, 284

Baker, Harold, 254

Baker, Josephine, 213, 254
Baker's Keyboard Lounge, 2, 272–273
Ball, Marcia, 148, 159, 277, 339, 341
"Ball and Chain," 312
Ballard, Hank, and the Midnighters, 267
Barbieri, Gato, 138
Barefield, Eddie, 242, 298, 358
Barefield, Spencer, 278
Barker, Danny, 14, 26
Barnes, Bootsie, 167, 168
Barnet, Charlie, 118, 344–345
Barrell House Blues Supper Club, 287
Barron, Arthur, 96, 97
Barron, Kenny, 136, 162, 378
Barton, Lou Ann, 148, 346
Bartz, Gary, 184, 189
Basie, Count, 10, 42, 81, 90, 96, 103, 104, 107, 112, 117, 118, 119, 121, 143, 152, 176, 188, 190, 211–212, 213, 229, 238–245 *passim*, 254, 269, 271, 282, 321
  residence site of, 241
Bass, Fontella, 256, 258
"Battles of the Bands," 104, 310
B. B. King's, 48, 51
B. B.'s Lawnside Bar-B-Q, 249
Beale Street, 38, 39–40, 41, 42, 45, 47, 48, 49, 51–52, 54
  special events on, 56
"Beale Street Blues," 39, 41
Beale Street Blues Museum, 41
Beaman, Lottie, 238
"Bear Cat," 46
Beatles, 112, 119, 264
Bechet, Sidney, 14, 19–20, 21, 117, 122, 123, 125, 152, 163, 216, 291
  home of, 21
Beiderbecke, Bix, 10, 19, 120, 208, 216, 254, 270
  grave of, 237
  home of, 236–237
Belgrave, Marcus, 274, 276
Bell, Carey, 232
Bellson, Louis, 236
Belushi, John, 133, 386
Bennett, Tony, 88, 225
Benson, George, 133–134, 174, 177, 181
Berne, Tim, 135
Bernsen, Randy, 98
Berry, Chuck, 217, 218, 219,

230, 241, 254, 256, 257–258, 261, 264, 381
  home of, 256
Bertha's, 189–190
Bert's Marketplace, 274–275
Betts, Keter, 7, 196
Beulah's Red Velvet Lounge, 264
Big Bopper, 320
Big Maceo, 209, 267, 269
Billington, Johnny, 60, 66
Billy Berg's, 354, 355
Billy Blues (Austin), 348
Billy Blues (Dallas), 329
Billy Blues (Houston), 317
Billy Blues (San Antonio), 337
Bird, *see* Parker, Charlie
Birdland (Kansas City), 248
Birdland (1674 Broadway, New York), 104, 120
Birdland (2745 Broadway, New York), 129, 136, 142
Birdland West, 362
Bird of Paradise, 274, 279–280
Bix Beiderbecke Festival, 237
"Black, Brown and Beige," 110, 118
Black Artists Group, 254–255
Blackwell, Francis "Scrapper," 280
Blake, Eubie, 6, 19, 111, 149, 150, 177, 184, 187–188, 271
  National Museum and Cultural Center, 187
Blakey, Art, 174, 178
  Jazz Messengers of, 374
Blanchard, Terence, 15, 130, 145, 172
Bland, Bobby "Blue," 37, 38, 40, 41, 42, 77, 329, 334, 336, 342, 343, 382
Blayney's, 251
Blind Willie's, 87, 88, 89, 91
Blueberry Hill, 264–265
Bluebird Inn, 273
Blue Bonnet Hotel, 332, 333–334
Blue Cat Blues, 328
Blue Chicago, 231
Blue Devils, 238, 257, 321
Blue Diamond Lounge, 60, 61, 63, 66
Blue Note (New York), 129, 130–131, 147, 149
Blue Note (Philadelphia), 162, 170
Blue Room (New York), 121–122

Blue Room (Vicksburg, Mississippi), 81
Blues, 380
B.L.U.E.S., 209, 222, 229–230
Blues Alley (Minneapolis/St. Paul), 304
Blues Alley (Washington, D.C.), 194, 199, 200
Blues Brothers, 148, 158, 386
Blues City Café/Band Box, 48, 49, 51–52
B.L.U.E.S., Etc., 230
Blues Foundation, 41, 42, 56
Blues Hall, 52
Blues Harbor, 88, 89, 91–92
Blues Palace, 329
Blues Saloon, 299, 303
Blue Wisp, 5, 290, 292, 293
Bluiett, Hamiet, 136, 254
Blythe, Arthur, 355
Boardwalk Bistro, 336
Boatner, Edward, home of, 22
Bob & Barbara's, 170
Bob's Bar-B-Que & Cabaret, 262–263
"Body and Soul," 119, 213
Bogart, Deanna, 189, 192, 199
Bojangles, 388
Bolden, Buddy, 14, 19
  home of, 24–25
Bollenback, Paul, 189, 199
Bollin, Zuzu, 321
Bo-Mac's, 275
Bone, 328
"Boogie Chillen," 269
Booker, James, 29
Booker T. and the MG's, 38, 45, 52
Bop Shop, 221, 227
Boston Globe Jazz Festival, 161
Bottom Line, 129, 133
Bowie, Lester, 1, 254
Brackeen, Joanne, 157, 355
Bradford, Bobby, 343, 360, 361
Bradley's, 5, 129, 132
Bradshaw, Tiny, 254, 289
Brady's Blues Lounge, 234
Braff, Ruby, 154
Braggs, Al, 321
Branch, Billy, 222, 231, 234
Brasserie Montmartre, 387
Braxton, Anthony, 209, 375
Bread of Life, 97, 98
Brecker, Randy, 137, 169
Brenston, Jackie, 46, 65, 218

Brewery, The, 55
Bristol Lounge, 157
Brittenum's Corner Lounge, 54
Broadbent, Alan, 360, 363
Broadway Oyster Bar, 261
Brooks, Roy, 266, 274
Broonzy, Big Bill, 117, 125, 209, 219, 220
Brother Jimmy's BBQ, 232
Brown, Charles, 289, 375
Brown, Clarence "Gatemouth," 148, 293, 305, 311, 334, 342
Brown, Clifford, 162, 170, 177, 292
Brown, Donald, 38
Brown, James, 213, 289, 291, 342
Brown, Nappy, 145
Brown, Piney, 240, 241
Brown, Pud, 26, 27, 29
Brown, Ray, 154, 174, 178, 259
Brown, Ruth, 113, 195, 394
Brubeck, Dave, 25, 131, 372
Brunious, John, 26
Brunious, Wendell, 26
Bruno's Texas Star, 340
Buck, George, 29
Buford, Mojo, 48
Bulls, The, 221, 227–228
Bunker's Music Bar & Grill, 305
Burbank's Real Bar-B-Que, 296
Burke, Solomon, 145, 382
Burnett, Chester, see Howlin' Wolf
Burrell, Kenny, 217, 266
Burton, Gary, 154, 161
Butler, George, 115
Butts, Jimmy, 113
Byard, Jaki, 142, 152
Byas, Don, 113
Byrd, Charlie, 192, 224
Byrd, Donald, 170, 266
Byrd, Emry ("Moose the Mooche"), 354
Byrd, Henry Roeland, see Longhair, Professor

Cables, George, 134, 375
Cabooze, 299, 303
Café Bohemia, 105, 125
Café Brasil, 30
Café Carlyle, 141
Café du Nord, 377
Café Lautrec, 202
Café Luxeford, 301–302
Café Ricardo's, 275

Café Society, 105, 125
Café Tattoo, 191
Café 290, 91, 92
Cajun, 129, 138
Caldezo, Joe, 139
"Caldonia," 289
Caliban, 138
Calle, Ed, 96
Calloway, Blanche, 184, 195, 211
Calloway, Cab, 85, 106, 112, 131, 184, 243, 284, 323, 324, 334
    room, 188
Campise, Tony, 346, 347
Candlelight Room, 389
Cantab Lounge, 157, 159–160
Capp-Pierce Juggernaut, 360
Caravan of Dreams, 9, 325–326
Cardwell Dawson School of Music, 178–179
Carlton, Larry, 365
Carmichael, Hoagy, 19, 208
Carnegie Hall, 110, 117–118, 149
Carr, Barbara, 256, 258
Carr, Leroy, 280
Carr, Sam, 60, 72
Carrollton Station, 36
Carson, Norma, 385
Carter, Benny, 117, 155, 169, 193, 201, 354
Carter, Betty, 138, 266, 279, 301, 378
Carter, Ron, 257
Carver Jazz Festival, 338
Caston, Baby Doo, 298
Catalina Bar & Grill, 361
Catfish Station, 347, 351
Cat's Eye Pub, 190, 192
Celestin, Papa, 14
Center for Southern Folklore, 43
Central, The, 396
Central Avenue, 357
Cephas, John, 193, 199
Cezanne, 315
Chaloff, Serge, 152
Chambers, Paul, 174, 266
Charles, Ray, 24, 79, 112, 131, 312, 332, 358, 391, 392
Charlie's Playhouse, 343
Chatterbox Tavern, 285
Cheatham, Doc, 131
Checkerboard Lounge, 11, 219, 231, 232–233
Chelsea Commons, 138–139

Cherry Blossom, 7, 243–244
Chess, Leonard, 216, 217–218
Chess, Phil, 216, 217–218
Chess Records, 217–218
Chestnut Cabaret, 167, 171
Chestnut Room, 129, 142
Chevy's Four Seasons Restaurant, 77
Chris' Café-Bar, 169
Christian, Charlie, 1, 113, 114, 117, 310, 321, 322
Chubby's Club LaSalle, 287
Cibolo Creek Country Club, 337–338
City Blues Bar, 203
City Light, 246, 247
Clapton, Eric, 71, 230
Clarke, Kenny, 104, 113, 174
Clay, James, 325, 326
Clayton, Buck, 113, 118, 120–121, 123, 357–358
Cleopatra's Needle, 143
Climmie's Western Inn, 263–264
Club Alabam (Chicago), 216
Club Alabam (Los Angeles), 358
Club Brasserie, 362
Club Café, 181
Club Ebony, 76
Club Hangover, 374
Club Indianola, 77
Club La Veek, 313
Club M, 99, 101
Club Memphis, 51, 55
Club Mingo's, 314, 316
Club Paradise, 42, 54
Club Penta, 275–276
Club Second Line, 28
Cobb, Arnett, 310, 311, 313
Cobb, Jimmy, 163, 193, 212
Cobb, Joyce, 48, 49
Cobbs, Willie, 66, 68
Coco's, 294
Cody's Jazz Bar & Grill, 316
Coe, Jimmy, 282, 284
Cole, Nat "King," 85, 94, 96, 143, 177, 312, 329, 354, 358, 359, 360, 385
Coleman, George, 38, 136, 169
Coleman, Ornette, 105, 124, 321, 358, 374
Collette, Buddy, 354
Collins, Albert, 99, 148, 171, 249, 262
Colon, Willie, 132, 378
Coltrane, Alice, 266

Coltrane, John, 6, 105, 124, 130, 149, 162, 163, 165, 188, 212, 248, 273, 292, 374
   home of, 166, 167
Columns Hotel, 27, 31
Concord Jazz Festival, 384
Condon, Eddie, 72, 122, 125, 208, 214
"Confession Blues," 392
Confer, Gene, 385
Congo Square, 14, 18
Congress Hotel, 214
Connick, Harry, Jr., 14, 15, 19, 134, 387
Connick, Harry, Sr., 29
Connie's Inn, 106, 111
Continental Club, 350
Cook, Joe, 154, 160
Cooke, Sam, 61, 85, 95, 187
Cookery, 124
Copacetics, 143
Copeland, Johnny, 91, 145, 171, 303, 310, 329
Corea, Chick, 130
Cornelia Street Café, 135
Coryell, Larry, 392
Cory's, 292, 295
Cosmopolitan Club, 7, 257–258
Cotton, James, 46, 58, 60, 100, 148, 171, 182–183, 191, 210, 220, 229, 232, 233, 277
Cotton Club (Chicago), 223–224
Cotton Club (Lenox Avenue, New York), 3, 106, 110, 129
Cotton Club (125th St., New York), 144
Cotton Inn, 77
Country Blues Lounge, 67
"Cousin Mary," 166
Cowens, Herbie, 325
Cranston, Lamont, 300
Crawford, Hank, 38
Crawford, Jimmy, 38
Crawford Grill, 177, 179
Cray, Robert, 134, 148, 249, 392
Crayton, Pee Wee, 341, 371, 375
Criss, Sonny, 38, 228, 354, 359, 372
"Crossroads Blues," 60, 332
Crudup, Arthur "Big Boy," 47, 209, 218
Crystal Caverns, 165, 195
C.T. Peppers, 281, 287
Cuddle Inn, 233–234

Cullum, Jim, 333, 335
Cunningham, Bradley, 132
Curtis, James "Peck," 69, 70

Dakota Bar & Grill, 299, 301
Dameron, Tadd, 114
Dandelion Pub, 389
Dan Lynch's, 129, 145
Dan Lynch's on 10th Avenue, 146
Dante's Down the Hatch, 89–90
Davenport, Wallace, 26, 29
"Davenport Blues," 237
Davis, Miles, 105, 115, 118, 120, 121, 124, 127–128, 130, 132, 133, 152, 163, 170, 212, 213, 254, 257, 264, 273, 292, 355
   apartment of, 115
Davis, Quint, 23
Davis, Tyrone, 3, 82, 99, 329
Davison, Wild Bill, 133, 152
Davis's Bar-B-Q, 319
Dawn Club, 373
Deanna's Café, 138
Decade, 182–183
Decatur Street, 86–87
Dee Felice's, 292, 294
Deems, Barrett, 222, 223
Deep Ellum, 309, 321, 322–323
Delta Blues Museum, 62, 63, 66
Delta Cultural Center, 69, 70
Desmond, Paul, 132, 372
Dew Drop Inn Café and Bar, 24
Dewey Square, 113
Dick's Last Resort (Chicago), 225
Dick's Last Resort (Dallas), 327
Dick's Last Resort (San Antonio), 337
Diddley, Bo, 210, 217, 220, 230, 338, 339
Dimitriou's Jazz Alley, 393–394
Dirty Dozen Brass Band, 2, 15, 100
Dixon, Willie, 58, 80, 171, 210, 217, 218, 303
D'Lugoff, Art, 131
Doc Dammer's Saloon, Bar & Grill, 99
Dockery Farms, 58, 67, 75
Dr. John, see Rebennack, Mac
Dr. Rib, 92
Dodds, Baby, 19, 208
Dodds, Johnny, 14, 21, 208, 215
Doggett, Bill, 162
Dolphy, Eric, 124, 355

Domino, Fats, 14, 15, 31, 92, 358
  home of, 22
Domino, Floyd, 346
Donegan, Dorothy, 384
Dorham, Kenny, 341
Dorsey, Georgia Tom, 84, 86
Dorsey, Jimmy 324
Dorsey, Tommy, 44, 104, 116, 157, 211, 236, 324, 350
Dorsey brothers, 241
Downbeat, 119
Downtime, 129, 146
Dukes of Dixieland, 28
Dupree, Big Al, 325
Durham, Bobby, 162
Durham, Eddie, 238, 322
Durst, Lavada, 341, 343
Dusen, Frankie, 19
Duskin, Big Joe, 292
Dyer, Johnny, 360
Dylan, Bob, 117, 148, 230, 298

Eagle Saloon, 19–20
Eaglin, Snooks, 26, 35
Earl, Ronnie, 154
Earle Theater, 164, 165
Early, Frank, 18
Eblon Theatre/Cherry Blossom, 243–244
Eckstine, Billy, 113, 174, 196, 270, 282, 325
Economy Hall, 18
Ed Sullivan Theater, 119
Edwards, Honeyboy, 78, 220
Edwards, Teddy, 354, 359, 360, 362, 363, 364
8X10, 189, 191
1815 Club, 221
1860 Saloon, 262
Eileen's Bar & Zebra Room, 175, 182
Eldorado Ballroom, 312–313
Eldridge, Roy, 114, 118, 174, 241, 387
Electric Lady Studios, 125–126
Elephant Room, 346, 347
Eli's Mile High Club & Restaurant, 11, 375, 379, 381
"Elite Syncopations," 256
Ellington, Duke, 1, 6, 8, 24, 25, 106, 108, 110, 112, 116, 118, 121, 128, 152, 163, 188, 193, 196, 201, 213, 215, 217, 236, 271, 298, 334, 357–358, 374, 385
  apartment of, 110
  birthplace of, 198
  boyhood home of, 197
  grave of, 127–128
  statue of, 116
Ellington, Mercer, 193
Ellis, Big Chief, 193
Ellis, Herb, 156, 169
Ennis, Ethel, 184, 189, 192
"Entertainer, The," 256
Epicurean Lounge, 248
Ernestine's and Hazel's, 53
Ertegun, Ahmet, 196
Estes, Sleepy John, 344
Esther's Breakfast Club, 375
Etta's Lounge & Restaurant, 318
Europe, James Reese, 117, 193
  home of, 198
Evans, Bill, 156
Evans, Gil, 118, 121, 131
Evans, Herschel, 243, 310, 322, 332
Evening Star Jazz Bar, 199, 201

Fabulous Satellite Lounge, 319
Fabulous Thunderbirds, 329, 349
Faces Midtown Night Club, 286
Fais Do Do, 368
Famous Ballroom, 188
Famous Coachman, 274
Famous Door, 103, 104, 119
Fantasy Lounge, 68
Farlow, Tal, 169
Farmer, Addison, 359
Farmer, Art, 131, 169, 201, 354, 357, 359
Fat Matt's Rib Shack, 92
Fats, Tuba, 26, 36
Fat Tuesday's (New York City), 126, 129, 135
Fat Tuesday's (Washington, D.C.), 204
Fender, Freddie, 318
Fenix Café, 396
Ferguson, Maynard, 159, 177
Fields, Mickey, 189, 190
Fieldstones, 48, 54
Fifth Amendment, 382
55 Bar, 129, 134
Fifty-second Street, 118–119
Filipiak, Carl, 189, 191
Fine Line Music Café, 304
First Avenue, 304–305

Fitzgerald, Ella, 24, 88, 96, 104, 106, 112, 113, 188, 196, 218, 282, 298, 314
Fitzerald's, 229, 232
5-4 Ballroom, 358
Five Spot (St. Mark's Pl.), 105, 124, 129
Five Spot (31st St.), 139
Flamingo Lounge, 144
Flanagan, Tommy, 132, 266, 378
Fogerty, John, 79
Ford, Frankie, 82
Ford, Fred, 48, 50
Fortune, Sonny, 134, 142, 162, 189
Foster, Frank, 289
Fountain, Pete, 16, 25, 26, 30
Fourth Ward, 312
Four Tops, 272
Fox Theatre (Atlanta), 93
Fox Theatre (Detroit), 269, 279
Fox Theatre (St. Louis), 266
Francis, Panama, 94
Frank Early's Saloon, 18
"Frankie and Johnny," 253
Franklin, Aretha, 117, 343
Freeman, Bud, 208, 216, 217
Freeman, Von, 222, 223, 227, 228
French Quarter Festival, 36
"Friar's Point Shuffle," 72
Friesen, David, 385, 386, 387
Frishberg, Dave, 378, 386
Frog Island Festival, 278
Frost, Frank, 60, 67, 72
Full Moon Saloon, 191
Fulson, Lowell, 360, 371, 375, 379, 381
Funderburgh, Anson, and the Rockets, 321, 329

Gaines, Grady, 314, 318, 319
Gallant Knight, 316
Garland, Red, 132, 162, 321, 324
Garner, Erroll, 113, 118, 119, 174, 178
Garner, Honeymoon, 48, 50
Garrison, Jimmy, 94
Geddins, Bob, 371
Gee, Jack, 164, 166
Geller, Lorraine, 385
Gensel, John Garcia, 149
Gerri's Palm Tavern, 212, 229
Gershwin, George, 44, 122
home of, 114
Get Me High Lounge, 221, 227

Getz, Stan, 100, 161, 225, 378
Gibbs, Marla, 364
Gibson, Banu, 26
Gillespie, Dizzy, 6, 88, 90, 104, 109, 112, 113, 118, 119, 127, 131, 132, 138, 143, 161, 163, 164, 165, 166, 170, 178, 188, 201, 213, 216, 223, 241, 243, 314, 325, 354, 355, 358, 378
New York apartment of, 113
Gilly's, 292, 297–298
Gist's Music Company, 70–71
Gleason, Jackie, 94
Golden Lily, 212–213
Goldkette, Jean, 120, 267, 270, 272
Gold Star Sardine Bar, 224–225
Golson, Benny, 162, 165, 172
Gonsalves, Paul, 152
Goodman, Benny, 104, 107, 108, 117, 118, 119, 122, 157, 208, 211, 214, 215, 236, 241, 284, 324, 340
Goodman, Freddy, 214–215
Gordon, Dexter, 130, 132, 190, 223, 248, 354, 358, 359, 372
Gordon, Lorraine, 130
Gordon, Max, 5, 130, 385
Gordon, Roscoe, 40
Gordy, Berry, Jr., 271
Grace Cathedral, 374
Graceland, 39, 47
Grand Avenue Bar, 5–6, 353, 360, 363
Grand Emporium, 246, 249
Grand Terrace Ballroom, 211–212
Grant Park, 216
Granz, Norman, 118, 313–314, 354
Graystone Ballroom, 267, 270–271, 272
Graystone International Jazz Museum, 271, 278
Great American Music Hall, 384
Great Grizzly Bear, 261–262
Green, Al, 55, 70, 329, 375
Green, Clarence, 314, 317
Green Mill, 9, 221, 225–226
Green's Lounge, 2, 48, 49, 53–54
Greenstreets, 99
Greenwich Tavern, 292, 293–294
Grey Ghost, 341, 346, 350
home of, 343–344
Grove Street Stompers, 133

Gruene Hall (New Braunfels, Texas), 339
Guaraldi, Vince, 372
Guinan, Texas, 226
Guitar Shorty, 360
Guitar Slim, 24, 314, 317
Guy, Buddy, 126, 152, 171, 182, 220, 222, 329, 345
legends of, 231–232
New Checkerboard Lounge of, 231, 232–233

Hackett, Bobby, 125
Hal & Mal's, 82
Hall Brothers, 300
Hamilton, Chico, 354, 359
Hammond, John, 52, 65, 100, 107, 117, 149, 171, 172, 176, 211–212, 238, 339
home of, 117
Hampton, Lionel, 42, 82, 89, 104, 131, 143, 329, 332, 359
Hampton Sisters, 280, 284
Hancock, Herbie, 152, 325, 378
H&M Bar-B-Que, 250–251
Handy, W. C., 6, 37–38, 39, 40–41, 42, 43, 44, 46, 50, 56, 57, 58, 73, 117, 119, 159, 199, 253
birthplace, 57–58
grave of, 127, 128
homes of, 41, 64
Handy Park, 40, 42
Hanna, Sir Roland, 142, 266
Haque, Fareed, 226
Hardin, Lil, see Armstrong, Lil Hardin
Hargrove, Roy, 136, 259, 321, 326
Harling's Upstairs, 250
Harmonica Fats, 360
Harper, Danny, 88
Harper, Walt, 177, 179, 180
Harper's Ferry, 159
Harris, Barry, 134, 266, 267, 273
Harrison, Donald, 15, 32, 145
Harrison, Nelson, 8
Hart, Clyde, 113
Hart Plaza Blues Festival, 278
Harvelle's, 369
Hastings Street, 269
Hawes, Hampton, 354, 359
Hawkins, Coleman, 118, 119, 213, 241, 243–244

Haynes, Roy, 143, 152
Heath, Jimmy, 149, 162, 169, 172
Heath, Percy, 162
Heath, "Tootie," 162
Heathman Hotel, 388
Hemphill, Julius, 172, 254, 321
Henderson, Fletcher, 83, 104, 107, 108, 109, 111, 119, 125, 212, 214, 243, 267
home of, 93–94
Henderson, Horace, 93–94
Henderson, Joe, 375, 378
Henderson, Skip, 78, 79
Hendrix, Jimi, 112, 125–126, 237, 391, 392
Hepcat, Dr., see Durst, Lavada
Herman, Woody, 118, 196, 213, 215, 225
"Herman at the Sherman," 215
"He's Got the Whole World in His Hands," 22
Heywood, Eddie, 83
Hiatt, John, 285
Hickory House, 119
Hicks, Johns, 134
Higgenbotham, J. C., 83
Higgins, Billy, 355, 363, 364
Hi Hat, 152
Hill, Andrew, 361
Hill, Blind Joe, 360
Hill, Buck, 193, 199, 201
Hill, Chippie, 211
Hill, Teddy, 113
Hill, Z. Z., 321
Hines, Earl, 173–174, 176–178, 211, 270, 371, 374
Hines, Frank, 298
Hines, Gregory, 141
Hinton, Milt, 112, 134, 208
Hirt, Al, 28
"Hitch Up My Pony, Saddle Up My Black Mare," 75
"Hitler Blues, The," 344
Hodes, Art, 123, 214, 215, 217
Hodges, Johnny, 127
Hole in the Wall, 351
Holiday, Billie, 6, 104, 107, 110, 111–112, 113, 117, 118, 119, 121–122, 125, 165, 184, 186, 187, 198, 226, 268, 269
New York apartments of, 107, 114–115
statue of, 187
Holly, Buddy, 320
Holmes, Johnny, 342–343

Hood, Bill, 385
Hooker, John Lee, 58, 61, 100, 132, 171, 249, 267, 269, 277, 289, 329
Hopkins, Claude, 193
Hopkins, Lightnin', 310, 317, 344
Horizons, 30
Horne, Lena, 94, 96, 112, 113, 125, 196, 291, 358
Hors d'Oeuvrerie, 139
Horton, Walter, 46, 220, 229
Horvitz, Wayne, 135
Hotel Dunbar, 357–358
Hothouse, 221, 226–227
"Hound Dog," 47, 312
House of Blues (Boston), 154, 158
House of Blues (Los Angeles), 367
House of Blues (New Orleans), 26, 33
House of Blues (New York City), 147
Houston International Festival, 320
Houston International Jazz Festival, 320
Howard Theater, 196
Howell, Peg Leg, 84, 86
Howlin' Wolf (Chester Burnett), 6, **38**, 46, **58**, 68, 75, 79, 152, 210, 217, 218, 221, 233
grave of, 221
Hubbard, Blues Boy, 343, 346
Hubbard, Freddie, 89, 155, 280, 376
Huey's, 49, 50, 55
Huggins, Speedy, 246
Hughes, Joe, 314, 317, 318, 319
Hull House, 214–215
Humphrey, Hey Hey, 226
Humphrey, Percy, 27, 29
Humphrey, Willie, 27
Humphrey Brothers, 26, 27
Hunter, Alberta, 38, 39, 49, 52, 55, 113, 124, 149, 196, 208
Hunter, Ivory Joe, 24, 320, 371
Hurricane, The, 251
Hurt, Mississippi John, 58
Hutcherson, Bobby, 376
Hyman, Dick, 378

"I Hear a Symphony," 272
Indiana Avenue, 280, 282–283

Indiana Avenue Jazz Festival, 288
Indiana Roof Ballroom, 283–284
Indigo Jazz Lounge, 366
Inferno, 251
Ink Spots, 282
International Academy of Jazz Hall of Fame, 178
Interstate Grocer Company, 71
Ivery, Marchel, 324, 325, 326

Jack's Bar, 375, 380
Jack's Sugar Shack, 367–368
Jackson, Franz, 222, 228
Jackson, Grady "Fats," 88, 91
Jackson, Michael, 272
Jackson, Tony, 17, 18
Jacquet, Illinois, 130, 142, 310
Jaffe, Allan, 27
Jaffe, Sandra, 27
Jagger, Mick, 230
Jamal, Ahmad, 163, 178, 183, 273, 301, 361
James, Elmore, 58
James, Etta, 218, 303, 375
James, Harry, 44, 324
James, Skip, 81
James Street, 182
Jarrett, John "Pigmeat," 294, 295
Jarrett, Keith, 90, 152
Jazz: A Louisiana Kitchen, 348
Jazz and All That Art on Fillmore Fair, 384
Jazz at Pearl's, 377
Jazz at the Philharmonic (JATP), 313–314, 354
Jazz Bakery, 362
Jazz Cooker, 286
Jazz de Opus, 387
Jazz Foundation of Memphis, 55
Jazzmobile, 149
Jazz Oasis, 224
Jazz Passengers, 135
Jazz'SAlive, 338
Jazz Showcase, 5, 221, 222–223
Jazz Workshop (Boston), 152
Jazz Workshop (North Beach), 374
Jefferson, Blind Lemon, 6, 310, 321, 322
grave of, 331
Jefferson, Eddie, 174, 273
Jefferson, Thomas, 29
Jefferson, Wesley, 60, 66, 67
Jelly Roll's, 28
Jenkins, Bobo, 267, 274
Jenkins, James, 8, 271

Jenkins, Slim, 371
Jennings, Joe, 88, 89
Jimmie's Cocktail Lounge &
    Nightclub, 382
Jimmy Ryan's, 119
Jimmy Walker's, 129, 141
J.J. & His Bad Boys, 368
J.J.'s Grotto, 6, 169
Joe's Cozy Corner, 31
Joe's Generic Bar, 349
Joe Tex, 343
John Coltrane Festival, 370
Johnny D's, 154, 157, 158–159
Johnson, Big Jack, 60, 66, 67
Johnson, Bunk, 123
Johnson, Claude, 324, 325, 326
Johnson, James P., 117, 125
    residence of, 109
Johnson, James "Stump," 254
Johnson, Jimmy, 230
Johnson, J. J., 280, 282, 284
Johnson, Johnnie, 258
    Sir John's Trio, 257–258
Johnson, Lonnie, 209, 254, 289,
    322
Johnson, Luther "Guitar Junior,"
    154
Johnson, Luther "Houserocker,"
    88, 91
Johnson, Robert, 58, 60, 61, 63,
    68, 81, 158, 332, 333–334
    memorial monument, 78
    tombstone of, 78
Johnson, Snuff, 346
Johnson, Tommy, 44, 58, 75, 81
Jones, Arthneice "Gas Man," 60,
    66
Jones, Carmell, 246
Jones, Elvin, 266
Jones, Etta, 228
Jones, Floyd, 220
Jones, Fritzy, see Jamal, Ahmad
Jones, Hank, 132, 142, 266
Jones, Jonah, 112
Jones, Philly Joe, 162
Jones, Quincy, 392
Jones, Thad, 266
Jones Hall for the Performing
    Arts, 320
Joplin, Janis, 166, 312, 320, 340,
    343, 344, 345–346
Joplin, Scott, 6, 10, 253, 256,
    310
    boardinghouse of, in New
        York, 121
    home of, in St. Louis, 255–256
Jordan, Louis, 76, 81, 289

Jordan, Stanley, 297
Josephson, Barney, 124, 125
Joyce Cobb's, 49–50
Jubilee Jam, 83
"Jumpin' at the Dew Drop," 24
Juneteenth Blues Festival,
    320
Jungle Club, 195–196
Junior Kimbrough's Houseparty,
    49, 57, 60, 75
Just Jazz (Atlanta), 88, 89
Just Jazz (St. Louis), 258, 259

Kala-Kala, 202
Kaldi's Coffeehouse & Bookstore,
    294
Kansas City Blues & Jazz Festi-
    val, 252
Kansas City Red, 65
Kater Street, 163
"Kater Street Rag," 163
Katz, Dick, 184
Kelley, Peck, 310, 311, 332
Kelly, George, 94
Kelly's Pub, 99
Kelly's Stable, 119
Kemp's, 32
Kenton, Stan, 196
Keppard, Freddie, 208
Key, Troyce, 371, 376, 381
Keyhole Inn (Mississippi Delta),
    76
Keystone Korner, 374
KFFA Radio (Helena, Arkansas),
    64, 69–70
Kiki's Bon Ton Maison, 250
Kimball's, 375, 376
Kimball's East, 375, 378
King, Albert, 40, 48, 51, 52, 54,
    58, 76, 132, 303
King, B. B., 33, 37–53 passim,
    58, 75–76, 79, 82, 99, 119,
    126, 132, 133, 146, 213,
    219, 233, 297, 313, 315,
    317, 318, 334, 342, 358,
    382
    home of, 76
King, Freddie, 321, 343
King, Little Jimmy, 51
King Biscuit Blues Festival, 69
"King Biscuit Time," 69
King of France Tavern, 188–
    189, 192
King Records, 289, 291
King's Palace Café, 55
Kingston Mines, 222, 230
Kinsey Report, 229, 277

Kirk, Andy, 112, 238, 239, 242, 358

Kirk, Rahsaan Roland, 212

Kirkland, Kenny, 360, 362

Knickerbocker Restaurant, 134

Knitting Factory, 129, 135

Koenigswarter, Baronness "Nica" de, 116

Koester, Bob, 234

Koncepts Cultural Gallery, 383–384

Konitz, Lee, 355

Krupa, Gene, 214, 217, 236, 241

La Carrousel, 89, 90

La Cave on First, 141

Lacy, Steve, 131, 361

La Famille Restaurant, 143–144

Lafayette Theater, 110–111, 121

Laine, Jack, 19
home of, 21

Lake, Oliver, 254, 278, 384

La Louisiane, 336

Lambert, Dave, 152

Lamb's Café, 215

La Menthe, Ferdinand, *see* Morton, Jelly Roll

Land, Harold, 311, 354, 360, 362, 363, 364

Landing, The, 335

Larkin, Milton, 310, 311, 313, 314

LaRocca, Nick, 117
home of, 22–23

Larry Blake's R&B Café, 383

Larry's Greenfront, 396

LaSalle, Denise, 3, 54, 251, 297, 329, 382

Last of the Blue Devils (film), 243

Lateef, Yusef, 163, 223, 266, 273

Laury, Booker T., 48, 52

Lawson, Hugh, 266

La Zona Rosa, 350

Leadbelly, 130, 310, 321, 322

Le Café, 365

Lee, Frankie, 371, 382

Lee, George, 238, 242

Lee, Julia, 238, 242

Lee, Peggy, 298

Lee, Roosevelt, 289

Lee, Spike, 286

Lee's Unleaded Blues, 233

Left Bank Jazz Society, 188, 192

Legends of Hollywood, 364–365

Lennon, John, 298

Leon Springs Café, 339–340

Levee, The, 248

Leviev, Milcho, 360

Lewis, Furry, 37, 39, 41, 48, 52, 158

Lewis, George, 27, 373–374

Lewis, Meade "Lux," 117, 125

Lewis, Mel, Big Band, 130

Lewis, Ramsey, 89, 90, 139, 394

Liberty Lunch, 350

Lighthouse Café, 359

Lilly's, 222, 231

Lincoln High School (Dallas), 324–325

Lincoln High School (St. Louis), 256–257

Lincoln High School Jazz Band (St. Louis), 259

Lincoln Theater (New York), 104, 107, 110

Lind, Dale, 149

Lipscomb, Mance, 341

Little Hatch, Provine, 246, 248, 249

Little Milton, 46, 77, 251, 303, 313

Little Richard, 24, 42, 85, 303

Little Walter, 217, 220, 263

"Livery Stable Blues," 117

Living Room, 366

Local Charm, 318

Local 1207, 292, 295

Lockwood, Robert, Jr., 69, 76

Lone Star Roadhouse, 129, 147

Long Beach Blues Festival, 370

Long Beach Jazz Festival, 370

Longhair, Professor, 14, 15, 34
home of, 23–24

Longhorn Ballroom, 329–330

Loring Café & Playhouse, 302

Los Fairlanes, Beto y, 347

"Louisiana Blues," 209

Louisiana Community Bar & Grill, 129, 138

Lou's Pier 47, 381

Lucas, Lazy Bill, 298

Lucille's Paradise Band Box, 242

Lulu White's Saloon, 17

Lunaria, 363

Lunceford, Jimmie, 38, 359

Lynn, Gene, 260

Mabry, Esther, 375

McBeth, Ida, 246, 250

McClain, "Diamond Teeth" Mary, 100

McClinton, Delbert, 329, 380

McCormick, Mack, 345
McCracklin, Jimmy, 371, 375, 380
McCrae, Carmen, 201, 325, 378
McDuff, Jack, 293, 299, 378
McFerrin, Bobby, 213, 254
McGary, Jimmy, 290
McGriff, Jimmy, 156, 162
Mack, Lonnie, 91, 148, 297, 304
McKenna, Dave, 132, 152, 154
McKenna, Larry, 169
McKinney's Cotton Pickers, 267, 270, 271
McMinn, Don, 48, 52
McMurry, Lillian, 81, 82
McNeely, Big Jay, 145, 354, 357, 359
McPartland, Jimmy, 118, 208, 214, 216
MC's Bar and Grill, 251
McShann, Jay, 238, 239, 242, 246, 247, 340
McTell, Blind Willie, 84, 86, 87, 88, 91
McVey, Girard, 48
Madame Walker Urban Life Center, 283
Madigan's, 36
Magic Bag Theatre Café, 276
Maher, Big Joe, and the Dyna-flows, 199
Mahogany Hall, 17
Maison Bourbon, 28–29
Majestic Theatre, 323–324
Mallard's, 49, 50
Malone, J. J., 371, 381
Manchester Craftsmen's Guild, 183
M&M Lounge, 389
Manne, Shelly, 355, 359
Mannish Boys, 262, 346
Manny's Car Wash, 129, 148
Manone, Wingy, 217
Mansion Hill Tavern, 292, 295
Maple Leaf Bar, 35–36
"Maple Leaf Rag," 255
Maramosa, Dodo, 174
"March Majestic," 256
Margaret's Blue Diamond Lounge, *see* Blue Diamond Lounge
Marketplace Café, 157
Marla's Memory Lane, 364
Marmalade's, 51, 52
Marsalis, Branford, 15, 25, 360, 363

Marsalis, Delfeayo, 15, 25, 191, 362
Marsalis, Ellis, Jr., 25, 26, 30, 31
Marsalis, Ellis, Sr., 25
Marsalis, Wynton, 15, 25, 169, 297
Marsalis family, 14, 19
Marsalis Motel, 25
Martin, Sara, 211
Martini's, 327
Masekela, Hugh, 135, 138, 159
Maxwell, Jimmy, 29
Maxwell's Toulouse Cabaret, 27, 29
Maxwell Street, 209, 220–221, 235
Maybeck Recital Hall, 375, 378
"Maybellene," 218, 219
Mayfield, Percy, 10, 354
Mayfield, Tina, 10
Mayweather, "Earring" George, 154
Melrose, Lester, 74, 209
"Memphis Blues," 42
Memphis Horns, 47
Memphis James, 52
Memphis Minnie, 37, 41, 58, 60, 68, 209
Memphis Music Fest, 56
Memphis Music Hall of Fame, 41
Memphis Slim, 37, 132
Metheny, Pat, 152, 155, 161, 262
Metropole (New York), 120–121
Meyers, Augie, 332, 337
Mezzrow, Mezz, 111, 216
Michael's Pub, 141
Mickey's Mardi Gras, 317
Mid-City Lanes, 27, 35
Middle East Restaurant, 154, 156–157
Midway Café, 160
Mike & Min's, 261
Milburn, Amos, 289
Miller, Glenn, 122, 324
Miller, Punch, 27, 213
Millinder, Lucky, 85, 165, 195, 197
Millions, Kenny, 96, 98
Mills, Florence, 111
Milneburg Lighthouse, 14, 26
Milt Trenier's Lounge, 225
Minger, Pete, 96, 97, 98
Mingo's, *see* Club Mingo's

Mingus, Charles, 105, 120, 124, 130, 132, 137, 152, 177, 354, 358, 374
loft of, 124
Mint Lounge, The, 367
Minton's Playhouse, 7, 104, 110, 113–114, 119
Miss Catie's, 292, 296
Mississippi Nights, 262
Mississippi Valley Blues Festival, 237
Missouri Bar & Grill, 265
"Misterioso," 289
Mr. Johnnie's Place, 66
Mr. Lou's Rhythm & Blues, 278
Mitchell, Andrew "Sunbeam," 42, 52, 54
Mitchell, Billy, 266, 273
Mitchell, Blue, 94
Mitchell, Paul, 88, 89
Mitchell, Roscoe, 209, 226–227
Mitchell's Hotel, 42, 53, 54
Moby Dick's, 274, 277–278
Modern Jazz Quartet, 131, 141
MoJazz Café, 96, 97
Molly's, 261
Monarch Club, 41
Mondo Cane, 146
Monk, Thelonious, 104, 109, 113, 124, 130, 142, 152, 163, 177, 199, 289
apartment of, 115–116
Monroe's Uptown House, 104, 110
Montgomery, Buddy, 280
Montgomery, Wes, 280, 282
Moody, James, 170, 217
Moonlight Gardens Ballroom, 291
Moore, Alex, 321, 322
Moore, Arnold "Gatemouth," 40, 44
Moore, Clarence "Gatemouth," 61, 320
Moore, Glen, 385
Moosehead Bar & Grill, 224
Moose Lounge, 260
Morgan, Frank, 168, 359
Morgan, Lee, 162
Morganfield, McKinley, *see* Muddy Waters
Morgan's, 169
Morton, Jelly Roll, 14, 17, 21, 193, 195–196, 199, 208, 217
home of, 22
Mosby, Curtis, 358

Moten, Bennie, 164, 211, 238
residence site of, 242
Motown Museum, 271–272
Mt. Hood Jazz Festival, 390
Muddy Waters (club), 35
Muddy Waters (musician, McKinley Morganfield), 43, 46, 58, 61, 64, 65, 68, 133, 152, 209, 210, 217, 218–219, 233, 344
birthday of, 68
homes of, 63–64, 219
Mulligan, Gerry, 130, 355
Murphy, Mack "Guitar," 92, 146
Murphy, Mark, 156, 180, 293, 394
Murphy, Turk, 371, 373
Murphy, Willie, 298, 300
Murray, David, 1, 136, 226, 355
Murray, Sunny, 162
Music Hall (Houston), 313–314, 320
Musicians Exchange Café, 96, 100
Music Mart, 75
Music Room, 98
Musselwhite, Charlie, 99, 145, 182–183, 381, 388
Mustafa, Milton, 98
Mutual Musicians Foundation, 9, 242–243, 246, 247
Myers, Sam, 325

"Nagasaki," 241
Nasser, Zaid, 48
Natalie's Lounge, 170
Nathan, Syd, 291
National Negro Opera Company, 178–179
Navarro, Fats, 94
Needham, Theresa, 220
Neely, Bill, 341
Neely, Frances, 46
Negri, Joe, 179, 181
Nelson, Chicago Bob, 88
Nelson, Willie, 344
Nepper, Jimmy, 142
Netto, Rene, 29
Neville, Charles, 24
Neville, Charmaine, 26, 30, 159, 262
Neville Brothers, 34
New Apartment Lounge, 215, 228
Newborn, Calvin, 38, 48, 51
Newborn, Phineas, Jr., 38, 52

New Checkerboard Lounge, 231, 232–233
New Haven Lounge, 188, 189, 192
Newman, David "Fathead," 8, 172, 321, 324–325
New Orleans Creole Restaurant, 394
New Orleans Jazz and Heritage Festival, 23, 25, 36
New Orleans Jazz Club Collections, 19
New Orleans Room, 375, 376–377
Newport Jazz Festival, 161
New Regal Theater, 207, 212, 213, 235
New Vegas Lounge, 204
New York, New York, 326–327
New York Swing Dance Society, 129, 150
Nighthawk, Robert, 60, 61, 65
Nightingale, Ollie, 54
Nightmoves, 252
Nix, Willie, 40
Nona's, 336
North End, 49–50, 55
North Star Bar, 171
Nostalgia, 301
Not Just Jazz, 327

O'Day, Anita, 226, 227
Off Broadway, 262
O'Gara's Bar and Grill, 305
O'Hara's Pub, 96, 97–98
OK Hotel, 394, 395
Okoshi, Tiger, 156
    and Tiger's Baku, 154
Old Absinthe House Bar, 33
Old City Auditorium, 313
Old Timers' Café, 396–397
"Ole Miss Blues," 41
Oliver, Jimmy, 162, 167
Oliver, Joseph "King," 14, 17, 107, 127, 128, 208, 212
Olson, Sev, 298
Omar and the Howlers, 339, 346, 351
O'Neal, Jim, 58, 68, 78, 79
"One O'Clock Jump," 321
One Step Down, 199, 200
Onyx, 104, 119
Orbison, Roy, 46, 148
Orchestra Hall (Detroit), 270
Oregon, 385
Original Dixieland Jazz Band, 14, 22–23, 104, 117
Ortlieb's Jazz Haus, 167, 168

Ory, Kid, 373–374
Osborne, Walter, 80
"Oscar for Treadwell, An," 289
"Oska T.," 289
Otis, Johnny, 354, 362, 383
Otter Crest Jazz Festival, 390
Ovations, 315
Overtown Square, 94, 95–96
Owens, Tary, 343–344

Page, Oran "Hot Lips," 114, 118, 122, 216, 238, 310, 321, 322
Page, Walter, 238
Palace Theater, 41–42, 47
Palm Court Jazz Café, 27, 29
Palmieri, Eddie, 138, 393
"Pantin' in the Panther Room," 215
Paradise Valley, 267, 269
"Parchman Farm Blues," 74
Parchman Penitentiary, 74–75
Parham, Truck, 222
Park Central Hotel, 118
Parker, Charlie (Bird), 1, 6, 104, 108, 109, 110, 113, 118, 119, 120, 122, 133, 152, 165, 178, 209, 238–246, 270, 273, 282, 289, 321, 354, 355, 385
    apartment of, 123
    and Birdland, 104, 120
    death of, 116
    grave of, 245–246
Parker, Junior, 46, 61, 79, 311
Parlan, Horace, 174
Parris, Rebecca, 154, 155
Paschal's Motor Hotel and Restaurant, 90
Pat and Pete's Bonton Room, 317
Patton, Charley, 58, 60, 61, 67, 73, 75, 78, 81
    grave of, 79
Paul, Les, 136
Paul's Mall, 152
Paycheck, Johnny, 147
Payne, Felix, 241
Payne, Sonny, 70
Payton, Nicholas, 26
Payton, Perry, 79
Payton, Walter, 26, 31, 32
Peabody Hotel, 5, 44
Pearl, Bernie, Blues Band, 360
Pearl's Oyster Bar, 346, 349
Pearson, Duke, 83
"Pea Vine Blues," 75

PeeWee's, 42
Pendergast, Thomas J., 239, 240
  home of, 245
Pennsylvania Avenue, 185–186
"Pennsylvania 6-5000," 122
Pepper, Art, 354, 358, 359
Perkins, Pinetop, 69, 159, 203,
  229–230, 380
Perry's Flowing Fountain, 79
Perseverance Hall, 19
Person, Houston, 228
Pete Fountain's, 30
Peterson, Oscar, 131, 201, 217,
  387
Petit, Buddy, 21
Pettiford, Oscar, 125, 298
Phillips, Sadie, 177
Phillips, Sam, 38, 44, 45–46, 218
Phoenix Piano Bar & Grill, 246,
  247
Pickett, Wilson, 145, 213
Pieces of a Dream, 224, 293
Pierson, Leroy, 258
"Piney Brown Blues," 240
Pitchford, Lonnie, 68
Place 2-B, The, 54
Plough & Stars, 159
Poindexter, Buster, 148
Point, The, 250
Polk, James, 343, 346
Pollack, Ben, 118
Ponder, Jimmy, 179, 181
Pontchartrain, Lake, 14–15, 26
Pontiac Jazz Festival, 279
Poor David's Pub, 328–329
Pope, Odean, 162, 167, 172
Pops for Champagne, 228
Porter, Sid, 385
Powell, Bud, 120
Powell, Richie, 162
Powers, Michael, 146
"Preachin' the Blues," 87
Preer, Andy, 106
Preservation Hall, 13, 27, 36, 52
Presley, Elvis, 38, 45, 46, 47,
  112, 119, 264–265, 312
"Pretty Baby," 18
Price, Jesse, 241
Price, John, 60, 77
Price, Sam, 238, 321, 322
Pride, Charlie, 64
Prince, 133, 304–305
Principato, Tom, 189, 193, 199
Pryor, Snooky, 220, 339
Puente, Tito, 132

Queen of Hearts, 73, 82–83

Rachell, James "Yank," 285
Radcliff, Bobby, 148
Radiators, 34, 52
"Ragtime Dance, The," 256
Rainbow & Stars, 140
Rainbow Room, 129, 140
Rainey, Gertrude "Ma," 38, 131,
  322
  home of, 93
Raitt, Bonnie, 298
Ramada Renaissance Hotel,
  120
Ramey, Gene, 310, 340
Ramsey's II, 181
Randi, Dan, 365
Randle, Eddie, 257, 264
Rasselas, 377
Rattlesnake Club, 276
Rawls, Lou, 285, 375
Razaff, Andy, 111, 193
"Reachin' Pete," 68
Rebennack, Mac, 14, 15, 34,
  133, 145, 249, 303, 304
ReBirth Brass Band, 15, 26,
  34
Red, Hot & Blue (Mississippi
  Delta), 83
Red Blazer Too Restaurant, 129,
  140
Redding, Otis, 38, 44
Reddi Room, 318
Red Onion, 20–21
"Red Onion Blues," 21
Red's, see South End Disco
Reed, A. C., 262
Reed, Jimmy, 58
Reed, Lou, 133
Regal Theater, 213
Regattabar, 6, 154, 155, 156
Reinhardt, Django, 125
Reisenweber's Restaurant, 104,
  117
Reisner, Robert, 122, 123
Rena, Kid, 19
Renaissance Ballroom and Ca-
  sino, 108
Reynolds, Marie, 289
"Rhapsody in Blue," 44, 122
Rhodes, Sonny, 167, 171, 371
Rich, Buddy, 100, 118, 313
Rick's Café Américain, 285–
  286
Ritenour, Lee, 365
Ritz-Carlton (Buckhead), 91
RiverBlues, 172
Rivers, James, 26
River West, 232

Roach, Max, 90, 113, 131, 177, 183, 223, 301, 361, 363, 393
Robert Mondavi Winery, 384
Roberts, Luckey, 177
Roberts Hotel, 213
Robey, Don, 311, 312
Robillard, Duke, 148, 153, 159, 182–183, 191
Robinson, Bill "Bojangles," 111, 141
Rockefeller's, 315, 319
Rockefeller's West, 315–316
"Rocket 88," 46, 65, 218
Rodgers, Jimmie, 346
Rogers, Jimmy, 231
Rogers, Shorty, 355, 359
Roker, Mickey, 162, 167, 168
Rolling Stones, 148
Rollins, Sonny, 5, 105, 128, 130, 163, 168, 178, 262, 387
Roof Restaurant, 157
Roomful of Blues, 92, 148, 153, 203, 339
Rosa's, 222, 230–231, 235
Rose, Al, 14–15, 18, 22
Rosebud, 181
Roseland Ballroom, 94, 119–120, 129, 140–141
Rose's, 96, 97
Ross, Annie, 114
Ross, Diana, 272
" 'Round About Midnight," 124
Rouse, Charlie, 125, 193
Rowles, Jimmy, 360
Rowles, Stacy, 360
Royal Peacock, 85, 92
Royal Roost, 104, 120
Royal Theatre, 186
Royston's, 144–145
Rum Boogie Café, 52, 53
Rumsey, Howard, 355, 359
Rush, Bobby, 303
Rush, Otis, 132, 217, 220, 221, 230, 396
Rushing, Jimmy, 238
Rushing Winery, 73
Russell, George, 152, 289
Russell, Pee Wee, 122, 125, 152, 254
Ryles, 155

Saffire, The Uppity Blues Women, 199
Sahm, Doug, 332, 337

Sain, Oliver, 254, 258, 262
  studio of, 256
St. Cyr, Johnny, 217
St. John's African Orthodox Church, 374–375
"St. Louis Blues," 57, 253
St. Louis Blues Heritage Festival, 266
St. Peter's Lutheran Church, 149
Salgado, Curtis, 389
  & the Stilettos, 386
Saloon, The, 381
Saluté, 336–337
Salute! in Citta, 394, 395
Sambuca Mediterranean Café & Jazz Bah, 326
Sanborn, David, 254, 260
Sanchez, Bobby, 199
Sandbar, 31–32
San Francisco Blues Festival, 384
San Francisco Jazz Festival, 384
Santana, Carlos, 372
Santizzi, Ray, 154
Savoy, 104, 106–107, 188
Sazerac House, 129, 135
Scarlet Tree, 397
Schenley High School, 177–178
Schooner's, 328
Schwab's, A., 43, 56
Scott, Clifford, 332
Scott, Isaac, 393
Scott, Shirley, 162, 167, 174
Scott, Tom, 353
Scott-Heron, Gil, 138, 201
Scullers, 154, 156
Seals, Larry, 199
Sears, Al, 108
Segal, Joe, 5, 222–223
Selvidge, Sid, 48, 50
708 Club, 220
Seventh Street, 375
"Seventh Street Boogie," 371
Shadyside Balcony, 180
Shakespeare Pub, 318
Shank, Bud, 355
Shaw, Artie, 121, 157, 196, 324
Shaw, Charles "Bobo," 254
Shaw, Eddie, 221
Shaw, Robert, store and home of, 345
Shearing, George, 118, 217
Shepp, Archie, 162
"Sherman Shuffle," 215
Shields, Harry, 25
Shields, Lonnie, 60, 66, 68, 72
Shines, Johnny, 68
Short, Bobby, 116, 141, 225, 271

Shorter, Wayne, 378
Showboat, 163–164
Showman's Café, 11, 129, 143
Silver, Horace, 132, 149, 378
Silvercloud, 258
Simon Rodeo Music and Arts
    Festival, 370
Sims, Zoot, 228
Sinatra, Frank, 225, 358
Singleton, Zutty, 111, 122, 125
Sissle, Noble, 111, 177, 198,
    280, 283, 284, 291
Slim's, 375, 380
Slippery Noodle Inn, 286–287
Smalls, Ed, 108, 156
Smalls' Paradise, 107–108, 137,
    156
Smith, Bessie, 6, 10, 38, 43, 64–
    65, 84, 86, 87, 93, 100, 111,
    112, 117, 162, 163, 164,
    322
    family home, 164
    grave of, 166
Smith, Big Walter, 300
Smith, Buster, 242, 310, 321,
    322
Smith, Huey "Piano," 15, 82
Smith, Jabbo, 162, 215
Smith, Jimmy, 90, 136, 273, 313
Smith, Lonnie, 96, 97
Smith, Mamie, 289
Smitty's Corner, 218–219
Smitty's Red Top Lounge, 61,
    66–67
Snowden, Elmer, 184
Snug Harbor, 27, 29–30
S.O.B.'s, 138, 234
"Soda Fountain Rag," 197
Son House, 58, 61, 75
Son Seals, 203, 230, 231, 262
Soulard Mardi Gras, 266
Soup Kitchen Saloon, 274, 277
South Eddie, 216
South End Disco, 60, 66
South Street, 163
Spanier, Muggsy, 125
Spanish Fort, 26
Spann, Otis, 82
Speckled Red, 44
Sphinx Club, 187
Sportsmen's Lounge, 190, 192
Springsteen, Bruce, 117, 133,
    152, 381
Squire, 129, 138
Stackhouse, Houston, 58, 69
Stackhouse/Delta Record Mart,
    58, 61, 68

Stanhope Hotel, 116
Staton, Dakota, 144, 156, 170,
    174, 201
Stax Recording Studios, 39, 45
Steamboat Natchez, 36
Stephen Talkhouse, 96, 100
Stern, Mike, 134, 156
Stewart, Rod, 261
Sticky Mike's, 160
Stitt, Sonny, 22, 152, 190, 215,
    217, 228, 254, 260, 273
Stolen Moments, 180, 182
Storyville (Boston), 152
Storyville (New Orleans), 14, 16–
    17, 18, 20, 28
Stovall plantation, 63–64
Strachwitz, Chris, 345
Straight Ahead Band, 274, 276
"Strange Fruit," 125
Strayhorn, Billy, 148, 173–174,
    178
Strehli, Angela, 5, 310, 341, 349
Strictly Tabu, 326
Striver's Row, 108–109
Strozier, Frank, 38
Stubbs, George, 133
Studio One 83, 98–99
Subway Club, 241
Subway Lounge, 83
Sullivan, Ira, 94, 96, 97, 98, 193,
    223
Sullivan, Maxine, 174
Sully's, 274, 277
Sunflower River Blues Festival,
    68
Sunnyland Slim, 68, 210, 220,
    222, 229, 277
Sun Ra, 162, 223, 249, 384
    and his Arkestra, 136
Sun Records, 218
Sunset Café, 211
Sunset Social Club, 368–369
Sun Studio, 39, 44, 45–46, 65,
    218
Sushi Blues Café, 96, 97, 98
Sutherland Show Lounge, 212
Sweet Basil, 129, 131
Sweetwaters, 143
Sykes, Roosevelt, 68, 254
Sylvia's, 144

Tabby's Blues Box & Heritage
    Hall, 37
Taj Mahal, 91, 99, 100
Takoma Station, 199, 201
Tam, 157, 159
Tampa Red, 209, 267

Tapscott, Horace, 359, 360, 361, 363
Tate, Buddy, 228
Tate, Erskine, 211
Tatum, Art, 118, 119, 125, 273, 311, 354, 370, 371
Tavern on the Green, 142
Tavern 213, 99
Taylor, Billy, Dr., 142, 149, 193
Taylor, Cecil, 124
Taylor, Hound Dog, 220–221
Taylor, Koko, 222, 229, 230, 231, 277, 305
Taylor, Little Johnny, 54, 329, 342
Taylor, Mick, 98
T-Bone, 383
Teagarden, Jack, 118, 165, 226, 310, 311, 332
exhibit, 331
Terilli's Restaurant, 327
Terra Blues, 129, 146
"Terraplane Blues," 332
Terry, Clark, 142, 178, 215, 228, 254
Terry, Doc, and the Pirates, 258, 261
Teschemacher, Frank, 216
Thackery, Jimmy, and the Night-hawks, 193
"That's All Right, Mama," 46–47
Theresa, Hotel, 112
Theresa's Tavern, 220
Thigpen, Ed, 359
Third Ward, 312
1369 Club, 153
Thomas, Carla, 38
Thomas, Erroll, 50
Thomas, Gary, 189
Thomas, Irma, 14, 15, 26
Thomas, Kid, 27
Thomas, Robert "Honeyboy," 44
Thomas, Rufus, 38, 41, 44, 46, 48, 54, 91
Thomas Jefferson High School, 359
Thomas's Lounge, 67
Thompson, Roach, 96, 101
Thornhill, Claude, 226
Thornton, Willie Mae "Big Mama," 47, 310, 312, 344
Threadgill, Henry, 157, 209
Threadgill, Kenneth, 344, 346
Threadgill's, 345–346
Three Deuces, 104, 119

Three Rivers Arts Festival, 184
"Thrill Is Gone, The," 44
Tibbs, Andrew, 216
"Tiger Rag," 23
Time Café, 137
Times, The, 301
Timmons, Bobby, 162
Tin Angel, 172
Tipitina's, 2, 24, 26, 34–35
Tjader, Cal, 372
T-Model Ford, 60, 77
TOBA (Theatre Owners Booking Association), 238
Tobacco Road, 96, 97, 99–100
Todd, Tommy, 385
"Tom Rushen Blues," 73
Too Sweet, 182
Torin, Symphony Sid, 120, 132
Tornado Alley, 199, 203
Torres, Nestor, 96
Tough, Dave, 118, 214
Toussaint, Allen, 14, 24
Towner, Ralph, 385, 393
Town Hall, 122, 149
Townhouse, 366
Townsend, Henry, 258
Tramps, 129, 145
"Trav'lin' All Alone," 107
Treadwell, Oscar, 289
Trenier, Milt, 225
Trent, Alphonso, 310, 321, 324
Tristano, Lennie, 245–246
Trombone Shorty's, 26, 27, 30–31
Trumbauer, Frank, 254
Trumpet Records, 81, 82
Tuba, The, 250
Tubby's Red Room, 257, 263
"Tune Town Shuffle," 254
Turner, Big Joe, 24, 117, 329, 334
Turner, Ike, 38, 46, 61, 65, 254, 258, 382
home of, 258
Turner, Joe, 113, 125, 238, 240, 241, 375
Turner, Tina, 254, 256
home of, 258
Turpin, Tom, 253
Turrentine, Stanley, 155, 174, 177, 224, 325
Twin's Restaurant and Lounge, 9, 199, 201
219 Restaurant/Basin Street Lounge/Bayou, 202
Tyner, McCoy, 131, 161–162, 292, 301, 378

Underground Atlanta, 84, 87–88
Underground Wonder Bar, 224
"Union Man Blues," 216
Uptown, 260
Uptown Rhythm Kings, 189, 199
U Street, 193, 194–195, 197
U2, 46

Valens, Ritchie, 320
Valentine, Cal, 321
Vaughan, Jimmie, 5, 341, 346
Vaughan, Sarah, 113, 118, 125
Vaughan, Stevie Ray, 5, 52, 249, 310, 341, 349, 351
Vega, Suzanne, 133
Velvet Lounge, 228–229
Venuti, Joe, 267
Vic's Kangaroo Café, 33–34
Victory Grill, 340, 342–343
Viking Bar, 300, 303
Village Bar & Grill, 369
Village Corner, 129, 133
Village Gate, 124, 129, 131–132, 149
Village Vanguard, 1–2, 5, 105, 109, 129, 130, 385
Vincent, Johnny, 81, 82
Vine Street Bar & Grill, 361–362
Vinnegar, Leroy, 280, 386, 387
Vinson, Eddie "Cleanhead," 310, 311
Vinson, Mose, 40, 48
Visiones, 134
Vulcan Gas Company, 40, 48, 344

Wade, Theo "Bless My Bones," 44
Walden, Donald, 273, 274, 276
Walker, Earl, 282
Walker, Junior, 135, 303, 329
Walker, Madame C. J., 282, 283
Walker, T-Bone, 310, 321, 323–324, 354
"Walking Blues," 332
Wallace, Beulah "Sippie," 211, 273, 310
Waller, Fats, 104, 107, 108, 109, 110, 111, 112, 114, 117, 118, 138, 186, 215, 271, 358
Wally's Café, 152, 155–156, 160
Walton, Cedar, 321, 324, 363
Walton, Wade, 64
Waluhaje Club, 85, 88
Warehouse Café, 27, 32, 34

Washington, Albert, 292
Washington, Dinah, 5, 24, 81, 88, 130, 163, 187, 196, 213, 283, 371
    apartment of, 109
Washington, Grover, Jr., 134, 155, 162, 178, 326
Washington, Walter, 26, 30, 35
Water Front Blues Festival, 390
Waterloo Ice House, 347–348, 351
Waters, Ethel, 106, 162, 163, 196
Watson, Bobby, 172
Watters, Lu, and his Yerba Buena Jazz Band, 371, 373
Watts, Jeff, 360
Waxie Maxie record stores, 197
WDIA (Memphis), 39, 44, 46–47
Webb, Chick, 104, 106–107, 108, 113, 184, 187
    Memorial Recreation Center, 188
Webster, Ben, 193, 238, 243–244
Webster, Katie, 384, 394
Webster Hotel, 217
Wein, George, 152
Wells, Junior, 152, 220, 222, 231, 233, 249
Wells, Ronnie, 199
West End Gate, 142–143
Western Front, 157
"West Helena Blues," 68
Westin William Penn, 176, 181–182
Westinghouse High School, 178
Wharf, The, 204
"What a Difference a Day Makes," 109
Wheatstraw, Peetie, 254
"When the Saints Go Marching In," 22, 48
Whiskey Junction, 303
White, Bukka, 37, 39, 58, 61, 74, 158
White, Jesse, 274, 278
White, Josh, 125, 130
White, Leroy, 298
White Horse Café, 169–170
Whiteman, Paul, 44, 104, 122, 216
Whitted, Pharez, 280, 284
Wiggins, Phil, 193, 199
Wilkerson, Ed, 209
William Penn Hotel, see Westin William Penn

Williams, A. C., 44
Williams, Big Joe, 37
Williams, Clarence, 17, 211
Williams, Claude "Fiddler," 246, 247
Williams, Joe, 362
Williams, Mary Lou, 109, 118, 173, 178, 238, 239, 242, 243–244, 245
apartment of, 109
Williams, Nat D., 41, 44, 47
Williamsburg Bridge, 128
Williamson, Sonny Boy, I (John Lee "Sonny Boy" Williamson), 1, 58n, 209
site of death of, 218
Williamson, Sonny Boy, II (Rice Miller), 1, 10, 58, 58n, 65, 69, 70–71, 76, 82
boarding house of, 71
grave of, 74
Willow Jazz Club, 156
Wilson, Cassandra, 145
Wilson, Kim, 71, 148, 277, 310, 341, 349, 380
Wilson, Nancy, 212
Wilson, Teddy, 114, 117, 118, 125, 149, 213, 214, 298, 310, 340
Winnah's Circle, 32
Winter, Bob, 154
Winter, Johnny, 344

Witherspoon, Jimmy, 136, 156, 354, 360, 383
Wonder, Stevie, 133, 271
Woodlawn Cemetery, 127–128
World Music Institute, 150
World Saxophone Quartet, 131, 379
World Stage, 363–364
Wright, Early, 62–63, 68
Wright, Marva, 26, 28, 35
WROX (Mississippi Delta), 62–63
Wylie Avenue, lower, 176–177

Yardbirds, 71
Yardbird Suite, 129, 136–137
"Yellow Dog Blues," 41
Yoshi's, 375, 378
Young, Lee, 354, 358
Young, Lester, 108, 112, 118, 125, 238, 243–244, 245, 298, 354, 358
Youngblood, Lonnie, 143
Young Olympians Brass Band, 26
Your Place Too, 382

Zanzibar, 134–135, 136
Zanzibar Blue, 167, 168
Zinno, 134
Zoo Bar, 203
Zorn, John, 135
Z.Z. Top, 62